# PERCEPTUAL PROCESSING

THE CENTURY PSYCHOLOGY SERIES

*Kenneth MacCorquodale*
*Gardner Lindzey*
*Kenneth E. Clark*
*editors*

# Perceptual Processing

## *stimulus equivalence and pattern recognition*

*edited by*

PETER C. DODWELL
*Queen's University*



APPLETON-CENTURY-CROFTS
Educational Division
New York MEREDITH CORPORATION

ACKNOWLEDGMENTS

I.1 From Heinrich Klüver, *Behavior Mechanisms in Monkeys*. Copyright 1933 by the University of Chicago Press. All rights reserved. Reprinted with permission.

I.2 From *Visual Mechanisms: Biological Symposia* Vol. VII, ed. Heinrich Klüver (Lancaster, Pa.: The Jaques Cattell Press, 1942): pp. 301–321. Reprinted with permission. A paper presented in the Symposium on "Visual Mechanisms" at the Fiftieth Anniversary Celebration of the University of Chicago, September 24, 1941.

I.3 From *Bulletin of Mathematical Biophysics*, 1947, 9, 127–147. Reprinted with permission. The authors wish to express their great indebtedness to Professor Elizabeth Crosby for her generous assistance. This work was aided by grants from the Josiah Macy, Jr. Foundation and the Rockefeller Foundation.

I.4 From von Halst, E., and H. Mittelstaldt. Das reafferenz prinzip. In: *Die Naturwissenschaften*. 37 Jg., S. 464–476. Berlin-Gottingen-Heidelberg: Springer, 1950. Reprinted with permission. Footnotes renumbered. Lecture given on June 1, 1950 at a Symposium on Behavioral Physiology held at the Max Planck Institute at Wilhelmshaven. Points raised by H. Böhn, K. Lorenz, and W. Metzger have been taken into account in the extension and revision of the original presentation.

I.5 From *The Mechanization of Thought Processes* (London: HMSO, 1959). Reprinted with permission.

II.1 From *British Journal of Psychology*, 1955, *46*, 30–37. Reprinted with permission.

II.2 From *Nature*, 1957, *179*, 11–13. Reprinted with permission. The author wishes to thank the Royal Society for grants from the Broine Research Fund which made the experimental work possible, Professor J. Z. Young for invaluable advice and encouragement, and the director and staff of the Stazione Zoologica, Naples, for the hospitality and facilities afforded him there.

II.3 From *Nature*, 1969, *185*, 443–446. Reprinted with permission. The author wishes to thank Professor T. H. Bullock for discussion and encouragement, Professor J. Z. Young for helpful correspondence and neuroanatomical data, Dr. N. S. Sutherland for discussion of his results, and Dr. G. A. Horridge for helpful comment.

II.4 From *Psychological Review*, 1969, *71*, 148–159. Reprinted with permission.



71 72 73 74 75/10 9 8 7 6 5 4 3 2 1

Library of Congress Card Number: 70-167686

PRINTED IN THE UNITED STATES OF AMERICA
390-27035-0

II.5 Reprinted from *Sensory Communication,* edited by W. Rosenblith, by permission of the M.I.T. Press, Cambridge, Massachusetts. Copyright © 1961 by The Massachusetts Institute of Technology.

III.1 Excerpted from *Journal of General Psychology,* 1938, *18,* 123–193. Reprinted with permission.

III.2 Courtesy of *Journal of Experimental Psychology,* 1938, 22, 497–523. The author wishes to record here his gratitude to Professor Wolfgang Köhler for his helpful criticisms in connection with the preparation of this manuscript.

III.3 From *Psychonomic Science,* 1970, *18,* 5–7. Reprinted with permission. This research was supported by Grant APA 44 from the National Research Council of Canada to the first author, which is gratefully acknowledged.

III.4 From *Science,* 1963, *139,* 209–210. Copyright 1963 by the American Association for the Advancement of Science. Reprinted with permission. The experiments were performed at California Institute of Technology, where the author received support from grants made to R. W. Sperry by the National Institute of Health and the Frank P. Hixon fund of the California Institute of Technology. The work forms part of a project on "stimulus analyzing mechanisms" financed by the Office of Naval Research (contract N 62558–2453). The author also acknowledges a travel grant from the Wellcome Trust and thanks Gene Mercer for assistance in running the experiment.

III.5 From *Psychonomic Science,* 1967, 9, 519–520. Reprinted with permission. This research was supported by grant APT 109 of the National Research Council of Canada to the first author.

III.6 Ingle, D. "Two visual mechanisms underlying the behavior of fish." In: *Psychologische Forschung,* Bd. 31, S. 44–51. Berlin-Heidelberg-New York: Springer, 1967.

III.7 Schneider, G. E. "Contrasting visuomotor functions of tectum and cortex in the golden hampster." In *Psychologische Forschung,* Bd. 31, S. 52–62. Berlin-Heidelberg-New York: Springer, 1967. During the period of reported research, the author was supported by a U.S. Public Health Service predoctoral fellowship. Additional support was received from the National Institute of General Medical Sciences under their Training Grant ST1 GM 1064-04 BHS.

III.8 From *Journal of Physiology,* 1966, *187,* 437–445. Reprinted with permission. This investigation was supported by a United States Public Health Service research grant (NB 06046–01). J. J. K. was generously supported by the British Council.

III.9 From *Vision Research,* 1967, 7, 999–1013. Reprinted with permission. The author would like to thank Professor D. M. MacKay for frequent and invaluable discussions of the experiments as they progressed, and Professors H. B. Barlow and G. Westheimer for many constructive comments upon the presentation.

IV.1 Reprinted from *Sensory Communication,* edited by W. Rosenblith by permission of the M.I.T. Press, Cambridge, Massachusetts. Copyright © 1961 by The Massachusetts Institute of Technology. The quantitive analysis of inhibitory interaction reviewed here was supported by a research grant (B 864) from the National Institute of Neurological Diseases and Blindness, Public Health Service, and by Contract Nonr 1442(00) with the Office of Naval Research.

IV.2 From *Nature,* 1960, *186,* 836–839. Reprinted with permission. The research reported in this communication has been sponsored in part by the United States Air Force Office of Scientific Research. The author is greatly indebted to the Nuffield Foundation for continual support and to Dr. P. Dohrn and the staff of the Zoological Station at Naples for their help.

IV.3 From *Proceedings of the Institute of Radio Engineers,* October 1959, pp. 1940–1951. Reprinted with permission. This work was supported in part by the U. S. Army (Signal Corps), the U. S. Air Force (Office of Sci. Res., Air Research, and Dev. Command), and the U. S. Navy (Office of Naval Research); and in part by Bell Telephone Labs., Inc. The authors are particularly grateful to O. G. Selfridge whose experiments with mechanical recognizers of pattern help drive us to this work and whose criticism in part shaped its course.

IV.4 From *Journal of Neurophysiology,* 1953, *16,* 37–68. Reprinted with permission. This investigation was supported by a research grant from the National Institute of Health, U. S. Public Health Service. The author is grateful to Dr. S. A. Talbot for his help, particularly in the design of the optical and electronic instruments, which made this study possible. Thanks are also due to Mr. Albert Goebel for constructing the optical apparatus.

IV.5 From *Journal of Physiology*, 1962, *160*, 106–154. Reprinted with permission. The authors wish to thank Miss Jaye Robinson and Mrs. Jane Chen for their technical assistance. They are also indebted to Miss Sally Fox and Dr. S. W. Kuffler for their helpful criticism of this manuscript. The work was supported in part by Research Grants B–2251 and B–2260 from the United States Public Health Service, and in part by the United States Air Force through the Air Force Office of Scientific Research of the Air Research and Development Command under contract No. AF 49 (638–713. The work was done during tenure of a U. S. Public Health Service Senior Research Fellowship No. SF 304-R by D. H. H.

IV.6 From *Journal of Physiology*, 1967, *193*, 327–362. Reprinted with permission. Many refinements of the methods used in this work were developed in the Department of Physiology, Sydney, and W. R. Levick, to whom we are also indebted for help and discussion. This work was supported by Grant No. NB–05215 from the United States Public Health Service, and was performed when one of the authors (H. B. B.) held a Miller professorship.

V.1 From *EEG and Clinical Neurophysiology*, 1954, *6*, 479–494. Reprinted with permission. The author wishes to thank Mr. D. A. Sholl for giving him a sense of proportion about cortical structure, Dr. W. Grey Walter and Dr. I. C. Whitefield for valuable discussions and for permission from the latter to reproduce figure 11, and Professor J. Z. Young for encouragement and advice. Acknowledgement is made to the Chief Scientist, the Ministry of Supply, and the Controller of H. British M. Stationery Office for permission to publish this paper. British Crown Copyright Reserved. Fig. 10. Reproduced with permission from Galambos and Davis, in *Journal Neurophysiology*, 1943, *6*, 39–57.

V.2 From *Proceedings of the Institute of Electrical Engineers*, 1959, *106*, 210–221. Reprinted with permission.

V.3 Reprinted from *Models for the Perception of Speech and Visual Form*, edited by W. Watheu-Dunn by permission of the M.I.T. Press, Cambridge, Massachusetts. Copyright © 1967 by The Massachusetts Institute of Technology.

V.4 Reprinted from *Models for the Perception of Speech and Visual Form*, edited by W. Watheu-Dunn by permission of the M.I.T., Cambridge, Massachusetts. Copyright © 1967 by The Massachusetts Institute of Technology. This work was supported in part by the Joint Services Electronics Program under Contract DA 36–039–AMC–03200(E); in part by the National Science Foundation (Grant GP–2495), the National Institute of Health (Grants MH–0437–04 and NB–04332–02), the National Aeronautics and Space Administration (Grant NSG–496), and in part by the U. S. Air Force Cambridge Research Laboratories, Office of Aerospace Research, under Contract AF 19(628)–3325.

Figures in Part IV

Fig. A, p. 327. Adapted from F. E. Cady and H. B. Dates, *Illumination Engineering* 2d Ed., New York: Wiley, 1928.

Fig. 3, p. 278. Reproduced with permission from Hartline, Wagner, and Ratliff, *Journal of General Physiology*, 1956, *39*, 651–673.

Fig. 4, p. 280, and Fig. 7, p. 284. Reproduced with permission from Hartline and Ratliff, *Journal of General Physiology*, 1957, *40*, 357–376.

Fig. 5, p. 281. Reproduced with permission from Hartline and Ratliff, *Journal of General Physiology*, 1958, *41*, 1049–1066.

Fig. 6, p. 283, and Fig. 8, p. 285. Reproduced with permission from Ratliff and Hartline, *Journal of General Physiology*, 1959, *42*, 1241–1255.

Fig. 11, p. 289. Reproduced with permission from Ratliff, F., and Mueller, C. "Synthesis of On-Off Responses in a Visual Neural System," *Science*, Vol. 126, pp. 840–841, Fig. 11, 25 October 1957.

# Contents

## III. EXPERIMENTAL EVIDENCE ON PATTERN RECOGNITION



## IV. THE NEUROPHYSIOLOGY OF VISUAL PATTERN CODING

# *Preface*

Books of readings seem to be appearing at an accelerating pace these days, a development which is on the whole to be welcomed. The advantages of such collections to supplement—or even substitute for—textbooks of the recognized form are that they expose students to the work of scientists who are actively engaged in the process of creating new knowledge; also they can (or should) serve to organize the salient features of a field without the necessity of the neophyte's wading through an everincreasing torrent of journals, monographs and books such as now appear in many areas of psychology. A major deficiency of many books of readings, however, is that they give the student very little help in evaluating or interpreting the contents of individual papers. Also, in attempting to be comprehensive, they may cover too small a range of topics within any one field to give the novice a clear understanding of what the relevant issues are and how they have been tackled.

I have tried to avoid these pitfalls by presenting a series of papers in a more limited domain. They are divided into five parts, each one presenting work of a particular type. A number of the papers are not by psychologists, but I have attempted to place such papers within a context which brings out their relevance for the questions and problems which interest psychologists. All the readings are accompanied by a fairly extensive commentary which is aimed at providing that context, evaluating the major points of each paper, and holding together the common threads running through each section, and also between sections.

Although I have tried to achieve some sort of balance, my personal convictions about the more important developments in this field have certainly biased the selections. No doubt some of the interpretations and discussions I give in the commentary would be disputed in certain quarters. Some bias is inevitable, and I believe it is well to admit it right away: I also believe that it can serve a useful pedagogical function, since the provision of a viewpoint at least gives the reader a position to attack or defend. One danger in a book of readings can be that it turns out to be too bland, or too diffuse, to convey a convincing picture of a field of work. My purpose is rather to develop the basis for a particular way of looking at perceptual processing, which is further elaborated in my *Visual Pattern Recognition* (Dodwell, 1970).

Several of the papers are quite difficult, and quite technical (particularly in the fourth section, on neurophysiology), and some thought was given to the question of cutting and simplification. I decided that it was probably more useful to give the unadulterated original versions of papers, and to give a commentary that would try to make these originals understandable to the nonspecialist, rather than to water them down. Modern scientific research in visual pattern recognition is a highly specialized and technical field, and the fact should not be concealed.[1] I hope also that the strategy of presenting the unedited version will make the readings useful for more advanced students too, although the main aim is to present material that is suitable to the undergraduate major level.

The only change from the original versions of papers, apart from those mentioned in the footnote, is that the reference sections have been corrected (a surprisingly extensive task in some cases!), completed and put into a common form, so far as possible. A few references could not be traced, and references which only occurred in the deleted sections of papers have not been included.

Selecting papers for a book of readings is bound to pose difficult choices, and this is particularly true when the choices range over several fields of scientific investigation. Apart from the question of theoretical relevance and balance between different points of view, I have been somewhat influenced, particularly so far as the first and last parts of the book are concerned, by availability. That is to say I have chosen several papers which are not at present available in easily accessible sources, but whose importance justifies their wider dissemination. The paper by von Holst and Mittelstaedt in Part I is a translation of their now classical *Das Reafferenzprinzip* which first appeared in 1950. Although a brief English presentation of von Holst's ideas has been available for some time (von Holst, 1954), this is the first time that a fuller exposition has appeared. The translation is my own, but I received invaluable help on points of technical detail and interpretation from Horst Mittelstaedt, which I gladly acknowledge.

Some of the preparation of the book was done at the Center for Advanced Study in the Behavioral Sciences, some at Queen's and some while I was Visiting Professor at Harvard. The support of all three institutions is acknowledged, and I am particularly grateful to Priscilla Jones, Dick Lewis, Margaret Morris, Agnes Page, Eleanor Rosenberger, Barbara Savoy, and Nigel Smith who assisted with various stages of the book's preparation.

All the living authors (or senior authors) of readings were kind enough to give permission to use their material, and are duly thanked for their courtesy. Acknowledgment to the various copyright holders is made on the copyright page.

Professor U. Neisser gave some advice on the selection of readings for

[1] One concession is made in that paragraphs containing technical details or special mathematical formulation, the understanding of which is not central to a general grasp of the paper, and paragraphs which are not particularly difficult but of subsidiary interest, are set in small type. Where inessential material made it possible, some of the papers have been shortened, but such cuts are always indicated.

the final part of the book. Thanks are due to him also, although I mention his name with hesitation since I did not follow his advice in all respects. I scarcely need add, in conclusion, that the responsibility for such deficiencies as there may be in the book is solely mine.

P. C. D.

## *REFERENCES*

Dodwell, P. C. *Visual pattern recognition.* New York: Holt, Rinehart & Winston, 1970.

Holst, E. von Relations between the central nervous system and the peripheral organs. *British Journal of Animal Behaviour,* 1954, 2, 89-94.

## A Note on Referencing

Each of the readings is identified as to source and date of publication on the page on which it starts. Full bibliographic references can be found on the copyright page (the reverse of the title page). Works cited in the introduction and commentary are all referenced in the same place at the end of the book together with a list of suggested further reading.

# Introduction

For decades, psychologists have puzzled over the question of stimulus equivalence. Put in one of its simpler and more usual forms, the question is this: How does an organism *abstract* from the rich and continually changing flux of sensory impressions to which it is subjected, certain attributes or features to which it will respond in a particular way? We might also say: How does an organism *categorize* events in its environment? or, perhaps less concretely: How does an organism recognize *patterns?*

One can attempt to answer such questions at a variety of different levels, by investigating physiological properties of the visual (or other sensory) system, by studying discrimination behavior, by observing animal activities in the natural environment, by synthesizing mechanical systems that "recognize" patterns, and so on. A great part of the fascination of this field lies in the fact that its questions are so general and can be looked at from several different points of view. In this book of readings I shall illustrate both points, by showing that many different questions have been asked about pattern recognition, and how several different disciplines have converged in the field. Happily we shall see that the sorts of questions asked are not so disparate that we cannot relate the research efforts in different disciplines to each other. In fact, one of the major purposes of the book is to attempt to document the convergence; hence, the subtitle *Stimulus Equivalence and Pattern Recognition.* By including the term stimulus equivalence I hope to suggest the types of approach on which I shall concentrate. One might almost have used the term *stimulus control* rather than *stimulus equivalence*—except that the former has a rather special connotation now within the Skinnerian tradition—since one way to rephrase our main question is this: What are the effective stimuli to which an organism responds? Or: What stimuli are effectively equivalent in eliciting a given response?

Even with this apparently more restricted version of the original question, there are many different ways of seeking answers. One may look with the ethologist for patterns of environmental stimuli which "release" certain kinds of built-in behavior; or with the neurophysiologist for the "pattern coding" system of the brain; or with the psychologist for the conditions of training that render two patterns equivalent or not. By taking stimulus equivalence as the major facet of pattern recognition and organizing the readings around it, I have attempted to achieve a certain unity despite the diversity of techniques and interpretations which are inevitable in passing from one discipline to another.

The different parts of the book are organized more or less by discipline, but more accurately in terms of the approach to a specific question or area of research. The first part is largely a historical introduction with selections from the writings of three psychologists, two biophysicists, and two biologists which put the major questions in perspective and set the stage for the later treatment. Part II contains papers on a fairly restricted, although central topic, the coding of patterns and pattern elements in different sorts of visual system. The papers in this part are all concerned with specific coding models. Part III comprises a number of papers describing experiments on pattern recognition, mainly on animals, but also including two reports on human vision. In the fourth part some of the major contributions in the neurophysiological literature are included, and the fifth and final part consists of papers on pattern recognition by machines, modeling, and computer simulation.

Although the topic of pattern recognition is presented mainly in terms of stimulus coding, or analysis, and pattern classification, some space has been devoted to the relation between stimulus input and motor output—the *modes* of response of an organism to its environment. This is done to avoid a certain danger; the danger that too rigid a devotion to the input side of things will result in too passive a conception of the organism to the view that all we need to explain about organisms is the way in which they classify stimuli. Curiously enough too strong an emphasis on *output* (overt responses) in the past led the Behaviorists of the 1920s and 1930s to a similarly passive model of the organism, in which stimuli "elicited" responses and, in the extreme form, *all* behavior was thought of simply as "movements reflexly elicited by stimuli." So, although we want to know about stimulus categorization and about the "form" or "structure" of an organism's world, we want to do this as a step in the process of understanding growth, development and adaptation to that world, not simply as an end in itself. To attempt to understand the basic or "initial" conditions of perception, to try to understand how perceptual development depends on—or grows from—these, and to relate that process to concept formation and intellectual growth in general is to span many of the most challenging questions in psychology (see Dodwell, 1970b). However, such a large purpose is beyond the scope of this set of readings. If the student is convinced by what is presented here that questions about stimulus equivalence, about coding, and about pattern recognition in general are central to an understanding of the subject-matter of psychology, the book will have achieved its objective.

# I

# HISTORICAL PERSPECTIVE: THE SORTS OF QUESTIONS RAISED, AND SOME IDEAS ABOUT ANSWERING THEM

*One of the charms of selecting a set of readings is that it allows one to resurrect papers which, although often quoted, are probably extremely seldom read by the present-day student. This is particularly true if the papers happen to be in books or journals which are out of print or otherwise not readily available. Some of the issues raised in the writings of thirty or forty years ago may seem archaic to us today, but we cannot afford to be too patronizing about them. To the extent that psychologists of an older generation were willing to raise and discuss very general questions about behavior, they may seem somewhat naïve to the person steeped in the specialized modern approaches to experimental psychology. Yet we may be in danger of an opposite lack of sophistication: by refusing to consider the broader issues we may be isolating ourselves from legitimate questions which it should be within our province and power to answer.*

*The first selection in this part is from Heinrich Klüver's introduction to his* Behavior Mechanisms in Monkeys, *often referred to as the classical statement of the problem of stimulus equivalence. Reading this statement today, a psychologist is likely to find it particularly striking that what Klüver tended to treat as one question we now divide into a number of topics. He raises questions about the following matters: sensory coding, learning that two or more different objects can be treated as equivalent for some special purpose, the "measuring" of objects and events, cultural conditioning; even epistemology and semantic problems in the definition of equivalences. To see the question of stimulus equivalence in this broad way is perhaps useful as a starting point. Yet not all sides of the matter will receive equal treatment in what follows. Not all aspects of the question have been pursued vigorously—at least not by experimental psychologists. But in raising the question in this general way Klüver at least gives us the chance to think about which avenues of inquiry are likely to be most fruitful, or which are likely to be amenable to experimental analysis.*

# The Problem of Equivalence in the Sensory Field

H. KLUVER

In the present study we have been primarily interested in demonstrating characteristic forms of behavior which remain unaltered in the presence of pronounced changes in the environmental stimulus constellation. We believe that the *analysis* of such objectively demonstrable forms of behavior will throw light on "mechanisms" which are truly "fundamental" or "basic" in behavior.

A person is still the "same" person although we see him at a distance of 100 feet standing on his head; a square is recognized as the "same" square although it is represented by only four dots; the reactions of a given male bird (*Melopsittacus*) to the female may remain the "same" despite the fact that the female has been painted red (Tirala, 1923). Notwithstanding certain changes in the stimulus situation the stimuli are in some way "identical" or "similar"; they call forth the "same" response; they are, from the point of view of the reaction produced, "*equivalent*." It is possible of course, to introduce changes which destroy this "equivalence": upon the introduction of such changes the stimuli become "*non-equivalent*."

The question at once arises as to how far we can go in changing the properties of the stimulus situation without affecting the consistency of the response. In this study we are not merely interested in the fact that under certain conditions we find an equivalence of stimuli; we are far more interested in determining the *equivalence range*. In fact, most of the experiments reported in this volume deal with the determination of equivalence ranges. Of course, the question as to how far we can go in changing the stimulus situation can only be experimentally answered.

It is clear that in systematically introducing changes in the stimulus situation a great deal depends on *what stimulus properties we consider effective in making heterogeneous situations "similar."* We are dealing here with one of the central problems of modern psychology: the problem as to what the properties or characteristics really are which account for the "identity" or "similarity" of heterogeneous stimulus constellations. It could be easily shown that the solution of this problem is of fundamental im-

Reprinted from *Behavior Mechanisms in Monkeys,* 1933.

portance not only for the psychology of perception but also for investigations in the fields of emotion, motivation, personality, and character. The constancy of the response, the fact that a certain form of behavior remains unaltered in spite of striking changes of the stimulus can, of course, be explained only by assuming that certain aspects of the stimulus situation have remained constant; in some respects the stimuli must be "identical" or "similar." The fact that under certain conditions a circle and an ellipse are "similar" whereas under different conditions they are "dissimilar" is of less interest to us than the question as to why there is "similarity" or "dissimilarity."

At this point we shall be content with indicating, in a very general way, that in certain instances it may seem easy whereas in other instances it may seem extremely difficult to define those stimulus properties which are responsible for the "similarity" or "identity" of the stimuli and, therefore, for the constancy of response. It should be remarked that theoretically we are at every point confronted with exactly the same difficulties. But at first sight it seems that we can easily define the properties which account for the similarity between a square consisting of a homogeneously colored area and a square represented by four dots, between a bright yellow and a neutral color, e.g., a certain light gray. It may seem less easy to state in what respect there is a similarity between a live monkey baby and a dead rat. And, to turn to humans, it may seem still more difficult to determine why the "same" response is made to the face of a woman, a melody, a rhythm, a "nonsensical" configuration of lines, a word, and a landscape. What seems to be of fundamental importance is to recognize, first of all, that there must be some properties capable of bringing about "similarity" even between stimuli (and not only between "sensory" stimuli) which are as different as the stimuli just mentioned, and secondly, that such properties not only affect behavior and impart certain directions to behavior but, in fact, are very potent in influencing behavior. To make certain assumptions concerning the characteristic which supposedly accounts for the "similarity" between the above-mentioned stimuli and to say, for instance, that they share the property of being "bright and cheerful" is, to be sure, not equivalent to demonstrating experimentally that it is actually this property which is effective in determining the response.

About ten years ago I conducted certain experiments on school children in Berlin and on students at Stanford University, California. The subjects had to decide, for instance, which one of several colors "goes with" a certain melody, a certain configuration of lines, etc. It was found that there are certain colors, rhythms, sentences, poems, curves, pictures, etc., which "belong together." In this connection it is of little interest that there was such a remarkable consistency in the responses of subjects with different habits and background; what is remarkable is that it should be possible at all to find, for instance, certain melodies and certain lines which "belong together" or are "similar." Incidentally, I did not ask the subjects to explain why they considered the stimuli as similar. Since then the problems considered here have been dealt with in a number of experimental and theoretical investigations (cf. for instance Arnheim, 1928; Köhler, 1929; Krauss, 1930; Werner, 1926; Wolff, 1929). It should be recalled also that the "color impression of vowels" was one of the problems which attracted the attention of Fechner (1897).

It is clear from a number of observations and experiments recently reported that there are stimulus properties which are very definite in the sense that they determine, for instance, our *reactions* to, and our *understanding* of, other persons but which are very indefinite in the sense that they do not seem to be "objectively" measurable. If we find that different stimuli elicit the same response because of being red it appears that in this case the similarity rests upon an aspect which is objectively measurable; if a person entering my laboratory, a sample of handwriting, and a voice coming from a phonograph elicit the same response because of being "aggressive" or "energetic" it appears that the similarity between the stimuli rests upon a property which is not objectively measurable. It may happen that in experiments in which the subjects have been asked to determine which one of a number of individuals represented by photographs has written, for example, a certain word or sentence, some subjects do not assign the handwriting which is lying before them to the "right" person. It cannot be emphasized too much that in this connection it is of no importance at all whether or not "errors" are made; what is of real importance in understanding human behavior is the fact that there are properties which make it at all possible to find a similarity between a picture and a handwriting.

It is, of course, nonsensical to say on the one hand that what counts in determining our response to a number of "red" stimuli is an "objective" property and to say on the other hand that what counts in determining our response to the stimuli we have termed "aggressive" or "energetic" are "subjective impressions." Both responses, to be sure, are "subjective" in the sense that they are responses of a particular organism under particular conditions. The fact that "redness" can be objectively measured, that is, identified by radiometric, photometric, and other methods does not permit any conclusion as to whether a particular organism is capable of being affected by "color"; the fact that "aggressiveness" cannot be objectively measured in such a way does not permit us to conclude that properties of such kind are not effective in influencing the organism. Indeed, there is no doubt that our behavior is often strikingly influenced by such properties. One may react to the fact that the face of a person is "sad" just as readily or more readily than to the fact that his nose is "red." It is possible to determine the "redness" of the nose by recourse to physical measurements (in fact, values of the reflection of light of various wave lengths from the human skin have been obtained in a number of recent studies) although it is not possible to produce an instrument for measuring the "sadness" of the face. Yet whether or not an object, for instance, to the right of me or opposite me, is "sad," "ugly," "attractive," "repulsive," "restless," etc., may radically influence the course of my behavior.

It is clear that in a sense it is just as impossible to measure "redness" as it is impossible to measure "sadness," "attractiveness," etc. All that we can do by way of "measuring" red is to determine the effect of certain forms of radiation on a bolometer or a photoelectric cell or some other physical instrument. And vice versa, it is just as possible to "measure" sadness, restlessness, and the like as it is possible to meaure red since we are able to identify the physical data producing such effects. There is nothing surprising in the fact that in the case of reactions to "red" objects we find one set of physical data and in the case of reactions to "attractive" objects we find another set or other sets of physical data. It is off the point to remark that in general the appearance of "redness" is always linked up with the same physical data whereas "attractiveness" may be produced by utterly different sets of physical data. It is also beside the point to consider that the objective conditions which are linked up with "attractiveness" today may be linked up with "ugliness" tomorrow whereas such variability does not exist in the case of "redness." We should not confuse "objective" properties with the effects produced by them and we should sharply distinguish constancy and variability in the objective conditions from constancy and variability in the effects. What is of real significance to the student of behavior is not so much the fact that such effects as "blueness," "loudness," "aggressiveness," "ugliness," "restlessness," etc., are produced, as is the possibility of demonstrating experimentally that "blueness," "restlessness," "ugliness," etc., are reacted to as the properties of *objects* in perceived space.

Another point is to be considered in this connection. Phenomenal properties may be very effective in influencing my behavior; yet scientifically they do not exist and cannot exist, in the sense that the "red" I am experiencing can be shown to be the "same" phenomenal red that someone else is experiencing and that the "restlessness" I see can be shown to be the "same" restlessness someone else finds in his phenomenal world. All that matters scientifically is that there is nothing in the observable reactions of the particular organism which is incompatible with the hypothesis that the organism in question is reacting to something which, in my experience, appears phenomenally as "red," "attractive," "aggressive," etc. It is of little interest if we find somebody able to determine "introspectively"—or rather "extrospectively"—that his actions are definitely determined by the phenomenal properties of objects; it is of far-reaching importance, however, if we approach the study of behavior by hypothetically assuming the efficacy of certain phenomenal properties. There is just as little sense in inquiring into the exact phenomenal *experiences* of a human as in inquiring into the phenomenal experiences of a bee or a dog. The problems involved here do not permit of a solution. There is some sense, however, in studying the effects of various forms of radiation on humans or insects. At the same time there is no doubt that without the appearance of light or color in our phenomenal world no attempts would have been made to determine the "photosensory" responses of insects. The fact that we start a certain line of inquiry by assuming the efficacy of certain phenomenal properties does not mean that we should ever be interested in attempting a reconstruction of the way phenomenal objects are *experienced*.

The starting point for the above discussion, it will be recalled, was the fact that heterogeneous stimulus constellations frequently elicit the same characteristic response. At this point it should be emphasized that in the present study we have been primarily interested in determining *how great* —and have been interested only slightly in determining *how small*—the differences may be without affecting the consistency of a given response. In other words, *we have been concerned more with finding stimulus situations which are still "identifiable" than with finding stimulus situations which are still discriminable.* Of course, the fact that an animal is not affected by certain differences does not mean that it is incapable of being affected by these differences, and vice versa, the fact that an animal reacts differentially to certain stimuli does not prove that it is incapable of "identifying" these stimuli. The fact that under certain conditions monkeys as well as insects are not affected by differences in the shape of luminous stimuli loses nothing of its importance if it is found that under different conditions monkeys are able to distinguish stimuli differing in shape whereas insects are not.

The significance of what has been said above will be more readily grasped if we assume, for example, that the properties in terms of which different situations are "identifiable" are spatial characteristics such as "to the right of," "nearer," etc., or temporal characteristics such as manifest themselves in "rhythms," "changes," and the like. It is obvious that the most diverse sensory objects may be "alike" or "similar" in that they are perceived as "to the right of" or "nearer" than something else. The "same" temporal property, for instance, "sudden change," may be exhibited by "visual" and "auditory" stimuli. But why should properties such as are referred to by the words "smoothness," "sadness," etc., be different from properties such as "greater distance," "change," etc? *In all these instances we are dealing with characteristics which permit of "identifying" heterogeneous situations.* That a melody or face is "sad" may be as effective in imparting certain directions to my behavior as the fact that the sounds come "from the right" or the face is "nearer" than a given object. The student of behavior must take into account recent developments in *general* sensory physiology: it has been recognized that by erecting unsurmountable barriers between the different "senses" certain facts are left out of the picture.[1] Consequently the problem of "suprasensory" properties has attracted widespread attention.

Not to complicate matters we have confined our discussion to considering the relation between the organism and the environmental stimulus situation; that is, we have been primarily concerned with the relation between the organism and what has been called the "outer field" (Lewin, 1926). The fact that in the "outer field" there are objects which have the properties of "redness," "hardness," "sadness," "restlessness," etc., and the fact that such properties become effective in influencing behavior does not necessarily mean that the tendency of the organism to react in terms of such properties is non-existent in the *absence* of external stimulation.

Just why, in most of our experiments, we have studied reactions to *sensory* stimuli will not be discussed here at any length. The "sensory" world is of interest not only to the student of sensory physiology and biophysics. There are such sensory objects as dollar bills and pistols. To say that "hexagons" and "squares" are "meaningless" geometric forms whereas "pistols" are "meaningful" objects does not solve any problems. A monkey may react to a "hexagon" because it "means" the possibility of getting food; a human may react to a "pistol" because it "means" the attempt to get food from him. A monkey may refuse to react to a box the front side of which shows an intermittently appearing light because of the fact that "intermittence" means "no food"; a human may quickly react and pull a pistol when noticing that the face of a certain person is "restless" or, to adopt Köhler's expression, "flickery" because being "flickery" or "restless" means "danger." What is of interest to us is that among the properties affecting our behavior there is, for example, such a property as "flickery" or "restless." Of course, one may be interested in the different "meanings" certain properties have, that is, in the fact that they are differently reacted to under different conditions. But this does not mean that there are ever "meaningless" objects. The fact that the "redness" of an object is reacted to tells us something about the reaction systems of the organism in question or, more specifically, about its "visual analyzers," to use Pavlov's term; the fact that the very same object is reacted to as "dangerous" tells us also something about the modes of reaction in this organism. Of course, we may be interested in how certain modes of reaction came about. We may wish to find out whether a given individual reacts to a certain object as "dangerous" because of his being "instinctively" afraid of snakes or because of some "learning" that took place. But it should be realized that the problem of whether or not an organism is capable of certain modes of reaction is of an entirely different nature than the problem of the genesis

[1] In his "Introduction to the Physiology of the Senses" von Weizsaecker (1926) makes the statement that from a certain point of view there are not different senses, there is only one sense, that is, a *Sinnlichkeit*.

of these reaction tendencies. An animal or a human may react in many different ways to the same object and in the same way to a large number of different objects, yet basically only one mechanism may be involved. To us it seems that the genesis of certain forms of behavior cannot be profitably studied without first learning something about the mechanisms involved. To be sure, we may not be forever satisfied with simply knowing that an animal, in reacting to its environment, is able to fall back on certain mechanisms; we may want to know whether it has always been able to throw these mechanisms into gear; we may want to know something about the ease or quickness with which it falls back on certain modes of response. But for the time being, it should be insisted upon, we must seek clarity as to what it is which may or may not be effective in determining behavior.

That under certain conditions certain "mechanisms" are operative in the behavior of monkeys does not prove that the monkey is an automaton which, under the stress of different stimulus constellations, simply throws different response mechanisms into play. Experimentally we can do nothing but show types of response to be dependent on certain properties of the stimulus situation. But it is clear that the response mechanisms do not exist *because* of certain conditions in the "outer field" although the only way of demonstrating the existence of such mechanisms is to observe reactions to different conditions in the "outer field." We may infer the character of a response mechanism from the differential effect of certain stimuli; we may infer the kind of stimuli an animal is confronted with from our knowledge of certain response mechanisms. But to say that one aspect "determines" the other is not justifiable or, if justifiable, it is so only in certain attempts to present intelligently the results of an experimental analysis.

The point may be raised that many of the stimulus situations introduced in our experiments are "artificial" or "unnatural" and that consequently no insight can be gained into the mechanisms operative in behavior. There is no doubt that the purpose of our experiments has not been to "duplicate" events outside the laboratory. The question is not whether the arrangements made by the experimenter are "artificial"; the only question is whether all the variables and the right variables involved in a certain event have been taken into consideration in setting up the experiment. An experimental situation is always "artificial," the more artificial the better. In fact, the degree of artificiality is probably proportionate to the number of variables we are able to identify or to measure.

To sum up: in the present study we have been concerned only with what we consider to be the first step toward determining "mechanisms" which are truly "fundamental" in behavior. We have been interested in those properties which make heterogeneous stimulus constellations "equi-valent" or "identifiable" and which set off the "equivalent stimuli" from others, here referred to as "non-equivalent" stimuli. On the *stimulus* side we have been interested, not in sensory stimuli in general, but only in the properties of stimuli in the "outer field," more specifically, in those stimulus properties which are significant in connection with the problem of what von Kries (1923) calls "objectification of sensations." On the *behavior* side we have been primarily concerned with certain facts of motor behavior. It should be distinctly understood, therefore, that in this investigation we do not deal with behavior in general but only with certain aspects of motor behavior in their relation to different properties in the sensory field.

## *REFERENCES*

Arnheim, R. Experimentell-psychologische Untersuchungen zum Ausdrucksproblem. *Psychologische Forschung,* 1928, *11,* 2-132.

Fechner, G. T. *Vorschule der Aesthetik.* (2nd ed). Leipzig: Breitkopff & Hartel, 1897.

Kohler, W. *Gestalt psychology.* New York: Liveright, 1929.

Krauss, R. Über graphischen Ausdruck. *Zeitschrift für angewandte Psychologie,* 1930, *48,* VI & 141.

Kries, J. von. *Allgemeine Sinnesphysiologie.* Leipzig: Vogel, 1923.

Lewin, K. *Vorsatz, Wille und Bedürfnis.* Berlin: Springer, 1926.

Tirala, L. G. Die Form als Reiz. *Zoologisches Jahrbuch: Abteilung für allgemeine Zoologie und Physiologie der Tiere,* 1923, 39, 395.

Weizsaecker, V., Freiherr von. Einleitung zur Physiologie der Sinne. *Handbuch der normalen und pathologischen Physiologie,* 1926, *11,* 1-67.

Werner, H. *Einführung in die Entwicklungspsychologie.* Leipzig: Barth, 1926.

Wolff, W. Gestaltidentität in der Charakterologie. *Psychologie und Medizin,* 1929, *4,* 32.

*The next paper, by K. S. Lashley, perhaps the outstanding neuropsychologist of the first half of this century, poses sharply the first major problem we have to face specifically: that is to say, the problem of explaining abstraction of relevant characteristics from variable stimulus patterns, of reconciling the facts of stimulus generalization and equivalence with the fact that a particular pattern must stimulate a particular set of receptors. If the recognition of the pattern is to be independent of the particular set of receptors stimulated on a given occasion, then surely there must be some general property of the nervous system which will account for that fact? Lashley's posing of the right questions turned out to be more important for the progress of scientific psychology than the answers he proposed to those questions. Indeed, he was fully aware of the inadequacy of his own solutions to the problems. This state of affairs should not surprise us; extremely few questions in psychology (or any other science) are definitely settled within a single generation. The people who make progress possible are the ones who pose the right questions, and start the move in search of adequate solutions.*

# The Problem of Cerebral Organization in Vision

K. S. LASHLEY

With the development of the cerebral cortex of mammals, many activities which are mediated by midbrain and thalamic structures in submammalian species are taken over, in part or wholly, by the new cerebral structures. After removal of the cerebral cortex or of the limited striate areas of the occipital lobes the capacity for visual responses is enormously reduced. In primitive mammals there remain only the pupillary and optokinetic reflexes, discrimination of intensities of light, and possibly some very crude remnants of detail vision, mediated by the tectum or pretectile region (Tsang, 1937; Marquis, 1934; Smith, 1933). The anthropoid apes have lost even such slight capacities for independent activity of the thalamus and midbrain as persists in lower mammals. The visual cortex of the primate brain is essential for any reaction to the spatial properties of a visual stimulus. Thus practically the entire repertoire of visual functions of mammals is dependent upon the activity of the occipital cortex.

Study of the integrative functions of the visual cortex plunges the investigator at once into definitely psychological problems. The adequate stimulus for an optic reflex can usually be described as a simple change in intensity of light, but the characteristic cerebral responses are based upon the distribution of intensities of light within the visual field. An analysis of the effective stimulus for such reactions regularly reveals a selective organization or abstraction of effective elements and a certain degree of generalization, even in the most primitive mammals. Thus for the rat, as for man, visual impressions consist of organized objects, seen against a less coherent background. Discriminative reactions, when analyzed, are found to be based upon certain generalized features of the stimulus. Analysis of the properties of stimuli which determine reaction shows that in every case there is functional equivalence between a rather wide range of

Reprinted from *Visual Mechanisms: Biological Symposia*, 1942.

objects which have in common only certain general or relational characters which cannot be reduced to terms of stimulation of identical nervous elements (Lashley, 1938a, 1938b). Such perceptual generalization is typical of every differential response and may be traced by graduated steps, without change in fundamental principle, from the discriminative reactions of the rodent to the human insight which leads to important scientific generalizations.

The questions posed by such activities must be faced by the student of cerebral physiology. It has been customary to say that psychological processes of this sort are so complex that they defy immediate physiological analysis, and to hold to the faith that continued study of elementary nervous activities will eventually lead to an understanding of the complexities of organization. Generalization, insight, and reasoning have been regarded as aggregates of more elementary processes, built up by a combination of the activities of sensory fields brought about by transcortical association or by the activities of higher coördinating centers.

In contrast to such a view of intellectual functions as composites of simpler neurological processes, there is some reason for believing that generalization is one of the primitive, basic functions of organized nervous tissue. For example, the transposition of reactions along a stimulus dimension has been found in all organisms which are capable of differential response. That is, when an animal is trained to choose the larger or brighter of two objects and is then confronted with a still larger or brighter he chooses on the basis of relative size or brightness. Such generalizations, transpositional responses, are universal, from the insects to primates. They persist in the rat after total destruction of the striate cortex (Hebb, 1938) and thus seem to be as primitive as is discrimination.

In fact, the gross structural evolution of the nervous system may be largely disregarded when considered in relation to problems of sensory perception. The laws governing the organization of elements into coherent units of figure and ground, the determination of similarities for visual form, the whole organization of the visual field is fundamentally the same for the bird, the rodent, and man and it is very probable that the same general principles will be found to apply to insects and cephalopods, when these have been adequately studied. In spite of the enormous differences in structural arrangement of the visual systems of different animal classes, the functional activity seems essentially the same.

Visual tests for use with animals may be constructed to present a series of perceptual or logical relations of graded difficulty, after the manner of Thurstone's "figure classification test" (Thurstone, 1938). The most difficult task of this character which it has been possible to teach a normal rat is that which I have called the "conditional reaction," in which a positive or negative reaction to the same stimulus is required, according to the character of the background upon which it is displayed. Destruction of non-visual areas of the cortex or incisions along the margins of the striate areas, separating them from adjacent parts of the cortex, do not interfere with the establishment of this reaction. No part of the cerebral hemisphere except the visual area is essential for solution of any problem of this type which a normal animal can solve. In fact, if enough striate cortex remains to permit of any detail vision, that part seems able to mediate the most difficult perceptual generalization (Lashley, 1942). Transcortical association or control by higher intellectual centers seems to be ruled out by such experiments, which point to the conclusion that the receptive areas of the cortex are themselves capable of processes of generalization not fundamentally different from "higher" intellectual activities.

Such facts as these indicate that the explanation of perceptual generalization is to be sought in the primitive organization of nervous tissue, rather than in any elaborate construction of transcortical associative connections or of higher coordinating centers. Every discriminative reaction involves a process which is basic for all generalization and intellectual functions; all imply a common neurological problem. This may be illustrated by equivalence of reactions in the so-called transposition experiment. The principle involved is that the reaction is determined by relations subsisting within the stimulus complex and not by association of a reaction with any definite group of receptor cells.

The same principle is inherent in the recognition of every visual object. Visual fixation can be held accurately for only a moment, yet, in spite of changes in direction of gaze, an object remains the same object. An indefinite number of combinations of retinal cells and afferent paths are equivalent in perception and in the reactions which they produce. This is the most elementary problem of cerebral function and I have come to doubt that any progress will be made toward a genuine understanding of nervous integration until the problem of equivalent nervous connections, or as it is more generally termed, of stimulus equivalence, is solved. Therefore, rather than review the disconnected and somewhat unintelligible details of experimental studies on the visual cortex, I propose now to survey the possibilities of an explanation of stimulus equivalence in terms of present knowledge of the nervous system and with special reference to detail vision.

Neurologically, the problem is clear enough. The first experience of a stimulus excites a certain number of neurons in a definite pattern (Fig. 1, *bc–f*). An associated reaction (*y*) is formed as a result of this stimulation. Thereafter, the excitation of any similar pattern of neurons (*ce–k*) will elicit the associated reaction. The later stimulation need not, and practically never does, involve the original combination of sensory cells. It preserves only certain proportions or relations among the elements of the stimulus pattern.

It must be assumed that the first stimulation leaves some trace in the

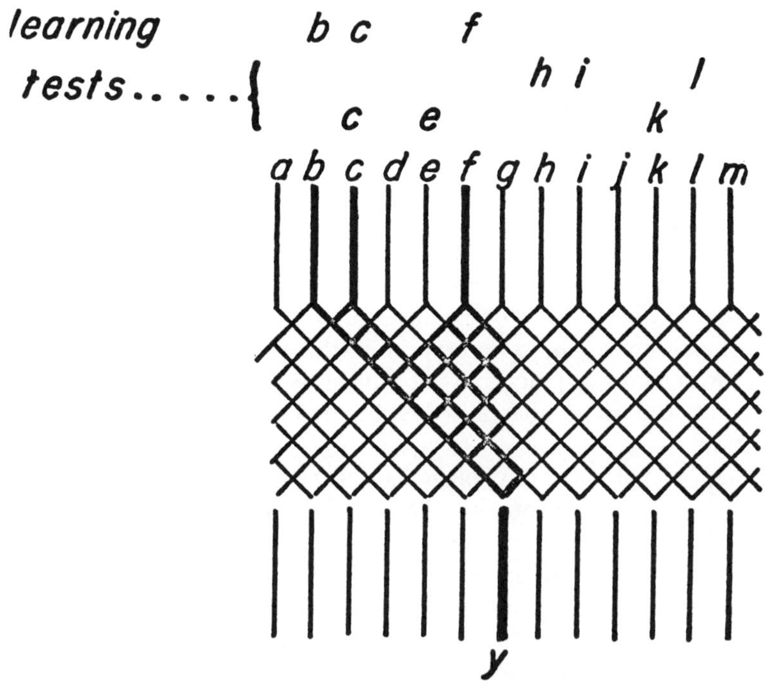


Fig. 1. Diagram to illustrate the problem of stimulus equivalence. An association is formed with *y* by stimulation of receptor cells *bc–f*. Thereafter any similar pattern of receptors (*ce–k*) will excite reaction *y*. A fixed trace, as indicated by the heavy lines, fails to account for such equivalence.

nervous system which determines the subsequent reactions. The difficulty for neurological theory arises when an attempt is made to localize this trace. It cannot be restricted to the neurons originally excited or to their immediate connections, for they need not be reactivated in order to elicit the reaction again. It cannot be in any other restricted group of cells, for after a single experience, any part of the macular field can mediate the reaction. The memory trace somehow becomes a property of the whole system. This inference from the nature of stimulation is borne out by experimental and clinical studies which have uniformly failed to localize specific memories.

Here is the dilemma. Nerve impulses are transmitted over definite, restricted paths in the sensory and motor nerves, and in the central nervous system from cell to cell through definite intercellular connections. Yet all behavior seems to be determined by masses of excitation, by the form or relations or proportions of excitation within general fields of activity, without regard to particular nerve cells. It is the pattern and not the element that counts. What sort of nervous organization might be capable of responding to a pattern of excitation without limited, specialized paths of conduction? The problem is almost universal in the activities of the nervous system and some hypothesis is needed to direct further research.

## *THEORIES OF STIMULUS EQUIVALENCE*

The possibility of any physiological explanation of stimulus equivalence has been denied by vitalists like Driesch and McDougall. An especially detailed analysis of the problem and criticism of physiological theories of association has been given by Becher (1911). The vitalistic approach has been valuable in emphasizing aspects of the problem which are ignored in the formulation of practically all biological theories of memory, but it should not lead us to abandon the search for the neurological basis of association.

Few students of nerve physiology have attempted to deal with the problem of stimulus equivalence in relation to memory but some half dozen different theories have been proposed to account for generalization of the stimulus. None of these has been developed in any detail. They appear rather as suggestions interpolated in discussion of other matters or merely by implication in general theories of nervous organization, so that I may be doing some injustice to their authors in elaborating such statements to fit these particular problems. However, the possibilities suggested must be considered.

Pavlov (1927) attempted an explanation of generalization based upon his theory of nervous irradiation. Briefly, he assumed that the effects of stimulation spread through the cortex from the point of primary excitation, so that adjacent points, as well as the primary one, become associated with the conditioned reaction. Fig. 2 illustrates the theory as applied to the discrimination of two objects of different size. A field of positive association is formed around the excited field of the larger, and of negative association around that of the smaller. New objects of different size would elicit positive or negative reactions according to the relative areas of the two association fields which they excite. Obviously, however, the theory of irradiation completely fails to account for constancy of figure with changes in visual fixation and for transfer to similar figures differing in size, since simple irradiation generalizes the figure only for one retinal position. Some of Pavlov's followers have modified his theory by omitting its assumptions concerning the spatial spread of excitation and have assumed instead that irradiation is along dimensions of similarity (Spence, 1937; Hull, 1939); the conditioned reaction spreads to similar objects. This, of course, simply begs the question of the nature of the generalizing process, since it assumes that generalization is a function of similarity whereas similarity is an unexplained result of generalization.

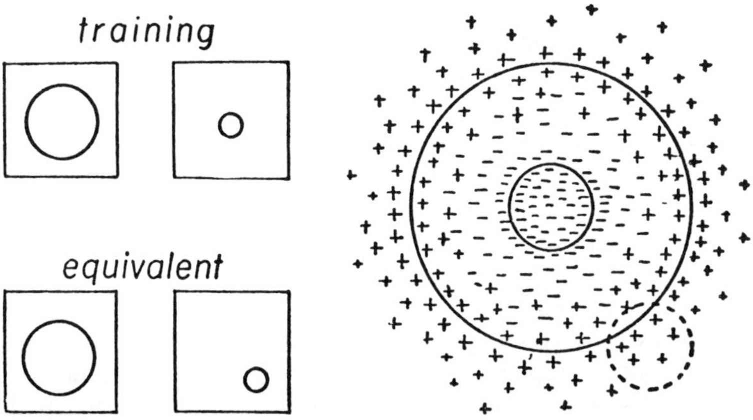


Fig. 2. Diagram to illustrate the neurological implications of Pavlov's theory of generalization. Differential training with the large circle as a positive stimulus is assumed to establish a cortical field of positive association for the larger, of negative for the smaller. Irradiation of the effects of stimulus constitutes generalization. Obviously any change in the point of fixation would render the mechanism inoperative.

A second suggestion has been derived by analogy with the selective switches of an automatic telephone system. The successive levels of nervous structure, constituting a series of relay stations between sense organ and muscle, seem adapted for some such action of selective switching. The idea has not been elaborated. I myself have not been able to work out a model on this principle without assuming definitely localized memory traces which are contradicted by experimental facts; or assuming an innate exact reduplication of intercellular connections such as is precluded by the irregularities of nervous growth.

The possibility of chemical sensitization as a basis for memory has given rise to some speculations but, again, has not been elaborated. As applied to the problem of stimulus equivalence it would seem to require the assumption that each pattern of excitation gives rise to a specific chemical compound to which the final common path is sensitized; that a combination of excitations in the form of a triangle produces the same compound, no matter where it occurs; and that the degree of similarity of the compounds produced (proteins or what not) varies with the degree of similarity of the patterns of stimulation. Such results of stimulation seem impossible in the light of what is known concerning the chemistry of the nerve impulse.

Much of the recent experimental work on sensory equivalence and the organization of percepts has been carried out by members of the Gestalt school and has led to the formulation of the so-called field or vector theories. These assume that the pattern of sensory excitation in the cortex gives rise to a field of force, perhaps electrochemical in nature, for which generally the perimeter of the figure forms a boundary separating areas of different potentials (Köhler, 1940). The behavior of elements in perception is interpreted in terms of the interplay of forces in a simple physical medium. The interrelations of figures in perception, the dominance of figure over background and the phenomena of illusions and apparent movement may be somewhat clarified by the theory. I suspect, however, that the success of field theory is more apparent than real. Its application to specific problems frequently involves specific, *ad hoc* assumptions, and its explanations turn out to be only elaborate tautologies.

No attempt has been made to deal with stimulus equivalence in terms of field theory. The assumption is implied that similar force-fields give rise to similar conscious experience and the theory has not been carried beyond this point. It seems still to be one of psycho-physical interaction. Interpreted in neurological terms it is subject to the same criticism as was applied to Pavlov's conception of irradiation, since it assumes a brain field corresponding in its spatial characteristics to those of the sensory surface, with forces spreading according to the pattern of sensory excitation.

Some years ago I suggested that differential excitation might give rise to electrochemical gradients within the medium surrounding the neurons and that the latter might be so modified as to respond to the direction of the gradient (Lashley, 1929), thus making reaction dependent upon relative intensity of activity in different regions rather than upon specific nervous connections. It is doubtful, however, whether energies produced within such gradient fields, if they exist, are sufficient to modify the activity of the neurons.[1] Such gradient fields would necessarily be of considerable area, corresponding in dimensions to the striate cortex and in such a field the fall in potential across the dimensions of a single cell would be exceedingly small. It is also impossible to deal with complicated figures in terms of such a simple notion of gradients.

None of these proposed explanations is then adequate in its present form to account for stimulus equivalence, nor does any one of them suggest a mechanism which seems capable of development to meet the requirements of the problem.

## *CHARACTERISTICS OF CEREBRAL ACTIVITY*

In seeking a more satisfactory hypothesis certain general considerations must be given weight.

[1] Gerard (1941) has shown that nervous activity in one region of the brain may start waves of potential change which traverse the cortex and excite nervous activity in other regions without transmission of impulses through intervening cells. The significance of these phenomena for integrated activity is not yet clear, but it is difficult to conceive that such potential differences can be characteristically different for different complicated visual patterns.

1. Keith Lucas has written: " . . . we should inquire first with all care whether the elementary phenomena of conduction, as they are to be seen in the simple motor nerve and muscle, can give a satisfactory basis for the understanding of central phenomena; if they cannot, and in that case only, shall we be forced to postulate some new process peculiar to the central nervous system." The statement of Lucas is a statement of the principle of parsimony, but direct studies of action currents within the brain have only confirmed the view that the transmission of nervous impulses from cell to cell forms the basis of all integration. Any hypothesis concerning the mechanism of generalization must start from the established facts of nerve conduction and must weave them into its texture.

2. The number of nervous elements activated by any stimulus must be estimated in millions or hundreds of millions. The receptive layer of the visual cortex, in an animal even so primitive as the rat, contains half a million cells, all of which are subject to continuous excitation from the retina, and this half million serves only to initiate the chain of cerebral activities. In any such system the contribution of a single nerve cell can have little influence upon the whole. Behavior is essentially the statistical outcome of nervous activity. The memory traces upon which stimulus equivalence is based must involve the modification of large numbers of neurons.

3. With the best techniques available, students of the histology of the visual cortex have failed to demonstrate long transcortical connections between the striate areas and other architectonic fields, except the peristriate, nor are there long connections within the striate area itself (Clark, 1941). It is probable therefore that the integrative functions of the visual cortex are carried out by transmission over short internuncial fibers within the cortex.

4. The exact topographic projection of the retina and of the cutaneous surface upon the striate areas and the sensory cortex respectively has led to what may be an oversimplification in conceptions of the spatial relations of nervous activity underlying perception. Pavlov assumed an irradiation of excitation over a surface in the brain corresponding in its dimensions to the surface of the skin. Field theories, as developed by psychologists, postulate forces acting according to the geometry of the retina or of the objects in the visual field. Actually nothing is known of the functional significance of topographic projection of sensory surfaces on the cortex. The assumption that accurate projection of the cutaneous surface and the retina is important in providing a spatial reproduction of the sensory surfaces at an integrating level is rendered questionable by the fact that the anterior thalamic nuclei have an equally precise cortical projection for which no functional correlate is apparent (Lashley, 1941). Interconnections within the retina and the lateral geniculate nuclei may modify the sensory pattern profoundly before it reaches the cortex and within different cortical layers

the effective pattern of organization may be reconstituted. There is no reason to believe that the effective integrative forces of the cortex act within a field which is a geometrical reproduction of the sensory surface. The geometry of nervous integration may be something quite different from the geometry of the stimulus.

5. The functional equivalence of different combinations of sensory fibers is paralleled by other natural phenomena: the diffusion gradient, the formation of crystals, and the regeneration of form by living tissue. In each of these examples any part can exhibit the same functions as any other part within limits with which the reader is familiar. The parts are, in the terminology of Driesch, equipotential. In these analogous cases the substratum, or active substance, is a system composed of reduplicated structural elements; the distribution of molecules in the diffusion gradient, the reduplicated molecular structure in the crystal, and the identical chromosomal mechanisms in different cells of the organism. That is, in all instances of which we have knowledge the equipotential system appears to be a system composed of a number of identical elements. It is to be expected, therefore, that the memory trace is likewise reduplicated throughout the system (striate area, or what not) concerned in stimulus equivalence.

These considerations, especially the intercellular transmission of nervous impulses, the involvement of many elements, and the reduplication of functional mechanism as the basis of equivalence of parts, suggest probable characteristics of the memory trace. By what possible mechanisms might a pattern of stimulation, exciting one restricted group of nerve cells, set up a reproduction of itself, reduplicated throughout the whole cerebral area into which those nerve cells discharge?

## *REDUPLICATION OF ASSOCIATIVE MECHANISMS*

The anatomic studies of Lorente de Nó (1934) have revealed a system of cross connections in the cortex which will permit the spread of excitation in any direction along the surface. Many adjacent neurons are capable of mutual excitation and the whole system is organized as a network, with loops of various lengths and complexity, capable of transmitting impulses from cell to cell across the cortex, or of reexciting initial points of stimulation by the action of return circuits having diverse characteristics.

From such a structural organization functional properties may be inferred with some confidence. Excitation started at any point must spread from that point throughout the system, since extinction (through building up of activity in reverberatory circuits) will occur only after the passage of the initial impulse. If the system is uniform throughout, a series of radiating waves should be produced, since the first wave of excitation will be followed by a wave of extinction, with excitation following again, either from successive volleys arriving over sensory pathways or by reexcitation at the retreating margin of the zone of extinction. The timing of the waves should be uniform, since it is dependent upon the speed of conduction and the refractory periods of the elements of the system. With several or many points of excitation, interference patterns will be formed.[2]

Disregarding for the moment the effects of return circuits in order to get a simplified picture, the action should be somewhat analogous to the transmission of waves on the surface of a fluid medium. Interference of waves in such a system produces a pattern of crests and troughs which is characteristic for each spatial distribution of the sources of wave motion and which is reduplicated roughly over the entire surface. A somewhat similar patterning of excitations in the plane of the cortex is to be expected. Spatially distributed impulses reaching the cortex from the retina will not reproduce the retinal pattern of excitation in the cortex but will give rise to a different and characteristic pattern of standing waves, reduplicated throughout the extent of the functional area. An immediate objection is that the excitation of one part of the field may render that part refractory to impulses coming from other parts, and so block the formation of a uniform pattern. However, if the transcortical paths or reverberatory circuits are of random length, as they apparently are, not all in any region will be simultaneously in a refractory state and blocking will not occur.

The analogy with wave motion in a homogeneous liquid cannot be applied seriously to the cortical activity, since the cortical tissues have inherent characteristics as a transmitting mechanism quite different from those of a fluid. The analogy is presented only to give a conceptual picture of a reduplicated system which may serve as a starting point for a more adequate conception of the structure of the memory trace.

The cortex, built up as it is of millions of transmitting loops of various lengths and refractory periods, actually consists of an indefinite number of resonators. Each minute area may respond to any of a number of frequencies of excitation, establishing a resonance to that frequency and inhibiting momentarily the activity of other circuits of different characteristics. The effects of excitation at one point should spread through the cortex, activating successively circuits having the same characteristics as that initially excited. With the excitation of two or more points interference effects would change the pattern and establish dominant circuits having other characteristics than those elicitable from either point alone. Without more complete knowledge of the details of cortical structure and the characteristics of its reverberatory circuits than is now available, it is impossible

[2] The conception of interference patterns as the basis of integration has been suggested by Goldscheider (1906), Horton (1925), and others. These authors have not attempted to deal with the problem of stimulus equivalence and seem to have assigned the memory trace to a definite limited locus.

to construct any clear picture of cortical activity, but it is not improbable that for any pattern of stimulation a stable resonance pattern, not unlike the interference effects of simple wave motion, would be established.

The problem of formation of intercellular connections is perhaps simplified by consideration of the fact that visual stimuli generally take the form of figures, that is, grouped masses of excitation of which the boundaries are the effective attributes for behavior. Interference patterns arising from such figures may have a simpler structure than those produced by a number of isolated points of excitation. Thus a linear stimulus should produce parallel waves throughout the excited area; neurons lying in parallel rows will be simultaneously excited and a sort of polarization of the area produced. Under such conditions, the associative connections required for a generalization of "direction" in the visual field are quite simple. Simultaneously excited rows of neurons may acquire functional connections. It is perhaps significant that the reaction to the direction of lines is the visual association readily acquired by lower mammals.

It is futile at present to speculate concerning the interplay of more complicated patterns but certain of the simpler phenomena of visual perception can be predicted from such a theory of cerebral organization. For example, increase in frequency of excitation and increase in area of excitation produce similar changes in the interference pattern of spreading waves, corresponding to the fact that, under certain conditions, luminous intensity and surface area are equivalent for behavior. The filling in of interrupted outlines and the completion of simple geometrical figures follow also from the characteristics of interference patterns.

Except for hypnagogic and after-images, which constitute a unique problem, the visual memory image is lacking in detail. After brief exposure of a nonsense figure, such as an ink blot or pattern of intersecting lines, memory of it is likely to consist only of a vague impression of direction of lines, or a single detail of intersecting lines (Woodworth, 1915). Memorization of the entire figure requires that it be broken up and learned piecemeal. Its recall will then consist, not of a concurrent reproduction of the whole, but a serial reconstruction of one part after another. Such facts, together with the visual behavior of lower mammals, indicate that primitive visual memory is a matter of fixation of a direction or combination of few directions in visual space. In other words, the pattern or organization effective for behavior at any given moment is a relatively simple element in the total temporal pattern of excitation. This fact has significance for the next stage of integration. I shall make no attempt here to deal with the temporal pattern or serial ordering of activities. That is a problem for which no clue is as yet provided by neurological research. The evidence suggests, however, that, at the receptive level of the cortex, the stimulus is integrated into a relatively simple pattern of excitation in which the dominant feature may be a directional association of elements, a sort of polarization. The structural organization of the cortex is such that the formation of a reduplicated pattern after the analogy of a wave interference pattern is not impossible, and such a reduplication of the memory trace seems to be the only postulate by which we can account for the phenomena of stimulus equivalence.

## *TRANSMISSION OF PATTERNS TO THE MOTOR SYSTEM*

Such a theory of integration is still useless without some picture of the transition from the sensory pattern to the pattern of motor activity. What sort of connection from the sensory field to the neurons of the final motor path would permit of a constant reaction to the reduplicated patterns postulated in the theory? A reduplication of patterns throughout the sensory area, such as I have postulated, would permit the formation of similar associative connections within all parts of the area, since cells in definite spatial patterns would be simultaneously excited.[3] If efferent fibers from all parts of the sensory area play upon the final motor mechanism, equivalence of function of different parts of the sensory area would be provided. But such a mechanism of transmission is precluded by the plasticity and functional equivalence of motor reactions. Motor habits are no more rigidly restricted to a small number of specialized cellular elements than is sensory perception. The learned reaction is not a combination of just those movements which are exercised during the learning, but is an adaptive pattern, shifting from one to another group of muscles according to the demands of the moment. The learned reaction can be described only as a sequence of movements in relation to the axes of the body. Movement is determined by direction in relation to the body and not by the training of specific muscles. This fact is well illustrated by handwriting which retains its essential characteristics, even when produced by combinations of muscles which have not before been employed for such purposes. Fig. 3 shows the writing of two individuals, blindfolded, using right and left hands in various positions, as well as other muscle groups, unpracticed. In spite of clumsiness, the general features of the writing, individual differences in the forming of letters and the like, are characteristically maintained. The mechanics of writing is a sequence of movements in relation to bodily position, not a set pattern of special groups of muscles.

Usually the adaptive movements imply a still more general frame of reference; the coordinate system which constitutes the organism's orienta-

[3] Temporal contiguity is the only one of the "laws" of learning which approaches universality. Not all simultaneous activities of the nervous system become associated but apparently some temporal overlap is essential for association.

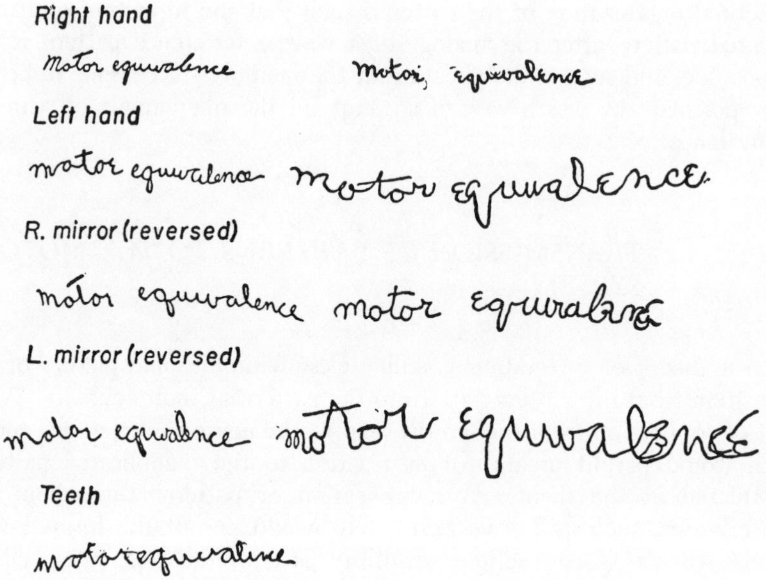


Fig. 3. Writing of two blindfolded subjects with practiced and unpracticed groups of muscles. Mirror writing has been reversed for comparison with normal script.

tion to its environment. When the rat learns the maze, he learns, not a stereotyped sequence of movements, but a series of distances and turns, which can be performed by unpracticed muscle groups, as when a cerebellar lesion forces him to roll through the maze. Maze performance is related to a system of coordinates still more plastic than the axes of the body. It is not unlike the achievement of the blindfolded chess player, who can rotate the board before his mind's eye, and play alternately from either side.

Not only is the equivalence of motor expressions a characteristic of behavior, but the motor control shows the same independence of limited conduction paths as does perception. The efferent path activating an adaptive pattern is no more restricted to specific fibers than is the recognition of a visual pattern dependent upon a single group of fibers in the optic nerve. In lower mammals double hemisection of the spinal cord does not preclude the performance of habitual manipulative acts and even in lower primates motor patterns survive the destruction of the pyramidal and other long spinal tracts (Brown, 1916).

The transition from the visual perceptual to the motor level thus appears to be, primitively, the translation of one system of space coordinates into another. Direction is dominant in visual memory and the reaction reduces to a sequence of directions of movement. Intervening between these is the system which constitutes spatial and postural orientation. Such a view of sensorimotor connections requires a revision of current conceptions of motor organization. The analyses of postural tonus made by Sherrington and by Magnus have shown that the tonic activity of each spinal motor center is influenced by almost every sensory stimulus to which the organism is subjected, including proprioceptive and cutaneous from all regions of the body, as well as vestibular and visual. The mechanism of this postural control is usually pictured in terms of specific connections from sense organ to muscle (Sherrington, 1911, p. 148). Such a conception implies the separate connection of every sensory cell with every motor center, although such interconnections have not been explicitly claimed. The effects of spinal lesions lead rather to the conclusion that the connections are more diffuse and it seems probable that the receptors pour their impulses into a common pool or network which acquires a more or less uniform polarization or dynamic pattern throughout and which in turn determines local reactions by the general characteristics of that organization. Cerebral influences may alter either the whole character of the pattern or produce local alterations through more direct paths. Local motor effects on activity of flexors and extensors may be exerted either through differential effects of the general interference pattern upon reciprocally connected motor centers or by more restricted interference in excitation of the many end buds on a single cell.

Obviously such a picture of nervous organization is almost as much oversimplified as were older diagrams of direct reflex arcs through the cortex. The dominance of one organization over others, as illustrated by the facts of attention, the mutual influences and distortions of perceptual forms which has been dealt with chiefly by field theories, and especially the temporal aspects of behavior apparent in the serial ordering of activities have not been touched upon.

The way seems open, however, for the extension of the same explanatory principles to such phenomena. A pattern of excitation in a cortical field may form a relatively stable and permanent foundation, modifying the effects of later excitation, as attention determines the selection of stimuli. That is, in cortical activity there must be postulated a persistent substratum of tonic innervation upon which are superimposed the fluctuating patterns resulting from current stimulation, in the same way that the innervation of voluntary movement is superimposed upon the spinal pattern of postural tonus. In the light of experimental evidence concerning the nature of nervous activity it seems most probable that the various patterns of integrated activity in successive levels of the nervous system have the form of tuned resonating circuits.

Such a speculative discussion is justified only by the prime importance of the problem of generalization and the inadequacy of current theories to deal with the problem. Bartley (1941) has recently contrasted the analytic approach which characterized studies of nervous transmission with the tendency to emphasize holistic concepts which is dominant in studies of perceptual organization, and has pointed out the need for some unifying principle which will bring these two opposed views together. The scheme of nervous organization which I have sketched makes no assumptions concerning elementary nervous activities beyond those established in studies of reflex conduction. It suggests a mechanism for action of the system as a whole which is also subject to analytic treatment in terms of nerve transmission. In this respect it is a substitute for field theory and, if of lesser immediate predictive value, is more consistent with elementary nerve physiology and is more open to experimental examination.

Details of the theory are of little immediate importance. But the principles of the establishment of interference patterns at successive levels in the nervous system, of the modification of these patterns by superimposed patterns from earlier stages in the series of levels, from retina to motor cells, and the reduplication of memory traces as a consequence of the properties of the interference pattern are, I believe, reasonable conclusions from the organization of behavior and the structure of the nervous system. The visual system is primarily concerned with spatial orientation and for it the transition from a sensory to motor pattern can be most adequately conceived as an interplay of polarized systems or of interweaving dynamic patterns in which the spatial properties of the visual stimulus are translated by integration at a series of levels into modifications of the general pattern of postural organization.

## *REFERENCES*

Bartley, S. H. *Vision*. New York: Van Nostrand, 1941, pp. xv & 350.

Becher, E. *Gehirn und Seele*. Heidelberg: Winter, 1911, pp. xiii & 405.

Brown, T. G. Studies in the physiology of the nervous system, XXVII. On the phenomenon of facilitation, 6. *Quarterly Journal of Experimental Physiology*, 1916, *10*, 103-143.

Clark, W. E. LeGros Observations on association fibre system of visual cortex and central representation of retina. *Journal of Anatomy*, 1941, *75*, 225-235.

Gerard, R. W. *Ohio Journal of Science*, 1941, *41*, 160-172.

Goldscheider, A. *Neurologisches Zentralblatt*, 1906, *25*, 146.

Hebb, D. O. The innate organization of visual activity III. Discrimination of brightness after removal of the striate cortex in the rat. *Journal of Comparative Psychology*, 1938, *25*, 427-437.

Horton, L. H. *Dissertation on the dream problem*. Philadelphia: Cartesian Research Society, 1925, pp. 115-169.

Hull, C. L. The problem of stimulus equivalence in behavior theory. *Psychological Review*, 1939, *46*, 9-30.

Köhler, W. *Dynamics in psychology*. New York: Liveright, 1940, pp. 1-158.

Lashley, K. S. *Brain mechanisms and intelligence*. Chicago: University of Chicago Press, 1929, pp. xiv & 186.

Lashley, K. S. Experimental analysis of instinctive behavior. *Psychological Review*, 1938, *45*, 445-471. (a)
Lashley, K. S. The mechanism of vision: XV. Preliminary studies of the rat's capacity for detail vision. *Journal of General Psychology*, 1938, *18*, 123-193. (b)
Lashley, K. S. Thalamo-cortical connections of the rat's brain. *Journal of Comparative Neurology*, 1941, *75*, 67-121.
Lashley, K. S. The mechanism of vision XVII. Autonomy of the visual cortex. *Journal of Genetic Psychology*, 1942, *60*, 197-221.
Lorente de Nó, R. Studies of the structure of the cerebral cortex II. *Journal für Psychologie und Neurologie*, 1934, *46*, 113-177.
Marquis, D. G. Effects of the removal of the visual cortex in mammals. *Association for Research on Nervous Diseases, Proceedings*, 1934, *13*, 558-592.
Pavlov, I. P. *Conditioned reflexes*. Oxford: Oxford University Press, 1927, pp. xv & 430.
Smith, K. U. Visual discrimination in the cat: VI. The relation between pattern vision and visual acuity and the optic projection centres of the nervous system. *Journal of Genetic Psychology*, 1933, *53*, 251-272.
Spence, K. W. The differential response in animals to stimuli varying within a single dimension. *Psychological Review*, 1937, *44*, 430-444.
Sherrington, C. S. *The integrative action of the nervous system*. New York: Scribner, 1906.
Thurstone, L. L. Primary Mental Abilities. *Psychometric Monographs*, 1938, No. 1, pp. viii & 121.
Tsang, Yü-Chüan. Visual sensitivity of rats deprived of visual cortex in infancy. *Journal of Comparative Psychology*, 1937, *24*, 225-262.
Woodworth, R. S. A revision of imageless thought. *Psychological Review*, 1915, *22*, 1-27.

*Lashley criticized the Gestalt school of perceptual psychologists and the attempts by its members to explain sensory equivalence and organization; in this paper he even went so far as to characterize its explanations as "only elaborate tautologies." Those are strong words, and we should inquire whether or not they are justified. What, in fact, was the Gestalt solution to the problem of stimulus equivalence? It is contained in the so-called theory of isomorphism, which has as a basic postulate the assertion that what is perceived (e.g., as a visual pattern) is equivalent to a particular pattern of cortical excitation, or brain state. Indeed, isomorphism means "having the same form," and the theory just asserts that the identity of form holds between the cortical pattern and the perceived pattern. Now the problem of stimulus equivalence is "solved" in this theory by saying that the equivalence of two perceived patterns is explained by the similarity, or equivalence, of the isomorphic cortical patterns for the two. But then it seems reasonable to ask how the two brain states are recognized as equivalent—and there is no satisfactory answer. We can scarcely explain their similarity by pointing to the "equivalence" of the two perceived patterns, for this is precisely what needs explaining! On the other hand, we do not want to say that there is a little man (homunculus) sitting in the brain inspecting the various cortical patterns: apart from anything else we should have to explain his recognition of "equivalent patterns" by another homunculus in his brain, and so on . . . in an infinite regress. So it seems that the Gestalt psychologists really did no more than to state that two brain states are equivalent if they are equivalent—a tautology, as Lashley rightly pointed out.*

*Unfortunately very much the same criticism can be aimed at Lashley's theory of interference patterns, since he was not able to specify by what operations two interference patterns could be recognized as similar (equivalent) or different. That is, he was not able to say: interference patterns are generated in this particular way, so that these patterns will be treated as equivalent, but those will not—in fact, the theory is too vaguely specified to be testable by experiment. It is only fair to add that Lashley was well aware of the shortcomings of his theory, and recognized that it did little more than re-pose the problem of stimulus equivalence in a form which is more plausible to the neurophysiologist than are the electrical fields of force postulated by some Gestalt psychologists (Lashley, 1951). Incidentally, Lashley was instrumental in showing that, even if the theory of isomorphism were correct in postulating field forces in the brain, the forces could not be electrical field forces on the surface of the brain cortex. Lashley, Chow, and Semmes (1951) showed that implanting gold pins in the visual cortex of monkeys or placing gold foil over the cortical surface, disrupted visual discriminations very little. This proves the point, because if the discriminations were mediated by electrical fields, they would have been severely distorted by the presence of the pins or foil (see also Sperry, Miner, and Myers, 1955).*

*The next selection manifests a different approach to the question of stimulus equivalence. Lashley argued, it will be recalled, that the equivalence (for perception and memory) of different parts of the cortex indicates that their patterns of activity must be reduplicated in some way. In this paper Pitts and McCulloch argue from a somewhat different point of view: they ask how a network of "neurons"[1] can compute an invariant output from a variable input. This question is held to be formally the same as the question of stimulus equivalence as we have come to understand it, since the invariant output can be considered as the analogue of a particular pattern in the input—say a square or a triangle. Lashley was attempting to reconcile constancy of pattern with change in location (in the brain) by reduplication: Pitts and McCulloch reconcile the two by demonstrating*

[1] These "neurons" or modules, are really artificial models of the real neurons of nerve tissue. They have some of the main characteristics of their real counterparts, and McCulloch and Pitts showed in an earlier publication how they can be put together to form computing networks.

the possibility of a constancy of computation. As such, their paper represents an important advance in the history of ideas about stimulus equivalence. The reader should be warned in advance that the writing style is sometimes exotic, not to say obscure.

# How We Know Universals: The Perception of Auditory and Visual Forms

W. PITTS AND W. S. MC CULLOCH

*Two neural mechanisms are described which exhibit recognition of forms. Both are independent of small perturbations at synapses of excitation, threshold, and synchrony, and are referred to particular appropriate regions of the nervous system, thus suggesting experimental verification. The first mechanism averages an apparition over a group, and in the treatment of this mechanism it is suggested that scansion plays a significant part. The second mechanism reduces an apparition to a standard selected from among its many legitimate presentations. The former mechanism is exemplified by the recognition of chords regardless of pitch and shapes regardless of size. The latter is exemplified here only in the reflexive mechanism translating apparitions to the fovea. Both are extensions to contemporaneous functions of the knowing of universals heretofore treated by the authors only with respect to sequence in time.*

To demonstrate existential consequences of known characters of neurons, any theoretically conceivable net embodying the possibility will serve. It is equally legitimate to have every net accompanied by anatomical directions as to where to record the action of its supposed components, for experiment will serve to eliminate those which do not fit the facts. But it is wise to construct even these nets so that their principal function is little perturbed by small perturbations in excitation, threshold, or detail of connection within the same neighborhood. Genes can only predetermine statistical order, and original chaos must reign over nets that learn, for learning builds new order according to a law of use.

Numerous nets, embodied in special nervous structures, serve to classify

Reprinted from *Bulletin of Mathematical Biophysics*, 1947. Part of the paper (pp. 137–146 of the original) has been deleted, since it deals with a problem which is not of primary concern in the present context.

information according to useful common characters. In vision they detect the equivalence of apparitions related by similarity and congruence, like those of a single physical thing seen from various places. In audition, they recognize timbre and chord, regardless of pitch. The equivalent apparitions in all cases share a common figure and define a group of transformations that take the equivalents into one another but preserve the figure invariant. So, for example, the group of translations removes a square appearing at one place to other places; but the figure of a square it leaves invariant. These figures are the *geometric objects* of Cartan and Weyl, the *Gestalten* of Wertheimer and Köhler. We seek general methods for designing nervous nets which recognize figures in such a way as to produce the same output for every input belonging to the figure. We endeavor particularly to find those which fit the histology and physiology of the actual structure.

The epicritical modalities map the continuous variables of sense into the neurons of a fine cortical mosaic that strikingly imitates a continuous manifold. The visual half-field is projected continuously to the *area striata*, and tones are projected by pitch along Heschl's gyrus. We can describe such a manifold, say $\mathcal{M}$, by a set of coordinates $(x_1, x_2, \cdots, x_n)$ constituting the point-vector $x$, and denote the distributions of excitation received in $M$ by the functions $\phi(x, t)$ having the value unity if there is a neuron at the point $x$ which has fired within one synaptic delay prior to the time $t$, and otherwise, the value zero. For simplicity, we shall measure time in mean synaptic delays, supposed equal, constant, and about a millisecond long. Indications of time will often not be given.

Let G be the group of transformations which carry the functions $\phi(x, t)$ describing apparitions into their equivalents of the same figure. The group G may always be taken finite, as is seen from the atomicity of the manifold; let it have N members. We shall distinguish four problems of ascending complexity:

1. The transformation $T$ of G can be generated by transformations $t$ of the underlying manifold $\mathcal{M}$, so that $T\phi(x) = \phi[t(x)]$; e.g., if G is the group of translations, then $T\phi(x) = \phi(x + a_T)$, where $a_T$ is a constant vector depending only upon $T$. If G is the group of dilatations, $T\phi(x) = \phi(a_T x)$, where $a_T$ is a positive real number depending only upon $T$. All such transformations are linear:

$$\begin{aligned} T[\alpha\phi(x) + \beta\psi(x)] &= \alpha\phi[t(x)] + \beta\psi[t(x)] \\ &= \alpha T\phi(x) + \beta T\psi(x). \end{aligned}$$

2. The transformations $T$ of G cannot be so generated, but are still linear and independent of the time $t$. An example is to take the gradient of $\phi(x)$, or to replace $\phi(x)$ by its average over a certain circle surrounding $x$.

3. The transformations $T$ of G are linear, but depend also upon the time. For example, they take a moving average over the preceding five synaptic

delays or take some difference as an approximation to the time-derivative of $\phi(x, t)$.

4. Not all $T$ of G are linear.

Our special nets are essays in problem 1. The simplest way to construct invariants of a given distribution $\phi(x, t)$ of excitation is to average over the group G. Let $f$ be an arbitrary functional which assigns a unique numerical value, in any way, to every distribution $\phi(x, t)$ of excitation in $\mathcal{M}$ over time. We form every transform $T\phi$ of $\phi(x, t)$, evaluate $f[T\phi]$, and average the result over G to derive

$$a = \frac{1}{N} \sum_{\substack{\text{all} \\ T \in G}} f[T\phi]. \tag{1}$$

If we had started with $S\phi$, $S$ of G, instead of $\phi$, we should have

$$\frac{1}{N} \sum_{T \in G} f[TS\phi] = \frac{1}{N} \sum_{\substack{\text{All } T \\ \text{such that} \\ TS^{-1} \in G}} f[T\,\phi] = a, \tag{2}$$

for $TS^{-1}$ is in the group when, and only when, $T$ is in the group; that is, the terms of the sum (1) are merely permuted.

To characterize completely the figure of $\phi(x, t)$ under G by invariants of this kind, we need a whole manifold $\Xi$ of such numbers $a$ for different functionals $f$, with as many dimensions in general as the original $\mathcal{M}$; if we describe $\Xi$ by coordinates $(\xi_1, \xi_2, \cdots, \xi_m) = \xi$, we may fulfill this requirement formally with a single $f$ which depends upon $\xi$ as a parameter as well as upon the distribution $\phi$ which is its argument, and write

$$\phi_{f,G}(\xi) = \frac{1}{N} \sum_{T \in G} f[T\phi\xi]. \tag{3}$$

If the nervous system needs less than complete information in order to recognize shapes, the manifold $\Xi$ may be much smaller than $\mathcal{M}$, have fewer dimensions, and indeed reduce to isolated points. The time $t$ may be one dimension of $\Xi$, as may some of the $x$, representing position in $\mathcal{M}$.

Suppose that G belongs to problems 1 or 2 and that the dimensions of $\Xi$ are all spatial; then the simplest nervous net to realize this formal process is obtained in the following way: Let the original manifold M be duplicated on N—1 sheets, a manifold $\mathcal{M}_T$ for each $T$ of G, and connected to M or its sensory afferents in such a way that whatever produces the distribution $\phi(x)$ on $\mathcal{M}$ produces the transformed distribution $T\phi(x)$ on $\mathcal{M}_T$. Thereupon, separately for each value of $\xi$ for each $\mathcal{M}_T$, the value of $f[T\phi\xi]$ is computed by a suitable net, and the results from all the $\mathcal{M}_T$'s are added by convergence on the neuron at the point $\xi$ of the mosaic $\Xi$. But to proceed entirely in this way usually requires too many associative neurons to be plausible. The manifolds $\mathcal{M}_T$ together possess the sum of the dimensions of $\mathcal{M}$ and the degrees of freedom of the group G. More important is the number of neurons and fibers necessary to compute the values of $f[T\phi, \xi]$, which depends, in principle, upon the entire distribution $T\phi$, and therefore requires a separate computer for every $\xi$ for every $T$ of G. This difficulty is most acute if $f$ be computed in a structure separated from the $\mathcal{M}_T$, since in that case all operations must be performed by relatively few long fibers. We can improve matters considerably by the following device: Let the manifolds $\mathcal{M}_T$ be connected as before, but raise their thresholds so that their specific afferents alone are no longer able to excite them; cause adjuvant fibers to ramify throughout each $\mathcal{M}_T$ so that when active they remedy the deficiency in summation and permit $\mathcal{M}_T$ to display $T\phi(x)$ as before. Let all the neurons with the same coordinate $x$ on the $N$ different $\mathcal{M}_T$'s send axons to the neuron at $x$ on another recipient sheet exactly like them, say $Q$—this $Q$ may perfectly well be one of the $\mathcal{M}_T$'s—and suppose any one of them can excite this neuron. If the adjuvant neurons are excited in a regular cycle so that every one of the sheets $\mathcal{M}_T$ in turn, and only one at a time, receives the increment of summation it requires for activity, then all of the transforms $T\phi$ of $\phi(x)$ will be displayed successively on $Q$. A single $f$ computer for each $\xi$, taking its input from $Q$ instead of from the $\mathcal{M}_T$'s, will now suffice to produce all the values of $f[T\phi, \xi]$ in turn as the "time-scanning" presents all the $T\phi$'s on $Q$ in the course of a cycle. These values of $f(T\phi, \xi)$ may be accumulated through a cycle at the final $\Xi$-neuron in any way.

This device illustrates a useful general principle which we may call the *exchangeability of time and space*. This states that any dimension or degree of freedom of a manifold or group can be exchanged freely with as much delay in the operation as corresponds to the number of distinct places along that dimension.

Let us consider the auditory mechanism which recognizes chord and timbre independent of pitch. This mechanism, or part of it, we shall suppose situated in Heschl's gyrus, a strip of cortex two to three centimeters long on the superior surface of the temporal lobe. This strip receives afferents from lower auditory mechanisms so that the position on the cortex corresponds to the pitch of tones, low tones exciting the outer and forward end, high tones the inner and posterior. Octaves span equal cortical distances, as on the keyboard of a piano. The afferents conveying this information from the medial geniculate slant upward through the cortex, branching into telodendria in the principal recipient layer IV, which consists of vertical columns of fifty or more neurons concerning the course of whose ramifying axons there is no certain knowledge except that their activity eventually excites columns of cells situated beneath the recipient layers. Their axons converge to a layer of small pyramids whose axons terminate

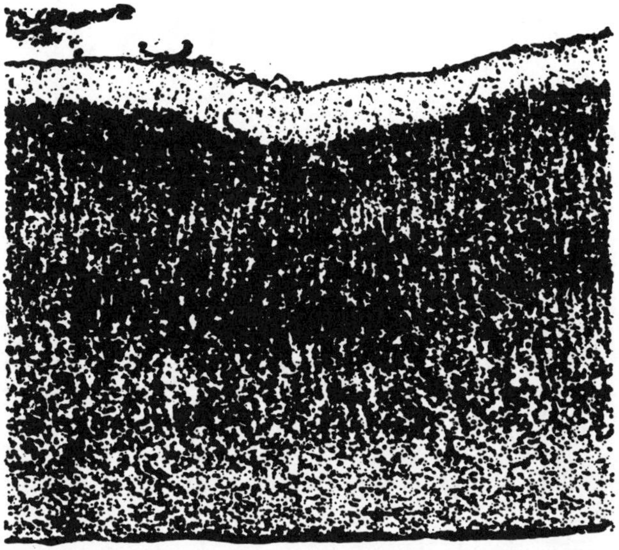

Fig. 1. Vertical section of the primary auditory cortex in the long axis of Heschl's gyrus, stained by Nissl's method which stains only cell bodies. Note that the columnar cortex, typical of primary receptive areas, shows two tiers of columns, the upper belonging to the receptive layer IV and the lower, lighter stained, to layer V.

principally in the secondary auditory cortex or adjacent parts of the temporal lobe. To the layers above and below the receptive layers also come "associative" fibers from elsewhere in the cortex, particularly from nearby. There is no good Golgi picture of the primary auditory cortex in monkeys, but unless it is unlike all the rest of the cortex, it also receives nonspecific afferents from the thalamus, which ascend to branch indiscriminately at every level. A picture of the primary auditory cortex stained by Nissl's method is given in Figure 1, and a schematic version in Figure 2.

The secondary auditory cortex has separate specific afferents and the same structure as the primary except for possessing some large pyramids known to send axons to distant places in the cortex such as the motor face and speech areas.

In this case, the fundamental manifold $\mathcal{M}$ is a one-dimensional strip, and $x$ is a single coordinate measuring position along it. The group G is the group of uniform translations which transform a distribution $\phi(x, t)$ of excitation along the strip into $T_a\phi = \phi(x + a, t)$. The group G is thus determined by adding the various constants to the coordinate $x$, and therefore belongs to problem 1. The set of manifolds $\mathcal{M}_T$ is a set of strips $\mathcal{M}_a$ that could be obtained by sliding the whole of $\mathcal{M}_a$ back and forth various distances along its length. The same effect is obtained by slanting the afferent fibers upward, as in Figure 2, and in the auditory cortex itself

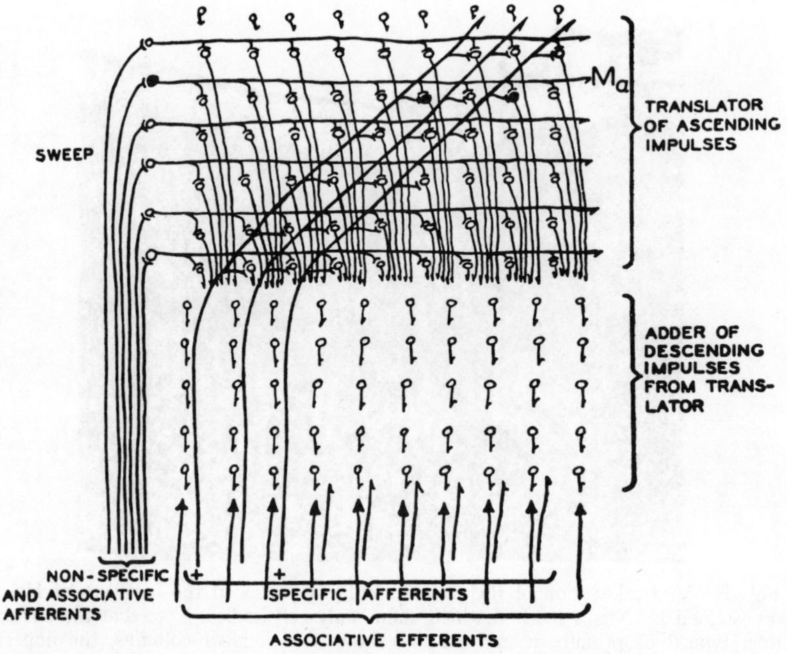


Fig. 2. Impulses of some chord enter slantwise along the specific afferents, marked by plusses, and ascend until they reach the level $M_a$ in the columns for the receptive layer activated at the moment by the nonspecific afferents. These provide summation adequate to permit the impulses to enter that level but no other. From there the impulses descend along columns to the depth. The level in the column, facilitated by the nonspecific afferents, moves repetitively up and down, so that the excitement delivered to the depths moves uniformly back and forth as if the sounds moved up and down together in pitch, preserving intervals. In the deep columns various combinations are made of the excitation and are averaged during a cycle of scansion to produce results depending only on the chord.

where the levels in the columnar receptive layer constitute the $\mathcal{M}_T$. These send axons to the deeper layer, a mass capable of reverberation and summation over time, that may well constitute the set of $f(T\phi, \xi)$ computers for the various $\xi$, or part of them.

To complete the parallel with our general model, we require adjuvant fibers to activate the various levels $\mathcal{M}_a$ successively. It is to the nonspecific afferents that modern physiology attributes the well-known rhythmic sweep of a sheet of negativity up and down through the cortex—the alpha-rhythm. If our model fits the facts, this alpha-rhythm performs a temporal "scanning" of the cortex which thereby gains, at the cost of time, the equivalent of another spatial dimension in its neural manifold.

According to Ramón y Cajal (1911), Lorente de Nó (1922), and J. L. O'Leary (1941), the specific visual afferents originate in the lateral geniculate body and travel upward through the calcarine cortex, to ramify horizontally for long distances in the stripe of Gennari. This is called the *granular layer* by Brodmann from Nissl stains, and is also called the *external stria of Baillarger*, from its myeloarchitecture. (Zunino, 1909). It is the fourth, or receptive, layer of Lorente de Nó. It may be divided into a superior part IVa, consisting of the larger star-cells and star-pyramids, and an inferior part IVb, consisting of somewhat smaller star-cells, arranged in columns, although the distinction of parts is not always evident (O'Leary, 1941, p. 141). The stripe of Gennari is the sole terminus of specific afferent fibers in the cat and higher mammals, although not in the rabbit. Its neurons send numerous axons horizontally and obliquely upward and downward within the layer; others ascend to the plexiform layer at the surface or descend to the subjacent fifth layer of efferent cells; and axons from the larger star-pyramids even enter the subjacent white matter.

The electrical records of J. L. O'Leary and G. H. Bishop (1941) indicate that the normal response of the striate cortex to an afferent volley is triphasic, commencing in layer IV, shown by a surface-positive potential. Next it rises to the surface, making it negative; then as the surface becomes positive, it descends first to the third layer to project to other cortical areas, and then reaches the fifth layer, whence it goes to the pulvinar, the superior colliculus (Barris, Ingram, & Ranson, 1935), and tegmental oculomotor nuclei, especially to the para-abducens nucleus, which subserves conjugate deviation of the eyes. (Personal communication from Elizabeth Crosby.) This triphasic response, having the period of the alpha-rhythm, is too long to be easily envisaged as a single cycle of purely internal reverberation in the striate cortex. This opinion is confirmed by the superimposed faster response to more intense afferent volleys. It is more reasonable to regard efferents to undifferentiated thalamic nuclei and nonspecific afferents from them (Dempsey and Morrison, 1943) as responsible for the sustention of this triphasic rhythm. As in the auditory mechanism, we assign them the function of "scanning" by exciting sheets seriatim in the upper layers of the cortex.

A version of the visual cortex which agrees with these facts and which constitutes a mechanism of the present type for securing invariance to dilatation and constriction of visual forms is diagrammed in Figure 3. For comparison with this scheme some drawings by Cajal (1900) from Golgi preparations are shown in Figure 4 with the original captions.

Figure 3 is a diagram of part of the neurons in a vertical section of cortex taken radially outward from that cortical point to which the center of the fovea projects. The lowest tier of small cells in IVb is the primary receptive manifold $\mathcal{M}$; the upper tiers of internuncials in I, II, and III, to which the upper tiers of layer IVa separately project, constitute the manifolds $\mathcal{M}_a$ for uniform constriction of all the coordinates of an apparition by factors $0 < a < 1$. This reduplication of the layers of IVa in additional upper internuncial tiers is of course unnecessary since the nonspecific

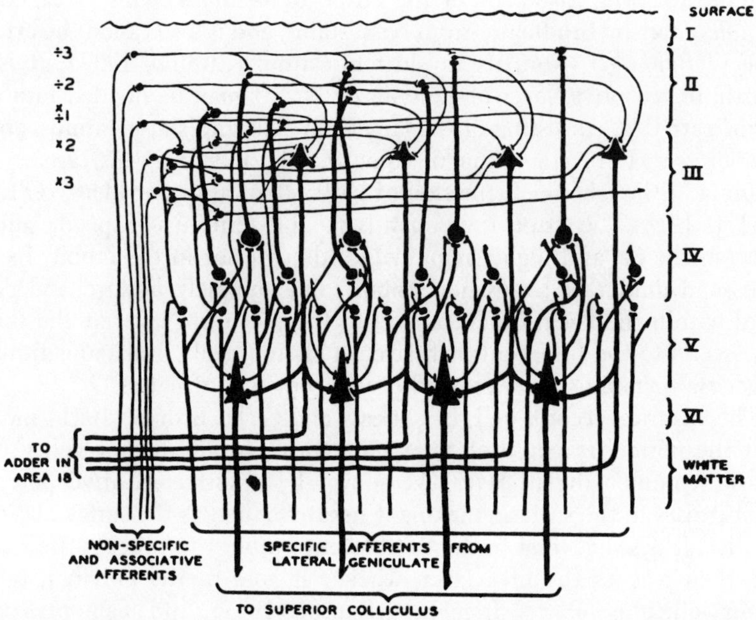


Fig. 3. Impulses relayed by the lateral geniculate from the eyes ascend in specific afferents to layer IV where they branch laterally, exciting small cells singly and larger cells only by summation. Large cells thus represent larger visual areas. From layer IV impulses impinge on higher layers where summation is required from nonspecific thalamic afferents or associative fibers. From there they converge on large cells of the third layer which relay impulses to the parastriate area 18 for addition. On their way down they contribute to summation on the large pyramids of layer V which relays them to the superior colliculus.

afferents might equally well scan the layers of star-pyramids themselves. The magnifications of the apparition are represented on the internuncial tiers drawn beneath the efferents in the third layer. It is quite likely that these are in reality the small star-cells of IVb, or even the long horizontal extensions of the specific afferents within the outer stria of Baillarger. Histological sections of the visual cortex are now being cut radial to the projection of the center of the fovea and perpendicular to it. It is evident that many details of this and the other hypothetical nets of this paper might be chosen in several ways with equal reason; we have only taken the most likely in the light of present knowledge. The sheet of excitement from nonspecific afferents sweeping up and down the upper three layers, therefore, produces all magnifications and constrictions seriatim on the efferent cells of layer III, traveling from there to the parastriate cortex where the functionals *f* are made of them and the results added.

It is worth observing again, when special example can fix it, that the group-invariant spatio-temporal distribution of excitations which represents

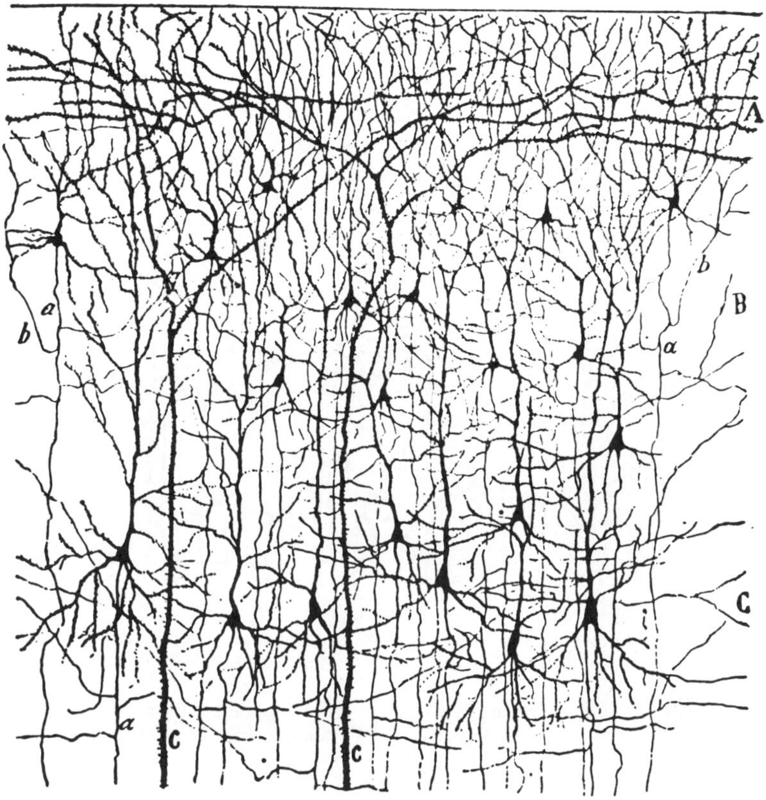


Fig. 4*a*. The following is the original caption.
Kleine und mittelgrosse Pyramidenzellen der Sehrinde eines 20 tägigen Neugeborenen (Fissura calcarina). *A*, plexiforme Schicht; *B*, Schicht der kleinen Pyramiden; *C*, Schicht der mittelgrossen Pyramiden; *a*, absteigender Axencylinder; *b*, rückläufige Collateralen; *c*, Stiele von Riesenpyramiden.

a figure need not resemble it in any simple way. Thus, purely for illustration, we might suppose that the efferent pyramids in the layer III of our diagram project topographically upon another cortical mosaic, which only responds to corners, and accumulates over a cycle of scansion. A square in the visual field, as it moved in and out in successive constrictions and dilatations in Area 17, would trace out four spokes radiating from a common center upon the recipient mosaic. This four-spoked form, not at all like a square, would then be the size-invariant figure of square. In fact, Area 18 does not act like this, for during stimulation of a single spot in the parastriate cortex, human patients report perceiving complete and well-defined objects, but without definite size or position, much as in ordinary visual mental imagery. This is why we have situated the mechanism of Figure 3 in Area 17, instead of later in the visual association system. This also makes it likely that one of the dimensions of the apperceptive manifold

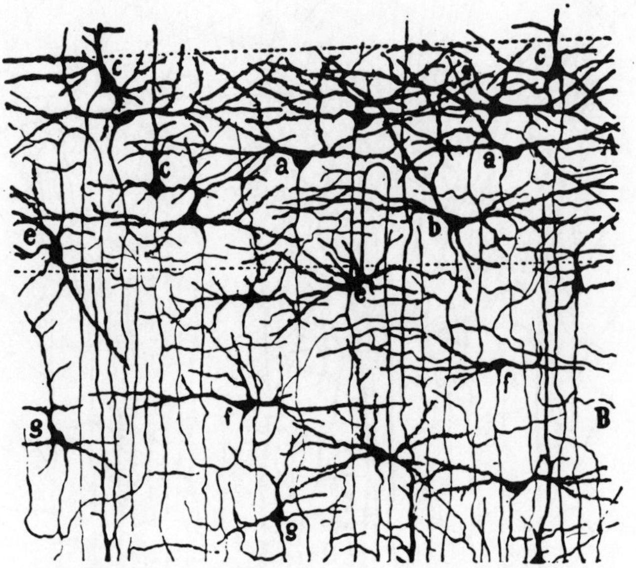


Fig. 4*b*. The following is the original caption.
Schichten der Sternzellen der Sehrinde des 20 tägigen Neugeborenen (Fissura calcarina). A, Schicht der grossen Sternzellen; *a*, halbmondförmige Zellen; *b*, horizontale Spindelzelle; *c*, Zellen mit einem zarten radiären Fortsatz; *e*, Zelle mit gebogenem Axencylinder; *B*, Schicht der kleinen Sternzellen; *f*, horizontale Spindelzellen; *g*, dreieckige Zellen mit Starken gebogenen Collateralen; *h*, Pyramiden mit gebogenem Axencylinder, an der Grenze der fünften Schicht; *C*, Schicht der kleinen Pyramiden mit gebogenem Axencylinder.

$\Xi$, upon whose points the group-averages of various properties of the apparition are summed, is time.

This point is especially to be taken against the Gestalt psychologists, who will not conceive a figure being known save by depicting it topographically on neuronal mosaics, and against the neurologists of the school of Hughlings Jackson, who must have it fed to some specialized neuron whose business is, say, the reading of squares. That language in which information is communicated to the homunculus who sits always beyond any incomplete analysis of sensory mechanisms and before any analysis of motor ones neither needs to be nor is apt to be built on the plan of those languages men use toward one another. . . .

We have focussed our attention on particular hypothetical mechanisms in order to reach explicit notions about them which guide both histological studies and experiment. If mistaken, they still present the possible kinds of hypothetical mechanisms and the general character of circuits which recognize universals, and give practical methods for their design. These procedures are a systematic development of the conception of reverberating neuronal chains, which themselves, in preserving the sequence of events while forgetting their time of happening, are abstracted universals of a kind. Our circuits extend the abstraction to a wide realm of properties. By systematic use of the principle of the exchangeability of time and space, we have enlarged the realm enormously. The adaptability of our methods to unusual forms of input is matched by the equally unusual form of their invariant output, which will rarely resemble the thing it means any closer than a man's name does his face.

## *REFERENCES*

Apter, J. The projection of the retina on the superior colliculus of cats. *Journal of Neurophysiology*, 1945, 8, 123-134.

Apter J. Eye movements following strychninization of the superior colliculus of cats. *Journal of Neurophysiology*, 1946, 9, 73-85.

Ariëns-Kappers, C. V., Huber G. C., & Crosby, E. C. *The comparative anatomy of the nervous system of vertebrates*. New York: The Macmillan Co., 1936.

Barris, R. W., Ingram, W. R., & Ranson, S. W. Optic connections of the diencephalon and midbrain in cat. *Journal of Comparative Neurology*, 1935, 62, 117-144.

Dempsey, E. W., & Morison, R. S. The electrical action of a thalamo-cortical relay system. *American Journal of Physiology*, 1943, *138*, 2, 283-296.

Lorente de Nó, R. La Corteza Cerebral del Raton. *Trabajos del Laboratorio de investigaciones biologicas de la Universidad de Madrid*, 1922, 20, 41-78.

O'Leary, J. L., & Bishop, G. H. The optically excitable cortex of the rabbit. *Journal of Comparative Neurology*, 1941, 68, 423-478.

Ramón y Cajal, S. *Histologie du système nerveux*. Paris: Maloine, 1911.

Ramón y Cajal, S. *Die Sehrinde*. Leipzig: Barth, 1900.

Zunino, G. Die Myeloarchitektonische Differenzierung der Grosshirnrinde beim Kaninchen. *Journal für Psychologie und Neurologie*, 1909, *14*, 38-70.

*The very great specificity of Pitts and McCulloch's treatment, as compared to that of Klüver, scarcely requires comment. It should be noticed that their networks are quite clumsy in the sense that a tremendous amount of computing has to be done on each and every input pattern to extract the invariant property, which is always an average taken over all the possible linear transformations of the original input pattern. The Pitts-McCulloch model has been criticized on these grounds, by Lashley and others, and in fact it turns out to be untestable too, since it makes no specific predictions about which sorts of pattern should be classified together, which mis-classified, and so on. If no such prediction can be made, how could one ever* decide whether the model were true or false? As a matter of fact, so far as I know, no empirical behavioral tests of this sort were ever attempted, and in this sense the ideas did not lead to specific new research. However, despite these negative remarks, the model must be recognized for what it is: an important milestone on the road to adequate treatment of the topic of stimulus equivalence. Two features deserve special mention in this regard. The first is the attempt to correlate the postulated functions with what was then known of the anatomy and neurophysiology of sensory systems, the second is their formal specification of what the model actually does. Pitts and McCulloch's importation of a new standard of rigor into the field can scarcely be overrated in importance. It should also be mentioned in passing that together Pitts and McCulloch broke important new ground in the theory of logic circuits and automata, work which was fundamental to the development of the modern field of computers.

The next paper, von Holst and Mittelstaedt's "The Principle of Reafference," is of a different genre and perhaps needs a word of justification since it is not exactly on the topic of pattern recognition. It is included for three reasons: (1), It has something important to say about the responses of organisms to patterns of stimulation, about their orientation in the world and the stabilization of a perceptual field. (2), It is a nice demonstration of the new concepts of central nervous activity which explicitly reject the notion of the central nervous system (CNS) as a merely passive switchboard between "incoming stimuli" and "outgoing responses". (3), It serves to bridge the gap between the psychologists' typical interest in mammalian visual systems and the wealth of data of a rather different sort which have been collected on submammalian and invertebrate species. There are very real differences between different phylogenetic levels as we shall see, not least of which is the degree of "fixity" of stimulus control demonstrated by different types of organisms. But some of the principles of control may be surprisingly constant at all levels.

# *The Principle of Reafference: Interactions Between the Central Nervous System and the Peripheral Organs*

E. VON HOLST AND H. MITTELSTAEDT

## *INTRODUCTION*

A major question for the physiology of the central nervous system (CNS) has always been this: what lawful relationships hold between impulses which are generated by external stimulation and travel inward into the CNS and those which—either directly or indirectly—reemerge from it; that is, the question of the relations between *afference* and *efference*? The CNS has been characterized as a sort of automat, which reflexly delivers a given ticket when a particular coin is inserted in it. For simple protective reflexes—like sneezing and withdrawal from painful stimuli—this idea is easy to accept; for more complicated reactions such as balancing and orienting responses, the same conceptual scheme has been advocated. Even rhythmic locomotor patterns can be understood in these terms, if one assumes that each single movement reflexly evokes its counterpart, that each component sets off its successor in time (reflex chain theory). The higher forms of behavior, which are modifiable through experience, are subsumed under the same rubric by way of "conditioned" reflexes.

This "classical reflex theory" largely still holds sway, although there are many facts which are inconsistent with it. We know that the breathing centre maintains its activity without external rhythmic stimulation, that the central locomotor rhythms of many invertebrates remain intact in the absence of afference (von Holst, 1932, 1933, 1938), that in fish (von Holst, 1935; Lissman, 1946) and amphibians (Weiss, 1941; Gray, 1946, 1950) only a very small part of the afferent innervation is sufficient to ensure that all parts of the body can continue to locomote properly. The reflex chain theory cannot handle such facts. The analysis of *relative coordination* in anthropods, fish, mammals and humans has taught us to recognize central forces of organization—of coordination and control—whose interplay leads to the establishment of laws which are formally quite similar to those laws of perception which were discovered by Gestalt psychology.

Reprinted from *Die Naturwissenschaften,* 1950.

These newer findings defy description in terms of reflex terminology. It is therefore understandable that they have remained unassimilated to the mainstream of the physiology of the CNS, although they have had a certain influence on research in comparative behavior (Lorenz, 1950; Tinbergen, 1951, for example) and in human psychology (Metzger, 1953). Even recent textbooks are based entirely on the classical reflex theory. For many physiologists the idea that the CNS is an active entity in which orderly occurrences are possible without external stimulation, that rest and sleep are but special forms of CNS activity, seems to be unscientific. The "cause" of every central occurrence is still held to be "the stimulus."[1]

This position is quite understandable; no one would want to give up a simple theory until he had a better one—especially if on account of its great age that theory has come to be taken as established fact. A new theory must encompass both old and new findings, and allow predictions beyond the areas previously encompassed. Some recent experimental results have led us to develop a conceptual framework which, within specified limits, may satisfy these conditions. This is laid out in the following pages by means of examples, and its viability established in terms of known, but hitherto unexplained, phenomena. The chief characteristic of this new conception is a complete reversal of the usual way of looking at the system. We do not enquire into the relations between a given afference (input) and the efference (output) to which it gives rise (i.e., the reflex arc) but rather start with the efference and ask: what happens after the efference has caused changes in the organism *via* the effectors, and then is reverberated back into the CNS by way of the receptors, as afference? This type of afference which is caused by the efference itself we shall call *reafference*.

## *REAFFERENCE*

### Introductory Example

Let us start with an example: if a hollow cylinder, the inner surface of which is painted with vertical black and white stripes, is placed over a stationary insect such as the fly *Eristalis*, and rotated, the insect starts to turn in the same direction. It attempts to maintain, or stabilize, its visual field (Fig. 1a). This well-known optomotor reflex is readily elicited at any time. However, if the insect starts to move *itself* within the (stationary)

[1] This misunderstanding is probably psychologically motivated, in the sense that it reinforces the naive attempt to explain every visible bodily movement in terms of a specifiable environmental event, rather than in terms of invisible transformations within the CNS. The latter seem to have too mystic a quality.

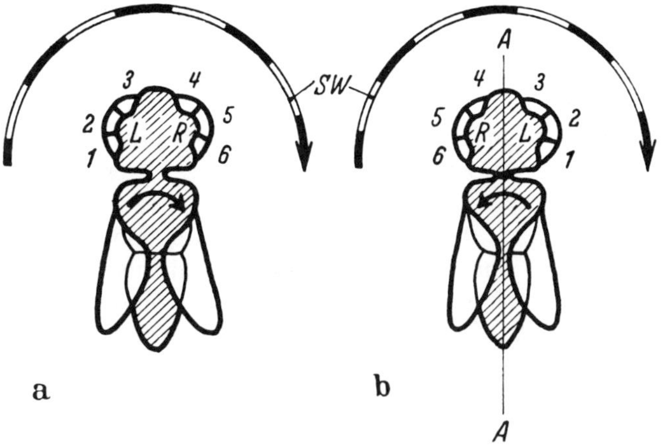


Fig. 1. Behavior of the insect *Eristalis* when a striped cylinder SW is rotated past the eyes from left to right. *a,* Normal insect, *b,* following rotation of the head by 180° about the axis A-A. R = right eye, L = left eye (each ommatidium is numbered). The arrow on the thorax indicates the direction of active turning.

cylinder, normal voluntary movement occurs just as in an optically unstructured environment. The question now is why the optokinetic reflex does not force the fly back into its starting position, as soon as it begins to turn, since the movement of the image of the cylinder across the retina is the same as in the former case (rotating cylinder, fly stationary). The answer of reflex theory is that during spontaneous locomotion the optokinetic reflex is inhibited. But that answer is wrong! *Eristalis* has a slender and flexible neck which can be rotated through 180° about its longitudinal axis. If this is done, and the head glued to the thorax, the positions of the two eyes are reversed (Fig. 1b; see also Mittelstaedt, 1949). In this way a clockwise rotation of the cylinder produces image movement across the retina which under normal circumstances would be produced by counterclockwise rotation. The stationary fly responds to rightward movement of the cylinder by turning itself promptly to the left. If the optomotor reflex were indeed inhibited during "voluntary" movements, the free movement of the fly within a stationary cylinder should occur normally, as in an intact insect. That only happens, however, in an optically homogeneous environment. In the striped cylinder things are no longer normal; *Eristalis* turns continuously to the left or right in tight circles, or else short sharp turns to the left and right follow one another in rapid succession, until the insect eventually stops, "freezing" in an atypical posture. If the head is returned to its original orientation, behavior is once again restored to normal.

This finding contradicts the reflex inhibition hypothesis; it shows that contour movement across the retina influences locomotion, both when the insect moves itself, as well as when the cylinder moves. As a first formulation we can say: the moving insect "expects" a very specific change in retinal stimulation which, insofar as it occurs, is "neutralized" in some way. But following interchange of the two eyes there is retinal motion opposite to that which is expected, and the optomotor response is immediately evoked. This movement, however, magnifies the unexpected retinal motion, and thus the process is self-reinforcing. Every time the insect starts to turn, it is forced further around in the same direction by the optomotor response. If it attempts to move in the opposite sense, it faces the same dilemma. The result is clearly a central catastrophe!

If this account of things is correct, we must ask ourselves how the CNS "knows" which type of retinal image motion to expect. There are two possibilities; either the CNS retains information for a certain time about the efference which has been sent to the limbs, information which is stored as a central record to be compared to the subsequent retinal changes; or if the CNS does not have this simpler capacity, it must rely on the reafference from the receptors of the moving limbs, calculating the direction and speed of body motion in order to compare them with the retinal reafference. Both alternatives are possible, and we shall leave the question of which one is correct open for the moment, turning our attention instead to another example for clarification.

## *SHARPER DEFINITION OF THE PROBLEM*

Each labyrinth of the vestibular organs of every vertebrate contains a flat body, the *utriculus otolith.* When the head is in its normal orientation this body lies horizontally on a sensory surface, and is responsive to gravity. Experiments with fish, recently reported (von Holst, 1949, 1950), show that the adequate stimulus to this receptor is a force parallel to the above-mentioned sensory surface. This *shearing* force increases sinusoidally as the head tends away from the normal position, and causes a sinusoidally increasing central imbalance in activity, a "central turning tendency" which initiates motor activity to bring the animal back to its normal posture. The system works with great precision without adaptation or fatigue. In the words of reflexology: the organism maintains its normal posture by virtue of its "postural reflex." Now one can readily observe, in all animals and in man, that it is possible to maintain *other* postures for shorter or longer periods of time. Fish, for example, position themselves practically vertically, facing up or down, turn on their sides, etc., when seeking food, following prey, in fighting, or copulation.

How are these variations in maintained posture possible, in view of the ever-ready "postural reflex"? Reflexology answers as before, that the postural reflex is wholly or in part inhibited. It is easy to show that this notion is wrong. The "intended" or "goal" postures which differ from the norm are themselves maintained against external perturbations by exactly the same kind of corrective movements which serve to maintain normal posture!

One might suppose that the reflexes are maintained in operation, but shunted through different pathways by a superordinate control mechanism. The higher center merely activates the control points which determine what the route is to be from afference to efference (the "redirected reflex" —*gelenkte Reflexe*—of W. R. Hess). This conception leads to an experimentally testable consequence: simple switching points do the same job, however light or heavy the traffic they bear. In other words, the operation of this reflex governor, or switching mechanism, should be independent of the amount of afference. However, that is simply not the case.

One can magnify the force exerted by the statolith on its receptor surface in a centrifugal field of force. If the weight of the statolith is doubled in this manner, the shearing stimulation produced by departures from the normal posture is also doubled. If the frequent spontaneous deviations (nose up, or down) of a free-swimming fish are recorded, it will be observed that they become smaller, the heavier one makes the statoliths. "Voluntary movements" show themselves to be dependent on the returning stream of afference which they themselves cause!

Another example: fish position the main body axis in the direction of water flow by "latching on" to the optically static environment. This is true in the main also if the current flows at an angle, or vertically from above (or below); the more the fish is able to point its nose into the current, the more easily can it maintain its posture against perturbations without fatigue (von Holst, 1949). Investigating the behavior of a free-swimming fish in a tank subjected to a constant water current, one finds that increasing the weight of the statoliths makes it more and more difficult for the fish to maintain its posture against the current flow as that flow approaches the vertical (Fig. 2). It now attempts to maintain a *dorsal* posture to the direction of the current, but can do so only imperfectly, and tires rapidly. This difference disappears if the statoliths are removed: in that case the proper orientation to the current flow can be maintained, no matter what the mechanical field forces are.

We see, then, that the higher central system which is activated by deviations from the "goal posture" is not simply a switching mechanism, since the reafference caused by its activation has a quantitative influence on the resulting posture itself. Despite this refutation of the concept of "redirected reflex," the following exposition is closely related to the research of W. R. Hess (although his methods are quite different)—both in terms of problem statement and mode of thought. However, *this* switching (points) system must work harder, the more traffic passes through! How is that to be explained?

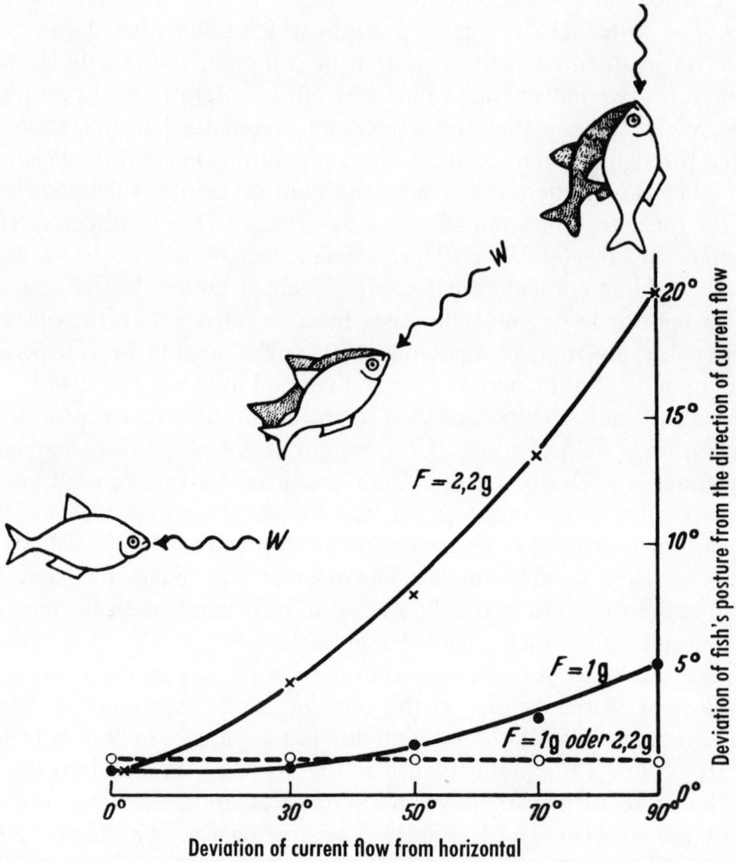


Fig. 2. Postural adjustment of a fish swimming freely in a tank through which water flows with constant velocity. Parameter indicates gravitational field force, F. ("Vertical" is here the resultant of gravitational and centrifugal forces.) ● and X are for intact fish, O for fish from which the statoliths have been removed. The white fish indicates the behavior of an intact organism under F = 1g, the grey one under F = 2.2g. W = direction of water flow (speed of current approximately one fish length per second). Hydrostatic pressure was held constant. Means for 5 experimental runs each with 3 fish (*Gymnocorymbus* and *Hypessobrycon*).

We can picture the matter quite simply by keeping in mind two well-established and basic physiological facts:

1. The sensory cells of the labyrinth have, like other (and perhaps most) receptors, a basal spontaneous firing rate even in the absence of a shearing stimulus. The shearing stimulation of the statoliths increases or decreases that firing rate, depending on the direction of shear. This automatic response of the receptors has been confirmed both by our own investigations on fish, and by direct electrical recording from the afferent fibers (O. Lowenstein, 1950) and from the vestibular nuclei in the brain (Adrian, 1943).

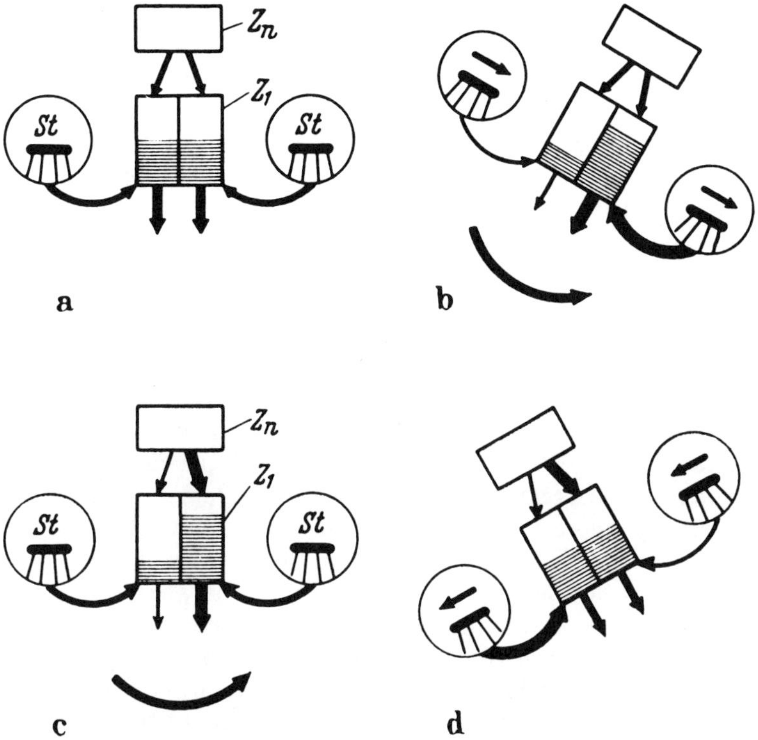


Fig. 3. Schema for the elucidation of the coordinated activity of higher centres ($Z_n$) with the lower postural centre ($Z_1$) and the Statolith apparatus (St) in postural orientation of the fish (about its longitudinal axis). The thickness of the arrows indicates the strength of a stream of impulses (number of impulses per unit time) flowing from one point to another. The shading in $Z_1$ indicates the strength of activity within its two halves at any given instant. St = statoliths, the arrows in *b* and *d* indicating the direction of shear; the large middle arrows in *b* and *c* show the direction of turning. *a*, Normal situation; *b* and *c* show the direction of turning. *a*, Normal situation; *b*, tendency to return to the normal posture after the fish has been passively tipped to the side; *c*, active (spontaneous) turning to the left, *d*, its result the intended "goal posture."

2. A steady stream of impulses flows between higher and lower centers even in the absence of external motor activity. This also has been established by electrophysiological investigation for many different central areas, and can be inferred from the large and abrupt decline in activity when certain descending central connecting fiber bundles are severed. The "spinal shock" of lower motor centers after destruction of the vestibular-spinal tract corresponds to the "shock" which the left vestibular nucleus suffers on destruction of the left labyrinth. In both cases a steady activating stream of impulses is interrupted.

These two prerequisites are needed to substantiate the model sketched in Figure 3. The "position center," a complex of neural ganglia (whose spatial distribution is not our present concern) consists of two halves, both of which receive impulses from the statolith epithelium and from higher centers. If both halves are equally "weighted" (both in the same condition of activation) then they send equally strong trains of impulses to the lower motor centers of the spinal cord (Fig. 3a), which result in the well-known "tonus" effect of the labyrinth (Ewald; see also von Holst, 1949). If the fish is tipped passively to the right (Fig. 3b), then, as has been experimentally proven (von Holst), the shearing effect in the right statolith produces an increase in afference, but in the left statolith a decrease. The resulting difference in levels between the right and left "position centers" entails inequality in the trains of impulses to the spinal cord, and this sets in action the motor apparatus to produce a turning movement to the left. This, in the classical terminology, is what is called the "postural reflex."

A corresponding difference in levels can also occur as a result of unequal input from higher centres (Fig. 3c, d); the result is the same motor pattern as before.[2] These occurrences are known as "voluntary movements" in physiology. It appears that the resulting "goal posture" or "intended posture" is just as efficiently maintained in the presence of passive external disturbances as the "normal" posture, and in exactly the same manner in terms of the afference arising from the statolith apparatus; every passive change in position leads to a difference of levels in the postural centres and hence to a "postural reflex" without the involvement of higher centers.

Let us consider some of the testable consequences of this model:

1. Destruction of the left statolith apparatus must result in an immediate fall in the level in the postural center, and hence produce a continuous tendency to turn to the left. And this must reach a maximum when the organism is turned on its right side (strongest afference from the right), a minimum when it is turned on its left side. This turns out to be true for all vertebrates, and has been measured quantitatively in fish (von Holst, 1949). The same is true if the postural center itself is damaged or destroyed, as is already known (Spiegel & Sato, 1927).

2. Once the left postural center has recovered from the immediate postoperative disruptive effects of statolith removal, and is again under normal load or "weight,"[3] the tendency to turn in response to changes of posture only reaches half its former value, since the left-hand input remains constant and only the right-hand input responds to changes of position. This has been confirmed quantitatively in fish (von Holst).

3. Raising of the mechanical field force, and thereby of the afference from the stato-apparatus, must increase the influence of the stato-apparatus on the postural system in comparison to the effects of other processes con-

[2] The idea that higher centres have the function of controlling the balance of activity in lower antagonistic centres was first developed in connection with the relative coordination of rhythmic locomotor patterns of movement (von Holst, 1936). It has recently been further confirmed by electrophysiological studies (Bernhard and coworkers, 1947).

[3] Our coworker L. Schoen (1949) has studied these central effects quantitatively; we shall not consider them further here.

cerned with posture, such as visual afference in fish. This also has been proven quantitatively (von Holst). Doubling of the mechanical field force, for example, compensates exactly for a missing statolith (point 1).

4. After removal of the higher centers there should be no active deviations from the normal posture. This also is known to be true (Magnus, 1924, among others).

5. The stronger the field forces, and hence the shearing stimulation of the statoliths, the less should spontaneous changes of "goal posture" or those mediated by afference via other higher centers, affect postural adjustments. On this important point, too, as we saw, the prediction is confirmed: the adjustment of the postural centers is mediated by the shearing force; that is, the heavier the statoliths, the smaller the angle of adjustment attained by the organism (see Fig. 2).

6. Conversely, after bilateral interruption of the afferent pathways, small inequalities in the inputs from higher centers will lead to exaggerated movements since, mechanically speaking, if the reafference is removed, the feedback signal, which is used to estimate when movements should be terminated, is destroyed. This phenomenon can readily be observed in free-swimming fish and amphibia, and has often been described. Organisms with bilaterally removed labyrinths exaggerate any intended change of position so strongly that frequently they can do no more than reel and stagger around.[4] In terrestrial animals such behavior is less noticeable, on account of the general lack of tonus which follows loss of the labyrinths and because of the large part the muscle receptors play in movement control (see Fig. 5b,c). Even so, it can be observed after partial loss of the balance receptors; following destruction of both horizontal canals, for instance, horizontal to-and-fro motions of the head can readily be observed during execution of an intentional movement (especially in birds).

A number of the inferences to be drawn from our model thus prove to be correct, and concern matters which, to a degree, cannot be understood in terms of the concepts of reflexology.

## *GENERAL EXPOSITION OF THE PRINCIPLE OF REAFFERENCE*

The essential point in the examples of the previous section is the role played by reafference, the afference which is itself caused by active movement. The reafference compensates for changes brought about by move-

[4] Schöne (1950) reports a closely analogous observation on insect larvae. The *Dytiscus* larva normally positions itself with its back to the light, but will do backward somersaults in swimming upwards if the backward and forward facing eyes have been blinded. Apparently this happens because the reafferent signal which normally would inhibit its corrective movements (stronger illumination of the anterior eyes) is missing (Schöne's own explanation follows similar lines.)

ment commands from higher centers in such a way that equilibrium is reestablished. If by experimental manipulation this afference is removed, made too great or too small, or reversed in sign (the rotated head of *Eristalis*), predictable changes in motor behavior will result.

We shall first give a general exposition of this principle, and then establish its validity by applying it to a number of different neuromotor systems.

Consider some center $Z_1$ (Fig. 4) which services an effector EFF, having both sensory and motor connections to it. This effector could be a muscle, a limb, or the whole body. There is a number of superordinate centres $Z_2 \ldots Z_n$ above $Z_1$. Some command K from $Z_n$, that is, some change in the flow of impulses from $Z_n$ to $Z_1$, produces in $Z_1$ a sequence of efferent impulses E. In addition to the efference E, however, it causes a strictly correlated neuronal process (e.g., by a change of activity which spreads, after a certain temporal delay, into the neighboring ganglia) called the *efference copy* (EK). The efferent stream of impulses flowing out into the periphery sets its effector in motion, and this gives rise to the afference A. This, in turn, interacts with the efference copy. We shall arbitrarily label the efference and its copy positive (+), the reafference negative (—). The efference copy and reafference compensate for each other exactly in $Z_1$. The original command from $Z_n$ can therefore flow down without modification as efference. Should the total afference become too great or too small however, as a result of external influences in the effector, $Z_1$ will show a positive or negative residual bias. This residual is fed back, often—as we shall see—to the highest centers; we shall call this a *report*, M. This ascending report may—but need not—branch collaterally into $Z_2$, where it can again be summated with the descending command. In this case the system consisting of $Z_2$ and the lower units becomes a *feedback control system* in the technical sense.[5]

Let us suppose that some influence on the effector EFF causes an increase in afference in $Z_1$, and consequently, an increase in the report to $Z_2$; the (negative) report will *decrease* the positive command output from $Z_2$ until a balance is again struck. Similarly an externally caused decrease in afference will result in a positive residual bias in $Z_1$, a positive report to $Z_2$, and consequently an increase in the positive command output from $Z_2$. In other words, in both cases the efference is modified until no further report is received from $Z_1$.[6] In the example of postural orientation we have already been introduced to such a control system.

[5] We are grateful to Dr. Böhm for pointing out the kinship to control theory (see also Böhm, 1950).

[6] It should be emphasized that this "negative feedback" (*negative Rückkoppelung*) of the Anglo-Saxon literature is not a necessary component of the principle of reafference, and should not be confused with it! The essential point for our principle is the mechanism which distinguishes between reafference and exafference. This distinction plays no part in feedback control technology.

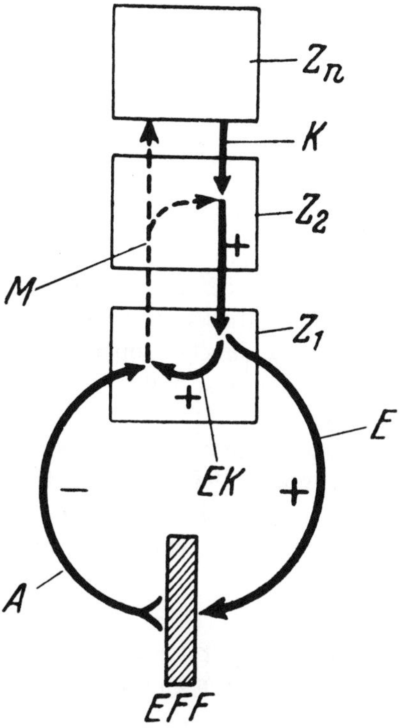


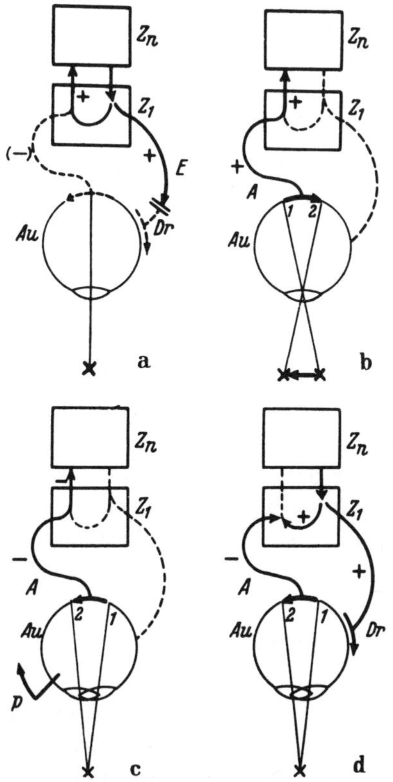


Fig. 4 (*left*). General schema for the principle of reafference; explanation in text.

Fig. 5 (*right*). Explanation of movement perception by the eye under normal and experimental conditions in terms of the principle of reafference. *Au* = eye (in primary position, seen from above), $Z_1$ lowest, $Z_n$ highest optical centre. The efference E which goes to the eye musculature and the afference A which results from image motion on the retina are labelled analogously to the schema of Fig. 4. In *a* the paralyzed eye receives the command signal to turn to the right (turning moment Dr towards the right): in *b* the observed object X itself moves to the right, and the retinal image moves from 1 to 2; in *c* the eye is passively (mechanically) moved, as indicated by the arrow P, and the retinal image of the stationary X moves from 1 to 2; in *d* the eye makes an active (voluntary) movement to the right (turning moment Dr, as in *a*), at which the retinal image of the stationary object X moves from 1 to 2. Further elaboration in text.

We shall define every change in afference which is *not* a direct consequence of efference, but rather results from *external* stimulation, as exafference; this exafference occurs in both proprioceptors and exteroceptors. Exafference, then, according to our schema, is that positive or negative residual in $Z_1$ which ascends from $Z_1$ to higher centers as a report.

The proposed schema makes two physiological assumptions:

1. The consequences of different impulses (signals) can be mutually (additively) reinforcing or antagonistic. This point is well documented:

for example, in the field of motor behavior the superposition of two motor rhythms of different frequencies in relative coordination (von Holst, 1939) where summation or compensation is possible, according to the phase relations between two rhythms. An example from the field of sensory coordination is the exact linear superposition of statically and optically caused central changes in activity, and similarly, the purely additive positive or negative effect produced by manipulating changes in activity in the postural control center of fish (von Holst, 1949).

2. Efferent output from a lower center leaves behind it a specific change of state, or "copy." This assumption is plausible a priori for the higher centers, and now may be taken as established for lower centers also. Recent work on action currents in the spinal cord using antidromic stimulation (which causes action potentials to propagate in a direction opposite to the normal one) suggests that the normal discharge of a motor ganglion cell is propagated not only over the efferent axons, but also over the small dendrites which interconnect with neighboring internuncial neurons, in which they may cause local changes of state. Tonnies (1949) describes this action as "central feedback" and ascribes great significance to it in the regulation of spinal excitation. For us it is sufficient to see that our assumption is at least plausible physiologically.

## *APPLICATION OF THE PRINCIPLE OF REAFFERENCE TO SEVERAL DIFFERENT NEUROMOTOR SYSTEMS*

### Eye Movements

We shall now try to find out to what extent certain facts that cannot be understood in terms of classical reflexology can be explained by the principle of reafference. In order that we may use perception as a source of evidence, we start with man, and consider the visual system. Here we may expect to find that conditions are simple, since the eye lies within a protective socket in the head, and is not normally subjected to external mechanical disturbance.

Reafference for the active eye can have two sources: (1) movement of the image on the retina and (2) impulses from the receptors in the eye muscles. Only the first of these is available to conscious perception; the part played by the second can at best be inferred. Let us start with a crucial—because unexpected—prediction: if the eye is immobilized and the muscle receptors put out of action (Fig. 5a), then, on the command "look right" (turn the eye: all directions are considered from the subject's point of view), the efference copy will return undiminished from the lowest center as report, in the absence of any reafference from the retina or the eye muscles. Moreover, this report must be identical with that which, if the eye remained stationary, would normally be caused by a congruent movement of the environment in the same direction (Fig. 5b).[7] "The total visual field 'jumps' to the right." This prediction is correct! It has long been known of patients with paralysis of the eye muscles that intended eye movements give rise in perception to a shift of the visual field in the same direction. Moreover, the extent of the jump appears to be equal in magnitude to the intended eye movement. This point has been carefully confirmed by Kornmüller (1931) who anaesthetized his own eye muscles to do the experiments. The apparent shift of the visual field cannot be distinguished from a true visual change—understandably so, according to the reafference principle, since in both cases the identical report is fed back. In this experiment, the *efference copy itself* is, so to speak, made visible.

Since Hering's day (cf. Trendelenberg, 1943, p. 240ff.) this phenomenon has been attributed to "shift of attention" during eye movements. A plausible physiological explanation has been lacking until now. We shall see presently that "attention" has nothing to do with the matter, since the same effect occurs even with eye movements of which the subject is unaware. Perception is here simply a convenient indicator for a physiological process which is otherwise difficult to monitor.

One gets the same experience of movement as above, but in the opposite sense (to the left) if the eyeball is moved passively, by means of forceps, to the right (Fig. 5c). In this case there is no command to move, and the retinal exafference ascends without modification as a report, thereby evoking an "illusory" perception, which is: "the visual world jumped to the left."

Let us now combine the first condition with the second, namely, move a paralyzed eye passively at the very moment when the movement command is given (and in the same direction). Or—obviously, so much easier—let us make a normal eye movement with the *intact* eye: in either case, there are indeed two complementary trains of impulses (Fig. 5d); an efference copy which on its own makes the visual scene move to the right, and an afference[8] which on its own makes it move to the left. Since, however, these two cancel each other out at the low level of $Z_1$ no report ascends higher and we see neither movement; as witnessed by our everyday experience, the environment remains stable. And that, in the present instance, is objectively correct. The "right" perception turns out to be the sum of two opposite "false" perceptions.

[7] This is to be expected since in such an environmental shift the *opposite* displacement of the retinal image occurs to that which would be occasioned by an eye movement to the right. The reversal of direction is represented in our schema by a reversal of the sign of the afference, from negative to positive so that a positive report, that is a report having the same sign as the efference copy, is fed back.

[8] In the first case (forced movement) this afference is, in our terminology, an exafference, in the second case (normal eye movement) a reafference.

This central apparatus has, like all technical structures, definite limits of precision. It works reliably only at medium-sized eye deviations and moderate eye velocities. If one turns the eyes far to the right, for example, and scans rapidly up and down a vertical corner of a room, there is a noticeable "apparent rotation" of the field (Hoffman, 1924). According to our interpretation, this means that the efference copy of the movement (a rotation, according to Listing's law) cannot completely annul the afference which it causes, so that some report is fed back to higher centers. Also, the visual world seems to move to and fro (and in the opposite sense) if the eyes are moved rapidly right and left; in this case, it seems that the efference copy builds up too slowly, so that a small report gets through.

The fact that both passive movements of the normal eye as well as the intention to move a mechanically fixed eyeball can give rise to powerful apparent movements of the visual world (as Helmholtz already knew) demonstrates that the afference of the eye muscle receptors can be of little, if any, significance here. If these receptors signaled the position of the eyeball, in the way that certain receptors monitor limb position (see also the section on limb movements, pp. 58–63), then it should only be possible to get apparent movement of the visual world after they had been eliminated (as in Kornmüller's experiment). The role of the eye muscle receptors has been much overemphasized up to now—as we shall soon see below—because reflexology took no account of internal feedback processes.

The principle of reafference is valid not only for the so-called "voluntary" movements, but also for those involuntary movements in which the eye "scans" the visual field, fixating first one point and then another, moving rapidly between them. This scanning occurs both in active eye movements, as when reading a book (in which every line requires four or five fixations) as well as when the head and body are turned (labyrinthine nystagmus) or the visual world moves before us (optomotor nystagmus). In all these cases, we normally notice nothing of the to-and-fro movements of the retinal image, but rather see the environment moving steadily in one direction or indeed (as when reading) remaining still. According to orthodox reflex physiology, these phenomena are to be explained as follows: when the visual world passes before our eyes (as in looking out of the window of a train) the eye is "reflexly" driven along with it. The eye muscles therefore move, and their receptors signal the velocity of the moving environment; the movement of the retinal image cannot do so since there is little or no visual movement relative to the retina. When the muscle tension reaches its maximum, there is a "reflex" movement in the opposite direction—the rapid phase of nystagmus. During this rapid phase, the afference resulting from rapid movement of the retinal image is "inhibited," or does not reach consciousness because it is so rapid.

This explanation is contradicted, among other things, by the following observations: Fixation of a bright cross produces a retinal after-image;

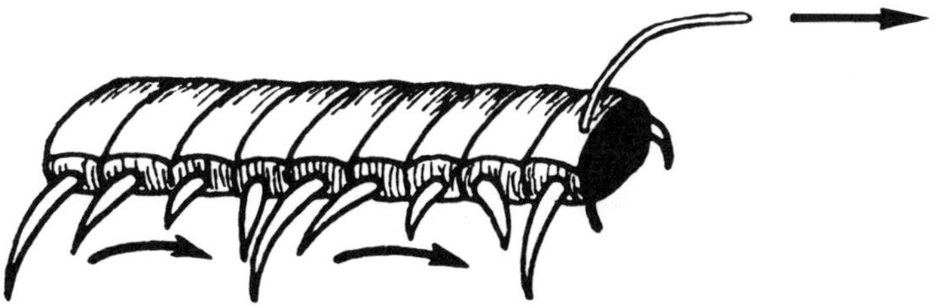

Fig. 6. Short segment of the arthropod *Geophilus* which is pulled forward by means of a hook attached at the anterior end. The legs which are off the ground swing forward actively (→) in such a manner that each leg lands exactly in the footprint of its predecessor; the spoor is the same as that of a two-legged organism.

this image remains visible for some time in the dark and when a labyrinthine nystagmus is induced can be observed to move slowly in one direction, and rapidly in the other (some practice in self-observation is needed). That is to say, the image is *not* eliminated in the rapid phase of nystagmus (Fischer, 1926). However, this behavior is to be expected, as we shall presently see, on the basis of the principle of reafference.

The much-debated mechanism of nystagmus can best be understood by taking quite literally our characterization of it as an "optical pacing" apparatus. Consider by way of comparison the locomotor apparatus of an arthropod, *Geophilus* (von Holst, 1933) following ablation of the higher centers (Fig. 6). The insect can be activated by continuous excitement (e.g., electrical) of the ventral cord, in which case the legs step out in an orderly fashion, just as a steady train of impulses from higher centers sets off nystagmus. But it can also be activated—like nystagmus—by moving the "fixated visual world," namely by pulling the insect along the ground at a variable speed. The legs then move *actively*; even those which at any moment are off the ground and thrusting forward at a speed which is determined by the speed of the legs which are *on* the ground and being driven by the speed of forced motion. The "support" phase corresponds to the slow phase of nystagmus; legs and eyes "fixate" the substrate, and are governed by exafference. The forward thrust phase corresponds to the rapid phase of nystagmus; legs and eyes lose fixation and take a step in the opposite direction. In both instances, higher centers need have no information about the individual steps; the stream of pulses downward is continuous, just as is the ascending report which signals the relative velocities of subject and environment. The pacing apparatus fails to operate if the moving substrate is undifferentiated (*Geophilus*: surface of quicksilver; eye: homogeneous field of view), or if the movement is too rapid. In the latter case, legs and eyes both remain "stuck" in the extreme driven position.

Let us try to understand this central optical pacing system more exactly: the visual world starts to move past the eye, say, to the right, and therefore causes retinal image movement. The image movement generates

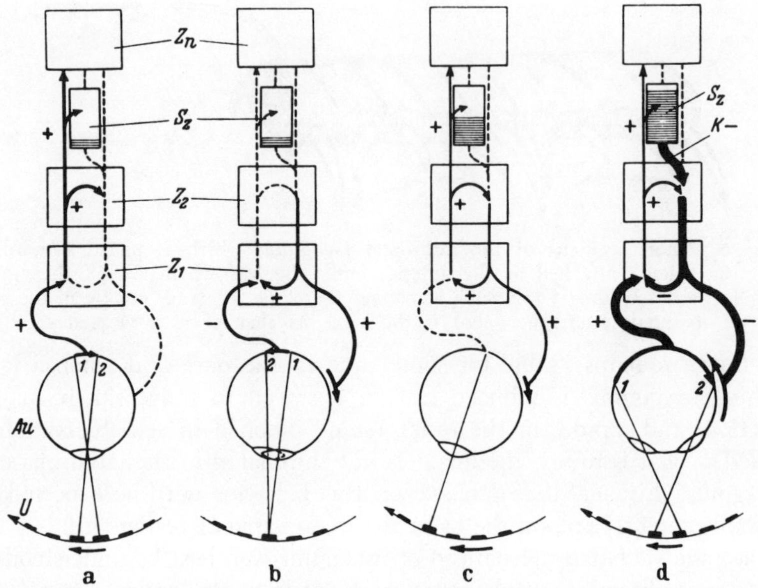


Fig. 7. Explanation of the pacing movements of the eye *Au* in the case of optomotor nystagmus as the environment *u* moves. The schema follows the pattern of Figs. 4 and 5. $Z_1$ and $Z_2$ are lower movement centers, SZ is the pacing center which is responsible for the rhythmic movements of nystagmus, $Z_n$ is a higher optical center. In *a* the eye is at rest, the environment moves a bit, and an (arbitrarily chosen) element of the retinal image moves from 1 to 2. In *b* active following has been initiated, and the given element is back at its original retinal position. In *c* the eye moves with the same angular velocity as the environment, and the retinal image remains stationary. In *d* the pacing centre SZ discharges, causing a powerful movement command K in the opposite direction; during this rapid movement, the environment continues to move; an arbitrary element of the retinal image moves from 1 to 2. Thickness of the arrows indicates strength of impulse trains. Further elaboration in text.

a positive signal which proceeds to higher centers, including both $Z_2$ and the "pacing" center SZ (Fig. 7a). This positive signal returns downwards immediately as efference and initiates eye movement. Thereby the image is restored to its original location on the retina, but at the same time there is a negative afference which cancels the positive efference copy in $Z_1$. The eye movement would stop at once (Fig. 7b) were it not for the fact that the process of 7a immediately recurs. The system eventually reaches a state of equilibrium (Fig. 7c); the eye responds so rapidly that no retinal movement (or almost none) is registered, and the whole control system is self-maintaining. As this happens the pacing center SZ is gradually being "loaded" until eventually it discharges explosively like a relaxation oscillator,[9] and returns the eye to its original position (Fig. 7d); this is the

[9] A. Bethe (1940) in particular has done important experiments on relaxation-oscillators as models for physiological processes.

rapid phase. As it occurs the efference copy and afference cancel each other out, except for the small residual exafference caused by the movement of the visual world; this signal ascends as a report which is thus independent of the change of phase (see Fig. 7c). And now the process recycles.

The reader may convince himself that this whole apparatus is by no means a reflex mechanism, for, in the presence of sufficient self-activation or stimulation from $Z_n$ it should go into an autorhythmic state, *even in the absence* of all afference (cf. Fig. 7c); such states can in fact be observed under certain experimental and pathological conditions.

## Accommodation

Let us turn from eye movements to another phenomenon: accommodation. The relaxed (single) eye is accommodated to optical infinity, since the elastic lens is flattened by its suspensory ligaments. Near accommodation is achieved by contraction of a sphincter muscle which opposes this tension and allows the lens to bulge, thereby decreasing its focal length. This system mediates perception of the approximate size and distance of visual objects projected on the retina, although it is not their sole determinant. Two equal, and equally sharp, retinal images will be judged as distant and large, or near and small, according to the state of accommodation, or as the usual formulation has it: the "subjective size" depends on the "apparent distance."

Reflexology can only explain this by supposing that receptors in the accommodation system have a "reflex" effect on the percept which depends on their own state of excitation. This possibility can be discounted by a well-known fact: if the mechanism of accommodation is knocked out with Atropin and one unsuccessfully attempts to accommodate for near vision, everything appears diminished in size (*micropsia*) although the paralyzed peripheral mechanism cannot produce any "reflex." Conversely, everything appears enlarged if one attempts far vision when the accommodation muscle is fully contracted by application of Eserin (*macropsia*). The reafference principle can explain these relationships.

We start with a simple example, (a): suppose that there is a sharp after-image of a cross on the retina, which was seen in near vision; the eye then focusses on a distant wall. The signal for far accommodation causes a particular efference to the musculature from the lowest center, together with its corresponding efference copy. Since the image of the cross remains as large and as sharp as before on the retina, there is no reafference, the unmodified efference ascends and mediates a distinctive and definite perception: "the cross is now much larger." Consider a second case, (b): the direct observation of a large cross first of all, followed by a smaller one at the same distance from the eye. Here there is no signal to change accommodation, and in the absence of an efference copy the exafference ascends simply as a report which again mediates a definite perception: "The (second) cross is smaller." Then (c): we take the larger cross, first observe it in near vision and then move it away until its retinal image is exactly the same size as was that of the small cross in (b) before. Now we have *first* the report [as in (a)] which on its own would mediate the perception "cross is larger" and *secondly* the report [as in (b)] which on its own would mediate "cross is smaller." The efference copy and the exafference cancel each other out in a lower center and *no* report ascends to higher centers. The perception must therefore be: "the cross remains the same size"—which it does! That is, a "correct" perception is attained as the result of mutual compensation by two "false" perceptions.

This explanation is readily applied to the micropsia and macropsia discussed above: if the peripheral musculature cannot respond to its efference, there can be no retinal reafference, and the efference copy therefore ascends as a report which mediates perception of a change in size.

It is worth noting again that there are limits to the precision with which efference copy and reafference cancel each other out. When accommodation ceases to operate, as in very close or very distant vision, one does indeed see things grow smaller or larger, as is to be expected. Similarly, the mechanism follows rapid changes in distance somewhat sluggishly, so that a rapidly approaching visual object may appear to grow in size.

The principle for monocular distance setting which we have given can also be applied to the binocular distance-measuring function, namely to convergence of the eyes, which increases as a fixated object approaches them. We shall not follow up this example since we do not as yet know whether, or to what degree, reafference from the eye muscles is involved in the process.

## Limb Movements

Consider another system, the moving extremities of the body. Here one may expect to find greater complexities because, in contrast to the well-protected eye, all sorts of passive (mechanical) changes of position occur, about which the CNS must be precisely informed in order to operate properly. We can perceive at least four different types of mechanical influence: touch, pressure, tension ("force"), and position. The first two, as we know from everyday experience, shade into one another. The difference between tension and limb position is vividly experienced under increases in the gravitational field, as in a centrifuge. If one's weight is doubled in this fashion, for example, an amazing effort is required to lift the arms—despite the absence of any external pressure on them—but at the same time one senses correctly their positions. Visual checks of a limb movement that was not visually guided yields no surprises.[10] The position sense is provided mainly by receptors within connective tissues which are external to the muscles[11]; measurement of tension, on the other hand, is achieved by receptors in the muscle fibers and tendons. Together they mediate the so-called "deep sensibility."

Let us start with a concrete question: how would a muscle which has an external load imposed on it behave, given that the efferent and afferent arrangements between the tension sensors in the tendons and the higher controlling centers are similar to those we have learned about in the postural control of fish? The lightly tensed muscle is stretched so that the tension increases (Fig. 8a). The increased negative afference (exafference) rises to $Z_2$ and there reduces the magnitude of the previous efference: the muscle relaxes actively. On relaxation flexion the opposite occurs: the positive efference copy rising from $Z_1$ to $Z_2$ increases the total efference; the muscle contracts actively (Fig. 8b). However strong the muscle tonus, the

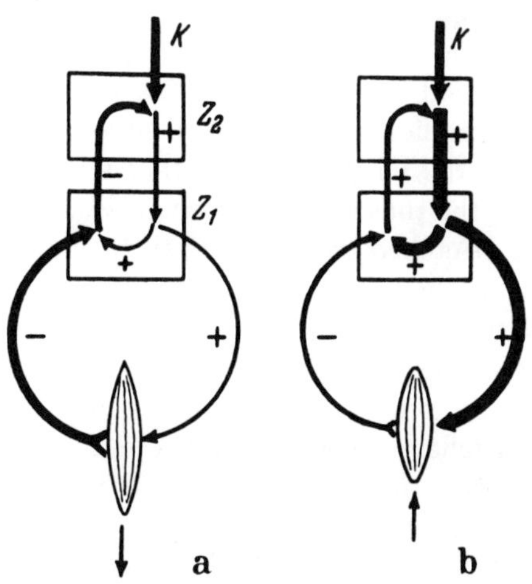


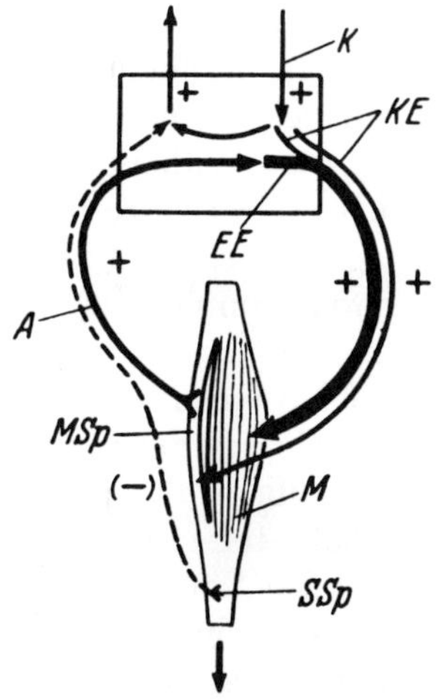


Fig. 8 (*left*). Explanation of the behavior of a muscle under tension during externally imposed (passive) extension (*a*) and contraction (*b*). The muscle actively follows the imposed movement while higher centers maintain tonus by means of the command K. See text for detailed explanation.

Fig. 9 (*right*). Behavior of a muscle, maintained in slight tension by the higher command K, in response to an externally imposed load. In this case, the central apparatus is so arranged as to oppose actively the external load (↓) by contraction. Msp = muscle spindles (tension sensors); KE = efference to the muscle and spindle fibres, determined by command from higher centers; EE = the efference added to KE as a consequence of the afference from the muscle spindles; Ssp = tension sensors in the tendons ("tendon spindles") which have higher thresholds and which switch in the mechanism described in Figure 8.

[10] Personal observation in an enclosed experimental room operated as a centrifuge.

[11] Comment: Subsequent research indicates that the relevant receptors are situated *in or at the joints,* thus confirming the expectation of finding them outside the musculature (Mittelstaedt).

externally imposed movement is followed "spastically" by the limb. Mechanisms of this sort are common and can be observed in pathological conditions in pure form. An example of this type is the active response of *Geophilus* (Fig. 5a) to imposed movement. The same thing can be observed in vertebrates (dog, toad) following thoracic section of the spinal cord; the hind legs start to walk if the surface supporting them is pulled backwards.[12]

In the actively innervated muscles of intact warm-blooded animals, however, the reaction to an imposed load is normally just the opposite of this: the muscle contracts strongly enough to balance the load. This much-studied "stretch-reflex" (*Eigenreflex*) (cf. P. Hoffmann, among others) is mediated by a direct arc from sensory to motor neuron and works without the intervention of an efference copy or the activity of higher centers. Its receptors are the muscle spindles, delicate contractile fibers which have sensory and motor innervations (and make up about 1 percent of the muscle fibers, the remainder of which have only motor innervation). If we assume that the afference from the muscle spindles is led directly to the motoneurons controlling the rest of the muscle bundle, the behavior of the stretch reflex can be understood (Fig. 9). If the muscle contracts or expands freely without extrinsic load, the spindles remain "silent" so long as their lengths change in the same way as the lengths of the other muscle fibers. If an external load is imposed on the muscle (either when relaxed, or during contraction) the spindles are stretched and "fire" until they are relieved of tension by the contraction of the rest of the muscle fibers.[13] The CNS prescribes the intended position or movement, and the stretch reflex achieves the desired objective, even against external obstacles. We may ascribe to the tension receptors in the tendons, which have a higher threshold, the task of switching off this reflex mechanism in the event of overloading, and switching on the adaptive mechanism described in the previous paragraph, in order to avoid muscle damage.

By this elegant device, Nature achieves maintenance of balance as a self-regulating muscular mechanism. If a stationary animal is pushed from the left, so that it bends over to the right, then—even before the labyrinths can come into play—the extensors of the leg(s) on the right side stiffen as a result of the increased load. The organism gets just the required support at the required time and place, whether standing or walking and remains as well-balanced as if set on delicate springs. The economy in higher control signals and muscle energy which this arrangement affords can well be imagined.

We see, then, that the principle of reafference is replaced by a different,

[12] Of course, some additional locomotor activity must be present to sustain the forward (thrust) phase of leg movement.

[13] We thank Dr. Lissmann of Cambridge and Professor Hoffmann of Freiburg for supplying important data concerning proprioceptor functioning not contained in the literature available to us.

peripheral, mechanism in the case of the stretch reflex, but in other respects still plays a role in limb movement. Let us see to what extent perception—as with the eye—can help us to look further into this.

Section of the afferent pathways (dorsal roots) of a limb, say the arm, does not lead to "apparent movements" when that limb is actively moved, despite the absence of reafference. At first glance, this would seem to argue against the validity of the reafference principle in this case. But the argument does not hold, since any conceivable perception of apparent movement of an object presupposes the perception of a real object, which, in the case of the arm, is probably mediated by touch and pressure afference; in this instance however the afference is also cut off. In a precisely analogous way, the feedback of an efference copy from the actively moving eye *in darkness* naturally does not lead to "apparent movement of unperceived objects." In both cases, the perceptual substrate itself is simply not there. It is certainly true, on the other hand, that a man whose arm has been amputated still has "control" over its central representation, can open and close the "phantom hand," and knows how he moves it.[14] However, as many a witness has stated, these things occur in an "imaginary" space which interpenetrates the "real" space, that is, the one built up by the remaining normal afference.

To avoid these difficulties, let us rather limit our consideration to instances in which we can make *concrete predictions* for changes of limb perception on the basis of the principle of reafference.

If the deep sensibility of a limb has been impaired, a distinctive sensation should be expected to accompany active movement against a firm substrate or support (apart from extinction of the stretch reflex and the drop in muscle tonus which accompanies it); because there is too little reafference from the tension receptors, each time the limb is moved under tension the efference copy must ascend as a report: "The substrate is moving away." This prediction is confirmed! For example, in polyneuritis the deep sensitivity of the leg extensors is sharply reduced; it appears to the patient as if the floor "sinks down elastically" when he steps down, say, from a bench onto the floor.[15] Analogous reports of *Tabes dorsalis* patients, that the ground is "like rubber" are probably to be explained similarly.

Conversely, from the motor aspect of the matter, one would expect active movements to lead to greater excursion of the limb than was intended. As we already saw in the case of postural orientation, if reafference is reduced there is too little "peripheral feedback" in the lowest centre, normal equilibrium is not achieved so that efference continues, and too great an excursive movement results. The exaggerated ataxic movement of patients suffering from *Tabes dorsalis* demonstrate this very clearly.

[14] Unfortunately, the important question of whether motor impulses proceed into the stump of the limb at such times has apparently not yet been investigated.

[15] Personal communication of K. Lorenz and others.

Another example: according to the reafference principle, the perceptions which arise from a difference in pressure to the soles of the feet should be very different when they are produced by active movement on the one hand, or by passively pressing a surface against the soles on the other. In the first case, one should notice no change in pressure, but in the second case a clear difference should be observed. To a great extent this has been confirmed also. Katz (1948) discovered that the difference threshold is *twenty times higher* if the pressure on the soles is changed through active alternations of weight distribution, as in bending the knees, supporting oneself on one's arms, etc., compared to the threshold found when the subject lies down and the soles of the feet are subjected passively to different pressures.[16]

Thus, again, we see that perception demonstrates the validity of the principle of reafference. In the last example the mechanism should be sought at quite high central levels since it coordinates and controls all four limbs in concert.

## Reafference and Locomotion

We can measure the extent to which reafference is built into a neuromotor system as an *integrative element* by observing how much greater in amplitude and yet much less precise a movement is following destruction of the sensory pathways. In this connection there are some interesting phylogenetic differences: in the lower swimming and crawling species (fish, amphibians) locomotion is still quite normal following deafferentation; in walking mammals it is very ataxic, and the complicated chains of movement of the human hand can only occur in ragged, exaggerated and uncoordinated fragments (Foerster, 1936). From this it follows that in the lower forms the CNS operates in principle independently, and thus is "automatic" in character (von Holst, 1936; Weiss, 1941), whereas higher forms of movement require reafference, although not necessarily reflex-eliciting stimuli. In the series: swim, crawl, walk, climb, grip, touch (hand, tongue), we have first of all movements which require no afference; then types which are mediated and controlled through reafference, and at the end those which depend on exafference![17]

From this viewpoint the old arguments about whether movements of the limbs are reflexive or automatic can be laid aside; the alternatives were wrong! To put things metaphorically: the fin movements of a swimming fish proceed blindly in the dark, but the moving hand needs an illuminated environment. The deafferented hand is like a blind person who cannot find

[16] The author of these experiments sought to explain the findings in terms of "Gestalt experience of the whole body."

[17] The tongue lacks proprioceptive receptors, as do certain facial muscles; in the fingers, proprioceptors are the most important mediators of exafference.

his way because he does not know where he is. But this hardly means that his readiness to initiate coordinated movement is smaller than is the fish's! And just as the blind help themselves through the sense of touch, so too the eye can come to the aid of the "sensorily crippled" hand. In both cases, the ancillary afference improves matters greatly.

## Interaction of Several Types of Afference

The situation in the CNS is more complicated when afferent streams from different parts of the body work simultaneously to control posture and movement. To take a simple example:

The direction of movement in arthropods is controlled by nerve ganglia in the head. If the right-hand circumoesophageal connections are severed, thereby cutting out operation of the right-hand sensory center (supra-oesophageal ganglion), there is a tendency for the organism to turn towards the left (analogous to the tendency produced by unilateral removal of the vestibular nuclei in vertebrates). In attempting to move forward, the insect bends toward the left, and in attempting to move backwards, bends toward the right; that is, in both cases the path of movement is counterclockwise (von Holst, 1934).

If we make the justifiable assumption that the commands which control tonus in the body segments come from a higher center (suboesophageal ganglion) then according to the reafference principle we should expect that reducing the number of segments should lead to more pronounced torsion in the remainder. This is to be expected because, in order to balance out the too great difference in levels in the higher command center, a certain amount of reafference is needed, which following loss of reafference from the severed segments, has to be generated by more vigorous bending of the remaining segments. This expectation is in fact met by the outcome; if a many legged arthropod is shortened (for instance, *Lithobius*) by cutting off a posterior section, the bending becomes progressively greater (Fig. 10 and 11) so that the half-centipede runs in a circle scarcely half the diameter of the circular path of the intact specimen: surely a singular result, so far as reflexology is concerned (von Holst, 1934)!

We should expect, moreover, that passively bending the hind end of the intact insect (in the absence of other disturbance) should lead to an active and opposite bending of the anterior end, because the exafference from the rear must be compensated by an opposing afference from another place in order to maintain the correct summated afference rising to higher centres. This sort of behavior is well known in certain arthropods, and goes by the name "homostrophic reflex" (Fig. 12).

Now let us consider a less straightforward case: the postural orientation of higher vertebrates and man. In the fish, postural orientation is fairly

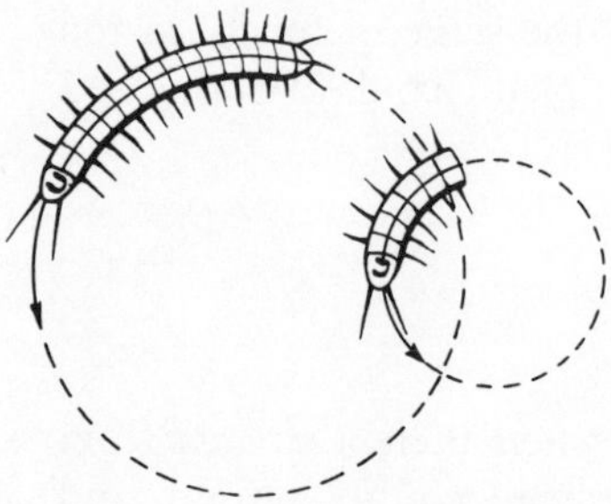

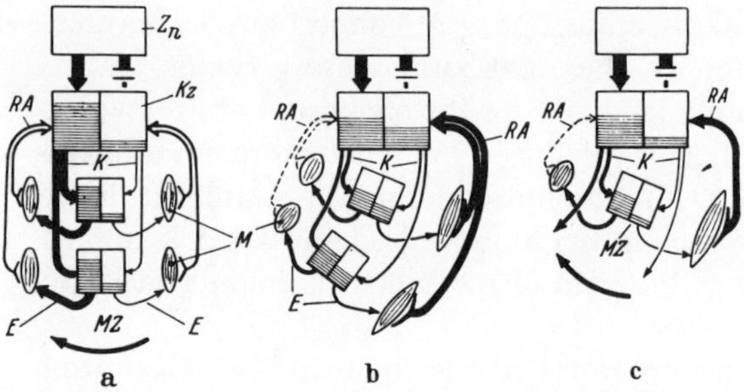


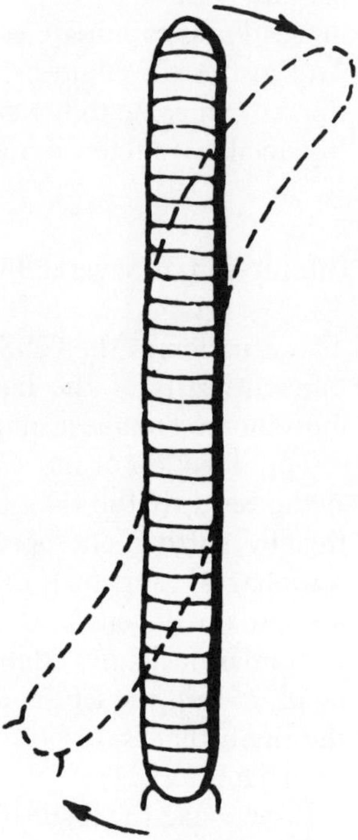

Fig. 10 (*upper left*). Arthropod (*Lithobius*) runs in circles of a specific diameter following section of the right circumoesophageal connections. *a*, otherwise intact insect, *b*, insect with posterior portion removed.

Fig. 11. Schema to explain Fig. 10. $Z_n$ = higher sensory centre supraoesophageal ganglion; $K_z$ = command center suboesophageal ganglion; K = command to the lower motor centers of the body segments MZ (of which only two are shown); E = efference to muscles M; A = afference; RA = reafference from the position sensors in the body joints. The thickness of the arrows indicates the strength of impulse trains. The righthand stream of impulses from $Z_n$ to $K_z$ has been interrupted. In Fig. 11*a*, the asymmetrically innervated command center $K_z$ causes a similarly asymmetrical input to the motor centers, whose efference leads to a bending (alteration in tonus) to the left (lowest arrow). Fig. 11 *b* shows how the reafference from this bending stimulates the command center in the *opposite* sense, so that a balance is struck between asymmetrical innervation from above and reafference from below. If one of the motor centers is removed, as in *c*, the reafference becomes too small to balance the efference from above, and a further bending, or change in tonus, has to occur (lowest arrow).

Fig. 12 (*right*). Arthropod (*Julus*) bent passively to the left at the posterior end, responds with active bending of the anterior end to the right ("homostrophic reflex").

easy to comprehend, since the head which carries the otoliths is fairly rigidly connected to the body. Also, the motor system does not have to make permament active contributions to the *maintenance* of a goal posture once it has been attained, since mechanically, the fish is in a state of indifferent (passive) equilibrium with its supporting medium. *Our* upright posture, on the other hand, is labile, the maintenance of every goal posture requires

Fig. 13. Schematic indication of the correctional movements of the limbs and eyes in warm-blooded animals (mammals, birds) which are elicited by passive (imposed) changes in position (direction of tipping is labeled from the animals' point of view). *a,* Normal position; *b,* body and head tipped to the right; *c,* body only, *d* head only turned to the right. In *e* the same situation is shown as in *d,* head only turned to the right. In *e* the same situation is shown as in *d,* except that in this case the labyrinths have been removed (compare with *d* and *e* of Figure 4).

particular active patterns of innervation, and moreover the head, body and extremities are mobile independently of one another. Active or passive movement of the head alone must *not* be accompanied by reflex movements of the limbs initiated by the labyrinths, since this would only disturb the body's balance! Let us consider the system's actual behavior (compare Fig. 13 a–d).

A stationary animal is turned passively, body and head together, to the right; it makes compensatory righting movements with the limbs (Fig. 13b). If the head is held still and only the body moved, the same movements are elicited (Fig. 13c). If the head is turned by itself, the attempt is made to right it alone, and the rest of the body remains passive (Fig. 13d). These observations are most easily understood by assuming that the positional receptors are in the torso, as has often been postulated (Trendelenberg, 1916, 1907; Fischer, 1926). But the behavior of the eyes is not consistent with this; in condition (b) they rotate slightly to the left, in (c) slightly to the right, and in (d) strongly to the left so that they maintain approximately the same relation to the body as before—which is quite analogous to the behavior of anterior and posterior body segments in the "homostrophic reflex."

The simplest explanation of the whole behavior is that (at least) two afferent inputs are involved in postural control of the torso, head and eyes. One of these stems from the statolith apparatus, in the head, the other from the positional receptors of the neck. The two streams of impulses are mutually subtractive so far as the position of the body is concerned, but are additive with respect to the eyes (Fig. 14a). If this explanation is correct, then the reafference principle predicts a very precise dysfunction as soon as the afference from the two sides of the neck is artificially unequalized. The CNS would have to interpret such an event as "turning of the body, the head remaining upright," and would set in motion a compensatory set of movements in the limbs. This is just what

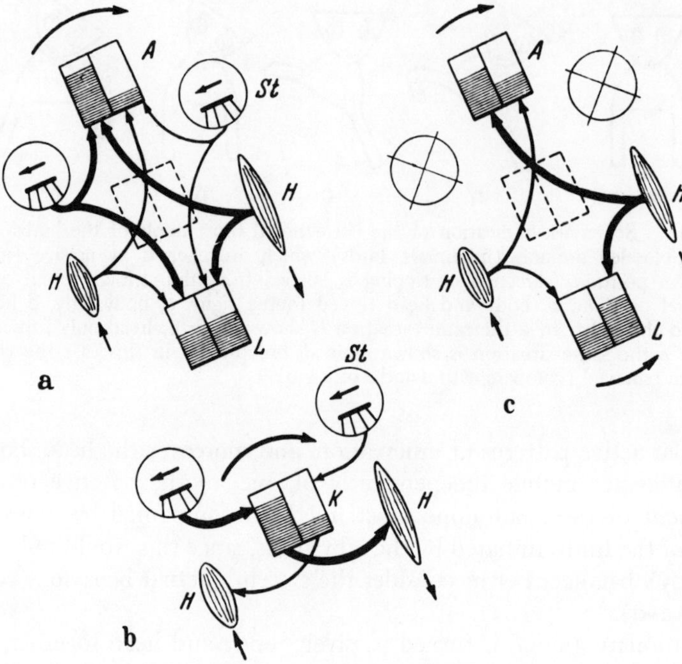


Fig. 14. Schemata (analogous to Fig. 3) to explain the behavior of a warm-blooded animal with statoliths (*a*, *b*) and without (*c*) in the event of passive sideways bending of the head (compare 13 *d*, *e*—Fig. 14 *a* and *b* are also valid for active head movements). L = positional center for the trunk, A for the eyes, K for the head. H = neck muscles. For clarity's sake, K has been omitted from *a*, but is shown in *b* (in *c* it has also been left out). The strength of afference from the statoliths and positional sensors of the neck muscles is indicated by the thickness of arrows, as before. The unequal stimulation of the eye centres (A in *a* and *c*), of the head centre (K in *b*), and of the trunk centre (L in *c*), cause an impulse to turn as indicated in each case by the curved arrows. Further elaboration in text.

happens: if a cold cloth is held against the left side of the neck below the *os petrosum*, a hot one on the right side (so that the impulse frequency of the assumed neck afference is diminished on the left, increased on the right), the expected limb movements are elicited.[18]

The reafference principle predicts exactly the same misinterpretation if the head is moved, actively or passively, following bilateral removal of the labyrinths. In this case too the CNS must "believe" that the head remains upright and the body is in a rotated position, since no report of head rotation occurs; it therefore should attempt to correct for the rotated position.

[18] This phenomenon was first described by Griesman (1922) and confirmed by Fischer and Wodak (1922). Goldstein (1925) used it as an argument for a general plasticity theory of the CNS. So far as we know no physiological explanation has been given before.

This is precisely what happens, as has long been known (Dusser de Barenne, 1924; Magnus, 1924; cf. Fig. 13a and 14c).

Although these sorts of "neck reflexes" have long been known—they were discovered by Barney (1906)—they were assumed to be absent in normal people, since we can move our heads without eliciting "reflexes" in the body. That this conclusion has been so widely accepted must apparently be held against reflexology, since according to it any stimulus must elicit some response; but in this case the response (movement) does not occur.

The proposed mutual cancellation of afference from the labyrinths and the neck is valid only for control of the trunk and limbs, not for the eye. In that case, the two components are additive. Rotating the head to the left causes an opposite rotation of the eyes to the right—as can readily be observed in a mirror. The amplitude of the eye rotation is equal to the sum of the amplitudes obtained by (1) tipping the whole body while the neck remains motionless and (2) bending the neck as the head remains upright (e.g., turning the body to the right), as Magnus and his co-workers already knew.[19] By means of this summation the eyes tend to maintain their relationship to the vertical, and therefore help to stabilize the visual field when the head moves.

The behavior of the head itself is easy to understand in terms of its afferent-efferent arrangements: the center for "head position" receives afference from the labyrinths and sends efference to the neck muscles. The head, together with the neck muscles, is comparable to the fish and its whole musculature (Fig. 4b). The head rights itself after being passively bent, but can also be actively moved (by command of higher centers). In both cases the reafferent streams which flow from the labyrinths and from the positional receptors of the neck muscles to the centers for head and eye position are equal. Therefore, we see that so far as the trunk and eyes are concerned, active and passive head movements are equivalent. One can now give a plausible account of how the trunk and limbs can be brought actively into any desired posture, while the head maintains its spatial position independently.

## *CONCLUSION*

The picture here presented is a first crude outline. But even so it has perhaps made clear the ways in which the principle of reafference is an advance on earlier conceptions. Reflexology describes everything which results from stimulation with one and the same word. There would be no objection to this—we too need generalized concepts—if it were not the case that behind

[19] The relative contributions of the two afferences, shown here (Fig. 13) equally big, *can* be unequal so far as the eyes are concerned.

the word stands the misleading concept of the reflex arc, which nearly always leads to false interpretations. The opposite of reflexology, the doctrine of *plasticity* (Bethe, 1931) holds that everything is connected to everything else, and excitation in the nervous system spreads out as in a nerve net; it is doubtless correct in its rejection of pure reflex doctrine, but neither one can predict in concrete situations what will actually happen; and that is never "just anything."[20] The reafference principle makes definite predictions by which it is possible to assess the range of its validity. It is *one* mechanism among several and prejudges nothing with regard to automatisms, coordination and spontaneity. It seems rather to have the potential to reconcile various different approaches. Since the reafference principle applies throughout the CNS from the lowest phenomena (internal and external control of the limbs, relations of different parts of the body to each other) to the highest (orientation in space, perception, illusions), it can build a bridge between "low level" nerve physiology, and the "high level" science of behavior.

For example, it has often been asked whether an insect can discriminate between its own movements and movements of its environment. Mathilde Hertz (1934) answered the question positively—with a sure instinct—but could not plausibly explain how it could be so. Other investigators, like von Buddenbrock, have answered in the negative, arguing on the basis that the relative motion of insect and external world are identical in both cases. We recognize now that the *eye* does not distinguish between the two sorts of movement, but the *animal* does; for we recognize that the living creature has a CNS which consists of more than simply a set of connecting cables between receptors and muscles! By means of the principle of reafference it achieves a representation of the invariances in its environment.

In human psychology, phenomena relating to invariance play a large role. For instance, the fact that we see a stable environment during eye movements (space constancy), or that an object's size appears to us to be independent of its distance (size constancy), are well known examples. The principle of reafference, as we saw earlier, can explain them both. However, it cannot explain every invariance phenomenon; for example, the color constancy of visual objects, which depends on central processes; this is not a drawback, but rather an advantage of the principle. Because it makes concrete predictions, pseudoexplanations of a heterogeneous collection of different facts can be avoided.

The principle of reafference leads to a precise position on the question of the *objectivity of perception*. We saw in several instances that the

[20] Bethe is of the same opinion; this is shown in his various attempts to approach an understanding of the actual events by means of physical models. His principle of the mechanical "gliding coordination" (1931) is to our minds a good model; the expositions of Section 5 are indeed the detailed presentation of such a coupling.

"correct" report was the resultant of two "false" reports, and the latter—as we can demonstrate experimentally—each considered on its own have individually the same character as the "correct" report. For a lower center, which receives but one afference, all reports are equally "correct." The question of whether a perception is objectively correct or not can only be asked where several different afferent streams come together. "Objectively correct" then means nothing other than congruence of several reports. A report will only be evaluated as illusory if it is not consistent with other simultaneous reports. The lowest center is in this sense completely stupid, but we should not forget that the highest centers also cannot be more clever than their afferent inputs allow, every one of which can be deceived!

Let us hope that these pages will help to overcome, at long last, the tendency to describe and explain the functions of the most highly developed organ with a few crude notions. Up to now, the barrier between neurophysiology and the study of behavior—consider just terminology alone!—has seemed to be formidable. The sooner we recognize, however, that those complex higher functional entities, before which reflexology stands helpless, have roots in the simplest basic function of the CNS, the sooner will that barrier vanish into oblivion.

## *REFERENCES*


Adrian, E. D. Discharges from vestibular receptors in the cat. *Journal of Physiology*, 1943, *101*, 389-407.

Bethe, A. Die biologischen Rhythmus-Phänomene als selbständige bzw. erzwungene Kippvorgänge betrachtet. *Pflügers Archiv für die gesamte Physiologie*, 1940, *244*, 1-42.

Bethe, A. Plastizität und Zentrenlehre. *Handbuch der normalen und pathologischen Physiologie*. Bd. 15. Berlin: Springer, 1931, pp. 1175-1220.

Bernhard, C. G., & Skoglund, C. R. Slow positive and negative ventral root potentials accompanying extension and flexion evoked by medullary stimulation. *Acta physiologica Scandinavica*, 1947, *14* (47, No. 3), 1-12.

Bernhard, C. G., & Therman, P. O. Alternating facilitation and inhibition of extensor muscle activity in decerebrate cats. *Acta physiologica Scandinavica*, 1947, *14* (47, No. 7), 1-10.

Böhm, H. Vom lebendigen Rhythmus. Studium generale 1951, *4*, 28-41.

Buddenbrock, W. von. *Grundriss der vergleichenden Physiologie*. Bd. 1. Berlin, 1937.

Fischer, M. H. *Handbuch der normalen und pathologischen Physiologie*. Bd. 11. Berlin: Springer, 1926.

Foerster, O. *Handbuch der Neurologie*. Berlin: Springer, 1936.

Fulton, J. F. *Physiology of the nervous system*. (2nd ed.) London: Oxford University Press, 1943.

Goldstein, K., & Riese, W. Influence of sensitive skin stimuli on so-called vestibular reaction movements. *Klinische Wochenschrift,* 1925, *4,* 1201-1204; continued *4,* 1250-1254.

Gray, J. The role of peripheral sense organs during locomotion in the vertebrates. *Symposia of the Society for Experimental Biology, No. 4: Physiological Mechanisms in Animal Behavior.* New York: Academic Press, 1950, pp. 111-126.

Gray, J., & Lissmann, H. W. Further observations on the effect of deafferentation on the locomotory activity of amphibian limbs. *Journal of Experimental Biology,* 1946, *23,* 121-132.

Griessmann, B. Zur kalorischen Erregung des Ohrlabyrinths. *Internationale Zentralblatt für Ohrenheilkunde,* 1921, *19,* 336.

Hoffmann, F. B. Augenbewegungen und relative optische Lokalisation. *Zeitschrift für Biologie,* München, 1924, *80,* 81-90.

Holst, E. von. Untersuchungen über die Funktionen des Zentralnervensystems beim Regenwurm. *Zoologische Jahrbücher,* 1932, *51,* 547-588.

Holst, E. von. Weitere Versuche zum nervösen Mechanismus der Bewegung beim Regenwurm (*Lumricus terr. L.*). *Zoologische Jahrbücher,* 1933, *53,* 67-100.

Holst, E. von. Über das Laufen der Hundertfüsser (*Chilopoden*) *Zoologische Jahrbücher,* 1934, *54,* 157-159.

Holst, E. von. Zwei Versuche zum Hirnproblem der Arthropoden. *Pflügers Archiv für die gesamte Physiologie,* 1934, *234,* 114-123.

Holst, E. von. Über den Prozess der zentralnervösen Koordination. *Pflügers Archiv für die gesamte Physiologie,* 1935, *236,* 149-158.

Holst, E. von. Vom Dualismus der motorischen und der automatisch-rhythmischen Funktion im Rückenmark und vom Wesen des automatischen Rhythmus. *Pflügers Archiv für die gesamte Physiologie,* 1936, *237,* 356-378.

Holst, E. von. Zentralnervensystem. *Fortschritte der Zoologie,* 1937, *3,* 343-362.

Holst, E. von. Über relative Koordination bei Säugern und bei Menschen. *Pflügers Archiv für die gesamte Physiologie,* 1938, *240,* 44-59.

Holst, E. von. Entwurf eines Systems der lokomotorischen Periodenbildungen bei Fischen. *Zeitschrift für vergleichende Physiologie,* 1939, *26,* 481-528.

Holst, E. von. Die relative Koordination als Phänomen und als Methode zentralnervöser Funktionsanalyse. *Ergebnisse der Physiologie,* 1939, *42,* 228-306.

Holst, E. von. Über relative Koordination bei Arthropoden. *Pflügers Archiv für die gesamte Physiologie,* 1943, *246,* 847-865.

Holst, E. von. Von der Mathematik der Nervösen Ordnungsleistung. *Experientia,* 1948, *4,* 374-381.

Holst, E. von. Die Arbeitsweise des Statolithenapparates bei Fischen. *Zeitshrift für vergleichende Physiologie,* 1950, *32,* 60-120.

Holst, E. von. Die Tätigkeit des Statolithenapparates im Wirbeltierlabyrinth. *Naturwissenschaften,* 1950, *37,* 265-272.

Hertz, M. Zur Physiologie des Formen- und Bewegungsehens I. Optomotorische Versuche an Fliegen. *Zeitschrift für vergleichende Physiologie,* 1934, *20,* 430-449.

Kornmüller, A. E. Eine experimentelle Anästhesie der äusseren Augenmuskeln am Menschen und ihre Auswirkungen. *Journal für Psychologie und Neurologie,* 1931, *41,* 354-366.

Katz, D. *Gestaltpsychologie* (Rev. ed.) Basel: Benno-Schwabe, 1948.

Lissmann, H. W. The neurological basis of the locomotory rhythm in the spinal dogfish II. The effect of de-afferentation. *Journal of Experimental Biology,* 1946, 23, 162-176.

Lorenz, K. Z. The comparative method in studying innate behavior patterns. *Physiological Mechanisms in Animal Behavior* (Symposium of the Society for Experimental Biology, IV) 221-268. Cambridge: Cambridge University Press, 1950.

Lowenstein, O. Labyrinth and equilibrium. *Symposia of the Society for Experimental Biology, No. 4: Physiological Mechanisms in Animal Behavior.* New York: Academic Press, 1950, pp. 60-82.

Metzger, G. *Gesetze des Sehens* Frankfurt: Kramer, 1953.

Magnus, R. *Körperstellung. Experimentell-physiologische Untersuchungen.* Berlin: Springer, 1924, p. 740.

Mittelstaedt, H. Telotaxis und Optomotorik von Eristalis bei Augeninversion. *Naturwissenschaften,* 1949, 36, 90-91.

Schoen, L. Quantitative Untersuchungen über die zentrale Kompensation nach einseitiger Utriculusausschaltung bei Fischen. *Zeitschrift für vergleichende Physiologie,* 1950, 32, 121-150.

Schöne, H. Die Augen als Gleichgewichtsorgane bei Wasserkäferlarven. *Naturwissenschaften,* 1950, 37, 235-236.

Spiegel, E. A., & Sato, G. Experimentalstudien am Nervensystem. Ueber den Erregungszustand der medullaren Zentren nach doppelseitiger Labyrinthausschaltung. *Pflügers Archiv für die gesamte Physiologie,* 1926, *215,* 106-119.

Tinbergen, N. *The study of instinct.* Oxford: Clarendon Press, 1951.

Trendelenberg, 1943, p. 240.

Wodak, E., & Fischer, M. H. Ueber die Arm-Tonus Reaktion. *Zeitschrift für Hals, Nasen und Ohrenheilkunde,* 1922, 3, 215-220.

*Von Holst and Mittelstaedt conceive of the reafference principle as applying principally to the rather specific and fixed systems of orientation and balance control, and of the responses of lower organisms to particular environmental events such as predation (Mittelstaedt, 1962) types of response which also tend to be rather stereotyped and probably unmodifiable by learning as that process is generally understood by psychologists. It is of some interest to note that the principle has been taken over by psychologists, principally by Richard Held, and modified and extended to form the basis for a model of human perceptual lability and adaptation (Held, 1962). Also, it should be noted that the reafference principle can only work given that there is also stimulus equivalence; for instance, for the feedback control of a fly-catching mechanism to work, it is necessary that the fly be recog-*

nized as such in different positions and at different times. In a later section a fairly specific neurophysiological basis for such equivalence will be outlined.

The final paper in this part, Sutherland's "Stimulus Analysing Mechanisms," reverts once more to our central topic, and does so from a particular point of view. Sutherland considers the question of the sorts of analyzing, or coding, system which should be looked for by scientists interested in the equivalence of stimuli and pattern discrimination. On the one hand, there is a certain appeal in looking for a general-purpose system, and on the other, certain pieces of evidence tend to favor the view that rather specific types of coding and analysis occur, particularly in lower visual forms. This paper is included to present the two sides of the argument and to illustrate a point of very real significance in the development of ideas about pattern recognition. Although Sutherland supported the notion of specific analysing systems, he was able to adduce singularly little evidence in its favour a dozen years ago (the paper was first presented in 1958). Had he been writing today, he could have told a very different story, one which will be quite fully documented in the following sections of the book.

# Stimulus Analysing Mechanisms

N. S. SUTHERLAND

*Two distinct approaches to the problem of stimulus analysing mechanisms in organisms are outlined. The first, often adopted by engineers, is to assume that there is a very general analysing system at work for each modality which in principle is capable of categorising stimuli in all possible ways. The second approach is to assume that specific analysing mechanisms are at work and that stimuli can only be categorised in a limited number of ways by these specific mechanisms.*

*If the first sort of system were correct it would be impossible to make predictions about how stimuli would be categorised based merely on the system: such predictions could only be made from a knowledge of previous inputs to the system. Evidence is produced to show that it is highly probable that some stimulus analysis is performed by specific mecha-*

About half the original paper is presented. Pages 585–588 and 591–596 have been cut, since they are not too relevant to our discussion. Reprinted from *The Mechanization of Thought Processes,* 1959.

*nisms, at least in sub-mammalian organisms where many categorisations seem to be innate. The evidence for mammals is inconclusive, but suggestions are made for how it would be possible to test for the existence of the general type of analysing mechanisms in mammals. The existence of specific analysing mechanisms would not only be economical in terms of the number of nerve cells required, but it would account for many facts of animal and human behaviour, particularly if we envisage the possibility that the same specific analysing mechanisms may actually be used in different ways of categorising stimuli in one sensory modality and that some of the analysing mechanisms may be common to more than one modality. Thus competition for specific analysing mechanisms would explain why the human being seems to function as a single information channel, it would give a rationale for recent neurological findings on the peripheral blocking of incoming stimuli, and it would account for findings on animals which suggest that animals learn not merely to attach a response to a stimulus but also learn which analysing mechanisms to switch in on a given occasion. Some of the difficulties in using behavioural evidence to set up hypotheses about specific analysing mechanisms are discussed, and the difficulty of deciding what sorts of coding mechanisms are at work in the central nervous system is discussed with reference to a particular example of a simple discrimination. It is suggested that engineers might profitably turn their attention to the design of specific analysing mechanisms intended to account for some of the ways in which animals are known to classify stimuli.*

## *INTRODUCTION*

This paper will be concerned with the problem of how ideas based on engineering concepts can best be applied to help solve some of the problems which arise when we consider how patterned stimuli are classified by organisms. The paper will deal mainly with visually presented patterns.

There are two different kinds of theoretical mechanism which have been proposed to explain what organisms do. The first kind is one which attempts to give a very general explanation of what organisms do by postulating a broad model or type of connectivity, and then pointing to some very general features of the model's behaviour which are said to be shared by animals. Examples of this type of theory are those of Hebb (1949), Uttley (1956), Taylor (1956), Ashby (1952). The second kind of theory is of a more specific sort and is designed to explain a limited range of behaviour by putting forward a model whose parts are highly differentiated: examples of this kind of model are those put forward by Deutsch (1955),

Dodwell (1957), and Sutherland (1957) to explain certain features of shape recognition, or by Tinbergen (1951), to explain certain features of instinctive behaviour. In the specific type of mechanism, the parts are arranged in a highly systematic way. In this sort of mechanism, information contained in the input can be selectively lost so that this sort of system is potentially more economical than general analysing mechanisms. This gain in economy is offset by a loss in flexibility. Wherever the classification of stimuli can be shown to be innate, the existence of a specific analysing mechanism is implied. Specific analysing mechanisms could, however, arise out of an initially randomly connected network as a result of learning: a small initial bias in part of the system could in theory lead to a highly specific system being developed out of an initially randomly connected network. For example, Sutherland (1957), has suggested that the tendency of the octopus to move its head up and down while viewing shapes could lead through a learning process to the development of a visual analysing system in which the vertical extents of shapes are counted at different points on the horizontal axis, while other information is lost.

In what follows the two types of theory will be discussed in detail, and an attempt made to specify their characteristics. The rather general type of system will be considered first, and it ought to be said at the outset that I am perhaps prejudiced against this type of system. The rationale of this prejudice will be made clear later. In general it is typical of the first sort of system that it is put forward by engineers who know little about psychology, it is typical of the second sort that it is put forward by psychologists who know little engineering: Hebb is an exception on this rule.

## *CHARACTERISTICS OF GENERAL ANALYSING SYSTEMS*

If the neural mechanisms mediating stimulus classification are highly unspecific, this sets a severe limitation on the possibility of discovering what the neural mechanisms are and working from knowledge of the mechanisms to predictions about what animals will actually do. This can be illustrated with reference to Hebb's theory of shape recognition. According to Hebb the connections from the primary visual projection area in the brain are initially random: thresholds at synapses will presumably vary in a random way from moment to moment according to such factors as how recently the post-synaptic nerve cell has fired. This means that when a given shape is first projected onto the retina, it is impossible to predict what output the system will give: initially any shape is as likely to produce a given output as any other. However, once a shape has given a certain output the chance of its giving the same output on the next occasion of presentation will be increased (provided it stimulates the same retinal cells), since it is postulated that the probability of a given synaptic connection being used increases every time it is in fact used. Moreover, given that a given shape falling on a given part of the retina excites a given cell assembly as a result of an increase in the probability of transmission at specific synapses, any shape projected onto the retina in close temporal contiguity with the initial shape should come to excite the same cell assembly through the mechanism of spatial summation in the nervous system: of the random connections which the new shape might excite the ones it will be most likely to excite are those already excited by the initial shape. Thus the two shapes will come to have a cell assembly in common—they will tend to give a common output. Since the same shape will be constantly being shifted across the retina from moment to moment, this means that the same shape projected to different parts of the retina should come to give the same output.

An interesting paradox arises. When Hebb's theory was first put forward it was hailed as showing how it might be possible to account for behaviour in terms of plausible neurophysiological mechanisms: it was thought that Hebb had demonstrated the possibility of explaining the findings of psychology in physiological terms. However, a moment's reflection shows that, if he is right, what he has really succeeded in doing is to demonstrate the utter impossibility of giving detailed neurophysiological mechanisms for explaining psychological or behavioural findings. According to Hebb the precise circuits used in the brain for the classification of a particular shape will vary from individual to individual with chance variation in nerve connectivity determined by genetic and maturational factors, they will vary within the individual with chance variations in the threshold at synapses at times when a given shape is first seen and during the succeeding presentations, and they will vary according to the frequency and temporal order of shapes projected onto the retina when learning is occurring. This means that even if we knew the precise sequence of shapes an animal has been subjected to in its previous history, it would be impossible to translate the effects of that sequence into actual brain circuitry and then work from the brain circuitry to predictions about subsequent behaviour: the circuits will be so complex, so scattered over different parts of the brain and, above all, they will vary so much from individual to individual that trying to take the intermediate steps for translating the effects of early experience of shapes into actual brain circuitry becomes an impossibility. Different individuals will achieve the same end result in behaviour by very different neurological circuits. If we wish to make predictions about individuals we must concentrate on correlating differences in early environment with differences in later behaviour, and translating these differences in early environment into differences in brain circuitry and then working from there to predictions about subsequent behaviour becomes impossible. If Hebb's general system is right, it precludes the possibility of ever making detailed predictions about behaviour from a detailed model of the system underlying behaviour. This seems to me a most unfortunate consequence since the explanation of complex phenomena in terms of a simpler system is something which is intellectually satisfying, and which is in some ways more exciting than the working out of statistical correlations between early stimulus sequences and subsequent behaviour. This is clearly not a reason for rejecting the account given by Hebb, but it is certainly a good reason for looking to see whether it is possible that the initial system is less randomly organised than Hebb supposes.

The same sort of consideration would apply if Taylor's model for classification were correct or if Uttley's were. Taylor is in fact trying to discover whether a system of the general sort Hebb proposes would have the properties Hebb attributes to it, by actually building a model of it. This is one of the cases in which building a physical model of a system is useful, because it is impossible to predict whether or not Hebb's system will have the properties he attributes to it, and it would be impossible even if some of the variables in the system were precisely specified because the equations necessary for a solution would be too complex to solve. Thus as more and more shapes occur together on the retina it seems possible on Hebb's system that all cells will ultimately be connected up with all other cells so that any shapes will eventually fire all cell-assemblies: Milner (1957) has recently proposed a most ingenious solution to this problem, but in order to do so he has to assume considerably more specificity in the arrangement of cortical cells than Hebb envisaged.

In the discussion of Hebb's theory so far, no account has been taken of the specific mechanisms which he alleges may be present from birth. The most important of these is the alleged tendency of animals to fixate successively the corners of figures, which in the case of rectilinear figures would result in the scanning of the contours. This mechanism would result in the equivalence of figures of different sizes since if corners are successively fixated the successive patterns at the fovea will be identical for the same shape irrespective of size and also eye movements will occur in the same directions though they will be of different lengths. Unfortunately Hebb never bridges the gap between recognition occurring in this way and recognition occurring without eye movements and when shapes are projected to different parts of the retina, although it is quite certain that human beings are capable of recognition under both these conditions (Collier, 1931). It should be noticed that in order for the eye movements to occur at all there must be a specific mechanism in the brain for reading off the position of a point relative to another in order to send the appropriate message to the eye muscles, and this is already a considerable limitation on the randomness of further connections from the primary projection area. If such a specific mechanism exists then logically it might play a part in shape recognition without the eye movements occurring. Since this is a limitation on the operation of a general mechanism which could according to training discriminate any shape from any other shape, and since evidence about the role of eye movements in shape recognition is almost entirely lacking, it will not be further discussed here. The possibility of using the way information is coded to determine some primitive response (such as fixation) to throw light on possible coding mechanisms in use to perform more complex functions (such as shape discrimination) will, however, be further discussed below.

Uttley (1956) has proposed a system of classification based on the principles of set theory. Input units are connected to ouput units in such a way that each possible combination of input units is connected to one output unit: whether or not a given combination of input units is firing can then be detected by reading off whether the appropriate output unit is firing. With some limitations, the same result can be achieved with an initially random connection of input and output units. Such a system will not mediate generalisation where the generalisation involved is not from a given input pattern to a pattern of which it is a subset. Uttley postulates a further system which works out conditional probabilities of one unit firing given that another unit has fired: connections between units are altered in such a way as to represent conditional probabilities. Such a system could account for generalisation occurring between pattens one of which was not a subset of the other. Once again, the detailed model would be of little use in prediction: we could predict only by knowing the details of the previous inputs to the system, and our predicitions would not involve following tranformations of an input through a mechanism to arrive at an output, but merely considering previous inputs in terms of their class relationships of inclusion and exclusion and the working out of conditional probability relationships between different sets.

It should be noticed that all three theories make the assumption that the actual classificatory mechanism used by animals arises wholly as a result of learning. This is not accidental: in any general system of this kind where initial connections are random or are arranged in all possible ways, it would be very hard to account for any innate classification. For example on Hebb's system it cannot be determined at birth what cell assembly will be used for what classification: thus it would be impossible genetically to specify any connections which would lead to a given response being given to a given stimulus. Even if some such system as Hebb, Taylor and Uttley suggest is at work in parts of the brain—and from the degree of perceptual relearning that can occur in human beings as evidenced by studies with distorting lenses (Kohler 1951) it seems likely that a system of this sort may operate—it would be extremely interesting to discover what its limitations are: these limitations indicate non-randomness of connections and therefore suggest analysing mechanisms of the specific kind at work which will explain and predict behaviour and which do not vary from individual to individual in a given species. It is important therefore to examine the evidence for stimuli innately producing specific reactions since any examples of this must severely limit the applicability of the general system I have been describing, and open the way to the postulation of more specific systems.

## *EXPERIMENTAL TESTS FOR GENERAL ANALYSING SYSTEMS*

### Innate Stimulus-Response Connections

Evidence has been accumulating that at least in many sub-mammalian organisms there is a considerable degree of specificity in the classificatory mechanisms at work. The studies cited by Tinbergen (1951) on innate fright reactions of gallinaceous birds to a figure moving in the direction of the short arm, and on other innate releasing stimuli often of a complex configurational kind are well known. Unfortunately, there is still some doubt about their validity because often these reactions were not studied under strict laboratory conditions and in only a few cases were precautions taken to exclude the possibility of the reaction coming into being as a result of early learning. However, more recent studies are not open to these objections and have confirmed that some classification can occur without learning. Thus Fantz (1957) has shown unequivocally that dark reared chicks exhibit a preference in their pecking behaviour for round objects as opposed to square or triangular ones, under conditions where the preference could not have been influenced by rewards and punishments. Wells (1958) has shown that newly hatched Sepia have a very specific preference for attacking Mysis, a small crustacean with a complex and specific form; although unrewarded for their attacks, the latency of attacks decreased with the number of attacks made, and it was difficult to persuade them to attack any other shape. Rheingold and Hess (1957) have shown that chicks' preference for water is determined by its visual properties, and that chicks rely upon the same visual properties before and after experience with water.

By fitting chicks with prisms, Hess (1956) has demonstrated that the direction and distance at which a chick will peck to a stimulus are both innately determined. Some years ago Sperry (1942, 1943, 1944) demonstrated that fly catching behaviour in the newt was determined by a highly specific neural organisation: if the eye ball was rotated through 180° and the optic nerve severed and allowed to regenerate, reactions to objects moving in the visual field were made to a position 180° from the position of the stimulus in the visual field. If the severed optic nerve can re-establish connections with such precision despite their biological uselessness to the animal, this suggests that the original connections may have had the same degree of specificity. Thus there can no longer be any question but in many submammalian species there is a degree of specificity present in the arrangement of the connections in classificatory mechanisms which means that theories of the general type cannot satisfactorily account for stimulus classification in these animals.

## Perceptual Deprivation

The situation with regard to mammals is still not resolved. Several investigators—Riesen (1949, 1950, 1951), Riesen, Kurke and Mellinger (1953), Riesen and Mellinger (1956), Chow and Nissen (1955) have demonstrated that some mammals (cats and chimpanzees) discriminate less well between visually presented shapes if they have been brought up without prior experience of patterned light. Although this is sometimes taken to mean that these animals have to learn to classify stimuli or more specifically to build up specific connections out of initially random ones, this conclusion is far from forced upon us by the evidence. Thus there are at least four alternative explanations for why animals brought up without pattern vision should learn a given visual discrimination less readily than a normally reared animal. These are: (1) Possible degeneration in the system due to lack of use: it is impossible to know whether this has been eliminated even where animals have been brought up in diffuse light rather than total darkness. (2) The disruptive effects on learning of emotional responses given to completely novel stimuli: Miller (1948) found that rats brought up in the dark and trained on a maze habit in the dark actually performed worse when run in the light. (3) The possibility that there are specific connections present initially, but that they become more specific only with use, and irrespective of how they are used. This possibility is underlined by the experiments of Wells (1958) and Hess (1956): Hess found that the pecking response increased in accuracy with use, even in the case where because of distortion introduced by a prism in front of the eye the increase in accuracy merely led to the chick pecking consistently in the wrong spot. It is also suggested by an experiment of Chow and Nissen (1955): they found incomplete interocular transfer where chimpanzees had been brought up with one eye receiving pattern vision, the other diffuse light: this suggests that the anatomical overlap of fibres from opposite eyes is at first incomplete, but that it becomes complete with use. The conditions necessary for its completion, however, do not include knowledge of results since it is completed if patterned light is given alternately to either eye. Riesen and Mellinger (1956) obtained a similar result with cats. (4) The possibility that increased learning time for a visual discrimination is brought about because animals have learned to switch in analysing mechanisms for other sensory modalities through previous experience: animals might switch off the input from vision when it first appeared because it could not initially be useful in solving a problem and would only interfere with a solution achieved through some other sensory modality. Recent results on the peripheral blocking of sensory input from a modality to which the animal is not attending (e.g., Sharpless & Jasper, 1956) underline this possibility. These results will be referred to in more detail below.

The upshot of this is that at the moment there is no reliable evidence on the extent to which the classificatory system is of the extremely general sort suggested by Hebb and others in mammals, and on how far the actual classificatory system used in later life develops only as the result of learning. If mammals have few innate responses to stimuli and if the type of experiment which has been performed on perceptual learning to date is inconclusive, it must be asked whether it would be possible to obtain evidence which would help to decide how far the classificatory mechanisms at work in mammals were of the very general sort proposed by Hebb, how far they were more specific. . . .

## *EVIDENCE FOR SPECIFIC ANALYSING MECHANISMS*

### Economy of Specific Analysing Systems

Some of the evidence which has already been presented suggests that specific analysing systems must be at work at least in the case of certain submammalian organisms which exhibit innate responses to some classes of stimuli. Although the crucial experiments have not been performed on mammals there is evidence from other directions that some specific classifying mechanisms must be at work even here. Both behavioural and physiological evidence indicate that part of what is involved in discriminating shape is the switching in of an appropriate analysing mechanism. In what follows, I shall argue that within any sensory modality, there are probably different specific ways of processing incoming information: these different methods correspond to different ways of classifying incoming information. Probably part of what an animal faced with a discrimination task learns is to switch in the correct analysing mechanism: a second part is to attach a response according to which output the mechanism switched in is giving. This general idea has some plausibility on the grounds of economy. Presumably many of the operations to be conducted on incoming data will be the same from one sense to another and also for different ways of classifying information from any one sense, though here the sequence of operations may differ from one method of classifying to another. If this is the case it would presumably be most economical to use the same actual analysing mechanisms in a variety of different classifications rather than to have a separate analysing mechanism for each classification (the latter is implicit in the general type of theory put forward by Uttley). Thus in the use of computers it is most economical to have one computer capable of carrying out operations on different kinds of data and of varying the sequence of the operations it carries out according to the way in which it is programmed, rather than to have different computers for every variety of information which is to be fed in and for every variation in the sequence of operations to be carried out. To summarise this crudely, in the model envisaged the brain is being viewed as containing at least three different boxes: (1) A number of different analysing mechanisms. (2) A control centre which determines which of these mechanisms shall be switched in on any given occasion and in what sequence they shall be switched in. (3) A further box which is responsible for selecting the response to be attached to the output from the analysing mechanisms. This is obviously a gross oversimplification and in practice the boxes may turn out to be not so very discrete, but it is worth seeing how far available evidence supports this conception.

## Evidence for Specific Analysing Mechanisms

One consequence of this crude model is that the nervous system would not be able to process information in two different ways at once, since there would then be competition for the common analysing mechanisms. There is plenty of evidence to suggest that this is in fact the case. Thus Mowbray (1953) found that when the eye and ear are presented with complex stimuli at the same time, the information presented to one or the other is made effective in the response but not the information presented to both: Mowbray points out that this finding is against the type of theory put forward by Hebb. Broadbent (1954) shows that digits simultaneously presented to the two ears are not accepted by the analysing mechanisms in their temporal order of presentation but all digits presented to one ear are accepted and then all presented to the other ear; he has extended this finding to digits presented simultaneously to ear and eye (Broadbent, 1956). To explain the finding that information presented simultaneously on two channels can be accepted although it is accepted successively not simultaneously he postulates a short term memory store in which information can be stored until the central analysing mechanisms are ready to receive it. The idea that the same central analysing mechanisms may be used in processing information from different modalities gives a rationale for the finding that it is not possible to accept information from two channels at once. Davis (1956, 1957) has shown that where two stimuli requiring different but peripherally compatible responses are presented with intervals of less than about 200 milli-seconds, the response to the second one is delayed: in an ingenious series of experiments involving different modalities, he has shown that the amount of delay is approximately the same as the amount of overlap between the time the first stimulus occupies central pathways and the time the second stimulus would have occupied central pathways if it could have been accepted immediately: this suggests that the second stimulus cannot get access to central analysing mechanisms until the first one is cleared.

A second line of evidence suggesting the same general conception of the working of the central nervous system is that provided by recent studies on the recticular formation and on the peripheral blocking of input on sensory pathways. Since there have been a number of recent reviews of this evidence (e.g., Lindsley, 1957), it is unnecessary to go into it in detail here. Hernandes-Peon, Scherrer, and Jouvet (1956) found that a click given to a cat's ear evokes a markedly reduced potential at the cochlear nucleus if the cat is simultaneously shown a mouse or given a whiff of fish. This suggests that stimuli unimportant for the animal can be blocked at a peripheral level if more important stimuli are being received: the blocking is itself under central control possibly mediated by the reticular formation (Hernandes-Peon & Scherrer, 1955). Once again the rationale behind this can only be that central analysing mechanisms can only be set in one way at a time, and if different stimuli were given access to them simultaneously their efficiency in dealing with any one stimulus would be impaired. In addition to giving support for the existence of specific analysing mechanisms used for a variety of stimuli, such experiments suggest in themselves a considerable degree of specificity in the innate organisation of the central nervous system and thus constitute evidence against the very general systems proposed to carry out stimulus analysis. It should futher be noted that the existence of analysing mechanisms which although specific could be used for a variety of purposes is in line with the findings on mass action, i.e., the failure of lesions outside the primary sensory and motor areas of the cortex to produce loss of some specific functions only. In addition the idea that the same analysing mechanisms might be used in processing information from different sensory modalities may account for some examples of synaesthesia. . . .

There is one further point which may be worth making about specific systems of shape recognition. It seems likely that any such system must operate by comparing relative quantities somewhere in the nervous system rather than by taking into account any absolute quantity at any given stage. This is indicated not only by the fact that in all species tested it has been found that having learned to discriminate between shapes of a given size they will transfer the discrimination readily to shapes of different sizes, but by more general considerations about the operation of the nervous system. Any discrimination task which necessarily involves the storage of information about absolute quantities is in fact very poorly performed in terms of the information which can be extracted on any one presentation of the stimulus. Thus Garner (1953) showed that when human beings were asked to make judgments of absolute loudness, judgments were most accurate as measured by the amount of information transmitted per judgment where only five categories were used: increasing the number of categories led to a decrease in accuracy which was not compensated for in terms of extra information transmitted by means of the additional number of categories used. Similarly Eriksen and Hake (1955) found that where subjects were asked to judge the size of squares, increasing the number of categories used above five did not lead to any increase in the amount of information transmitted per judgment: it led to a decrease in the accuracy of judgments which was partially compensated for by the increase in number of categories used. In both studies about 2.1 bits of information per stimulus were transmitted. It is obvious that in human beings and many animals very much more information per stimulus can be transmitted where visual patterns are being classified, particularly if there are no severe limitations on the length of time the stimulus is exposed or the length of time within which a response must be made. This can only mean that the nervous system performs more efficiently in terms of information transmitted where it is analysing relationships between quantities simultaneously present in it, than where it is analysing one absolute quantity. The explanation of this feature of the nervous system may have to do with changes in state of adaptation: it may be impossible to analyse accurately absolute quantities due to changes in states of adaptation of parts of the nervous system, but the changes in states of adaptation might be such that the relation between different quantities of excitation is preserved provided they are transmitted over the same parts of the nervous system. A mechanism for distinguishing shapes which depends upon an analysis of relative quantities is therefore more plausible than one which depends upon an analysis of absolute quantities.

## *CONCLUSION*

It has not been the purpose of this paper to examine in detail any specific theories of how the nervous system classifies shapes. I have tried to show that the very general type of analysing system which engineers have tended to propose for pattern recognition may not correspond to the way in which the nevous system works, and to give reasons for supposing that there are in fact more specific and more economical analysing systems at work. I have also tried to suggest ways of testing between the two alternatives, and ways of working out what the more specific analysing mechanisms are.

The engineer could obviously be of enormous help to the physiologist and the psychologist in setting up hypotheses about specific analysing mechanisms, but to do so he would have to start by taking into account the known facts about which shapes are classified together and which are classified apart, and to develop theories about analysing mechanisms in collaboration with experimentalists who could test the specific predictions made from this type of theory.

## *REFERENCES*

Ashby, R. C. *Design for a brain*. Chapman & Hall: London, 1952.

Broadbent, D. E. The role of auditory localisation in attention and memory span. *Journal of Experimental Psychology*, 1954, *47*, 191-196.

Broadbent, D. E. Successive responses to simultaneous stimuli. *Quarterly Journal of Experimental Psychology*, 1956, 8, 145-152.

Chow, K. L., & Nissen, H. W. Interocular transfer of learning in visually naive and experienced infant chimpanzees. *Journal of Comparative and Physiological Psychology*, 1955, *48*, 229-237.

Collier, R. M. An experimental study of form perception in indirect vision. *Journal of Comparative Psychology*, 1931, *11*, 281-289.

Davis, R. The limits of the "psychological refractory period." *Quarterly Journal of Experimental Psychology*, 1956, 8, 24-38.

Davis, R. The human operator as a single channel information system. *Quarterly Journal of Experimental Psychology*, 1957, 9, 119-127.

Deutsch, J. A. A theory of shape recognition. *British Journal of Psychology*, 1955, *46*, 30-37.

Dodwell, P. C. Shape recognition in rats. *British Journal of Psychology*, 1957, *48*, 221-229.

Eriksen, C. W., & Hake, H. W. Absolute judgments as a function of the stimulus range and the number of stimulus and response categories. *Journal of Experimental Psychology*, 1955, *49*, 323-332.

Fantz, R. L. Form preferences in newly hatched chicks. *Journal of Comparative and Physiological Psychology*, 1957, *50*, 422-430.

Garner, W. R. An informational analysis of absolute judgments of loudness. *Journal of Experimental Psychology*, 1953, *46*, 373-380.

Hebb, D. O. *The organization of behavior*. New York: Wiley. 1949.

Hess, E. H. Space perception in the chick. *Scientific American*, 1956, *195*, 71-82.

Hernandes-Peon, R., & Scherrer, H. Inhibitory influence of brain stem reticular formation upon synaptic transmission in trigeminal nucleus. *Federation Proceedings*, 1955, *14*, 71.

Hernandes-Peon, R., Scherrer, H., & Jouvet, M. Modification of electric activity in the cochlear nucleus during "attention" in unanesthetized cats. *Science*, 1956, *123*, 331-332.

Kohler, I. *Über Aufbau und Wandlungen der Wahrnehmungswelt.* Vienna: Rohrer, 1951.

Lindsley, O. R. Psychophysiology and motivation. In Jones (Ed.), Nebraska Symposium on Motivation. V, 1957, pp. 44-105.

Miller, M. Observation of initial visual experience in rats. *Journal of Psychology,* 1948, *26,* 223-228.

Milner, P. M. The cell assembly: mark II. *Psychological Review,* 1957, *64,* 242-252.

Mowbray, G. H. Simultaneous vision and audition: the comprehension of prose passages with varying levels of difficulty. *Journal of Experimental Psychology,* 1953, *46,* 365-372.

Mowbray, G. H. The perception of short phrases presented simultaneously for visual and auditory reception. *Quarterly Journal of Experimental Psychology,* 1954, *6,* 86-92.

Rheingold, H. I., & Hess, E. H. The chick's "preference" for some visual properties of water. *Journal of Comparative and Physiological Psychology,* 1957, *50,* 417-421.

Riesen, A. H. The development of visual perception in man and chimpanzee. *Science,* 1947, *106,* 107-108.

Riesen, A. H. Arrested vision. *Scientific American,* 1950, *183,* 16-19.

Riesen, A. H. Postpartum development of behavior. *Chicago Medical School Quarterly,* 1951, *13,* 17.

Riesen, A. H., Kurke, M. I., & Mellinger, J. C. Interocular transfer of habits learned monocularly in visually naive and visually experienced cats. *Journal of Comparative and Physiological Psychology,* 1953, *46,* 166-172.

Riesen, A. H., & Mellinger, J. C. Interocular transfer of habits in cats after alternating monocular visual experience. *Journal of Comparative and Physiological Psychology,* 1956, *49,* 516-520.

Sharpless, S., & Jasper, H. Habituation of the arousal reaction. *Brain,* 1956, *79,* 655-680.

Sperry, R. W. Reestablishment of visuomotor coordination by optic nerve regeneration. *Anatomical Record,* 1942, *84,* 470. (Abstract 52)

Sperry, R. W. Visuomotor coordination in the newt (*Triturus veridescens*) after regeneration of the optic nerve. *Journal of Comparative Neurology,* 1943, *79,* 33-55.

Sperry, R. W. Optic nerve regeneration with return of vision in anurans. *Journal of Neurophysiology,* 1944, *7,* 57-69.

Sutherland, N. S. Visual discrimination of orientation and shape by the octopus. *Nature,* 1957, *179,* 11-13.

Taylor, W. K. Electrical simulation of some nervous system functional activities. In Cherry, C. (Ed.), *Information Theory. Third London Symposium.* London: Butterworths Publications, 1956, pp. 314-327.

Tinbergen, N. *The study of instinct.* Oxford: Clarendon Press, 1951.

Uttley, A. M. Conditional probability machines and conditioned reflexes. In Shannon, C. E. & McCarthy, J, *Automata Studies.* Princeton, N.J.: Princeton University Press, 1956, pp. 253-275.

Wells, M. J. Factors affecting reactions to *mysis* by newly hatched *sepia.* *Behaviour,* 1958, *13,* 96-111.

*The purpose of this first introductory part of the book was to set the stage and to give some perspective on the sorts of questions which have been posed about stimulus equivalence. First of all, the very general topic of the nature of categorization and classification was raised (Klüver), followed by a more specific outlining of the question which is really our major topic (Lashley). This is the question of stimulus coding and pattern recognition and how these can be conceived of as processes which go on in the brain. The next paper (Pitts and McCulloch) shows how an explicit, but very general, solution could be obtained; but at least as important is their demonstration of a new method of modeling brain functions in terms of computing networks. The von Holst and Mittelstaedt paper is also an explicit essay in modeling central nervous system functioning, which brings to the fore the question of movement and orientation control, and within their general schema the question of stimulus control can be considered as a particular case. Finally, we have Sutherland's proposals for the sorts of system it would be fruitful to look for. In closing this part, I should like to remind the reader that most of the earlier part of Sutherland's discussion is concerned with the theoretical position of D. O. Hebb. While there is no direct quotation from Hebb's work in this book, his ideas and theories have played a very strong role in the development of ideas in the field of perceptual learning and stimulus equivalence. From time to time through the commentary those ideas will be touched on and related to the present readings; one assumes that every reader will be to some extent familiar with his contributions already, if not through* The Organization of Behavior *then at least through one of the accounts contained in nearly every contemporary textbook of psychology. While it can be argued that Hebb's treatment of pattern recognition was not altogether successful, his ideas have been a profound stimulus to others to find satisfactory solutions to problems in the field.*

# II

# SOME SPECIFIC MODELS FOR STIMULUS CODING

*During the 1950s there was a spurt of interest among psychologists in the question of stimulus coding and the specific operations which might mediate shape and pattern recognition. This renewed debate on stimulus equivalence (in one of its aspects) undoubtedly was caused by a proposal put forward by J. A. Deutsch in 1955. In contrast to Lashley, and to Pitts and McCulloch, Deutsch suggested that pattern coding for shape might be based on a very simple process which occurs locally at one place in the brain and which entails a straightforward computation concerning the relative positions of contours within a shape. A measure of these relative positions (or inter-contour separations) is transformed, or mapped, into a sequence of pulses of varying amplitude and temporal pattern, fed into a single transmission line, which is hence independent of the position on the retina at which the shape was imaged. Independence of position is achieved without requiring the activation of the whole cortex or a whole cortical area. This proposal seems to be almost disarmingly simple; yet it has some powerful advantages for explaining stimulus equivalence which will be made explicit both in Deutsch's paper, which is the first selection in this part, and in the later commentary.*

*Perhaps a word should be said at this point about the use of the word "model." I shall use the term to refer to those rather specific proposals for explaining a limited range of phenomena which are typified in this section. Usually the process of constructing such a model goes through the following stages: (1) a specification of the to-be-explained behavior is made; (2) a system of elements or units is devised which have certain well-specified properties and relations with one another; (3) these elements are put together into a structure that has properties which in given respects mirror the real system that is to modeled. The behavior of the system is then predicted on the basis of deductions made from the model and its properties. Such explanatory devices can be distinguished from theories, which generally may be of wider scope but also more vague in their predictions. Deutch's system, although he calls it a theory in his title, is a prime example of the sort of structural model I have just characterized.*

# *A Theory of Shape Recognition*

J. A. DEUTSCH

## *INTRODUCTION*

The purpose of this paper is twofold. First, it is intended to show by another practical example the fruitfulness of a view of psychological theory put forward in another paper (Deutsch, 1953). In this the author proposed a theory of motivation and learning which was of a particular logical nature. It was argued that the task of a theory in psychology is to infer the system or mechanism which is producing the phenomena of behaviour without necessarily giving the embodiment of such a system. That such a policy was practically feasible at this stage was shown by the construction of a system whose properties tallied closely with those of a motivated learning organism. Further, to show that this theory was really the description of a mechanism in general terms and not a re-description of the behaviour of an animal in highfalutin language, a machine was actually built embodying the system. It is intended here to give another example of such a theory and to show how this approach is of use in the study of perception.

The second object is partially to fill what many felt to be a gap in the previous theory. The system described in the previous paper dealt with and acted on information which had already been digested. The process of classifying environmental stimulation was taken for granted. In what follows an attempt is made to elaborate a mechanism of shape perception which is complementary to the behaviour system. Though there have been previous attempts in this direction, none of the models suggested has had properties which tallied sufficiently with the known peculiarities of shape recognition in animals. Nor was it possible to put them to test as they made no particular further prediction about behaviour. Accordingly they have more the status of inventions than of explanatory theories.

## *THE PROBLEM*

What are these known peculiarities which any theory concerning the subject must explain?

Reprinted from *British Journal of Psychology*, 1955.

There are six main facts:

(*a*) Animals can recognize shapes independent of their location in the visual field. It is not necessary to fixate the centre of a figure in order to recognize it nor need the eyes be moved around the contours of a figure.

(*b*) Recognition can be effected independently of the angle of inclination of a figure in the visual field. (By this is not meant tilt of the figure in depth such as occurs in shape constancy experiments, but the tilt of an image in two dimensions.)

(*c*) The size of a figure does not interfere with the identity of its shape. This of course does not hold at the extremes of size for reasons which seem sufficiently obvious.

(*d*) Mirror images appear alike. Both rats and human beings tend to confuse these. This would tend to rule out any 'template' theories of shape recognition. According to these a contour is rotated in two dimensions until it coincides with one of the many patterns already laid down. But such a superimposition cannot take place in the case of mirror images and no room is left for this particular type of confusion.

(*e*) Visually primitive organisms such as the rat and the octopus find it hard (perhaps impossible) to distinguish between squares and circles. This does not seem to be a limitation imposed by the peripheral characteristics of the optical systems. It appears to be a more central defect as these organisms can distinguish shapes which are far more alike geometrically. This type of evidence tends to cast doubt on theories which base themselves on the angular properties of figures. To quote Lashley (1938): 'The pair of figures giving greatest difficulty of discrimination where the element of acuity might play a part are the square and the circle. In several experiments these have required from 60 to 300 trials for learning and only one-fourth of the animals have shown any improvement above chance. Yet acuity is certainly not the chief limiting factor in this case.'

(*f*) These abilities, which appear to be mediated by the striate cortex, survive the removal of the major part of it. It is therefore reasonable to suppose that this ability to disentangle shape is common to all parts of the striate area and that one part of the striate area is not essential in helping the next one to operate.

This consideration would tend to rule out notions based on a scanning process. It is difficult to see how a regular scan could be maintained in the presence of extensive damage. Further, any system which requires the fixation of the centre of a figure so that it coincides with the centre of the visual field must also be ruled out. The ability is maintained even when there are extensive scotomata of central origin.

In what follows a system is proposed which will abstract from and yet satisfy the above specifications. It will also lead to fresh predictions about the discriminability of certain figures. It is therefore testable.

It is not suggested that it is the only system concerned in recognition.

There must be other systems devoted to the recognition of brightness, location and size. This makes many experiments on pattern discrimination difficult to assess from the point of view of evidence for the mechanism of shape discrimination pure and simple.

## *THE SYSTEM*

Let us assume that there is an array of units (or cells) arranged in two dimensions, each unit having many neighbours. This plane composed of cells has messages arriving on it from light receptors (or the retina). Each group of cells is joined to a particular retinal element in such a way that neighbouring retinal elements also excite neighbouring groups of cells on this two-dimensional array. But it is assumed that only a particular source of excitation is passed on from the retina. This is excitation from contours, the regions of the sharpest change.

Thus when a ball is focused on the retina the contour of this ball is projected on this two-dimensional array. Excitation in the form of a circle will appear on it. Thus we have the first rule.

1. Each unit on the two-dimensional array can be excited by a contour falling on the region of the retina to which it is joined.

2. When such excitation from the retina arrives each unit will pass on a pulse down what will be called a final common cable. It will also excite its neighbour. This neighbour will pass it on in its turn. Therefore when a contour is projected on the two-dimensional array two things will occur: a message consisting of one pulse will be passed down the final common cable by each cell or unit on which that contour lies. Thus a measure of the total number of cells stimulated will be passed down.

3. Second, the contour will excite all the cells which lie next to it on the two-dimensional array. These will pass the excitation on to their neighbours but not down the final common cable. The assumption is made that a cell will pass on its excitation at right angles to the contour of which it happens to be a component. Thus for instance the excitation produced by a straight line will be a line equal and parallel to it and gradually moving away. In the case of a curve, for instance an arc of a circle, it will be also an arc of a circle moving away 'parallel' to it, but gradually decreasing as it draws away, coming to a point and then fanning out again, this time reversed (since all the advancing points of excitation move at the same speed from the point of their origin).

4. As such lateral excitation from a point in a contour advances another message will be sent down the final common cable as soon as it coincides with another point in a contour imposed on the two-dimensional array.

This message down the final common cable will at each moment give a

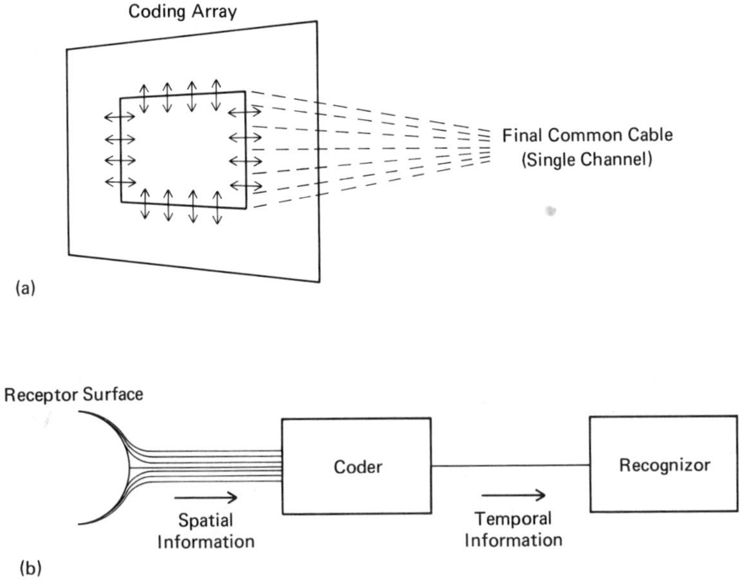


Fig. 1. (a) Shows the coding array and final common cable in perspective view with a square projected to the center of the array. (b) Shows schematically the relationship between receptors, coder, and recognition system.[1]

measure of the number of points thus brought into coincidence. For example, if the figure is a rectangle, the first set of pulses sent down the final common cable will be a measure of the total number of cells excited lying on the contour (rules 1 and 2). The second set of pulses down the final common cable will be sent when the excitation travelling in a parallel line (rule 3) coincides with the two longer sides.

As these two sides are parallel to each other the excitation and the contours will coincide simultaneously and send a number of pulses proportionate to the length of these sides down the final common path all at the same instant of time. Some time later the disturbance from the two shorter lines will reach each of these lines and another message will be sent down the final common cable, indicating that a smaller number of cells have been fired off this time but also all simultaneously. Thus the message sent down the final common cable for any rectangle will consist of three sharp volleys, the proportions of the last two being governed by the ratio of the longer to the shorter sides. The message generated by a square will be two sharp volleys, both equal in magnitude. As the two pairs of sides are equidistant the advancing disturbances will hit the sides simultaneously. As they are parallel, the disturbance generated and the contours will over-

[1] Figure 1 is not in the original paper, but is inserted here to help the reader to visualize the model—Ed.

lap all along their length at the same instant of time, causing the cells representing the contour to fire down the final common path together.

Oddly enough a circle too would generate two sharp volleys, both equal in magnitude. All the pairs of points lying opposite each other are equidistant. Therefore the disturbance travelling across would reach all the opposite parts of the contour simultaneously—a sharp pulse equal to the first, when the circular contour first arrived on the two-dimensional array. Thus, if we agree that this is the number and relative size of the pulses that is made use of at the next stage in primitive organisms in distinguishing shapes, then circles and squares will be treated as identical. Thus the theory so far would predict the fifth finding (fact *e*) about the confusion between squares and circles. There is another group of predictions which appear *prima facie* unlikely and which have not been tested. This is that a pentagon and all odd-sided regular polygons, till there is a breakdown of acuity (central and peripheral) ought to be discriminable from a circle by these organisms where a square, a hexagon, etc., would not be.

To make the logic of this deduction clear let us consider an equilateral triangle, the simplest of the regular polygons without parallel sides. As soon as this is projected on the two-dimensional array a message will be sent down the final common cable giving a measure of the total length of contour. Immediately after this the three sides will propagate lines of disturbance parallel to themselves. As these lines of disturbance meet the contours of the triangle, there will be another message sent down the final common cable. But this time the cells on the contour will not fire off all together as the disturbance will pass across them obliquely. Their firing will be staggered according to the angle at which the disturbance and the contour interact. Thus in the case of the equilateral triangle, there will be a large initial or sharp volley followed immediately by a much smaller continuous discharge which will suddenly cease.

In the case of the pentagon then there will be a large and sudden first spike (as with all figures) followed by a gap (before the disturbances make contact with the opposite sides). There will then be a message of a much smaller magnitude and spread out in time, following it as the disturbance meets the opposite contours obliquely. The pentagon then, given this system of encoding and decoding ought to be quite easily discriminable from both a circle and a square, whilst these latter appear the same.

In spite of this interesting confusion it would seem that this system would derive fairly distinctive messages from most shapes which cannot be superimposed. There are two exceptions to this which are again important. This is the case of mirror images (fact *d*), another interesting property which seems accounted for. The same message will be sent down the final common cable as long as the relations of angle to length of side remain the same internal to the figure.

The second relates to figures with highly complex and irregular contours and internal lines. Unless there is some regularity of geometrical arrangement within complicated figures, the messages down the final common cable generated by these will tend to approximate with growing complexity. There would be a very large initial spike followed by a continuous signal as the many disturbances set up by contours hit other contours continuously. Any feature of equal or parallel spacing, which we normally call regularity, would set up messages which were synchronous and thus additive or sharp, giving rise to distinctive peaks in the message. Absence of these would lead to the opposite. This tallies with Lashley's (1938) experimental findings. 'The indications are that a somewhat larger number of animals fail to discriminate irregular than regular geometrical figures, but those which do discriminate require no longer to learn the one than the other type. There is evidence that those animals which learn do so by isloating some simpler cue or part figure.'

The system outlined would also display the properties of sending the same message down the final common cable whatever the inclination or position of the figure on the two-dimensional array (facts $a + b$). The message generated depends entirely on the properties of the figure itself and not on its relation with some external axes.

So far only one fact of the original six is left unexplained. This is the animal's ability to recognize shape independent of size (fact $c$). The encoding two-dimensional array will of course pass on information derived from differences in size though it discards differences in position. However, the same proportions between the components of the message passing down the final common cable will be preserved provided that the shape alone is constant. The problem of reducing messages of identical proportions to the same message or having a detector which is only sensitive to the proportions independent of size must therefore be separately considered if we adopt this scheme. A way of doing this can be envisaged, especially as the first part of the message in the system outlined above could provide an indication of the scale of the figure. The difficulty is to decide between possible alternatives as there are hardly any clues. There is a constant relationship between the initial pulse giving the length of the contour, and the size of the rest of the following message for each particular figure. This relation may be used to reduce the message for each figure to the same size, whatever the original size of this figure. If the size of the second part of the message is always divided by the size of the first, the crests of the message for a given shape will not only be of the same proportions but also of the same absolute height. (The problem of the recognition of a figure now becomes merely the problem of recognizing pulses of identical height.)

How could such a scheme be worked? For instance, the measure of the total number of cells involved signalling the length of the contour could pass on ahead. It could then act on a section of the final common cable through which the whole message would soon pass on its way to the final detector units. It would throw this section of the final common cable into a state of refractoriness proportionate to the magnitude of this measure. It would thus alter its threshold of response to the following message to differing degrees. Only a very small proportion of a message following a large pulse would survive. A large proportion of the measure after a small pulse had set the 'resistance' would pass. Thus if both these messages were derived from the same shape, let us say at different distances, they would both give rise to a message the height of whose pulses was physically identical. Hence they would pass to the final stage whither we shall not follow them. We should pass too far into the realms of speculation to give an answer to what no longer seems a problem.

So far a mechanism has been suggested to reduce a purely relational entity, a shape regardless of its location, size and inclination, to a unique set of physical events. This mechanism also shares some other rather peculiar properties with an animal's shape-recognition mechanism. It is therefore supposed that such a mechanism is in fact that used by an animal.

This mechanism has other properties which follow as predictions.

1. It should prove easier to discriminate between a square and a rectangle than between a square and a rectangle both with one side missing.

2. There should be an almost perfect transfer from an equilateral triangle to another with one side missing. This agrees with Lashley's findings, but this type of transfer should be worse in the case of other triangles, where the removal of a side should make a great difference. For instance the removal of the hypotenuse in the case of a right-angled triangle should militate more strongly against transfer.

3. Shallow curves should be undistinguishable from straight lines in the absence of other contours in the vicinity. (It may be that the factor of a change of direction in the case of the curve may provide a cue here.)

4. If shallow curves and straight lines are indistinguishable, their addition to otherwise identical figures should make these discriminable. For instance, the substitution of a curved side in a rectangle, should differentiate it from the normal rectangle. This effect should be smaller for most triangles.

5. A 'mixture' of a square and a circle should be distinct from these even though they are not distinct from each other. In fact transfer to a rectangle ought to be easier in some circumstances, for instance, where two arcs of a circle complete a square with two opposite sides missing.

6. A scotoma of central origin when falling wholly inside a figure, where there are no contours in the vicinity, should prevent identification of the shape.

7. The prediction concerning regular polygons with an odd number of sides has already been made. It will be noted that all these predictions are independent in the sense that it would be difficult to subsume any two

under a single generalization. If to the writer's greatest surprise some of these predictions receive experimental confirmation, it may be worth drawing a few more deductions from the theory.

There are, however, some difficulties.

(i) Such a mechanism could only handle one figure at a time. Consider the effect on the message down the final common cable of a square and a triangle in two different parts of the field. The two messages would be inextricably mixed up or superimposed as they would be sent down at one and the same time. They should therefore mask each other to a certain extent. But they are in fact recognized easily and separately except in one interesting condition. This is when the contours actually touch or cross. It is therefore suggested that figures are passed to the two-dimensional array on the following principle. Assume that the points in the visual field are arranged in an arbitrary order of precedence. The stimulated point which is highest in order will inhibit all the others, preventing their passage until another signal (such as might arise from the final identification apparatus) is sent up. Then the next point in order of precedence will be dealt with. Now consider the case where such points have neighbours. Assume that the effects of this inhibition are overcome by a supervening excitation passed on from this point which is inhibiting all others to those of its neighbours (if any) that were also excited, and passed on by these. (It is assumed that interrupted contours are completed.) In this way a whole contour is passed on (and others are kept in 'cold storage') until it is dealt with. If this was the case, masking of one figure by another would occur as soon as their outlines touched. They would now be dealt with as one complex figure. Something of the sort is borne out by everyday experience and Gottschaldt's experiment (1926). In any case this is merely to show that this property of being able to handle only one shape at a time can be circumvented by an additional hypothesis.

(ii) Higher forms can distinguish squares from circles. There is no evidence that human beings have any difficulty at all in this. It would be more plausible to propose a mechanism which would preserve a phylogenetic continuity. The present scheme cannot be made to distinguish between squares and circles as it stands. But there can be quite a simple 'evolutionary' development of it to work with greater precision and to make this distinction. The encoding part of the mechanism can be kept the same and the same message sent down the final common cable. But the message must be sent to a detecting mechanism which is sensitive not merely to absolute differences in the height of the successive pulses. A mechanism is incorporated which is sensitive to the relation between the height of the pulses and their spacing in time. These will of course depend on each other for each particular form or figure. But their proportions may vary from figure to figure, even though the proportions of the successive pulses generated by these figures may be identical. This is in fact so in the case of the square and the circle. A circle's boundary is shorter than that of a square when the distance to be travelled by the laterally spreading disturbance from contour to contour is the same. Therefore, though the two pulses sent down in each case are of the same height, there will be a greater distance between the two pulses even though they are of the same height. The analysis of the encoded information by two different means would probably improve the accuracy of recognition even where no radical confusion was possible. Such a possibility of improving the system by further development without any basic change perhaps gives the whole suggestion an enhanced biological plausibility.

(iii) It will doubtless be objected that nothing has been done to explain the lateral spread with the convenient properties postulated for it. No *modus operandi* has been suggested. This is admittedly a weakness of the hypothesis logically speaking. We ought in principle to state what family of machine performs this task, what interrelationships we postulate among our elements. On the other hand from the point of view of practical science to suggest possible networks of some complexity merely because they are required theoretically would be somewhat foolish, especially as there is nothing to distinguish between rival possibilities. It is really only necessary to ask whether it is plausible to assign such a property to the nervous system. Has anything like it in fact been found?

Motokawa claims to have found evidence for a laterally spreading effect on the retina, which he calls 'retinal induction'. 'For all these phenomena to take place it would be necessary that some process is propagated in a successive manner from one part to the next contiguous part. . . . In other words, the front of propagated induction may be supposed to proceed with a certain velocity through the retina, leaving a field of retinal induction behind it' (Motokawa, 1951). The processes of what Motokawa calls indirect induction show some of the features of the lateral spread which are postulated and which seem in many ways the least plausible physiologically. This is the ability for two types of indirect induction to cross over each other without interference with each other's spread. This property is clearly brought out in the phenomena of neutralization. Here the two processes generated by complementary colours invade each other's territory and neutralize each other. They do not form a contour as would happen if they nullified each other.

The fact that similar processes appear to take place on the retina would argue for the ease and simplicity with which the proposed system could be embodied in the central nervous system. Though no great weight is put on this analogy, it does show that the postulation of a process with somewhat similar properties in a structure of greater possible complexity is not too far fetched. It is true that what is so far known of this retinal induction indicates a greater crudity of operation than that which has been postulated for the central process. The further objection that such a central spreading process has not been suggested on anatomical grounds can be answered by saying that no one suspected retinal induction on anatomical grounds either.

Of course until more work is done on retinal induction this possible analogy cannot be stressed too much. Perhaps the most one should say about it is that such a laterally propagated retinal process is being considered by some neurophysiologists.

## *SUMMARY*

A theory of form recognition, complementary to a previously published theory of motivation and learning is put forward. A number of facts which any theory must account for, is given. These are ability to abstract form independent of place, inclination or size, equivalence of shape of mirror images and of squares and circles in some species, and lastly the survival of these abilities following extensive lesions of the striate area.

A mechanism which displays the requisite properties is suggested. This mechanism is also seen to have further properties which ought to manifest themselves in behaviour if the appropriate tests are made.

Lastly various objections are discussed. Aspects of the mechanism are not entirely without neurophysiological plausibility.

## *REFERENCES*

Deutsch, J. A. A new type of behaviour theory. *British Journal of Psychology*, 1953, *44*, 304-317.

Gottschaldt. Ueber den Einfluss der Erfahrung auf die Wahrnehmung von Figuren. *Psychologische Forschung*, 1926, 8, 261-317.

Lashley, K. S. The mechanism of vision. XV. Preliminary studies of the rat's capacity for detail vision. *Journal of General Psychology*, 1938, *18*, 123-193.

Motokawa. Propagation of retinal induction. *Journal of Neurophysiology*, 1951, *14*, 339-351.

*In a remarkable way Deutsch's model overcomes two objections to earlier notions about stimulus coding and equivalence. One objection, to both the Lashley and the Pitts–McCulloch models, is that they were too general to be testable by experimental means. They made no prediction about which shapes should be readily discriminable from each other, or which* ones should be easily confused, for example, nor did they make any predictions about the coding of specific features—which cues in a shape should be salient, for instance. A second objection, which applies to the Pitts and McCulloch model, is that it was too cumbersome, and required too much computing even for the simplest shapes to be recognised. The first objection quite evidently does not apply to the Deutsch model, since some very specific predictions are made. The second objection also is inapplicable, since the computations required are simple for simple shapes, and the coded output is simple for them too. The assumption that complicated shapes generate more complicated codes seems to be reasonable.

The gain in power, plus the feature of simplicity, are achieved by not requiring that the coding model preserve all the features of the original input. One may well ask whether the advantages have been bought at too great a price—whether too much is thrown out by restricting the computations in this way. I shall leave that particular question for the moment, but return to it later in the section. The next two papers illustrate a development which is clearly related to the Deutsch model, a development which is due to Sutherland's initiative in studying shape discrimination in the octopus, as part of the program of intensive study of the octopus by J. Z. Young and his associates, working at the Naples Zoological Station. Sutherland looks for and finds evidence for a quite simple coding process which can explain many features of the octopus's ability to discriminate between different shapes. His paper is followed immediately by a second paper of Deutsch's, which attempts a further move in the direction of understanding stimulus classification by relating shape discrimination behavior to a plausible neurophysiological "computing" process.

# Visual Discrimination of Orientation and Shape by the Octopus

N. S. SUTHERLAND

The experiments reported here were undertaken in an attempt to discover the mechanism responsible for visual discrimination of orientation and form in octopus. If for any animal we knew enough about the ways in which that animal classifies shapes, it should be possible to formulate hypotheses about the neurological mechanism which performs the classifi-

Reprinted from *Nature*, 1957.

cation. This was the approach followed in the classic experiments of Lashley (1938) and Fields (1932) on rats in the 1930's: their results have never been adequately followed up. The rat is not an ideal animal for such experiments, since in the situation normally used for training rats on form discrimination the rat has been shown frequently to respond in terms of parts of the form only, or in terms of the relationship between the form and the backgrounds; it is often difficult to be sure which properties of the forms the rat is using to discriminate between them. This is not true of the octopus in the situation devised by Boycott and Young (1956); *Octopus vulgaris* Lamarck was therefore used in the present series of experiments.

The training situation used is fully described elsewhere (Sutherland 1957). Octopuses were trained individually to discriminate between pairs of shapes: a different group of octopuses was trained on each pair of shapes used. Each member of a pair was presented separately, and octopuses learned to attack one shape (the positive shape) for food reward and not to attack the other shape (the negative shape) in order to avoid an electric shock. The shape which was made positive was changed for the two halves of each group of animals trained on any given pair. Positive and negative shapes were presented in a randomized order. The scores to be presented here represent the percentage of correct responses a group of animals made to the shapes over a given number of trials. A score of 50 per cent is a chance score and shows that animals were not discriminating between the two shapes of a pair. Higher scores measure the relative ease with which octopuses could discriminate between different pairs of shapes, or the extent to which the classificatory mechanism in the octopus's brain gives a different output for the two members of each pair. In certain cases transfer tests were performed after animals had learned to discriminate between a given

TABLE 1.
PERFORMANCE ON DISCRIMINATION OF
ORIENTATION OVER FIRST SIXTY TRIALS

| *Shapes* | *Dimensions* | *No. of Animals* | *Per cent Correct Responses* |
|---|---|---|---|
| ❘ vs. — | 10 cm. × 2 cm. | 6 | 81 |
| ❘ vs. / or \ | ” | 8 | 71* |
| — vs. / or \ | ” | 8 | 65•5 |
| ⊤ vs. ⊥ | Long stroke, 10 cm × 2 cm. Tail, 4 cm. × 2 cm. | 6 | 59* |
| ⊢ vs. ⊣ | ” | 7 | 56 |
| / vs. \ | 10 cm. × 2 cm. | 6 | 50* |

Asterisks indicate that the difference in level of performance between two adjacent groups is significant at better than the 0•05 level of confidence.

pair of shapes; in the transfer tests, further shapes were presented, but octopuses were not rewarded or punished for attacking them. A measure was thus obtained of how far the classifying system treats new shapes as equivalent to the ones on which the animal was originally trained.

The main results for ease of learning different orientations are set out in Table 1. It will be seen that vertical and horizontal rectangles were very readily discriminated, whereas two oblique rectangles were scarcely if at all discriminated. A vertical and oblique, or a horizontal and oblique, could clearly be discriminated; but discrimination was more difficult than for a horizontal and a vertical. In view of the fact that two obliques differ from one another by a 90° rotation, whereas a horizontal or vertical and an oblique differ from one another by only a 45° rotation, this result may well seem surprising. It can only mean that in the classifying system of the octopus vertical and horizontal axes have a peculiar status not shared by oblique axes. The results with *T* figures are a further indication that the octopus can discriminate differences both along the vertical co-ordinate and along the horizontal co-ordinate.

On the basis of these results, the following classificatory mechanism is proposed. The excitation produced by the shapes on the retina is relayed to an array of nerve cells representing a projection of the retina in the optic lobes. The outputs from this array are so arranged that the cells of each column and each row have connexions to further cells specific to each column and row (see Fig. 1). The amount of firing in the output from the cells connected with the columns will now represent the height of the figure, and the amount of firing in the output from the rows will represent the lateral extent of the figure. Such an arrangement of nerve cells is plausible on several grounds. Many of the bodily movements of the octopus are horizontal, and the head is held in a fixed orientation by the statocysts; this means that the same point in the environment will stimulate successively different cells in one row when the octopus is in movement. It is

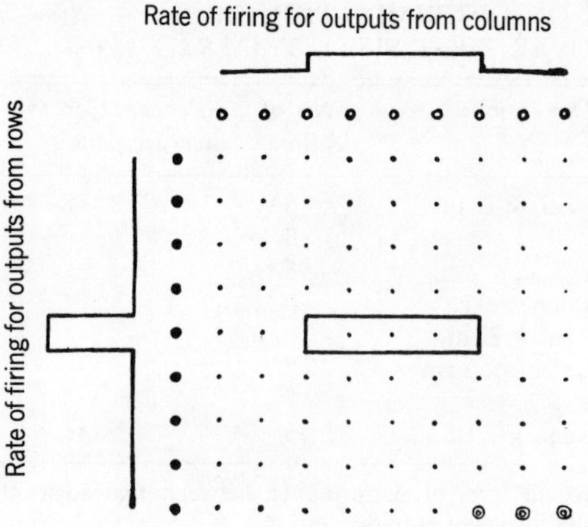


Fig. 1. Dots represent array with horizontal rectangle projected on it. Open circles: cells specific to each column. Filled circles: cells specific to each row. Each cell in the array is connected to the output cell for its own row and the output cell for its own column.

probable that this would result in all cells in any one row developing a common output (cf. Eccles 1953, Hebb 1949). When the octopus is stationary, its head movements are usually made in a vertical direction; by a parallel argument this would lead to cells in the same column developing a common output. On this system, discrimination can be performed by comparing two quantities in the nervous system. A further analysing mechanism is needed to analyse and compare the size of outputs from points on rows and columns; such a mechanism presents no difficulty of principle, but for reasons of space no suggestions about it are made here. Because the system works by comparing quantities of excitation, it is unnecesasry for the nervous system to store information about absolute quantities when a discrimination is being learned. It also follows that the importance of specific nervous pathways is reduced, and that exact locus of stimulation on the retina is not important in discrimination.

The main confirmation for the existence of a classificatory mechanism of the kind proposed is that it accounts fully for the results reported here and those of other workers in this field. Fig. 2 shows the excitation patterns predicted by the theory in the outputs from rows and columns for the shapes so far discussed. If height of excitation alone is considered, it will be seen that the difficulty the octopus experiences in discriminating the orientations of rectangles used is fully accounted for: vertical versus horizontal produce large differences in output; vertical or horizontal versus

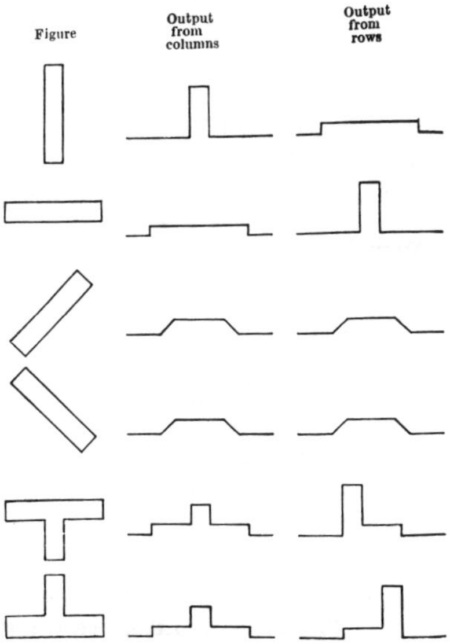


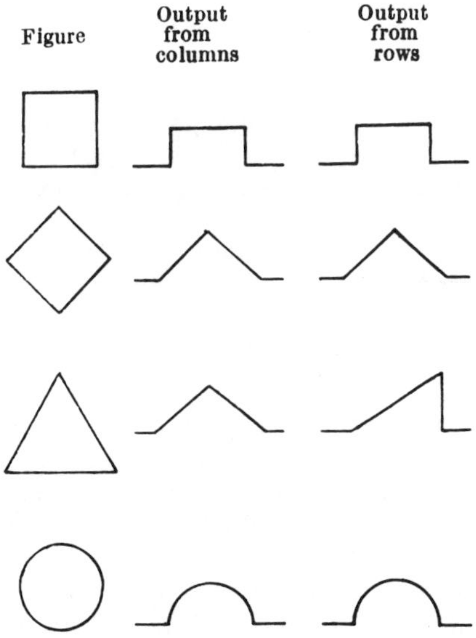


Fig. 2 (*left*). Figures used for investigating discrimination of orientation, with outputs predicted by theory.

Fig. 3 (*right*). Figures used in investigation of shape discrimination with outputs predicted by theory.

oblique produce smaller differences; there is no difference in output between two obliques, hence the confusion between these forms.

The mechanism proposed would produce certain further results on transfer tests. For example, (1) because the proposed system works by comparing quantities of excitation, octopuses should generalize a given discrimination to shapes of different sizes; thus octopuses should treat vertical and horizontal rectangles of different sizes and (within limits) of different ratios between long and short sides as equivalent; (2) having learned to discriminate between a vertical and an oblique, an octopus should treat a horizontal as equivalent to the oblique (the original discrimination depends upon greater excitation in the output from the columns in the vertical than in the oblique, and vice versa for the rows, and horizontal as compared with the vertical produces the same result in an exaggerated form); these predictions were verified in the transfer tests.

The mechanism proposed also accounts for the fact that discrimination of *T* figures is more difficult than vertical versus horizontal discrimination, but easier than discrimination between two obliques. The same operation is involved in the *T* figure discrimination as in the vertical–horizontal discrimination; but in the case of the *T* figures an additional analysing step is necessary in order to discriminate between them; namely, that account must be taken of the direction of the high excitation in relation to the low excitation on the output from either rows or columns (see Fig. 2).

Results of experiments with further pairs of forms are summarized in Table 2. Differences in ease of discrimination are again in accordance

TABLE 2.
PERFORMANCE ON SHAPE DISCRIMINATION
OVER TRIALS 41-120

| *Shapes* | *No. of Animals* | *Per cent Correct Responses* |
|---|---|---|
| □ vs. △ or ▽ | 4 | 85 |
| ◇ vs. △ or ▽ | 4 | 67* |
| ○ vs. △ or ▽ | 5 | 67 |
| ○ vs. □ | 5 | 69 |
| ○ vs. ◇ | 4 | 74 |

All shapes were 25 sq. cm. in area. The difference in performance between the first two groups was significant at better than the 0•05 level of confidence.

with expectations based on the theory (see Fig. 3). Thus a square is more readily discriminated from a triangle than a diamond from a triangle (Table 2); the excitation pattern produced in the outputs from rows and columns is more similar for diamond and triangle than for square and triangle. Again, a square and a circle are as readily discriminated as a triangle and circle, though other theories would predict that this would not be the case (Hebb, 1949; Deutsch, 1955). Transfer tests again showed excellent generalization to figures of different sizes.

While it is certain that the theory advanced here represents a considerable over-simplification of the mechanism for shape discrimination in the octopus, it is felt that the way it fits with the results described here and with those of Boycott and Young indicates that at the very least a mechanism similar to that proposed is operating. The theory will also account for many of the findings of workers on shape discrimination in the rat, although these are open to the difficulties of interpretation mentioned above. It is worthy of note that Dodwell, on the basis of some recent work (unpublished), concludes that rats also in discriminating visual forms classify them by a system in which vertical and horizontal co-ordinates are of primary importance. It seems probable from the evidence we have that something like the system proposed here may operate in human beings; but in humans it would almost certainly be only one classifying system operating among several others. It is interesting that in humans, in order to bring a point in the environment into the centre of the field of vision, information about the position of that point seems to be divided into the two co-ordinates, horizontal and vertical, in order to give an appropriate output to the eye muscles.

## *REFERENCES*

Boycott, B. B., & Young, J. Z. Reactions to shape in Octopus Vulgaris Lamarck. *Proceedings of the Zoological Society of London*, 1956, *126*, 491-547.

Deutsch, J. A. A theory of shape recognition. *British Journal of Psychology*, 1955, *46*, 30-37.

Eccles, J. C. *Neurophysiological basis of mind.* Oxford: 1953.

Fields, P. E. Studies in concept formation. I. The development of the concept of triangularity by the white rat. *Comparative Psychology Monographs*, 1932, 9 (2).

Hebb, D. O. *The organization of behavior*. New York: Wiley, 1949.

Lashley, K. S. The mechanism of Vision XV; preliminary studies of the rat's capacity for detail vision. *Journal of General Psychology*, 1938, *18*, 123-193.

Sutherland, N. S. Visual discrimination of orientation by octopus. *British Journal of Psychology*, 1957, *48*, 55-71.

# *The Plexiform Zone and Shape Recognition in the Octopus*

J. A. DEUTSCH

It is the purpose of this article to suggest a possible structural basis for shape recognition in the octopus. The octopus is now the best-investigated animal in respect of its discrimination of visual shape, and this is chiefly due to the work of N. S. Sutherland. This author has also put forward a theory to account for his findings (Sutherland, 1957a, b), but this theory was criticized by Dodwell (1957) on grounds which seem to me to be substantially correct. The cephalopod visual system has also been studied from the neuroanatomical viewpoint by Kopsch (1896), Lenhossek (1896) and Cajal (1917). The present work is an attempt to infer the way the well-defined neural structures, uncovered chiefly by Cajal, result in the behavioural properties which the octopus displays when discriminating shape.

## *THE SYSTEM*

The basis of the system is an arrangement which converts the distance between two points into an output, the size of which is inversely proportional to the distance. That is, the larger the distance between two imposed points the smaller will be the output, and the smaller the distance between the two points the larger the output.

This operation is performed by an arrangement of the following form. There is a set of lines running parallel to each other. Each line is interrupted at randomly chosen points, so that each line is divided into a number of segments of varying size.

Into this set of parallel segments enter at right angles a set of other lines (to be called retinal receptor fibres). These enter the layer of segmented lines at equally spaced intervals and penetrate the layer of the segmented lines to its other boundary.

Now let us assume that the retinal receptor fibres become active when

Reprinted from *Nature,* 1960.

they have been stimulated by a boundary discontinuity. The distance between two retinal receptor fibres reflects the distance between two points on a boundary. Let us also assume that the line segments in the parallel line layer also become active only when two or more than two simultaneously active retinal receptor fibres cross them. It will then follow that the closer together the two active retinal receptor fibres are, the greater the number of line segments will become active. The sum of active line segments in the parallel line layer will correspond in inverse ratio with the distance apart of the active incoming retinal receptor fibres.

The arrangement which has been described corresponds with what can be seen of the histology of the 'zona plexiforme' of the deep retina as described and illustrated by Cajal (1917). Fig. 1 shows the terminations of the incoming retinal fibres. Fig. 2 shows some of the fibres which may be identified with the segmented parallel line layer of our arrangement. It is to be seen that each of the segments in the section has an output leading out of the 'zona plexiforme' farther into the optic nervous system. We simply have to assume that the fibres in this figure act as a 'coincidence gate' or a spatial summator. If we make this assumption, then arrangements such as these have the function of converting distance between fibres into numbers of impulses. Distances or intervals can then be handled in the same way as intensities. Such a transducer of relational properties does not rely on 'scanning', with its high requirements of timing accuracy and overall precision. Such an arrangement would therefore have implications in the phenomena of neural integration beyond those of cephalopod vision.

So far, the arrangement described would transform the distance between

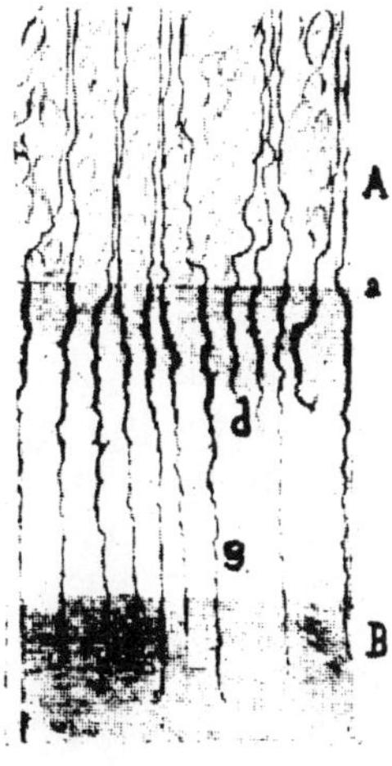


Fig. 1.

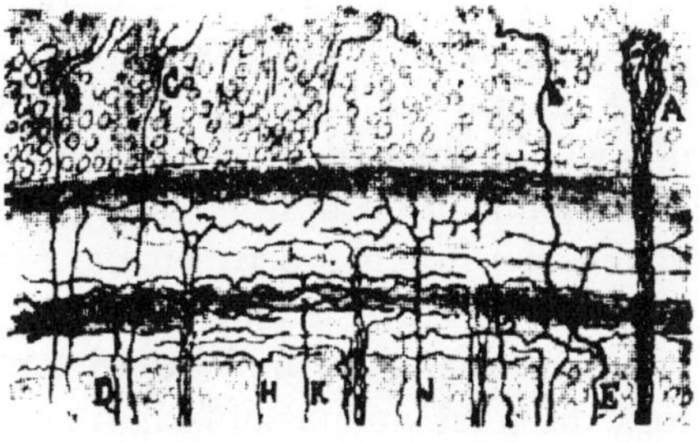


Fig. 2.

a pair of points into an amount of neural activity. The shapes to be discriminated, however, are composed of a great number of pairs of points. It is assumed that these pairs lie on lines parallel to each other and that each pair is measured by an arrangement such as was described above. This is done by having many such arrangements side by side, parallel to each other, running in the vertical visual axis. It is assumed that the total amount of excitation generated by the whole set of these arrangements gives the octopus its chief cue to the discrimination of shape. Different shapes are in this way translated into a single continuum of amount of activity. The problem of discriminating between them becomes one of differentiating between various levels of activity in a single channel.

Before proceeding, I should make clear that for the purposes of prediction two accessory assumptions must be made: (1) that vertical lines produce little or no output, because excitations on the same vertical arrangement inhibit each other over a small distance, and (2) that the octopus can also discriminate relative vertical positions of the output converted in the above way. This second appears to be a residual factor left when we have explained the rest of Sutherland's results. We may assume that it is an independent channel which signals these differences also as differences in quantity of output. It should also be stated that the present system has been left quantitatively flexible. It has been assumed, for example, that the vertical distance between two points leads to an output which is the reciprocal of this distance.

There is no reason for supposing that the conversion is precisely this. The theory only has to assume that the conversion is something like this, and then perhaps not over the whole range (for example, the system may collapse over very large visual angles).

## *PROPERTIES OF THE SYSTEM*

(1) *Transfer to Different Sizes of the Same Shape.* Let us take two parallel lines and their scale enlargement, and place them at right angles to the arrangements described above (that is, in the horizontal visual axis). The total amount of discharge from the system outlined above for the two figures will be the same. If we double the vertical distance between the lines, the amount of firing from each pair of points will halve. However, as we double the distance between the two lines, we also double their length. If we double their length we measure from twice the number of arrangements (as they run parallel to each other in the vertical direction). Therefore, the total amount of output given of both sets of lines separately will be the same. Transfer should therefore be excellent in the case of this shape.

Transfer from one size to another will depend on two factors: (*a*) the shape used; and (*b*) the other member of the pair from which the octopus has learnt to make the discrimination.

As regards the first point, it will be readily seen that, if we take a V shape lying on its side and a scale enlargement of it, the scale enlargement will produce a greater output. The small V shape is a part of the larger V shape. Such reasoning will apply to diamonds and triangles, *inter alia*. However, any scaling down (or scaling up) will subtract only the pairs of points (or add pairs of points) which are the most distant from each other on the vertical axis. These will be contributing disproportionately little to the total amount of output.

This brings me to the second point. If the total amount of output from the shape to be discriminated from the other member of the pair was larger, then the increase in output due to the enlargement of this shape will not destroy the discrimination, because the effective distance along the continuum is increased. (". . . the octopus, having been trained to discriminate between vertical and oblique, treats the horizontal in transfer tests as equivalent to the oblique (and vice versa for animals initially trained to discriminate between horizontal and oblique)"—Sutherland, 1958a, p. 456.) There may actually be an improvement if the other parameters which the octopus derives from the stimulus also increase the distance between discriminanda.

Sutherland has frequently noted that the octopus is capable of maintaining a discrimination between two shapes even when their size is altered (within certain limits) (for example, Sutherland, 1957a, p. 65, 1957b, p. 13). He has noted that a decrease in size shows a smaller transfer than

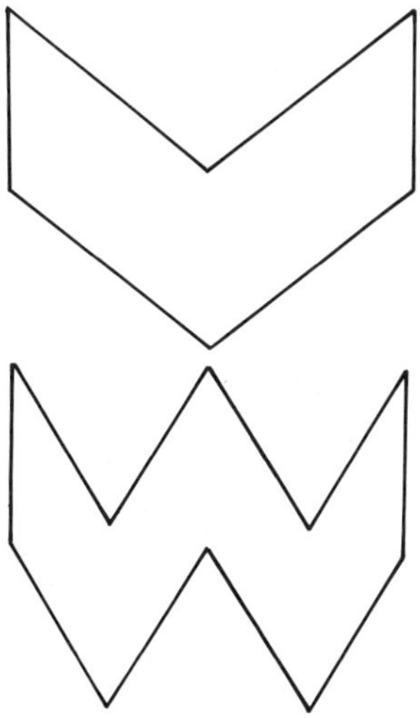

Fig. 3.

an increase. This would be predicted on the present theory with certain pairs of figures where the distance along the continuum of output was decreased.

However, a breakdown of the size transfer data according to the shapes to be discriminated has not been considered. A search of Sutherland's data, however, reveals that there is a difference in the predicted direction (Sutherland, 1958). The animals were trained to discriminate between a square and a triangle, both 25 sq. cm. in area. Transfer tests to larger squares (36 sq. cm.) show 65 per cent correct responses. (The accuracy of responding to the original square under the same conditions is 65 per cent.) The figure for transfer to a small square is 67·5 per cent. However, transfer to larger triangles yields a score of 88 per cent in the case of the larger and 67·5 per cent when the triangle is made smaller (changes in area equal to those made in the case of the squares). As a triangle of the same area produces a much larger output than the square, an increase in the size of the triangle will increase the difference in the amount of output between the triangle and the square. Changes in the size of the square will not produce changes in output, if we assume (assumption 1) that its vertical lines produce little or no output. Transfer here should not vary with the direction of the change of size.

The theory is thus in agreement with what is known of the ability to transfer from one size to another in the octopus. Further testing of the theory should examine the relation between shape and the capacity to transfer to other sizes, and also the relation between size transfer and the other member of the pair to be discriminated. We should expect on this theory not only transfer of size to be relative to the other member of the stimuli to be discriminated. Even if the present theory is wrong, it will have been important if it directs attention to these two factors, which so far have been neglected.

(2) *Difficulty of Discrimination Between Shapes*. The difficulty of discrimination on this theory should be proportionate to the difference in the quantity of output generated by the two shapes to be discriminated. Each pair of points on the boundary of the shape where it cuts a vertical arrangement will produce an output which will be inversely proportional to the distance of the two points. The sum of the outputs produced by all the pairs of points will characterize the shape for the octopus. The shape, regarding this mechanism only, will be represented as a quantity, or a number on a single dimension. The calculation of similarity can therefore be made with rigour. An index of similarity will be the difference between the two quantities generated by the two shapes to be discriminated. (Such a formulation assumes that the message on all other visual discrimination mechanisms is kept constant, such as that mentioned in assumption 2 (below). There are also others such as brightness, but these are easy to keep constant.)

(1) Sutherland (1958a, b) finds that horizontal rectangles are easily discriminated from vertical of the same proportions. This is readily explained. The horizontal rectangle stimulates a large number of vertical arrangements with a set of points relatively close to each other vertically. It is to be remembered that points close to each other produce a larger output than points farther apart. However, the vertical rectangle stimulates a relatively smaller number of vertical arrangements and by pairs of points farther from each other. There should, therefore, be a very large difference (1:25) between the outputs if the rectangles are 10 cm. × 2 cm.

"Perfect transfer occurred where the ratio of long to short sides was altered from 10 : 2 to 7 : 2 or 7 : 1" (Sutherland 1957a). This would be an alteration of 1 : 25–4 : 49 and 1 : 49 in the amount of output in the discrimination. However, the absolute quantities of output would be different here also. As the direction of the ratios and of the difference remains the same here, this result does not count against the theory and, if anything, supports it. It is a result worth quoting because it shows that in circumstances where the differences among the two discriminanda are large, transfer occurs within a wide margin. It is as if the octopus was simply learning larger–smaller output differences. What would happen if larger numbers of shapes had to be retained in the same experiment by the octopus would be of interest. Further, these results show that if the two shapes to be discriminated give large differences of output, 'size-constancy' for the octopus does not need to be notably accurate .

(2) Sutherland (1958a) finds that two oblique rectangles (⁄ and ∖) are indiscriminable. Here the sums of the outputs in the vertical arrangements are the same.

(3) Furthermore he stated (1958a): "The finding that a vertical rectangle is more readily discriminable from an oblique than is a horizontal was unexpected". Such a difference is readily predicted from the present theory. The horizontal rectangle would produce a much greater output than the vertical rectangle. The output of the oblique rectangle would not be intermediate as might at first sight appear because the tilt of the figure would produce a set of points close to each other at the corners on the vertical axis. It is predicted that if the corners of the horizontal figure were altered to make it into a parallelogram with the short sides parallel to the vertical visual axis (the area being kept the same) the differential discrimination would disappear.

(4) Sutherland (1959) has found that V and W shapes (Fig. 3) of the same height, width and area can be discriminated with great difficulty or not at all (accuracy 53 per cent) when the figures are in this orientation. An inability would be predicted on the present theory. The total vertical distances are the same in both cases. However, it would be predicted that the same shapes would be more discriminable when both are tilted through 90°. With ≲ the vertical distance is divided into more short segments

than in the case of $<$. Therefore, as short segments produce more output than long, and there are here more short segments, output should be larger for $\lesssim$ than $<$.

(5) Sutherland (1959) has found that $\vee$ is indiscriminable from $\wedge$ (accuracy 50 per cent). This can be predicted in a straightforward way. He has also found that $<$ can be discriminated from $\wedge$ (though only with an accuracy of 56 per cent). The $<$ shape would cut the vertical arrangements at points closer to each other than the $\wedge$ shape, thus producing more excitation. However, M is discriminated from $>$ with greater ease (69 per cent accuracy) and the present theory cannot readily account for this or the quantitatively small success of the octopus with $<$ against $\wedge$. (There are, however, assumptions about the sensitiveness to alterations in output with equal inaccuracies of verticality which differ for the shapes used and the amount of the shape deleted due to assumption 1 which could be made.)

(6) Sutherland (1958a) has found that octopuses have more difficulty in discriminating a diamond (a square with base at 45° to the horizontal) from a triangle than in discriminating a normal square from a triangle. This again is in accordance with the calculations of differences of magnitude of output derived from the theory. Though the other findings on the discriminability of the standard geometrical shapes (circles, triangles, etc.) show good agreement with the theory, differences in height (assumption 2) equally well account for some of the findings, as shapes of equal area were used. A further point to be borne in mind is that so far the assumption has usually been made that the placing of the shape on the receptor field of the octopus relative to the vertical has been geometrically exact, and departures from this have not been considered. However, the output of some shapes is much more affected by deviations. It is possible that the octopus uses this magnitude of oscillation about a mean to effect some discrimination. This supposition could be tested by imposing known and differing degrees of rotation in one direction and then the other in quick succession on the same shape, one amount serving as the positive signal and the other as the negative.

(7) It is found that the octopus can discriminate some up–down mirror images. This would be covered by assumption 2. However, left–right mirror images are indiscriminable, and this agrees with the theory.

## *DISCUSSION*

In the previous section, the salient reported findings on the shape discrimination of the octopus have been discussed in relation to the proposed system. The reader must be the judge of the success of the system in accounting for these findings. Predictions have also been made which allow the theory to be tested behaviourally.

However, the theory is not simply behavioural, and in this sense it is of much wider scope. A functional significance is suggested for a neuronal network of a kind to be found in many other places. It is proposed that this network converts relative distance into an output simply of quantity, and a simple *modus operandi* is given. In this way a look at the neurohistology may give a clue to the component operations on information in neural systems the overall function of which is already known. Direct work correlating visual input with events in the cephalopod optic lobes can also be used to check the correctness of my surmise.

On a more general plane it is conjectured that the octopus breaks down its visual information into various 'components' or dimensions of which the system put forward is only one. Each of these 'components' (given varying visual input) will vary only in amount. This amount for each 'component' is presumably represented as a quantity of excitation leaving the optic lobes, via one of the nerve fascicules. If this is correct, then sectioning one of these bundles, while conducting behavioural tests, would reveal the kind of classification or breakdown of the visual environment which the octopus performs by noting resulting confusions. Similarly, recording from these nerve bundles (should this prove feasible) while the eye is stimulated with various inputs should prove revealing. It is indeed possible that the transformation of shape into a simple quantitative continuum may prove to be a paradigm of the way that the problem of perceptual classification is dealt with in other organisms. In this way a given environment could be translated into a set of levels of activity in a number of channels. Thus a state of affairs for the organism could be represented as a point in an $n$-dimensional space.

## *REFERENCES*

Cajal, S. R. Contribución al conocimiento de la retina y centros ópticos de los cefalópods. *Trabajos del Laboratorio de investigationes biologicas de la Universidad de Madrid,* 1917, *15,* 1-82.

Dodwell, P. C. Shape discrimination in the octopus and the rat. *Nature,* 1957, *179,* 1088.

Koffsch, F. Das Anozenganglion der Cephalopoden. *Anatomische Anzeiger,* 1895, *11,* 361-369.

Lenhossek, M. *Archiv für mikroskopische Anatomie,* 1896, *47,* 54.

Sutherland, N. S. Visual discrimination of orientation by *Octopus. British Journal of Psychology,* 1957, *48,* 55-71. (a)

Sutherland, N. S. Visual discrimination of orientation and shape by *Octopus. Nature,* 1957, *179,* 11-13. (b)

Sutherland, N. S. Visual discrimination of the orientation of rectangles by *Octopus vulgaris* Lamarck. *Journal of Comparative and Physiological Psychology,* 1958, *51,* 452-458. (a)

Sutherland, N. S. Visual discrimination of shape by *Octopus.* Squares and triangles. *Quarterly Journal of Experimental Psychology,* 1958, *10,* 40-47. (b)

Sutherland, N. S. A test of a theory of shape discrimination in *Octopus vulgaris* Lamarck. *Journal of Comparative and Physiological Psychology,* 1959, 52, 135-141.

*It should be stated that the ideas presented in the previous two papers do not represent any final solution to questions about how shapes are classified by the octopus. Sutherland has revised his ideas several times (e.g., Sutherland, 1963), and Deutsch, too, has subsequently suggested other possible models (e.g., Deutsch 1962). However, the papers give a good idea of the state of theoretical notions at that time. In one sense the proposals were far too ambitious, and in another they lose their interest unless they can be related very closely to the empirical evidence. They were far too ambitious in supposing that the proposed coding systems could be quite general, and applicable for instance to octopus, rat, and man. Looking over the possibilities today, it seems absurd to suppose that one and the same model or system could fit visual systems with such very different properties. The force of this remark will perhaps only become clear in Part IV, where those differences are described in some measure. But, it also may be noticed that Deutsch's paper on the plexiform zone of the octopus contains the seed of the destruction of that overambition, since it seeks to tie the coding system rather closely to known anatomical and physiological arrangements within the organism's visual system. Of course it is possible to have a "formal" model which lacks support from physiological sources; as long as such a model is in harmony with the behavior of the system it seeks to explain, it cannot be faulted. Yet clearly a model will gain greatly in plausibility if one can identify at least the probable anatomical and/or physiological bases for its elements and structure. This point leads directly back to the second remark made about structural models, namely, that they rapidly lose interest unless they can be tied closely to the data.*

*This is important because rapid and spectacular advances in our understanding of the structure and functioning of visual systems have taken place in the past few years. Whereas ten years ago it was reasonable to postulate models for shape and contour coding and analysis which were purely formal, that is no longer true today. As we shall see in Part IV, the constraints which knowledge of visual physiology now places on the classes of models to be looked at are quite considerable and are different for different orders of visual systems. Also, the question of solving the problem of* stimulus equivalence is no longer pressing, and just any solution will not do. Since the general mode of solution is now clear (Deutsch provides a good example, and many other models could now easily enough be devised) what one needs is a class of models which fit particular sorts of visual systems well, both with regard to the known structure and physiological function of such systems and with respect to the behavioral evidence on pattern recognition. It has to be admitted that the latter is meagre for most species, but is not nonexistent, as we shall see in Part III.

I proposed a coding model (Dodwell, 1957) which was overambitious in the same sense as those presented in this section so far, but at least it had the merit of seeming to fit the experimental data for the rat rather better than the Deutsch model (the old arguments on this point need not be gone into). It subsequently turned out, by good fortune, that the sort of coding principle I had suggested, and at least the outline of how such coding might be attained, received rather strong support from neurophysiological researches which were undertaken quite independently.

The observant reader already may have asked himself the question of how the sorts of coding models discussed so far can deal with perceptual change, adaptation, and learning. Surely we know enough about the importance of such factors, at least for higher organisms, to require that they should not be excluded completely from consideration. It can be suggested that the coding models represent a fixed, primary step in the processing of visual information about patterns—to anticipate yet again, we shall find in Part IV good evidence of such a primary detection system—that the modeling of perceptual learning should be treated separately, and as an additional feature, in some way to be hooked up with the coding model. This is the position I have argued, and I attempted to model the two processes simultaneously and in such a manner that they can be fitted together. Doing things in this way has some very real advantages, which will be discussed further following the paper in which the combined system is outlined.

# *A Coupled System for Coding and Learning in Shape Discrimination*

P. C. DODWELL

*A system for coding visual information about shape is described. It is shown how the output from this coding system can be coupled to a classifier, or recognizer, in such a way that shape equivalence is preserved. A major weakness of previous coding-type theories of shape recognition is remedied, in that a memory system is built into the recognizer, which becomes self-organizing in terms of stimulus regularities in the environment. This is shown to be a logical basis for perceptual learning and perceptual constancy. Recent confirmatory neurophysiological findings from direct recordings in the striate cortex of cat are briefly considered, and the possibility of coupling the recognition system to a response system is outlined.*

## *INTRODUCTION*

It has been argued elsewhere (Dodwell, 1961c) that the orthodox probabilistic approach to constructing theories of discrimination learning is weak, because of the ambiguity with which the term "stimulus" is used in such theories. An ambiguous term in an abstract theory may have functions similar to those of a *deus ex machina,* and should be regarded with suspicion. It was also argued that a more precise definition of the term was needed, and that one way of defining stimulus would be in terms of a system for coding or classifying sensory input. Indeed, for some types of visual discrimination, such as shape recognition, there is now considerable behavioral evidence to indicate the general principles on which such classifying systems may work in fairly simple visual systems (e.g., Deutsch, 1960; Dodwell, 1957, 1960, 1961a, 1961b; Sutherland, 1957, 1959, 1960, 1963). This evidence has recently been supplemented by neurophysiological findings obtained by direct recording from individual neurons in the visual cortex of cat (Hubel & Wiesel, 1962).

The concept of shape coding, as originally suggested by Deutsch (1955), can be held to be unsatisfactory because it does not allow for the operation

Reprinted from *Psychological Review*, 1964.

of perceptual learning. This criticism can be leveled at a shape coding theory as a theory of shape recognition, that is, as a *complete* theory about how shapes are recognized, but there is no reason why the output from a coding system should not be coupled to a learning system or "response probability generator" to yield a more complete and logically satisfactory theory. In fact it is the purpose of this paper to show that it can be done, and to show that the coupled system is not open to the sorts of criticism which can be made of either component (i.e., the shape coding system and the probabilistic discrimination learning model) on its own.

The system to be described consists of an elaborated version of a shape analyzing system proposed earlier to explain shape discrimination in rats (Dodwell, 1957), connected to a signal classification system suggested by Uttley (1954). This dual system does not directly predict response probabilities in the way stochastic models do, but a straightforward extension of the double system can do so. This combined model gives a good fit to most of the behavioral data on shape discrimination in the rat and octopus, and also incorporates many of the features discovered in the direct neurophysiological exploration of the striate cortex of cat.

## *THE SHAPE CODING SYSTEM*

The system envisaged consists of a two-dimensional array of units arranged in parallel chains, so that each unit has two neighbors, except for the end units of each chain, each one of which has only one neighbor. The chains are functionally independent except in two important respects: one set of end units (Set A) is so arranged that if one of them fires, they all fire simultaneously, and each one of the other set of end units (Set B) is connected to a single tranmission line, called the final common cable (fcc). Each chain has the same number of units (this is not a necesssary condition of the working of the system, but its introduction simplifies the exposition). Each unit is connected to a receptor, or group of receptors, on the retina, and when the receptor (or group of receptors) is stimulated this activates the unit to which it is connected. Such a unit is "active"; when a unit is not so activated it is "passive." An active unit does not affect any of its neighbors by transmitting "activation" to them. It is assumed that only excitation from regions of sharp change in stimulation (contours) activates the array, and that adjacent receptors (or groups of receptors) activate adjacent units. Thus, when the image of a sphere is focused on the retina, a set of units corresponding to a circular contour is activated on the array. "Corresponding" is used advisedly since, although a one-to-one correspondence between receptors (or groups of them) and units is postulated, this does not imply any simple geometrical similarity in the mapping of the points in the two regions. However, an important assumption is made about horizontal straight lines: it is assumed that (with the retina in normal orientation) stimulation by a horizontal line will activate units all on the same chain.

A second process in the units, called *excitation,* originates in the firing of the End-set A, and results in a "sweep" across the array, since each unit can pass excitation from itself to its neighbor in the direction of the End-set B. All units of this set discharge into the fee. This excitation is not to be confused with activation of units by receptors, or groups of receptors, to which they are connected. The transmission of excitation from unit to unit involves a small delay, the length of which is determined by whether the transmitting unit is active or passive. Only the two states are envisaged, and the delay for each is constant, say $Ta$ and $Tp$. For convenience let $Ta > Tp$.

Each unit can pass excitation to one neighbor only, and excitation always travels from A towards B. The time for excitation to traverse a chain of $n + 1$ units, all of which are passive, is $n(TP)$. If the units of the array are passive, the traverse times will be equal, and there will be a single large discharge into the fee, since all the A units fire together and excitation reaches all the B units simultaneously.

When some units are active, some passive, the traverse time for any particular chain will depend only on the number of active and passive units on it, and can be written in the form $n(Ta) + (n - r)(Tp)$. The added delay involved when $r$ units are active on a chain is obtained by subtracting $n(Tp)$ from this expression:

$$\begin{aligned} r(Ta) + (n-r)(Tp) \\ - n(Tp) = r(Ta - Tp) \end{aligned}$$

Let the additional time for transmission through an active unit be $\Delta T$. Thus $T = Ta - Tp$, and the added delay on a chain with $r$ active units is $r\Delta T$. This may be called the "delay function" for a single chain. The delay function for an array of N chains will be made up of a set of terms of this form. Effectively, the system transforms spatial information into a function of a single variable, $t$. Thus, the characteristics of the delay function are independent of which particular chains, or which units on those chains, are activated. That is, the signal in the fee is independent of the signaled shape's position (but not its orientation) on the array.

Sets may be formed for chains having equal values of $r$. One of these will be the set for which $r = 0$, which may be written $[q_o, nTp]$, where $q_o$ represents the number of chains in the set, and hence the amplitude of the initial volley in the fee. The total signal, for one "sweep" will be the *union,* or logical sum, of these sets. The set for any one value $r = r_k$ contains two components, $q_k$, and $r_k\Delta T$. The former is a measure of the amplitude of pulse generated in the fee, the latter a measure of the time at which the pulse is generated, measured from the initial pulse (when $r = 0$) as base line. The delay function for the array is sufficient for deducing the important characteristics of a signal if, as would often be the case, the number of empty chains and the size of the initial volley are unimportant. In general it is necessary that there should be either at least one large set with equal $r$, or at least one chain with a value of $r$ that is atypical, for a distinctive signal to be generated (either $q_k$ or $r_k$ or both, identify a set).

It has already been stated that the array is assumed to be so arranged that chains represent, functionally, one of the principal axes of the visual field; stimulation of receptors by a horizontal line will activate units all on one chain. Which chain this is will be immaterial as far as the signal in the fee is concerned; the delay function is simply $[1, r\Delta T]$, and the distinctiveness of the signal is due to this one atypical value of $r$ (for all other chains, $r = 0$). Two horizontal lines would be distinguished from one by a doubling of the amplitude of the delayed discharge, and so on.

In general, the system will yield distinctive signals for different shapes, and is sensitive to changes in orientation (rotation in the frontal plane). Simple geometric considerations show that this sensitivity is greatest for small rotations of a horizontal straight line (provided the density of units on the array is uniform) whether or not this part of a shape, such as the base of a square or triangle. The same considerations show that it is least sensitive to rotations near the vertical. However, as it stands the system will not yield distinctive signals for some pairs of shapes which one would expect to be readily discriminable, such as a diamond and a pair of vertical lines. This difficulty can be overcome by postulating two systems, functionally perpendicular to each other, so that in the second a vertical line in the visual field activates units all on one chain. Such a dual system will explain fairly satisfactorily most of the data on shape discrimination in the rat and in the octopus. For instance, it will explain the fact that both species can readily discriminate horizontal from vertical straight lines, but have difficulty with mutually perpendicular lines set at 45° to the horizontal; the fact that mirror images tend to be confused, that transfer tends to be easy (for the rat) when the transfer shape shares a horizontal contour with the training shape and that rotation of shapes in the sagittal plane tends to upset discrimination. Detailed evaluations of the empirical evidence for this, and for other shape coding systems, have been published elsewhere (Dodwell, 1957, 1961b) and will not be repeated here. While it is true that some facts about shape recognition are not compatible with the theory, it should be remembered that other means of discrimination, such as by brightness distribution, may enter as contaminating factors (see Dodwell, 1961b). The important feature to be brought out at the moment is that the primary information processing postulated in the coding system is the first step in the specification of a logically satisfactory theory of shape recognition. The features of the system that are important in this respect are, first of all, the fact that in it spatial information is transformed into a temporal analogue, and secondly, that this analogue consists of sequences of pulses of different amplitudes and latencies which all occur in a single transmission line. It is not claimed that this is the only suitable way of coding information about shape for further processing, but it has two major advantages.

The first advantage is that the information about shape is coded independently of the position on the array (and hence on the retina) at which the shape was present. This means that the system overcomes the problem of identification of a shape in different locations—which has always been a major difficulty for neural theories of shape discrimination—in a simple fashion. The second advantage is that it makes possible an attempt to solve the problem of stimulus equivalence in general (recognition of shape independently of position is, of course, also part of the problem of stimulus equivalence, but is a rather special case). Explicit separation of the operations of "coding" and "recognizing" allows one to reformulate the problem of stimulus equivalence into the question: which outputs from the coding system are classified in the same way by the "recognizer"? To answer this question one must consider how the recognizer operates on the outputs from the coding system.

## *THE RECOGNIZING SYSTEM*

How can "recognition" be defined in a formal system of the type here envisaged, which is to be equated, in some sense, with neural processes in the brain? One may define recognition as the registration of some constant pattern of activity, or activity at some constant locus, for a given input pattern or class of input patterns. Such a system will now be described.

The recognizer accepts and classifies the output from the coder, which in the present system consists of sequences of pulses of varying frequency and amplitude, all occurring in a single transmission line (or in two lines for the double system; the single system will be described, since the problem is in principle identical, but more complicated, for the double system). A system has been outlined by Uttley (1954) which, with slight modifications, will classify inputs of this type. As it stands, Uttley's system classifies temporal patterns of discrete pulses of equal amplitude, and is thus a digital system. The outputs of the coding system described above are analogues of the geometrical properties of shapes; however, Uttley (1954) indicates a simple analogue-digital conversion system, of a type which might be used in a computer, which could occur in a nervous system (p. 486). There is evidence that analogue-digital conversion does occur in certain neural structures (e.g., Hilali & Whitfield, 1953), so it is not implausible to suggest that some such conversion occurs between the outputs of the coder and the recognizer. The particular form of analogue-digital conversion suggested requires that the recognizer have a number of inputs, and is as follows: each volley in the coder output gives rise to a "unit" impulse in one of the inputs to the recognizer. If $l$ different amplitudes are to be discriminated, there must be $l$ inputs in the recognizer: each input fires for one and only one value of amplitude $q_k$, or for only a small range of such values. For the simplest case, where only two different amplitudes are recognized, two inputs to the recognizer are required, inputs $j$ and $k$, say. These two inputs are connected to counters which register either (*a*) the initial arrival of unit impulses in either input, or (*b*) the temporal patterns of impulses on either or on both inputs. This is achieved by feeding each input into a series of delay units, and then to the counters, as shown in Figure 1. (The recognizer can be imagined as either a nerve network or as an electrical system; however, its properties are specified independently of any particular embodiment.) Except for the first two counters ($j$ and $k$), a counter will only register when two impulses arrive at it simultaneously or within an arbitrary small interval of time. To see how this occurs, consider the counter labeled $jj'$ in Figure 1. It will register if, and only if, an impulse in the $j$ input is followed by a second impulse in the same input after the time $\tau$, where $\tau$ is the delay induced by the first delay line on input $j$. Similarly, the adjacent count $jk'$ registers only when an impulse on $j$ is followed by an impulse on $k$ after time $\tau$. (The primes refer to the number of delay units separating a pair of impulses.) Assuming $\tau = h\Delta T$, where $h$ is an integer, the time intervals required to activate different counters will be simply related to the output from the coder. It can be seen that the recognizer of Figure 1 will discriminate all possible patterns for the two inputs $j$ and $k$, up to time delays of $3\tau$. For patterns involving more than two impulses, more than one counter (excluding the initial $j$ and $k$ counters) will register. A simple higher order type of recognition can easily

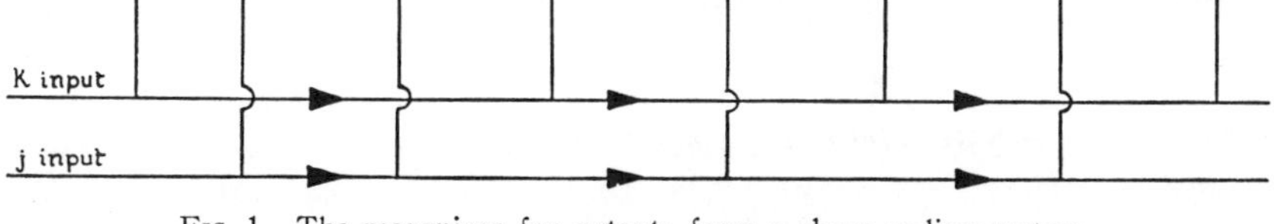

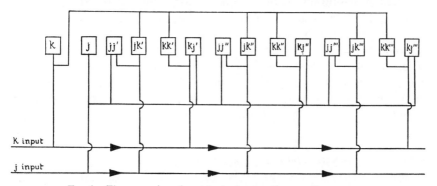

FIG. 1. The recognizer for outputs from a shape coding system.

Fig. 1. The recognizer for outputs from a shape coding system. (For explanation, see text.)

be added, whereby a counter $jj'kk''$, for example, will only register when both $jj'$ and $jk''$ are registering. $jj'$ and $jk''$ fire simultaneously if, and only if, an impulse in $k$ is followed by one in $j$ after time $2\tau$, followed by a second impulse in $j$ after a further time $\tau$. In this case the counter $jk'''$ would also fire, of course, so that at a third level of classification a counter $jj'jk''jk'''$ would register. This hierarchical system of classification can be continued to any desired level of complexity, according to the number of inputs, and the number and complexity of patterns to be classified. The only restriction required is that $U\tau < n\Delta T$ where $U$ is the number of delay units in the recognizer, and $n$, as before, is the number of units per chain in the array.

"Equivalent stimuli" can now be defined as inputs from the receptors which give rise to the activation of the same set of counters in the recognizer. It may be thought that little is gained by introducing a recognizer of this form—that in fact the original information about shape has been lost almost beyond recovery, and that no compensating advantage has been secured. However, it should be noted, in the first place, that original signal information is contained unambiguously in the system of registers that are activated: if the system were reversed, so that the counters became signal generators, the original input signal would be perfectly reproduced for a given constellation of registers, but now as an output from the system (Uttley, 1954). Secondly, a distinct advantage has been secured in the sense that a structure is set up by which a constant local pattern of activity is a necessary consequence of a spatial pattern, at the receptors, which is *not* location specific. As Ayer (1957) points out, the occurrence of a necessary consequence is in all respects equivalent to a sufficient condition for the antecedent's occurrence; i.e., the occurrence of a given pattern at the recognizer is sufficient to ensure that a particular pattern *did* activate the receptors. The only exception here is the fact that certain different patterns may give rise to identical or nearly identical patterns from the coder, in which case perceptual confusion arises. The question of whether or not "perceptual confusion" is to be equated with "perceptual equivalence" is taken up in the next section of the paper. Before taking up this question, it may be noted that an information-reducing system such as the coder, interposed between the receptors and the recognizer, serves to remove an objection that has been raised against the Uttley-type recognizer. This is the objection that, to be effective, such a classificatory system would need an impossibly large number of units to deal with all combinations of receptor activation patterns (Uhr, 1963).

## *PERCEPTUAL LEARNING*

The coupled system so far described has no "memory"; its performance is entirely independent of its own previous states. As such, therefore, it is deficient as a model for perception. To show how the system can be modified to incorporate a type of perceptual learning, the notion of a conditional probability computer can be introduced. The idea is, again, due to Uttley (1956, 1958, 1959). Consider the hierarchical classification system of Figure 2. The lines *a, b,* and *c* represent inputs, the open circles represent, as in Figure 1, coincidence counters. Simultaneous inputs at, for instance, *a* and *b* will activate the three counters *a, b,* and *ab*. Simultaneous inputs at *a, b,* and *c* will activate all the counters. Suppose now that each counter has a limited memory, such that each time it counts, its state is altered stepwise, but gradually tends to revert to its initial condition. (A simple physical analogue is a leaky condenser, to which a standard charge is applied, each time the unit counts.) Suppose, further, that in this system two counters in approximately the same state (with equal charges) will count if either one of them is activated. For example, if *b* has almost always occurred at the same time as *a*, then if *a* is activated (but not *b*) the *b* and *ab* counters will also be activated. By choosing a suitable criterion for "same state" such a system computes conditional probabilities at a specified level. (The probability that *b* occurs, given *a*, determines whether or not the *b* and *ab* counters register when *a* occurs alone.) The details of these computers, and the related conditional certainty computers, are given by Uttley (1956, 1958, 1959) and will not be repeated here, except to note that by building in suitable short- and long-term decay characteristics, rather good an-

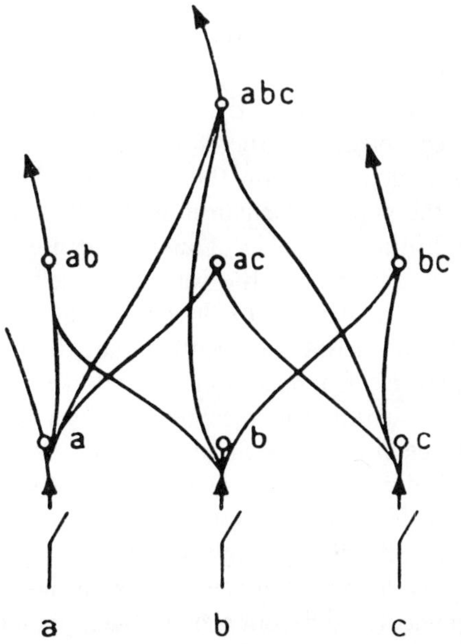


Fig. 2. A recognizer with three levels of classification. (For explanation, see text.)

alogues of the main features of classical conditioning can be produced. In any case it is clear that such computers will "recognize" patterns, conjunctions of patterns, and conjunctions of patterns occurring in rapid succession. Such conjunctions of patterns must lead to "generalization" or "inference" by the machine, and this is all that is needed to complete the type of perceptual learning required for the coupled system of coder and recognizer. For, in its normal environment, an organism is in constant visual contact with stimuli which fluctuate in size, shape, locus of stimulation of the retina, and so on. How does it come to "organize" or "recognize" a stable visual world? The usual answers are either that it learns to perceive the regularities amongst stimuli and conjunctions and sequences of stimuli, or that such perceptions are built in—both answers which nicely beg the question at issue when couched in such general terms.

The coupled system offers a solution which is not so flagrantly question begging. If one imagines a particular object in the early environment of an organism, say a circular disk, then as the organism approaches the object, moves around, over or away from it, the size, shape, orientation, etc. of the object will change, but these changes will be orderly, and will give rise to orderly changes in the output from the coder, and hence to orderly sequences of counts in the units of the recognizer. Many of these sequences will occur in fairly rapid succession (as when the organism locomotes) and, eventually, will give rise to "inferential learning" when the conditional probabilities become high enough, and stable enough. (In the interests of reasonable conciseness these conditions have not been enumerated; Uttley (1956, 1958) discusses them.) That is, when one member of the sequence is counted by the recognizer, if that counter's state is sufficiently close to the states of some other counters in the system, these will also register. The recognizer will therefore build up a system of internal classification which is dependent on the organism's history, to the extent that regularities in the perceived environment will be matched by regular patterns of activity in the recognizer. Thus, one can envisage two types of stimulus equivalence, one due to the ways in which the coder processes incoming patterns, which gives rise to "low order equivalence" because outputs from the coder are identical or very similar, the other due to experience of regular sequences of signals from the coder, which builds up higher orders of equivalence within the recognizer. Thus, for example, in this system the equivalence of a pair of circular contours is explainable in terms of the nearly identical outputs they generate in the coder. On the other hand, the "equivalence" of different perspective views of a circular disk, which may generate quite different outputs from the coder, is explainable in terms of "perceptual learning," which means, in this context, the regular conjunction of sequences of different signals. Such higher-order equivalence can even be thought of—rather speculatively—as the basis for perceptual constancy. It may be noted that this system offers an explicit and quite precise solution to the problems which Hebb's cell assembly theory was designed to meet. Hebb's explanation of "superordinate activity" as a basis for equivalence is vague, and in fact circular (Hebb, 1949, p. 98). The present system incorporates both the feature of low-level "preset" recognition of simple visual elements, and the feature of learned equivalence on the basis of repeated contiguous stimulation, but explains these as consequences of the initial coding system and the self-organizing properties of the recognizer, respectively. The first of these two deals satisfactorily with an awkward feature of Hebb's theory, namely that of explaining just how a *primitive* feature—a line, or angle in his argument—is initially "equivalent" for different retinal stimulus locations, and the second allows us to give an unambiguous definition of what Hebb calls "superordinate activity," that is to say, the constant physiological event that mediates perceptual recognition and generalization. The gain in precision leads to a more powerful theory of perceptual learning, which means of course one that is more amenable to experimental verification.

The testable consequences of this theory stem mainly from the properties of the coding system, and these predictions have been made, and some of them tested, in other places (e.g., Dodwell 1957, 1960, 1961a). However, the combined system does allow one to make a specific statement about perceptual equivalence, perceptual confusion, and the limits of discriminability. By the definition of the system, any pair of similar outputs from the coder are "equivalent," at the lowest level, for the recognizer. In view of the inferential character of the recognizer's operation, it is clear that, after some perceptual learning has occurred, a pair of similar outputs from the coder will activate a set of higher-order counters in the recognizer. If the pair of outputs actually are consequents of the reception of two different shapes, then perceptual confusion has occurred. However, any one shape (or object) will, in general, be capable of generating a number of different outputs from the coder, as explained above, and it is the set of these possible outputs that defines final, learned, recognition. Only in a case where *all* the possible outputs generated by a pair of shapes are the same would one have to admit the logical necessity of equivalence by confusion. Otherwise, successive discrimination of differences can occur in the system with prolonged visual inspection and search, as the two sets of units corresponding to the two shapes are organized in the recognizer. It should now be clear, too, that the system can handle contextual effects.

## *SOME NEUROPHYSIOLOGICAL EVIDENCE*

The model presented in the previous three sections was devised and in part published some time ago (Dodwell 1957, 1958), but at that time there was behavioral evidence bearing only on the form of the coding system in any direct way. The recognition system was elaborated to complete the model for perception in a logically satisfactory way, as indicated in the Introduction above. It did no violence to the facts, yet there was no solid evidence in its favor—it was speculative. However, quite recently some neurophysiological findings which bear directly on this system have been reported, findings which confirm quite strikingly that the main features of the proposed coding and recognition system are correct, although modification in detail may eventually be required.

Hubel and Wiesel (1959, 1960, 1962) in a number of publications have reported on their method of direct recording from individual neurons in the striate cortex of cat. Their principal early finding (1959) was that many of these neurons have well defined retinal receptive fields, which have a *specific orientation,* in contrast to retinal receptive fields at the lateral geniculate body, which tend to be circular. Moreover, such cortical cells characteristically are maximally sensitive to a stimulus which consists of a rectilinear contour falling on the midline of the receptive field, and in its orientation. Small changes in the orientation of the line relative to the retina are accompanied by rapid decreases in sensitivity, and small changes of position on the retina give rise to sharp changes in the firing pattern of the cortical neuron, since typically the receptive field consists of a narrow excitatory band, surrounded by a wider inhibitory field, or vice versa. It is *contour* rather than *surface* that activates these neurons; blanketing a receptive field with a surface leaves the neuron inactive. These so-called "simple" fields can be mapped out with small spots of light, to define their excitatory and inhibitory areas, and knowledge of these areas is sufficient to interpret the response of the neuron to more complex stimuli, such as a rectilinear contour, in terms of summation of excitation and inhibition from different parts of the field.

Clearly the simple receptive field represents a stage of processing sensory input which is very similar to the stage postulated for the coder described above. The latter's principal feature is that contours generate specific signals according to their orientation and position on the two-dimensional array. It will be recalled that these signals are taken into a function of a single variable, *t,* in the final common cable, in such a way that information about contour orientation is preserved, but positional information is not. Contours thus become *equivalent,* so long as they are in the same orientation, and this is represented in the model by the fact that such equivalent contours all activate the same unit in the recognizer. Interestingly enough, Hubel and Wiesel (1962) have identified cortical neurons having exactly this property also; namely, that they are activated only by rectilinear contours in specific *orientations,* but the *position* of that contour on the retina can vary considerably, in some cases over a field subtending an angle of up to 32° at the eye. This clearly represents a further stage in the coding process, beyond the simple fields. To be specific:

> The cell . . . failed to respond to round spots of light, whether small or large. By trial and error with many shapes of stimulus it was discovered that the cell's firing could be influenced by a horizontally oriented slit ⅛° wide and 3° long. Provided the slit was horizontal its exact positioning within the 3°-diameter field was not critical. When it was shone anywhere above the centre of the receptive field . . . an 'off' response was obtained; 'on' responses were evoked throughout the lower half, . . . one might have expected wider slits to give increasingly better responses owing to summation within the upper or lower part of the field, and that illumination of either half by itself might be the most effective stimulus of all. The result was just the opposite: responses fell off rapidly as the stimulus was widened beyond about ⅛°, and large rectangles covering the entire lower or upper halves of the receptive field were quite ineffective. . . . On the other hand, summation could easily be demonstrated in a horizontal direction, since a slit ⅛° wide but extending only across part of the field was less effective than a longer one covering the entire width. One might also have expected the orientation of the slit to be unimportant as long as the stimulus was wholly confined to the region above the horizontal line or the region below. On the contrary, the orientation was critical, since a tilt of even a few degrees from the horizontal markedly reduced the response, even though the slit did not cross the boundary separating the upper and lower halves of the field . . . for this cell the strict requirements for shape and orientation of the stimulus were in marked contrast to the relatively large leeway of the stimulus in its ordinate position on the retina [Hubel & Wiesel, 1962, pp. 114-115].

At the same time it must be stated that these authors have found quite a variety of receptive fields, although the two types described appear to be the main ones. They find no evidence for a preponderance of neurons with receptive fields in horizontal and vertical orientations. No evidence on this point is available for the rat, but there is anatomical evidence of dominance in the octopus (Young, 1960), and there is probably a genuine species difference between the cat and rat in this respect, since Sutherland (1963) has recently shown that cats have no difficulty in discriminating between mutually perpendicular contours set at 45° to the horizontal, in contrast to the marked difficulty of this discrimination for the rat and for the octopus.

## *THE RESPONSE SYSTEM*

Nothing has been said so far about responses, or the way classification in the system is related to response probability. There are two different problems to be faced. The first is: How are responses related to stimulation during the acquisition of hierarchical classifications in the recognizer?

The second is: How are responses related to stimulation for an already formed (stable) classification system or subsystem? It would go beyond the scope of this paper to try to deal with these questions in detail, but a brief outline of a possible system might be as follows:

At some level of the classification system "response generators" are connected to the counters in the recognizer. These response generators have the property that, if activated, they produce a particular response or class of responses. Initially, all counters at the level in question have an equal probability of activating any one of the response generators (only one of which can be activated at a given time). The probability of a particular response generator's being activated by a particular counter on subsequent trials is raised or lowered according to the history of successes or failures of that response to the stimulus in question; there is ample scope here for deployment of the operators of stochastic models for learning. The relation of response generators to counters would be a one-many relation, both within and between different levels of the classification system. In this way discrimination learning would be possible at differing levels of complexity and abstraction. Early learning would occur principally at the lowest levels of the classification system (responses would only be made consistently to simple aspects of the environment), where adult learning could be in terms of more general, complex or abstract features. While this component of the system is indicated only in the briefest way, it at least shows that the initial suggestion made in this paper, of hooking together a coding and perceptual learning system with a response generating system, is quite feasible, and should lead to a more realistic characterization of discrimination learning processes than has previously been possible. Finally, it may be noted that perceptual learning in the proposed system is by contiguity alone, but that reinforcement of instrumental responses would certainly affect the contingencies through which perceptual learning and organization occur.

## *SUMMARY*

The study of shape discrimination and discrimination learning has progressed from two different, but not contradictory, points of view. Theories of shape discrimination have concentrated on the problem of coding or analyzing the properties of shape as a basis for explaining the behavior of organisms with simple visual systems in discriminatory training and transfer situations. This approach has neglected the importance of perceptual learning. Theories of discrimination learning, couched in probabilistic terms, have neglected problems of stimulus classification and stimulus equivalence. A theory of shape classification (coding) is described, together with a system for recognition of the outputs of the coder, which is self-organizing in terms of regularities in the perceived environment. That is to say, the system incorporates the principle of perceptual learning. A possible method of connecting this coupled system to a response generating system is also briefly outlined. Taken together, these three systems—coder, recognizer, and response generator—constitute a logically satisfactory model for shape discrimination and discrimination learning.

## *REFERENCES*

Ayer, A. J. *The problem of knowledge.* London: Penguin Books, 1957.

Deutsch, J. A. A theory of shape recognition. *British Journal of Psychology,* 1955, *46,* 30-37.

Deutsch, J. A. The plexiform zone and shape recognition in the octopus. *Nature,* 1960, *185,* 443-446.

Dodwell, P. C. Shape recognition in rats. *British Journal of Psychology,* 1957. *48.* 221-229.

Dodwell, P. C. Visual discrimination of shape in animals and men. Unpublished doctoral dissertation, Bodleian Library, Oxford University, 1958.

Dodwell, P. C. Discrimination of small shapes by the rat. *Quarterly Journal of Experimental Psychology,* 1960, *12,* 237-242.

Dodwell, P. C. Visual orientation preferences in the rat. *Quarterly Journal of Experimental Psychology,* 1961, *13,* 40-47. (a)

Dodwell, P. C. Facts and theories of shape discrimination. *Nature,* 1961, *191,* 578-581. (b)

Dodwell, P. C. Coding and learning in shape discrimination. *Psychological Review,* 1961, *68,* 373-382. (c)

Hebb, D. O. *The organization of behavior.* New York: Wiley, 1949.

Hilali, S., & Whitfield, I. C. Responses of the trapezoid body to acoustic stimulation with pure tones. *Journal of Physiology,* 1953, *122,* 158.

Hubel, D. H., & Wiesel, T. N. Receptive fields of single neurones in the cat's striate cortex. *Journal of Physiology,* 1959, *148,* 574-591.

Hubel, D. H., & Wiesel, T. N. Receptive fields of optic nerve fibres in the spider monkey. *Journal of Physiology,* 1960, *154,* 572-580.

Hubel, D. H., & Wiesel, T. N. Receptive fields, binocular interaction and functional architecture in the cat's visual cortex. *Journal of Physiology,* 1962, *160,* 106-154.

Sutherland, N. S. Visual discrimination of shape by *Octopus. British Journal of Psychology,* 1957, *48,* 55-71.

Sutherland, N. S. Visual discrimination of shape by *Octopus:* Circles and squares, circles and triangles. *Quarterly Journal of Experimental Psychology,* 1959, *11,* 24-32.

Sutherland, N. S. The visual discrimination of shape by *Octopus:* Squares and rectangles. *Journal of Comparative and Physiological Psychology,* 1960, *53,* 95-103.

Sutherland, N. S. Cat's ability to discriminate oblique rectangles. *Science,* 1963, *139,* 209-210.

Uhr, L. Pattern recognition computers as models for form perception. *Psychological Bulletin*, 1963, *60*, 40-73.

Uttley, A. M. The classification of signals in the nervous system. *Electroencephalography and Clinical Neurophysiology*, 1964, *6*, 479-494.

Uttley, A. M. A theory of the mechanism of learning based on the computation of conditional probabilities. *Proceedings: First International Congress on Cybernetics*, Namur, 1956.

Uttley, A. M. Conditional probability computing in a nervous system. In: *The mechanization of thought processes*, Her Majesty's Stationery Office, London, 1958.

Uttley, A. M. The design of conditional probability computers. *Information and Control*, 1959, *2*, 1-24.

Young, J. Z. The visual system of *Octopus*. *Nature*, 1960, *186*, 836-839.

*It may be pointed out that the hooked-up model presented in this paper gives a rather explicit solution to the problem of recognition of coded outputs. One major problem for the Gestalt psychologists, for Lashley, for Pitts and McCulloch, and for Hebb, was that none of them could say how particular input classes were mapped into specified outputs—or in other words how particular patterns could be recognized. Their solutions were either tautologous (circular) or too general to be testable. If one can specify the actual processing steps in going from the input pattern to a particular unit in the recognizor this problem is solved; but it must be admitted that the vagaries of perceptual learning could make the identification of equivalences rather difficult. At least it should be possible to find experimental evidence for the two sorts of equivalence proposed (e.g., in differences in types of stimulus equivalence in young and older organisms), although such evidence is presently lacking.*

*In the postulation of a primary detector system and a "higher order" associational system which integrates the information about pattern features in terms of spatial and temporal contiguity, the combined model starts to look like a newer version of the notion Hebb put forward on perceptual learning (Hebb, 1949). While the empirical support for this sort of model of visual perception is not absolutely conclusive or overwhelming, it is pretty strong. Since it is not our main purpose here to go into questions of perceptual learning to any extent, the evidence will not be assessed now (a good deal of it is presented and discussed in Dodwell, 1970a), but one point about the interpretation does require further discussion. The Deutsch-type model gains its power through simplification of the processing of contour information. The question was raised earlier of whether this sort of move involves oversimplification. We shall find that the neurophysiological evidence supports the notion of simplicity of computation (see Part IV); but this very fact, and the finding that such computations are fairly fixed* (apparently they do not change much with age, for example), simply reinforces the point that the coding can only be one step—perhaps the first and no doubt a most important step—in "building up" the perception of whole patterns, of Gestalten. So, the simplicity of the coding itself need not be considered a flaw in this type of model; rather, we should be aware that steps involved in analyzing and classifying stimuli beyond that coding need to be investigated.

The final paper in this part is by Werner Reichardt and is a rather complete departure from the line of work we have been following so far. It demonstrates a very different approach to a problem in pattern recognition, and is clearly related to the von Holst and Mittelstaedt paper in Part I. Indeed, basically it is included here for the same three reasons. As I have hinted several times already, and as will become abundantly clear in Part IV, there are very big differences in anatomical and other visual organization between vertebrates and invertebrates; in particular there are important differences between mammals and insects. Many insects have compound eyes which consist essentially of a number of discrete receptor units, called ommatidia, which seem to function to some degree independently of one another (this statement has to be strongly qualified, as Ratliff's paper in Part IV well demonstrates). In some respects, therefore, we can expect the principles of operation of a compound eye in response to externally imposed patterns of stimulation to be more easily inferred than the corresponding principles for the more complex vertebrate organ. Reichardt's analysis of the optomotor reflexes of the beetle Chlorophanus is a beautiful demonstration that this is so. In an obvious way the analysis goes much deeper than the models described earlier in this part and gives a more complete and explicit explanation for a particular sort of behavior. Yet, this degree of refinement is only possible because the optomotor response is, in a real sense, simple: it is fixed, "preprogramed," predictable and reproducible. The visual behavior of higher animal forms is less regular; it is labile, adaptable, and so on. Add to this the higher level of anatomical and physiological complexity of the visual systems of vertebrates and the more elaborate forms of computation these must embrace, and it is perhaps not too surprising that we have been able to make only a few steps in the direction of modeling them adequately.

All this is said not to detract from Reichardt's work, but rather as an apologia for the less sophisticated state of the art of modelling mammalian systems. The details of the mathematical treatment given by Reichardt will not be of primary interest to most psychologists, provided it is accepted that the graphed functions shown in some of the figures really follow from the mathematical expressions. However, the general features of correlational systems can be grasped without the mathematical derivations.

# *Autocorrelation: A Principle for the Evaluation of Sensory Information by the Central Nervous System*

W. REICHARDT

Many animals react to optical stimulation by moving the eyes, the head, or even the whole body. These reactions are called "optomotor responses." They are continuously graded functions of optical stimulation.

Figure 1 illustrates how optomotor reactions can be elicited (Hassenstein and Reichardt, 1956a, b, 1959). The animal (Chlorophanus) sits inside a hollow cylinder which is composed of perpendicular black and white stripes. When the cylinder rotates, the animal tries to follow the movement. For the insect, this response to the movement observed reduces the relative speed of the surroundings to a residual speed—the slip. Insect and surroundings together form a feedback loop.

The direction and intensity of the optomotor responses have been used as an indicator of the perception processes involved in the central nervous system (CNS) of the experimental animal. In the experiments the feedback loop has been cut off by fixing the animal in the center of the cylinder in such a way that its optomotor reactions could be observed by the experimenter without influencing the position of the animal itself in relation to its optical environment. The experimental procedure is shown in Fig. 2 (Hassenstein, 1951). The beetle's back is glued to a piece of cardboard which is held by a clip, and the clip is fixed to a stand. The beetle is thus freely suspended in air. Then the beetle is given the Y-maze globe which it carries of its own free will. The Y-maze globe consists of six pieces of curved straw that join at four points to form Y-like junctions. When the beetle starts to walk it remains fixed, but the Y-maze globe performs the negative of the movements the beetle would perform if it were walking freely. After a few steps the beetle reaches a Y junction, or rather a Y junction reaches the beetle, and it has to choose right or left. After passing the junction, the animal is in the same situation as before. After the next few steps it has to choose again, and so on. For the beetle the Y-maze globe is an infinite Galton probability apparatus. In a given situation of optical stimulation, the ratio of choices has been proved to be a sensitive quantitative measure of optically induced (optomotor) turning tendencies.

Reprinted from *Sensory Communication*, 1961.

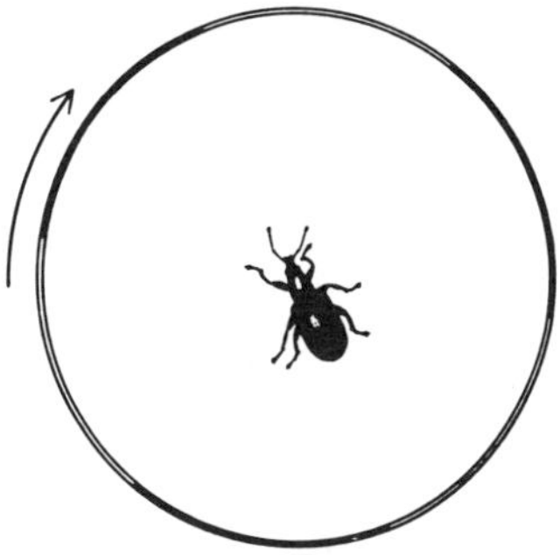

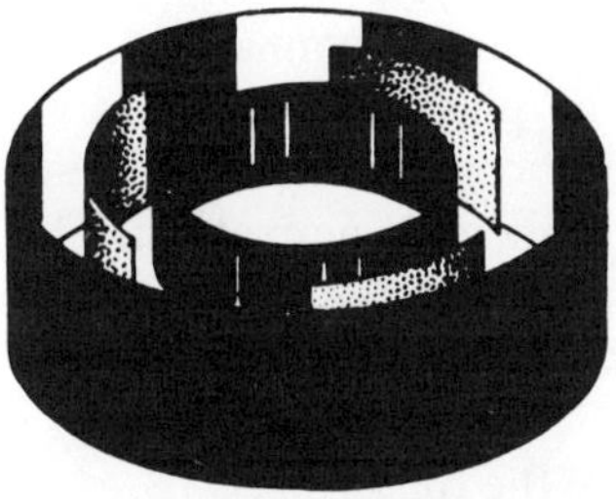

Fig. 1 (*upper left*). Diagram of striped-cylinder experiment in which optomotor responses can be elicited.
Fig. 2 (*right*). The animal (Chlorophanus) during the experiments.
Fig. 3 (*lower left*). Experimental arrangement for the production of sequences of light change.

The intensity of the reaction has been measured by the ratio:

$$R = \frac{W + A}{W - A} \tag{1}$$

where *W* indicates the number of choices "with" and A the number of choices "against" the direction of cylinder motion during the experiments. Statistical considerations have shown that *R* is practically a linear function of the turning tendency as long as *R* is smaller than 0.7. The number of choices that has to be taken into account depends on the intensity of reaction. This has been explained in full detail elsewhere (Hassenstein, 1951, 1958a).

In order to check the relations between stimuli and reactions, successions of narrow linelike light stimuli were delivered to the eyes of the experimental animal. Figure 3 presents one of the experimental arrangements used in the various tests (Hassenstein, 1958b). The set-up consists of three concentric cylinders. During the experiments the beetle with the Y-maze globe is suspended in the center of the cylinders. The inner cylinder is fixed and contains perpendicular slits. The outer cylinder is made up of black and white stripes so arranged that—looking from the beetle's position —the background of each slit consists of either a black or a white field. A "rotating cylinder" of separated gray screens is located between the inner and outer cylinders. If the gray screens are rotated, their leading and trailing edges generate an alternating sequence of running light changes in the slits of the inner cylinder. If light changes from dark to lighter are designated by a plus sign (+) and those from lighter to darker by a minus sign (—), and the slits are labeled X,Y,Z, . . . , the arrangement of Fig. 3 produces sequences + in X, — in Y, + in Z, or — in X, + in Y, — in Z, and so on. With similar arrangements, programs involving nearly any light change can be produced and used for different stimulations of single ommatidia in the beetle's eye.

If we use A, B, C, D, E, . . . to designate adjacent ommatidia in a horizontal row of the facet eye, and if again the plus sign represents an illumination change from darker to lighter, we can describe with the formula $S^{+\,+}_{A\,B}\,(t_1, t_2)$ a succession of two stimuli in adjacent ommatidia. The first stimulus is received by ommatidium A at time $t = t_1$, the second stimulus by ommatidium $B$ at $t = t_2$. The reaction of the animal to this stimulation $S^{+\,+}_{A\,B}$ is represented by $R^{+\,+}_{A\,B}$.

The results of stimulation to the ommatidia are the following:

1. The most elementary succession of light changes that is able to release an optomotor response consists of two stimuli in adjacent ommatidia.

2. In generating optomotor responses, the stimulus received by an ommatidium can interact only with the stimulus received by the immediately adjacent ommatidia or by those once removed. No physiological interaction exists between ommatidia separated by more than one unstimulated ommatidium.

3. The maximum reaction is elicited with a time interval $\triangle t = t_2 - t_1$ of about ¼ sec between the two stimuli. The strength of reaction decreases with both greater and smaller time intervals. The maximum time interval between stimuli producing small reactions was found to measure slightly more than 10 seconds. The physiological interaction takes place between the after-effect of one stimulus and the effect of a following one.

4 The combined stimulus $S^{+\,+}_{A\,B}$ leads to the reaction $+R^{+\,+}_{A\,B}$. This means that the animal follows the direction of stimulus successions.

5 Stimulus $S^{-\,-}_{A\,B}$ produces $R^{-\,-}_{A\,B}$. We have found that $+R^{-\,-}_{A\,B} = +R^{+\,+}_{A\,B}$.

6 Successions of stimuli in adjacent ommatidia produce the reaction $R^{+\,+\,+\,+\,\cdots}_{A\,B\,C\,D\,\ldots}$. This reaction turns out to be the sum of the partial reactions $R^{+\,+}_{A\,B}$, $R^{+\,+}_{B\,C}$, $R^{+\,+}_{C\,D}$, $\cdots$ and $R^{+\,+}_{A\,C}$, $R^{+\,+}_{B\,D}$, $R^{+\,+}_{C\,E}$, $\cdots$. More precisely, $R^{+\,+\,+\,+\,+\,\cdots}_{A\,B\,C\,D\,E\,\ldots} = R^{+\,+}_{A\,B} + R^{+\,+}_{B\,C} + R^{+\,+}_{C\,D} \cdots + R^{+\,+}_{A\,C} + R^{+\,+}_{B\,D} + R^{+\,+}_{C\,E} \cdots$.

7. Stimulating the facet eye with alternating light sequences as $S^{+\,-}_{A\,B}$ or $S^{-\,+}_{A\,B}$ leads to reactions *opposite* to the direction of stimulus successions. In

other words, $R^{+-}_{AB}$ is equal to $R^{-+}_{AB}$ is equal to $-R^{++}_{AB}$ is equal to $-R^{--}_{AB}$: $R^{+-}_{AB}$ and $R^{-+}_{AB}$ result in "negative" optomotor responses.

The experimental results reported in 5 and 7 show clearly that the relation between stimulus input and reaction output is in accordance with an algebraic sign multiplication.

TABLE 1.
ALGEBRAIC MULTIPLICATION

| | $S_A^+$ | $S_A^-$ |
|---|---|---|
| $S_B^+$ | $+R$ | $-R$ |
| $S_B^-$ | $-R$ | $+R$ |

8. A cylinder of gray stripes on a white background releases weaker optomotor responses than a cylinder of black stripes on a white background that rotates at the same angular speed. The intensity of optomotor reactions depends not only on the speed of moving patterns but also on the absolute amount of the individual light changes of which the stimulus situation consists. In one of the experiments the time intervals of stimulus successions were constant, and the stimulus intensities were varied by screens of different shades of gray (Fig. 4). This was done in such a manner that the sum of stimulus intensities was also kept constant. When ommatidium $A$ received the stimulus amount $x$, $B$ received the amount $-(1-x)$. The result of the experiment, as plotted in Fig. 4, showed that the reaction is a quadratic function of stimulus intensities, namely, $R$ is proportional to $-x(1-x)$.

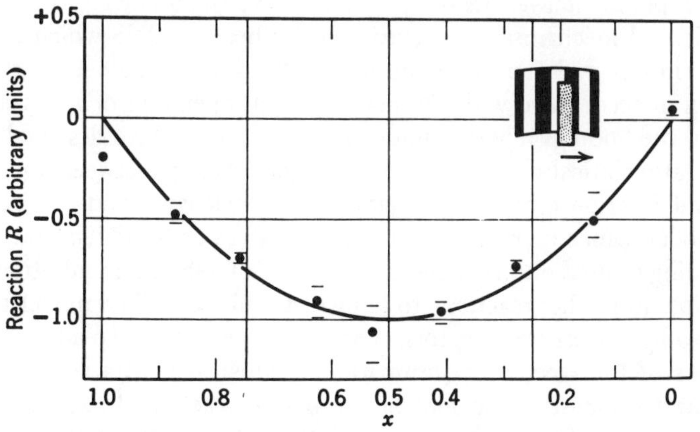


Fig. 4. The intensity of optomotor reactions to movements of different gray screens in front of black and white strips. On the ordinate, the maximum intensity is equal to −1. On the abscissa, $x$ represents differences in reflected-light intensities between moving screens and black cylinder fields; the black-white interval equals 1.

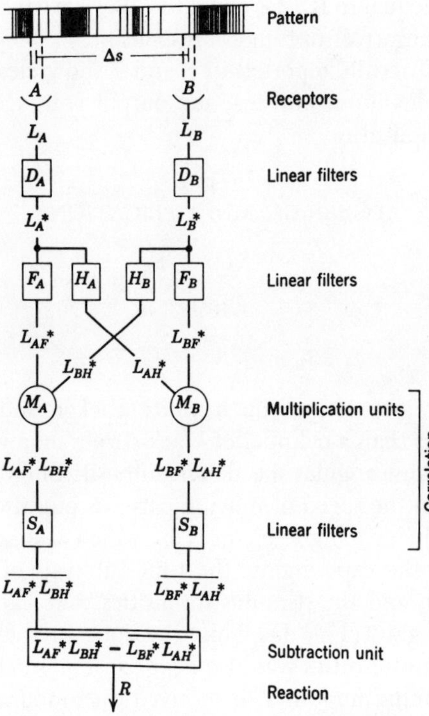


Fig. 5. Mathematical model describing stimulus-reaction relations of optomotor responses in Chlorophanus.

The experimental results of 5, 7, and 8 have the following consequence: physiological mechanisms must exist in the beetle's CNS which cause the sensory inputs and the motor output to be linked together by a process working in accordance with the mathematical operation of multiplication.

From the findings reported under 1 through 8, we have designed a minimum mathematical model that describes the relations between stimulus inputs and reaction output (Reichardt, 1957; Reichardt and Varjú, 1959). The model, which is presented in Fig. 5, enables us to understand the corresponding evaluation principle in the beetle's CNS and in addition makes it possible to predict reactions to known stimulations. The model contains only two light-sensitive receptors, *A* and *B*, representing two adjacent visual elements of the facet eyes (ommatidia). This takes in account that the optomotor response is the sum of the partial reactions to stimulations of adjacent ommatidia and those once removed. The receptors A and *B* transform the space- and time-dependent processes of the optical surroundings into the time functions $L_A$, $L_B$. When we shift the light pattern in front of the receptors from left to right (see Fig. 5), the light-intensity values of the pattern are received first by receptor A and, after a time interval $\Delta t$, by receptor $B$. If $\Delta s$ designates the angular distance between A and $B$, the time interval is connected with the velocity of the pattern by the relation $\Delta t = \Delta s/w$. The time functions $L_A$ and $L_B$ feed information channels which are linked together in the multiplier units $M_A$, $M_B$. The time functions $L_A$, $L_B$ are linearly transformed by the units $D$, $F$, and $H$. We call these units linear filters in accordance with expressions used in control engineering (see, for instance, Laning & Battin, 1956).

The multiplier and low-pass filter units $M_A$, $S_A$ and $M_B$, $S_B$ process the transformed time functions $L_{AF}^* \, L_{FH}^*$ to the time average $\overline{L_{AF}^* \, L_{BH}^*}$ and $L_{BE}^* \, L_{AH}^*$ to the average $\overline{L_{BF}^* \, L_{AH}^*}$. Since multiplication and time averaging of two time functions is called first-order correlation (see, for instance, Wiener, 1949), we speak of the correlator units. The outputs of the correlator units are subtracted from each other in the subtraction unit. The output of the last-mentioned unit controls the motor output of the animal (see Fig. 5).

The symmetry of optomotor reactions to pattern movement from left to right, and vice versa, requires symmetry of the model, which means that

$$D_A = D_B = D;$$
$$F_A = F_B = F;$$

and

$$H_A = H_B = H \tag{2}$$

We now consider, as an example, the movement of a one-dimensional light pattern in Fig. 5 from left to right. This pattern is thought to be built up of perpendicular stripes with shades whose reflection values are measured in the center of the cylinder and are called L. The value L covers a range of $0 \leqq L \leqq L_{max}$. The distribution of L values can be of very different types. In the irregular case, for instance, L is a stochastic variable. The time functions $L_A$, $L_B$ are considered to be the sum of the time average C and the fluctuating light component $G(t)$:

$$\begin{aligned} L_A &= C + G(t) \\ L_B &= C + G(t - \Delta t) \end{aligned} \tag{3}$$

In other words, G is defined in such a way that its average value is zero. The time functions $L_A$ and $L_B$ are transformed by the filters $D$, $F$, and $H$. Since the experimental results have shown that these filters are linear ones, the transformed time functions $L^*$ can be written as convolution integrals of $L$. We consider the input functions of the filters to be built up of narrow pulses. If a unit pulse ($\delta$-function) with the properties

$$\delta(t - t_0) = \begin{cases} \infty & t = t_0 \\ 0 & t \neq t_0 \end{cases} \qquad \int_{-\infty}^{+\infty} \delta(t - t_0)\, dt = 1 \tag{4}$$

stimulates a filter input, the output responds with the time function $W(t)$. ($W$ is the weighting function of the filter.) For an arbitrary input function $F(t)$, the output of the filter can be written as a convolution integral

$$F^*(t) = \int_0^{+\infty} W(\xi)F(t-\xi)\, d\xi \tag{5}$$

If we call $W_{DF}$ the weighting function of the vertical and $W_{DH}$ the weighting function of the cross channels in Fig. 5, then we obtain at the correlator inputs the time functions

$$L_{AF}^* = \int_0^{+\infty} W_{DF}(\eta)L_A(t-\eta)\, d\eta$$

and similarly

$$L_{BH}^*,\quad L_{BF}^*,\quad L_{AH}^* \tag{6}$$

After straightforward calculations the output $R$ was found to be

$$\begin{aligned} R = &\int_{\eta=0}^{+\infty} W_{DF}(\eta)\, d\eta \\ &\int_{\xi=0}^{+\infty} W_{DH}(\xi)\Phi_{GG}(\eta-\xi-\Delta t)\, d\xi \\ -&\int_{\eta=0}^{+\infty} W_{DH}(\eta)\, d\eta \\ &\int_{\xi=0}^{+\infty} W_{DF}(\xi)\Phi_{GG}(\eta-\xi-\Delta t)\, d\xi \end{aligned} \tag{7a}$$

In Eq. 7*a* $\Phi_{GG}$ designates the autocorrelation function of $G(t)$. This function is defined as follows:

$$\Phi_{GG}(\xi) = \lim_{T\to\infty} \frac{1}{2T} \int_{-T}^{+T} G(t)\, G(t-\xi)\, dt \tag{8}$$

The relation in the frequency domain equivalent to Eq. 7*a* was determined as

$$R = \tfrac{1}{2} \int_{-\infty}^{+\infty} Y_D Y_D^* [Y_F Y_H^* - Y_F^* Y_H] S(\omega)\, e^{+i\omega\Delta t}\, d\omega \tag{7b}$$

In the equation $Y_D$, $Y_F$, and $Y_H$ are the transfer functions of filters $D$, $F$, and $H$ (they are related to the weighting functions by Fourier transforms); $Y^*$ designates the conjugated complex of $Y$; $S(\omega)$ is the spectral density of $G(t)$; $S(\omega)$ and $\Phi_{GG}(\xi)$ are Fourier pairs of each other; $\omega$ is connected with the wave length $\lambda$ of a sinusoidal light pattern and its speed $w$ by the relation $\omega = (2\pi/\lambda)w$; $i$ designates the imaginary unit $\sqrt{-1}$.

Equations 7*a* and 7*b* describe the relation between stimuli and reactions as far as the model has been determined by the experiments reported here.

But there remain still to be investigated quantitatively the linear transformations of filters *D*, *F*, and *H*.

In order to analyze these transformations, we have studied experimentally the reaction *R* as a function of cylinder speed *w* to a sinusoidal light pattern with wave length $\lambda = 4.7\Delta s$ (Hassenstein, 1959). The results of this experiment are shown by the points in Fig. 6. With rising speed the intensity of optomotor reactions increases, reaches a maximum, and finally falls again to zero. In the semilogarithmic plot, the reaction curve is symmetrical with respect to its maximum. From this reaction curve we have determined the filter transformations. This analysis (Reichardt and Varjú, 1959) can be presented here in rough outline only.

The spectral density of the sinusoidal component $G(t)$ was determined as

$$S(\omega) = \sigma^2 \left[ \delta \left( \omega - \frac{2\pi}{\lambda} w \right) + \delta \left( \omega + \frac{2\pi}{\lambda} w \right) \right] \tag{9}$$

In this equation $\sigma^2$ equals $A^2/2$; A designates the amplitude of the sinusoidal component. Taking into account Eq. 9, we obtain as the result of integration in Eq. 7*b*

$$R = i|Y_D|^2 (Y_F Y_H^* - Y_F^* Y_H) \sigma^2 \tag{10}$$

where

$$\omega = \frac{2\pi}{\lambda} w = \frac{2\pi}{4\Delta s} w$$

Since the transformations in the filters *D*, *F*, and *H* have been proved to be linear and constant in time, the input-output relations of the filters can be described only by linear differential equations with constant coefficients.

In principle, these equations can be of the ordinary or partial type. The results of the analysis—on the basis of the optomotor responses indicated in Fig. 6—have shown that the transforming properties of the *F* and *H* filters can be described by first-order linear differential equations, whereas the *D* filters respond in accordance with a partial differential equation of the one-dimensional diffusion type. From these findings we derived the filter transfer functions of the model, which are in the Laplace domain.

$$Y_F = \frac{\pm b_{oF}}{a_{oF} + p} \tag{11a}$$

$$Y_H = \frac{\pm b_{oH}}{a_{oH} + p} \tag{11b}$$

$$Y_D = \pm b_{oD} \sqrt{p}\, e^{-\sqrt{b_{1D} p}} \tag{11c}$$

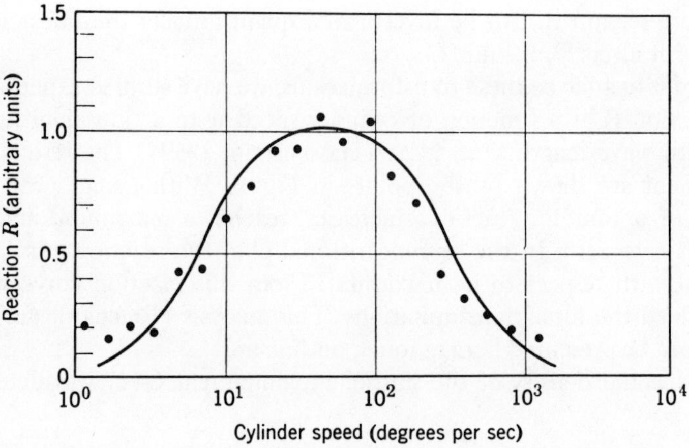


Fig. 6. The intensity of optomotor reactions as a function of cylinder speed $w$. In this experiment a sinusoidal pattern with wave length $\lambda = 4.7\Delta s$ was used. On the ordinate, the maximum intensity is equal to +1.

In Eq. 11, $p$ designates the variable of the Laplace domain. Finally, the time constants of the filter transformations have been determined from the measurements plotted in Fig. 6. They are

$$\tau_F = \frac{1}{a_{oF}} = 1.6 \text{ sec},$$

$$\tau_H = \frac{1}{a_{oH}} = 0.03 \text{ sec},$$

$$\tau_D = b_{1D} \leqq 10^{-4} \text{ sec} \qquad (12)$$

The solid curve in Fig. 6 was calculated by Reichardt and Varjú (1959) from Eqs. 10 and 11 and the time constants $\tau_F$, $\tau_H$, and $\tau_D$.

Up to this point the results of experiments reported here have been used to design a mathematical model that describes in quantitative terms the relations between stimuli and observed optomotor responses. It remains as a challenge to prove that this model (Fig. 5) enables us to predict optomotor responses of Chlorophanus to movements of any patterns mathematically analyzable.

We can proceed here in the following way. A one-dimensional cylinder pattern is selected and mathematically described; more precisely, the $G(t)$ function is determined. Introducing $G(t)$ into Eq. 7*a* or 7*b* and considering Eq. 11, we can predict the intensity of optomotor responses to different speeds of the selected pattern. The results are compared with experiments carried out with the same pattern.

This procedure can be combined with an even more rigorous test of the model. We have already shown that the optomotor responses depend on the autocorrelation or spectral density of $G(t)$ and not on $G(t)$ itself, as is expressed in Eqs. 7*a, b* which describe the relations between stimuli and responses in the time and frequency domain. The one-dimensional light patterns and, in addition, the time functions $G(t)$ can be decomposed into components of Fourier series. Each sinusoidal component is determined by its frequency, amplitude, and phase shift. Since the transformations by the filters $D$, $F$, and $H$ are linear, the Fourier components interact with each other only in the correlator units of the mathematical model. It is well known that the output of the correlator unit is not influenced by phase shifts between sinusoids at its inputs. This property of a first-order correlation process has an important consequence (Reichardt & Varjú, 1959) for optomotor responses of Chlorophanus: the class of all patterns that differ from each other only in the different phase relations of their Fourier components should produce the same optomotor responses for any pattern velocities.

In order to test this predicted property of the beetle's CNS, we have selected the two periodic cylinder patterns of Figs. 7*a* and 7*b*. The patterns consist of equally spaced black and white stripes with wave lengths $\lambda = 90$ degrees and $\lambda = 22\frac{1}{2}$ degrees. We superimposed (Varjú, 1959; Hassenstein, 1959) the two patterns in two ways. (1) Each contour edge of the

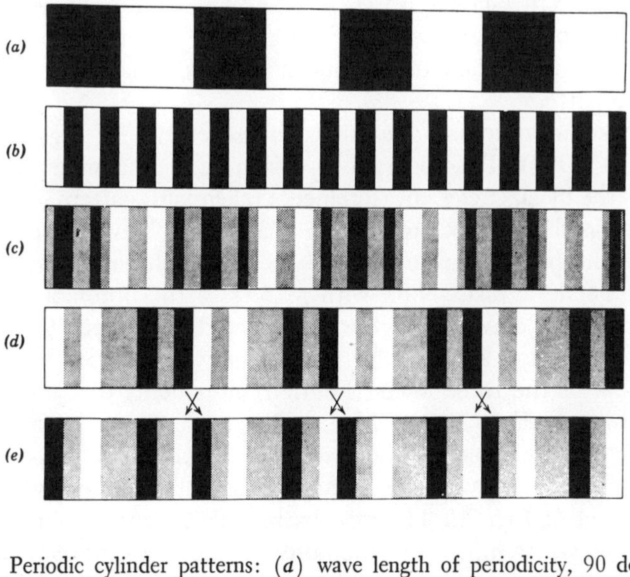


Fig. 7. Periodic cylinder patterns: (*a*) wave length of periodicity, 90 degrees; (*b*) wave length of periodicity, 22½ degrees; (*c* and *d*) constructed by superposition of patterns (*a*) and (*b*), in accordance with the mixing rules for pigment colors (black + black = black, white + white = white, black + white = gray); pattern (*e*) was derived from pattern (*d*) by the reversal of one pair of black and white stripes in each period.

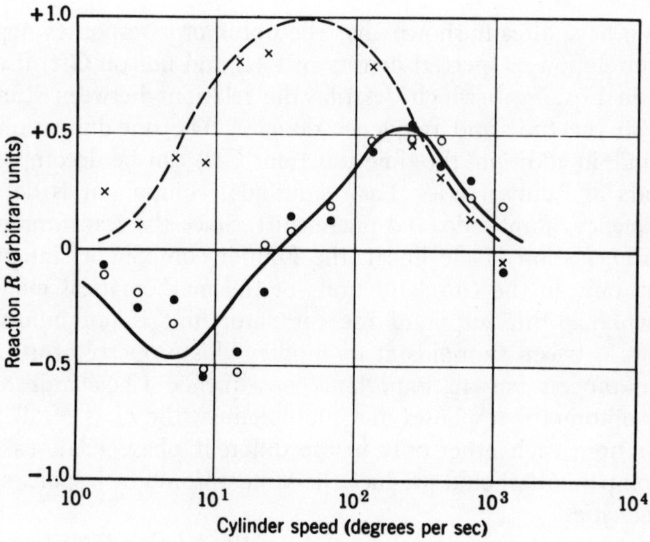


Fig. 8. The intensity of optomotor responses as a function of cylinder speed *w*. The reactions were measured with patterns in Figs. 7*c*, *d*, and *e*. The maximum intensity of the dashed curve equals +1.

90-degree pattern was placed in the middle of two contour edges of the 22½-degree pattern (shown in Fig. 7*c*). (2) The contour edges of the two patterns are superimposed without any shift (Fig. 7*d*). The patterns of Figs. 7*c* and 7*d* differ, therefore, by only a 90-degree phase shift of the short wave-length pattern.

Figure 8 shows optomotor reactions to movements of Figs. 7*c* and 7*d* (Hassenstein, 1959). The open circles designate measurements taken with pattern 7*c*, the black circles, measurements taken with pattern 7*d*. The reactions show clearly the predicted effect: phase shifts between periodic components of the pattern do not change the optomotor responses. In other words, the beetle is phase-blind with respect to the optomotor reactions. The solid response curve in Fig. 8 was calculated from Eqs. 7*b* and 11, and the time constants of Eq. 12. The calculations were carried through with consideration of the three lowest Fourier components that are contained in the patterns of Figs. 7*c* and 7*d*. In order to demonstrate that only the phase shift is responsible for the generation of the same response curves to patterns 7*c* and 7*d*, we have reversed a pair of black and white stripes in each period of Fig. 7*d*. The new pattern is presented in Fig. 7*e*. The measured (Hassenstein, 1959) optomotor responses to movements of pattern 7*e* are contained in Fig. 8 and are designated by crosses. The corresponding broken-line reaction curve was calculated (Varjú, 1959) from Eqs. 7*b*, 11, and 12, and the lowest five Fourier components of pattern 7*e*. It is obvious from the reaction curve for pattern 7*e*, that the slight altera-

(*a*)

(*b*)

Fig. 9. Cylinder patterns consisting of random light sequence. (*a*) Width of stripes, 7 degrees; (*b*) width of stripes, 1 degree.

tion in pattern 7*d* resulted in a drastic change in the reaction curve. This is because the reversal of one black and white stripe per period changes not only the phase relations in pattern 7*d* but also the amplitude distribution of the Fourier components. Since the predicted reaction curves to movements of patterns 7*c*, *d*, and *e* are in accordance with the measurements, we conclude that the mathematical model of Fig. 5 describes the perception processes in the beetle's CNS with respect to optomotor reactions.

Finally, we shall consider another property of the optomotor response predictable from the model in Fig. 5. Up to this point we have studied only responses to moving periodic patterns. These patterns are rich in redundancy, since one period of light distribution determines the whole pattern. But the natural environment of the beetle is not made up of pure periodicities; it consists of a distribution of "spots" with different degrees of reflection. These distributions demand a statistical description (Reichardt, 1957). The limiting case of such a surrounding is given if the degree of reflection of each spot is statistically independent of the degrees of reflection of all other spots. A one-dimensional pattern of this type can be built up by purely random sequences of small stripes with different degrees of reflection. Figure 9 contains samples of random patterns. The angular width of the equally spaced stripes in Fig. 9*a* was selected as 7 degrees, whereas in the pattern of Fig. 9*b* the width of the stripes amounts to 1 degree. Both are random sequences, but pattern 9*b* is a much better approximation to the case that involves "white noise," since the smaller the stripes, the closer we approach a constant spectral density.

Figure 10 contains optomotor responses measured (Hassenstein, 1959) with the patterns of Fig. 9. The black points were obtained from measurements using pattern 9*a* and the crosses from pattern 9*b*. The solid curve was calculated from Eqs. 7*b*, 11, and 12 under the assumption that the randomly constructed pattern is "white noise." This reaction curve reveals a curious property: at very low pattern velocities the optomotor response turns out to be opposite to the direction of pattern movement. This predicted effect (Reichardt & Varjú, 1959) is found experimentally with pat-

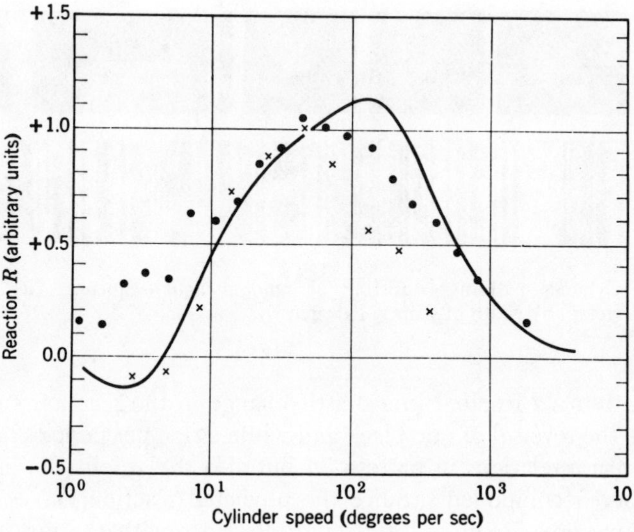


Fig. 10. The intensity of optomotor reactions as a function of cylinder speed $w$. Points, reactions to pattern in Fig. 9*a*; crosses, reactions to pattern in Fig. 9*b*. Maximum intensity of measured values equals +1.

tern 9*b* which approximates the white-noise limiting case much better than does pattern 9*a*, since the angular width of stripes is only 1 degree. With increasing velocities the experiments done with pattern 9*b* (crosses) follow the calculated reaction curve until the optomotor response reaches a maximum. For higher velocities the responses decrease more rapidly than the predicted values. This is because the random pattern was glued on a cylinder. Therefore the white-noise assumption is violated at high velocities, since the longest wave length in the pattern is 360 degrees and not infinity. We have shown that the negative part of the reaction curve at low velocities is due to the kinetics of the *D* filters (Reichardt & Varjú, 1959).

## *SUMMARY*

Like many other animals, the beetle Chlorophanus responds with optokinetic reactions to relative movement of its optical surroundings. These reactions are elicited not only from the movement of figures distinguishable against their backgrounds but also from the movement of randomly constructed patterns of shades from white through black. The most elementary succession of light changes that is able to release an optomotor response consists of two stimuli in adjacent ommatidia of the facet eye. A stimulus received by one ommatidium can interact only with a stimulus received by the adjacent ommatidia or by those once removed. The stimuli received by the ommatidia are linearly transformed, and their interaction in the central nervous system is in accordance with the principle of first-order correlation. As a consequence of this evaluation principle in Chlorophanus, the class of all optical surroundings that differ from each other by different phase relations of their Fourier components produce the same optomotor responses for any pattern velocities.

## *REFERENCES*

Hassenstein, B. Ommatidienraster und afferente Bewegungsintegration. *Zeitschrift für vergleichende Physiologie*, 1951, 33, 301-326.

Hassenstein, B. Die Stärke von optokinetischen Reaktionen auf verschiedene Mustergeschwindigkeiten. *Zeitschrift für Naturforschung*, 1958, *13b*, 1-6. (a)

Hassenstein, B. Über die Wahrnehmung der Bewegung von Figuren und unregelmässigen Helligkeitsmustern. *Zeitschrift für vergleichende Physiologie*, 1958, *40*, 556-592. (b)

Hassenstein, B. Optokinetische Wirksamkeit bewegter periodischer Muster. *Zeitschrift für Naturforschung*, 1959, *14b*, 659-674.

Hassenstein, B., & Reichardt, W. Functional structure of a mechanism of perception of optical movement. *Proceedings of first International Congress on Cybernetics, Namur*, 1956, 797-801. (a)

Hassenstein, B., & Reichardt, W. Systemtheoretische Analyse der Zeit-, Reihenfolgen- und Vorzeichenauswertung bei der Bewegungsperzeption des Russelkafers Chlorophanus. *Zeitschrift für Naturforschung*, 1956, *11b*, 513-524. (b)

Hassenstein, B., & Reichardt, W. Wie sehen Insekten Bewegungen? *Die Umschau*, 1959, *10*, 302-305.

Laning, I. H., & Battin, R. H. *Random processes in automatic control.* New York: McGraw-Hill, 1956.

Reichardt, W. Autokorrelationsauswertung als Funktionsprinzip des Zentralnervensystems. *Zeitschrift für Naturforschung*, 1957, *12b*, 447-457.

Reichardt, W., & Varjú, D. Übertragungseigenschaften im Auswertesystem für das Bewegungssehen. *Zeitschrift für Naturforschung*, 1959, *14b*, 674-689.

Varjú, D. Optomotorische Reaktionen auf die Bewegung periodischer Helligkeitsmuster. *Zeitschrift für Naturforschung*, 1959, *14b*, 724-735.

Wiener, N. *Extrapolation, interpolation, and smoothing of stationary time series*. New York: Technology Press and Wiley, 1949.

*What lessons can be learned from the papers in this part? Perhaps first and foremost, we have learned that model building can lead to new ideas about what to look for in discrimination experiments. Second, the interpretation of behavioral findings is often not too easy, in the sense that different explanations are sometimes available for the same set of facts; knowledge of anatomy and physiology of the relevant visual system may be an aid in choosing between alternative models. Third, ideas about coding alone are insufficient, at least for mammalian visual systems, to account for visual perception; some principles of perceptual learning and adaptation are required in addition. Fourth, even rather simple ideas about how patterns might be processed can lead to interesting predictions and insights into the sorts of computation that may go on in the brain (or, to avoid a mistake in overgeneralization perhaps one should say: the sorts of computation that may go on in a variety of different brain types).*

*In conclusion, I should mention again that there are other approaches to questions of pattern recognition and stimulus equivalence which attempt to define the effective cues or dimensions very precisely. Ethological work on stimulus control and the "release" of predetermined behavior patterns has already been mentioned (for a recent review of this work, see Hinde, 1966). Another relevant, although very different, approach has been taken by psychologists working with operant conditioning techniques. The reader interested in exploring this field of research might wish to look at the reviews contained in Honig (1967).*

# III

# EXPERIMENTAL EVIDENCE ON PATTERN RECOGNITION

*Most of the papers presented in this part are of rather recent date, but two classical accounts of experiments in pattern recognition in rats are presented at the start. The first of these, by K. S. Lashley, is rather long even in the reduced version given here (nearly half the material of the original has been omitted), and contains a wealth of information on several different aspects of pattern vision. There are findings on specific properties of detail vision in the rat, and also data on relational learning and perceptual organization. We tend to take it for granted that visual organization in infra-human species is similar to that found in man, but reading Lashley's arguments and experimental analyses of more than thirty years ago can serve to remind us that this is a question which we should not neglect entirely.*

*Lashley's paper is classical also in the sense that his methods and procedures for doing experiments on discrimination learning and pattern recognition have become standard in the field. Even the jumping stand, usually modified so as to make it less punishing, is still used occasionally, although newer methods employing operant conditioning techniques are tending to supplant it. (Some examples of the newer methods are given later in the section.)*

*The parts of the paper that have been cut are those which have the least to do with pattern recognition in the sense of shape recognition. Thus, the sections on brightness and size discrimination, while obviously relevant to questions of stimulus equivalence, have been excluded on these grounds. Similarly, sections on relative and absolute factors in size discrimination, peculiarities of rats' visual reactions (mostly to do with finding suitable methods of training), and on simultaneous contrast have been left out. Unfortunately it was necessary to take out some sections of closer relevance to our main themes, in the interests of reasonable conciseness. These sections are discussed in the commentary which follows the paper.*

# *The Mechanism of Vision: XV. Preliminary Studies of the Rat's Capacity for Detail Vision*

K. S. LASHLEY

## *INTRODUCTION: OBJECTIVES OF THE EXPERIMENT*

The discrimination of visual patterns and the recognition of similarities between visually presented objects may involve a wide range of functions from a direct tropistic reaction up to the recognition of intricate logical relations subsisting among the objects compared. The study of visual discrimination in animals thus offers not only an approach to problems of sensory acuity but also a method for study of the nature and limits of capacity for generalization. Current notions of the intelligence of animals are based largely upon their behavior in situations calling for motor adaptation through manipulative or orienting movements, as in experiments with puzzle boxes or mazes. The equal or greater value of studies of perceptual organization for a science of comparative psychology has been demonstrated by Klüver's investigations with monkeys (1933), but such methods have not been used extensively with lower mammals.

This study of the rat was undertaken primarily to establish norms of behavior as a basis for later experiments on visual amnesia and agnosia after cerebral lesions. Tests were therefore restricted to forms which would be practicable for use with operated animals; speed rather than great accuracy in measurement of thresholds, daylight adaptation, and the selection of stimuli giving maximal rates of learning were stressed, and these requirements limit the range of the investigation. In spite of such restrictions, the picture of visual organization is rather more complete than has been reported for any other animal below the primates and may serve both to illustrate the usefulness of the method and to suggest some of the early steps in the evolutionary development of sensory organization and of processes of abstraction.

For an understanding of integration in behavior a knowledge of the

Reprinted from *The Journal of General Psychology,* 1938.

essential nature of the stimulus is necessary. Descriptions of behavior in terms of stimulus-response relations are futile so long as the stimulus is defined only in terms of the total environmental situation, as "the maze" or "a paper triangle." Not until the adequate stimulus, the part, element, or property of the total situation which is effective in eliciting behavior, is known will it be possible to infer from stimulus-response relations anything concerning the intervening coordinative processes which constitute the real problem of psychology. Most of the experiments reported below are attempts to discover the adequate stimulus in the total complex of light rays reaching the retina. From the results it seems possible to infer certain general principles concerning the properties of the objective stimulus which are effective in behavior, although admittedly the range of experiments is too limited to prove the conclusions beyond question.

The range of tests of capacity for generalization which have been applied is too small to give any real insight concerning the ability of the animal. It is difficult to devise a graded series of tests covering a narrow range of ability, since we do not know beforehand what the successive steps in evolution of intelligence may have been and cannot say with certainty whether development has been by continuous quantitative change or by large, qualitatively different steps. The results at least emphasize the need for intensive investigation in this direction.

There are many studies of motor performance in instinctive behavior. The accuracy with which the web of the spider or nest of the bird conforms to the species-type has been stressed, but the possible implications of these facts for the perceptual organization of the animals has been neglected. Is the nest form determined by mechanical limitations of the animal's structure, as Bethe proposed in his theory of the building of the honeycomb, or by perceptual factors, by the fact that only a certain form "looks right" to the animal? There is a little evidence that complex sensory patterns are "recognized" independently of experience (Lashley and Russell, 1934; Lashley, 1915; Stone, 1922; Borovski, 1936; Hebb, 1937, a,b,c,d). It is quite possible that perceptual organization, the patterns of stimuli readily perceived, may vary widely in different species and be responsible for certain instinctive activities. The question is especially intriguing when applied to higher mammals. Much of the Gestalt theory of perception implies a belief that the things we see are determined by our innate organization rather than by experience (Gottschaldt, 1929; Koffka, 1935).[1] If such an interpretation is correct, "instinct" may be as dominant in human behavior as in the life of the bee. Thorough investigation of sensory organization in various animals is thus important as providing a possible clue to the rôle of innate differences of perception in directing or limiting behavior. A major interest of this study was therefore to discover traits of vision peculiar

[1] The results of Djang (1937) are less favorable to such a view than the earlier ones of Gottschaldt.

to the rat. Failure to discover such traits and the close correspondence of data on the rat to the facts of human perception argue somewhat against the ascription of organized motor patterns of behavior to perceptual factors.

The study has extended over a period of six years, with the accumulation of too great a number of experiments to be reported in full. I have therefore selected for description those tests which seem the most significant and, if at times the conclusions drawn go beyond the scope of the experiments, this is at least in part due to the fact that the work reported is seen against the background of a more comprehensive mass of data. The tests have been largely exploratory and restricted to a few animals in each case. They therefore lack statistical reliability, yet the behavior of the animals when discriminating is so precise that there is little room for doubt of their failure or success in any given test. I have not attempted to present detailed records of the majority of experiments, since the space requirements would be too great. The few tables included illustrate the general character of the data.

In discussing the work I have not hesitated to use anthropomorphic terminology. There is little choice between the Scylla of reflexological dogma and the Charybdis of mentalistic implication. The most significant recent studies of sensory organization have been made by members of the Gestalt school, and for the present it is more important to recognize that the same sensory problems are common to the lower animals and to man than to try to phrase these problems in a deceptively objective language. So long as we recognize that the terminology is merely one of classification of problems, the danger of reading more into the animal's behavior than the objective facts of differential reaction and transfer can be avoided.

The greater part of the work was done at the University of Chicago and was aided by a grant from the Otho S. A. Sprague Memorial Institute.

I am indebted to Dr. John D. Layman for training animals on the Thorndike figures and to Dr. Maria Zebrowska of the University of Warsaw for the data on liminal differences in discrimination of brightness.

## *EXPERIMENTAL METHODS*

In the work a modified form of the apparatus previously described (Lashley, 1930) has been used. This requires the animal to jump against stimulus cards from a distance of 20 cm. with the reward of food for a correct choice, and punishment by a fall into a net for an incorrect. The jumping platform and stimulus cards are arranged as indicated in Figure 1. Enclosing sides and a glass cover limit the animal's activities. A projecting fin between the cards forces choice of one or the other and there are no exposed edges or projections to which the rat can cling. The lower feeding

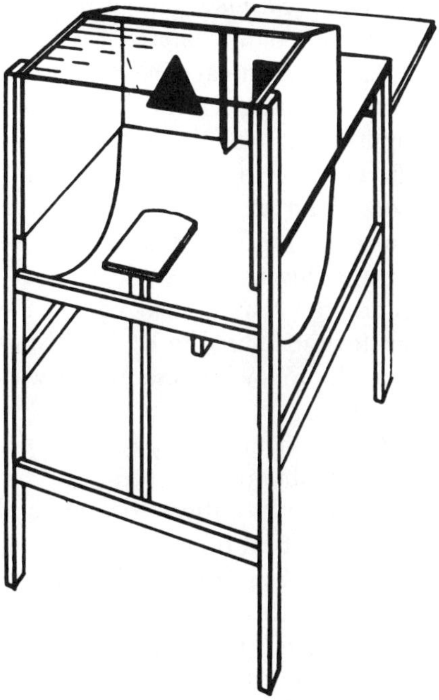

Fig. 1

platform at the rear reduces soiling of the fallen card by food. In some tests a box of similar structure presenting three stimulus cards equidistant from the jumping platform was used.

Except where indicated, the stimulus figures were cut from white paper and pasted on mat black cards. They could be readily renewed when soiled or in control tests.

The animals used were mature rats, with fully pigmented eyes, from an inbred strain derived by crossing Wistar albino stock with trapped wild. . . .

In the earlier training and testing series the cards were alternated in an irregular order corrected for position but not for alternation habits. Since 1933 the series devised by Gellermann (1933) has been used. This gives chance scores for alternation, double alternation, and position habits. Except where contraindicated by the purpose of the experiment, all animals were first trained to jump to the open doors of the apparatus, then to a 10 cm. white square vs. a black card, then to horizontal vs. vertical striations of 20 mm. width, followed by acuity tests, before specific training on the problem for which they were used.

In the figures the stimulus cards are reproduced on a scale of 1/12th. In the apparatus they were, of course, completely surrounded by a black ground formed by the cloth net, sides and top of the box.

*The Method of Equivalent Stimuli.* The principal method used in the experiments is a combination of the preference tests of earlier students with preliminary training. The animal is first trained to choose one of a pair of stimulus patterns (training figures) and to avoid the other, with reward (food) and punishment (fall) as incentives. He is then suddenly confronted with a different pair of patterns and is allowed a free choice between them, receiving food at every trial, regardless of the pattern chosen. These preference tests, without punishment, will be referred to as "critical trials," following Klüver's terminology. A significant preference for one of the new figures after training may be taken as evidence that it is in some way equivalent for the animal to the positive training figure.

As a formal procedure the following tests were carried out in all critical trials.

1. Practice on the training figures with 10 trials per day until 20 consecutive errorless trials were obtained.
2. On subsequent test days 10 critical trials with the training figures, followed immediately by 10 critical trials with the new pair of figures.
3. Twenty-four hours rest. Ten critical trials with the training figures followed by 10 critical trials with the new figures.
4. In case of failure of transfer, 10 critical trials with the training figures immediately following the failure.

This sequence gives for comparison 20 trials with the training figures and 20 critical trials with the new figures. In case of failure of transfer the 10 critical trials with the training figures control any loss of the original habit. Twenty trials are usually adequate to give clear evidence of transfer or lack of transfer of training. The majority of animals in critical trials either choose one of the pair of figures in more than 80 per cent of the trials or assume a position habit and make chance scores. I have generally varied both the positive and negative figures. Pache (1932) substituted parts of the positive figure for the negative until the reaction broke down. His method is superior in some respects for discovering the properties of the positive stimulus which determine reaction.

Certain difficulties of the method are unavoidable. The new figures, even when identified with the familiar ones, introduce a disturbing element. The animal hesitates for long periods, turning back and forth from one card to the other. Errors are most often made in the first trials, as if the animal were trying out both figures before settling down to a consistent selection of one. In a long series of tests for equivalence of a variety of patterns, especially after some failures of transfer, the animal apparently learns that no choice is necessary when new figures are presented and promptly adopts a position habit whenever figures other than the training series are introduced, even with figures which in earlier tests gave perfect transfer. Thus after a time the animals seem to become sophisticated in the tests and give less consistent results than others which have had less experience with the visual stimuli.

The effects of previous training may also persist over long periods and distort the results of later tests. I have not carried out systematic studies of retention, but three experiments illustrate the effects of previous training.

1. Two animals were trained on horizontal (positive) vs. vertical striations and on an upright (positive) vs. an inverted equilateral triangle. They were left for six months without training and when tested again made no errors in selection of the horizontal striations and erect triangle. Fields (1935, 1936) has reported similarly good retention over periods up to seven months.

2. In training tests with ink blots two animals showed from the first an absolute preference certainly referable to previous training on triangle vs. circle, although for the experimenter the blots had no resemblance to these figures.

3. In the tests reported on page 160 the earlier training on striations dominated the effects of later training on geometrical figures.

4. There are also transfer effects of training when no equivalence of the stimuli is involved. The data of Lashley and Frank (1934) show that previous training on horizontal and vertical striations reduced the learning scores on erect and inverted triangles by 50 per cent.

Such observations made it advisable to discard each group of animals after the completion of a series of tests and to train a new group for each new problem, rather than risk unpredictable effects of earlier training. Except where indicated, therefore, each test series involves animals not recorded elsewhere.

Fields (1932) has claimed that with the jumping apparatus the animal is chiefly influenced by the positive stimulus; ". . . the avoiding reaction to the negative figure which was found with the running apparatus is almost totally lacking when the jumping apparatus is used." The tests upon which this conclusion is based consisted of opposing the positive and the negative stimulus cards singly with a black card. Reaction to the positive card persisted, whereas chance scores were obtained with black vs. the negative figure. Fields' animals, however, had previously been trained to avoid a black card and even though as many as a thousand trials of training with pairs of figures had intervened before the tests with negative figure vs. black card, our data on retention indicate that this previous training would carry over. That the negative stimulus is effective is shown by critical trials in which the combination of a negative stimulus with a positive disrupts the reaction (pp. 160 ff.).

The use of pairs of figures, positive and negative, makes it somewhat more difficult to interpret some of the experiments on equivalence of stimuli than if the reaction were to a single figure, but this latter condition is really impossible of attainment and the differences between the positive and negative stimuli serve to define the basis of reaction far better than the properties of the positive stimulus alone.

*Tests for Relative "Identifiability" of Figures.* Discrimination problems vary in difficulty and this variation throws some light on the interrelations of discrimination, retentiveness, and recognition in the performance of the differential reaction. To measure the relative difficulty of discrimination problems a routine training technique was followed. The animals were trained to jump to the food platform with both doors open. They were next trained, with 10 trials per day, to jump to a white card and avoid a black. Pairs of stimulus cards to be tested were then presented and training continued with 10 trials per day until the animal made 10 consecutive correct choices on each of two consecutive days. These 20 consecutive errorless trials were accepted as a criterion of learning. Scores are recorded as the total number of trials and of errors preceding the 20 errorless.[2]

For the most part the scores are based on the records of separate groups of animals, but when it was desired to compare the difficulty of two pairs of figures the animals were sometimes divided into two equal groups which were then trained in inverse order on the two pairs of figures, and the average scores of the two groups were taken as a measure of comparative difficulty. This is the usual procedure to control effects of transfer of training. It assumes that such transfer occurs equally in either direction. Actually this turns out to be incorrect in some cases, e.g., if animals are trained to choose the largest of three white figures, they will immediately choose the brightest of three gray figures of equal size but, if trained first on brightness, they do not transfer to size. Thus results with this method may be less reliable than with separate groups. In any case the reliability of these comparative tests is low.

*The Influence of the Experimenter.* The use of controls for cues from the experimenter, as for secondary cues from the apparatus, has become a routine procedure. They have been introduced systematically in these experiments and for the sake of brevity will not be reported in detail. Animals do learn to react to the way in which they are placed on the platform, they may be guided by the position of the experimenter behind the apparatus, by noises in shifting the cards, and the like, but these cues are readily eliminated and in no case reported has a consistent reaction been disrupted by any control except a change in the visual properties of the stimulus cards.

[2] By a trial is meant the behavior from the time the animal is placed on the platform until he jumps to the positive stimulus and receives food. By an error, such a trial in which the animal jumped one or more times to the negative card before choosing the positive. The method seems the best one to express the behavior in relation to chance performance. When the animal is first placed on the platform the chances of his jumping to one or other card, which may or may not have been shifted after the last trial, are equal. Five errors in 10 trials therefore represents chance performance. If the cards may be shifted after every jump, whether right or wrong, the animal is not permitted to correct his own errors and a different learning situation is introduced. If all wrong jumps are reported as errors, correct jumps must also be reported to give a means of estimating superiority of the score over chance. We do not know the relative influence of success and error in learning, so any method of counting scores is largely arbitrary.

A more subtle influence of the experimenter arises from the fact that the work must be planned from the human point of view. If the general characteristics of visual organization are the same in animals as in man, then experimental tests derived from an analysis of human vision may give a fairly complete picture of the animal's capacity. But if the animal's vision is organized upon an unknown, different principle, the discovery of this organization will be largely a matter of chance, since experiments cannot be devised beforehand to reveal it. Lashley (1916) has reported a little evidence that the unity of spectral colors is not the same for the fowl as for man and Hertz (1929, 1935) has reported that coherence of visual patterns is different for the facet eye of the bee and for the human eye. Except for these two studies, experimenters have usually made the assumption that the principles of integration are the same throughout the phylogenetic series, and have sought for the presence or absence of human capacities rather than for different modes of organization.

In all of the work especial attention has been paid to aberrant behavior in the hope of picking up clues to unique visual traits. Certain peculiarities of behavior, the dominance of remote stimuli in orientation, the ineffectiveness of small figures well above the visual threshold, and an apparent ready suppression of vision seem to distinguish the rat from man. These and certain other peculiarities of the rat's behavior in the experimental situation will be discussed in a later section.

*Individual Variation.* In tests of elementary sensory functions, thresholds, difference limens, etc., consistent results are obtained from the majority of animals, but whenever the experiments require the discrimination of stimuli which differ in several attributes, marked individual differences in the behavior of the animals appear. I have carried out a large number of experiments attempting to discover what elements in a given pair of figures determined the discrimination. Thus, after training with white triangles on a black ground (Figure 2) all animals transfer in critical trials to outlines (Figure 3), the majority to two sides (Figure 4), a few to the bases (Figure 5), about one in ten to the lower angles (Figure 6), and one animal only was disturbed by changing the position of the center of

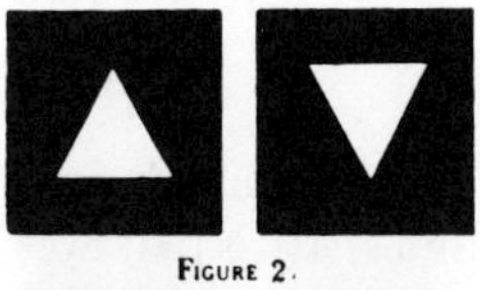

FIGURE 2.

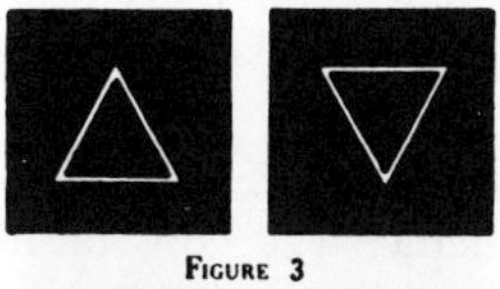

FIGURE 3

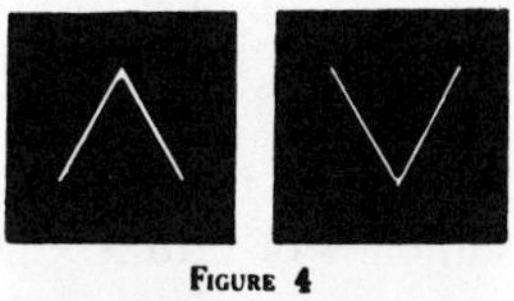

FIGURE 4

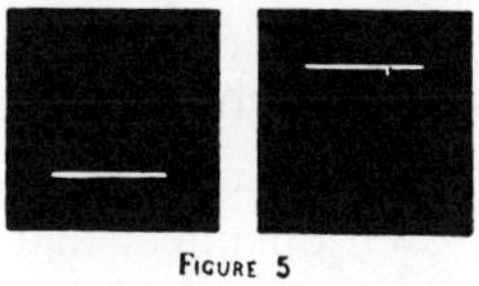

FIGURE 5

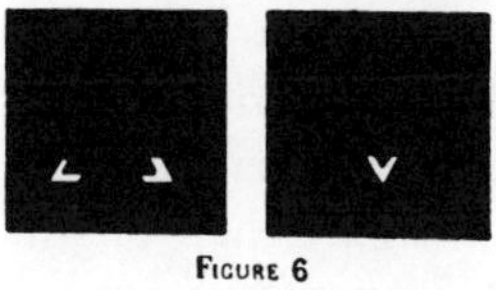

FIGURE 6

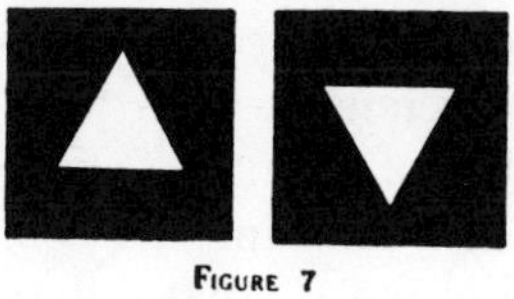

FIGURE 7

FIGURE 8

FIGURE 9

FIGURE 10

area of the figures (Figure 7). Munn (1930b) has reported other tests of the adequate stimulus from these figures.

Occasionally animals have reacted to the distance of the lower corner of the figure from the inner edge of the card; to the slope of the inner line; or to discolorations on old cards. A few animals have transferred without error from horizontal striations (Figure 8) to the horizontal base of the erect triangle.

The results are much like those of a human experiment in testimony; for each subject particular aspects of the situation are conspicuous and the reports of no two may stress the same details. Such individual differences, due to chance in what is noted, are to be expected with complex situations. They lead to apparently contradictory results with different animals, so that norms cannot be established. Nevertheless, the contradictions do not invalidate clear cut results with individuals, although they decrease the reliability of any negative findings.

## *LIMITING CONDITIONS FOR DISCRIMINATION*

As a preliminary to study of organization within the visual field, data concerning acuity and differential thresholds must be available, so that we may be sure that the test conditions involve differences which are supraliminal for the animal. No attempt has been made in this study to determine the optimal conditions of adaptation and illumination for vision. Interest was directed rather to the limits of discrimination set by differential thresholds under conditions practicable for tests of the animal's ability to deal with complex visual situations. The tests were therefore made wth light adapted animals under diffuse daylight illumination, with light reflected from mat surfaces.

Since in tests of detail vision it was desirable to train the animals to a standard of errorless performance (20 consecutive errorless trials), it was necessary to determine what differences could be discriminated with this degree of accuracy. The threshold was therefore arbitrarily defined as that difference which the animal could distinguish without error in 20 consecutive trials after not more than 150 trials of training at the given interval. The constants are somewhat higher than might have been obtained, had the more usual criterion of 75 per cent correct after unlimited training been adopted. The difference is probably not great, however, if the indications from studies of acuity can be taken as representative. Extensive tests have been made with striated fields and neither long training nor a criterion of 70 per cent reduces the threshold significantly. It seems likely that the jumping technique forces a maximum of attention, so that the relatively large steps in the series of threshold tests do not reveal the limited range of uncertainty.

*Visual Acuity.* In an earlier study (Lashley, 1930) tests of visual acuity on three albino and five pigmented rats were reported. These placed the acuity of pigmented animals under daylight illumination with black and white striations at between 26 and 52 minutes of arc, and that of albinos between one and two degrees. Similar tests with striations have been carried out with 10 additional pigmented animals. Threshold tests were made with the animal at such a distance that he could bring his eyes not closer than 15 cm. to the stimulus cards. The test objects were cards ruled with alternate black and white lines of equal width. The animals were trained to jump to horizontal and avoid vertical stripes. In training, stripes 2 cm. in width were used (Figure 8). Successive tests were made with 5, 2, 1.5, 1, 0.8, 0.6, and 0.3 mm. lines, with training until the animal failed to make better than chance score in 100 trials. Five animals discriminated 1.5 mm. lines and failed with 1 mm.; three failed at 0.8 mm.; two discriminated at 0.3 mm. striations.

We have found it difficult to rule large areas with fine lines uniformly enough to avoid secondary lines through fusion at threshold limits. This effect was controlled by reducing the size of the stimulus cards from 15 x 25 cm. to 5 x 5 cm. The two animals which had discriminated 0.3 mm. striations failed under these conditions to discriminate lines narrower than 1.5 mm. They had evidently been reacting to some irregularities in the ruling. Reduction in the size of the targets also disturbed other animals which had been discriminating below 1 mm.

The figures confirm the results of the previous study. The threshold for the majority of animals lies between 24 and 35 minutes of arc and it is probable that all records better than this are due to irregularities in ruling the cards.

Ten albinos were tested under similar conditions. The majority discriminated 3.5 mm. lines. None discriminated 3 mm. lines. This again confirms the earlier result, with the threshold located between 1 degree, 10 minutes and 1 degree, 20 minutes.

Tests have also been made with pigmented animals for perceptible distance of separation of solid areas such as those shown in Figures 9 and 10. A horizontally as well as vertically divided square was used, and a single broken circle versus a continuous one. With these figures no animal discriminated when the separation was less than 5 mm. and the majority failed below 5.5 mm. This gives a threshold of approximately two degrees for resolution of large white objects on a black ground under average conditions of daylight illumination.

The majority of rat eyes show marked astigmatism (Lashley, 1932). In human vision astigmatism seems to exaggerate the apparent difference in the striations of Figure 8 and to obscure the differences of Figures 9 and 10, unless the black spaces coincide with the axis of sharpest focus. The marked difference in thresholds with the two sets of test objects may thus be due to defects of refraction.

*Discrimination of the Direction of Striae.* Five animals were trained to discriminate horizontal and vertical striated fields with alternate black and white stripes 1 cm. in width, forming a circular field. They were then tested with horizontal versus sloping striations of the same width at angles of 45°, 22°, 12°, and 6° from the horizontal. All animals transferred without error to the 22° slope, one to the 12° slope. When failure of transfer occurred the animals were trained until they discriminated or until they showed no improvement in 150 trials. One failed to discriminate the 12° slope, 4 reached the criterion of 20 errorless trials with this angle. All failed to discriminate at 6°. The figures discriminated at 12°, by 4 of the 5, are shown in Figure 11.

FIGURE 11

FIGURE 12

FIGURE 13

Fields (1935) estimates the threshold for discrimination of an equilateral triangle with horizontal base from one slightly rotated as between 10° and 5°, which corresponds closely to that found for striations. Johnson (1916) reported a threshold between 2° and 5° for a cebus monkey and between 25° and 40° for a fowl, under somewhat different conditions of training. . . .

*The Discrimination of Visual Distance.* The experiments of Russell (1932), Lashley and Russell (1934), and Lashley (1937) have agreed in placing the rat's threshold for depth discrimination over a range of from 20 to 50 cm. at somewhere near 2 cm. This is almost as good as human achievement under comparable conditions, where the subject is required to take an initial set for visual distance, then to touch the stimulus object with eyes closed, eliminating current control by vision. No new data on depth discrimination are presented in this study, since the discrimination apparatus uses a constant distance, but the data should be kept in mind in later discussion as evidence of the high development of the rat's vision for spacial orientation.

## ORGANIZATION OF THE VISUAL FIELD

### Figure-Ground Relations

Many of the studies of vision in animals have been dominated by the concepts of "pattern," "shape," and "form" which were formulated by Hunter (1913) and Bingham (1914) in the early days of the discrimination experiment. Hunter suggested that the most primitive level of visual perception might involve no differentiation of figure from background but merely the differentiation of one total visual field from another. Thus in the discrimination box the animal might learn to react differently to such fields as are shown in Figures 12 and 13, not by distinguishing the triangles as objects, but because the total field of Figure 12 differs from that of Figure 13. To this hypothetical form of organization Hunter applied the term "pattern vision."

Bingham differentiated between "shape" and "form." He defined shape as the specific distribution of light in the visual field. Thus an equilateral triangle with the base horizontal presents a different distribution of light from one with the base inclined. This constitutes a difference in shape. The recognition of the triangle in any orientation constitutes a recognition of its "form" and involves a further step in generalization beyond that required for differential reaction to shape.

These concepts had only a speculative basis and represent only a few of many possible steps in the evolution of visual organization. Moreover, there is no evidence that pattern or shape, as defined, are ever the basis of reaction. In the most primitive eyes capable of giving a differential distribution of light on the visual elements, the rhabdomes are divided into two groups whose stimulation determines antagonistic reflexes (Taliaferro, 1920; Mast, 1924). Thus the most primitive organization appears to be one in which stimulation of a specific part of the retinal surface initiates a specific reaction; a condition just the reverse of that postulated for pattern vision. In the progressive levels of disintegration of vision described by Poppelreuter (1923) the ability to identify position within the visual field appears as the lowest stage of detail vision. This condition involves differential reaction to different parts of the visual field rather than a reaction to different total fields. Thus neither phylogenetic studies nor evidence from pathology reveals pattern vision as a primitive function.

The logical distinction of form as corresponding to an indefinite series of shapes is no assurance that shape is the more primitive type of organization. If the mechanism of reaction were one of point-to-point correspondence of reflex paths, then shape should be the more primitive. But if seeing the outline of a figure involves some such processes of organization

Figure 14

Figure 15

as those postulated by Rachevsky (1935), then form should be more primitive than shape. Actually, as will appear in the following sections, the ability to recognize a figure in any orientation is only one of a variety of abstractions concerning figures of which the animal is capable and which require an accurate appreciation of the outlines of the figure. Failure to identify a rotated figure does not mean that the animal is reacting to the absolute distribution of light on the retina, for the animal which fails this problem may give evidence of reaction to other relational properties of the figure.

*Figure vs. Total Situation.* Most of the experiments reported in the following sections of this paper give evidence that the rat responds immediately to organized visual objects as such and, without special training, disregards the characteristics of the background. They show also that the adequate stimulus is almost always some relational property of the figure such as direction, size, or relative proportion of parts and that some elementary generalization is involved in all visual discrimination. The following two experiments show the figural properties of the adequate stimulus and its independence of the concrete pattern of the total situation.

TABLE 1
SCORES IN CRITICAL TRIALS WITH FIGURES 16 TO 27 FOR TWO ANIMALS

| *Figure No.* | *Description* | *Animal* A | *Animal* B |
|---|---|---|---|
| 16 | Outlines | 17 | 20 |
| 17 | Gray ground | 20 | 20 |
| 18 | Black on white | *13* | *12* |
| 19 | Small figures | 18 | 20 |
| 20 | Patterned ground, figures centered | 18 | 18 |
| 21 | Patterned ground, figures excentric | 16 | 16 |
| 22 | On 2 cm. striae | *8* | *12* |
| 23 | Encircled figures | 17 | 20 |
| 24 | Reduplicated figures | 18 | 20 |
| 25 | Reduplicated lines | *16* | *10* |
| 26 | Figures rotated 90 degrees | *10* | *8* |
| 27 | Simple, reduplicated | 19 | 18 |

The columns at the right give the number of times that the triangle was chosen in 20 critical trials. Chance scores are italicized.

1. Four animals were trained with cross and triangle (positive) vs. circle and triangle (Figure 14). Learning was slow, requiring an average of 140 trials with 49 errors. Critical trials were given with the cross and circle alone, centered on the cards. The animals selected the cross 16, 17, 19, and 10 times respectively in 20 trials. With the one animal which made a chance score in the critical trials, the figures were changed to the position off-center which they had occupied when combined with the triangles. In critical trials with this change he selected the cross in 19 of 20 trials. Without further training he then made a perfect score with the figures centered on the cards.

Other experiments have shown that the triangle is one of the most readily identifiable of figures for the rat. Nevertheless in this experiment the triangle was entirely disregarded and the animals came to react only to those elements with respect to which the cards differed.

2. Two animals were trained with triangle (positive) and cross (Figure

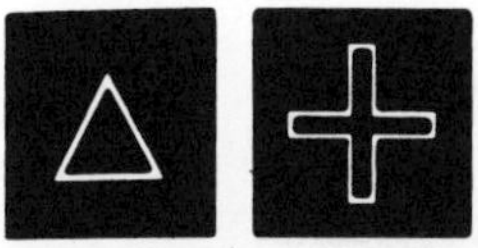
Figure 16

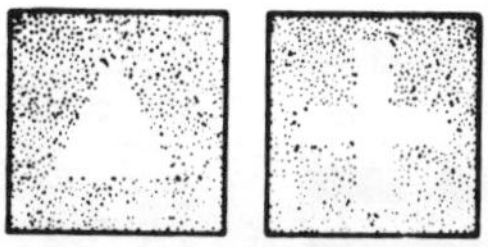
Figure 17

Figure 18

Figure 19

Figure 20

Figure 21

Figure 22

Figure 23

Figure 24

Figure 25

Figure 26

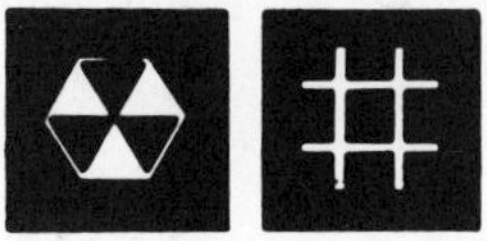
Figure 27

15). They were then given critical trials with the patterns shown in Figures 16 to 27. Their scores in these trials are given in Table 1. Twenty trials with the training figures, with an average above 95 per cent correct, intervened between each test with new figures and the next. Failure of transfer occurred with the reversal of brightness (Figure 18), with coarsely striated ground (Figure 22), with reduplicated lines (Figure 25) and with rotated figures (Figure 26). Successful transfer to the other figures shows that the animal reacts to a limited part of the total visual field and is relatively indifferent to the surrounding ground (Figures 20, 21, and 23), that the exact retinal distribution of light is unimportant (Figures 16, 19, and 24), and that some property of the figure can be identified when the figure is masked in a different total pattern (Figures 23, 24, and 27). . . .

*The Relation of Figure to Surrounding Patterns.* Once a reaction is established to a definite figure, indifferent patterns in the ground do not disturb the reaction.

1. The animals were trained to choose an erect and avoid an inverted triangle. The triangles were then mounted on cards ruled with 5 mm. striations (Figure 30) and presented in critical trials. All animals chose

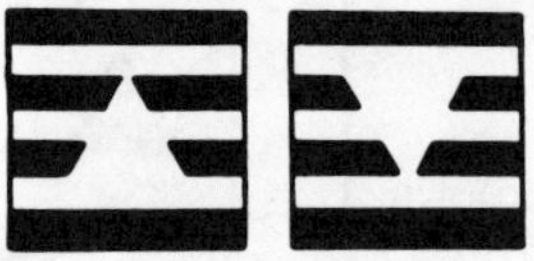

FIGURE 29

FIGURE 30

the erect triangle. Unfamiliar figures and changes in the shade of the ground delay but do not disturb the accuracy of reaction, as is shown by the transfer of reaction to Figures 17, 20, and 21, summarized in Table 1.

2. When markings on the ground distort the outlines of the figure beyond undefined limits, reaction is abolished. With the two animals trained on erect and inverted triangles, which had been undisturbed by the 5 mm. striated ground, two cards having the ground ruled with 20 mm. striations (Figure 29) were presented in critical trials. Both animals made chance scores. The same result was obtained with the triangle and cross of Figure 22.

FIGURE 31

FIGURE 32

If the ground contains a pattern which has previously served as a basis for reaction this pattern may dominate the figure, or the combination may interfere with reaction to either, as shown in the following tests.

3. Four animals were trained to choose horizontal and avoid vertical striations of 10 mm. width. They were then trained to choose a cross and avoid a circle. These test objects were then combined so that the cross and circle appeared on striated fields. With the cross on the vertical striations (Figure 31), the positive figure on the negative ground, the scores of the four animals in 20 critical trials were:

| | No. 1 | No. 2 | No. 3 | No. 4 |
|---|---|---|---|---|
| Cross (vertical striae) | 10 | 7 | 10 | 10 |
| Circle (horizontal striae) | 10 | 13 | 10 | 10 |

The cross was next placed on the horizontally striated field (Figure 32). The scores under these conditions were:

| | No. 1 | No. 2 | No. 3 | No. 4 |
|---|---|---|---|---|
| Cross (horizontal striae) | 10 | 18 | 16 | 16 |
| Circle (vertical striae) | 10 | 2 | 4 | 4 |

Without retraining the animals were given critical trials with the original cross and circle and with the striations alone. All made 90 per cent or better in the selection of the originally positive figures. This experiment shows an interference between figure and surroundings when both have acquired significance for reaction in previous training. This result is confirmed by the experiments on the relations of internal and external position of the figure, reported below. . . .

*The Influence of Continuity of Figure.* The importance of continuity of contour or surface in determining figure has been frequently stressed. The following tests show that for the rat as for man continuity of surface or closed contour contributes to identification of figures, though it is not a prime essential.

1. Six animals were trained on horizontal striations (positive) vs. vertical striations, 2 cm. in width (Figure 8). They were then given critical trials with single lines, either continuous (Figure 33) or interrupted by 2 cm. gaps (Figure 34). The three animals tested with the continuous lines chose the horizontal 20, 18, and 20 times respectively in 20 trials. The other three, tested with the interrupted lines, chose the horizontal 19, 18, and 17 times respectively. Interruption of the line interfered slightly, but not significantly with the transfer.

2. Four animals trained on horizontal (positive) and vertical striations, 2 cm. in width, were all given critical trials with the variously interrupted lines shown in Figures 35, 36, 37, and 38. All chose the two horizontal lines

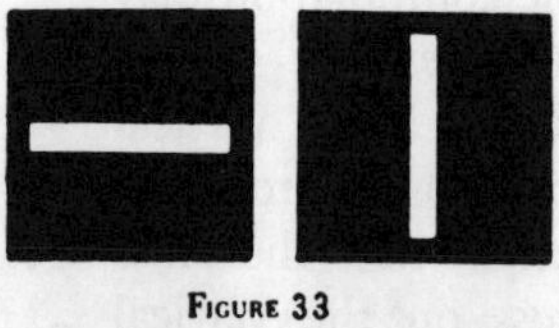

Figure 33

Figure 34

Figure 35

Figure 36

Figure 37

Figure 38

of Figure 35. One animal chose the narrow horizontal stripes (right side of Figure 36) in 18 of 20 trials. All did better than chance with Figure 37. Only chance scores were made in all other tests with Figures 36, and 38.

3. The four animals used in the foregoing test were next given critical trials with the zigzag lines shown in Figure 39. All made chance scores.

Figure 39

The same result was obtained in other tests with narrower lines and with wavy lines, whenever the deviations from a straight line exceeded the width of the striations.

In these tests with striations, direction of the lines is the determining factor. The width of the lines may be reduced to nearly threshold value or their contrast reduced by half without affecting the accuracy of response. The interrupted figures are equivalent to the striations, so long as they show a dominant direction of masses. Continuity of line, on the other hand, is not alone sufficient to determine direction.

4. Two animals were trained on cross (positive) vs. circle (Figure 40).

Figure 40

Figure 41

Figure 42

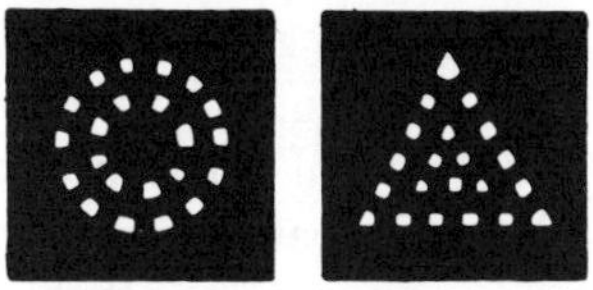

FIGURE 43

FIGURE 44

They were then given critical trials with the interrupted cross and circle of Figure 41. Both made chance scores. The interrupted circle was then rotated 45 degrees (Figure 42) and 20 critical trials given. One animal made a chance score, the other chose the interrupted circle, now a Maltese cross, 20 times.

5. In various experiments animals have been trained with continuous contours such as those shown in Figure 3 and comparison groups with similar figures in which the outlines were interrupted by 1 cm. gaps. In brief, no consistent difference in rate of learning under these conditions has been found. There is no consistent difference between learning of solid figures and outlines in the tests made.

6. Four animals were trained on the interrupted circle (positive) and triangle of Figure 43, four others with the irregular dots of Figure 44, and four with solid white circle and triangle as controls. There was no significant difference in the learning of the solid and interrupted regular figures. No animal made better than chance scores with the irregular dots of figure 44 in 150 trials.

7. Two animals were trained with the pairs of dots of Figure 45. Both then chose the sloping line of Figure 46 in 18 of 20 critical trials. Direction, rather than pattern, was the determining factor.

8. Two animals were given initial training on solid erect triangle (positive) vs. inverted (Figure 2) and two others on outlines (Figure 3). They were then given critical trials with the other pair of figures. From outlines to solid figures both animals made no errors. From solid figures to outlines one animal made 4, the other 3 errors in 20 trials. Transfer from outlines to solid figures thus seemed somewhat more certain than the reverse.

The data here are not sufficient to define the conditions under which separate elements are combined into a figure equivalent to a continuous one. Closeness of approximation of the dots is apparently a factor. With

FIGURE 45

FIGURE 46

geometrically simple figures continuity of outline is apparently not of great importance for recognition. With the striations the animals seem to react to direction, disregarding other attributes of the figures. As will appear in many of the experiments described later, most visual reactions seem to be determined by some such abstraction. Where a pattern of discrete elements might be learned as a pattern, some more general attribute of the figure is likely to form the basis of the reaction, as in Experiment 7 above. Certain types of organization, such as direction and perhaps some simple forms, seem most readily achieved and identifiability of figure depends more upon the closeness with which arrangement of elements conforms to these abstract forms than upon the number of elements which are combined.

*Relation of Internal and External Figures.* Fields (1932, 1935) has reported for the rat that the external of two superimposed figures dominates reaction. Koffka (1935, p. 199) is uncertain about the matter for man. The following experiments show that other factors are more important than internal or external position and that the latter may not be a determining factor of itself.

1. Four animals were trained successively on horizontal (positive) vs. vertical striae (Figure 8), on solid triangle (positive) vs. square (Figure 47), on outline triangle (positive) vs. outline square (Figure 48), and on cross (positive) vs. outline circle (Figure 49). They were then given critical trials with a combination of triangle with circle vs. cross with square,

FIGURE 47

FIGURE 48

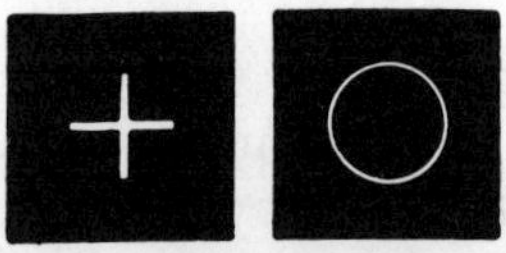

FIGURE 49

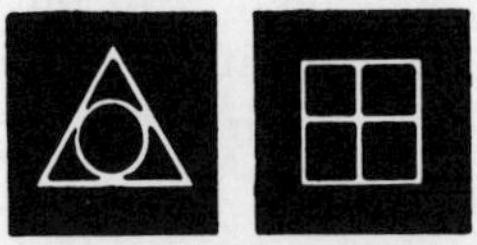

FIGURE 50

FIGURE 51

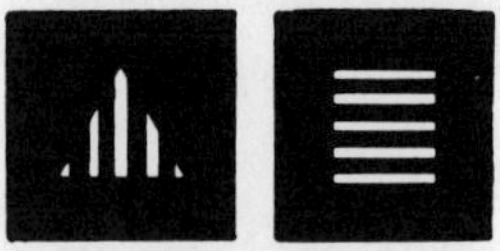

FIGURE 52

FIGURE 53

FIGURE 54

FIGURE 55

arranged so that one positive figure was external, the other internal to a negative figure (Figure 50). The enclosing triangle was chosen 20, 16, 16, and 14 times in 20 trials by the four animals. Definitely, the outer figure dominated.

The white circular outline was next blocked in solid (Figure 51) and critical trials again given. The triangle-enclosing-circle was now chosen 8, 10, 20, and 9 times in 20 trials by the four animals. For three of the four the more conspicuous solid circle, though not previously seen, interfered with the positive reaction to the outer figure.

2. The animals were retrained to 20 errorless trials with the solid triangle and square (Figure 47). They were next given critical trials with these figures combined with internal striations. They had been trained positive to horizontal striations at the beginning of the experiment, but had not seen the striated cards for 90 days or more.

With the triangle (positive) striated vertically (negative) and the square horizontally (Figure 52) the triangle was chosen 0, 0, 2, and 8 times in 20 trials by the four animals respectively. The striations, dominated over the external form of the figure. With the positive striations combined with the positive triangle (Figure 53) all animals chose the triangle without error.

3. Solid white triangle and square were next presented on striated grounds, combining positive figure with negative ground (Figure 54), and positive figure with positive ground (Figure 55). With Figure 54 (positive figure on negative ground) the animals chose the triangle 10, 10, 10, and 7 times respectively in 20 trials. With Figure 55 (positive on positive) the triangle was selected 10, 18, 12, and 16 times. Immediately after these tests the animals made errorless scores with striated fields and with triangle and square on black ground. The combined patterns therefore interfered, even when positive was combined with positive. The external figure interfered with but did not dominate the reaction.

When either the figure or the ground was striated, the striations tended to determine the reaction. With the outlines of Experiment 1, the outer figure dominated until a more conspicuous inner figure was introduced, whereupon the dominance of outer figure was abolished. In the transfer experiment with Figure 23 a white circle around each familiar figure did not disturb reaction.

In the experiment on simultaneous contrast the reaction of the animals was in direct opposition to what it would have been had they transferred their reaction to brightness to the outer figure. Clearly the dominance of inner or outer position of a figure in a complex is secondary to other factors which cannot at present be defined. . . .

*Definition of "Figure" in Comparative Psychology.* Are we justified in attempting to extend the conception of figure-ground relations developed from studies of human perception to interpretation of animal behavior? Figure is generally described as something perceived as coherent and unitary in contrast to ground, which is somewhat lacking in this property. We cannot, of course, apply such a subjective definition in comparative studies but, if we seek a definition of unity in perception, we may reach an objective expression. Unity is the exhibition of properties which are not inherent in the component parts of an unorganized system and which arise only when the parts are grouped in a functional aggregate. Thus size or direction are properties of a figure which must be distinguished as a unit, if the properties are recognized. With this definition it is quite legitimate to apply the concept of figure-ground relations to the animal's visual field, when a reaction is found to a property which can be derived only from a total aggregate of elements in the stimulus.

The experiments described in this section have shown that the animal reacts to a limited part of the total visual field and disregards variations in the remainder. They have shown that the constants to which he reacts in an otherwise variable situation are properties which can be derived only from a total figure, hence that his reaction is dependent upon some sort of unification of the elements within a part of the field. They have shown that some of the same factors are instrumental in determining this unification as are at play in the production of "figure" in human perception. . . .

*Discrimination of Symmetrical Pairs of Figures.* In human reading confusion of symmetrical letters is often reported. Confusion of horizontal symmetries is more frequent than of vertical. Thus *b* and *d,* and *p* and *q* are confused; *b* and *p,* and *d* with *q* rarely. Mirror writing is common, inverted writing rare.

FIGURE 64

The confusion of symmetries may represent a more primitive level of organization than their differentiation; an effectiveness of the configuration of excitation, irrespective of its orientation. Or differentiation may represent the lower level, with tendency to confusion arising with the development of symmetrical movement systems in turn controlled by some mechanism of hemisphere dominance, as postulated by Orton (1925).

Tests of the ease of discrimination of symmetrical pairs of figures have been carried out with a number of rats.

1. Fifteen animals were trained on each of the patterns shown in Figures 65 to 68, triangles and *U* patterns in horizontal and vertical reversal. The

FIGURE 65

FIGURE 66

FIGURE 67

FIGURE 68

FIGURE 69

FIGURE 70

learning scores for the four groups were the following: the averages based only on cases which reached the criterion in 150 trials or less.

| | Trials | Errors | No. failed |
|---|---|---|---|
| Triangles, vertical reversal (Figure 65) | 42.0 | 10.3 | 0 |
| Triangles, horizontal reversal (Figure 66) | 33.0 | 7.4 | 0 |
| *U*-figures, vertical reversal (Figure 67) | 70.5 | 14.3 | 2 |
| *U*-figures, horizontal reversal (Figure 68) | 119.4 | 32.6 | 5 |

The learning scores with the symmetrical figures do not significantly exceed those for non-symmetrical pairs of figures of the same order of complexity. The difference in difficulty between triangles and *U*-figures is greater than the difference of horizontal and vertical symmetry.

The greater difficulty of the horizontally reversed *U*-figures is significant and may indicate a confusion introduced by the symmetry. It is more probably due to the identity of base-line of these particular figures.

2. Five animals were trained on each of the *N*- and *S*-designs shown in Figures 69 and 70: five others on each pair rotated 90 degrees. None of the 20 animals discriminated these figures in 150 trials.

3. Two animals were trained on a clockwise vs. a counterclockwise involute of a circle. Neither made better than chance scores after 300 trials.

The figures in Experiments 2 and 3 lack conspicuous identifying elements, other than relative position of parts which are remote from the frame of reference provided by the edges of the cards. Symmetry was probably of less importance than lack of distinct identifying features in determining the failure to differentiate these pairs. In general, there is no clear evidence that the normal animal confuses mirror-image figures.

*Complexity of Figure and Situation.* The term complexity is very freely and loosely used in current psychological literature. It most often refers to the number of items which the experimenter can discover and enumerate in the situation, but frequently the only basis for the judgment of complexity is the apparent psychological difficulty of the task. Viewed as a whole, which is the more complex, Figure 21 or Figure 24, or Figure 64? In each case one of the figures contain more lines, and more recognizable part figures than the other but these are arranged in a repetitive pattern. If complexity is defined as number of elements, then the regular figures are the more complex. But if lack of conformity to a conceptual plan containing few elements is taken as the criterion, then the irregular figures are the more complex. It is in the latter sense that most judgments of complexity are actually made.

There is little evidence that the number of items influences the identifiability to any great extent. The reduplicated lines of Figure 25 rank with triangle vs. square in ease of learning for the rat and are significantly easier than *H* vs. 5-pointed star. Where increase in items seems effective, as in the difference between cross vs. circle (30 trials, 11 errors) and cross plus triangle vs. circle plus triangle (140 trials, 49 errors) the difference may be ascribed to other causes—the fact in this case that the figure nearest the center bar of the apparatus was alternately significant and nonsignificant. Where the pattern contains many items, the animal solves the problem by disregarding most and reacting to a part-figure.

Number of variables in the total situation does apparently increase its difficulty. Thus cross vs. circle in the 2-card apparatus requires 30 trials with 11 errors, whereas cross vs. 2 circles, in the 3-card apparatus requires 150 trials with 49 errors, and size discrimination with 3 circles requires 4 times as much practice as with 2 circles. These results are the opposite of those reported by Fields (1935) who found that apparatus presenting 5 cards gave more rapid learning than the 2-card apparatus. Our apparatus and methods of training are so different that it is impossible to interpret this contradiction. The results are in agreement with those of Grether and Wolfle (1936), who report a progressive increase in learning time in a brightness discrimination experiment with increase in number of stimulus cards from two to five.

*Conformity with a Frame of Reference.* Next to presence vs. absence of a figure, the horizontal and vertical striations of Figure 8 have been most readily learned by all animals. Other figures in which conspicuous lines differ clearly in direction are also easily learned. A certain correspondence of these directions to the vertical and horizontal axes is important. Thus Figure 8 is learned very quickly but, if the lines are sloped 45 degrees in opposite directions, the difficulty is increased, and the contrast is still more pronounced, if circular frames like those of Figure 11 are introduced.

In experiments with horizontal vs. vertical striations more than half of the animals studied have reached the criterion of 20 consecutive jumps to the horizontal lines without once jumping to the vertical. With training positive to the vertical no animal has ever made better than chance scores in the first ten trials.

In training experiments to establish reactions to numerical relations, where several variable figures were displayed on each card the animals most readily learned to react to the direction of the black spaces between the figures, whenever these had a determinate direction.

Next to direction, distance from the dividing partition between the doors of the apparatus seems most readily identified, and is likely to provide the cue to discrimination. When marked differences in size or surface area of the figures exists, the animals are likely to disregard form entirely and transfer to any figures which differ similarly in size. When the figures contain many elements, the animal either disregards the elements when they conform to a regular geometrical plan, as in the case of Figure 43, or reacts to some limited part.

Although the evidence is very sketchy, it all seems to point in the same direction. The identifying feature is conformity to a more general frame of reference, either spacial orientation or position in a linear quantitative series. We have seen that with very complex or interrupted figures a regularity of geometrical arrangement facilitates learning, and this regularity also introduces dominance of direction or other means of relating the figure to some frame of reference. With very complex irregular figures, the basis of discrimination is a part-figure; the response is to some limited cue and the remainder of the figure is ignored. The part selected seems to be determined by its relation to the boundaries of the stimulus card, again a dominance of direction and distance. Thus recognition seems never to be specific but always the identification of some property of the figure with a more general reaction tendency.

## Primitive Forms of Abstraction

An organism may give the same reaction to various objects because it lacks sensory or integrative capacity to distinguish between them. This may give rise to a false appearance of generalization, if to the human observer the objects differ widely except for a single common attribute. The orientation of Euglena may be determined by the relative intensities of two lights, because, in spiral course the avoiding reaction to shading orients it to a direction in which the least change in intensity of light on the eyespot is brought about by its spiral course (Mast & Johnson, 1932). The insect may react more readily to radiating flower patterns (Hertz, 1929, 1935), not because the flower forms are generalized as biologically significant objects, but because the facet eye is maximally stimulated by the flicker produced by involved contours (Wolf, 1933, 1935). Reaction to a single stimulus in otherwise nonstimulating situations requires only a simple reflex mechanism, and does not raise the problem of generalization or abstraction as it appears in human behavior.

When, however, an organism is variously stimulated by constellations of forces in two situations and reacts only to those forces which are common to the two, some mechanism in addition to a simple sensory-motor connection must be postulated. There is selective reaction to the common properties of the two situations and an inhibition of reaction to other properties determined by the internal organization of the reacting system. In the conditional reflex experiment on differentiation of the stimulus this internal organization is developed by a series of combined stimulations in which reaction to the stimulus or attribute to be differentiated is reinforced and that to others subjected to experimental extinction. In the discrimination experiment much the same thing seems to happen. Presented with a pair of stimuli, the animal reacts to first one, then another attribute. There is reinforcement of reaction to one, inhibition of reaction to others by punishment, until the significant character is isolated from the total complex of stimuli. But perceptual organization and discrimination must always have occurred before the differential training can be effective. Once such a reaction has been established the animal will identify the familiar attribute among a group of unfamiliar stimuli.

A review of the experimental literature on abstraction and the formation of concepts reveals that these expressions are used to designate just such a process as this. In his study of the "evolution of concepts" Hull (1920) required his subjects to discover the identical element in a series of Chinese characters and applied the term "generalizing abstraction" to the recognition of the identical element. In his "simple to complex" method the procedure was essentially the same as in our tests with Figures 15 to 27. Other investigators have sought to exclude the recognition of identical elements from the concepts of generalization and abstraction and to limit the terms to cases in which the common element is relational or propositional. Thus the stress which has been laid upon the animal's ability to develop a "generalized conception of form" seems to derive from the notion that this particular sort of generalization marks a sharp inflection in the evolution of intelligence.

In contrast to such a view, I wish to emphasize that the sort of generalization implied in Bingham's definition of form is only a particular instance in continuous series of generalized abstractions. It is more difficult for the animal than the recognition of direction but less difficult than the discovery of the common attribute of size, when the brightness relations of figure and ground are reversed. The fundamental process, the identification of the common properties in two or more constellations of elements, seems to be almost universal among animals, appearing wherever a differential reaction is established. In the course of evolution this basic process of isolating and identifying common properties of objects has changed little, if at all. By both rat and man, a variety of properties of objects are immediately perceived and behavior is associated with those found by trial and error to have functional significance. The problem of the evolution of the capacity for generalization is really a question of the kinds of properties or of relations between objects with which animals at different evolutionary levels can deal.

Identical reaction to the identical existential elements in different situations is logically the simplest form of generalized reaction. That it is physiologically the simplest or most primitive is doubtful, but that question may be ignored for the present. Plenty of evidence has been presented to prove that the rat can give a consistent reaction to a constant figure on a varied ground. It has also been shown in equivalence tests that the basis of reaction is not the identical existential element but the presence of some more abstract common property.

What kinds of relations can the animal perceive and what is their comparative difficulty? For the rat, after presence vs. absence of object, direction seems the most easily distinguished of all properties and to be the one which dominates reaction when situations differ in several respects. Next in order of difficulty seems to be the relative position in a linear, directional series. Relative size, brightness, or distance seem to form the basis for a very primitive reaction. . . .

*Generalized "Concepts" of Form.* The series of experiments with Figures 15 to 27 show that once an animal has learned a differential reaction to a pair of figures he is able to recognize them in spite of alterations in size, in continuity of surface, or of outline, and is able to discover the figure in various combinations with irrelevant lines. In this there must be some primitive generalization of form which goes beyond the recognition of identical elements. The reaction is independent of any characteristics of the patterns except those contained in the internal proportions of the figure.

Fields found that, without special training, the rat is unable to identify a triangular figure when it is rotated more than 10 degrees from the position in which it had been learned. Only after long training with triangles in many positions did his animals learn to identify a triangle irrespective of its orientation.

Failure to recognize figures rotated through 90 degrees has been confirmed in several experiments, as with the cross and triangle of Figure 26. However, with very unlike figures the opposite result has been obtained.

Two animals were trained to choose a large *H* (positive) and avoid an X of equal surface area and length of major axes (Figure 82). The cards were then rotated through 90 degrees (Figure 83) and 20 critical trials given. One animal chose the rotated *H* in 18, the other in 20 of the 20 trials. Control tests with fresh cards and with cards bearing other designs assured that the reaction was to the visual properties of the figures. Beyond this no attempt was made to analyze the basis of the reaction.

Figure 82

Figure 83

Gellermann (1933a) has listed 6 requirements for proof that the animal can discriminate form "per se." These, formulated for triangularity, are:

1. A subject must be able to learn to discriminate a triangle from other forms.

2. He must be able to maintain the discrimination throughout *rotation* of the triangle.

3. His discrimination must be independent of absolute or relative size.

4. He must be able to respond to all *types* of triangles, as well as to the particular one upon which he was trained.

5. He must be able to respond to *outlined* triangles as well as to solid figures.

6. His discrimination of the triangle from other forms must be independent of the particular *backgrounds* in which the forms appeared.

In one or another test reported in the foregoing sections the rats have met every one of these criteria. We may therefore conclude with Fields that the rat has a conception of form *per se*. The importance of this particular test of ability to generalize has, however, been considerably exaggerated, as if there were only one kind of generalization which must be either present or absent. Actually there seems to be no difference in principle between the abstraction of *size* and of *form per se*. Both involve the discovery of relational properties common to several stimulating situations. Transposition in a brightness series is easier for the rat than is the recognition of a rotated figure, but the latter is easier than is transposition for width of striations or in a numerical series. The rat can find the common difference in the figures on page 162, but he would never find the identical elements in Hull's Chinese ideographs. We are not justified in assuming that abstraction or the formation of concepts appears as a sudden advance or unique trait in the evolutionary scale. It appears rather that the fundamental process of generalization is involved in all discrimination and that evolutionary development has been concerned chiefly with the application of the process to particular kinds of material or of relations.

*Generalizations of a Second Order.* In all of the tests reported it has been possible to vary the stimulus figures through a fairly wide range without disturbing the reactions. The adequate stimulus seems always to be some relational property of direction, distance, size, proportions, or the like. In generalizations at this level the rat is not markedly inferior to higher mammals. When, however, the problem requires a reaction to a combination of properties the limits of his capacity are approached. Difficulty arises when two variables must be reacted to simultaneously or when one variable determines the reaction to another.

Reaction to the "intermediate" of three figures in a directional series seems to require simultaneous reaction to both "larger than" and "smaller than." I have failed to obtain this. The experiment of Wolfle (1936) may have involved it, though the reactions in that case were more probably on an absolute basis.

Borovski (1930a and b) has reported experiments in which the reactions to one property of the stimulus were determined by another. He succeeded in training rats concurrently to choose the larger of two circles and the smaller of two triangles. In this case the form of the figure presumably determined the sign of the reaction to size. He also attempted to train animals to choose, of a triangle and circle, the triangle when on a white ground, the circle when on a black. In this task the animals failed.

Borovski's experiment was not well controlled, as Munn (1933) points out. His apparatus allowed the animals to crawl through holes, forming the figures to be tested, and he did not demonstrate that the reaction was visual. He did not show that the reactions were to size rather than to the position of the lower edge of the openings. In the experiment with black and white grounds the figures occupied a constant position and the animals failed to make the discrimination. This confirms the suspicion that in the successful experiment the animals were not reacting to the visual properties of the figures. We cannot, therefore, accept his experiments as conclusive.

The generalization required in Borovski's experiment was conditional, of the order, *if a, then b*. Two other methods have been tried to establish generalizations of this type at a still higher level of complexity. In the first of these the animal was required to compare the stimuli with a separate model and to choose the one like the model.

1. The three-door apparatus was arranged so that the middle door was always locked and the animals were trained to jump to the lateral doors. The cross and circle, figures easily discriminated by the rat, were chosen for the experiment. These figures were irregularly alternated between the lateral frames. A similar cross or circle was exposed at each trial in the middle frame. The animal was required to choose the one of the two lateral figures which was like that in the middle frame.

The animals readily learned to jump only to the lateral frames. Their training records for 200 trials are summarized in Table 2.

The reduction in number of false jumps during the tests is due to elimination of the tendency to jump more than once to the wrong figure in any single trial. The slight improvement in percentage correct choice resulted from an increased tendency to alternate between the doors which, with the order of shifting cards used in this experiment, gives a slightly better

TABLE 2
TRAINING SCORES OF ANIMALS REQUIRED TO SELECT THE ONE OF TWO FIGURES LIKE A THIRD

| | *No. 1* | | *No. 2* | |
|---|---|---|---|---|
| *Trials* | *Per cent Correct* | *False Jumps* | *Per cent Correct* | *False Jumps* |
| 1-50 | 44 | 54 | 38 | 45 |
| 51-100 | 38 | 42 | 38 | 36 |
| 101-150 | 46 | 30 | 52 | 27 |
| 151-200 | 48 | 30 | 54 | 25 |

score than does a position habit prevailing in the first hundred trials. The data give no indication that the animals could solve the problem.

In other experiments the comparison figure was located above or below the dividing panel of the two-card apparatus, but in all cases the results were the same. In the first trials the animals jumped to the comparison figure as well as to the stimulus cards but, after a few falls resulting from this, they confined their reactions to the stimulus cards and did not again make movements of fixation toward the comparison card.

2. Animals were trained in an attempt to establish the generalized reaction described by the clause, *that one of any three figures is correct which is different from the other two*. Klüver (1933) has observed spontaneous selection of the different figure by the monkey and Robinson (1933) has established a similar consistent reaction by training. With apparatus presenting three stimulus cards different groups of animals were trained in the following ways:

(*a*) To choose 1 cross vs. 2 circles (Figure 84). Next to choose 1 circle vs. 2 crosses (Figure 85). Alternate training was continued in the hope that the animals might eventually come to choose whichever figure was presented singly. Instead, after the third to fifth reversal all animals became confused and either refused to jump or jumped persistently to one figure in spite of scores of bumps and falls.

(*b*) To choose a cross and avoid two triangles, to choose a circle and avoid two crosses, to choose a striated card and avoid two circles, and so on through a series of different pairs of figures. Some animals learned as many as 10 such pairs, but never showed any tendency to choose the single

Figure 84

Figure 85

figure of a new pair, either when it was opposed to formerly positive figures, as above, or when both figures presented were entirely new.

*(c)* With apparatus presenting two stimulus cards, a card bearing two circles was opposed to one bearing circle and triangle. Training was continued with a number of like combinations of figures in the hope that the animals might ultimately learn to choose any card bearing two unlike figures. All animals failed.

*Limits of Generalization.* The experiments reported in this section form a very incomplete analysis of the rat's capacity to deal with complex visual situations. They do indicate an upper limit of generalization beyond which the rat cannot go and which is relatively easy for the lower monkey. They suggest some types of generalization of which the rat is capable. The experiments have been incidental to other work and the chief excuse for reporting them is their suggestiveness for a more systematic analysis and classification of possible types of generalization.

The conception of generalization is a broad category which does not designate a unitary psychological process but rather a certain class of logical relations. As Heidbreder (1924) has said, ". . . most of the words used in describing thinking are merely collective terms and . . . do not refer to processes, but only to results produced." There is no satisfactory analysis and classification of the processes by which different kinds of generalizations are reached, nor is there an adequate classification of the end products.

The discovery of identical elements in a series of figures was designated by Hull (1920) as "generalizing abstraction." In the study of Fisher (1916) the characters generalized were sometimes relations among the parts of the figures. Heidbreder (1924) required generalization of a conditional relation, *if a, then b.* These by no means exhaust the possible types of abstraction, nor can we say how many diverse integrative processes may be involved in them. The whole problem is closely tied up with that of perceptual organization, and limits of capacity are set by the latter as well as by the types of organization which are described in formal logic. The rat can discover a triangle as the common element in a series of patterns. He certainly could not discover any of the identical symbols in Hull's series of Chinese ideographs. The result, the discovery of the identical element, can be described by the same logical formula, but evidently a greater complexity of perceptual organization is required for the solution of Hull's figures.

What determines the relative difficulty of such tasks? We speak of complexity but usually find ourselves involved in a circle in which complexity is really only a synonym for psychological difficulty. To what extent is ability a continuous function, varying with the amount of "neural energy" available, as interpreted by Spearman? To what extent an aggregation of qualitatively diverse functions (capacities for specific insights) as implied by Gestalt psychologists? Is each "insight" a unique event or is there a limited number of types of insight each mediated by a particular kind of nervous organization? No conclusive answers can be given to these questions at present and only a comprehensive analysis of the nature of the adequate stimuli in a great variety of situations will provide decisive evidence. . . .

## *THE NATURE OF THE RAT'S VISUAL ORGANIZATION*

Aside from any interpretation of the experiments reported here, one must be impressed by the similarity of the rat's discriminative behavior to the perceptual impressions of the human observer. If a series of patterns is ranked in order of the conspicuousness of the figures for the human eye, that order will have a high predictive value for the rate at which the rat can learn the figures. Stimuli to which the rat transfers in equivalence tests are those obviously similar for man. Figure-ground relations seem to be determined in much the same way for both. Both distinguish complex figures by discovering limited part-figures as cues.

I do not believe that this result is an artifact arising from the design of the experiments by *Homo* rather than by *Mus*. In addition to those reported I have run equivalence tests with scores of figures, often quite at random, to see if the rat might find similarities which were not evident to the experimenter. In only one instance did this seem to occur. Two rats insisted for 40 trials each that Figure 63*a* is a circle and 63*b* a triangle. Repetition of this test with other animals gave negative results and in every other case where two figures were equivalent for the rats they were obviously similar for the experimenter. In no case has there been any indication that the rat perceives relations which are not obvious to the human observer. Even though we are not able to define the organizing forces satisfactorily, it seems clear that they are essentially the same in the rat and in man.

Whenever the attempt has been made to discover to what characteristics of the stimulus pattern the rat is reacting, by eliminating parts of the pattern or by testing for equivalence with new patterns, the adequate stimulus has been found to be some rather simple perceptual relation within the pattern. The animal never responds to pattern as defined by Hunter or shape as defined by Bingham, nor to an exact form which must be a replica of the training figure, but always to some more general property which differentiates the positive from the negative training figure.

The range of these general properties revealed by equivalence tests seems quite limited. Presence or absence of a figure, direction, relative distance, relative brightness or size, and geometrically simple proportions probably exhaust the range. Yet by using these and by isolating part-figures the animal is able to identify configurations of almost any degree of irregularity and numerical complexity of elements. Perhaps man employs no greater range of abstractions in his visual perception.

Figures which the rat fails to differentiate, aside from those presenting only liminal differences, are the ones in which differentiating features are subordinate to general similarities of form, such as the symmetrical S's of Figure 70.

The basis for more generalized recognition of form is still obscure. I have found immediate transfer to *H*- and X-figures on 90 degree rotation but not to triangle and cross. Fields has shown that with long training this can be acquired. Evidently success in such tests depends not only on the capacity for generalization but on the particular forms as well. We can identify a white with a black triangle in any orientation, but how many people can identify a negative portrait, or even an inverted one? At present we can only specify what the rat can do in two particular situations and neither from these nor from human data of a similar nature can we infer what factors set a limit to such generalization.

The experiments reported stress the tendency of the rat to base his reactions upon such relations as distance, or direction, where a human subject identifies a total geometrical figure. It must be borne in mind that the jumping apparatus emphasizes the relation of the figure to the frame of the card and that this may determine the property to which the animal reacts. A ski jumper is more likely to note the distance of a spectator from the slide than the shape of his hat. Nevertheless, the care with which the animals inspect the figures before jumping, and the readiness with which such properties as brightness are perceived, which do not involve relation to the frame, argue for the validity of the data.

Observations of the rat in the maze and free-field have suggested that the chief function of vision in the animal's adaptive reactions is for general orientation, with little or no visual identification of specific objects. This is consistent with the dominance of distance and direction in the discrimination of figures. The contrast between the rat, on the one hand, and the cat and monkey with respect to the readiness of transfer to rotated figures, as revealed by the experiments of Fields (1932), Smith (1936), and Gellermann (1933a, b) also shows a correlation between this behavior and the use of vision in daily life. Finally the behavior which I have interpreted as a suppression of vision, the importance of remote cues, especially the direction of the source of light, for orientation, and the accuracy of perception of depth in the visual field, all point to a visual system primarily organized for adjustment in space rather than for identification of objects.

So long as the problem is the discovery of differences or resemblances between specific figures which can be generalized in terms of spacial relations the rat is able to solve it readily. When, however, the problem requires a combination of such generalizations or when one generalization is conditional upon another, the limits of his capacity are approached. The experiments with size indicate that the animal is able to generalize simultaneously several properties which are later differentiated, but such a generalization as "intermediate" has proven impossible. Borovski's experiment, which is not adequately controlled, has given positive evidence of a conditional generalization, but other tests involving the same principle have given only negative results. The variety of tests carried out at this level is too limited to justify the conclusion that they are beyond the rat's capacity, but the failure to learn to choose the one of three figures which is different from the others definitely distinguishes between the rat and monkey.

## *THEORETICAL CONSIDERATIONS*

The discrimination experiment presents the animals with a definite situation, then with another having different characteristics, and ultimately establishes a different reaction to each situation. What is the basis for this differential reaction? For a stimulus-response psychology the one situation is associated with approach, the other with withdrawal: $S_a \rightarrow R_a : S_w \rightarrow R_w$: all simple and neat. Unfortunately this formula does not include the essential feature of discrimination, the fact that the efficacy of each stimulus is dependent upon the character of the other; $S_a = FS_w$. The moment we examine the concept of stimulus critically, the inadequacy of such general formulations becomes apparent.

*The Nature of the Adequate Stimulus.* Analysis of the differential response reveals the following facts concerning the character of the effective stimulus:

1. The positive or negative reaction is determined by some fraction of the total visual situation. In every case the total situation may be broken down into an effective part, the figure, and an indifferent part, the ground.
2. The effective fraction of each situation is always some character which differentiates the negative from the positive stimulus. The animal trained to the larger of two circles chooses the larger of other figures, but not a circle from other forms of equal area.
3. The differentiating characters are always abstractions of general relationships subsisting between figures and cannot be described in terms of any concrete objective elements of the stimulating situations.
4. In isolating these characters the animal itself is an important factor, since in identical situations no two animals may react on the basis of the same properties.

These conclusions, which are amply supported by the experimental evidence, show that the description of discrimination as a mere combination of a positive and a negative reaction misses the essential features of the process, which are the isolation of figure, the discovery of differences, and the generalizing character of the response. These are prior to and not a result of the training.

*The Fractioning of the Visual Field.* Physically, visual stimulation of the rat consists of the excitation of some 28 millions of structurally independent rhabdomes with various intensities of light. The light rays reaching the individual rhabdomes are the elements of the stimulus. Any functional relations of pattern or form must be determined by the interaction of impulses from the rhabdomes at some central level. Studies of figure-ground relations show that there are certain general principles of organization applicable to the isolation not only of familiar but of new figures. The general effectiveness of continuity of figure, contrast, or conformation to a regular geometrical arrangement in determining the structure of figure cannot be accounted for in terms of trial-and-error learning except by the postulation of some capacity for generalization which begs the question at issue between nativistic and habit-system theories. The experiments of Turner (1935), Lashley and Russell (1934) and Hebb (1937a, b) and the data on the congenitally blind with restored vision (Senden, 1932) all point to the conclusion that the isolation of figure occurs at the first moment of visual stimulation. The fractioning of the visual field into coherent units must then be recognized as an immediate product of organic structure and an indicator of the character of the integrative mechanism. . . .

*Identical Elements or Abstract Relations.* For many years the doctrine has been urged upon psychologists that a recognition of identical existential elements in different situations is the most primitive and simple of reactions and therefore to be preferred among alternative explanations of similarity. During the controversies concerning the value of formal discipline the theory of transfer of training through the presence of identical elements reached the height of its vogue and won a practical victory, even though its proponents finally admitted that identity after all is not identity and elements are relations.

The assumption that reaction to identical elements is physiologically a simple process is a consequence of the connectionist or telephone theory of integration. If cerebral integration occurs by the interaction of dynamic fields (Köhler, 1924), then reaction to abstract relations should be the most immediate and direct form of response, whereas the recognition of the identity of existential elements should require the combined recognition of all of the common properties of the situations. It is time that we realize that the doctrine of transfer through identical elements has no greater a priori claim to explanatory value or simplicity than has any relational or organismal theory.

Equivalence tests show that so long as the abstract property which differentiates the positive figure from the negative is preserved, differential reaction persists. No physical identity of stimuli is necessary for transfer nor is there any evidence that even in successive identifications of the same figure, physical identity is the determining factor.

*The Limits of Abstraction.* The relational properties which form the basis of the rat's reactions seem to be quite limited in number and to be chiefly those arising from the relation of the figure to the animal's orientation in space. Relative distance is quickly learned, relative number not at all; direction far more easily than specific pattern. What determines this limitation of the rat's capacity in comparison with the cat, monkey, or man? Is it past experience or structural organization? Is the predilection to see certain relations a result of the rat's mode of life, or is the mode of life determined by such limitation of capacity? Questions of this kind are of fundamental importance for understanding the evolution of behavior. There is no decisive evidence upon which an answer can be based, but both comparative and clinical material is consistent with the view that the relational framework within which generalization occurs is determined by innate structural or physiological organization.

I must take sharp issue with the view of Smith (1936, p. 51) that such speculations concerning constitutional determiners of activity do not further our knowledge of behavior. They do not, of course, provide any immediate explanation but they do formulate a definite problem which offers a meaningful alternative to a theory of redintegration, such as he proposes, and which is capable of solution by experimental means.

Perhaps the most significant result of this study is the indication that the development of ability for generalization or abstraction does not present a few well marked and easily defined steps, such as a capacity to abstract relations, a capacity to generalize form, or a capacity for eduction of relations, but rather that material and process cannot be sharply separated. The eduction of a size relationship differs in difficulty according to the figures used and differs also from eduction of a number relation. The processes involved may have only logical, not physiological similarity. Once we recognize this, stop trying to fit the animal's behavior into a few a priori logical categories, and turn to detailed analysis of relational behavior and of the conditions limiting abstraction and generalization the way is opened for an adequate account of the evolution of intelligence.

## *SUMMARY*

This study has been concerned with an analysis of the properties of the stimulating situation which form the basis for discrimination of visual objects. After estimation of differential thresholds for the chief variables with which later work is concerned, experiments were directed to determine the characteristics of stimulus objects which are effective for discrimination.

Evidence was obtained that the figure-ground relation exists in the animal's visual field and that the segregation of figure is determined by at least some of the same factors which are effective in human vision. Discrimination was found to be based upon the abstraction of certain general properties of the figure which are then recognized in non-identical figures. Ease of discrimination depends upon the presence of certain relational properties, such as predominant direction, in the figures.

Differences in the ease of discrimination and recognition of different figures indicate that the rat's visual system functions most efficiently in spacial orientation—the recognition of relative distance and direction—and that the identification of objects or forms, though possible, is secondary to a system of space coordinates.

The bearing of the observations upon the general problem of the nature and evolution of intelligence is discussed.

## *REFERENCES*


Bingham, H. C. A definition of form. *Journal of Animal Behavior*, 1914, *4*, 136-141.

Borovski, V. M. Experimentelle Untersuchungen über den Lernprozess: IV. Über Labilität der Gewohnheiten. *Zeitschrift für Vergleichende Physiologie*, 1930, *11*, 549-564.

Borovski, V. M. Experimentelle Untersuchungen über den Lernprozess: V. Zur Analyse des Sitzungsbegriffs. *Biologisches Zentralblatt*, 1930, *50*, 566-572.

Borovski, V. M. The relation of the gull to its nest, eggs, and young. (Russian). *Refleksi, Instinkti, Naviki*, 1936, *2*, 139-174.

Djang, S. The rôle of past experience on the visual apprehension of masked forms. *Journal of Experimental Psychology*, 1937, *20*, 29-59.

Fields, P. E. Studies in concept formation. *Comparative Psychology Monographs*, 1932, 9 (2) 1-70.

Fields, P. E. Studies in concept formation: II. A new multiple stimulus jumping apparatus for visual figure discrimination. *Journal of Comparative Psychology*, 1935, *20*, 183-203.

Fields, P. E. Studies in concept formation: III. A note on the retention of visual figure discrimination. *Journal of Comparative Psychology*, 1936, *21*, 131-136.

Fisher, S. C. The process of generalizing abstraction and its product, the general concept. *Psychological Review Monographs*, 1916, *21* (90) v & 213.

Gellermann, L. W. Form discrimination in chimpanzees and two-year-old children: I. Form (triangularity) *per se*. *Journal of Genetic Psychology*, 1933, *42*, 3-27. (a)

Gellermann, L. W. Form discrimination in chimpanzees and two-year-old children: II. Form versus background. *Journal of Genetic Psychology*, 1933, *42*, 28-50. (b)

Gellermann, L. W. Chance orders of alternating stimuli in visual discrimination experiments. *Journal of Genetic Psychology*, 1933, *42*, 206-207. (c)

Gottschaldt, K. Ueber den Einfluss der Erfahrung auf die Wahrnehmung von Figuren. *Psychologische Forschung*, 1926, 8, 261-371; 1929, *12*, 1-87.

Grether, W. F., & Wolfle, D. L. The relative efficiency of constant and varied stimulation during learning: II. White rats on a brightness discrimination problem. *Journal of Comparative Psychology*, 1936, 22, 365-374.

Hebb, D. O. Innate organization of visual activity: I. Perception of figures by rats reared in total darkness. *Journal of Genetic Psychology*, 1937, *51*, 101-126. (a)

Hebb, D. O. Innate organization of visual activity: II. Discrimination of size and brightness by rats reared in total darkness. *Journal of Comparative Psychology*, 1937, *24*, 277-299. (b)

Hebb, D. O. Studies of organization of behavior: I. Behavior of the rat in a field orientation. (In preparation.)

Heidbreder, E. An experimental study of thinking. *Archives of Psychology*, 1924, No. 73, 1-175.

Hertz, M. Das optische Gestaltproblem und der Tierversuch. *Verhandlung der deutschen Zoologischen Gesellschaft*, 1929, 23-49.

Hertz, M. Zur Physiologie des Formen- und Bewegungssehens: III. Figurale Unterscheidung und reziproke Dressuren bei der Biene. *Zeitschrift für Vergleichende Physiologie*, 1935, *21*, 604-615.

Hull, C. L. Quantitative aspects of the evolution of concepts. *Psychological Monographs*, 1920, *28* (123), 1-86.

Hunter, W. S. The question of form perception. *Journal of Animal Behavior*, 1913, *3*, 329-333.

Johnson, H. M. Visual pattern discrimination in vertebrates: V. A demonstration of the dog's deficiency in detail vision. *Journal of Animal Behavior*, 1916, *6*, 205-221.

Klüver, H. *Behavior mechanisms in monkeys*. Chicago: University of Chicago Press, 1933.

Köhler, W. The problem of form in perception. *British Journal of Psychology*, 1924, *14*, 262-268.

Koffka, K. *Principles of gestalt psychology*. New York: Harcourt, Brace, 1935.

Lashley, K. S. Notes on the nesting activities of the noddy and sooty terns. Papers from the Department of Marine Biology, Carnegie Institute of Washington, 1915, 7, 61-83.

Lashley, K. S. The color vision of birds: I. The spectrum of the domestic fowl. *Journal of Animal Behavior*, 1916, *6*, 1-26.

Lashley, K. S. The mechanism of vision: I. A method for rapid analysis of pattern vision in the rat. *Journal of Genetic Psychology*, 1930, *37*, 453-460. (a)

Lashley, K. S. The mechanism of vision: III. The comparative visual acuity of pigmented and albino rats. *Journal of Genetic Psychology*, 1930, *37*, 481-484. (b)

Lashley, K. S. The mechanism of vision: V. The structure and image-forming power of the rat's eye. *Journal of Comparative Psychology*, 1932, *13*, 173-200.

Lashley, K. S. The mechanism of vision: XIV. Visual perception of distance after injuries to the cerebral cortex, colliculi, or optic thalamus. *Journal of Genetic Psychology*, 1937, *51*, 189-207.

Lashley, K. S., & Frank, M. The mechanism of vision: X. Postoperative disturbances of habits based on detail vision in the rat after lesions in the cerebral visual areas. *Journal of Comparative Psychology*, 1934, *17*, 355-391.

Lashley, K. S., & Russell, J. T. The mechanism of vision: XI. A preliminary test of innate organization. *Journal of Genetic Psychology*, 1934, *45*, 136-144.

Mast, S. O. The process of photic orientation in the robber-fly, *Proctacanthus philadelphicus*. *American Journal of Physiology*, 1924, *68*, 262-279.

Mast, S. O., & Johnson, P. L. Orientation to light from two sources and its bearing on the function of the eyespot. *Zeitschrift für Vergleichende Physiologie*, 1932, *16*, 252-274.

Munn, N. L. A note on Lashley's method for studying vision in the rat. *Journal of Genetic Psychology*, 1930, *37*, 528-530.

Munn, N. L. *An Introduction to animal psychology*. Cambridge: Houghton, Mifflin, 1933.

Orton, S. T. "Word-blindness" in school children. *Archives of Neurology and Psychiatry*, 1925, *14*, 581.

Pache, J. Formensehen bei Fröschen. *Zeitschrift für Vergleichende Physiologie*, 1932, *17*, 423-464.

Poppelreuter, W. Zur Psychologie und Pathologie der optischen Wahrnehmung. *Zeitschrift für die gesamte Neurologie und Pathologie*, 1923, *83*, 26-152.

Rachevsky, N. Outline of a physico-mathematical theory of the brain. *Journal of General Psychology*, 1935, *13*, 82-111.

Robinson, E. W. A preliminary experiment on abstraction in a monkey. *Journal of Comparative Psychology*, 1933, *16*, 231-236.

Russell, J. T. Depth discrimination in the rat. *Journal of Genetic Psychology*, 1932, *40*, 136-161.

Senden, M. v. Raum- und Gestaltauffassung bei operierten Blindgeborenen vor und nach der Operation. Leipzig, 1932.

Smith, K. U. Visual discrimination in the cat: III. The relative effect of paired and unpaired stimuli in the discriminative behavior of the cat. *Journal of Genetic Psychology*, 1936, *48*, 29-57.

Taliaferro, W. H. Reactions to light in *Planaria* maculata, with special reference to the function and structure of the eyes. *Journal of Experimental Zoology*, 1920, *31*, 59-116.

Turner, W. D. The development of perception: I. Visual direction; the first eidoscopic orientations of the albino rat. *Journal of Genetic Psychology*, 1935, *47*, 121-140.

Wolf, E. Das Verhalten der Bienen gegenüber flimmerenden Feldern und bewegten Objekten. *Zeitschrift für Vergleichende Physiologie*, 1933, *20*, 151-161.

Wolf, E. An analysis of the visual capacity of the bee's eye. *Cold Spring Harbor Symposia on Quantitative Biology*, 1935, *3*, 255-260.

Wolfle, D. L. The ability of the white rat to learn an absolute brightness discrimination. *Psychological Bulletin*, 1936, *33*, 728-729.

Specifically the parts of Lashley's paper which have been excluded, but which could be considered as rather relevant to our discussion are: (1) a section on the relative brightnesses of figure and ground, (2) a section on part-figure discrimination, and (3) a section on geometrical regularity as a factor in the rat's recognition of patterns. Lashley found that rats trained to discriminate, say, between upright and inverted equilateral triangles presented as white figures against a black background, failed to discriminate between the same shapes presented as black figures on a white background. This was generally true for other shapes; reversing the brightness relations led to disruption of discrimination. This finding has been widely quoted as being true for the rat, yet one should pause and consider carefully whether the evidence fully justifies the conclusion that rats cannot recognize patterns when the brightness relation of figure and ground is reversed. A variety of factors might be involved in discriminating the original white upright triangle from the inverted triangle. For instance, the rat might discriminate "brighter below" (the upright triangle) from "brighter above" (the inverted triangle), or if it only observed the bottom of the two shapes, the rat might simply go by which one was brighter. There are some other possibilities too. The fact is I do not want simply to criticize Lashley's methods but to emphasize just the same point Lashley himself made: what the discrimination looks like to us may be irrelevant to the actual discrimination the rat (or any other animal) really makes. That is one of the reasons why he was so concerned about general questions of visual organization. It is especially an important point as far as pattern recognition is concerned since patterns (shapes) are not really salient features for rats. That is to say, rats will learn to respond much more easily to differences in brightness (or smell, or position . . .) than to differences in shape; therefore, it is necessary to exclude such other cues when studying shape recognition. Actually it is really difficult to get unambiguous evidence on shape recognition as such in rats and other animals, and we shall see later that the recent tendency has been to use much simpler stimulus arrays than those (or some of those) used by Lashley. At least one of the reasons for this change has to do with the desire to have clear evidence on pattern and shape recognition as such, rather than evidence that could be interpreted in terms of shape recognition but might equally well have something to do with other forms of discrimination.

Lashley found good evidence for discrimination by parts of shapes (this is discussed in the second section which I have omitted). That is to say, rats trained to discriminate between two arrays would very often discriminate successfully on subsequent occasions when only parts of the original patterns were displayed (e.g., only the bottom or top halves). In the jumping stand the lower halves of shapes are usually most effective—a finding subsequently confirmed by others—presumably because rats learn to look at and aim for the base of a shape in the jumping stand. Another point is that particular features, such as straight lines, tend to make displays discriminable, as opposed to patterns which consist of more or less random squiggles or dots.

These points can be related to the requirements for confirmation—or otherwise—of the sorts of model discussed in Part II. In that part the assumption generally made was that the whole pattern displayed was the effective discriminandum (the "thing discriminated"), and that other cues such as brightness, or brightness gradient, were not the cues controlling preference for one stimulus over another. If these assumptions are wrong, then of course the coding models either get into difficulties with predictions about part-shape discriminations, or are simply irrelevant if the discrimination does not involve shape or contour characteristics. As far as possible one will try to exclude the possibility that cues other than contour and shape are available (if one wants to study shape recognition), and it is usually possible to assess whether some other sorts of cues are effective by appropriate "control" procedures. For example, if one wanted to know whether the discrimination of upright from inverted triangle mentioned earlier were really based on differences in brightness distribution (bright above vs. brighter below) one could test the experimental animals on a different pair of shapes having this characteristic, and so on.

This discussion is very relevant to our next paper, which reports an important and surprising experimental outcome. Krechevsky, like Lashley, was interested in general features of visual organization, and particularly in the conditions of motivation and learning which might affect them. In his introduction a very explicit discussion of the Gestalt school's ideas about visual organization and pattern recognition is given, and the experimental test of the principle of "proximity" is nicely justified. Although the theoretical orientation is rather different from that of today's psychologist, and certainly Krech (as he now is) would no longer subscribe to all its premises, it is instructive to see how a keen mind saw the problem of pattern recognition three decades ago, and how the logic of the experiment was developed.

# *An Experimental Investigation of the Principle of Proximity in the Visual Perception of the Rat*

I. KRECHEVSKY

## *INTRODUCTION*

The extent and even the existence of spontaneous grouping in sensory fields is a question of dispute between the *Gestalt* psychologists and the non-*gestalt* psychologists. For the *Gestalt* psychologist the existence of spontaneous groupings in sensory fields is of fundamental importance for all of their discussions of the perceptual process. Thus, for the *Gestalt* psychologist, the sensory units which make up perception are primarily determined by the specific field organization, to which the stimulus distribution gives rise. While not denying the influence, under certain conditions, of learning and experience, they do not conceive of the genesis of such perceptual units as being primarily due to learning. To use a very simple and rather common example, they point out that our perception of the dots in Fig. 1 is *perforce* a perception of a fairly well-defined grouping, rather than of an unorganized scatter of dots. Further, the factors making for this grouping are factors inherent in the sensory field itself—autochthonous factors of organization—and relatively independent of previous experience, reasoning, etc. The *Gestalt* psychologists are, of course, much more specific than this. They do not rest content with merely affirming the existence of some vague autochthonous principle of organization, but have discovered and defined several specific principles of organization which enable them not only to say that our perceptual unit will be an *organized* one, but also to predict the *specific form* of the resulting organization. Thus, to return to our illustration, we could not only predict that we will see the dots of Fig. 1 as an organized grouping of dots, but that we will see them as organized in *two horizontal linear distributions*, and not, say, in five short vertical linear distributions, or a number of diagonal distributions, etc. (This is not an invarient response, since certain changes in the surrounding field *can* result in a *predictable* change in the perception, but the above prediction holds for most

Reprinted from *Journal of Experimental Psychology*, 1938.

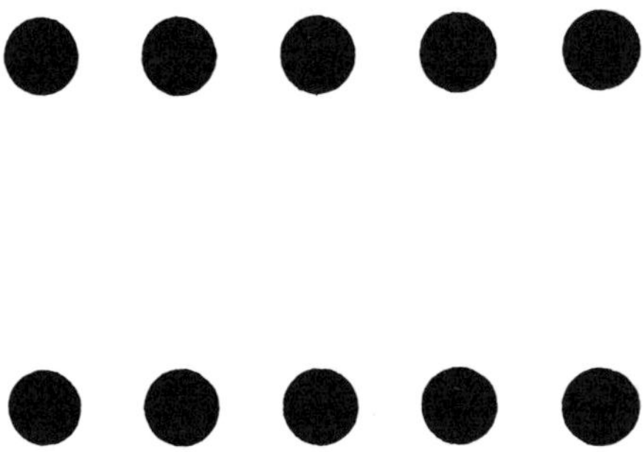

Fig. 1

cases.) The specific principle of organization which the *gestalt* psychologist would appeal to in making this specific prediction concerning our perception is the principle of Proximity. This principle supposes first the general factor that "group formation is due to actual forces of attraction between the members of the group" (Koffka, 1935, p. 165) and secondly, the more specific factor that "When the field contains a number of equal parts, those among them which are in greater proximity will be organized into a higher unit" (*Ibid.*). This principle of proximity would thus enable us to predict the actual perception obtained.

The critics of *Gestalt* theory, in this instance, would not deny that we *do* perceive the dots of Fig. 1 as two groups of horizontal distributions, but they would deny that there is anything 'necessary' about the perception, that the forces making for this perception are autochthonous. They would, instead, seek for an explanation in the past experience of the perceiving organism, in 'learning,' familiarity, etc. We are here, however, not interested in joining this debate, though we may parenthetically remark that in our opinion the *Gestaltists* have come off the victors on this question. What we were specifically interested in, in the planning of the present experiment were the following two questions: (1) Assuming the validity of the principle of autochthonous factors of organization in the sensory field, are these factors alone sufficient to account for the 'looks of things,' in all cases, or is some other set of factors necessary to make *effective* the operation of these principles? In other words, are the determining forces making for a particular organization to be found entirely within the sensory field, or are some of the essential determining forces making for a particular organization to be found outside of the specific sensory field in question and not derivable from the distribution of the field? (2) Assuming that the latter answer is the correct one for certain cases, then what is the nature of these necessary but non sensory-field forces, *i.e.*, what are the conditions which permit the functioning of the autochthonous principles of organization in these cases?

The general tendency of the *Gestalt* psychologist, in most of his experimental studies, has been to maximize the importance of the organizing forces within the sensory field and to minimize the importance of possible outside forces. (Exceptions to this general tendency will be discussed later in this paper.) To explain the horizontal groupings of the dots in Fig. 1 the *Gestalt* psychologist would, in general, not feel it necessary to go outside of Fig. 1. A complete analysis of the distribution of the dots in the figure would suffice for a prediction of the resulting perception.[1]

Without at all denying the existence of autochthonous organizing forces within a sensory field, it is still possible to answer the same question with a slightly changed emphasis. Tolman, in discussing what he believes to be the difference between his 'sign-*gestalt*' and the more orthodox *gestalt*, points out that

> According to a Simon-pure Gestalt-ist (. . . as we are conceiving such a one) these visual, kinesthetic and tactual stimuli will evoke a unique visual, tactual and kinesthetic configuration which will contain visual and tactual and kinesthetic qualities but will in addition present such properties as 'figure-on-groundness,' 'form,' 'solidity,' . . . etc. Finally, according to the Simon-pure Sign-Gestaltist . . . these same visual stimuli will be thought to evoke not just this configuration as a mere 'perceived' given, but rather some specific larger whole in which this merely pictured (*i.e.*, perceived) configuration will itself be embedded as one term in a larger means-end 'proposition' such, as that; 'that chair, if sat on, will lead to rest' (Tolman, 1933, pp. 394-95). And thus, argues Tolman, just as the *Gestaltists* have shown that the organization and form of the 'perceived' determines the very nature of the 'sensations' so is it the thesis of the Sign-Gestaltist that 'sign-*gestalts* determine Gestalten' (*Ibid.*, p. 410).

In simpler terms it seems to us what Tolman is saying is something like this: Just as we don't have 'pure sensations' divorced from organization and form, so don't we have 'pure organizations' in our perceptions divorced from certain immediately and concomitantly experienced 'propositions' concerning these 'perceptions.' This would mean that the particular orga-

[1] Assuming, of course, a given organism with a given nervous system to do the perceiving. In this connection, in order to avoid any misunderstanding, we are *not* suggesting that the *Gestalt* psychologists believe that *gestalten* exist outside the organism, that the forces of attraction, etc., operate 'out there' among the physical dots themselves, create segregated wholes, and then these 'wholes' project themselves into the nervous system of the organism. This is an erroneous reading of *Gestalt* psychology, but common enough an error to have caused Köhler to deny it specifically. "Organization in a sensory field," writes Köhler, "is something which originates as a characteristic achievement of the nervous system" (Köhler, 1929, p. 174); and again, "As a matter of fact the whole retina is a mosaic of indifferently related spots, and this is the case until sensory organization begins physiologically" (*Ibid.*, p. 177). Therefore, whenever we have occasion to use the phrase 'organizing forces within the sensory field' or 'forces of attraction between the members of the group' we mean, together with the *gestalt* psychologists, 'physiologically determined organizing forces within the experienced field.'

nization we would perceive would be a function of the autochthonous principles of organization as influenced by the needs, available means-end-readiness, etc., of the animal. Thus, bringing Tolman's argument to bear on the specific question concerning us here, he would say that in order to describe and predict the specific perception resulting from the stimulation of Fig. 1 he would not only want to make use of the principle of proximity but he would also want to know what the 'psychological situation' of the animal was at that moment. What were his needs, what did he know about the entire situation, etc. In other words, some of the forces determining the perception would derive from *outside* the particular sensory field.

Another way of describing these 'determining forces' deriving from without the sensory fields suggested itself to the present writer from some observations made in a previous experiment. In that experiment (Krechevsky, 1938a) we made a preliminary study of the operation of the principle of proximity in the perception of the rat. On the basis of the results obtained we concluded that the rat tends to group discontinuous stimuli according to the principle of proximity very much after the fashion of the relationship observed in the perceptual behavior of the human being. However, so strong did the 'forces of attraction' appear to be, that, after further consideration of our results, we were led to believe that some other factor than the principle of proximity must have been at work. In considering the possible factors (other than the organizational ones) which might be operating here, we made the following tentative analysis: The technique used in that experiment was to present the animal with what proved to be a difficult visual discrimination to solve. This discrimination could only be solved if the animal finally did achieve one specific visual organization rather than other possible organizations. In other words, the situation as a whole (the problem-situation) *required* that a given visual organization be made. Under those conditions of need the animal did finally achieve the organization in his perception. (Two visual patterns, one the positive and the other the negative, were used.) Phrasing the situation in terms of the *discrimination* to be made immediately implies that the rat's perception of the positive stimulus field might not be entirely a function of the sensory field obtained from that card, but somehow a function of the complex "Positive-Card-'A'-to-be-discriminated-from-negative-card-'B'." In other words, we would thus be suggesting that forces deriving from *the need to make the* A-B *discrimination* were in part responsible for the rat's perception, and these forces, of course, do not derive from the specific sensory field of card 'A.' This is merely an hypothesis, but one which could be tested. If we could devise an experiment where in one case the problem-situation did *not* force a particular organization, and in another case where the problem-situation *did* require that particular organization, but where, in both cases, the positive stimulus was the same, we could then test the influence of the differing problem-situations on the resulting perceptions of the identical positive stimuli.

We can now state our experimental question more specifically. Is the rat's perception of a given stimulus pattern of the type used in this experiment a function of the pattern alone, or is it also a function of the type of problem situation (discrimination) involved?

## *APPARATUS AND PROCEDURE*

The general experimental technique used was that of presenting two groups of animals with different visual discrimination problems, training them until they were able to make the necessary discrimination, and then running a series of test trials to obtain information on the nature of the rats' perceptions of the positive stimulus of each original pair. The apparatus used was the Lashley jumping-stand for visual discrimination learning.

Forty-two rats, divided into two main groups, were used as the subjects in the present experiment. These animals were all pigmented males, approximately three months of age at the beginning of the experiment, and were taken from the Swarthmore Psychological Laboratory stock. After an eight-day preliminary training period during which the animals were permitted to become accustomed to the apparatus and during which they were trained to jump through a white card as opposed to a black card, the two groups received the following training:

*Group I* (n = 19).—This group was given the 'difficult' discrimination. Immediately after the preliminary training period referred to above, these animals were started on the regular discrimination training. In order to control the possible effects of preference tendencies for certain visual patterns, the members of this group were divided into two sub-groups. Sub-group I*a* was presented with the discrimination set-up where Stimulus 'A' was the positive stimulus and 'B,' the negative stimulus (Fig. 2, 'Training Series'). For the rats of Sub-group I*b*, the card 'B' was the positive stimulus, and card 'A,' the negative one. Sub-group I*a* consisted of eight rats, and I*b*, of eleven rats. The training schedule

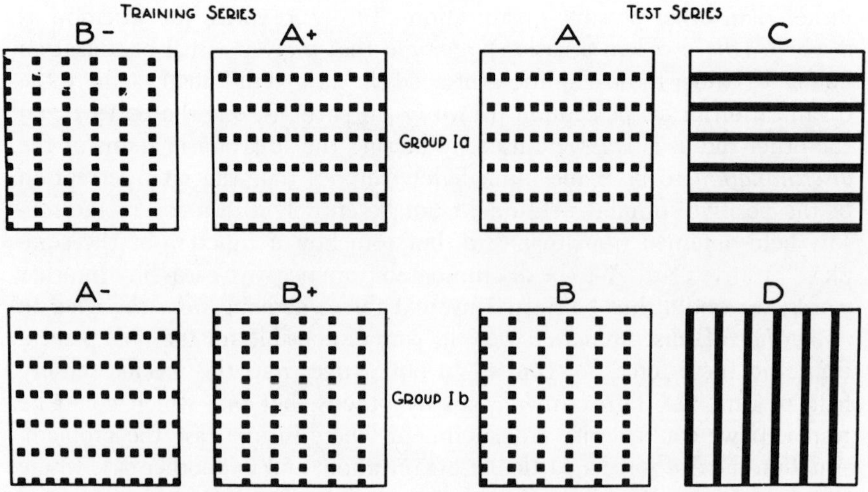


Fig. 2

consisted of ten trials per day until each animal met the criterion set up as indicating mastery. To meet this criterion, the animal was required to make at least eighteen correct choices on any two consecutive days, *i.e.*, 18 correct out of twenty, or 90 percent correct.

The order of right-left presentations of the correct stimulus was varied according to a pre-determined schedule so set up as to attempt to avoid favoring spatial habits. Each stimulus presentation was allowed to stand until the animal had made the correct response, or until the animal had made four repetitive errors on any one trial. In the latter case the correct card was removed after the fifth successive wrong jump, and the animal was allowed to jump through the open window to food. Each incorrect response was recorded as an error, thus the maximum number of errors an animal was allowed to make on any one trial was five. This arbitrarily and artificially decreased the total number of errors for the animals, but we were not, in this instance, primarily interested in the learning scores of the animals, and felt justified in adopting any procedure which would speed up the original learning of the discrimination. The same procedure was used, of course, for all the animals in this experiment.

On the very next day after the animals of Group I had met the criterion of mastery described above, the individuals of Sub-group I*a* were given the test discrimination between cards 'A' and 'C' (Fig. 2, 'Test'); while the rats of Sub-group I*b* were given the test discrimination between cards 'B' and 'D' (Fig. 2, 'Test'). In these test situations a choice of either of the cards of the pair was 'correct' and was rewarded equally. These test trials, also consisting of ten per day, were continued until the animal again met a criterion of consistency, *i.e.*, until he had chosen the same card, or the same side for at least 18 out of any twenty consecutive trials.

*Group II* (n = 23). This group was given the 'easy' discrimination. After the preliminary training these animals were started on their discrimination problems, and here also the animals were sub-divided. For Sub-group II*a* (eleven rats), stimulus-card 'A' was the positive stimulus and card 'E,' the negative: for Sub-group II*b* (twelve rats) stimulus-card 'B' was the positive stimulus, and card 'E,' the negative (Fig. 3). For Group II, as for Group I, the animals were run on the training schedule until they had mastered their discriminations and were then given the test series. The rats of Sub-group II*a* were given the test-discrimination between cards 'A' and 'C,' while the animals of Sub-group II*b* were tested with cards 'B' and 'D.' Thus the animals of Group II were given the same tests given the animals of Group I.

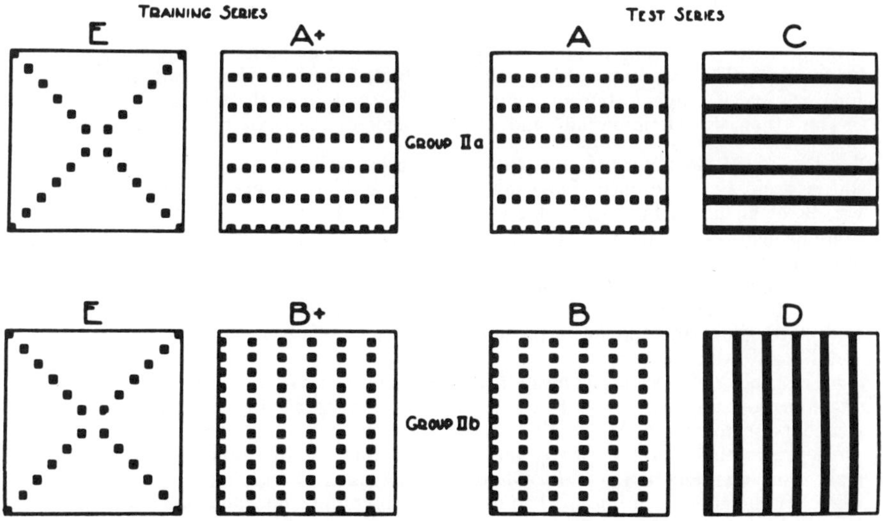


Fig. 3

The distribution of the discrete block squares on the stimuli cards used, and the test series, are such, we believe, as to provide for an adequate test of our experimental question. Considering first the cards used for the original training of Group I, we see that we have there two stimuli patterns of such a nature as to permit the operation of a definite autochthonous principle of organization—the principle of proximity (if such a principle is at all applicable to the perceptual process of the rat). It will be seen that any black square on card 'A' is nearer its neighbor to the right or to the left, than to its neighboring square above or below it. Just the reverse is true of the distribution of the squares on card 'B.'[2] In other words the principle of proximity would require that the squares on card 'A' be organized in a series of *horizontal* groupings, and card 'B,' in a series of *vertical* groupings. That this is what actually occurs in the perceptual process of the rat has already been shown (for cards with somewhat different dimensions) in a preliminary experiment (Krechevsky, 1938a). However, since the same kind of data will be available from this experiment, we shall reserve a more detailed discussion of this point until later in this report.

Further, not only are cards 'A' and 'B' of such a nature as to *permit* the formation of horizontal and vertical groupings (*i.e.*, permitting the principle of proximity to function), but, most importantly for the purposes of our experimental question, the *'A'—'B' discrimination situation* is one which *'forces'* such a grouping. Since both cards 'A' and 'B' are equal in all characteristics such as brightness values, number of discrete black squares, etc., the animal, if he is to discriminate at all between the two cards, must make such a discrimination on the basis of the differences in the spatial distribution of the black squares.[3] We have here, to repeat, *a discrimination situation* which forces discrimination in terms of a specific kind of perceptual grouping of the discrete stimuli on cards 'A' and 'B.'

If we consider now the stimuli cards used in the discrimination training given Group II, we find an altogether different situation. The positive cards 'A' and 'B' are identical with the positive cards used for Group I, and so, assuming the operation of the principle of proximity, we might expect a horizontal-vertical grouping for these cards, *but*, the negative stimuli-cards in these latter cases (Card 'E') differ from the positive cards, in at least *three* respects. That is, the animals of Group II could learn the discrimination problem set them either on the basis of the relative brightnesses of the positive and negative cards (Card 'E' having more white surface than card 'A' or 'B'), on the basis of the total number of black squares on each card (Cards 'A' and 'B' having more black squares than card 'E'), or on the basis of the different organizations possible in the two cards (Cards 'A' and 'B' giving a horizontal and vertical grouping respectively, and card 'E,' a set of crossing diagonal groupings). Any one of these discriminations would be 'correct.' The important thing here is that the *discrimination situation* does *not* force any specific organization or grouping for the solution of the problem.[4]

This, then, is the important and crucial difference between the two groups. For

[2] The actual dimensions for the stimuli cards are as follows: For both cards the black squares were ¼ × ¼ inch. For card 'A' the horizontal distance between the squares was ¼ of an inch, the vertical distance, ¾ of an inch. For card 'B,' the reverse relationship held. For cards 'C' and 'D,' the solid lines were ¼ of an inch in width, and were separated from each other by ¾ of an inch.

[3] The possibility of the animal's discriminating on the basis of extraneous cues peculiar to the specific cards used, was more or less eliminated by using different sets of cards throughout the training experiment. That is, we had alternate sets of 'A' cards and 'B' cards which were used.

[4] This does not necessarily mean that the animals of Group II could master their discrimination problem without making some sort of perceptual organization of the stimuli presented them. We could very well rephrase the differences between the two problem situations for the two groups by saying that for the animals of Group I to make the discrimination a vertical-horizontal grouping would have to be achieved, where for the animals of Group II to make their discrimination *some other visual grouping* (perhaps a more homogeneous one) would suffice. In other words, it isn't at all a question of visual organization being necessary for the rats of Group I and unnecessary for the rats of Group II, but simply one specific kind of organization being necessary for the animals of Group I and *another kind* of organization being adequate for Group II.

Group I the principle of Proximity *must* work, if the problem is to be solved, and for Group II, the principle of proximity need not operate in order for the rats to solve the problem. The next step in the procedure, as has been indicated, is to test the resulting perception of cards 'A' and 'B' for the two groups.

Observation of the patterns on test cards 'C' and 'D' (the two cards opposed to the positive cards used in the original training series for both groups of animals) at once reveals that what we have here is a *completed* or more perfect form of the grouping which would result from the operation of the 'forces of attraction' between the scattered squares on cards 'A' and 'B' respectively, if the principle of proximity did apply to the perceptual process of the rat. That is, where we have the possibility of perceiving the squares on card 'A' as consisting of a series of horizontal discontinuous groups, on card 'C' we have an actual and easily perceived series of horizontal lines.

The three following sets of results might appear on the test trials. (1) The animal might prefer the original card ('A' or 'B') to the new card ('C' or 'D'); (2) The animal might show *no* preference between the two cards, taking 'A' or 'C,' for instance, indiscriminately; (3) The animal might prefer the 'more perfect' card to the original card, *i.e.*, taking card 'C' in preference to card 'A.' If any rat should make the first type of response, we could then only say that some sort of grouping did take place (for Group I) but the 'forces of attraction' were not of such a nature as to permit of a shifting from the original card to the 'more perfect one,' *i.e.*, the rat still perceived the black squares on Card 'A' as discrete black squares. In the case of the rats of Group II, we could say one of two things, either their perception of card 'A' was identical with the perception of the rats of Group I, *i.e.*, they did group the squares in a series of horizontal lines, or else, the rats of Group II never did group the squares in that manner and had learned the discrimination between their stimuli on some other basis (with some other groupings) and therefore on the test trials preferred the known positive card to a 'strange' and unfamiliar card.

If the rats should make the second type of response (*i.e.*, showing no preference) then we could more certainly say that the animals *had* organized the squares into horizontal and vertical groupings and were therefore reacting indiscriminately to either card, but that here, also, the 'forces of attraction' generated by the operation of the principle of proximity were not enough to cause a preference for the 'more perfect' horizontal groupings as opposed to the original stimuli cards.

Finally, if the animals gave the third type of response (*i.e.*, showed a preference for cards 'C' and 'D' as opposed to cards 'A' and 'B') we could say much more than that. We could, it seems to us, conclude that not only do the forces of attraction among the squares operate in accordance with the principle of proximity, but that these forces thus generated, are of such a nature and of such a strength as to make for a perception which results in the preference of the organism for a stimulus-complex where the discontinuous members in fact coalesce as opposed to a stimulus-complex where the members are still, in some degree, discontinuous.

To summarize: Three types of response are possible in the test situation, and each of these types result from different perceptual processes. A comparison, therefore, of the responses of the rats in the two groups should enable us to say something about the effect of different discrimination-situations on the perception of a single member of the pair to be discriminated between. Should the perception of card 'A' (or 'B') be similar for both groups, then we would be forced to conclude that the perceptual process was for the most part conditioned by the autochthonous organizational factor of proximity; on the other hand, should we find a difference in the perceptions of the two groups, we would be forced to conclude that the autochthonous factor of proximity, in this case, is insufficient to account for the perceptual process.

## *DATA AND DISCUSSION*

It will be remembered that each of the two groups was split into two subgroups, in order to control the factor of a possible horizontal or vertical preference on the part of the animals. In making the following comparisons between the two major groups, we shall combine the results of each sub-group within each larger group, hoping thus to equate, in each group, for any possible preference difference. It might be pointed out, however, that no very decided preference for either 'A' or 'B' was discovered to exist, and for most of the measures Sub-group I*a*, for example, differs very little from Sub-group I*b*. A more complete analysis of the data in this respect will be made later (see appendix A) when the various measures will be more meaningful. In the following discussion, therefore, when we refer to the behavior of Group I with card 'A,' we are really referring to the combined results of the behavior of the animals of Group I*a* and I*b* with card 'A' and card 'B.' The same procedure will be used for Group II.

Considering now the initial learning records of the two groups we see immediately that the two discrimination problems differed in some very obvious respects. In the first place the discrimination problem for Group I proved to be a more difficult one to master than did the discrimination problem for Group II. This is true, however, if we limit ourselves to the criteria of total trials and 'initial' errors. The criteria of 'repetitive' errors and total errors seem to tell a different story. Let us first confine our discussion to the trials and initial-error scores. Where the animals of Group I took 164.2 trials and made 60.04 initial errors before mastery, Group II required less than half that number of trials (67.8) and made a little more than half that number of initial errors (31.70) (Table 1). Considering now the number of repetitive errors made, we find that Group II made many more such errors than did Group I, with the result that when we add the repetitive errors to the initial errors for both groups, the difference in favor of Group I is cut down considerably, and no reliable difference seems to exist. This apparent internal inconsistency in the performance scores of the two groups is definitely explained and becomes significantly meaningful for our analysis when we consider the following facts. (1) It will be remembered that as part of the standard preliminary training on the Lashley jumping-stand the animals of both groups were trained to jump through a white card as opposed to a black card. This

TABLE 1
LEARNING DATA FOR GROUPS I AND II

| | *Trials* | *Initial Errors* | *Repetitive Errors* | *Total Errors* | *Ave. Errors Trials 1-20* |
|---|---|---|---|---|---|
| Group I | 164.2 | 60.04 | 50.9 | 110.13 | 39.9 |
| Group II | 97.8 | 31.70 | 77.9 | 109.60 | 75.9 |
| Difference | 96.4 | 28.34 | 27.0 | .53 | −36.0 |
| DIFF. / $\sigma$ Difference | 9.62 | 8.91 | 4.25 | <1.0 | 8.91 |

was done in order to familiarize the animals with jumping through cards. But this training actually teaches the animal more than how to jump through cards, it trains him to react *positively* to the *brighter* of two stimuli. Now, when the animals of Group I, after this preliminary discrimination training, are presented with the experimental card (*i.e.*, when they start on their 'real' discrimination), this specific preliminary discrimination training can have very little influence on the distribution of their choices between cards 'A' and 'B,' since both these cards are equally bright. On the other hand, the situation is entirely different for the animals of Group II. In this latter case, as was pointed out above, the cards 'A' and 'E' differ from each other not only in the pattern or organization of their discontinuous stimuli, but also in brightness, *i.e.*, card 'E' is brighter than card 'A.' Thus, when the animals of Group II start in on their experimental discrimination, the distribution of their choices will be influenced by their preliminary discrimination training in such a manner as to make for a large number of incorrect responses, *i.e.*, they will, it can be expected, jump toward the brighter of the two cards (toward 'E') which in this case is the incorrect one. We thus have a situation where the animals of Group II would make many more errors than the animals of Group I at the very beginning of the regular training series. (2) In a previous experiment it was shown that for the Lashley jumping-stand, the first adjustment the animal has to make when attacking a discrimination problem, is that of learning not to repeat a response when it proves to be incorrect (Krechevsky, 1938). That is, at the beginning of his training on a discrimination problem the rat shows a very strong tendency to repeat his immediately previous jump, whether it had proved to be correct or not. This repetitive tendency persists with a considerable degree of strength for at least two days (twenty trials) after which it seems to be given up. It was shown in the experiment just referred to that half of all the repetitive errors made during a sixteen day training period were made during the first two days. (3) It is obvious that a 'repetitive' error cannot be made until an 'initial' error is made, and therefore if in a given situation some factor exists which would make for a large number of initial errors during the first two days, a correspondingly large number of repetitive (and therefore total) errors would result—much larger than in a situation where no factor 'forcing' initial errors were present. These two situations are exactly what we have here with our two groups. The former situation exists for our Group II and the latter for our Group I. A closer consideration of our data bears out this analysis. Where the animals of Group I made but 31.5 percent of all their errors during the first two training days, the animals of Group II made 69.3 percent of all their errors during the same period. In terms of average errors, the rats of Group I made an average of 39.9 errors during the first two days and the rats of Group II made an average of 75.9—or almost twice as many. And yet, despite this initial handicap the rats of Group II learned the discrimination much more rapidly (see trial scores) than did the rats of Group I. All of this leads to the following description of the learning processes for the two groups. The animals of Group I started off their experimental training knowing very little about the discriminanda involved and found it relatively difficult to finally solve the problem presented to them. The rats of Group II, on the other hand, were presented with what proved to be a simple discrimination to solve, but at the very start were prejudiced in favor of the brighter (and wrong) card. They therefore had to first 'unlearn' this discrimination, but once having learned to reverse the significates of the discriminanda, they proceeded very rapidly to master the discrimination. The very fact that the rats of Group II did respond to the brightness difference existing between cards 'A' and 'E' is of significance for us, since it immediately suggests that the differentia of brightness in this case was of behavioral importance for the rats and therefore they *could*, presumably, learn the 'A'–'E' discrimination on that basis alone (*i.e.*, on the basis of this simple organization) and never need achieve an horizontal-vertical organization of the two cards. This fact, of course, merely establishes the *possibility* of such a discrimination taking place, and we have yet to demonstrate that that is actually what occurred.

We are now ready for a consideration of the data obtained from the test trials.

It will be remembered that the animals were run in the test situation for ten trials per day until they had established some sort of well-defined preference, either for one of the two cards or for a response based on position, *i.e.*, to the right or to the left. In analysing the resulting records we have used four possible measures. The first measure of preference, and the one which in all test situations similar to the one used here is perhaps the most significant, is *the very first choice* made by the animal when presented with the test cards for the first time. The second measure we considered was based on the total number of choices made during the first day of the test trials, *i.e.*, the *first ten choices*. It so happened that some animals started off with one preference and about the second day, for one reason or another, shifted their preference, with the result that those animals which shifted their preference were continued until the second preference seemed to be established. This would mean that some animals were given more 'test trials' than others. Actually it might be argued that after a number of trials, say ten trials, we no longer had a significant preference-test situation, since the animals would have learned, by that time, that a certain response was rewarded and would be choosing on that basis rather than on a 'pure preference' basis. This would mean that our measures which took into account the performances of the rats after the first day were not as reliable indicators of preference as the other measures. With this analysis we would tend to agree, and we would put more faith in the two measures described above than in our following two measures, but all possible measures will be considered in analyzing our data. The third measure used, then, was based on all the responses of the animal until he had established some one habit 'preference.' The fourth measure is given in terms of the habit itself which was finally established by the rat. In this measure we ask the question "Disregarding the actual distribution of choices, how did the animal *finally* end up, did he establish, as a final pattern of response, an 'A'-positive response, a 'C'-positive response, or a spatial response?"

The data for all these measures are given in Table 2, and the most significant measures are summarized in graphic form in Fig. 4. In the second column of Table 2 are given the total number of 'C' card choices made on the very first test trial for both groups (Measure 1). The difference between the groups for this measure is striking. Of the nineteen animals of Group I, seventeen chose the continuous lines (card 'C') and three, the discontinuous lines (card 'A'). Of the twenty-three animals in Group II, only three made the 'C' choice! In terms of percentages these data indicate that where 89.4 percent of the rats of Group I chose the 'C' card, only 13.0 percent of the animals of Group II did likewise. When it is recalled that for both groups the 'A' card had been the positive card in the training series, the high score of Group I is strikingly significant. It may be argued, we believe, that this one measure is sufficient to establish a real difference between the two groups, since the first choice, in any preference test, is probably the 'purest' preference indicator.

In the third column of Table 2 are given the data for the second measure used. Here the total number of 'C' card choices made by the animals during the first ten trials are presented. Again the rats of Group I show a decided preference for the 'C' card, where the animals of Group II show a preference for the 'A' card. For Group I, 81.1 percent of all the choices made were 'C' choices, whereas for Group II, only 34.4 percent

TABLE 2
TEST DATA FOR GROUPS I AND II*

| | *1st Choice* | *Trials 1-10* | *Total Trials* | *Final Preferences* | | |
|---|---|---|---|---|---|---|
| | | | | *Spat.* | 'A' | 'C' |
| Group I | 89.4 | 81.1(3.62) | 74.6(2.09) | 9 | 0 | 10 |
| Group II | 13.0 | 34.4(3.27) | 38.7(2.00) | 20 | 3 | 0 |
| Difference / DIFF. | 8.12 | 11.04 | 12.50 | | | |
| σ Difference | 76.4 | 46.7 | 35.9 | | | |

* The data in the first three columns represent the percentage of 'C' choices made by the animals.

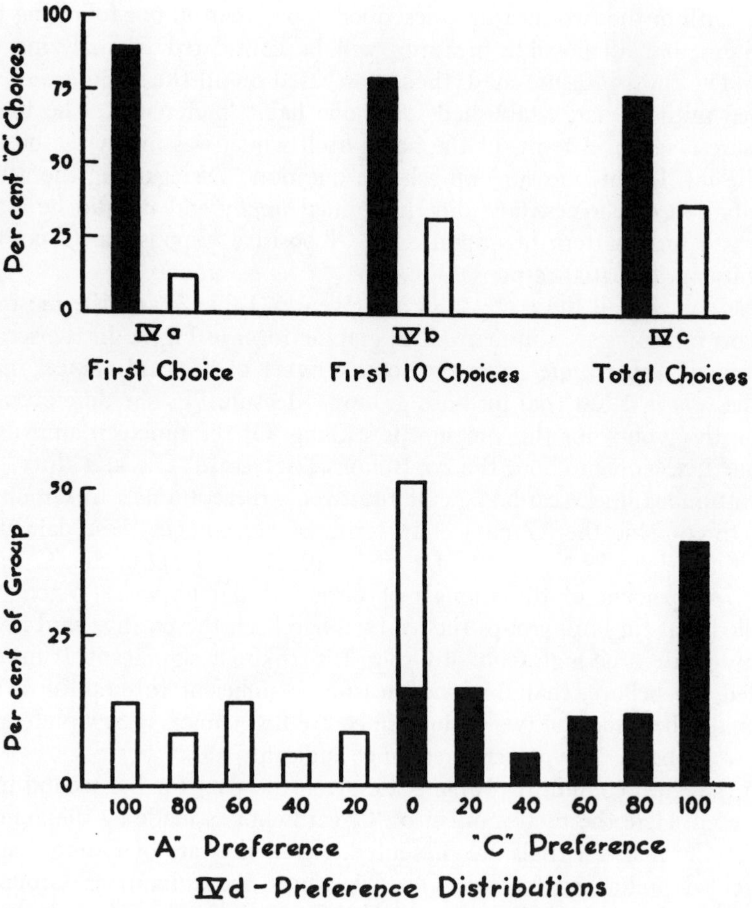


Fig. 4

were 'C' choices and the greater part of the choices (65.6 percent) were 'A' choices. The difference for 'C' choices between the two groups is thus 46.7 percent and that it is highly statistically reliable is indicated by a critical ratio of 11.04. In this connection we might ask another question. Granted that the difference between the two groups is a reliable one, is the preference of any one group reliably different from a zero preference? That is, are the scores of 81.1 percent for Group I and 34.4 percent for Group II, individually reliably different from a zero (or non-) preference score of 50 percent. Again referring to Table 2 we see that both these scores are reliably different from zero-preference (the figures in parentheses refer to the standard deviation of a 50 percent expectancy), and we therefore feel justified in concluding that the animals of Group I showed a real (statistically reliable) preference for Card 'C,' whereas the animals of Group II showed a real preference for card 'A.'[5] In the fourth column of Table 2 are given the data for the third measure used—the number of 'C' card choices for all the test trials. Again we find the same relationship between the two groups. Where 74.6 percent of all the choices made by the animals of Group I were choices of the 'C' card, only 38.7 percent of the Group II choices were to that card. This measure, of course, is not an independent measure, *i.e.*, it is highly correlated with our second measure, but is more inclusive. But here again the differences are reliable and each percentage taken by itself is reliably different from 50 percent. In the fifth column are presented the data for our final measure, the habit finally adopted by the animal. Again the same direction of differences between the two groups is noted. Nine animals of Group I ended up with position preferences, and ten animals with 'C' card preferences.[6] For Group II, there were twenty position preferences established and three 'A' card preferences.

Up to this point we have been considering only the *average* performance of each group for measures two and three. The difference between the two groups is much more striking when we make an analysis of the *individual* behavior of the animals. Doing that we find that *not a single animal of Group I showed even a slight preference of choices for the 'A' card and not a single animal of Group II showed even a slight preference for the 'C' card.* This is so whether we use the data from the second (1st ten trials) or the third (all the trials) measure. The distribution of the choices of the animals for the first ten trials are presented graphically in Fig. 4*d*. The scale on the abscissa ranges from 100 percent preference for the 'A' card (on the left of the scale) through zero preference (fifty-fifty choice) to a 100 percent preference for the 'C' card (on the right of the scale). The ordinate represents the percentage of animals in each group showing each indicated degree of preference. The black bars represent the scores of Group I and the white bars, the scores of Group II. Thus it can be seen that about 40 percent of the animals of Group I showed a hundred percent preference for the 'C' card, twelve percent showed an 80 percent preference, etc.; for the animals of Group II, about 14 percent showed a

[5] The following statistics were used in determining these reliabilities. The standard deviation of 50 percent for the total number of choices for Group I is 3.62 percent. That would mean that chance fluctuations from 50 percent would most probably not permit that percentage to go above 60.86 percent (*i.e.*, 50 percent plus three sigma of fifty percent). The actual obtained value was 81.1 percent, well above the limits indicated. Making a similar analysis for the choices of the animals of Group II, we find that the lower limit of a chance fluctuation from 50 percent would be 40.2, and the observed value was 34.4 percent.

[6] A number of these 'position' animals had started off with a 'C' preference, but during one trial or another would make a mis-step and fail to get through the 'C' card. They would then try the other side and from then on, persist in a spatial response to that side. It must be remembered that a spatial habit is much easier for the rat to establish than a habit based on a visual discrimination. The same thing occurred, of course, for the animals of Group II.

"hundred percent" preference for the 'A' card, ten percent showed an 80 percent preference for the 'A' card, etc., but no animal of Group I falls to the left of the preference scale (*i.e.*, the 'A'-preference side) and no animal of Group II falls to the right of the preference scale (*i.e.*, the 'C'-preference side).

On the basis then of all the measures used it appears that the animals of Group I, when presented on the test trials with a choice between the original card 'A' and a 'new' card 'C,' show a strong tendency to prefer the 'new' card 'C,' though some of the animals fail to show any preference whatsoever between the two cards. On the other hand it appears that when the same test is given to the animals of Group II, there is a strong tendency for the rats to prefer the original 'A' card while some of the rats show no preference between the two cards.

On the basis of our analysis of the three possible types of response in this test-situation (page 193) we would make the following interpretations concerning the perceptual processes of the two groups of rats resulting from stimulation by the 'A' card in the original training series. (1) *All* the animals of Group I organize the discontinuous visual stimuli on card 'A' according to the principle of proximity, very much after the fashion of the relationship observed in the perceptual behavior of the human being. (This interpretation is based on the fact that all the animals of this group displayed either the type 2 or type 3 response in the test trials.) (2) The perceptual process for *most* of the rats of Group I involve 'forces of attraction' between the discrete members of the visual group on card 'A' of such a nature as to cause the animals to prefer the continuous *gestalt* over that of the discontinuous *gestalt* even though the original training be on the discontinuous stimulus-complex. (This interpretation is based on the fact that most of the animals displayed the type 3 response in the test trials.) (3) *Some* of the rats of Group II also organize the discontinuous stimuli on card 'A' according to the principle of proximity. (This interpretation is also based on the fact that some of the Group II rats showed the Type 2 response in the test.) (4) Some of the rats *may* not have acquired this particular organization at all. (This interpretation is based on the fact that some of the rats gave the Type 1 response in the test.) (5) The perceptual processes of *none* of the rats of this group involved 'forces of attraction' of such a nature as to cause, in the test trials, a preference for the continuous *gestalt*.

It seems fairly conclusive, then, that the perceptual responses of the rats to the stimulus-complex 'A' differ for the two groups used in this experiment.

Returning now to the original questions asked in the Introduction we feel justified in making the following tentative answers.

1. Inasmuch as the positive stimulus cards for both groups were identical and yet the resulting perceptual response differed, we must answer

the first question posed by saying that the determining forces making for a particular sensory field are *not* to be found entirely within the sensory field, but instead it appears that some of the determining essential field-forces, in this case, derive from outside the given sensory field. This does not deny the existence of autochthonous organizing forces (actually the data of this experiment and the reasoning involved in our analysis *require* the existence of such factors) but it does deny their adequacy for explaining the 'looks of things' in this situation. Something else is required.

2. Since the only difference between our two groups was that of the difference between the two discrimination-situations and the resulting types of discrimination necessary, *i.e.*, in one case the situation was such as to make absolutely necessary a *particular* type of perceptual grouping and in the other case this was unnecessary, we might therefore say that only when the situation is such as to create a 'need' for a particular type of perceptual organization (as against other, and more simple, possible organizations) will that organization take place. And this 'need' derives, of course, from factors outside the sensory field—at least in part.

The word 'need' as used here is difficult to define clearly. That is a fault, perhaps, of the fact that the further we get away from the well-known and obvious 'needs,' such as the need for food, for sex, etc., the less clear-cut are our physiological correlates and the less clear-cut the behavior tests to be applied. We mean by this 'need' something like Tolman's 'subordinate goal.' That is, we are conceiving of a system of needs, an hierarchy of 'needs.' Let us assume that the first and fundamental need of the hungry rat in our problem situation is the need of food. The obtaining of food, if he is able to do so relatively immediately, he will do without making any other adjustments to the situation. The primary need of food can be satisfied without first satisfying other needs, *i.e.*, the need to be able to discriminate between lengths of path, position of correct paths, significates of certain visual stimuli, etc. If, however, he finds a barrier between himself and the food, other needs and other goals then and there become generated or begin to function. First there will be the need of making certain propositions about the consequences of certain responses to certain discriminanda, *i.e.*, he will begin to make 'hypotheses,' and just as the need for food immediately and intrinsically conditions the psychological forces affecting the animal, so the 'need' for determining the significates of certain visual discriminanda (in our situation) will immediately and intrinsically condition the so-called sensory field forces. Obviously the forces which will be generated by such a need (on the physiological level) are not the only forces which will condition the organization of the sensory field, there are other forces working at the same time and in an interdependent fashion—the so-called autochthonous forces of organization (also on the physiological level). Carrying our suggested analysis further we would then say that once this 'need' for discovering the significate of the discriminanda has been satisfied, one set of forces responsible for sensory organization no longer functions and further reorganizations of the field do not occur very readily. We would also have to assume that there exists an hierarchy of organizations, from the simpler, the more readily achieved to the more difficult. Thus, in our experiment, for Group II, one of the early, or more simple or more homogeneous organizations may have been that of 'many squares' versus 'few squares,' and it enabled the animal to satisfy the need of discovering the significates of the discriminanda involved and therefore the perception of card 'A' was a perception which might be described as an homogeneous organization or as 'a many squared card.' In the case of Group I a more articulated organization was necessary, since to perceive card 'A' as a 'many squared card' did not permit it to be differentiated from card 'B' and therefore did not satisfy the need involved. In this latter case, therefore, the need persisted until a 'working' perception did occur.

It seems to us that what we have been suggesting above, in a very loose manner perhaps, is the same sort of thing Tolman has been doing with his 'sign-*gestalt*.' The particular merit of Tolman's concept of 'sign-*gestalt*' lies in his continued and experimental insistence upon the interdependence of the forces we too often segregate under the two categories of 'motivation forces' (the forces Kurt Lewin works with, as well as Tolman) and 'perceptual organizing forces' (the forces which are the primary concern of the work of Köhler, Koffka, and Wertheimer). In very many cases both sets of forces operate simultaneously and on the same level. This does not mean, of course, that there are no cases where one set of forces is not the more significant or the more important set, but it does suggest that more experimental attention needs to be paid to the very many situations where both sets of forces are of equal and immediate importance.

At this point it may be of some value to compare the position we have just stated with the position of some *gestalt* psychologists.

Let us first state that it appears to us that there is no real or important difference involved, but that there may be a slight difference in emphasis. We pointed out in the Introduction that the general tendency of the *Gestalt* psychologist has been to maximize the importance of the organizing forces within the sensory field and to minimize the importance of possible outside forces. This kind of emphasis is, we believe, not necessarily due to a *theoretical* bias in favor of the importance of one kind of force as opposed to the other, but due, rather, to the choice of the *experimental problems*. That is, the type of problem the *Gestalt* psychologist has concerned himself with (excepting the work of Kurt Lewin and the work of Köhler with Apes) was one in which the 'organizing forces' were relatively more important than the 'motivational forces.' When, however, Köhler deals with psychological situations where 'motivational forces' could play a part, the interdependence of these two types of forces is very clearly recognized.[7] But, what we have been hoping to do with the analysis of the present experiment, is not merely to recognize that such forces must be dealt with in an interdependent fashion, but rather to experimentally define the specific interactions for at least one specific case. We have used a well-defined 'autochthonous principle of organization' and a fairly well-defined 'need situation' (a simple discrimination problem) and have investigated the inter-relations of the resulting forces. In other words we are suggesting the need for more experimental work which combines the 'motivational analyses' and the 'organizational analyses' with the hope that we shall then be able to arrive at certain well-defined and specific laws about the interrelations of the two types of forces under consideration here—laws as specific as the laws concerning the forces of organization or the 'need forces' of Lewin and Tolman.

## *SUMMARY AND CONCLUSIONS*

To test the assumption that under certain conditions the perceptual process of the rat is conditioned by forces of motivational origin as well as by certain 'autochthonous forces of organization,' an experimental situation was so set up as to present two groups of animals with two different discrimination situations, differing in difficulty of discrimination but having identical positive stimuli. In one case the positive stimulus could be differentiated from the negative stimulus only when one particular visual organization could be achieved by the subject; in the other case, the positive stimulus could be discriminated from the negative one without this particular organization taking place. Upon testing for the resulting perception of the positive stimulus it was discovered that the rats trained in the former situation did achieve the organization to be expected from the operation of the principle of proximity (used as the autochthonous organizational process in this experiment), whereas in the latter case a different (and perhaps more simple) organization had occurred. On the basis of the analysis thus made, the following conclusions are suggested:

1. Under certain conditions of need, such conditions being induced by the fundamental needs of the organism and conditioned by the specific

[7] In discussing some of his experiments with the Apes, Köhler writes, "After a short while we see the chimpanzee looking around for a stick. Evidently this attitude is not less determined in the total situation than was the direct tendency toward food. But again this new attitude has remarkable consequences upon the objects of the field. . . . The tree with its branches . . . may for a long time remain 'one thing,' too much a unit optically to let the functional value of a stick enter the branches, since these are not seen as optically real parts—at least by the chimpanzee. If finally this unit is destroyed under the pressure of the subjective attitude of 'seeking a stick,' we certainly have a case of a unit changed by the subjective attitude," (Köhler, 1925, p. 723).

problem situation and significate-attributes of the discriminanda, the rat tends to group discontinuous visual stimuli according to the principle of proximity.

2. The perceptual process, under those conditions of need, involves the operation of 'forces of attraction' between the members of a visual group of such a nature as to make the rat prefer the continuous *gestalt* over that of the discontinuous grouping even though the original training be on the discontinuous stimulus-complex.

3. When these conditions of need are not present, or present with lesser force, the data seem to indicate that the organization to be expected on the basis of the operation of the principle of proximity may not take place, under the conditions of our experiment.

4. The perceptual process which does occur, under the conditions of absence of specific need, is not of such a nature as to involve 'forces of attraction' between the members of a visual group which would cause the animal to prefer the continuous *gestalt* over that of the discontinuous one. Instead, it is suggested that the perception achieved may involve a less articulated, more homogeneous, organization.

## *APPENDIX*

The data for the comparisons between the sub-groups, I*a* vs. I*b*, and II*a* vs. II*b*, are presented in Tables 3 through 6. A consideration of the data there presented immediately shows the equivalence of the sub-groups for equivalent conditions, in all respects, but one. That is, it apparently mattered very little whether the correct stimulus were card 'A' or card 'B.' The learning time (in terms of trials or errors) and the test results were equivalent. The only statistically reliable difference is that obtaining between Sub-group I*a* and I*b* with respect to the percentage of 'C' choices over the entire testing period. Here the difference of 19.1 percent has a critical ratio of 4.88—obviously a reliable difference. However, it should be noted that *both* these sub-groups showed a real preference for the 'C' card. That is, the difference is not one of direction between the two groups, but one of degree of preference. Just what this means, if anything significant, we are not prepared to say, in the light of the fact that the other measures of preference for these two subgroups do not differ at all. Obviously, what happened was that the animals of Sub-group I*a* started off with a decided preference for the 'C' card, but then, for one reason or another, switched to a position preference. This may be a result of some uncontrolled condition existing during the training period for this group (each sub-group was run at different times).

In general, however, we find no significant difference between the two

TABLE 3
LEARNING DATA FOR GROUPS I*a* AND I*b*

| | *Trials* | *Initial Errors* | *Repetitive Errors* | *Errors Total* |
|---|---|---|---|---|
| Group I*a* | 167.5 | 62.1 | 54.2 | 116.3 |
| Group I*b* | 161.8 | 59.2 | 48.6 | 107.8 |
| Difference | 5.7 | 2.9 | 5.6 | 8.5 |

TABLE 4
TEST DATA FOR GROUPS I*a* AND I*b*

| | *1st Choice* | *Trials 1-10* | *Total Trials* | *Final Preferences* | | |
|---|---|---|---|---|---|---|
| | | | | *Spat.* | 'A' | 'C' |
| Group I*a* | 87.5 | 76.3 | 65.5 | 5 | 0 | 3 |
| Group I*b* | 90.9 | 84.5 | 84.6 | 4 | 0 | 7 |
| Difference | 3.4 | 8.2 | 19.1 | | | |

TABLE 5
LEARNING DATA FOR GROUPS II*a* AND II*b*

| | *Trials* | *Initial Errors* | *Repetitive Errors* | *Total Errors* |
|---|---|---|---|---|
| Group II*a* | 68.2 | 33.1 | 81.4 | 114.5 |
| Group II*b* | 67.5 | 30.3 | 74.8 | 105.1 |
| Difference | .7 | 2.8 | 6.6 | 9.4 |

TABLE 6
TEST DATA FOR GROUPS II*a* AND II*b*

| | *1st Choice* | *Trials 1-10* | *Total Trials* | *Final Preferences* | | |
|---|---|---|---|---|---|---|
| | | | | *Spat.* | 'A' | 'C' |
| Group II*a* | 9.0 | 34.6 | 35.5 | 9 | 2 | 0 |
| Group II*b* | 16.6 | 34.2 | 34.2 | 11 | 1 | 0 |
| Difference | 7.6 | .2 | 1.3 | | | |

sub-groups within each group, and this fact not only justifies our combining the two sub-groups for the major comparisons made in this report, but adds to the reliability of the differences between the two major groups, since each sub-group can be considered a repetition of the experiment, with different rats, at different times, but with the same results.

## REFERENCES

Koffka, K. *Principles of gestalt psychology*, New York: Harcourt Brace & Co., 1935.

Köhler, W. An aspect of *gestalt* psychology, *Journal of Genetic Psychology*, 1925, 32, 691.

Köhler, W. *Gestalt psychology*, New York: Liveright, 1929.

Krechevsky, I. A study of the continuity of the problem-solving process, *Psychological Review*, 1938, *45*, 107-133.

Krechevsky, I. A note on the perception of linear *gestalten* in the rat, *Journal of Genetic Psychology*, 1938, 52, 241.

Tolman, E. C. Gestalt and sign-gestalt, *Psychological Review*, 1933, *40*, 391.

*The really surprising finding in Krechevsky's experiment was that the animals in group I which were trained to respond to the "rows" (A) or "columns" (B) pattern as a positive figure subsequently preferred the smooth horizontal (C) or vertical (D) stripes. Every conventional theory of discrimination learning which talks of the "cues" in the positive and negative stimuli and the conditioning of responses to those cues (e.g., Hull, 1952; Spence, 1936) would surely predict that no new stimulus array can be more positive than the array which was positive in training. Finding a case of "anomalous transfer" where a new array is more positive than the training-positive pattern is, one would think, very strong evidence that the conventional so-called "continuity" theories must be wrong. From that point of view, it is surprising that Krechevsky's finding did not lead to further investigations along the same lines for nearly thirty years, and that in the meantime the continuity type of approach to discrimination learning remained the dominant theoretical position. (For a more extensive discussion of this point, see Dodwell, 1961.)*

*Although Krechevsky argues that the important difference between the transfer performance of his Group I (which displayed the "anomalous transfer" in preferring smooth stripes to the training-positive patterns) and Group II (which showed no anomalous transfer) lies in the conditions of training, and that the autochthonous[1] forces of organization in a sensory field cannot account completely for the result. To quote Krechevsky's own words: ". . . the determining forces making for a particular sensory field are not to be found entirely within the sensory field, but instead it appears that*

[1] The dictionary definition of autochthonous is: "formed or occurring in place where found." The forces postulated by the *Gestalt* psychologists were supposed to be innate, sufficient unto themselves, and not in need of explanation in terms of factors outside the immediate situation.

some of the determining essential field-forces, in this case, derive from outside the given sensory field" (from the Discussion, p. 519 in the original). An alternative, and perhaps simpler possibility is that rats in group II learned to discriminate in terms of an obvious difference in brightness between their training cards (E and A, or E and B), so that the pattern differences become irrelevant. At all events, the anomalous transfer found in Group I is by far the most interesting result, and the one that merits more discussion.

In the first place, one might argue that the anomalous transfer was not genuine transfer at all: it might have been due to a preference for smooth stripes which had nothing to do with the training to which the rats had been subjected. In that case might one not expect the same preferences in Group II? As was pointed out, the results for group II are confounded with a possible brightness discrimination, so are really uninterpretable as far as pattern discrimination is concerned. Even if the group II rats also had an initial preference for smooth stripes rather than interrupted stripes, this would only tend to show up when the animals were definitely responding in terms of contours and patterns rather than brightness. Another possibility—admittedly rather unlikely—is that the rats in Group I were responding to card C as a novel shape. Even though the possibility seems unlikely, it cannot be ruled out, except by experimental test.

Second, one could argue that if the anomalous transfer from the training-positive shape is a genuine property of the rat's visual organization, it should be possible to demonstrate an analogous effect with the training-negative shape. What should one expect the effect to be? I argued (before doing the experiment) that if there is an organizational, or coding, principle that makes horizontal stripes (C) more positive than "rows" (A) for rats trained with "rows" positive vs. "columns" (B) negative, then that same principle should make smooth vertical stripes "more negative" than "columns" (B). If that were true, animals trained on $A^+B^-$, and then given a transfer test in which the choice is between B and vertical stripes, should prefer B, the training-negative shape! Such a result would be even more surprising than the anomalous transfer with the positive shape, since it would mean that the animals preferred a "negative" pattern, which they had been consistently punished for choosing during training, to a new pattern which is to us (and to the rat) readily distinguishable from the negative one. Yet that is the way the experiment turns out: rats do show anomalous transfer with the negative pattern. That is to say they prefer it to stripes shown in the same orientation. This result was first reported some years ago (Dodwell, 1965) and has subsequently been replicated a number of times (Dodwell, 1970c). Fortunately the negative anomalous transfer effect can be used to eliminate the argument about novel patterns, because if in the positive case the choice of stripes had been a novelty effect, we should expect the same choice for stripes in the negative orientation too.

Krechevsky appealed to forces of organization in the sensory field to explain his anomalous transfer findings. I got interested in the topic because they can be explained in terms of the coding model described in the previous part (p. 114), which also predicts the negative effect. Clearly a model which codes for horizontal and vertical contour extents will yield stronger or more redundant signals for smooth stripes than for interrupted stripes like those in the "rows" and "columns" patterns. This sort of explanation of the transfer effects is given in more detail in the next paper by Dodwell, Litner and Niemi, but the postulated basis for contour detection is identified with coding principles which have been discovered by neurophysiologists. However, the full force of this identification will become evident only in Hubel and Wiesel's paper in Part IV.

# Anomalous Transfer Effects Following Pattern Discrimination Training in the Squirrel Monkey

P. C. DODWELL, J. S. LITNER, AND R. R. NIEMI

*Two squirrel monkeys* (Samiri scuireus) *were trained to discriminate between two patterns that were identical, except that their orientations differed by* 90 *deg. In subsequent transfer tests (a) the training-positive shape was shown with a novel shape having the same "positive" orientation, and (b) the training-negative shape was shown with the same novel shape in the "negative" orientation. Transfer choices were anomalous; the novel shape was preferred to the training-positive shape, and the training-negative shape was preferred to the novel "negative" shape. These results are held to be a function of the contour-coding processes of the mammalian visual system.*

Normally, one expects an organism that has been trained to discriminate between two stimuli to choose the training-positive stimulus if it is shown in a subsequent transfer pair or to avoid the training-negative stimulus if it is shown. Relational learning or transpositional discrimination, may be an exception to this generalization under some conditions, but in these

Reprinted from *Psychonomic Science*, 1970.

cases, the dimension along which the transposition occurs is usually unitary and easily identified. Krechevsky (1938) discovered an anomalous transfer situation, in which a novel shape was preferred to the training-positive shape but where the relevant stimulus dimension (if any) was not obvious. He trained rats to discriminate between square arrays of small squares arranged in "rows" or in "columns," as shown in Fig. 1, i.e., the horizontal center-to-center distance between squares is smaller than the vertical center-to-center distance in the "row" array, and vice versa for "columns." A group of rats trained with "rows" positive was subsequently presented with a choice between rows and an equally bright pattern of smooth horizontal stripes, and reliably preferred the stripes. Another group trained with "columns" positive subsequently preferred smooth vertical stripes to "columns." Dodwell (1965) replicated this finding (also with rats) and, moreover, showed that transfer preferences were anomalous with respect to the negative shape; rats trained with "rows" negative subsequently preferred "rows" to horizontal stripes and similarly for "columns" and vertical stripes. He also showed that the transfers were a genuine consequence of discrimination training and could not be explained in terms of either novelty or initial preferences between "rows," "columns," and stripes. The same effect has been demonstrated in squirrels and is sufficiently surprising to make it worth finding out whether or not it occurs in a primate visual system.

## *METHOD*

Two young squirrel monkeys (*Samiri scuireus*) were used, maintained on a 23-h food-deprivation schedule, being fed daily after the experimental session. The discrimination apparatus was a modification of the suspended monkey restraint platform described by Thompson, Seal, & Bloom (1959). The S faced a black plywood panel, in the center of which were two 3 x 2½ in. clear Plexiglas panels. Stimuli were back-projected onto a milk-glass screen ¾ in. behind the panels. A dipper-type feeder was placed immediately in front of and below the stimulus panels, and both panels and feeder could be reached comfortably with either hand. A response consisted of reaching out and touching one of the panels, a force of about 10 g being enough to activate a microswitch at the base of the panel. This turned on a light indicating to the E which panel had been chosen (at no time was he visible to the S during the experiment). Ss were shaped to press one panel, but not both, when the projector was turned on and the panels were illuminated. Such undesirable behavior as panel pressing between trials, or pressing both simultaneously, was effectively suppressed by introducing a time-out of 2 min following such behavior. Otherwise, the

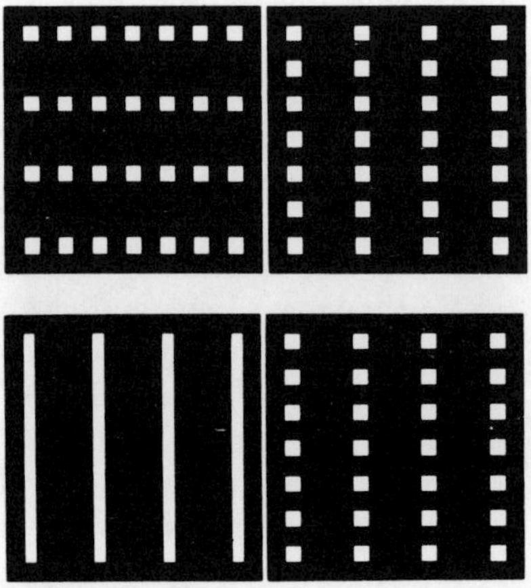

Fig. 1. (a) The training patterns, called "rows" and "columns." (b) A transfer pair; "columns" and vertical stripes.

intertrial interval was 30 sec, and food reinforcement was used. One S developed a side preference that was shaped out before further training.

Following shaping, "initial preference" tests were run without reinforcement. One S was presented with choice between "rows" and horizontal stripes of the same overall brightness, the other with choice between "columns" and vertical stripes, each for 40 trials. On the next day, the procedure was reversed so that the first S was presented with a choice between "columns" and vertical stripes, the second S with a choice between "rows" and horizontal stripes. There were no reliable initial preferences. During these preference sessions, and in all subsequent sessions, stimuli were randomized for side of presentation under the restriction that no stimulus was ever presented more than three times consecutively on the same side. Nonreinforcement of the preference trials led to sluggish responding, so both Ss were reshaped for 2 days before discrimination training began.

Discrimination training consisted of 40 presentations per day on the "rows" vs "columns" discrimination, the "rows" being positive (reinforced) for S1 and the "columns" positive for S2. The only punishment was a 2-min time-out after an incorrect choice; otherwise the intertrial interval was 30 sec, as in shaping, and reinforcement was given on 80% of correct trials (one in every five correct choices, chosen randomly, was not reinforced). S1 reached a very stringent criterion of 40/40 correct on 2 consecutive days after 340 trials, S2 after 520 trials.

Transfer tests were administered on the 2 days after S2 had reached criterion. On the 1st transfer day, the test was between "rows" and horizontal stripes, and on the 2nd day, it was between "columns" and vertical stripes; thus, S1 had a transfer test on its positive shape first, followed the next day by the test on its negative shape, and vice versa for S2. On both transfer days, each S was given 100 trials, which consisted of the original discrimination training procedure, with the 20 transfer tests (without reinforcement) substituted for the previously unreinforced 20% of correct choices. This was done in order to disrupt the original discrimination as little as possible and to insure vigorous responding to the transfer shapes.

## *RESULTS*

S1 preferred horizontal stripes to "rows" 19/20 times ($p < .01$ on an exact binomial test, with $p = q = \frac{1}{2}$) and "columns" to vertical stripes 18/20 times ($p < .01$), thus demonstrating very reliable anomalous transfer to both positive and negative training shapes. S2, on the other hand, preferred horizontal stripes to "rows" (its negative shape) on 13/20 trials (nonsignificant) but preferred vertical stripes to "columns" 19/20 times ($p < .01$) on the following day. S2 thus showed a very reliable positive anomalous effect but no negative effect, although responding to the negative shape was at a much higher level than on ordinary training trials. Both Ss maintained their discrimination between the training stimuli at nearly 100% correct on the transfer days.

It is surprising that one S should show such strong negative anomalous transfer, and the other S none. The order of presentation of transfer tests was balanced; S1 had transfer tests with the positive shape, followed by tests with the negative shape on the next day, but S2 had tests on the negative shape first. To find out whether or not this was relevant to S2's failure to show negative anomalous transfer, both Ss were retrained to criterion after several days' rest, and the transfer tests were administered in reversed order for the two monkeys. This time, S1 failed to show negative anomalous transfer when the transfer test with the negative shape was given first, but S2 did show it, and again, both showed reliable positive anomalous transfer. To make quite certain that this order effect was real, the whole procedure was repeated again, and with the same result: Provided transfer on the positive shape preceded the negative, the latter showed the anomalous effect but not otherwise. It is as if the system responsible for the anomalies has to be "primed" on the positive transfer before it will respond fully on the negative.

## *DISCUSSION*

How may the anomalous transfer effects be explained? They can be explained by a contour coding system that sums horizontal and vertical components in a display independently and evaluates the sums in a central "recognizor" (Dodwell, 1964), but they can also be interpreted in terms of what we know of the contour coding properties of retinal receptive field organization in the mammalian visual system. Hubel and Wiesel (1962, 1968) have found neurons in the visual cortex of cats and monkeys that fire selectively for contours or edges in particular orientations (and positions, in the case of their "simple" fields). These units not only detect contour orientation, but also detect contour extent, in the sense that a unit's output increases as the length of contour in the preferred orientation is increased, up to a limit set by the size of its receptive field on the retina.

Consider now the population of cortical units that fire selectively for horizontal contours (Set H) and those that fire selectively for vertical contours (Set V). Some members of each set will be activated by the "row" figure, but the H units will tend to have a stronger output. The reason for this is that the small squares in each row are closely spaced and will tend to produce summation of excitation in the horizontal fields. Summation of excitation in vertical receptive fields for the "row" pattern, on the other hand, will be much less, since contours are more widely separated in the vertical dimension. In fact, if the summation is linear, the output for H units should be about four times as great as for V units, since the spacing is in the ratio 4:1. An exactly analogous argument applies to the "column" figure; for it, V units should give a higher output than should H units. Thus, the original discrimination between "rows" and "columns" can plausibly be attributed to differential rates of firing for H and V units. For "rows," H output is higher than is V output, and for "columns," it is the reverse. It is clear that the smooth stripes will also affect H and V units differentially in the same sort of way, but the differences between H and V outputs for each shape will be even stronger than for the "row" and "column" patterns. In fact, we can show that the relative rates of firing give a very neat explanation of the anomalous transfer effects. Suppose S has been trained with "rows" positive, then the discrimination it has learned is: $\hat{H} > \hat{V}$ is positive and $\hat{V} > \hat{H}$ is negative, where $\hat{H}$ and $\hat{V}$ are the average outputs for H and V, respectively. The smooth horizontal stripes are now shown with the "rows." Since there is more H summation and less V summation for stripes, $H > V$ now implies that horizontal stripes are the "positive" shape; although both patterns give $\hat{H} > \hat{V}$, the difference is greater for stripes (the "positive" signal is stronger or more redundant for the stripes). There is almost no V output for horizontal stripes, but there is some for "rows"; since the "rows" pattern has the bigger V, it will tend to be treated as negative. The negative anomalous transfer can be treated in the same way. Here, $\hat{V} > \hat{H}$ implies negative, and vertical stripes give both a bigger output on $\hat{V}$ and a bigger difference between $\hat{V}$ and $\hat{H}$ than does the "column" pattern. When the two are shown together, the "column" pattern is preferred because the vertical stripes are "more negative."

Our paradigm is symmetrical with respect to horizontality-verticality, receptive-field properties, and positive-negative training conditions, so that a precisely analogous argument applies where "rows" are negative, "columns" positive, in initial training. The fact that neither monkey showed initial preference for smooth stripes in the same orientation as the "rows" or "columns" (nor preference for either of these over stripes) shows that the transfer results are genuine effects of the discrimination training. Also, "novelty" of the stripes can be ruled out, since an explanation in terms of a tendency to choose novel shapes would predict the opposite of what happened on negative transfer trials (see also Dodwell, 1970).

The anomalous transfer results are not compatible with any traditional "continuity" type of explanation of discrimination learning in which positive and negative "cues" are summed in the two patterns (Spence, 1936) or are "sampled" from trial to trial, as is proposed in stochastic learning models (Restle, 1955; Atkinson & Estes, 1963). On the other hand, the interpretation in terms of analysis by contour-detection units shows that the series *horizontal stripes-"rows"-"columns"-vertical stripes* forms a set of points on a single "horizontality-verticality" continuum, so that the anomalous transfers can be interpreted as cases of transposition behavior after all, in accordance with the classical analysis of Spence (1936). But the most important point to make is that the results can only be understood by taking account of the contour-coding system of the organism, which "structures" the stimulus input in a particular way.

We are puzzled by the fact that negative anomalous transfer only showed up after the positive anomaly had been elicited: No good explanation is readily apparent, but we hope to investigate the phenomenon experimentally in greater detail. The fact that anomalous transfers have been found in three species of mammal, using different apparatus and training techniques, suggests that this is not an isolated curiosity but a genuine function of the mammalian contour coding system. Yet it can scarcely be universal; one would not expect to get such transfer results with human adults. Transposition behavior is known to be influenced by the ability to attach verbal labels to discriminanda, however, so it would be interesting to know if the effects can be demonstrated in human infants.

## *REFERENCES*

Atkinson, R. C., & Estes, W. K. Stimulus sampling theory. In R. D. Luce, R. R. Bush, and E. Galanter (Eds.), *Handbook of mathematical psychology*. New York: Wiley, 1963, 121-269.

Dodwell, P. C. A coupled system for coding and learning in shape discrimination. *Psychological Review*, 1964, *71*, 148-159.

Dodwell, P. C. Anomalous transfer effects after shape discrimination training in the rat. *Psychonomic Science*, 1965, 3, 97-98.

Dodwell, P. C. Anomalous transfer effects after pattern discrimination training in rats and squirrels. *Journal of Comparative and Physiological Psychology*, 1970, *71*, 42-51.

Hubel, D. H., & Wiesel, T. N. Receptive fields, binocular interaction and functional architecture in the cat's visual cortex. *Journal of Physiology*, 1962, *160*, 106-154.

Hubel, D. H., & Wiesel, T. N. Receptive fields and functional architecture of monkey striate cortex. *Journal of Physiology*, 1968, *195*, 215-243.

Krechevsky, I. An experimental investigation of the principle of proximity in the visual perception of the rat. *Journal of Experimental Psychology*, 1938, 22, 497-523.

Restle, F. A theory of discrimination learning. *Psychological Review*, 1955, 62, 11-19.

Spence, K. W. The nature of discrimination learning in animals. *Psychological Review*, 1936, *43*, 427-449.

Thompson, T., Seal, D., & Bloom, W. A suspended platform for use in chronic restraint of monkeys. *Journal of the Experimental Analysis of Behavior*, 1966, 9, 146.

*I have devoted a good deal of space to presenting and discussing the anomalous transfer findings for several reasons: (1) Anomalous transfer is itself a very surprising phenomenon. (2) The papers demonstrate how experimental analysis of a problem can eliminate alternative explanations and hypotheses. (3) Taken together the two papers demonstrate quite well the progression in theorizing from rather abstract general principles to very specific notions about pattern recognition; from using a variety of stimulus arrays to get at "general principles" to the study of few arrays which differ on very few but readily identified dimensions, in this case orientation. (4) The explanation offered by Dodwell, Litner, and Niemi demonstrates the degree of convergence between neurophysiological and psychological experimentation and theorizing in this field. Last, but by no means least, that paper also shows how, in attempting to answer one question by experiment, a new question (or several) may emerge from the data and suggest further experiments which should be undertaken. The "order" effect in anomalous transfer was entirely unexpected, and trying to find out why it occurs should certainly lead to further understanding of mammalian pattern coding.*

*The next two papers are very short and report experiments on pattern recognition in animals which have features which are quite typical for such experiments these days. Simple patterns are used, specific hypotheses are tested, alternative explanations are considered and excluded by appropriate control procedures, and the behavioral results are related to neurophysiologi-*

cal findings. A word of caution is appropriate, however. There is a tendency to use Hubel and Wiesel's findings as if they were equally appropriate to any sort of visual system, but as we shall see in Part IV, their findings are only relevant really to vertebrate and particularly mammalian vision. The principles of anatomical organization in other biological orders are generally quite different; as yet there is no demonstration that the neurophysiological properties and coding systems are any less dissimilar than the anatomical.

# *Cat's Ability to Discriminate Oblique Rectangles*

N. S. SUTHERLAND

Abstract. *Cats were trained to discriminate either between a horizontal and vertical rectangle or between two oblique rectangles, one at 45°, the other at 135° to horizontal. All animals were first trained with both shapes (one in each orientation) presented together, and then retrained with only one shape shown at a time. Throughout the experiment the animals being trained with oblique rectangles performed as well as those being trained with horizontal and vertical rectangles. This finding is in marked contrast with results obtained from other species. The results suggest that the ability of a species to discriminate between rectangles in different orientations may depend upon the relative numbers of cells in the visual system having receptive fields in each orientation.*

Hubel and Wiesel (1962) have found that in the cat striate cortex there are neurons with long, narrow receptive field centers. Each of these neurons responds maximally to a rectangular shape projected on the retina in a particular orientation. Other neurons respond maximally to appropriately oriented boundaries between light and darkness. In the cat, different neurons have receptive fields in different orientations. Hubel and Wiesel found "no indication that any one orientation was more common than the others" (Hubel & Wiesel, 1962). Young (1962) has found that the dendritic fields of neurons picking up from incoming fibres in the optic lobe of octopuses are predominantly elliptical in shape. This may be the anatomical substratum for a similar type of coding device to that which Hubel and Wiesel have demonstrated in the cat. However, Young pre-

Reprinted from *Science,* 1963.

sents evidence which suggests that in the octopus there are more dendritic fields with orientations corresponding to the visual horizontal or vertical than with intermediate (oblique) orientations. Sutherland (1963) has suggested that this type of coding arrangement in the octopus brain would satisfactorily account for much of the behavioral evidence on how shapes are classified by *Octopus*. In particular, octopuses have great difficulty in discriminating between two oblique rectangles set at 45° and 135° to horizontal, whereas they discriminate very readily between a horizontal and vertical rectangle (Sutherland, 1957).

The explanation of the octopus's difficulty with the oblique rectangles may lie partially in the relative scarcity of dendritic fields in orientations corresponding to oblique orientations on the retina. If this account of shape discrimination in the octopus is correct, it should follow that if cats have about as many oblique fields as vertical and horizontal, they should discriminate between two oblique rectangles as readily as between a vertical and horizontal. My experiment was designed to test this prediction.

Four cats were trained to discriminate between a horizontal and vertical rectangle, and four between two oblique rectangles at 45° and 135° to horizontal. The rectangles were black, measured 3.5 by 0.7 inches, and were exposed against a white circular background 3.5 inches in diameter. The apparatus used was designed by Sperry, Miner, and Myers (1955). The stimuli were presented on doors to the left and right of a partition. The door bearing the positive stimulus was unlocked and the cats could obtain food by pushing against it. The door bearing the negative stimulus was locked and subjects running to it were pushed back into a start chamber and rerun. The interior of the apparatus was dark, and the stimuli were translucent and illuminated from the outside. The position of the positive and negative stimuli (to left or right) was determined by semirandom Gellermann type orders. Twenty trials a day were run in close succession, each trial concluded when the animal made the correct choice. All animals had been previously trained to push open the doors for food reward. The experiment was run in two stages.

*Stage I*. The two stimuli (a vertical and a horizontal rectangle for one group, two oblique rectangles in opposite orientations for the other) were presented simultaneously, and animals were run until they achieved a criterion of 38 correct choices out of 40 over a 2-day training period. The animals trained with vertical and horizontal rectangles averaged 11.0 days to reach criterion, (range 9 to 14 days); those trained with oblique rectangles averaged 10.75 days (range 8 to 13 days). The learning curves for the two groups are not shown since they were almost identical. Thus both groups learned equally fast to discriminate between the shapes presented simultaneously.

*Stage II*. The question arises whether the oblique group may have learned to discriminate in terms of the total pattern made by the shapes rather than in terms of the orientations of the two oblique rectangles. For example, they might have learned to run left when the tops of the oblique rectangles faced inward, and to run right when the bottoms faced inward. To control against this possibility both groups were retrained with one shape presented at a time. On half the trials the positive shape only was presented with a blank door on the other side, on half the negative shape only was presented. When the positive shape was shown, animals were rewarded for pushing the door on which it was exposed; when the negative shape was shown, they were rewarded for running to the door on the other side of the apparatus. All animals showed immediate transfer to this situation.

Thus on the first day of retraining with single shapes, animals trained with the horizontal and vertical rectangles ran correctly in 73 percent of the trials and those trained with the two obliques ran correctly in 78 percent of the trials. Training was continued in this way for 4 days, and although all animals ran consistently above chance their scores showed little sign of improvement. Thus on the fourth day animals trained with vertical and horizontal rectangles averaged 75 percent correct responses, and the other group 78 percent correct. The immediate transfer to the new situation strongly suggests that neither group had learned the original discrimination in terms of the total pattern made by the two shapes, but that they had learned independently the orientation of the positive and negative shapes. The fact that, when only one stimulus was presented at a time, the animals still discriminated as accurately between the oblique rectangles as between the horizontal and vertical rectangles was in marked contrast to my own powers of discrimination in relation to these shapes. In setting up the single oblique rectangles in the correct sequence, I had to proceed slowly and to double check every setting for fear of making an error. No such difficulty was experienced with the horizontal and vertical rectangles.

The finding that cats discriminate between two oblique rectangles as readily as between horizontal and vertical rectangles confirms the hypothesis that the relative ease with which animals discriminate rectangles in different orientations may depend at least partially on the number of neurons with receptive fields in particular orientations. The result is particularly striking when it is borne in mind that octopuses (Sutherland, 1957) and children under four (Rudel & Teuber, 1963) seem unable to solve the oblique discrimination at least with the training techniques so far used, while goldfish need about three times as many trials to learn to discriminate between two opposite oblique rectangles as they require to master the vertical-horizontal discrimination (Mackintosh & Sutherland, 1963). From an evolutionary standpoint it is difficult to say why the cat should differ from the other three species in this way. Accurate recognition of oblique orientations may be of special importance to an animal jumping from branch to branch.

## *REFERENCES*

Hubel, D. H., & Wiesel, T. N. Receptive fields, binocular interaction and functional architecture in the cat's visual cortex. *Journal of Physiology*, 1962, *160*, 106-154.

Mackintosh, J., & Sutherland, N. S. Visual discrimination by the goldfish; the orientation of rectangles. *Animal Behaviour*, 1963, *11*, 136-161.

Rudel, R., & Teuber, H.-L. Discrimination of live in children. *Journal of Comparative and Physiological Psychology*, 1963, *56*, 892-898.

Sperry, R. W., Miner, N., & Myers, R. E. Visual perception following subpial slicing and tantalum wire insertion in the visual cortex. *Journal of Comparative and Physiological Psychology*, 1955, *48*, 50-58.

Sutherland, N. S. Shape discrimination and receptive fields. *Nature*, 1963, *197*, 118-122.

Young, J. Z. The visual system of *Octopus* (i). Regularities in the retina and optic lobes of *Octopus* in relation to form discrimination. *Nature*, 1960, *186*, 836-839.

Young, J. Z. The retina of cephalopods and its degeneration after optic nerve section. *Philosophical Transactions of the Royal Society*, Series B, 1962, *245*, 1-58.

# Contour Separation and Orientation in Shape Discrimination by Rats

P. C. DODWELL AND R. R. NIEMI

*Several theoretical models to account for shape discrimination by rats have been proposed. A central issue has been the relative importance of contour separation or contour orientation as a major factor in the coding system. The models of Deutsch and Dodwell reflect this disagreement, Deutsch favoring the former variable and Dodwell the latter. Three stimulus figures were devised in such a way that two of them had equal and constant contour separation, and two had equal amounts of contour in the horizontal and vertical orientations. It was found that the pair with identical contour separation were readily discriminable from one another, but the pair with identical orientations were not. It was concluded that contour orientation is more important in the rat's pattern coding system than contour separation.*

Reprinted from *Psychonomic Science*, 1967.

A number of attempts have recently been made to account for shape recognition in such organisms as the rat and octopus (Deutsch, 1955, 1962; Dodwell, 1957, 1964; Sutherland, 1957, 1959). These attempts make the common assumption that spatial information on the retina is coded before recognition occurs, but differ in their proposals about the basis of coding. Deutsch has consistently employed the notion that a shape-coding system be based on the computation of intercontour distances, and cites anatomical evidence for the octopus and bee in favor of it. Sutherland's original model (1957), although based on separation of horizontal and vertical components in a pattern, also employs a system which computes, basically, intercontour distances. Dodwell (1957), on the other hand, has used the principle of coding by the extent of contours in different orientations—particularly horizontal and vertical—and subsequently cited supporting neurophysiological evidence from the visual system of the cat (Dodwell, 1964). There is no compelling reason to suppose that shape-coding systems in mammals are the same as in submammalian vertebrates and invertebrates; indeed there are anatomical and physiological grounds for expecting them to be different. Be this as it may, it seemed worthwhile to find out whether both contour separation and contour orientation have importance in shape recognition in the rat. The experiment reported here is also a test between the coding systems of Deutsch and Dodwell, although the oversimplifications inherent in both models are recognized.

The stimuli used are shown in Fig. 1. These patterns satisfy several criteria for a test of a shape-recognition system per se. That is, they have equal brightness, the same general orientation, and bilateral symmetry. Other factors may contaminate a test for properties of a shape-recognition system, e.g., difference in size (Fields, 1931) and the relation of figure edges to apparatus boundaries (Dodwell, 1957; Sutherland, 1961); however, these can be controlled by presenting white outline stimuli varying in size from trial to trial in a darkened apparatus, and by various part-figure tests.

The shapes A and C of Fig. 1 display contour orientation uniformity, but contour separation disparity. A and B display orientation disparity but separation uniformity. Although space precludes an exact derivation, it can be shown that for Deutsch's model A=B≠C, and for Dodwell's A=C=B. The experiment tests these predictions.

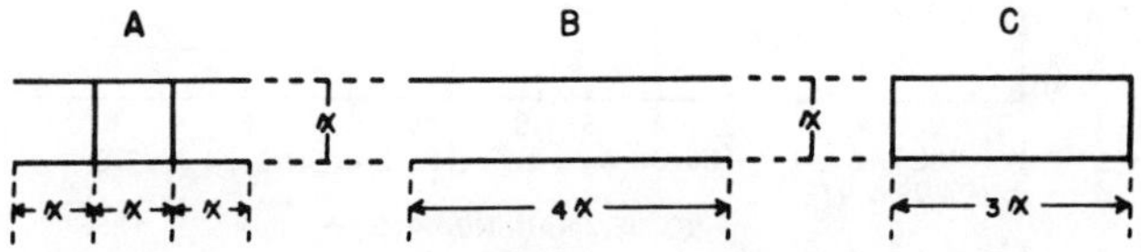


Fig. 1. Stimuli used in the experiment, shown in algebraic proportions. In the study, they were white outline figures on a black ground.

## *METHOD*

Ss were eight male hooded rats approximately three months old, maintained at 80% normal body weight, and handled for ½ h per day for seven days prior to experimentation. Ss were randomly assigned to two equal groups.

The apparatus consisted of a blackened, narrow chamber, 12 x 4 x 4 in. high. One end widened to 6 in. to contain two clear plastic panels 2 in. square and set 2 in. apart. Small cups delivering a standard food reinforcement pellet were located immediately beneath each panel. The other end of the chamber contained a horizontal bar.

Stimuli were white outline pairs of A and B or A and C on a black ground, mounted on slides and projected onto a ground glass screen behind the panels, one shape appearing behind each panel, in a Gellermann series. (The shapes provided the only illumination in the apparatus.) Sixteen pairs of stimuli were used, size varying by 24%. At the maximum viewing distance the contour width subtended 0.25°, i.e., well above the hooded rat's acuity threshold.

After shaping, the trial sequence was as follows. A bar press at the back of the box caused stimulus onset. A correct panel response (press) effected offset of the negative shape and presentation of food during 5 sec continued illumination of the positive shape. An incorrect response caused immediate offset of both shapes. The intertrial interval was 5 or 30 sec, for correct and incorrect responses, respectively.

After pretraining on a black-white discrimination, Group 1 was trained on A and B, then on A and C, 40 trials per day. For Group 2 the order was reversed.

Where learning occurred (80% correct responses per day or better), transfer tests for part-figure, brightness and size discimination were given. Where learning did not occur (400 trials without statistically observable effects), reversal of reinforcement value of the stimuli was tried, but had no observable effects. Retraining on a black-white discrimination was then

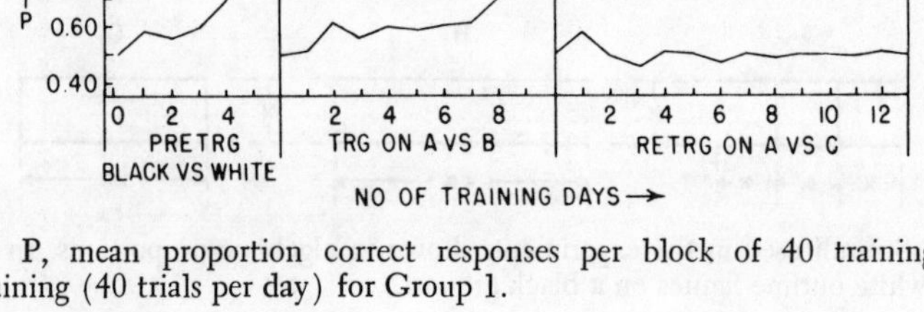


Fig. 2. P, mean proportion correct responses per block of 40 training trials vs days of training (40 trials per day) for Group 1.

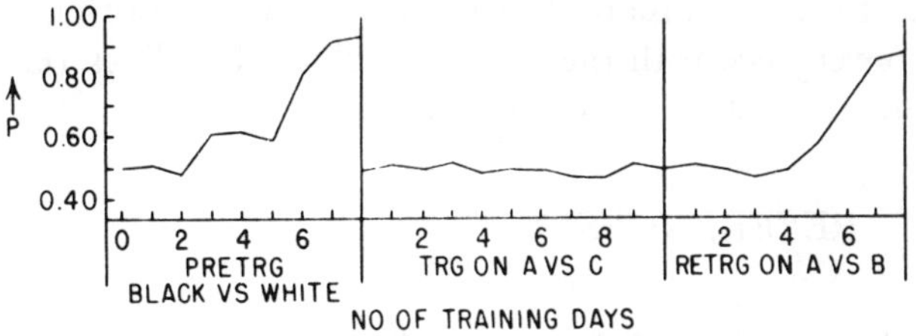


Fig. 3. P, mean proportion correct responses per block of 40 training trials vs days of training (40 trials per day) for Group 2.

instituted for non-learners. Reinforcement values of stimuli were appropriately counterbalanced. (Since part-figure etc. tests, and reinforcement counterbalancing etc. had no observable effects, these data are not reported.)

### *RESULTS*

Results are shown in Figs. 2 and 3 above. No statistical test of the reliability of the choice between A and B was deemed necessary, since all Ss reached the (stringent) criterion at Day 10 or better. No S displayed better than chance performance on A and C. No S showed reliable preference in the part-figure transfer tests (top halves, bottom halves), thus indicating that they were responding to the whole patterns.

### *DISCUSSION*

The findings lend strong support to the hypothesis that contour orientation plays an important role in rats' ability to discriminate shape. It also appears that contour separation, at least in this situation, is a much less effective cue, although it is not possible to prove that it is always entirely ineffective.

The test made is deemed unequivocal for the following reasons. First, confounding discriminatory factors such as brightness, size and general figure orientation were controlled, and appropriate transfer tests yielded no evidence suggesting that discrimination was based on part-figures, or other similar factors. Secondly, rats could discriminate A and B, but not A and C, irrespective of training order, although they displayed identical behavior in the two situations in other respects (thus "failure of attention" is ruled out).

Although work to date favors a contour orientation hypothesis in discrimination of shape by rats, neither this hypothesis nor the Dodwell model is supported to the exclusion of other possibilities. However, a surprising degree of convergence with the neurophysiological findings (e.g., Hubel & Wiesel, 1962) is evident, as in other situations (Dodwell, 1965).

## *REFERENCES*

Deutsch, J. A. A theory of shape recognition. *British Journal of Psychology*, 1955, *46*, 30-37.

Deutsch, J. A. A system for shape recognition. *Psychological Review*, 1962, *69*, 492-500.

Dodwell, P. C. Shape recognition in rats. *British Journal of Psychology*, 1957, *48*, 221-229.

Dodwell, P. C. A coupled system for coding and learning in shape discrimination. *Psychological Review*, 1964, *71*, 148-159.

Dodwell, P. C. Anomalous transfer effects after shape discrimination training in the rat. *Psychonomic Science*, 1965, *3*, 97-98.

Fields, P. E. Contributions to visual figure discrimination in the white rat. *Journal of Comparative and Physiological Psychology*, 1931, *11*, 349-367.

Hubel, D. H., & Wiesel, T. N. Receptive fields, binocular interaction and functional architecture in the cat's visual cortex. *Journal of Physiology*, 1962, *160*, 106-154.

Lashley, K. S. The mechanism of vision: XV. Preliminary studies of the rat's capacity for detail vision. *Journal of General Psychology*, 1938, *18*, 123-193.

Sutherland, N. S. Visual discrimination of orientation by *Octopus*. *British Journal of Psychology*, 1957, *48*, 55-71.

Sutherland, N. S. A test of a theory of shape discrimination in *Octopus vulgaris Lamarck*. *Journal of Comparative and Physiological Psychology*, 1959, *52*, 135-141.

Sutherland, N. S. Shape discrimination by animals. *Experimental Psychology Society Monograph No. 1*, 1961.

*The next two papers center on our subsidiary, but important, theme of postural orientation and visual control of the motor system. Up to this point the papers presented in this part are clearly relevant to questions of pattern coding and stimulus equivalence, but are within the restricted domain of learning to choose between a pair of stimulus arrays in a standard discrimination learning situation. By considering what functions pattern recognition must subserve in the organism's life, Ingle is able to make some novel suggestions about stimulus control of behavior. It is not necessarily the case that similar distinctions can be made for species more advanced than the goldfish with which Ingle works, but it is intriguing to find in Schneider's paper evidence for analogous differences in visual control func-*

*tions in the hamster, which are related to the functioning of different brain structures*[1] *(see also Held, 1971). This paper also illustrates the importance of the behavioral measures one chooses to record; two different sorts of response measures could lead to two quite different conclusions about visual deficits in this case, and as Schneider suggests, this probably accounts for some conflicting reports in the older literature.*

[1] Some description of the different structures of the mammalian visual system is given in Part IV.

# Two Visual Mechanisms Underlying the Behavior of Fish

D. INGLE

*Studies of motion-detection by fish reveal two separate processes, which are hypothetically linked to different kinds of behavior. Furthermore, studies of interocular transfer with "mirror-image" shape discriminations also indicate two distinct mechanisms for the representation of visual directions. From these two kinds of experiment, it seems that visual processes subserving* "orientation" *of the fish to a moving object should be clearly distinguished from processes by which the fish* "evaluates" *the identity or activity of the object.*

Speaking broadly, there are two ways to analyze the functions of the visual system:

1. a mechanistic analysis that begins with the receptors, and
2. a teleological approach that begins with the visually-guided *response*.

Using the first approach, neurophysiologists and psychophysicists have studied the peripheral visual system as it detects certain light fluctuations and selects important features of the surrounding world. According to the mechanistic approach, analysis of peripheral events has priority. By studying combinations of these events, it is assumed that more complex neural and perceptual entities will emerge in a lawful fashion. This faith has been bolstered by the elegant analysis of the cat neocortex by Hubel and Wiesel (1962, 1965). From these studies, we are led to believe that each afferent way-station provides a visual analysis that is further abstracted or refined

Reprinted from *Psychologische Forschung*, 1967.

at the next level. Presumably, a complete description of this afferent flow diagram will tell us what kind of information is presented to those central neural systems that control movements, store memories, and release feelings.

However, while unravelling the complex activities of the visual system, the second (behavioral) approach will also be useful. For example, the discrimination studies of Sutherland (in press) aim at describing ways in which fish classify visual shapes, so that the components of the analytic and storage systems can be theoretically modelled before actual physiological correspondences are sought. In the present article, we will ask a further question, "of what *use* is the visual information?" In this way, we hope to discover biologically relevant categories of visual coding. Fish have natural biases to snap at objects having certain colors, shapes, and sizes; they accurately identify members of their own species, whether for sake of love or war; and they show numerous movements that are guided by objects in their environment.

We have performed some experiments on the discriminatory capacities of fish hoping to develop a useful "model" of spatial vision relevant to higher vertebrates as well. On this point, the novelist, Herman Hesse, seems to agree:

> "Each man carries the vestiges of his birth—the slime and eggshells of his primeval past . . . frog, lizard, ant. Some are human above the waist, fish below" (Hesse, 1965).

I am inclined to say that we are human above the thalamus, and fish below. Neurologically speaking, we might regard a fish as man stripped down to his midbrain. The midbrain is concerned with sensory regulation of whole body posture and movements. The fish must "think" in terms of total relocations of his entire body in order to satisfy his smallest desire. In approaching the "internalized spatial representation" of man, we may learn secrets from the fish, who cannot help betraying his perceptions and intentions by overt responses.

## A *STUDY OF MOVEMENT-DETECTION*

The study of motion perception is a good beginning, since many vertebrates are conspicuously sensitive to those movements within their visual world that denote food or danger. Physiological studies by Jacobson and Gaze (1964) and Cronly-Dillon (1964) indicate that the motion-detectors of the goldfish retina are asymmetrically sensitive with respect to direction of motion. More units are sensitive to forward (nasalward) motion through their receptive fields than to backward motion. A behavioral study of movement perception was performed in order to test the inference that forward-moving spots would be more easily detected than those moving in the opposite direction. Conditioned deceleration of heart-rate was used as the

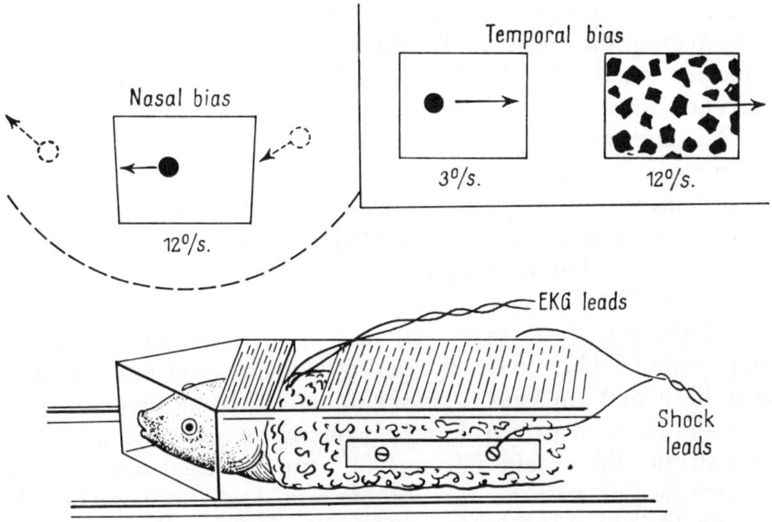


Fig. 1. Apparatus for cardiac conditioning of goldfish. Single or multiple dots move behind window of tank.

index of sensitivity as black spots moved—one at a time—through a window in the side of the training aquarium (Fig. 1). When a movement velocity was in the range employed by the physiologists (about 12°/second), the prediction was fulfilled: all subjects responded consistently more strongly to the nasalward moving spot.

However, two other groups of subjects showed surprising effects when certain parameters of stimulation were varied. With either single spot moving at 3°/second or a random-spotted field at 12°/second these subjects responded more strongly to motion in the backwards or temporal direction. Unlike the physiological experiments that restricted stimulus parameters, the behavioral data reveal *two* separate movement-detection processes. What common attribute can distinguish the two stimuli whose effective motion is temporal from the fast-moving single spot that is most effective when moving in a nasal direction? For the human observer, the latter stimulus seems to move from place-to-place, while the others appear to "flow" in a more diffuse manner. This subjective account recalls the hypothetical distinction of MacKay (1961) between detectors of "velocity" and of "position change" in man. This kind of dichotomy provides an agreeable hypothesis for the fish as well, provided that the two processes can be matched with different response categories through appropriate experiments.

It is easy to imagine that a fish would employ "change of position" analysis for orientation to moving prey. Some fish do wheel around in one rapid movement into a striking position when a small piece of food suddenly enters the lateral or temporal field. This initial movement is so accurate that they do not need to correct their orientation but immediately lunge forward to grasp the object. As the fish moves toward the food (the image now moving temporally), he obtains feedback as to his prediction of position. When food drops rapidly, the fish needs continuous feedback to judge the lunge and snap since under stroboscopic illumination at five flashes per second, it nearly always undercompensates for the falling movement and snaps too high. This account agrees in principle with that of human eye motion: a saccade is elicited by sudden change of position (Rashbass, 1961), but tracking of a moving object is governed by the "velocity" variable (Young & Stark, 1963).

Should the fish show directional bias in detecting the motion of a random-spotted field since it is not perceived as an object but as a surface? It seems likely that fish regulate swimming velocity by means of visual feedback produced by their own displacements. For example, in a backward-moving stream, fish require information from the visual surroundings to judge their own progress in a forward direction. Thus, our hypothesis links the nasally-biased mechanism to an orientation reflex, and the temporally-sensitive process to guidance of active movement via visual re-afference.

## *EXPERIMENTS ON THE CODING OF VISUAL DIRECTION*

Another type of experiment has also provided a basis for dissociating two kinds of coding process. This study concerned the interocular transfer of certain shapes that are left-right mirror-images of one another. Such an experiment requires the organism to judge the equivalence of stimuli, one presented to the left eye, the other to the right eye, that are differentiated only by the direction of their orientation. A series of experiments by Mello (1965a, 1965b, 1966) has demonstrated that pigeons peck most often at the "wrong" stimulus when given transfer tests, following monocular training on mirror-image pairs. From these experiments it is clear that such shapes were not seen by the pigeon primarily in their "left-right" orientation, since a left-pointing arrowhead seen via one eye was judged equivalent to a right-pointing arrowhead viewed by the other eye. These pigeons did show "front-back" equivalence, if we allow that mirror-image shapes pointing toward the binocular midline are each viewed by these subjects as pointing forward in the third dimension (as if projected on a sagittal plane).

Similar tests performed with goldfish give overtly different results: using oblique line pairs (45° vs. 135°) and arrowheads ($>$ vs. $<$), a goldfish shows left-right equivalence (Fig. 2). However, these shapes fill a visual angle of only 8 or 10°. When 15° sidewards T's (⊢ vs. ⊣) were used as discriminanda, the fish were suddenly converted to pigeons, and showed a

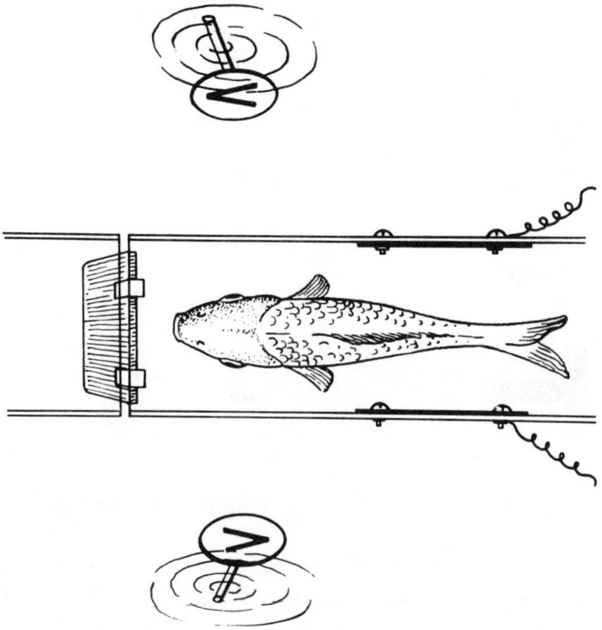

Fig. 2. Stimuli judged "equivalent" by goldfish during interocular transfer tests. During conditioned avoidance response, fish swims through door into identical box.

"front-back" mode of interocular equivalence. Using a stimulus consisting of red-plus-green squares separated by 22° (R-G vs. G-R), the same front-back equivalence was obtained, suggesting that interfield distance between the two parts of the stimulus is a critical variable in determining the kind of directional coding used in a particular case. These various kinds of stimuli are represented in Fig. 3.

It would seem that stimulus enlargement alters the coding principles by enhacing the "local sign" of the left and the right halves, while weakening the figural gestalt. With these larger figures, the interhemispheric commisures relay such information about the spatial position of two parts. For a lateral-eyed animal, it is reasonable that these separate positions of retinal impingement should denote the directions "front" vs. "back." With smaller figures, the shape is taken in as a unit, and the orientation is analyzed in terms of "relative" rather than "absolute" position of the parts. In any case, we may speak of a *shape-analyzing* process as distinct from an *orientation* process that takes (body-centered) spatial position into account.

The distinction between these two principles of coding can be made more concrete by envisioning a fish in the act of feeding. A novel food stimulus elicits a rapid orientation movement appropriate to the position of the object in the field. Only after orienting does the organism commit himself to a lunge and snap. Focal stimulation of the optic tectum, from

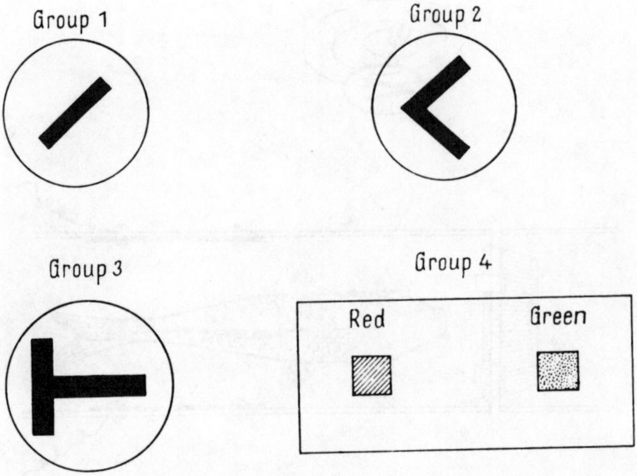


Fig. 3. Stimuli used for mirror-image discriminations.

fish to mammal, can induce similar orienting movements of body, head, or eyes—a "visual grasp reflex"—as Hess would call it. Electrophysiology of the peripheral system cannot distinguish units contributing to an orienting system from those involved in identification of the object as appropriate food. For example, the notorious "bug-detectors" described by Lettvin et al. (1961) in the frog retina may be saying to the brain, "look" rather than "OK . . . eat." This distinction is easily seen when a chameleon (*Anolis carolinensis*) turns only head and eye toward a dead insect on repeated tests, but moves with astonishing enthusiasm once a live bait appears in the same position.

It is not yet possible to relate the visual mechanisms that detect movement to those that distinguish spatial and directional relations between shapes. However, it is obvious that the mirror-image transfer procedure could be applied to moving objects or surfaces, such as those used in the first experiment. We can make a prediction from our broad hypothesis that responses form a basis for categorizing visual inputs. The single fast-moving spot has been identified as a moving prey object: as it moves across the midline from the right to the left eye's field, the right-left direction will be constant. The same turning movements required to follow the nasally-moving object will be predictive of its temporalward direction as it passed into the left field. Therefore, in a discrimination transfer test, a nasally moving spot on one side should be judged equivalent to a temporally-moving spot seen via the second eye. The opposite prediction emerges for the multiple spot stimulus; the re-afferent motion produced by the subject's forward motion is always backwards (temporalwards) for each eye simultaneously. Therefore, a forward-moving stimulus seen by one eye should be taken a equivalent to a forward-moving stimulus on the other side.

Our experiments indicate that at least two different processes underlie the

## *CONCLUSION*

coding of visual direction. Furthermore, two or more mechanisms exist for detection of visual motion, one of which may assist in guidance of the fish's own movements. The way in which these mechanisms impinge upon central neural systems for motor control poses one of the most intriguing problems confronting psychologists, neurophysiologists, and anatomists. Recently, data from these diverse areas is beginning to converge, and the importance of spatial perception for comparative and developmental psychology is now acknowledged with renewed enthusiasm.

Although my own experimental approach has been that of the laboratory, I should like to close my discussion with an appeal for a more naturalistic psychology of perception. I think that it is worth risking the wrath of those behaviorists who regard flirtation with teleology as an incriminating sin. This opinion which I have discussed more fully elsewhere (Ingle, in press) places strong priority on an analysis of the motor system and its requirements for visual guidance. The movements of an animal are not simply *elicited* by sensation—they frequently are performed in order to *obtain* stimulation. We hope to emphasize a psychology (indeed a physiology) of the active animal (Trevarthen, in press). The fish who manoeuvres through a complex terrain, who identifies dangerous predators, and who remains alert for a female companion must experience the visual and emotional decisions familiar to his more elevated vertebrate cousins. In the world of the fish we find the rudiments of selection, anticipation, exploration, and intelligence. In search of a psychology applicable to human beings we should not stop with a visit to the monkey house at the zoo, but reserve some thoughtful hours in a good aquarium.

## *REFERENCES*

Cronly-Dillon, J. R. Units sensitive to direction of movement in goldfish optic tectum. *Nature*, 1964, *203*, 214-215.

Hesse, H. Prologue to *Demian*. New York: Harper & Row, Bantam Books, 1965.

Hubel, D. H. & Wiesel, T. N. Receptive Fields, Binocular interaction and functional architecture in the cat's visual cortex. *Journal of Physiology*, 1962, *160*, 106-154.

Hubel, D. H. & Wiesel, T. N. Receptive fields and functional architecture in two non-striate visual areas (18 and 19) of the cat. *Journal of Neurophysiology*, 1965, *28*, 229-289.

Ingle, D. J. Visuomotor behavior of fish. In D. Ingle (Ed.), *The nervous system and fish behavior*. Chicago: Chicago University Press (in press).

Jacobson, M., & Gaze, R. M. Types of visual response from single units in the optic tectum and optic nerve of the goldfish. *Quarterly Journal of Experimental Physiology*, 1964, *49*, 199-209.

Lettvin, J. Y., Maturana, H. R., Pitts, W. H., & McCulloch, W. S. Two remarks on the visual system of the frog. W. A. Rosenblith (Ed.), *Sensory communication*. Cambridge, Mass.: M. I. T. Press, 1961.

MacKay, D. M. Interactive processes in visual perception. In W. A. Rosenblith (Ed.), *Sensory communication*. Cambridge, Mass.: M. I. T. Press, 1961.

Mello, N. K. Interhemispheric reversal of mirror-image oblique lines after monocular training in pigeons. *Science*, 1965, *148*, 252. (a)

Mello, N. K. Interocular transfer in pigeon: a comparison of colored left-right and up-down mirror-image patterns. *Proceedings of the American Psychological Association*, 1965, *1*, 137-138. (b)

Mello, N. K. Concerning the interhemispheric transfer of mirror-image pattern in pigeon. *Physiology and Behavior*, 1966, *1*, 293-300.

Rashbass, C. The relationship between saccadic and smooth tracking eye movements. *Journal of Physiology*, 1961, *159*, 326-338.

Sutherland, N. S. Shape discrimination in fish. In D. Ingle (Ed.), *The nervous system and fish behavior*. Chicago: Chicago University Press (in press).

Trevarthen, C. The process and the mechanism of vision in fish. In D. Ingle (Ed.), *The nervous system and fish behavior*. Chicago: Chicago University Press (in press).

Young, L., & Stark, L. Variable feedback experiments testing a sampled data model for eye tracking movements. *IEEE Transactions Human Factors Electr.*, HFE-4, No. 1, 1963, 38.

# Contrasting Visuomotor Functions of Tectum and Cortex in the Golden Hamster

G. E. SCHNEIDER

*Visually-guided orientation (spatial localization) and visual discrimination were dissociated by means of brain lesions in the golden hamster. After ablation of visual cortex, hamsters failed to discriminate visual patterns, but showed nearly normal ability to localize an object in space by means of vision. Ablation of the superior colliculus produced opposite effects: these animals were completely unable to orient to the position of a visual stimulus, but nevertheless showed excellent pattern discrimination.*

Some advantages of approaching the visual integrating systems from both ends—from the motor end as well as from the sensory (cf. Teuber, 1964)—

Reprinted from *Psychologische Forschung*, 1967.

have been illustrated in the previous paper from the study of visually-guided behavior in the fish. I hope to show by examples from the neuropsychology of the Syrian hamster that this dual approach may help add some needed pieces to an old puzzle, the central nervous mechanisms controlling visually-guided behavior in mammals. Investigators have agreed for a long time that this game is worth the candle but they have been hesitant to burn the candle at both ends.

## *ANATOMICAL AND HISTORICAL OVERVIEW*

There have been many investigations of the effects of ablating the principal projection areas of the visual system in mammals, namely, the visual cortex and the optic tectum (superior colliculus) of the midbrain. Before considering the conclusions of these studies, let us review the pathways followed by visually-initiated nervous impulses by referring to Fig. 1, which indicates the projections of the retina of the Syrian hamster (according to my own observations in Nauta-stained material). The arrows indicate the two largest pathways, going to the superior colliculus and to the dorsal division of the lateral geniculate nucleus of the thalamus, which projects to occipital neocortex. Other brainstem nuclei which receive direct retinal connections are also indicated in the figure, but these are less important at least in terms of gross size and the number of studies of their function, and will not be discussed in the present paper.

Early neurological studies depended on clinical methods of demonstrating visual responsiveness; later experimental studies have depended heavily on the technique of varying the properties of the stimulus in order to determine residual capacities for visual discrimination. Reports of the early

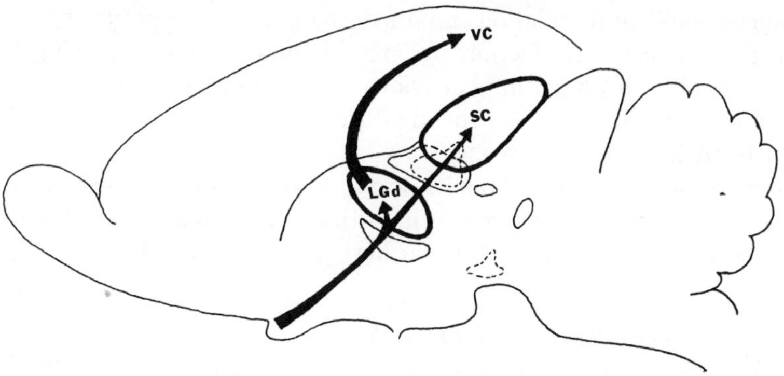


Fig. 1. Retinal projections in the hamster, depicted in a schematic side view of the brain with the thalamus and midbrain exposed. Arrows indicate the course of the two major pathways, going to the superior colliculus (*SC*) and to the dorsal part of the lateral geniculate nucleus (*LGd*). The latter project in turn to the visual cortex (*VC*). Smaller nuclei which also receive direct retinal connections are indicated by broken lines.

workers indicate that lesions either of visual cortex or of superior colliculus could result in animals which behaved as if blind in clinical tests (Flourens, 1842; Bechterew, 1884; Minkowski, 1911). But experimental analyses of animals deprived of visual cortex have shown that, although they are unable to learn the usual pattern discriminations (Lashley, 1931; Klüver, 1942), they retain an ability to discriminate differences in luminous flux (Klüver, 1942; Bauer & Cooper, 1964), and apparently even differences in amount of contour (Weiskrantz, 1963; cf. Klüver, 1941). Comparable experiments on animals with large tectal lesions have generally failed to reveal any deficits in visual discrimination (Layman, 1936; Ghiselli, 1937), leaving the apparent blindness reported in the early investigations, with their less formal tests, a puzzling anomaly.

### An Interpretation

These informal, quasi-clinical tests may have required of the animals quite different motor activities than those required by current laboratory tests of visual discrimination capacities. Therefore, to reach an understanding of the seemingly discrepant results obtained by investigators using different testing methods, it may be useful to employ both the earlier and later types of testing in studying the same brain-damaged animals. With this approach, both stimulus and response are varied. I have begun this type of analysis in a study of hamsters following ablations of the superior colliculus or the visual cortex.

At the risk of giving the erroneous impression that I was able to anticipate the results of this work, let me attempt to alter your perspective with a preview of the conclusions. Visual-cortex ablation leaves a hamster with only a minimal ability to tell *what* he is seeing, yet leaves nearly intact his ability to find *where* it is. In other words, he discriminates the identities of objects poorly, but can nevertheless orient to their positions in space.

Superior-colliculus ablation produces reciprocally opposite effects. A hamster with his optic tectum undercut knows *what* he is seeing but—when judged by his orienting behavior—acts as if he does not know *where* it is. That is, he discriminates the identities of objects very well but fails to orient to their positions in space.

This conclusion is put in such a strong form in order to underscore the implications, and to aid the reader in critically examining what follows (so that he can see in what respects I may have overstated the case).

## *GENERAL METHODS*

The hamster (*Mesocricetus auratus*) was chosen for this work partly because the superior colliculi are not covered at their caudal pole by cerebral cortex. This made it possible to undercut the entire structure by inserting a tiny vibrating knife passing just above the cerebellum and inferior collic-

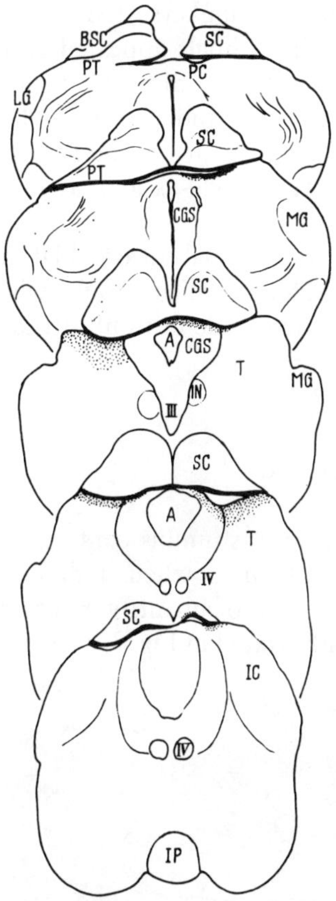


Fig. 2. Drawings made from Nissl-stained frontal sections through the superior colliculus of hamster RA-11. The most rostral sections appear at the top, showing the rostral pole of the colliculi at the level of the posterior commissure and caudal pretectum. The bottom section shows the most caudal pole of the superior and rostral end of the inferior colliculi. Stippling indicates gliosis due to vascular damage. *A*, The heavy line follows the cut under the optic tectum. aqueduct of Sylvius; *BSC*, brachium of the superior colliculus; *CGS*, central gray substance; *IC*, inferior colliculus; *IN*, interstitial nucleus of Cajal; *IP*, interpeduncular nucleus; *LG*, lateral geniculate nucleus; *MG*, medial geniculate nucleus; *PC*, posterior commissure; *PT*, lateral pretectal area; *SC*, superior colliculus (labelled at level of entering optic fibers, the stratum opticum); *T*, midbrain tegmentum; *III*, third nerve nucleus; *IV*, fourth nerve nucleus.

uli. The knife was held and guided by a stereotaxic instrument. The result is illustrated in Fig. 2, which represents a series of frontal sections through the midbrain of an animal with the superior colliculus totally undercut. The tectal tissue above such a surgical cut shows only a small amount of atrophy, even when virtually all of the input and output fibers have been severed. Visual cortex ablations were produced by suction, and resulted in marked atrophic changes in a major extent of the lateral geniculate nuclei.

Such brain-damaged animals and control groups of normal animals were subjected to repeated neurological examination, to a quantitative test of orienting responses, and to an analysis of visual discrimination abilities.

## *BEHAVIORAL PROCEDURES AND RESULTS*

### Neurological Tests: Tectal "Blindness"

Normal hamsters readily orient to sunflower seeds presented well beyond whisker distance in various parts of the visual field. (Klüver, 1937, called a somewhat similar technique which he applied to monkeys "food perimetry.") Without a normal superior colliculus, the animals appeared to be totally blind, making no orienting movement at all until the seed touched their whiskers. Only then would they localize the seed and seize it in their mouths. In the cases with the most complete lesions, there was no recovery from this symptom throughout the postoperative period—as long as seven months.

In marked contrast to this result, animals with visual-cortex ablations localized food objects normally, revealing a slight deficiency only when required to follow a seed moving rapidly from side to side in front of them.

## Further Analysis of Orienting Responses: Results Depend on Which Response is Observed

To confirm these results under conditions of greater stimulus control, and to discover whether similar results could be obtained when a different naturally-occurring response was observed, a method of quantifying orienting responses was devised, using the apparatus illustrated in Fig. 3.

Fig. 3. Apparatus used to elicit orienting responses to overhead movement. The animal walked on a small platform below a transparent plastic roof. The stimulus pattern, consisting of small black squares on a transparent plate, was suspended by thin wires below a large ceiling light, and was moved by hand. To test for responses to overhead sounds, the visual display was removed, and the roof covered by opaque cardboard.

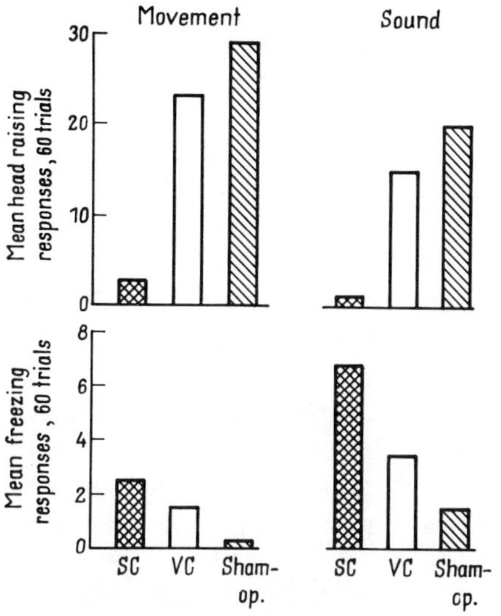


Fig. 4. Summary of results in the quantitative test of orienting responses. At the top are illustrated the mean numbers of head raising responses per subject in each group, at the left for the visual stimuli and at the right for auditory stimuli. The bottom graphs show mean numbers of freezing responses shown by the same subjects to the same stimuli. *SC*, 8 animals with superior colliculus lesions; *VC*, 7 subjects with visual cortex lesions; sham-op, 8 subjects with sham operations.

As the hamster walked around on a small platform, his responses to a suddenly moved pattern above a glass partition were recorded. When the glass roof was covered with an opaque card, responses to overhead sounds could be observed. Responses recorded included freezing as well as the more common head-raising responses. To prevent observer bias from producing spurious group differences, animals were coded so that the lesion was unknown throughout the periods of testing. Results are illustrated in Fig. 4, based on data from twenty-three hamsters.

Looking at the mean number of head-raising responses for sixty stimulus presentations per subject, you can see that the neurological results were confirmed. The fewest responses were shown by animals with colliculus lesions; in fact no responses at all were shown by the several subjects with total or near total damage to the optic tectum. This was true in the case of orienting to auditory stimuli as well as to visual. The group with visual-cortex ablations showed many more responses, slightly but insignificantly less than the normal group.

However, if one compares these scores to those for the freezing responses to the same stimuli, an opposite trend appears. Animals with tectal ablations, even when totally unable to orient to a movement or sound by moving the head toward it, actually showed significantly more freezing responses than the other two groups.

## Visual Discrimination Tests: Cortical "Blindness"

From the perspective created by the results of initial neurological testing, a surprising picture emerged from the analysis of visual discrimination performance. Sixteen hamsters were tested in this experiment with a two-choice apparatus in which a subject was required to push open and pass through a door displaying the positive stimulus in order to reach a water reward. The negative door was locked, and a push on this door was recorded as an error. Following an error, the animal was allowed to correct it by proceeding through the positive door to the water. At the beginning of this experiment, I predicted that the animals with tectal lesions which had failed to show visually-guided orientation in neurological testing would fail the more formal visual problems as well. But I had grossly underestimated the possibilities for the use of visually-guided responses other than these localization movements.

The initial series of tasks included discrimination of white from black, horizontal from vertical stripes, and a speckled pattern from diagonal stripes. The scores were in complete contrast to the neurological results. Animals with colliculus lesions showed excellent performance on these problems even when they were totally unable to localize an object in space by means of vision. But now the results for the group with cortex ablations revealed that, in agreement with Lashley's results for the rat, they were indeed lacking an important part of their visual mechanism. They were utter failures on the initial pattern problems; they showed good discrimination in only two problems: a bright, transilluminated door vs. a black door, and the speckled pattern vs. a gray of equal average reflectance.

## Resolution of a Paradox

The results raised a fundamental question: How could an animal that showed no ability to find anything by means of vision do so well on visual discrimination problems? A clue was provided by the unusual behavior of subjects with tectal ablations during problem solution. Fig. 5, which shows a top view of the visual discrimination apparatus, illustrates what follows. A normal hamster would leave the starting area and proceed down the center of the alley, moving his head from side to side as if he were deciding between alternatives. Then he would go directly toward the door to be pushed. Animals with large colliculus lesions, on the other hand, showed peculiar path habits. Let me describe the consistent behavior of one of them. He appeared to feel his way down the right-hand edge of the alley until he touched the door, then he would sit up and push the door or else move along the stimulus panel to the next door. Occasionally he would re-

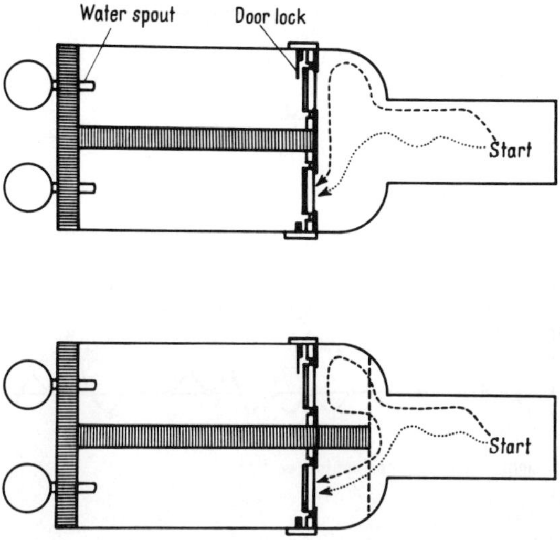


Fig. 5. Top views of the two-choice visual discrimination apparatus. The hamster walked down an elevated alley toward two doors displaying the stimuli. The door with the negative stimulus was locked; the door with the positive stimulus provided access to a water spout. In the lower drawing, the approaches to the two stimulus doors are separated by a divider. The dashed line indicates the path habitually followed by one subject with total ablation of the superior colliculus. The dotted line indicates a common path followed by a normal animal.

fuse to commit himself at either door, and follow the alley edge back to the starting point and begin the whole procedure again. Thus, it appeared likely that if the animal were required to move directly toward the correct door he might not do as well. I tried to impose such a requirement by slightly modifying the apparatus.

A small divider was placed between the two doors, thus forming two short parallel alleyways leading to the doors. With this divider present, a different method of recording errors could be applied. Recall that with the first technique, an error was recorded only when the subject actually pushed the wrong door. With the divider in place, an error could be recorded whenever an animal entered the wrong alley in front of the door. In retraining tests, errors were recorded both according to the initial technique and according to the new technique. The procedure can be described with reference to the lower part of Fig. 5, showing the modified apparatus and two possible paths to the correct door if it happened to be on the left. No errors were recorded if the animal stepped beyond the front edge of the divider only on the correct side (path indicated by dotted line). If the animal placed at least both front feet over this line on the negative side (dashed line), an "approach error" was recorded. In this case the subject could do one of two things: If he proceeded around the divider to the correct door, no further errors were recorded. Whenever, before doing this, he

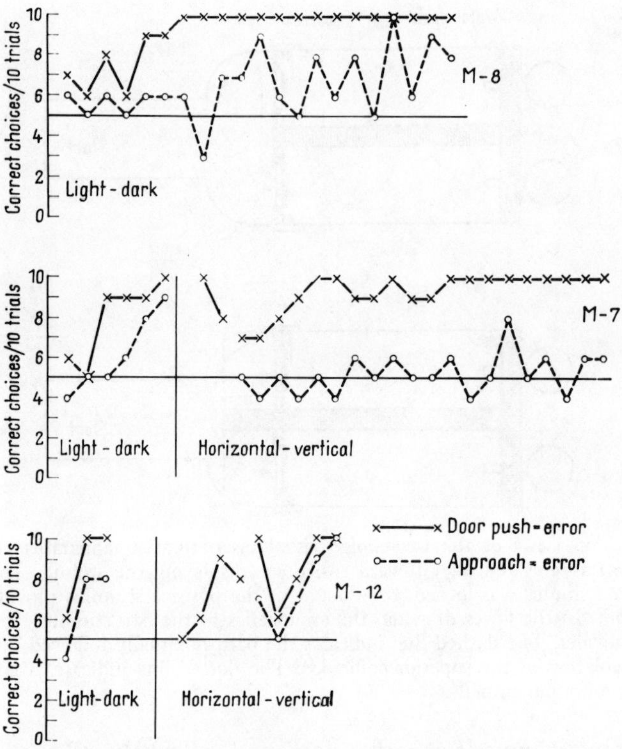


Fig. 6. Visual discrimination performance by two colliculus-operated subjects (M-8, M-7) and one normal (M-12), according to two different methods of scoring errors (see Key at lower right). Details of the procedure are explained in the text.

actually pushed the negative door, a second error—a "door push error"—was recorded.

When an entrance into the wrong approach alley was called an error, the severe handicap of the animals with superior-colliculus ablation revealed itself. Fig. 6 illustrates the results in the form of relearning curves for three subjects. The ordinate indicates the number correct in each block of ten trials, plotted separately for the two types of errors. For example, on a light-dark discrimination, subject M-8 (with a large tectal lesion) was soon performing at a level of 100% correct responses when a push on the wrong door was considered an error, but when entries into the wrong approach alley were called errors, he required 210 trials to reach a level of 80% correct responses. Subject M-7, with an apparently total superior-colliculus ablation, did better on the light-dark discrimination, but solved the horizontal-vertical stripes problem only according to the initial technique of recording errors. He persisted in approaching the incorrect stimulus about 50% of the time throughout retraining, for 200 trials. That this deficit was not the result of a myopia was shown by the ease with which this animal continued to push only on the correct side when the patterns were placed at some distance behind the transparent doorways.

Normal animals did not show this large difference in performance depending on the type of error, but consistently reached criterion levels of performance in either case (see bottom of Fig. 6).

This result appears to explain a controversial report on cats with superior-colliculus ablations. Blake in 1959 reported that such cats failed to perform a pattern discrimination postoperatively. Her method of testing was analogous to the modified technique I have used. Whenever the cats entered an alley leading to the incorrect stimulus, they were removed from the alley and an error was recorded. They were not allowed the choice of actually pushing or not pushing against the incorrect door. Blake's cats, and those in a later study by Sprague and Meikle (1965) showed orienting deficits similar to those I have found in hamsters, except that the clinical "blindness" in the hamster appears to be more complete and enduring.

My conclusion is that a hamster with the superior colliculus ablated could not orient to the position of a visual stimulus, but *could* decide whether to push or not to push a door on the basis of visual cues. Spatial orientation was apparently dependent on somesthesis and olfaction, but the starting and stopping of motor activity guided by other cues could be controlled by vision.

## *CONCLUSION: TWO VISUOMOTOR ABILITIES*

The foregoing analysis demonstrates the importance of experimental variation of the motor task as well as the stimulus in assessing the effects of brain lesions. Taken together, the experiments show a considerable dissociation between the ability to learn to identify a stimulus and the ability to orient to it in space. The superior colliculus of the hamster evidently plays a necessary role in the sensorimotor control of orientation—visuomotor at least, and to some extent audiomotor as well. The visual cortex, on the other hand, plays a supplementary role in visuomotor control which remains to be more fully defined.

By contrast, the performance of visual discriminative responses of the type described depends much more on the visual cortex, as has been suggested by many other investigators. The colliculus is necessary in this case only if the discriminative response includes visually-guided orientation to the location of the stimulus.

It seems possible that there may be certain categories of stimulus organization which hamsters could no longer discriminate once their spatial orientation is disturbed by tectal ablation—following the line of thinking suggested by Ingle in the previous paper. For example, could such animals learn to compare spatially separated stimuli? But such questions remain for future work to answer.

## *REFERENCES*

Bauer, J. H., & Cooper, R. M. Effects of posterior cortical lesions on performance of a brightness discrimination task. *Journal of Comparative and Physiological Psychology*, 1964, 58, 84-92.

Bechterew, W. Über die Function der Vierhugel. *Pflügers Archiv für die gesamte Physiologie*, 1884, 33, 413-439.

Blake, L. The effect of lesions of the superior colliculus on brightness and pattern discrimination in the cat. *Journal of Comparative and Physiological Psychology*, 1959, 52, 272-278.

Flourens, P. *Recherches experimentales sur les proprietés et les fonctions du système nérveux dans les animaux vertèbres* (2nd ed.) Baillière, Paris 1842.

Ghiselli, E. E. The superior colliculus in vision. *Journal of Comparative Neurology*, 1937, 67, 451-467.

Klüver, H. Certain effects of lesions of the occipital lobes in macaques. *Journal of Psychology*, 1937, *4*, 383-401.

Klüver, H. Visual functions after removal of the occipital lobes. *Journal of Psychology*, 1941, *11*, 23-45.

Klüver, H. Functional significance of the geniculo-striate system. *Biological Symposia*, 1962, 7, 253-299.

Lashley, K. S. The mechanism of vision: IV. The cerebral areas necessary for pattern vision in the rat. *Journal of Comparative Neurology*, 1931, 53, 419-478.

Layman, J. D. Functions of the superior colliculi in vision. *Journal of Genetic Psychology*, 1936, *49*, 33-47.

Minkowski, M. Zur Physilogie der Sehsphäre. *Pflügers Archiv für die gesamte Physiologie*, 1911, *141*, 171-327.

Schneider, G. E. Superior colliculus and visual cortex: contrasting behavioral effects of their ablation in the hamster. Unpublished doctoral dissertation, Massachusetts Institute of Technology, June 1966.

Sprague, J. M., & Meikle Jr., T. H. The role of the superior colliculus in visually guided behavior. *Experimental Neurology*, 1965, *11*, 115-146.

Teuber, H.-L. The riddle of frontal lobe function in man. In J. M. Warren and K. Akert (Eds.), *The frontal granular cortex and behavior.* New York: McGraw-Hill, 1964, 410-441.

Weiskrantz, L. Contour discrimination in a young monkey with striate cortex ablation. *Neuropsychologia*, 1963, *1*, 145-164.

*I have already made a number of references to the outstanding work of the neurophysiologists Hubel and Wiesel, and will continue to do so, even* more frequently, throughout most of the book. The final two papers in this part are addressed to questions of human pattern recognition which arise largely because progress has been made in the understanding of underlying neurophysiological processes; or at least one can say that the neurophysiological data suggested the sorts of perceptual effect which were sought. In a sense, then, the order of presenting the papers is wrong, since Hubel and Wiesel's major contributions are only described in the following section. This order was dictated by the desire to maintain regularity in the types of papers presented in each section, but some readers might want to read the Hubel and Wiesel paper in Part IV (p. 366) before proceeding to the end of this section.

The next paper, by Campbell and Kulikowski, addresses the question of whether evidence of interactions between contoured arrays in different orientations (in human vision) is consistent with Hubel and Wiesel's findings (in the cat and monkey) of cortical cells which are "selectively tuned" to respond to contours in specific orientations. The paper is somewhat technical, and may be easier to absorb if some of the specialized terms are explained.

The gratings referred to are simply arrays of parallel light and dark lines, in this case without sharp boundaries between them. Luminance means roughly what we would ordinarily term brightness (the exact definition does not matter here). Contrast refers (approximately) to the ratio of the brightest lines in the grating to the darkest lines (for the exact definition, see Figure I in the paper); the bigger this difference, the higher the contrast. Contrast sensitivity refers to the observer's ability to detect a change in contrast. This is measured by the increment threshold technique, in which a test stimulus (here the test grating) is flashed on and off; the increment threshold, as the name implies, is that value of the increment which gives rise to a just noticeable difference (j.n.d.) in contrast. The greater the contrast sensitivity, the smaller will be the increment threshold. The argument is that if changes in the relative orientations of two visual patterns (which are superimposed on each other) affect the ease with which contrast changes can be detected in one of them, this must be evidence for selective detection of contrast in sets of different detector units. Otherwise, if change in relative orientation had no effect, one would have to argue for a homogeneous, nonorientational system for contrast detection.

The section under the heading "method" is not essential to an understanding of the general purport of the paper.

# *Orientational Selectivity of the Human Visual System*

F. W. CAMPBELL AND J. J. KULIKOWSKI

*1. It is known that an object is less detectable when it is viewed against a background containing structures similar to the object. The effect of changing the orientation between the object and background is investigated.*

*2. Gratings of variable contrast were generated on two oscilloscopes; these were superimposed optically. The angle of orientation between them could be changed. The threshold of one grating, the test grating, was determined in the presence of the other, the masking grating.*

*3. When the gratings were presented with the same orientation (and locked in phase) the increment threshold of the test grating was found to be proportional to the suprathreshold contrast of the masking grating.*

*4. As the angle between the test and masking gratings was increased the masking effect fell exponentially.*

*5. At 12° on either side of a vertical test grating the masking effect was reduced by a factor of two with respect to its maximum value. This angle was independent of the contrast level of masking, the focus, and also the phase coherence of the masking grating.*

*6. If the test grating was presented obliquely the effect of masking was slightly less.*

*7. The narrow orientationally tuned channels found psychophysically by this masking technique are compared with the orientationally sensitive cells discovered electrophysiologically in the visual cortex of the cat.*

## *INTRODUCTION*

Hubel and Weisel (1959, 1962) have shown that many of the cells in the visual cortex of the cat respond only to lines with a certain orientation. Each cell has a particular angle to which it is most responsive. The population of this type of cell has representatives from all angles of orientation. Is it possible to demonstrate in man psychophysically a similar orientational sensitivity?

Reprinted from the *Journal of Physiology,* 1966.

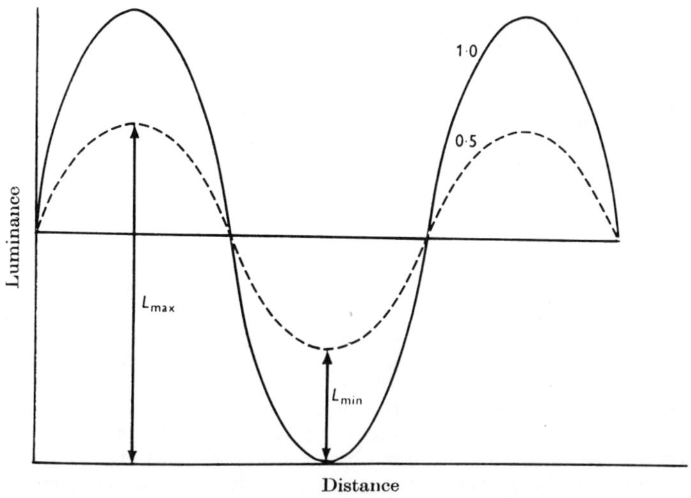


Fig. 1. Contrast is defined as $(L_{max}-L_{min})/(L_{max}+L_{min})$. Two values of contrast are illustrated: 1 and 0·5; the mean luminance level remains constant. Spatial frequency is defined as the reciprocal of the angular distance between successive maxima in the sinusoidal luminance distribution. Contrast sensitivity $= (L_{max}+L_{min})/(L_{max}-L_{min})$.

The experiment was designed as follows: A test target consisting of a fine grating was presented at a fixed orientation. The subject could adjust the contrast (Fig. 1) of the grating to a threshold value. A second masking grating of the same spatial frequency could be superimposed optically on the test grating; that is, it was added to the test grating without obscuring it. The contrast of the masking grating could be set to any level by the experimenter, and its angle of presentation could be altered relative to the test grating. The mean luminance of the combined test and masking grating was always constant and independent of their contrast settings. This apparatus enables us to evaluate angular interaction between the two gratings in terms of the contrast threshold of the test grating.

The reason for selecting gratings as test and masking stimuli was the expectancy that a large number of orientationally sensitive 'line detectors' from different parts of the visual field would be simultaneously involved, and thus thresholds might be determined with less variability.

## *METHODS*

Gratings were generated on each face of two oscilloscopes using the television technique of Schade (1956) and modified as described by Green and Campbell (1965). The first oscilloscope carried the test gratings which had a sinusoidal modulation of the contrast along one axis. The test grating frequency was always 10 c/deg of arc. Its contrast

(Fig. 1) could be varied by the observer. A second similar oscilloscope carried the masking grating, also with a frequency of 10 c/deg.

The observer looked at the test grating through an artificial pupil of 2·8 mm diameter and a spectacle lens to correct for the viewing distance. A beam-splitting cube was placed close to the spectacle lens and positioned so that the masking grating could be superimposed upon the test grating. In other words, the observer could see one grating added to the other. The superimposed gratings were contained in a circle subtending 2° and a screen subtending 10° surrounded this; the screen and the test field were matched in colour and had a luminance of 40 cd/m$^2$ as seen by the observer. The masking and the test gratings could be rotated through a range of 360° by two Dove prisms in the optic axis of each grating system.

As the screens of the oscilloscopes had an equal luminance, it is clear that the maximum contrast that can be achieved by the masking grating alone is 0·5, for its contrast is diluted by half the additional luminance from the test screen. In some experiments it was important to test the effects of high contrast levels of masking and this was done by decreasing the luminance of the test grating by the required amount. The luminances of the screens were measured with an S.E.I. (Ilford) photometer.

In order to generate a stationary grating of uniform spatial frequency and contrast, the beam intensity (Z-axis) of the oscilloscope was modulated with a pure sinusoidal frequency from an oscillator, and the time base controlling the X-axis was locked to the oscillator wave form. To generate a grating which did not have constant phase coherence, the Z-axis was supplied with a voltage from a noise generator which was passed through a tuneable narrow-band filter with a *Q* of 25. This produces a pattern like a grating, but in this case the position of each bar of the pattern is constantly moving in relation to the screen. The pattern has a constant mean spatial frequency and is easily recognized as a grating. The mean contrast of the grating is also constant, but each portion of it is continuously varying. In this way a masking pattern without spatial phase coherence was generated.

## *RESULTS*

In the initial experiment the test grating was vertically oriented and the masking grating was presented horizontally. The contrast sensitivity of the test grating (a reciprocal of the contrast threshold) was determined in the presence of different levels of contrast of the masking grating. The findings are shown in Fig. 2, results for 90°. Clearly, the threshold is not affected by the presence of a perpendicular masking grating even when its contrast is as high as 0·3. For higher contrasts there is only a slight effect. All contrast values are quoted relative to the combined luminance of masking and test gratings.

In the next experiment, the masking as well as the test grating were vertically oriented and were in phase with each other; that is, the contrast distribution was peak-on-peak and trough-on-trough. Findings are shown in Fig. 2, results for 0°. The arrow marks the contrast threshold for the masking grating, which is constantly present while the test grating appears for 1 sec every alternate 1 sec. When the masking grating has a contrast of less than 0·002 it does not produce a detectable effect on the contrast sensitivity of the test grating. From this contrast level up to 0·008, sensitivity is enhanced (i.e. contrast threshold decreases) in proportion to the contrast

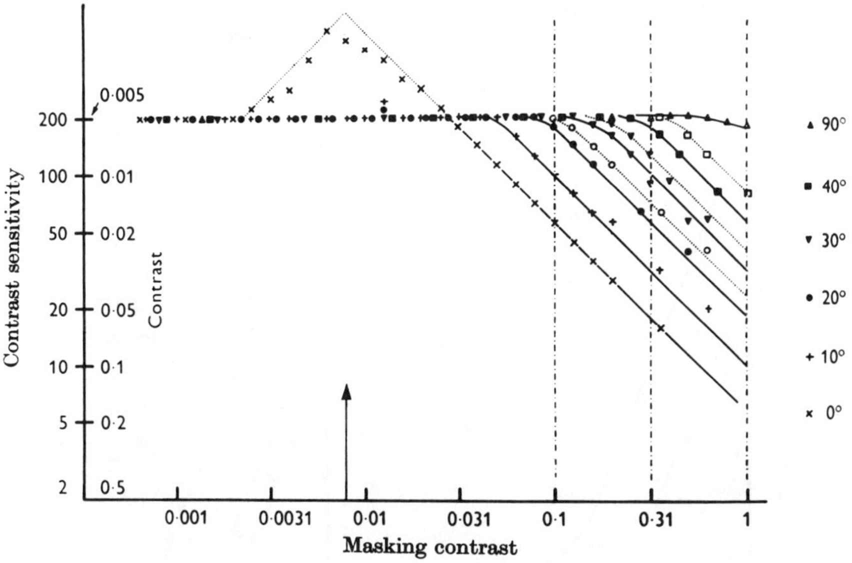


Fig. 2. Contrast sensitivity of the test grating as a function of masking contrast at different orientation angles: × 0°, + 10°, ● 20°, ▼ 30°, ■ 40°, ▲ 90°. Open symbols (○, ▽, □) and dotted lines denote results of measurements uncorrected for the reduction in contrast sensitivity of the masking grating.

of the masking grating. This is expected on physical grounds for the contrast of the two gratings must add optically. After this point it is possible to perceive the masking grating continuously. To determine thresholds at higher levels of masking contrast, the subject adjusted the test grating to a contrast level equal to a 'just noticeable difference' of contrast (j.n.d.). The absolute value of the j.n.d. increases in proportion to the masking contrast. *Effective masking* occurs with contrasts greater than 0·028, the point at which the j.n.d. reaches the contrast threshold of the test pattern. Thus, contrast sensitivity, the reciprocal of j.n.d., decreases in direct proportion to the masking contrast.

In the same manner, the contrast sensitivities for different amounts of masking contrast were determined for orientation angles of 20°, 30°, and 40°. The log contrast threshold of effective masking increases almost in proportion to the angle of orientation. It is well established that the contrast sensitivity for a grating in the oblique orientations is lower than that for a grating presented either horizontally or vertically (Campbell, Kulikowski & Levinson, 1966). In Fig. 2, the measured contrast sensitivities for these three orientations (open symbols) have been corrected for this effect (solid symbols). In all cases the corrected absolute value of the j.n.d. increases in proportion to the effective masking contrast.

To illustrate more clearly the effect of the angle of orientation of the

$$\log R = \log S_{\text{unmasked}} - \log S_{\text{masked}}.$$

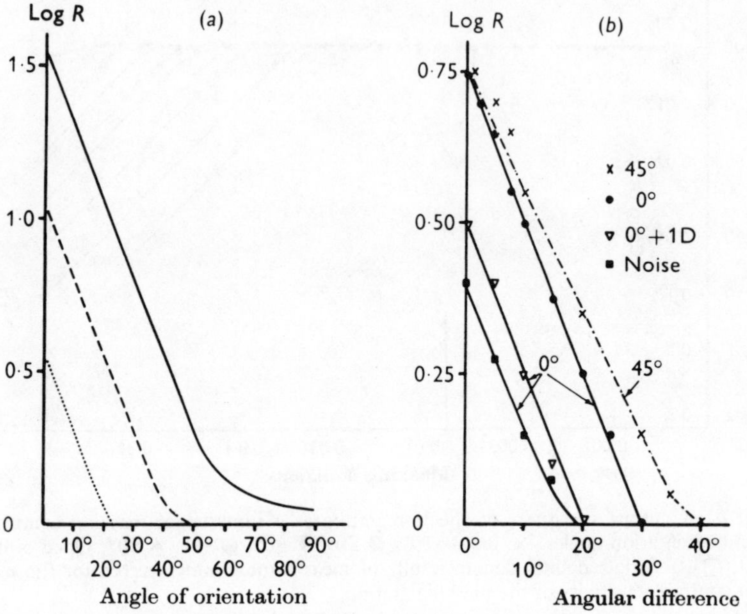


Fig. 3. The masking ratio, R, as a function of the orientation angle. (*a*) Results replotted from Fig. 2 for three masking-contrast levels of 1 (continuous line) 0·31 (interrupted line) and 0·1 (dotted line); these three levels of masking contrast are marked by three vertical lines in Fig. 2. (*b*) The masking ratio measured under different conditions—(1) vertical orientation of the test grating (0°): ● phase coherent sinusoidal masking grating, □ phase incoherent masking grating, ▽ test and masking gratings defocused +1 D; (2) oblique orientation of the test grating (45°): × phase coherent masking grating.

masking grating on the contrast sensitivity of the test grating, the results shown in Fig. 2 were replotted for three selected contrast levels of 1, 0·31 and 0·1 (vertical dot-dashed lines in Fig. 2) in terms of a masking ratio *R*. The masking ratio, *R*, was obtained from contrast sensitivities of unmasked ($S_{\text{unmasked}}$) and masked ($S_{\text{masked}}$) gratings by subtracting the logarithms of these sensitivities:

The $\log_{10}$ of these ratios are plotted against the angle of orientation on a linear scale, and illustrated graphically in Fig. 3*a*. It is evident that an exponential function adequately describes the angular effect of masking. Since the straight portions of the characteristics are parallel the exponent is constant for all levels of the masking contrast.

In the previous experiments, the masking and test gratings were in phase. The next experiment was designed to test the significance of phase location. This was done by generating a grating using a narrow-band noise source. In this way the position of each bar of the grating was arranged to change constantly. The resulting grating had a definite mean spatial frequency. Although it did not appear to vary in its spatial frequency, each bar varied constantly about its mean position and contrast. Thus, there was no constant relation between the phase of the masking grating and the fixed test grating. The effect of the orientation angle on the masking ratio is shown in Fig. 3*b* (squares).

For comparison the effect of a masking grating locked in phase on the masking ratio is also shown in Fig. 3*b* (circles) for a contrast of 0·2. It will be noted that the exponent for the two types of grating is similar. We may conclude that similar masking occurs with both in phase and changing phase gratings.

So far the masking ratio characteristics have had a constant exponent. Two further experiments were designed to find whether this slope could be changed. Since the resolving power for gratings is less in the oblique orientations (Campbell *et al.*, 1966), we examined the effect of a masking grating on a test grating presented obliquely (45°). The experiment was done in the same manner as described previously for the vertical grating. Results are shown in Fig. 3*b* (× and dot-dashed line). There is a well marked change in slope which indicates a reduction of the exponent amounting to 25%. Is this decrease connected simply with the reduction of resolving power associated with the oblique presentation? This may be tested by decreasing the resolving power in another way and again determining the masking ratio.

The resolving power of the eye was reduced by placing +1D lens in front of the artificial pupil. The resulting myopia decreased the contrast sensitivity of the test and masking gratings by 0·6 logarithmic unit, as could be expected from the findings of Campbell and Green (1965). The masking ratio was subsequently measured and results are shown in Fig. 3*b* (triangles). The exponent was found to be identical to a vertical test grating measured with an in focus eye.

## *DISCUSSION*

These experiments were designed to establish whether some channels in the visual system were sensitive to the angle of orientation of contours. Using gratings of variable contrast and a masking technique we have obtained some psychophysical results suggesting such organization. Figure 2 gives threshold values of contrast at which masking begins for various angles of orientation. The reciprocal of the masking-contrast threshold is plotted in Fig. 4*a*. We call this the masking sensitivity, $S_M$. It will be noticed that the upper part of this characteristic is identical to the masking ratio characteristic (Fig. 3*a*, continuous line). To illustrate this phenom-

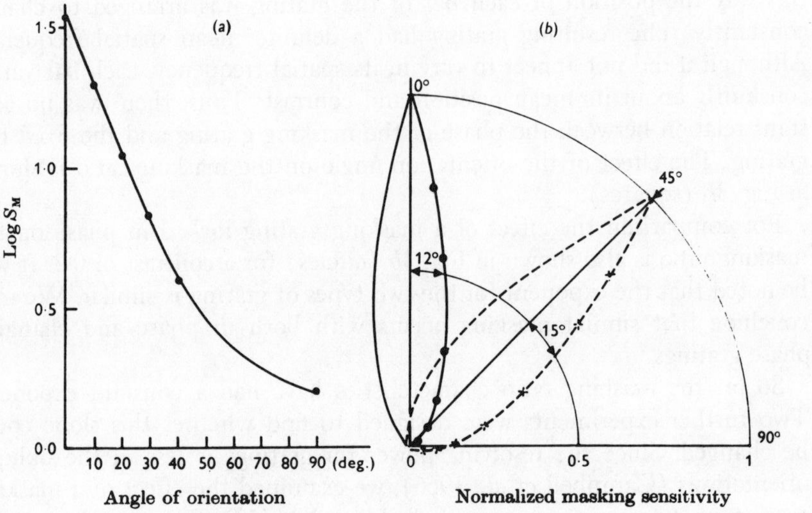


Fig. 4. Masking sensitivity as a function of orientation of the masking grating. (*a*) Logarithm of the masking sensitivity for the test grating vertically oriented. (*b*) Normalized masking sensitivity plotted in polar co-ordinates for two orientations of the test grating: ● vertical (0°) and × oblique (45°). Notice differences of the half width at half height of the characteristics: 12° for vertical and 15° for oblique presentations of the test grating.

enon more convincingly it is convenient to plot the masking sensitivity as a normalized quantity in a linear scale and in polar coordinates. This is shown in Fig. 4*b* for the two investigated orientations of test gratings, 0° and 45° (only one lobe of each is shown). At the half-value of the maximum masking sensitivity (0·5) the half-width of the characteristic is 12° for the vertical presentation and 15° for the oblique presentation. This is a convenient measure of angular selectivity.

It is, of course, not possible to argue convincingly from psychophysical data to neurophysiological description of the visual system. Nevertheless, it is interesting to compare the description of the orientational sensitivity of the cortical cells of the cat (Hubel & Wiesel, 1965) with our results. They found that most cells respond actively to straight-line stimuli, either a white or a dark line. This type of stimulus is effective only when presented in an orientation that is characteristic for the given cell. There is usually no response when the stimulus is presented at right angles to the optimum orientation. The range of orientations over which a response may be evoked is not more than 30° for a given cell. To give but one example taken from a description of a 'lower order hypercomplex cell' we quote: 'The orientation of the edge was critical, since changing it by more than 10°–15° produced a marked decrease in the response, and a 30° change made the stimulus ineffective.'

This semiquantitative description of the orientation sensitivity of cortical cells of the cat agrees surprisingly well with the angular selectivity found psychophysically. It should be possible to investigate electrophysiologically the angular selectivity of these cortical cells with a stimulation technique similar to that we have used. Such an investigation might establish more critically whether there is indeed any connexion between this psychophysical phenomenon and neurophysiological mechanisms.

The finding that the angular selectivity for the 45° presentation is 25% worse than that for the vertical orientation agrees quantitatively with the finding of other workers that the visual resolving power for a variety of test conditions (reviewed by Taylor, 1963) including an alignment task (Andrews, 1965) is also reduced approximately by the same amount. We find that degrading the optical image by defocusing by +1D does not change the angular selectivity. It may therefore be concluded that the poorer angular selectivity for the oblique presentation cannot be due to optical factors. Using a different method Campbell *et al.* (1966) also concluded that the orientational variation of the visual acuity was not due to optical factors. This suggests that these orientational effects are connected with a specific property of the visual nervous system.

The striking similarity of the findings with a wide variety of visual tasks suggest some common basic explanation. In the previous paper (Campbell *et al.* 1966), 90° orientational differences in visual resolving power might have suggested a Cartesian-co-ordinate system. However, we find the angular-selectivity characteristic much narrower than would be expected on a simple Cartesian-co-ordinate system. This implies that there must be numerous orientationally selective channels, closely separated in angle, in order to signal adequately all orientations. Hubel and Wiesel (1965) give a minimum estimate of 10–15 orientations originating from a given small retinal area. This suggests a maximum angular separation of 12°–15° between each channel, a value which would be adequate to represent all orientations.

## *REFERENCES*

Andrews, D. P. Perception of contours in the central fovea. *Nature,* 1965, *205,* 1218-1220.

Campbell, F. W., & Green, D. G. Optical and retinal factors affecting visual resolution. *Journal of Physiology,* 1965, *181,* 576-593.

Campbell, F. W., Kulikowski, J. J., & Levinson, J. The effect of orientation on the visual resolution of gratings. *Journal of Physiology,* 1966, *187,* 427-436.

Green, D. G., & Campbell, F. W. Effect of focus on the visual response to a sinusoidally modulated spatial stimulus. *Journal of the Optical Society of America,* 1965, *55,* 1154-1157.

Hubel, D. H., & Wiesel, T. N. Receptive fields of single neurones in the cat's striate cortex. *Journal of Physiology,* 1959, *148,* 574-591.

Hubel, D. H., & Wiesel, T. N. Receptive fields, binocular interaction and functional architecture in the cat's visual cortex. *Journal of Physiology,* 1962, *160,* 106-154.

Hubel, D. H., & Wiesel, T. N. Receptive fields and functional architecture in two nonstriate visual areas (18 and 19) of the cat. *Journal of Neurophysiology,* 1965, 28, 229-289.

Schade, O. H. Optical and photoelectric analog of the eye. *Journal of the Optical Society of America,* 1956, *46,* 721-739.

Taylor, M. M. Visual discrimination and orientation. *Journal of the Optical Society of America,* 1963, *53,* 763-765.

*The final paper in this section is the most difficult one for the nonspecialist to grasp, and its point depends to a large extent on an understanding of an earlier paper by Andrews (1967a) in which evidence for contour element detectors in human vision is reported. Since we have not room for both, the contents of that earlier paper will be summarized in such a way as to serve as an introduction to the one included here.*

*A variety of evidence shows that contour information in the visual system is "sharpened" in some way; for instance the optics of the eye make it certain that there must be some blurring of the retinal image, yet even very fine lines are seen in sharp detail, not as fuzzy images. This suggests that the visual system contains filters "tuned" to the detection of contours in specific orientations—a point which is strongly reinforced by Hubel and Wiesel's findings. Subjective reports of the appearance of very short line segments flashed briefly on a screen indicate that an observer may see a variable line, which can change in length, thickness, and orientation from occasion to occasion, and may even appear to rotate during a presentation. In a series of psychophysical experiments Andrews was able to estimate the characteristics of the response functions (both the average and the variability of response) of his observers to each particular stimulus configuration used (i.e., position, orientation, and duration of presented line segments). This led him to postulate that filters are indeed selectively tuned for specific orientations, that the tuning is most precise for orientations near the horizontal and vertical, and that the observer's response will be determined by the strongest output from one of a set of filters (ff) which are tuned for similarly oriented linc segments. It is reasonable to suppose that outputs will fluctuate over time, and this accounts for the variability of response to one and the same stimulus (one particular line segment). However, longer exposures, and longer line segments, give rise to more reliable (less variable) percepts, so there must be both temporal and spatial interaction between units (filters). Given longer exposure duration, it is held that processes of* mutual inhibition between different units will occur, and that perceived orientation will correspond to maxima in the inhibitory pattern. Similarly, longer line segments will be combined by some higher process in the system—but that is to anticipate the contents of the Andrews paper included here. There is evidence that the filter units have inputs from both eyes, and this too accords well with Hubel and Wiesel's findings on binocular interaction.

If the evidence on perception of short, briefly flashed line segments does support the notion of pattern-element detectors, specifically the notion that populations of such detectors "sample" visual input patterns—and I believe it does—then the question of how the detected elements can be "put together" into larger patterns or pattern features becomes of crucial importance. Andrews' approach to the problem is to compare human performance with that of an "ideal observer" which would put the information available together in the most efficient way. The experiments are restricted to cases of the simplest sorts of spatial integration, but their interpretation is pushed to the point of estimating several of the characteristics both of the units and the processes of combining their outputs. The experiments themselves are quite straightforward, although the interpretation and discussion become rather involved at times.

Explanation of some of the technical terms used may again be of some help. Acuity means the visual detection of detail. It is commonly measured by getting an observer to detect presence/absence of a fine line, or series of lines, at a specified position, orientation, and luminance. Vernier acuity is measured by the detection of misalignment between a pair of lines which are nearly collinear. Stereo acuity is measured by the detection of a difference in depth (distance from the observer) between two lines which are viewed binocularly (with both eyes) and where there are no other cues to depth present. A degree of visual angle is a measure of the extent of an element in the visual field, the degree being the same one that is familiar from geometry and trigonometry. The advantage of specifying elements in terms of degrees, minutes, and seconds of arc, is that this specifies extent on the retina, or in the visual field, independently of distance. Thus, a line 1 foot long seen at a distance of 6 feet will subtend the same visual angle as a line 2 feet long at 12 feet and will have the same "retinal image." A rough idea of the extent of 1° (degree) of visual angle is given by this: the thumbnail, viewed at arm's length, subtends about 1° horizontally to the eye. A minute of arc (1′) is 1/60th of a degree, and one second of arc (1″) is 1/60th of a minute. Actually Andrews sometimes specifies line lengths in terms of millimeters (mm) on the screen, sometimes in units of visual angle, and sometimes both, which might be confusing. So long as the screen is always viewed at a constant distance (which it was) the one measure is equivalent to, and can be converted into, the other.

# Perception of Contour Orientation in the Central Fovea: Part II. Spatial Integration

D. P. ANDREWS

## *INTRODUCTION*

The input to the visual system is a large number of signals that are separate in place and time. The output of the system is a continuous field displaying objects that are recognized. Spatial relations and other features can be 'read out' from the display on demand. In order to achieve this, the separate input signals must be related to one another. Any two objects can be related to one another spatially; therefore direct or indirect connections must exist between any two signal lines arising in the retina. This paper is addressed to the problem, how are the necessary connections effected?

It is unthinkable that every signal line should be directly connected to every other. There must be some simplifying system, in which signal lines are first related to neighbours, then the neighbours related to each other, and so on.

Anatomical and physiological observations support these notions; the latter indicate that small features of pattern in the retinal image elicit selective responses from units at a higher lever, and the higher up in the system the more complex the specification of the sufficient pattern. Physiological and psychophysical observations indicate that contours (loci of strong contrast) play a special role in vision. This allows less critical information to be rejected selectively, with resulting saving in channel capacity.

In Part I of the present work, Andrews (1967), it was assumed that there are units in the visual system that respond selectively to contours at particular orientations and positions in the visual field. Such units will be termed "*ff*". It was inferred from the experiments that *ff*:

(a) usually have inputs from both eyes
(b) respond more selectively when 'tuned' hear the horizontal and vertical directions
(c) are subject to long term adaptation which tends to distribute responses uniformly on average around the clock.

Reprinted from *Vision Research*, 1967.

The assumption that such units exist was initially based on physiological findings, especially of Hubel and Wiesel (1962, 1963), but the experiments in Part I also lend strong support: it would be difficult to explain the findings without proposing such units.

The present paper is concerned with the spatial integration involved in perceiving the parallelism of two straight lines. The experiments are designed to indicate the field-size of *ff* and how outputs from *ff* are combined.

The approach used in interpreting the results is to compare human performance with the best possible performance using the same receptor -response distribution. The ratio of observed to ideal performance constitutes a measure of efficiency of pattern processing. (This is not to be confused with the quantal or other efficiency of the receptors themselves). One can then ask whether efficiency varies with range of integration; if it does, then the manner of its variation may throw light on the integrative process. At the least, it will enable the processing losses to be described, should the interpretation be ambiguous.

The above approach defines the efficiency with which positional information in retinal patterns is integrated in psychophysical judgments. There are three basic questions one might ask about this integration:

(a) Are some features of the input, such as contour orientation, contour curvature, contour discontinuity, etc., processed more efficiently than others?

(b) How does efficiency vary with range of integration?

(c) Does the answer to (b) vary with the type of stimulus object, (e.g. curved lines vs. straight lines)?

All these questions can be approached by comparing human and ideal observer performances. The answers are likely to indicate whether there are other specialized filters besides *ff*, and whether they operate at the same or subsequent levels. Success depends on finding differences in efficiency, of course. If there were no differences, any sequence of lossless operations would fit the facts. The present paper is directed to answering question (b) in the perception of contour orientation.

There are several earlier studies in this general area. Question (a) is almost entirely untouched: in order to compare two performances, it is usually necessary that the same subjects serve for both at about the same time; only large differences can be established reliably by comparing different experiments. A paper by Berry (1948) does compare two performances, vernier acuity and stereoscopic acuity. He showed that vernier acuity suffers more than stereoscopic acuity when a gap is introduced between the test lines; this suggests the important conclusion that binocular disparities are processed earlier than contours.

Question (b) is not quite so neglected. Sulzer and Zener (1953) showed that acuity for parellelism increases with line length. This was confirmed by Rochlin (1955). These studies are closely related to the present one and are discussed further below. Ogilvie and Taylor (1959) have shown that acuity for a fine line increases with its length; corresponding results have also been established for vernier acuity (French, 1919–1920; MacKay, 1961) and stereoscopic acuity (Matsubayashi, 1938). Unfortunately, nearly all of these studies omit the very small stimuli which proved so revealing in the present experiments. Large stimulus objects also allow a confusion about the effects upon performance of eccentricity in the field and distance *per se*.

Question (c) could be approached by comparing studies such as those above, but the lack of data for very small stimulus objects prevents fruitful comparisons at present.

## *METHODS*

Procedures and apparatus were described in detail in Part I. The subject saw a bright line (*L*) against a less bright field 15° square, viewed at 1·5 m; *L* was 0·43 mm wide and of variable length. It was compared in orientation with a long black comparison line (*C*), which was always horizontal and constantly visible a few millimetres below *L*. The luminance of *L* was sufficient to allow optimal performance; this level was established for continuous and instantaneous presentation of *L* in a preliminary experiment.

The procedure was as follows in all the experiments:

The subject fixated the centre of *L*. His task was either to set *L* parallel to *C* (when using the adjustment method), or to judge the sign of their relative orientation (when using the method of constant stimuli).

The adjustment method was used when *L* was presented continuously. There were 18 settings in each run, the first of which was for settling in and was not recorded. The starting point was randomized after each setting. Each run took about 10 minutes. The mean ($\bar{x}$) and standard error ($s$) of the 17 observations was computed.

The method of constant stimuli was used with flash exposure (1msec). Runs consisted of approximately 120 presentations at intervals of about 7 seconds. Four stimulus orientations were used and succeeded in random order. There was a preliminary run before each recorded run to establish a suitable range of stimulus orientations.[1] The response frequencies were subject to probit analysis[1] to find the mean and s.e. ($\bar{x}$ and $s$) of the response error distribution.

For both methods, there was a break of at least two minutes between runs.

## *SYMBOLS*

The following symbols are used:

*L* A short bright line whose orientation is to be judged.

C A long horizontal black line near *L* which serves as a reference direction.

*d* The length of *L* in mm. (1 mm is equivalent to 2·3′ arc.)

[1] See Finney's "Probit Analysis" (1952) for further details and estimates of the s.e. of $x$ and $s$. For a standard run of 120 presentation, the s.e. of $\bar{x}$ and $s$ were about 0·25($s$) and 0·15($s$) respectively.

- *h* The height of *L* above C in mm.
- $\bar{x}$ The mean inclination of *L* when judged parallel to C, measured clockwise from the true orientation of C.
- *s* The standard deviation of a series of parallelism settings, measured in degrees. (When the method of constant stimuli was used, $\bar{x}$ and *s* were computed by the probit method.)
- *f* (plural *ff*). Units in the visual system which respond specifically to short lines at particular orientations and positions in the field.

## *EXPERIMENTAL RESULTS*

### Experiment I

This experiment was designed primarily to find the relation between line length (*d*) and acuity for parallelism (*s*), with L either continuously visible or presented instantaneously. The horizontal comparison line C subtended 15°.

Parts of this experiment were the first to be performed, and the results influenced the choice of *d* for all other experiments, including those in Part I. There were several parts to the experiment, not all of which are reported here; the experiment was exploratory, and, especially in the case of subject DPA, was spread over a considerable period.

The results of three series are reported here, in each of which a variety of line lengths were tested; (1) *L* presented continuously 11 mm above C; (2) *L* presented continuously 3 mm above C; (3) *L* presented instantaneously 11 mm above C. For series (1) and (2) the adjustment method was used, and for (3), the method of constant stimuli. In all cases, the subject was instructed to fixate the centre of *L*; there were two fixation points 5 mm apart symmetrically above and below the centre of L for series (3), and for series (1) when *d* was greater than 6 mm.

The various line lengths were tested in random order, with up to three consecutive runs at each line length. Results are shown in Figs. 1 and 2. Each data point represents the mean value of $\bar{x}$ and r.m.s. value of *s* for a group of consecutive runs at one line length. ($\bar{x}$ and *s* were computed for each run separately.) The number of consecutive runs varied with series and subject between 1 and 3 runs.

For subject DPA, series (1) and (2) were about a month apart. Both series were repeated about two years later, again about a month apart.

For subjects JS and DPA, a fourth series was run in which L was flashed and *h* was varied between 3 mm and 300 mm. A long and short line were tested. The results are not given below, because there was no evidence that $s^2$ varied according to *h*.

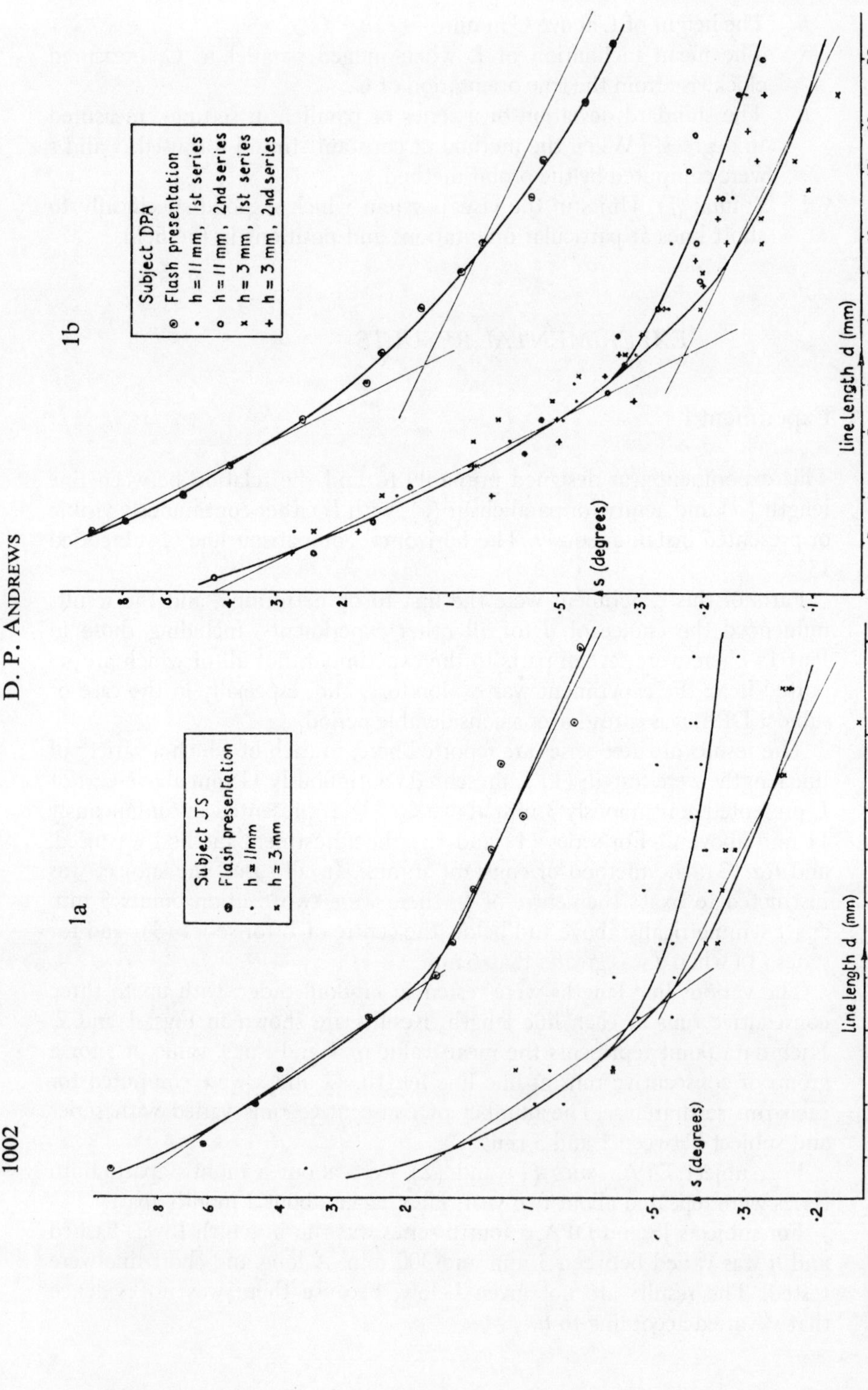
1002
D. P. Andrews
1a
Subject JS
Flash presentation
h = 11mm
h = 3 mm
s (degrees)
line length d (mm)
1b
Subject DPA
Flash presentation
h = 11 mm, 1st series
h = 11 mm, 2nd series
h = 3 mm, 1st series
h = 3 mm, 2nd series
s (degrees)
line length d (mm)

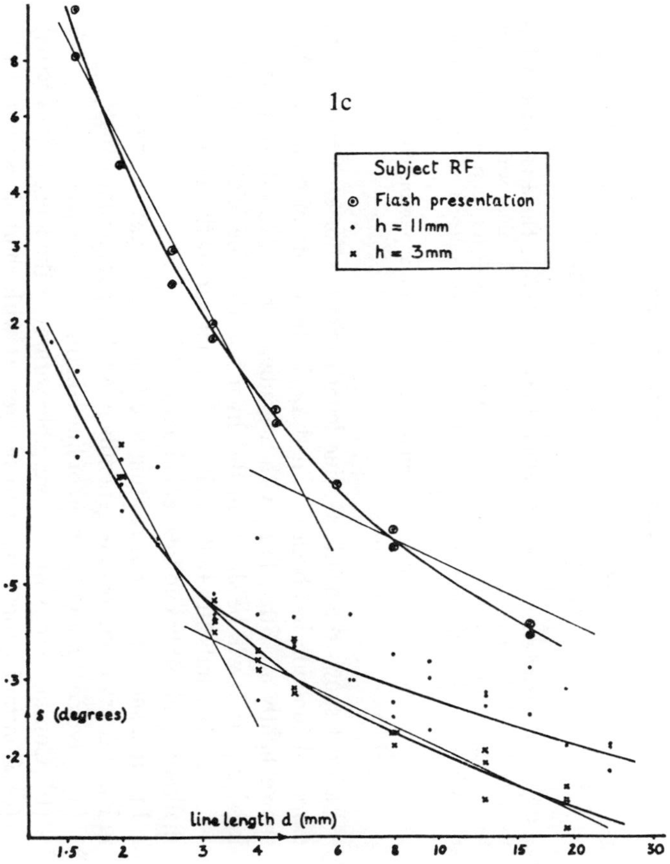


FIG. 1. Acuity for parallelism ($s$) between a short line and a long one, as a function of the length ($d$) of the short line.

There were three series for each subject:
(1) short line ($L$) continuously visible 11 mm above comparison line ($C$),
(2) $L$ continuously visible 3 mm above $C$,
(3) $L$ flashed instantaneously 11 mm above $C$. $C$ was horizontal and subtended 15° in length.
Empirical functions have been drawn in each case. $s$ was four to five times greater when $L$ was flashed, although the brightness of $L$ was set for optimal performance in each case. The thin lines have gradients $-3/2$ and $-1/2$, representing the relations $s^2 \propto 1/d^3$ and $s^2 \propto 1/d$.
Each data point represents the r.m.s. value of $s$ for up to three consecutive runs in the same condition. The s.e. of $s$ is about $\frac{0{\cdot}25s}{\sqrt{k}}$ in each case, where $k$ is the number of runs.

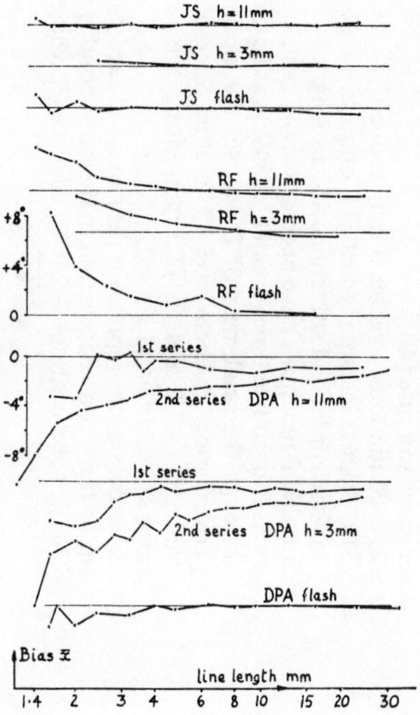


Fig. 2. Constant error ($x$) as a function of line length ($d$). The data correspond to those of Fig. 1. Each point represents the grant mean of all values with a given line length. The s.e. of $x$ is $0{\cdot}15s/\sqrt{k}$ for flashed presentation and $0{\cdot}25s/\sqrt{k}$ for continuous presentation, where $k$ is the total number of runs. Variation of $x$ over a period was much greater than this, of shapes of $x$ vs. $d$ functions can only be established approximately.

Figure 1 shows the acuity vs. line length relations for each subject. An empirical function has been drawn through the points in each case. Also shown lightly are fitted lines with a gradient of —3/2 and —½ on the log–log plot. It will be shown in the discussion that the relation $\log(s) = -3/2 \log(d)$ indicates that efficiency does not vary with line length. The shallower gradient has no theoretical basis.

Figure 2 shows functions relating line length and constant error ($\bar{x}$). As in Part I constant errors were generally present. Figure 2 shows that:

(a) $\bar{x}$ is a continuous function of line length.

(b) Constant errors were appreciable with even the longest lines tested.

(c) Constant errors tended to be greatest with short lines, and in the same direction for flashed and continuous exposure. For longer lines, constant errors were less predictable.

(d) Over a two-year period, $\bar{x}$ changed considerably, and the change itself varied as a function of line length.

The drifting of $\bar{x}$ exhibited in Fig. 2 was found over shorter periods also, and similar drifting was reported in Part I. All results showed that drift tends to increase with the time between test and retest.[2] Drift was also found to be greater for lines 4 mm or less than for longer ones; this is not a consequence of the greater sampling error of $\bar{x}$ for shorter lines.[2] No similar drifting of *s* was found.

## Experiment II

It can be seen in Fig. 1 that for longer lines $s^2$ is approximately proportional to $\frac{1}{d}$, but there is insufficient data to establish or reject this relation with confidence. It is also clear that *s* varies according to *h*, but the form of the variation is not known. Experiment II was designed to clarify these points. Also, the effect of fixating halfway between *L* and *C* was compared with the normal fixation at the centre of *L*.

With long lines, it is likely that *C* contributes an appreciable proportion of the error variance. In the present experiment *C* and *L* were made equal in length so that their contributions should be accountable. (It transpired that this reasoning oversimplifies the perceptual process.) *C* (and *L*) ranged in length from 9 to 30 mm, and *h* varied from 1·5 mm to 22 mm. Thus the whole of both lines fell within 1·1° of the fixation point.

*L* was always presented continuously, and the adjustment method was used. There were two runs at different times in each condition tested. Figures 3 and 4 show the r.m.s. value of *s* in each case, and indicate which conditions were tested. The fixation point was varied for subject DPA only; no significant variation of *s* was found.

Figure 3 shows the *s* vs. *d* functions for various values of *h*. There is no

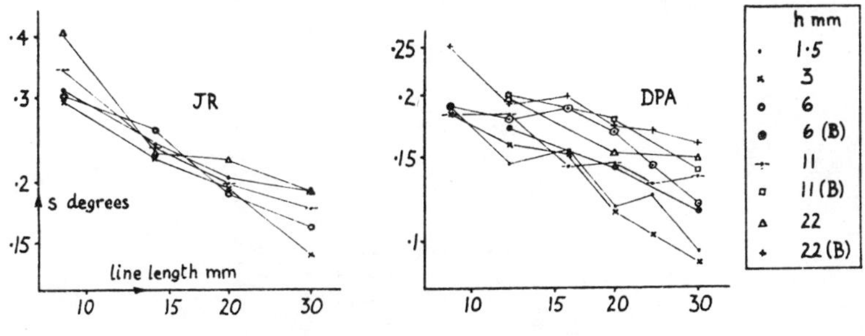


Fig. 3. Acuity for parallelism for two equal lines as a function of line length (*d*) for various separations (*h*). The comparison line (*c*) was horizontal, and the movable line (*L*) was adjusted to appear parallel. (*B*) indicates that fixation was midway between *L* and *C*; in all other cases, fixation was at the center of *L*. Each point is the r.m.s. of two values.

[2] Full details can be found in Andrews (1965).

evidence that the regression of $\log(s^2)$ on $\log(d)$ varied according to $h$ or fixation point.[2] The mean regression coefficient was $-0{\cdot}798$ for DPA and $-1{\cdot}074$ for JR. These coefficients differ from one another at the 1 per cent level of significance, and that for DPA differs from unity at the 5 per cent level.[2]

The $s$ vs. $d$ functions in Fig. 3 are at much the same level as in Experiment I. For DPA, $s$ was a little larger at $h=3$ mm and a little smaller at $h=11$ mm than in the previous experiment; on average, there is practically no difference. (JR was not a subject for Experiment I, so no similar comparison can be made.) This is surprising: it was anticipated that for a given line length $s$ would be rather larger in the present experiment, since C was shorter. Instead, it appears that the contribution of C to performance depends mainly on the length of $L$, and hardly varies with its own length. The probable explanation is that only the part of C in the neighbourhood of $L$ can be utilized effectively in the comparison process. (For short lines, the part of C that can be utilized still provides a much more accurate reference than $L$; this shown by the fact that performance did not vary with $h$.)

Figure 4 shows the relation between $s$ and $h$ for the various line lengths used. These functions are very shallow; in view of the sampling variation of $s$, there would be little value in trying to represent them by mathematical functions. However, for descriptive purposes only, the relation between $s$

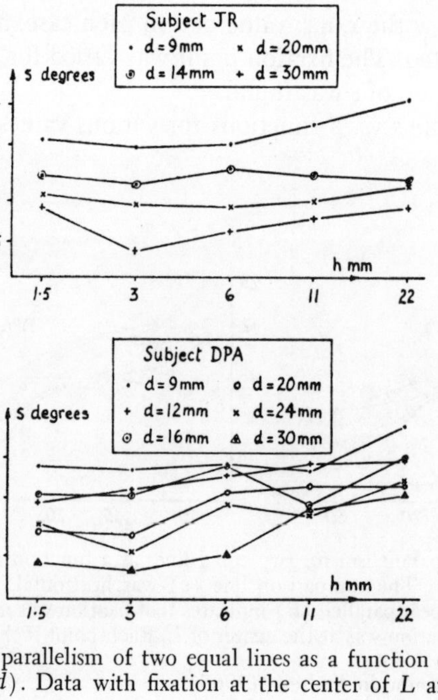


Fig. 4. Acuity for parallelism of two equal lines as a function of separation ($h$), for various line lengths ($d$). Data with fixation at the center of $L$ and between $L$ and C have been combined.

and $h$ is of order $s \propto \sqrt[5]{h}$ from $h=3$ mm to $h=22$ mm. There is an unexpected reversal of this gradient between the two smallest separations: in 9 cases out of 10, $s$ was higher at $h=1{\cdot}5$ mm than at $h=3$ mm. This accorded with subjective reports that the gap between $L$ and $C$ did not readily become wedge-shaped on turning the knob which caused $L$ to rotate. The case where $L$ and $C$ coincided was also tested informally, and the effect was much exaggerated: $L$ could be rotated a degree or so either way without visible result. The same result was obtained with two black lines.

Sulzer and Zener (1953) reported an experiment very similar to Experiment II. $L$ and $C$ were identical black lines which the subject had to set parallel. Line length was varied from ⅛ in. to 2 in. at a viewing distance of 30 in., (equivalent to the range 5·8 mm to 92 mm in my set-up.) Spacing $h$ was varied between 1/32 in. and 4 in. They found that $s$ was a linear function of $1/d$ and of $h$. This is not in agreement with my findings. Rochlin (1955) repeated the experiment, using line lengths of ¼ in. and 1 in. only, at the same viewing distance. He *reported* that the $s$ vs. $d$ relation was in agreement with Sulzer and Zener's findings; however, his data show that the variance for the 1 in. line was only twice that for the ¼ in. line, i.e. $s^2 \propto 1/d$. The findings of Experiment II fall between the two.

## Experiment III

The results of Experiment I suggested that up to a certain range in the visual field, integration of information is more efficiently carried out than over greater distances. (See Discussion.) This invites the question whether a line with a gap in the centre would be processed as efficiently as one without a gap. Experiment III was designed to answer this question.

$L$ was 11 mm above $C$, and had a gap in the centre which was varied from 1·2 mm to 20 mm. $C$ was horizontal and subtended 15°. The visible parts of $L$ ranged in length from 1 mm to 8 mm each. With flash presentation, there was a small fixation point at the centre of the gap. With continuous presentation, the subject was instructed to fixate the centre of the gap. The same three subjects served as in Experiment I.

The best indication of how a broken line is processed was given by its appearance when continuously presented. When the gap was 1·2 mm, the two parts of $L$ always appeared in line with one another. With gaps of 3·5 mm or more, the two parts of $L$ behaved independently; they did not appear to be in line, especially when the parts were short. When $L$ was rotated, it sometimes appeared to move like the two pans of a balance, and sometimes the inverse effect was observed. This never happens to the corresponding parts of an unbroken line. The reader is invited to check this for himself; the effect is best when lines and gap each subtend about 7′ arc. With flash presentation, the misalignment was also observed; ($L$ could not of course be rotated).

TABLE I. ACUITY FOR ORIENTATION OF A BROKEN STRAIGHT LINE

| Subject | Exposure | Gap length in mm | | | | | | | |
|---|---|---|---|---|---|---|---|---|---|
| | | 0·0 | 1·2 | 2·1 | 3·5 | 6·4 | 9·5 | 15·7 | 20·0 |
| D.P.A. | Continuous | 0·37 | 0·32 | 0·34 | 0·41 | 0·35 | 0·37 | 0·38 | 0·27 |
| J.S. | Continuous | 0·50 | 0·33 | 0·31 | 0·38 | 0·41 | 0·37 | 0·36 | 0·32 |
| R.F. | Flashed | 1·37 | 1·17 | 1·17 | 1·69 | 1·77 | 1·44 | 1·27 | 1·25 |
| J.S. | Flashed | 1·80 | 1·67 | 2·11 | 2·90 | 1·90 | 2·27 | 1·53 | — |

Entries show *s* as a function of gap length. The visible parts of *L* were each 2 mm long. Results for other line lengths were similar in that acuity was higher for a gap of 1·2 mm than with no gap; for greater gaps, acuity first decreased and eventually increased. The two parts of *L* did not usually appear in line to the subject. He was instructed to assess the overall gradient of the configuration, and judge its parrallelism to the long comparison line.

Results are shown in Table 1 for all cases when the visible parts of *L* were 2 mm long. Full results can be found in Andrews (1965). These results are typical, and can be summarized as follows: if a given line is parted in the middle (keeping the end-parts of constant length), acuity for orientation increases up to a gap-size of 1·2 mm. Thereafter, acuity falls or remains constant up to a gap of about 7 mm. For gaps of 10 mm or more, performance improves gradually. For an unbroken line, the *s* vs. *d* relation is monotonic.

Both the numerical results and subjective reports show that the two parts of a broken line have a degree of independence not observed in the corresponding parts of an unbroken line. It follows that the gap in *L* prevented some spatial interactions that would have taken place if no gap had been present. Very small gaps do not appear to prevent these interactions, though they may reduce them.

## *DISCUSSION*

### An Ideal Observer of Contour Inclination

Consider the case in which the image of a straight edge is stationary on the retina. The problem for the ideal observer is to estimate the orientation of the edge. Figure 5 illustrates the problem and the optimal solution. It shows a portion of the retinal mosaic in the human central fovea, traced from part of an enlargement of Fig. 40 in Polyak (1941). The edge to be detected is shown by a heavy line. It will be supposed for the present that the image is sharp, and that units crossed by the edge give an all-or-none response.

The information available to higher levels consists of the positions of unit centres plus a list of units that respond. The best estimate of the distal line's slope that the ideal observer can make is by fitting the line of least aquares through the centres of responding units, (or an equivalent operation if signals are otherwise coded.) This line is shown in Fig. 5 also.

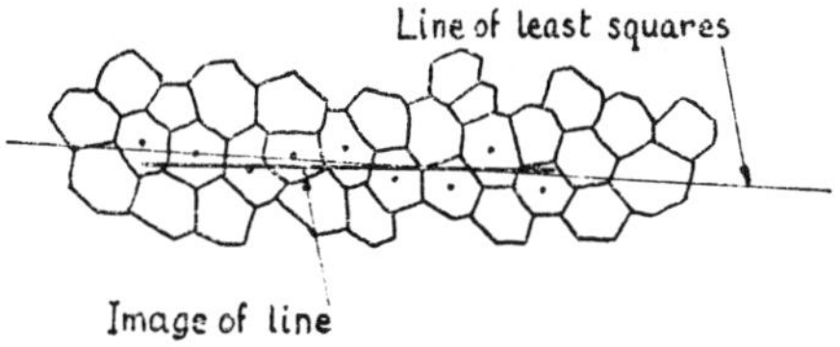


Fig. 5. The mosaic represents the retinal mosaic in the central fovea, and was traced from an enlargement of part of Fig. 40 in Polyak's "The Retina." The image of a line is shown crossing the mosaic, and a line of least squares has been fitted to the centers of the units on the line. The image and the line of least squares differ by an appreciable angle, whose probability distribution can be computed. (Actual retinal images are of course blurred, but the appropriate analysis is similar: see text.)

The regression of such a line is subject to sampling variation, since the image could fall anywhere on the retina. The variance of the regression ($V_b$) is given by $V_b = V_y\,(1 - r^2_{xy})/n.V_x$, where $n$ is the number of units responding, $V_x$ and $V_y$ are the variances of unit centres along and about the fitted line respectively, and $r_{xy}$ is the correlation of $x$- and $y$-coordinates of unit centres. $r_{xy}$ approximates to zero.[3] Now $V_y{=}c^2/12$ and $V_x{=}c^2n^2/12$, where $c$ is the average separation of unit centres. (The distributions of $x$- and $y$-coordinates are approximately rectangular, with maximum values of $cn/2$ and $c/2$ respectively.) Therefore, $V_b{=}1/n^3$ (rad.). The relation $V_b{=}1/n^3$ represents optimal use of positional information in determining the orientation of the edge.

A number of factors have been left out of account so far. The lines used in the experiment had two edges, and were viewed with two eyes; these factors would reduce $V_b$ by a constant if taken into account. Distribution of $x$- and $y$-coordinates are not quite rectangular, because cone separations vary; but whatever the distribution, $V_y \propto c^2$ and $V_x \propto c^2\,n^2$. Blur of the retinal image effectively increases the grain-size of the mosaic, and hence decreases $n$ by a constant. It was also assumed that units gave an all-or-none response; if instead they had $k$ distinguishable levels of response, $V_y$ would be divided by $(k-1)^2$. (The position of the image on a receptor can be estimated $(k-1)$ times more accurately.) The image was assumed stationary; in fact, the eyes move, which might allow several estimates of $V_b$ to be combined, and reduce it by a constant. However, if all such corrections were taken into account, the relation $V_b \propto 1/n^3$ would still represent an optimal integration of positional information.

A correction can be made to take account of the variation of receptor size with eccentricity. It was found[2] that this correction makes virtually no difference for lines up to 10 mm long (23′ arc), and would increase $V_b$ by only 20 per cent for a 20 mm line. A similar correction could be made to take account of the functional grain size of the retina, which is coarser than the receptor mosaic where several receptors share one output line. Assuming that grating acuity corresponds to functional grain-size, the appropriate correction is about the same as for receptor size within the foveal region.

One further correction should be made, to allow for errors in perceiving the comparison line. In Experiment I, $C$ was at least 7 times longer than $L$, so that $V_b$ for the com-

[3] In the retinal mosaic, serial correlations between cone centre ordinates are virtually zero for cones separated by seven rows or more, and only about 0·6 between immediate neighbours. Effective 'mosaics5 at higher levels are unlikely to be even so regular, as packing is not so tight. Correlations are based on an analysis of Figure 40 in Polyak (1941).

parison line should be less than 1 per cent of that for *L*. Total variance is simply the sum, and therefore little changed. In Experiment II, $V_b$ (for the model) should be the same for *L* and *C*, so the estimate of variance should be doubled. For an ideal processor, there is no loss in *relating* two orientations once each is fixed in relation to the mosaic.

The importance of the relation $V_b = k/d^3$ is that it allows a distinction between two types of error. Errors which affect all receptors equally, by losing information about intensity or position, leave $V_b$ proportional to $1/d^3$. A different kind of loss may occur if remote connections are fewer or less reliable than proximal ones, or if integration is performed in successive stages so that certain losses are peculiar to more extended figures. Losses of the second type will disturb the relation $V_b = k/d^3$.

## Constant Errors

Bias of perceived slope was found to increase as the short line was reduced in length, and this bias was in the same direction for flashed and continuous exposure. In Part I, two varieties of bias were distinguished: one component varied systematically according to orientation and exposure duration, changing sign between flashed and continuous exposure. There was also a bias which was independent of exposure duration, and subject to drift. The drift of constant error was found to be independent of exposure duration and affected both eyes similarly. The large biases found for short lines appear to be mainly of the second type.

In order to account for drifting of constant error, it was proposed in Part I that the relation between *f*-response and perceived orientation was subject to adaptation, such that perceived orientation in any small region is distributed uniformly on average around the clock. In Experiment I of the present series, constant error and drift of constant error were found to be greatest for short lines. Figure 2 illustrates this. This can also be attributed to adaptation which affects the scale of perceived orientation. The shorter the line, the fewer the *ff* which respond during voluntary fixation, and thus the smaller the region whose adaptive state determines constant error and its drift. For longer lines, adaptive states have a greater probability of cancelling out.

In Fig. 2, drift of constant error can be observed for even the longest lines. This may be due to a common adaptive error between many *ff*. However, it can more plausibly be attributed to adaptation affecting the space between *L* and *C*. Spatial adaptation is known to occur, and is discussed further below. Constant errors from this source and associated drift must have been present in all conditions.

## The Relation Between Line-Length and Acuity for Orientation

Figure 1 shows that there is a range of line lengths for which $s^2 = k/d^3$, between about 1·5 mm and 4 mm, (3·5–9′ arc). It was shown in Section

(1) that where the efficiency of transforming information into orientation signals is constant, this relation should hold.

It appears likely from this that the fields of *ff* are equivalent to at least 9′ arc in length. If *ff* had smaller fields, then their outputs would have to be combined without further loss to fit the facts. Lossless processing of positional information seems unlikely, though not impossible.

The present experiments offer no grounds for proposing two stages of orientation processing within a field size corresponding to 9′ arc. Hubel and Wiesel (1962) found no such process in the cat's visual system either although they did find that radially symmetric fields in the lateral geniculate body were subsequently combined into bar-detecting units. This fits well with the present results. The efficiency fall-off for lines less than 1·5 mm long can be attributed to the failure of two distinct lateral geniculate units to respond. The probability of this occurrence will increase rapidly at a certain line length, so that a point is seen instead of a line on most occasions. This fits the observed result precisely.

Up to a range of 9′ arc, efficiency is limited by range-independent losses, such as contrast-detecting accuracy, and the accuracy with which the geometry of the retinal mosaic is 'known' at the next highest level. The extent of these losses is not known because the information available in the input is not known; without it, one can compute the relative efficiency of two performances, but not the absolute efficiency.

When line length exceeds 9′ arc, efficiency of processing falls off rapidly. If optimal observed efficiency of processing is taken as 100 per cent (shown by the thin lines with gradient—3/2 in Fig. 1) then efficiency at 4 mm (9′ arc) averages around 75 per cent, but efficiency for an 8 mm line is only about 25 per cent; losses for still longer lines reduce efficiency by a factor of about 4 for every doubling in length. The 'knee' at about 4 mm is not sharp, but it is clear that processing efficiency is much lower for long lines than short ones and that the heavier losses commence at about this point. It is proposed that the knee marks the limit of receptive fields in *ff*, and that losses occur in combining the outputs of *ff*. One would not expect a very abrupt knee under this hypothesis, because two neighbouring units may sometimes respond when the line could be wholly accommodated within the field of one of them. The probability of this occurrence increases rapidly as the line length approaches the field size of a unit.

In order to demonstrate that the knee corresponds to the limit of receptive fields of *ff*, it must be shown that there is no loss in the integrative action of single *ff* which might cause the knee. Many such losses are conceivable; a detailed consideration of alternatives appears in ANDREWS (1965). Briefly: (1) Any loss which creates an absolute limit to performance is inconsistent with the observed reduction of $s$ as $d$ increases. (2) Possible effects of receptor size and functional grain size have already been discounted. (3) Distortions of the receptive field will add the same error variance for flashed and continuous presentation, whereas the error variance which gives rise to the knee is clearly different for flashed and continuous presentation.

It must also be shown that no other variety of loss causes the knee, (without reference to the field size of *ff*). One can exclude factors such as subjective criteria and manual skill under argument (1) above, and argument (3) excludes all factors that were constant between flashed and continuous stimulation, such as the comparison line or the distance between *L* and C. (The latter had some effect on knee position, and is discussed below.)

No factor has been found which could account for the knee which does not involve interactions between *ff*. Let us now consider how losses might occur when outputs from *ff* are combined.

Extended objects must excite a great number of *ff*. If these responses are to support shape recognition, then each response must advertize its *position* in relation to the others. It must also advertize the shape and orientation of the detail it is tuned to, but for the moment let us consider the coding of 'position'[4] only. If there are errors in the coding of 'position', then the perception of orientation will be greatly hampered when two or more *ff* are involved in one performance.

There are two ways in which 'position' signals will fall short of the ideal:

The first loss involves failure to identify the location of maximal response. Several *ff* may respond to a given stimulus in different degree, and it was proposed in Part I that weak responses are inhibited by mutual inhibition between *ff*. The result is that selectivity increases with exposure duration until inhibition reaches a steady level. (The need for this principle is clear in Experiment I also.) Now, weak responses must arise from *ff* with sub-optimal 'positions' as well as sub-optimal orientations. Thus, when a long line is presented briefly, the information concerning the positions of its parts is impoverished before ever it has to be combined. The net result is that acuities for flashed and continuous presentation bear a constant ratio whatever the line length.

The second loss arises from spatial adaptation. The metric of visual space is known to suffer continual changes as shown for example by figural aftereffects or the adaptation to distortion when wearing prismatic spectacles (Kohler, 1951). Spatial adaptation will set a limit to the precision of 'position' signals.[5] Adaptive errors will tend to accumulate, so that the loss of directional information for a given line will increase with its length, (com-

[4] 'Position' (in quotes) will be used to indicate the functional correlate of location in the visual field. Although the physical arrangement of neurones may be related to 'position,' it is not sufficient by itself. There must be some explicit correlate of location which is capable of influencing neural responses; otherwise, we should experience a fragmentary visual field.

[5] Andrews (1964) has proposed that the metric of visual space is determined by statistics of the visual input such that (1) average contour separation over a period is seen as uniform, and (2) average contour separation in any small region is seen as 'straight.' 'Position' signals are conceived by the writer to be prescribed in this way, although this is not essential to the present argument.

pared with ideal performance). Losses arising from adaptation can therefore account for the shallow gradients to the right of the 'knee' in Fig. 1. (The value of the gradient has not been predicted. This would require a precise description of the process of spatial adaptation, and of other errors which cause a measurable detriment to performance.)

There are undoubtedly other losses besides spatial adaptation which affect the accuracy of perceiving parallelism. One of these might set a lower ceiling to performance than does spatial adaptation. However, the fact that adaptation is observable argues against a still heavier loss. There are additional grounds for proposing spatial adaptation as the limiting factor in perceiving parallelism for lines which subtend over 9′ arc.

All losses can be divided into losses which arise in processing *L* itself and losses which arise because *L* has to be related to the comparison line *C*. Losses of the latter kind have been left out of account so far. They cannot account for the 'knee' in Fig. 1, since the comparison line was the same for flashed and continuous presentation. However, when *L* was continuously presented, the height of the *c* vs. *d* function and the position of the knee varied slightly according to the separation of *L* and *C*.

For each subject, the three functions can be made very similar in gradient and knee position by subtracting a variance from $s^2$ which depends on *h* alone. The same applies to Fig. 3. The implication of this is that losses which arise from relating *L* to *C* depend mainly on the distance between them. There is probably some dependency on the lengths of *L* and *C* also.

The loss which varied with *h* can also be attributed to spatial adaptation. Spatial adaptation of the space between *L* and *C* will reduce acuity for parallelism, and the loss will vary with their separation. Changes in spatial relations will also reduce the utility of line length in assessing parallelism: beyond a certain limit, one cannot distinguish real changes of gradient from volatile products of adaptation, so that the remoter parts of *C* cannot usefully be brought to bear on determining the relative slope of *L*. On the other hand, spatial adaptation tends to be cohesive, with neighbouring regions similarly affected; thus *C* and *L* may both appear bent but still be judged parallel if they are fairly close together. This would explain the finding that only the part of *C* opposite *L* can be utilized in judging parallelism.

## Integration of Outputs from Contour Detectors

The previous section was concerned with which errors set the ceiling to performance when the outputs from receptors or *ff* are combined. The present section is addressed to the positive problem of how the latter combination is effected. No final answers can be offered on available evidence. However, some progress is possible, and some of the problems can be made clearer.

Experiment III throws some light on the process. It was found that a broken line exhibits variability in its parts which is not observed in the corresponding parts of an unbroken line. It appears from this that outputs from neighbouring *ff* are combined in a way which does not occur between remoter *ff*.

Now, we can identify discontinuities, curvatures, or ends in lines, as well as straight portions. Therefore, the neighbour-integration process shown by Experiment III is not merely a matter of displaying straight lines of suitable mean gradient whenever neighbouring *ff* respond. Detectors of curvature, etc., must exist in some form.

There are at least three ways in which features may be recognized:

(1) By a variety of special-purpose filters. Evidence for this kind of processing has been found in the frog (Lettvin *et al.* 1959), but not yet in the cat or monkey.

(2) By combining the outputs of *ff* in logical combinations, so that 'end-of-line' for instance is recognized by units at a higher level when certain *ff* respond *and* certain other *ff* fail to respond. The work of Hubel and Wiesel (1965) indicates that this kind of processing occurs in the cat. Available evidence suggests that the human visual system is more like the cat's than the frog's.

There is a difficulty for this view in the present context. A vernier misalignment of about 2″ arc can just be detected; for optimum performance, each arm of the vernier must subtend at least 10′ arc. (MacKay, 1961). The corresponding optimum for slope detection in Experiment I was a height difference of 4″ arc between the ends of the line; the least s.e. was obtained with a line which subtended about 8′ arc. It appears from this that more positional information is available for perceiving detail of shape than for perceiving slope, whereas the reverse should be true if detail perception is a logical combination of outputs from *ff*. This strengthens the case for (1); however, there is a third way of recognizing pattern details, which squares much better with the physiological data.

(3) By statistical analysis of coincident responses. Some combinations of *f*-responses will occur more frequently than others, particularly in response to unbroken lines. Cases of vernier misalignment or other details are much less likely to occur in the distal pattern than a continuous contour. The most frequent coincidence of neighbouring f-responses can therefore be decoded as 'continuous contour', and other combinations decoded so that average frequency represents misalignment. The 'orientation' signals[6] are sufficient to determine whether the misalignment indicates curvature or parallel shearing.

The statistical detection of pattern features is an elaboration of (2); logical combination of *f*-outputs is still required, but detail discrimination is much better than would be possible by logical combination alone.

[6] *ff* have to signal both their 'position' and 'orientation' to be useful to higher mechanisms. It has been suggested that both signals are subject to adaptation.

The more accurate selection of response occurs only when the stimulus corresponds to a coincidence whose statistics have been stored. A broken line is processed as two objects unless the gap is small. Separate visual objects have to be related spatially by means of 'position' signals only.

We now have three forms of adaptation, which all operate in much the same way and affect the scales of 'position', 'orientation' and 'shape' (or degree of misalignment).

Experiment III shows that 'shape' adaptation is independent of 'position' adaptation. Experiment I shows that 'position' adaptation and 'orientation' adaptation are distinct: if the scale of 'orientation' was derived from 'position' values, then drift of 'orientation' should not increase for very short lines. Figure 2 shows clearly that it does. Lastly, 'shape' cannot determine 'orientation' scaling or vice-versa, because there is no sense in which one could prescribe the other.

These three features are sufficient for a display of visual space which has properties very like a geometrical space, although quite different on a small scale (and in coding). In the resulting response space, any small feature has 'shape', 'orientation' and 'position', and any number of such features can be related to one another simultaneously.

## *REFERENCES*


Andrews, D. P. Error-correcting perceptual mechanisms. *Quarterly Journal of Experimental Psychology*, 1964, *16*, 104.

Andrews, D. P. Psychophysical indications of visual contour-detecting mechanisms. Doctoral Thesis, University of London, 1965.

Andrews, D. P. Perception of contour orientation in the central fovea. Part I: Short lines. *Vision Research*, 1967, *7*, 975-997.

Berry, R. N. Quantitative relations among vernier, real depth and stereoscopic depth acuities. *Journal of Experimental Psychology*, 1948, *38*, 708.

Ditchburn, R. W. *Problems of Visual Discrimination*. Thomas Young Oration, University of Reading, 1959.

Finney, D. J. *Probit Analysis*. Cambridge: Cambridge University Press, 1952.

French, J. W. Height and width of vernier lines and separation. *Transactions of the Optical Society*, 1919-1920, *21*, 127.

Hubel, D. H., & Wiesel, T. N. Receptive fields, binocular interaction and functional architecture in the cat's visual cortex. *Journal of Physiology*, 1962, *160*, 106-154.

Hubel, D. H., & Wiesel, T. N. Receptive fields and functional architecture in two non-striate visual areas (18 and 19) of the cat. *Journal of Neurophysiology*, 1965, *28*, 229-289.

MacKay, D. M. Interactive processes in visual perception. In W. A. Rosenblith (Ed.), *Sensory Communication*. New York: Wiley, 1961, 335-339.

Matsubayashi, A. Forschung über die Tiefenwahrnehmung. V. *Acta Societa Ophthalmologica Japonica*, 1938, *42*, 2.

Ogilvie, J. C., & Taylor, M. M. Effect of length on the visibility of a fine line. *Journal of the Optical Society of America*, 1959, *49*, 898.

Polyak, S. L. *The retina*. Chicago: University of Chicago Press, 1941.

Rochlin, A. M. The effect of tilt on the visual perception of parallelness. *American Journal of Psychology*, 1955, *68*, 223.

Sulzer, R. L., & Zener, K. E. A quantitative analysis of relations between stimulus determinants and sensitivity of the visual perception of parallelness. *American Journal of Psychology*, 1953, *8*, 444.

*We have come a long way in this section, starting from the studies of Lashley on detail vision in the rat. One factor must have become increasingly clear: the more that is known about the neurophysiology of contour coding in visual systems, the more likely is such knowledge to affect both our theoretical predilections, and the sorts of experiment we will consider it worthwhile to undertake. It must also have become clear that one set of neurophysiological findings has had vastly more impact on psychological work on pattern recognition than any other, and I do not think that that impression is due to biased sampling of research reports in psychology on my part. Hubel and Wiesel's work certainly has had a remarkably warm reception. In the next part the picture will be broadened by presenting some of the other major findings in neurophysiology. Before doing that, it would be well to pause and consider the overall direction and emphasis of the work represented in this part.*

*In the first place, there has been a change of emphasis in research, which is probably common to all fields of psychology. Thirty years ago the tendency was to look for answers to broad issues, to have theories which would embrace, for instance, all of perception; today we tend to be satisfied with experimental analyses of a much more restricted nature, to look for confirmation of more specific hypotheses. This change may not have been entirely to the advantage of scientific psychology—that is an issue it would be difficult to judge objectively—but at least it is understandable in the sense that the more facts there are to be fitted together, the more difficult it becomes to do so if consistent patterns among the facts cannot be discerned. As a matter of fact the Hubel and Wiesel findings may present the key to the sorts of consistency we should like to find, since they restrict —and hence simplify—the areas in which it seems profitable to search. The majority of the selections in this section seem to favour that view, anyway.*

*How far can the sorts of work represented in this section be said to contribute to solutions to the problems of stimulus equivalence? By trying to find out what the nature of stimulus coding is, they should contribute to the broader question since, as Deutsch suggested, the form of coding is probably itself the basis for at least some of the forms of equivalence. As a matter of fact the theoretical question that so fascinated Lashley—and* which occupied him through much of his career—is now really solved. Recognition of spatial patterns independently of the groups of receptors activated can be handled in many ways. (There are numerous instances of this in pattern recognition by machines, for instance. See Part V.) The more immediate question now is: how can coding models, or neurophysiological and behavioural findings, help us to understand the concept of pattern? What are the relevant "dimensions" of shape? Attneave and Arnoult pointed out some years ago (1956) that we actually have very little conception of how shapes can be classified and specified meaningfully in psychological terms. So the more urgent question can be rephrased in this way: can principles of coding help us to understand the dimensions along which patterns (shapes) can vary? Some of the papers presented in this section have clearly initiated the search for answers to this sort of question. And, curiously enough, this brings us back to the more general questions of stimulus equivalence proposed by Klüver, as opposed to the restricted problem tackled by Pitts and McCulloch, and by Lashley (see Part I). A step in the direction of specifying a pattern dimension is taken in the explanation of anomalous transfer and the coding of "horizontality-verticality" for example (Dodwell and Niemi) and a different sort of step is taken by seeking to analyse the biological utility of some sorts of pattern coding processes (Ingle). Work of this type on human pattern vision is the most challenging and obviously the most difficult, but papers are beginning to appear in the literature which suggest that even here progress is beginning to be made, and once again the neurophysiological findings suggest a base from which to start.

Since discussion of neurophysiological findings has invaded the general commentary quite extensively by now, it seems appropriate at this point to turn to an explicit treatment of that important field.

# IV

# THE NEUROPHYSIOLOGY OF VISUAL PATTERN CODING

*The intention in this section is to present some of the major papers on the analysis of visual coding by electrophysiological methods. Physiological optics is a vast topic, and only the most salient matters will be discussed in the commentary; in fact, our interest will be confined almost entirely to work on the recording of electrical impulses from individual nerve cells or fibers within the visual system. The reason for this will become clear as we proceed.*

*Since neurophysiology and the comparative anatomy of visual systems are highly specialized fields, I will state right at the beginning what general knowledge in these matters will be assumed of the reader. Summaries of those other features needed to understand the subsequent papers and discussion will be presented when required.*

*1. It is assumed that the reader has an elementary knowledge of the generation and propagation of electrical signals in nerves, such as is found in any good introductory psychology text. That is to say, some understanding of the "spike" discharge, one-way transmission over synapses, frequency coding and temporal and spatial summation are assumed.*

*2. It is assumed also that the following facts about the anatomy and physiology of the visual system are known. (a) Light energy is transduced into neural energy at the retina, the complex of nervous tissue at the back of the eyeball of the vertebrate eye. (b) Neural signals ("spikes") are transmitted via the optic nerves to the visual (occipital) cortex of the brain in mammals, and to the visual lobe or the optic tectum in organisms with more primitive visual systems. (c) The detailed arrangements of visual anatomy does vary between different species which are closely related, but in general these variations are not great. (d) On the other hand, differences between different biological classes, such as between mammals and Arthropods (insects) are very great. (e) The major visual nerve pathways and structures have been identified by dissection, staining, and nerve degeneration techniques, as well as by electrophysiological methods which usually involve recording electrical responses of the system under study at different sites. (f) There are important differences between recording gross electrical responses [such as the electroretinogram and visual evoked (cortical) poten-*

tials] and recording from single units. (g) Generally speaking there is a close relationship between anatomical structure and physiological function, and knowledge of one will frequently throw light on the other.

Advances in electrophysiology are extremely dependent on electrical and electronic technology. It has been known that the eye responds to light stimulation with gross electrical discharges since the end of the nineteenth century, and forty years ago Adrian and Matthews (1927) recorded the overall responses of a vertebrate optic nerve to light signals, but the real breakthroughs started to occur when methods were developed for recording from individual units—nerve cell bodies or axonal fibres—within the visual system. This depended absolutely on the development of fine recording electrodes and methods of detecting and recording very small (of the order of millivolts) and very brief (millisecond) signals.

The first major success was achieved by Hartline and Graham, who in 1932 reported results of recording from individual fibers in the optic nerve of the horseshoe crab, Limulus. This organism is very convenient to work with, since it has a long optic nerve and the fibers in it are large. Also, the connections between the photoreceptors and the optic nerve fibers are rather direct, something which is common in simple visual systems but which is not true of vertebrate—and particularly mammalian—visual systems. The eyes of Limulus are called compound, since they are made up of numbers of apparently identical, and rather independent units, each one of which has its own optic nerve fiber. This compound arrangement is quite different from the organization found in higher forms.

The original work on Limulus has been followed by a long and distinguished series of researches, the highlights of which are reviewed in the first paper by Ratliff. It was stated above that each receptor unit (ommatidium) is a more or less independent entity, and this is true in the sense that in order to get electrical spikes in a given fiber its ommatidium must be stimulated by light: light shining on other ommatidia has no effect. However there are interactions between two or more ommatidia both (or all) of which are being stimulated. Apart from the elegant demonstration of the features of direct neural response to light stimulation, the work on Limulus is chiefly important for the thoroughness with which this sort of interaction has been explored.

# *Inhibitory Interaction and the Detection and Enhancement of Contours*

F. RATLIFF

The interplay of excitatory and inhibitory influences over interconnections within the retina yields patterns of optic-nerve activity that are more than direct copies of the pattern of external stimulation. Certain significant information is selected from the immense detail in the temporal and spatial pattern of illumination on the receptor mosaic, enhanced at the expense of less significant information, and only then transmitted to the central nervous system.

Among the most significant features of a pattern of illumination are the loci of transitions from one intensity to another and from one color to another. Indeed, if only these contours are represented—as in a line drawing or cartoon—much of the significant information is retained. This paper describes an integrative neural mechanism which plays a role in the detection and enhancement of such contours. A quantitative experimental analysis of the purely inhibitory interaction among retinal elements in the lateral eye of *Limulus* is reviewed in detail, and the physiological significance of inhibitory mechanisms is discussed briefly.

## *INHIBITORY INTERACTION IN THE EYE OF* LIMULUS

### Fundamental Properties of Excitation and Inhibition

The lateral eye of *Limulus* is a compound eye containing approximately 1000 ommatidia (Fig. 1*a*). Nerve fibers arise from the ommatidia in small bundles and come together to form the optic nerve. A plexus of nerve fibers interconnects these bundles immediately behind the layer of ommatidia (Fig. 1*b*).

Reprinted from *Sensory Communication*, 1961.

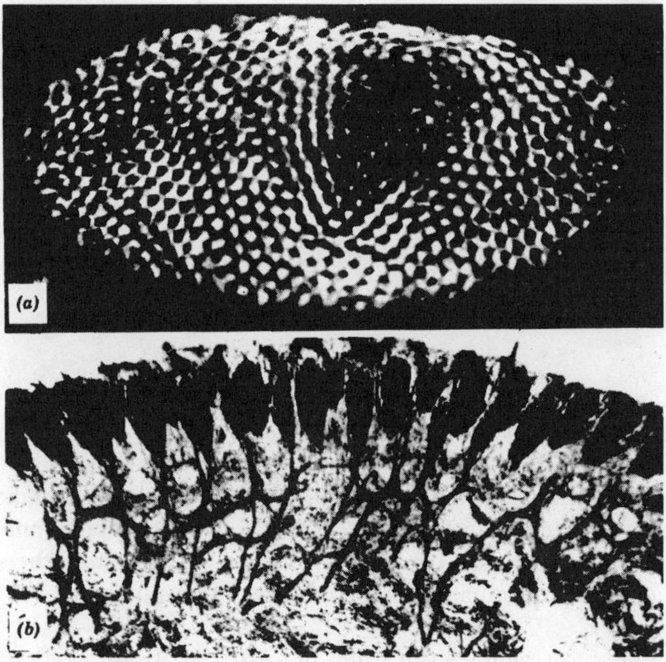


Fig. 1. The lateral eye of the horseshoe crab, *Limulus*. (*a*) Corneal surface. In a medium-sized adult each eye forms an ellipsoidal bulge on the side of the carapace, about 12 mm long by 6 mm wide. Each ommatidium has an optical aperture about 0.1 mm in diameter; the facets are spaced approximately 0.3 mm apart, center to center, on the surface of the eye. The optical axes of the ommatidia diverge, so that the visual fields of all those in one eye cover, together, approximately a hemisphere. The optical axes of the dark circular facets near the center of the eye are oriented in the direction of the camera. (*b*) Photomicrograph of a section of the compound eye of *Limulus* taken perpendicular to the plane of (*a*) at a slightly higher magnification. Samuel's silver stain. The cornea has been removed. The heavily pigmented sensory parts of the ommatidia are at the top of the figure. The silver-stained nerve fibers originating in the retinular cells and the eccentric cell of each ommatidium emerge as a bundle and join with similar bundles from other ommatidia to form the optic nerve. Small lateral branches of the nerve fibers form the network, or plexus, of interconnections immediately below the receptors. (Figure prepared by W. H. Miller.)

Each ommatidium (Fig. 2) contains approximately a dozen cells: a cluster of wedge-shaped retinular cells and one bipolar neuron, the eccentric cell (Miller, 1957). Both the eccentric cell and the retinular cells have axons that together make up the small bundle arising from the ommatidium; both types of axons branch profusely, and these branches constitute the plexus of interconnecting fibers (Miller, 1958; and Ratliff, Miller, & Hartline, 1958).

A small bundle containing a single active nerve fiber may be dissected from the optic nerve and placed on electrodes to record the action potential spikes (Hartline & Graham, 1932). Hartline, Wagner, & MacNichol (1952)

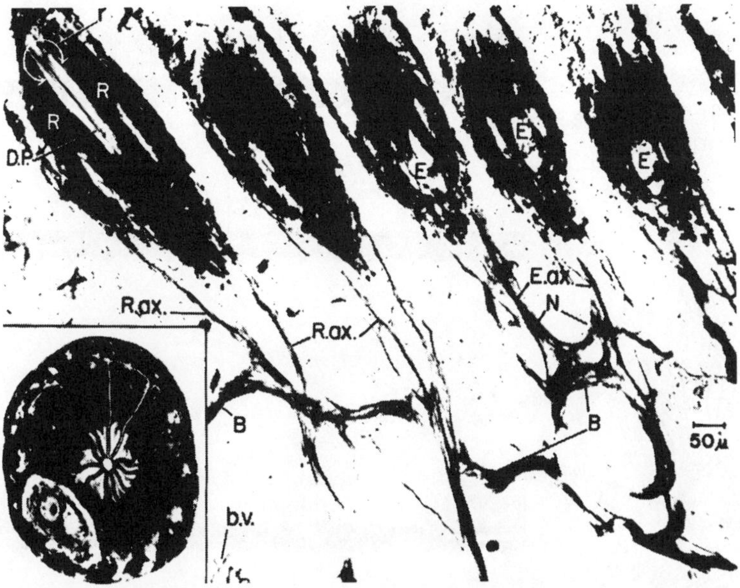


Fig. 2. Photomicrograph of a longitudinal section through several ommatidia. Samuel's silver stain. In one ommatidium (upper left) the dendritic distal process (D.P.) of an eccentric cell is seen extending up the axial canal of the rhabdom (r). This canal is formed at the junction of the medial portions of the retinular cells (R). The cell body of the eccentric cell of this ommatidium is not visible, but the eccentric cells (E) of other ommatidia to the right may be seen. The thicker, more densely stained fibers arising from the ommatidia are eccentric cell axons (E.ax.). The thinner, less dense fibers are retinular cell axons (R.ax.). Both types of axons give off small branches which form the bundles (B) of lateral interconnections that make up the plexus. These fine branches converge in regions of neuropile (N) in close proximity to eccentric cell axons (E). A portion of a blood vessel (b.v.) is shown at the bottom of the section.

The insert is a cross section of one ommatidium at the level of the eccentric cell body. Fixed in $OsO_4$ and stained by Mallory's aniline-blue method. One of the eleven retinular cells is outlined in white ink. Its axial border rests against the distal process of the eccentric cell which, at another level in the ommatidinm, is continuous with the eccentrically placed cell body shown in this section. The spokelike structures constitute the rhabdom, probably the site of the photosensitive pigment. Electron micrographs (Miller, 1958) show that the rhabdomeres are formed by microvilli projecting from the boundaries of the radially arranged retinular cells. (Figure prepared by W. H. Miller.)

have shown that the impulses recorded in this preparation originate in the eccentric cell, which seems to be a neuron rather than a true receptor (see also Waterman and Wiersma, 1954). This cell (Fig. 2) sends a dendritic distal process into the center of the rhabdom, which is made up of a dozen or so retinular cells and is in close juxtaposition with the specialized portions of the retinular cells (rhabdomeres) which are believed to be the photoreceptors (Miller, 1957). This whole assembly of cells appears to function as a "receptor unit."

The activity of one of these fibers in response to stimulation of the om-

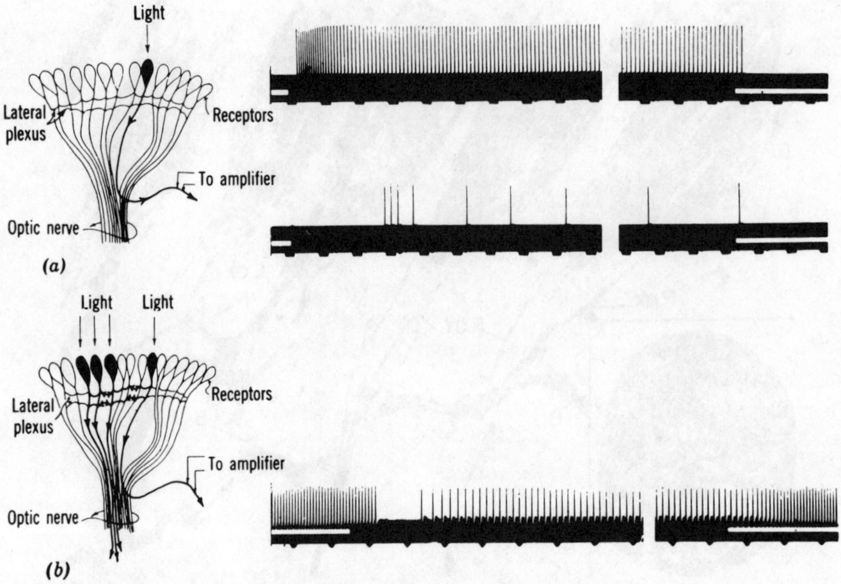


Fig. 3. Oscillograms of action potentials in a single optic nerve fiber of *Limulus*. The experimental arrangements are indicated in the diagrams at the left. (*a*) Response to prolonged steady illumination. For the upper record the intensity of the stimulating light was 10,000 times that used for the lower record. Signal of exposure to light blackens out the white line about the ⅕-sec time marks. Each record interrupted for approximately 7 sec. (Records from Hartline, Wagner, & MacNichol, 1952.) (*b*) Inhibition of the activity of a steadily illuminated ommatidium in the eye of *Limulus*, produced by illumination of a number of other ommatidia near it. The oscillographic record is of the discharge of impulses in the optic nerve fiber arising from one steadily illuminated ommatidium. The blackening of the white line above the ⅕-sec time marks signals the illumination of the neighboring ommatidia. (Record from Hartline, Wagner, & Ratliff, 1956.)

matidium from which it arises (Fig. 3*a*), is typical of the responses of many sensory nerves: there is a sizable latent period after the stimulus comes on before the first impulse is discharged; the frequency of discharge is relatively high at first; subsequently the frequency settles down to a lower steady level which may be maintained for long periods of time; and the frequency of discharge, particularly in this steady state, depends primarily on the intensity of stimulation. Responses to an abrupt increase or decrease in a steady level of stimulation are somewhat more complex, as will be shown later.

Illumination of other ommatidia near the ommatidium whose activity is being recorded produces no discharge in the eccentric cell axon of this ommatidium: activity in any one optic nerve fiber can be elicited by illumination of only the one specific receptor unit from which that fiber arises. Nevertheless, the sensory elements in this eye do exert an important influence on one another by way of the plexus of lateral interconnections. This interaction is purely inhibitory. The frequency of discharge of impulses in an optic nerve fiber from a particular ommatidium is decreased (Fig. 3*b*), and may even be stopped altogether, by illuminating neighboring areas of the eye (Hartline, 1949).

This inhibitory effect may be summarized as follows. The ability of an ommatidium to discharge impulses in the axon of its eccentric cell is reduced by illuminating other ommatidia in its neighborhood: the threshold to light is raised, the number of impulses discharged in response to a suprathreshold flash of light is diminished, and the frequency with which impulses are discharged during steady illumination is decreased. The magnitude of the inhibition, measured in terms of decrease in frequency, has been shown to depend upon the intensity, area, and configuration of the pattern of illumination on the retina: (1) the greater the intensity on neighboring receptors, the greater the inhibition they exert on the test receptor; (2) the greater the number of neighboring receptors illuminated, that is to say, the larger the area of illumination, the greater the inhibition exerted on the test receptor; (3) illumination of neighboring receptors near the test receptor results in greater inhibition than does illumination of more distant receptors (Hartline, Wagner, & Ratliff, 1956).

## Mutual Inhibition

The inhibitory influences are exerted mutually among the receptors in the eye of *Limulus:* the activity of each ommatidium influences, and is influenced by, the activity of its neighbors. If activity is recorded from two optic nerve fibers coming from two ommatidia not too widely separated in the eye, the frequency of their maintained discharges of impulses—in response to steady illumination—is lower when both ommatidia are illuminated together than when each is illuminated by itself. The magnitude of the inhibition of each one has been shown to depend only on the degree of the activity of the other; thus the activity of each is the resultant of the excitation from its respective light stimulus and the inhibition exerted on it by the other. Furthermore, it has been shown that, once a threshold has been reached, the inhibition exerted on each is a linear function of the degree of activity of the other (Fig. 4).

The responses to steady illumination of two receptor units (ommatidia) that inhibit each other mutually may thus be described quantitatively by two simultaneous linear equations that express concisely all the features of the interaction (Hartline & Ratliff, 1957):

$$r_1 = e_1 - K_{1,2}(r_2 - r^0_{1,2})$$
$$r_2 = e_2 - K_{2,1}(r_1 - r^0_{2,1})$$

The activity of the receptor unit—its response $r$—is to be measured by the frequency of discharge of impulses in its axon. This response is determined by the excitation $e$ supplied by the external stimulus to the receptor, diminished by whatever inhibitory influences may be acting upon

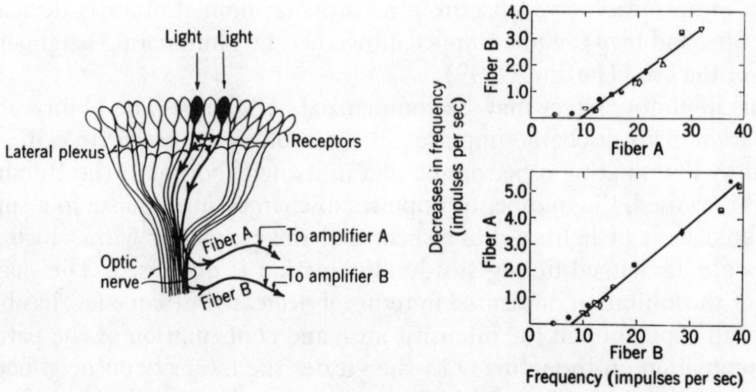


Fig. 4. Mutual inhibition of two receptor units in the lateral eye of *Limulus*. Action potentials were recorded from two optic nerve fibers simultaneously, as indicated in the diagram of the experimental arrangement. In each graph the magnitude of the inhibitory action (decrease in frequency of impulse discharge) of one of the ommatidia is plotted on the ordinate as a function of the degree of concurrent activity (frequency) of the other on the abscissa. The different points were obtained by using various intensities of illumination on ommatidia A and B, in various combinations. The data for points designated by the same symbol were obtained simultaneously. In the upper graph the slope of the line gives the value of the inhibitory coefficient of the action of receptor A on receptor B, $K_{B,A} = 0.15$; the intercept of the line with the axis of abscissas gives the value of the threshold $r^0_{B,A} = 9.3$ impulses per second. From the lower graph, $K_{A,B} = 0.17$; $r^0_{A,B} = 7.8$ impulses per second. (Reproduced from Hartline & Ratliff, 1957.)

the receptor as a result of the activity of neighboring receptors. (It should be noted that the excitation of a given receptor is to be measured by its response when it is illuminated by itself, thus lumping together the physical parameters of the stimulus and the characteristics of the photoexcitatory mechanism of the receptor.) The subscripts are used to label the individual receptor units. In each of these equations the magnitude of the inhibitory influence is given by the last term, which is written in accordance with the experimental findings as a simple linear expression. The "threshold" frequency that must be exceeded before a receptor can exert any inhibition is represented by $r^0$. It and the "inhibitory coefficient" $K$ are labeled in each equation to identify the direction of the action: $r^0_{1,2}$ is the frequency of receptor 2 at which it begins to inhibit receptor 1; $r^0_{2,1}$ is the reverse. In the same way, $K_{1,2}$ is the coefficient of the inhibitory action of receptor 2 on receptor 1; $K_{2,1}$, the reverse.

## Spatial Summation of Inhibitory Influences

The quantitative description given thus far is concerned only with the interaction of two elements. To extend the description to more than two elements, it is necessary to know how the inhibitory influences from different elements combine with one another. The spatial summation of inhibitory influences was analyzed by measuring the inhibition exerted on a test receptor separately by each of two small groups of ommatidia near it, and then by these two groups together (Hartline & Ratliff, 1958). It may be anticipated that in general the results of such an experiment will depend on the amount of inhibitory interaction between the two groups. A special case in which there is little or no interaction could easily be achieved experimentally since the interaction between ommatidia is less, the greater their separation. Consequently it was possible to choose two regions of the eye, on either side of the test receptor, that were too far apart to affect each other appreciably but were still close enough to the test receptor to inhibit it significantly. Under these conditions the inhibitory effects exerted by these two widely separated regions on the test receptor were undistorted by their own mutual inhibition, and the experimental results were quite simple. The inhibitory effects, when measured in terms of the decrease in frequency of the test receptor, combine in a simple additive manner: the arithmetical sum of the inhibitory effects that each group produces separately equals the physiological sum obtained by illuminating the two groups together (Fig. 5).

These results permit the extension of the quantitative description to include any number of interacting elements by expressing the total inhibition

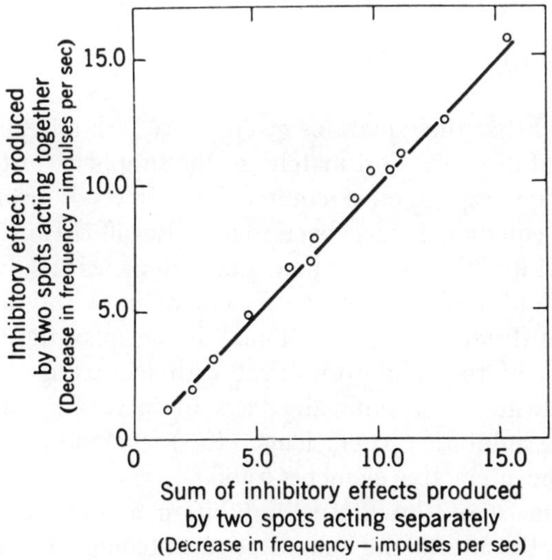


Fig. 5. The summation of inhibitory effects produced by two widely separated groups of receptors. The sum of the inhibitory effects on a test receptor produced by each group acting separately is plotted as abscissa; the effect produced by the two groups of receptors acting simultaneously is plotted as ordinate. (Reproduced from Hartline & Ratliff, 1958.)

exerted on any one receptor as the arithmetical sum of the individual inhibitory contributions from all the others (Hartline & Ratliff, 1958). Consequently, the activity of $n$ interacting receptors may be described by a set of simultaneous linear equations, each with $n - 1$ inhibitory terms combined by simple addition:

$$r_p = e_p - \sum_{j=1}^{n} K_{p,j}(r_j - r^0_{p,j})$$

where $p = 1,2, \cdots, n$; $j \neq p$; and $r_j < r^0_{p,j}$. In each such equation the magnitude of the inhibitory influence is given by the summated terms, written in accordance with the experimental findings as a simple linear expression.

These equations have been applied to experimental results obtained by illumination of three receptors whose optic-nerve responses could be recorded simultaneously. In these experiments (unpublished), the six thresholds and six coefficients of inhibitory action were first determined by illuminating the receptors by pairs, as in the experiment illustrated in Figure 4. On the basis of these experimentally determined constants, the responses expected from each member of the group of three, when illuminated together, were calculated. The observed responses of the group of three receptors illuminated simultaneously agreed satisfactorily with that predicted from the interaction observed when the receptors were illuminated in pairs.

## Diminution of Inhibition With Distance

It will be noted that the equations given above lack an explicit expression for the effects of distance. Fortunately for the simplicity of the quantitative treatment, no such expression is required. The effects of distance are already implicit in the equations: it has been found (Ratliff & Hartline, 1959) that the threshold of inhibitory action increases with increasing distance between the units involved, and that the coefficient of inhibitory action decreases with increasing distance (Fig. 6). Thus, in the quantitative formulation, the diminution of the inhibitory effect with increasing distance may be ascribed exactly to the combined effects of increasing thresholds ($r^0_{p,j}$) and decreasing inhibitory coefficients ($K_{p,j}$) that accompany increasing separation of the interacting elements $p$ and $j$.

The dependence of the mutual inhibition among receptors on their separation greatly affects the quantitative outcome of experiments with various configurations of interacting elements. Indeed, in many cases the law of spatial summation would seem to be called into question: often the inhibitory effect produced by the combined influence of several groups of receptors is *less* than the sum of the inhibitory effects produced by each

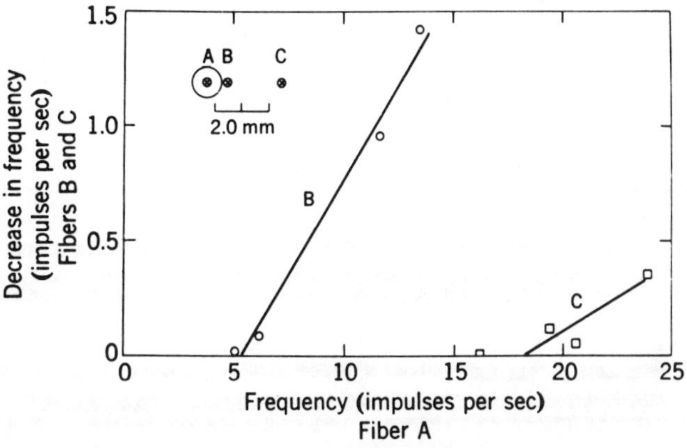


Fig. 6. The dependence of the magnitude of inhibition on distance. The inhibition (measured in terms of decrease in frequency) exerted by a small group of receptors (A) on two other receptors (B and C) is plotted as ordinate. As abscissa is plotted the concurrent frequency of the discharge of impulses of one of the receptors in group A. The geometrical configuration of the pattern of illumination on the eye is shown in the insert. The locations of the facets of the receptors whose discharges were recorded are indicated by the symbol ○. (Reproduced from Ratliff & Hartline, 1959.)

such group illuminated alone (Hartline & Ratliff, 1958). But this occurs simply because the inhibitory influence exerted by a receptor depends on its own *activity*. And since the amount of receptor activity in each of several groups close to each other is less when they are illuminated together than when they are illuminated separately because of the mutual inhibition, the inhibitory effect produced by the combined influence of these several groups acting together should be less than the sum of the inhibitory effects produced by each group illuminated alone.

This interpretation, as well as the quantitative description, is given even stronger support by experiments in which a third spot of light is used to provide additional inhibitory influences that can be controlled independently of the two interacting receptor units whose activity is being measured. When additional receptors are illuminated in the vicinity of an interacting pair, too far from one ommatidium to affect it directly but near enough to the second to inhibit it, the frequency of discharge of the first increases as it is partially released from the inhibition exerted on it by the second (Fig. 7). Such "disinhibition" simulates facilitation: illumination of a distant region of the eye results in an increase of the activity of the test receptor. This observed result is a direct consequence of the principle of interaction that was established above: the inhibitory influences exerted by a receptor depend on its own activity, which is the resultant of the excitatory stimulus to it and whatever inhibitory influences may, in turn, be exerted upon it.

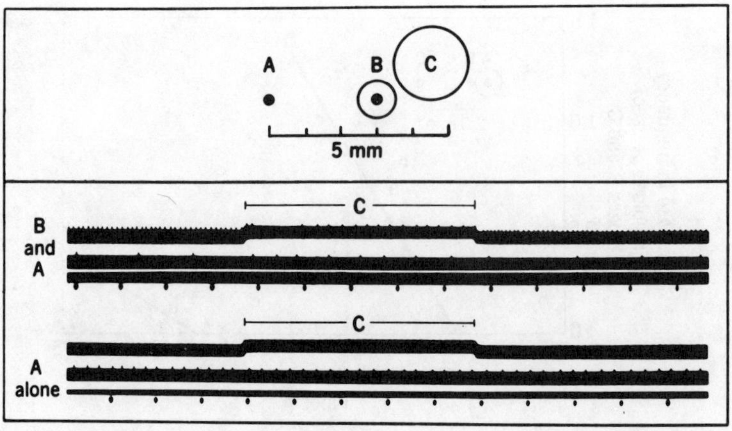


Fig. 7. Oscillograms of the electrical activity of two optic nerve fibers showing disinhibition. In each record the lower oscillographic trace records the discharge of impulses from ommatidium A, stimulated by a spot of light confined to its facet. The upper trace records the activity of ommatidium B, stimulated by a spot of light centered on its facet, but which also illuminated approximately 8 or 10 ommatidia in addition to B. A third spot of light C was directed onto a region of the eye more distant from A than from B. The geometrical configuration of the pattern of illumination is sketched above. Exposure of C was signaled by the upward offset of the upper trace. Lower record: activity of ommatidium A in the absence of illumination on B, showing that illumination of C had no perceptible effect under this condition. Upper record: activity of ommatidia A and B together, showing (1) lower frequency of discharge of A (as compared with lower record) resulting from activity of B, and (2) effect of illumination of C, causing a drop in frequency of discharge of B and concomitantly an increase in the frequency of discharge of A, as A was partially released from the inhibition exerted by B. Time marked in 1/5 sec. The black band above the time marks is the signal of the illumination of A and B, thin when A was shining alone, thick when A and B were shining together. (Records from Hartline & Ratliff, 1957.)

## Responses to Simple Spatial Patterns of Illumination

Although the activity of a system of interacting elements can conveniently be described without making explicit reference to their relative locations in the receptor mosaic and to the spatial pattern of illumination (since the dependence of the inhibitor influences on distance is implicit in the values of the thresholds and inhibitory coefficients), it is nevertheless clear that the strong dependence of the inhibitory thresholds and coefficients on the separation of the elements introduces a topographic factor that must be of considerable significance in retinal function. Any complete description of the spatial characteristics of the inhibitory interaction must, therefore, provide an explicit statement of the relations between these inhibitory parameters and corresponding distances on the receptor mosaic. At the present time, however, a sufficient number of measurements has not been made, covering the wide variety of locations, directions, and distances, to formu-

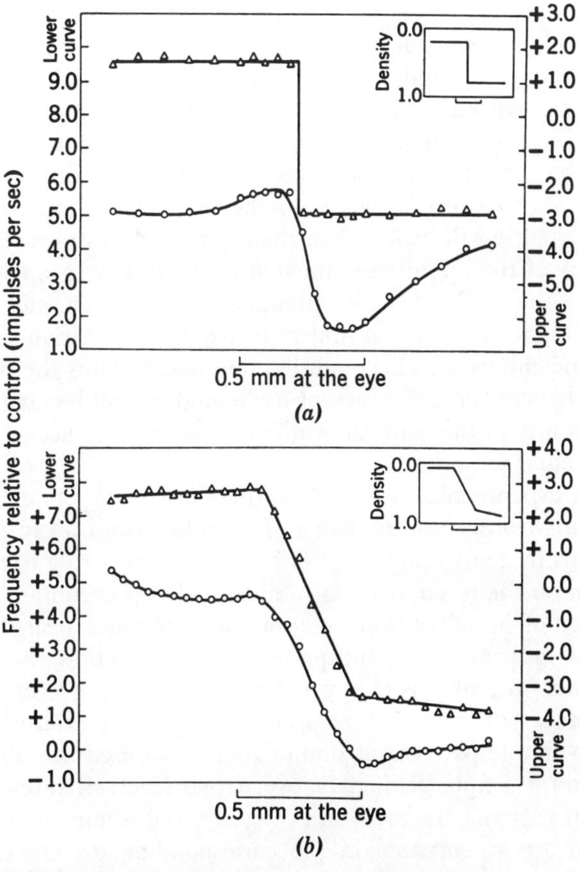


Fig. 8. The discharge of impulses from a single receptor unit in response to simple patterns of illumination in various positions on the retinal mosaic.

(*a*) "Step" pattern of illumination. The demagnified image of a photographic plate was projected on the surface of the eye. The insert shows the relative density of the plate along its length as measured, prior to the experiment, by means of a photomultiplier tube in the image plane where the eye was to be placed. The density of the plate was uniform across its entire width at every point. The upper (rectilinear) graph shows the frequency of discharge of the test receptor, when the illumination was occluded from the rest of the eye by a mask with a small aperture, minus the frequency of discharge elicited by a small control spot of light of constant intensity also confined to the facet of the test receptor. Scale of ordinate on the right. The lower (curvilinear) graph is the frequency of discharge from the same test receptor when the mask was removed and the entire pattern of illumination was projected on the eye in various positions, minus the frequency of discharge elicited by a small control spot of constant intensity confined to the facet of the receptor. Scale of ordinate on the left.

(*b*) A simple gradient of intensity (the so-called Mach pattern). Same procedure as in (*a*). (Reproduced from Ratliff & Hartline, 1959.)

late exactly such a law. Nevertheless, on the basis of a quantitative analysis of the inhibitory interaction, one can predict the general form of the patterns of response that will be elicited from the elements of the receptor mosaic by various simple spatial patterns of illumination.

Contrast effects, for example, may be expected to be greatest at or near the boundary between a dimly illuminated region and a brightly illuminated region of the retina. A unit within the dimly illuminated region, but near this boundary, will be inhibited not only by dimly illuminated neighbors but also by brightly illuminated ones. The total inhibition exerted on such a unit will be greater, therefore, than that exerted on other dimly illuminated elements that are farther from the boundary; consequently its frequency of response will be less than theirs. Similarly a unit within but near the boundary of the brightly illuminated field will have a higher frequency of discharge than other equally illuminated units that are located well within the bright field but are subject to stronger inhibition since all their immediate neighbors are also brightly illuminated. Thus the differences in activity of elements on either side of the boundary will be exaggerated, and the discontinuity in this pattern of illumination will be accentuated in the pattern of neural response.

The ideal experimental test of these qualitative predictions would be to record simultaneously the discharge of impulses from a great number of receptor units in many different positions with respect to a fixed pattern of illumination on the receptor mosaic. Since such a procedure is impractical, the discharge of impulses from only one receptor unit near the center of the eye was measured, and the pattern of illumination shifted between measurements, so that this one receptor unit assumed successively a number of different positions with respect to the pattern (Ratliff & Hartline, 1959). Two simple patterns of illumination were used: an abrupt step in intensity, and a simple gradient between two levels of intensity (the so-called Mach pattern). In each case (Fig. 8), transitions in the pattern of illumination are accentuated in the corresponding pattern of neural response: maxima and minima appear in the frequency of receptor discharge at the sides of the transitions.

## Temporal Aspects of Inhibitory Interaction

It is a fundamental characteristic of most receptors that not only do they signal the information about steady-state stimulus conditions, but they also respond vigorously to temporal changes in stimulus intensity. Both the excitatory and the inhibitory components of activity in the lateral eye of *Limulus* are marked by large transient responses to stimulus changes. The inhibitory transients may best be understood if the excitatory transients are examined first. MacNichol and Hartline (1948) found that a steady dis-

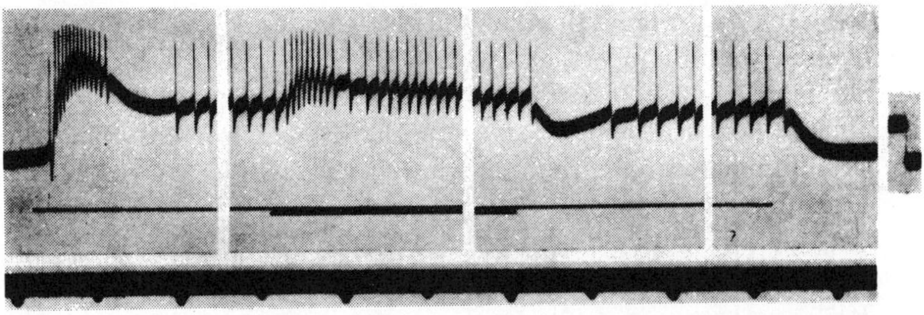

Fig. 9. Slow "generator" potentials and propagated action potentials arising within an ommatidium in response to transients in illumination. Recorded between a micropipette inserted into the ommatidium and an indifferent electrode in the solution covering the eye. Upward deflection of the trace indicates increasing positivity of pipette. Calibration signal, 10 mv; ⅕-sec time marks. Approximately 1 sec cut from each section of the record. Illumination is indicated by the dark line above the time marks. The shorter dark line near the center of the record indicates a step increment in the intensity of illumination. Under steady illumination the frequency of the spikes recorded by means of the microelectrode, as well as their concomitant propagated impulses, depends linearly upon the level of the slow potential (cf. MacNichol, 1956). During transients the frequency is less simply related to the slow potential changes; both the absolute level and the rate and direction of change of the slow potential determine the momentary rate of response. Any abrupt increase or decrease in the slow potential produced by a change in illumination is accompanied by a marked increase or decrease in the frequency of response.

charge to constant illumination by a single receptor unit in the eye of *Limulus* is modulated in the following manner by changes in the level of illumination: in response to a small step increase in the intensity of illumination, a large transient increase in frequency was produced—the frequency eventually subsiding to a steady level slightly greater than that preceding the change in illumination; a similar small decrease in intensity likewise produced a large decrease in frequency, followed by a gradual recovery to a level slightly below that preceding the change in illumination. Thus any change in the level of illumination is marked by a large transient change in frequency that is much greater than the comparable change from one steady-state frequency to the other. Transients such as these (Fig. 9) appear to depend upon both the rate of change and the absolute level of the slow "generator" potentials within the ommatidium (unpublished experiments).

These marked excitatory transients produce a similar but opposite effect in the frequency of response of neighboring elements on which the excitation has not been changed. Consequently, if the frequency of response of a particular element is compared with that of its neighbors, the excitatory transients will seem even larger, relatively speaking, since they produce this opposite effect on the neighboring elements. A typical example of such excitatory and inhibitory transients, recorded simultaneously from two optic nerve fibers, is shown in Fig. 10. Corresponding to the excitatory transient

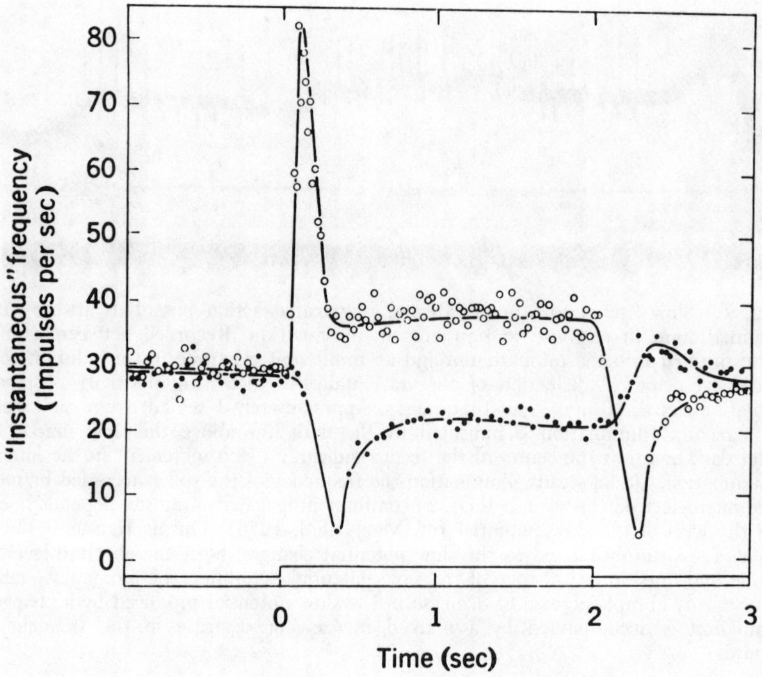


Fig. 10. Simultaneous excitatory and inhibitory transients in two adjacent receptor units in the lateral eye of *Limulus*. One receptor unit, black dots, was illuminated steadily throughout the period shown in the graph. The other unit, open circles, was illuminated steadily until time 0, when the illumination on it was increased abruptly to a new steady level where it remained for 2 sec and then was decreased abruptly to the original level. The added illumination produced a large transient increase in frequency of the second receptor, which subsided quickly to a steady rate of responding; the subsequent decrease in illumination to the original level produced a large transient decrement in the frequency of response, after which the frequency returned to approximately the level it had prior to these changes. Accompanying these marked excitatory transients are large transient inhibitory effects in the adjacent, steadily illuminated receptor unit. A large decrease in frequency is produced by the inhibitory effect resulting from the large excitatory transient; during the steady illumination the inhibitory effect is still present but less marked; and finally, accompanying the decrement in the frequency of response of the element on which the level of excitation was decreased, there is a marked release from inhibition.

in one element, but slightly later in time, there is a marked inhibitory transient in the other element. Corresponding to the decrement in the frequency of response of the element on which the level of excitation was decreased, there is a release from inhibition evident in the response of the other element, again slightly later in time than the excitatory transient. Such an increase in frequency due to this release from inhibition cannot exceed appreciably the level of response that this element would have shown if there had been no inhibition at all. That is to say, the uninhibited response of this element is the maximum response, since there are no excitatory interactions in this eye. Occasionally, however, there has appeared a very slight suggestion of an overshoot above the uninhibited level of response following inhibition, but such overshoots are always of extremely small magnitude. Although the inhibitory transients parallel the excitatory transients, they are probably not entirely dependent upon them. Tomita (1958) has shown that a large transient inhibitory effect can be produced by antidromic impulses of constant frequency. Apparently the initial phases of the inhibitory effects are inherently somewhat greater than the subsequent effects.

It is evident that the relatively simple discharge pattern typically observed in fibers of the optic nerve of *Limulus* (Fig. 3*a*) may be greatly modified by the combined action of the excitatory and inhibitory transients to produce a relatively complex response (Fig. 9). If this response is further modified by other means—such as exposure time, intensity of stimulus, and state of adaptation—it is possible to generate "on-off" and "off" responses in the individual fibers of the *Limulus* optic nerve (Ratliff & Mueller, 1957). These "synthesized" transient responses (Fig. 11) have the properties of the analogous responses in the vertebrate eye (Hartline, 1938): the

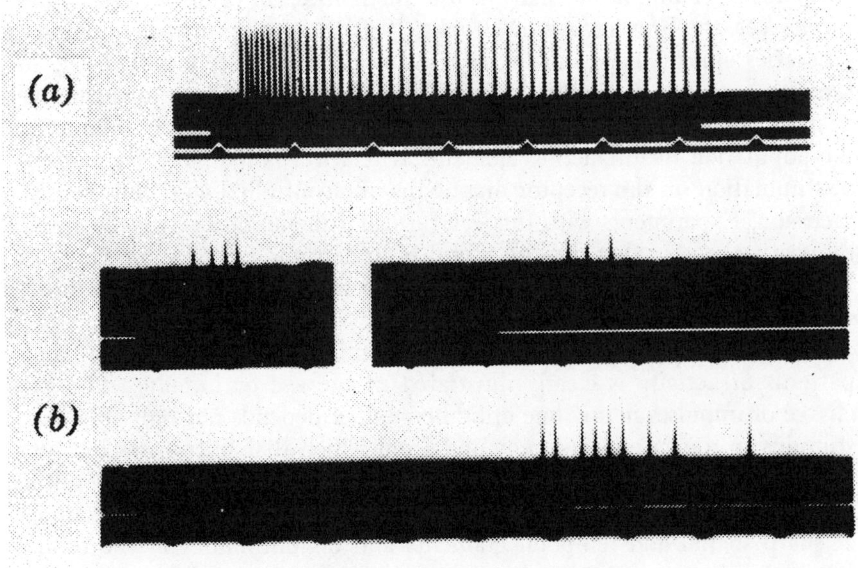


Fig. 11. Oscillograms of diverse types of impulse discharge patterns in single fibers of *Limulus* optic nerve. (*a*) Typical sustained discharge in response to steady illumination. (*b*) Upper record: a synthetic "on-off" response (approximately 1 sec was cut from the middle of this record). Lower record: a synthetic "off" response. Time is marked in ⅕ sec. Signal of exposure to light blackens the white line above the time marker. Fibers whose activity is shown in the two records of (*b*) gave a sustained discharge like that shown in (*a*) when the ommatidia from which they arose were illuminated alone. (Reproduced from Ratliff & Mueller, 1957.)

"on-off" responses are characterized by a burst of activity when the light is turned on, no further activity as the light stays on, and a final burst of activity after the light is turned off; the "off" responses do not appear until after the light goes off, and they may be inhibited by reillumination. These experiments lend considerable support to the view (Granit, 1933; Hartline, 1938) that "on-off" and "off" responses may be the result of the complex interplay of excitatory and inhibitory influences by showing that the experimental manipulation of these influences can, indeed, yield such transient responses.

The role of inhibitory interaction in generating specialized neural responses to *temporal* changes in stimulation may well be of greater physiological significance than the better known part it plays in the enhancement of contrast under steady-state conditions.

## DISCUSSION

Inhibitory interaction among neural elements is a fundamental neural mechanism common to many sense modalities, integrative levels, and species (cf. the brief review by Brooks, 1959); and its principal functional properties appear to be much the same wherever it is found. The eye of *Limulus* provides an especially favorable preparation for the quantitative analysis of these functional properties: the interaction is purely inhibitory; the population of interacting elements is relatively small; and the pattern of stimulation on the receptor mosaic may be controlled with considerable precision. Experiments with this eye furnish a model of a relatively simple integrative process that may be useful in understanding the more complex integrative processes in other parts of the nervous system and in other species.

The influence of inhibitory interaction among neural elements on their patterns of activity is clearly illustrated in the eye of *Limulus*. The discharge of impulses in any one optic nerve fiber depends not only upon the stimulus to the specific receptor unit from which that fiber arises but also upon the spatial and temporal distribution of the stimulation of the entire population of interacting elements. These interactions accentuate contrast at sharp spatial and temporal gradients and discontinuities in the retinal image: borders and contours become "crisp" in their neural representation. Thus, the pattern of optic-nerve activity that results is by no means a direct copy of the pattern of stimulation on the receptor mosaic; certain information of special significance to the organism is accentuated at the expense of less significant information.

Interaction in the vertebrate retina is more complex; it comprises both inhibitory and excitatory influences, which result in great diversity, and often lability of the patterns of optic-nerve activity. The one influence often obscures the contribution of the other. Nevertheless, it has been possible to parcel out some of the separate contributions of excitatory and inhibitory influences to the patterns of optic-nerve activity in the vertebrate visual system. For example, Hartline (1939) found that, in the eye of the frog, an "off" response elicited in a single fiber by illuminating one group of receptors may be inhibited by illuminating another group of receptors in the same receptive field. It has since been shown (Barlow, 1953) that light falling entirely outside but close to the receptive field of a particular fiber also has an inhibitory effect on that fiber's response. Kuffler (1953) has shown that in the eye of the cat certain areas within a single receptive field make either a predominant "on" or "off" contribution to the discharge pattern; and when two opposed areas within the receptive field interact, the responses of both through their common neuron become modified; the interaction is mutual. The possible role of inhibition in the modification of these responses in the retina is discussed in some detail by Barlow, Fitz-Hugh, and Kuffler (1957). Further modifications of the pattern of nerve activity take place at higher integrative levels in the visual pathway; for example, Baumgartner and Hakas (1959) have observed inhibitory interaction among neural units in the visual cortex of the cat.

Inhibitory interaction is undoubtedly the basis of a number of well-known visual phenomena such as brightness contrast and color contrast. Indeed, early psychophysical studies of these phenomena presaged the discovery of inhibitory interaction by electrophysiological methods. For example, Mach's quantitative formulation of the interdependence of retinal areas in the human eye (1866), based entirely on psychophysical observations, contains most of the important features of inhibitory interaction subsequently revealed by electrophysiological studies on lower animals nearly a century later! The visual significance of the contrast effects, too, has long been known. For hundreds of years artists have utilized these effects to brighten or subdue colors, or to alter their apparent hue, and—especially—to emphasize lines and contours. Indeed, it seems almost instinctive for the artist to accentuate the contours of an object he is representing; and he does this—as the eye does—at the expense of accuracy of representation of less significant features.

## *SUMMARY*

This paper reviews a quantitative analysis of the inhibitory interaction among receptor units (ommatidia) in the lateral eye of *Limulus*.

Activity in any one optic nerve fiber of the *Limulus* eye, isolated by dissection, can be elicited only by illumination of the receptor unit from which that fiber arises (there is no excitatory convergence in this eye). But the discharge of nerve impulses by any given receptor unit, nevertheless, is influenced by illuminating other receptor units in its neighborhood. This influence is purely inhibitory.

These inhibitory influences are exerted mutually among the interacting receptors; the activity of each is the resultant of the light stimulus to it and the inhibition exerted on it by the others. Under steady illumination the inhibition exerted by one receptor unit on a second receptor unit in its neighborhood is a linear function of the frequency of discharge of the first receptor unit. When several receptor units act on a given unit in their vicinity, the total inhibition they exert is determined quantitatively by the inhibitory influences of each, combined by simple addition. As a consequence, the responses of $n$ receptors interacting with one another may be described by a set of $n$ simultaneous equations, linear in the frequencies of the interacting units.

The inhibitory interaction between two receptors in the eye of *Limulus* is stronger, the closer they are to one another in the receptor mosaic. This factor has an important effect on the patterns of optic-nerve activity elicited by various spatial configurations of light on the receptor mosaic: contrast is accentuated in the vicinity of steep gradients in the retinal image. These effects resemble closely the analogous effects in human vision (Mach bands and border contrast).

The transient, dynamic phases of the inhibitory interaction accentuate the optic-nerve response to temporal changes in illumination. Indeed, by suitably pitting the excitatory influences of light stimulation of a receptor unit against inhibitory influences from some of its neighbors, transient discharges of impulses can be produced that resemble very closely the "on-off" and "off" bursts of impulses so characteristic of various optic nerve fibers of the vertebrate retina.

These experiments on the eye of *Limulus* furnish a model illustrating one mechanism that may contribute to spatial and temporal contrast effects in more highly organized visual systems, and that may be useful in understanding complex integrative processes in other parts of the nervous system.

## *REFERENCES*

Barlow, H. B. Summation and inhibition in the frog's retina. *Journal of Physiology*, 1953, *119*, 69-88.

Barlow, H. B., FitzHugh, R., & Kuffler, S. W. Change of organization in the receptive fields of the cat's retina during dark adaptation. *Journal of Physiology*, 1957, *137*, 338-354.

Baumgartner, G., & Hakas, P. Reaktionen einzelner Opticusneurone und corticaler Nervenzellen der Katze in Hell-Dunkel-Grenzfeld (Simultankontrast). *Pflügers Archiv für die gesamte Physiologie*, 1959, *270*, 29.

Brooks, V. B. Contrast and stability in the nervous system. *Transactions of the New York Academy of Science*, 1959, *21*, 387-394.

Granit, R. The components of the retinal action potential and their relation to the discharge in the optic nerve. *Journal of Physiology*, 1933, *77*, 207-240.

Hartline, H. K. The response of single optic nerve fibers of the vertebrate eye to illumination of the retina. *American Journal of Physiology*, 1938, *121*, 400-415.

Hartline, H. K. Excitation and inhibition of the "off" response in vertebrate optic nerve fibers. *American Journal of Physiology*, 1939, *126*, 527.

Hartline, H. K. Inhibition of activity of visual receptors by illuminating nearby retinal elements in the *Limulus* eye. *Federation Proceedings*, 1949, *8*, 69.

Hartline, H. K., & Graham, C. H. Nerve impulses from single receptors in the eye. *Journal of Cellular and Comparative Physiology*, 1932, *1*, 277-295.

Hartline, H. K., & Ratliff, F. Inhibitory interaction of receptor units in the eye of *Limulus*. *Journal of General Physiology*, 1957, *40*, 357-376.

Hartline, H. K., & Ratliff, F. Spatial summation of inhibitory influences in the eye of *Limulus*, and the mutual interaction of receptor units. *Journal of General Physiology*, 1958, *41*, 1049-1066.

Hartline, H. K., Wagner, H. G., & MacNichol, Jr., E. F. The peripheral origin of nervous activity in the visual system. *Cold Spring Harbor Symposia on Quantitative Biology*, 1952, *17*, 125-141.

Hartline, H. K., Wagner, H. G., & Ratliff, F. Inhibition in the eye of *Limulus*. *Journal of General Physiology*, 1956, *39*, 651-673.

Kuffler, S. W. Discharge patterns and functional organization of mammalian retina. *Journal of Neurophysiology*, 1953, *16*, 37-68.

Mach, E. Ueber den physiologischen Effect räumlich vertheilter Lichtreize, II. *Sitzber. Akad. Wiss. Wien.* (Math.-nat. KL.), Abt. 2, 1866, *54*, 131-144.

MacNichol, E. F., Jr. Visual receptors as biological transducers. In *Molecular structure and functional activity of nerve cells*. American Institute of Biological Science Publication No. 1, 1956, 34-53.

MacNichol, E. F., Jr., & Hartline, H. K. Responses to small changes of light intensity by the light-adapted photoreceptor. *Federation Proceedings*, 1948, *7*, 76.

Miller, W. H. Morphology of the ommatidia of the compound eye of *Limulus*. *Journal of Biophysical and Biochemical Cytology*, 1957, *3*, 421-428.

Miller, W. H. Fine structure of some invertebrate photoreceptors. *Annals of the New York Academy of Science*, 1958, *74*, 204-209.

Ratliff, F., & Hartline, H. K. The responses of *Limulus* optic nerve fibers to patterns of illumination on the receptor mosaic. *Journal of General Physiology*, 1959, *42*, 1241-1255.

Ratliff, F., Miller, W. H., & Hartline, H. K. Neural interaction in the eye and the integration of receptor activity. *Annals of the New York Academy of Science*, 1958, *74*, 210-222.

Ratliff, F., & Mueller, C. G. Synthesis of "on-off" and "off" responses in a visual-neural system. *Science*, 1957, *126*, 840-841.
Tomita, T. Mechanism of lateral inhibition in the eye of *Limulus*. *Journal of Neurophysiology*, 1958, *21*, 419-429.
Waterman, T. H., & Wiersma, C. A. G. The functional relation between retinal cells and optic nerve in *Limulus*. *Journal of Experimental Zoology*, 1954, *126*, 59-86.

*The significance of lateral inhibition in the compound eye for the enhancement of contour-detection is clear enough, and will provide a useful introduction to the study of similar processes in the vertebrate system. Before proceeding to that topic, however, a paper by J. Z. Young is presented, which summarizes some anatomical findings which are particularly interesting in suggesting a physiological basis for some of the properties of shape discrimination in the octopus. On the whole it is rare for an anatomist or physiologist to show enthusiastic interest in behavioral findings, however great the interest in the other direction, and Young is a pleasant exception to that generalization. The main reason for including the paper, however, is that the octopus eye and visual system is somewhere intermediate in structure and complexity between the compound eye and the vertebrate eye, and illustrates an additional stage in the evolution towards the enormously complex visual system which is found in mammals. Although the octopus eye has a lens and internal retina, the connections between the retinal elements and optic fibers are still rather direct, and the fibers feed straight into the optic lobe, where complex connections between a number of different sorts of cells are found. Anatomical mapping of cells and cell types has been done in great detail in the visual system of Octopus, but there is almost no information as yet on the functions which those cells subserve; for example no experiments have been done to show whether the inhibitory interactions which play such a big part in stimulus processing in Limulus—and presumably in other organisms with compound eyes—also occur, or occur in the same form, in the octopus or other organisms with similarly organized visual systems.*

# *Regularities in the Retina and Optic Lobes of* Octopus *in Relation to Form Discrimination*

J. Z. YOUNG

The capacity of an octopus to learn to make distinct reactions to differing visible shapes depends largely upon analysis of the vertical and horizontal extents of the figures (Sutherland, 1958). Certain regularities now found in the retina and optic lobes provide clues to the mechanism for computing in these two directions.

The cells of the optic lobes show a bewildering variety of shapes. Often it is not possible to distinguish clearly between dendrites and axons, or to establish histologically the probable sites of origin of action potentials or the direction of conduction of the cells. Some of the cells have orientated dendritic trees within which there may be complex interactions such as are known in neurons of somewhat similar form in Crustacea (Bullock & Terzuolo, 1957; Hughes & Wiersma, 1961). There are sufficient data to suggest that the shapes and anatomical arrangements of the cells are of fundamental importance in the coding system. Deutsch (1960) has proposed a hypothesis based on the general arrangement of the system as revealed by previous workers (Lenhossek, 1896; Cajal, 1917). Further study now provides additional evidence of regularities. It must be emphasized, however, that the forms of the cells are so complicated and difficult to investigate that much further work will be needed before it is certain which features are significant.

The outer segments of the retinal elements, directed towards the centre of the eye, form squares ('rhabdomes') as seen in tagential section, separated from each other by pigment granules (Schultze), Fig. 1). Further examination shows that the rhabdomes are orientated in the dorso-ventral and horizontal planes of the eye, as it is usually held with the pupil horizontal.

Each rhabdome contains four 'rhabdomeres', composed of piles of tubules (Wolken; Moody & Robertson, 1960), and these lie with their long axes approximately in the vertical plane in one pair and the horizontal

Reprinted from *Nature*, 1960.

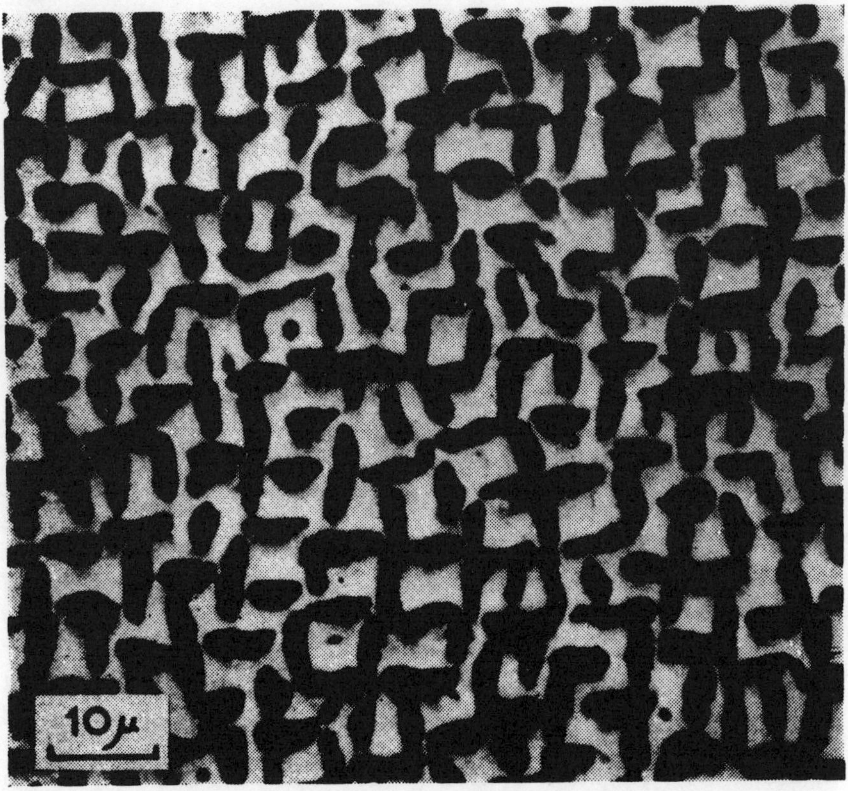

Fig. 1. Photograph of tangential section of retina of *Octopus*. Only the pigment shows, the rhabdomes being unstained. The long axis of the figure is dorso-ventral.

plane in the other pair in each rhabdome. The rhabdomes are connected to inner segments, each with a nucleus and nerve fibre, and counts show that there are twice as many nuclei as there are squares in the retina. Each rhabdome thus contains two receptor units (retinal cells), probably arranged as in Fig. 2. There are altogether $1–2 \times 10^7$ nuclei—a density of about 50,000 per mm.$^2$. There are no striking differences in density in the central and peripheral parts of the retina.

The processes of the retinal receptors pass through a plexus and then through a chiasma that inverts the display in the dorso-ventral plane. They end within the optic lobes mainly in a complicated plexiform layer, the deep retina. This layer shows the following features in Cajal and Golgi preparations:

(1) A marked layering; four layers of tangential fibres are recognized, separated by four in which they are mainly radial (Fig. 3).

(2) Each optic nerve fibre has endings at more than one depth in the

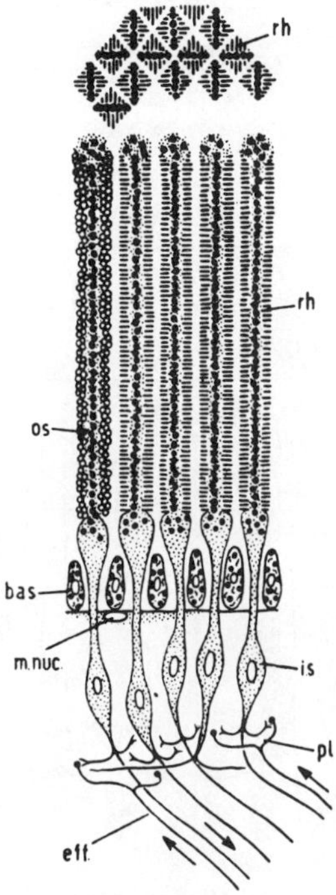


Fig. 2. Diagram of probable arrangement of the elements of the retina; above as seen in a tangential section, below in radial section. *bas.*, basal cell (which probably sends branches between the rhabdomes); *eff.*, efferent axon to the retina; *i.s.*, inner segment; *o.s.*, outer segment; *pl.*, plexus beneath retina; *rh.*, rhabdomes. It is calculated that each retinal unit (pair of rhabdomeres) subtends a visual angle of 1·3′.

plexiform zone. The endings are mainly either superficial or deep, but there are also intermediates.

(3) Numerous amacrine cells send processes that spread to increasing distances with increasing depth (Figs. 3 and 5). These cells often do not show one distinct process that could be called an axon, though it is possible that these are unseen with the light microscope. If these cells ensure that excitation occurs where their processes overlap they may produce activity in the more superficial layers for points near together on the retina and in deeper layers for those more distant, thus serving to produce a neural representation of length. However, without information as to the physiological characteristics of such cells, it is not possible to say exactly how they function. An alternative possibility is that they serve to produce inhibition when neighbouring retinal elements are active, sharpening the effect of contours.

(4) Deep to the plexiform layer are further layers of small cells. Some of these are amacrines. Others have numerous processes in the plexiform

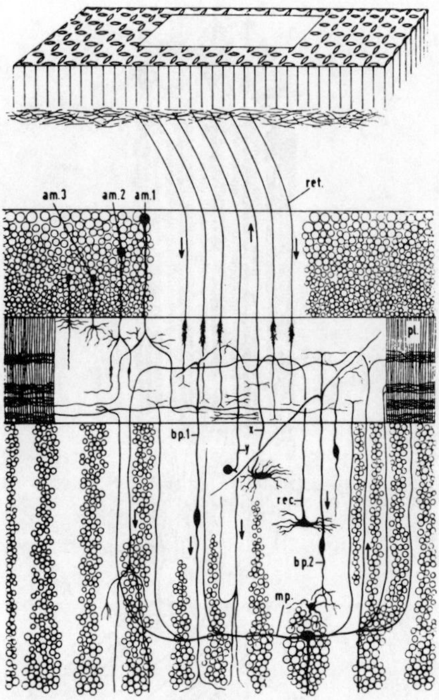


Fig. 3. Diagram of the structure of the outer part of the optic lobe of *Octopus*. The retina is shown above with the image of a small rectangle. *am*. 1, 2 and 3, amacrine cells; *bp*. 1 and 2, bipolar cells the dendrites of which at different levels in the plexiform zone are orientated in opposite directions; *mp*., multipolar cell with many dendrites reaching to plexiform layer; *pl*. plexiform layer; *rec*., cell with dendrites in plexiform layer and a recurrent axon; *ret*. retinal nerve fibre. *x* and *y* cells with efferent processes to the retina, *x* has short basal processes, *y* long ones. All the cells are shown very schematically. A rectangle of 20 cm.$^2$ seen at 1 m. would produce an image covering 14,000 retinal cells. A length of 100$\mu$ on the surface of the lobe corresponds to a visual angle of 40′, receiving some 30 optic nerve fibres.

layers and an axon that passes outwards into an optic nerve (Fig. 3) and presumably provides an efferent pathway to the retina. Collaterals have been described at the base of the inner retinal segments (Lenhossek, 1896; Cajal, 1917), and there are thus probably synaptic connexions in the plexus behind the retina, as in *Limulus* (Ratliff et al., 1958). The efferent cells to the retina also have basal processes, sometimes long (Fig. 3).

(5) Conduction inwards from the plexiform zone is by cells that can be called bipolars. They have numerous dendrites in the plexiform zone while the axon either proceeds from the base of the cell or as a recurrent fibre from one of the dendritic processes (Figs. 3 and 5). The dendrites may be in several of the layers or only in one layer. They extend over an appreciable portion of the lobe (1 mm.) and each is thus influenced by a wide angle of the visual field (see legend to Fig. 3). They do not run

TABLE 1

NUMBER AND LENGTHS OF FIBRES IN AN AREA OF 22,500$\mu^2$ IN THE PLEXIFORM LAYERS OF THE OPTIC LOBE OF AN OCTOPUS (CAJAL'S METHOD)

| | *Degrees from Horizontal* | | | | | |
|---|---|---|---|---|---|---|
| *Layer of Plexus* | 75-105 | 105-135 | 45-75 | 135-165 | 15-45 | 165-180 } 0-15 } |
| Second tangential | | | | | | |
| Number | 39 | 8 | 13 | 6 | 5 | 13 |
| Length ($\mu$) | 1,455 | 393 | 462 | 204 | 179 | 531 |
| Mean length ($\mu$) | 37 | 49 | 36 | 34 | 35 | 50 |
| Third tangential | | | | | | |
| Number | 24 | 18 | 11 | 16 | 11 | 19 |
| Length ($\mu$) | 625 | 447 | 373 | 490 | 445 | 664 |
| Mean length ($\mu$) | 26 | 25 | 34 | 31 | 41 | 35 |
| Fourth tangential | | | | | | |
| Number | 26 | 14 | 14 | 11 | 13 | 16 |
| Length ($\mu$) | 760 | 450 | 321 | 357 | 359 | 415 |
| Mean length ($\mu$) | 29 | 32 | 23 | 32 | 29 | 26 |
| Total | | | | | | |
| Number | 89 | 40 | 38 | 33 | 29 | 48 |
| Mean length ($\mu$) | 32 | 32 | 30 | 32 | 34 | 34 |

equally in all directions. Measurements on Cajal preparations show the greatest number and total length of dendrite to be in the vertical direction (Table 1). There are also many horizontal ones, but fewer obliques. The individual fibres are longest in the horizontal direction, and Golgi preparations show that many of the dendritic fields are oval, with the long axis horizontal (Fig. 4). However, others have the main axis vertical or oblique. It may be that where a cell has dendritic fields in several of the plexiform zone layers, these lie predominantly in different directions, as shown diagrammatically in Fig. 3. Since the fields can only be seen fully in tangential sections, it is difficult to obtain evidence on their orientation. That they have some relation to the main axes suggests a possible connexion with the fact that an octopus can discriminate between vertical and horizontal rectangles but not between obliques (Sutherland, 1957). Sutherland (1961) has provided evidence that octopuses discriminate between visual figures largely by taking account of some function of their vertical and horizontal extents. Cells with dendrites at different depths might be individually responsive to different ratios in these directions, if the amacrines ensure that excitation by contours of greater length occurs at greater depths.

(6) However, there is the further possibility that cells deeper in the optic lobes are sensitive to such ratios. Bipolar cells with oriented fields in one

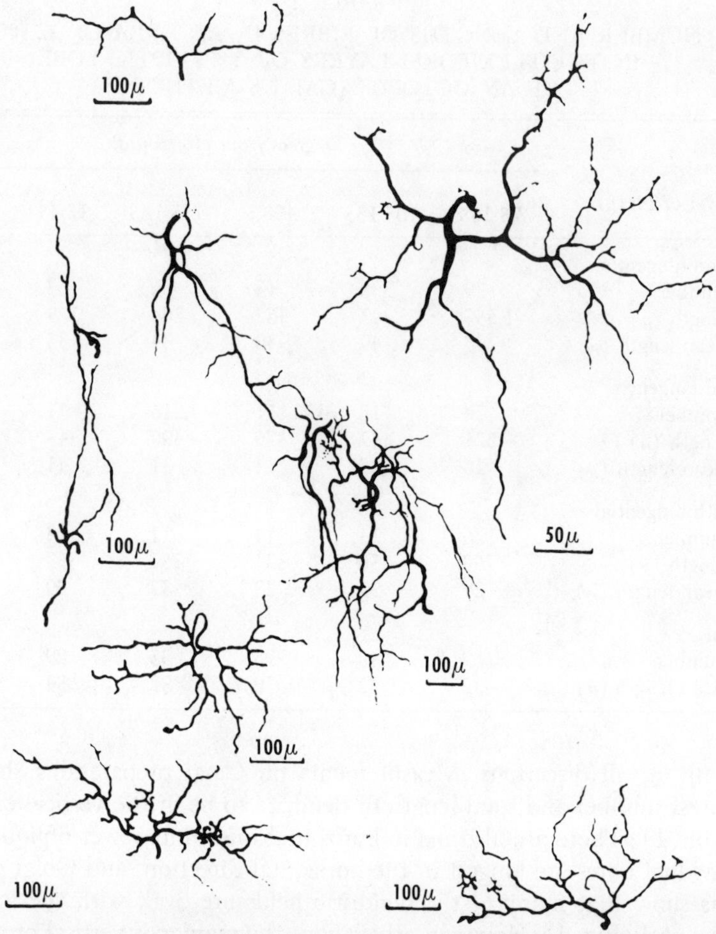


Fig. 4. Drawings of dendritic fields of some bipolar cells in the plexiform layer as seen in tangential sections of Golgi preparations. The fields are oval, with long axes directed mainly horizontally, but sometimes vertically.

plexiform layer only project to depths proportional to the sizes of their receptive fields (Figs. 5 and 6). Here they meet the dendrites of the cells of the medulla of the lobe, the fields of which have most elaborate forms. These are even harder to study than the flatter fields in the plexiform layer, especially as they extend through considerable depths. Some of them have many superficial branches and fewer at deeper levels, others the reverse. If the parts of the field at different depths lie in differing directions these cells might be specifically sensitive to excitation by shapes with particular vertical and horizontal extents.

Thus there are undoubtedly regularities in the distribution of the den-

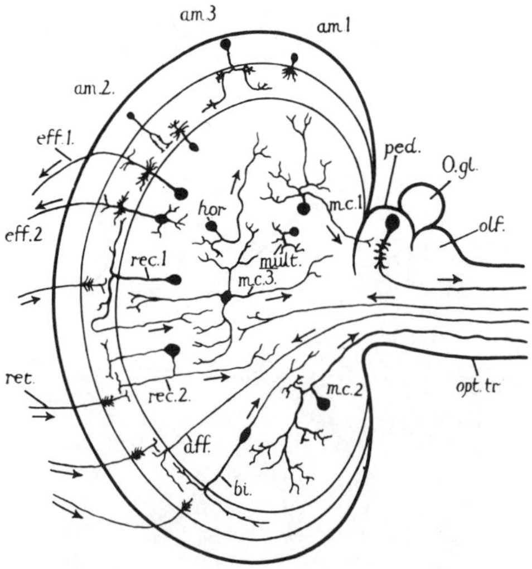


Fig. 5. Diagram to show further pathways through the optic lobe. *aff.*, fibres afferent to the lobe from the brain or opposite lobe; *am.*, amacrine cells; *bi.*, bipolar cell; *eff.*, cells with efferent fibres to the retina; *hor.*, horizontal cell; *m.c.*, cells of the medulla, some with axons leaving the lobe; *mult.*, small multipolar cell; *o.gl.*, optic gland; *olf.*, olfactory lobe; *opt.tr.*, optic tract; *ped.*, peduncle lobe; *rec.*, cells with recurrent axons. All the cells are shown schematically.

drites in the plexiform layer, and this may also be true throughout the lobe. The whole set of some 60 million cells would then provide a system able to learn to make appropriate responses to the vertical/horizontal extent of a moving figure.

The effect of visual stimulation of an octopus by an 'unknown' figure is to elicit attack only occasionally and after long delay. As a hypothesis it is suggested that if food reward occurs following showing of a given shape, the cells that were active become conditioned to produce attack. During the period immediately after presentation, pathways to other parts of the same and the opposite optic lobes and through the vertical lobes would ensure that further cells with appropriate structure become conditioned, in addition to those originally stimulated. This would allow for spread of the representation throughout the tissue and thus for generalization of the response to retinal regions other than that stimulated. Generalization for figures of different sizes might also be achieved in this way, but this requires further investigation. Conversely, a figure that was followed by a shock would come to produce an avoidance response. Learning would thus consist of the accumulation of a sufficient number of suitably conditioned cells to produce a reliable response.

If the learning of appropriate responses to shapes depends upon the presence of cells with pre-set orientations, then it may be expected that

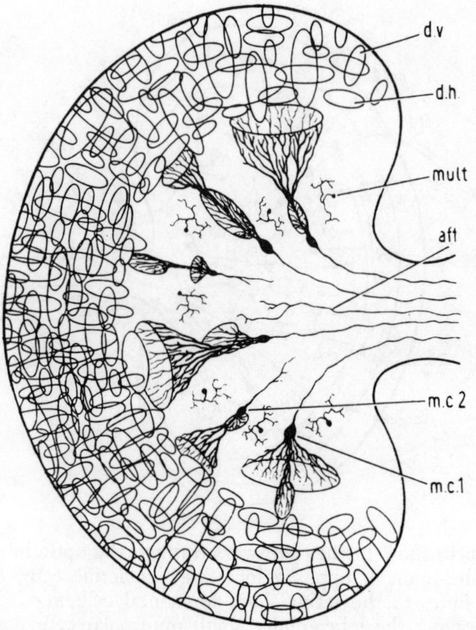


Fig. 6. Diagram of a thick horizontal section of the optic lobe to show probable arrangement of dendritic fields of some bipolar cells in single layers of the plexiform zone. Some run mainly vertically (*d.v.*), others horizontally (*d.h.*). The axons of the smaller cells end nearer the surface. The cells of the medulla have dendrites at many levels and these may run in different directions at different levels. Very diagrammatic. *aff.*, afferent fibres; *m.c.* 1 and 2, cells of the medulla with deep and superficial dendrites oriented in different directions and spreading to different extents.

training with several pairs of figures would produce confusions. This proves to be the case. After training in the relatively difficult discrimination between a square and a diamond octopuses discriminated between vertical and horizontal rectangles at a significantly lower level than normal (Sutherland, 1961). Other interpretations of this result are possible, and it cannot be claimed that it is proved that the mechanism operates as here suggested. It is interesting, however, that an animal that recognizes shapes largely by their vertical and horizontal extents shows elements in the retina and brain arranged in these directions.

There is a general similarity of the plan of organization of the visual system of *Octopus* with that of insects and vertebrates, which prompts the search for orientation of neuronal fields also in these animals. Indeed, some projections from the mammalian retina to the visual cortex are oval fields each with characteristic orientation (Hubel and Wiesel, 1959). The evidence serves to direct attention to the need for considering the form of the distribution of dendritic fields as a factor allowing coding by selection of particular features of an input.

## *REFERENCES*

Bullock, T. H., & Terzuolo, C. A. Diverse forms of activity in the somata of spontaneous and integrating ganglion cells, *Journal of Physiology,* 1957, *138,* 341-364.

Cajal, S. R. Contribución al conocimiento de la retina y centros ópticos de los cefalópods. *Trabajos del Laboratorio de investigationes biologicas de la Universidad de Madrid,* 1917, *15,* 1-82.

Deutsch, J. A. The plexiform zone and shape recognition in the octopus. *Nature,* 1960, *185,* 443-446.

Hubel, D. H., & Wiesel, T. N. Receptive fields of single neurones in the cat's striate cortex. *Journal of Physiology,* 1959, *148,* 574-591.

Hughes, G. M., & Wiersma, C. A. G. The coordination of swimmeret movements in the crayfish, *Procambarus Clarkii* (Girard). *Journal of Experimental Biology,* 1961, *37,* 657-670.

Lenhossek, M. Von. *Achiv für mikroskopische Anatomie,* 1896, *47,* 54.

Moody, M. F., & Robertson, J. D. The fine structure of some retinal photoreceptors. *Journal of Biophysical and Biochemical Cytology,* 1960, *7,* 87-92.

Parriss, J. R. (to be published).

Ratliff, F., Miller, W. H., & Hartline, H. K. Neural interaction in the eye and the integration of receptor activity. *Annals of the New York Academy of Science,* 1958, *74,* 210-222.

Sutherland, N. S. Visual discrimination of orientation by *Octopus. British Journal of Psychology,* 1957, *48,* 55-71.

Sutherland, N. S. Visual discrimination of the orientation of rectangles by *Octopus valgaris* Lamarck. *Journal of Comparative and Physiological Psychology,* 1958, *51,* 452-458.

Sutherland, N. S. Discrimination of Horizontal and Vertical Extents by Octopus. *Journal of Comparative and Physiological Psychology,* 1961, *54,* 43-48.

Sutherland, N. S. Visual discrimination of shape by *Octopus:* squares and rectangles. *Journal of Comparative and Physiological Psychology,* 1960, *53,* 95-103.

Young, J. Z. Failures of discrimination learning following removal of the vertical lobes in *Octopus. Proceedings of the Royal Society,* B, 1960, *153,* 18-46.

Young, J. Z. Unit processes in the formation of representations in the memory of *Octopus. Proceedings of the Royal Society, B,* 1960, *153,* 1-17.

*Further information on the anatomy of the octopus visual system, collation of that information with findings on shape recognition, and discussion of a number of related issues can be found in Young's book* A Model for the Brain *(1964). At the end of his paper, Young suggests that* the overall similarity in the plan of organization of the visual system of Octopus with those of insect and vertebrate should lead one to expect similar principles of anatomical mapping in them. I am rather sceptical of this suggestion, since the differences between these three types of visual system seem to be to be at least as impressive as their similarities. However, that is a point on which the reader may judge for himself after seeing the rest of the evidence presented in this section.

The next selection is a very celebrated paper, and rightly so, for it gives a clear and readable account of some truly outstanding research on properties of visual detectors in the frog. From the point of view of proceeding up the evolutionary scale, it is in the right place here since it is about the visual system of a submammalian vertebrate. Also, it is convenient to present it at this point since a good deal of the anatomy and physiology of the frog system—which is summarized at the beginning of the paper (see especially Figure 1)—is common to other vertebrates too. The paper was also written for nonphysiologists, so that all the necessary terms are explained, and the presentation is not unduly technical. From another point of view, it would have been sensible to precede it with the paper which actually succeeds it (Kuffler) since the latter was published earlier, and establishes some facts which are basic to the paper by Lettvin et al.

The reader should compare Young's Figure 2 (p. 297) with Lettvin et al.'s Figure 1(a) (p. 308) and Young's Figure 3 (p. 298) with their Figure 1 (d). The point of these comparisons is to emphasize the greatly increased complication of the cell types and arrangements of the retinal level in going to the vertebrate system on the one hand, and the apparently fairly similar sorts of anatomical complexity in the optic lobe (octopus) and tectum (frog) on the other. In the frog it appears that the apparatus for complicated information-processing at the retinal level exists, and we may well expect therefore to find that such processing occurs. In the octopus, on the other hand, it would be surprising to find complicated analyses occurring at the retinal level, given its much simpler anatomical organization.

# *What the Frog's Eye Tells the Frog's Brain*

J. Y. LETTVIN, H. R. MATURANA,
W. S. MCCULLOCH, AND W. H. PITTS

*In this paper, we analyze the activity of single fibers in the optic nerve of a frog. Our method is to find what sort of stimulus causes the largest activity in one nerve fiber and then what is the exciting aspect of that stimulus such that variations in everything else cause little change in the response. It has been known for the past 20 years that each fiber is connected not to a few rods and cones in the retina but to very many over a fair area. Our results show that for the most part within that area, it is not the light intensity itself but rather the pattern of local variation of intensity that is the exciting factor. There are four types of fibers, each type concerned with a different sort of pattern. Each type is uniformly distributed over the whole retina of the frog. Thus, there are four distinct parallel distributed channels whereby the frog's eye informs his brain about the visual image in terms of local pattern independent of average illumination. We describe the patterns and show the functional and anatomical separation of the channels. This work has been done on the frog, and our interpretation applies only to the frog.*

## *INTRODUCTION*

### Behavior of a Frog

A frog hunts on land by vision. He escapes enemies mainly by seeing them. His eyes do not move, as do ours, to follow prey, attend suspicious events, or search for things of interest. If his body changes its position with respect to gravity or the whole visual world is rotated about him, then he shows compensatory eye movements. These movements enter his hunting and evading habits only, *e.g.*, as he sits on a rocking lily pad. Thus his eyes are

Reprinted from *Proceedings of the Institute of Radio Engineers*, 1959.
A more extensive report on the work is contained in a paper by the same authors in the *Journal of General Physiology*, 1960, 43, No. 6, Part 2 (Supplement to July Issue), pp. 129-175.

actively stabilized. He has no fovea, or region of greatest acuity in vision, upon which he must center a part of the image. He also has only a single visual system, retina to colliculus, not a double one such as ours where the retina sends fibers not only to colliculus but to the lateral geniculate body which relays to cerebral cortex. Thus, we chose to work on the frog because of the uniformity of his retina, the normal lack of eye and head movements except for those which stabilize the retinal image, and the relative simplicity of the connection of his eye to his brain.

The frog does not seem to see or, at any rate, is not concerned with the detail of stationary parts of the world around him. He will starve to death surrounded by food if it is not moving. His choice of food is determined only by size and movement. He will leap to capture any object the size of an insect or worm, providing it moves like one. He can be fooled easily not only by a bit of dangled meat but by any moving small object. His sex life is conducted by sound and touch. His choice of paths in escaping enemies does not seem to be governed by anything more devious than leaping to where it is darker. Since he is equally at home in water and on land, why should it matter where he lights after jumping or what particular direction he takes? He does remember a moving thing providing it stays within his field of vision and he is not distracted.

## Anatomy of Frog Visual Apparatus

The retina of a frog is shown in Fig. 1(a). Between the rods and cones of the retina and the ganglion cells, whose axons form the optic nerve, lies a layer of connecting neurons (bipolars, horizontals, and amacrines). In the frog there are about 1 million receptors, 2½ to 3½ million connecting neurons, and half a million ganglion cells (Maturana, 1959). The connections are such that there is a synaptic path from a rod or cone to a great many ganglion cells, and a ganglion cell receives paths from a great many thousand receptors. Clearly, such an arrangement would not allow for good resolution were the retina meant to map an image in terms of light intensity point by point into a distribution of excitement in the optic nerve.

There is only one layer of ganglion cells in the frog. These cells are half a million in number (as against one million rods and cones). The neurons are packed together tightly in a sheet at the level of the cell bodies. Their dendrites, which may extend laterally from 50 $\mu$ to 500 $\mu$, interlace widely into what is called the inner plexiform layer, which is a close-packed neuropil containing the terminal arbors of those neurons that lie between receptors and ganglion cells. Thus, the amount of overlap of adjacent ganglion cells is enormous in respect to what they see. Morphologically, there are several types of these cells that are as distinct in their dendritic patterns as different species of trees, from which we infer that they work in different ways. The anatomy shown in the figures is that found in standard references. Further discussion of anatomical questions and additional original work on them will appear in a later publication.

## Physiology as Known up to This Study

Hartline (1938) first used the term *receptive field* for the region of retina within which a local change of brightness would cause the ganglion cell he was observing to discharge. Such a region is sometimes surrounded by an annulus, within which changes of brightness affect the cell's response to what is occurring in the receptive field, although the cell does not discharge to any event occurring in the annulus alone. Like Kuffler (1953), we consider the receptive field and its interacting annulus as a single entity, with apologies to Dr. Hartline for the slight change in meaning. Hartline found three sorts of receptive field in the frog: ON, ON-OFF, and OFF. If a small spot of light suddenly appears in the receptive field of an ON-cell, the discharge soon begins, increases in rate to some limit determined by the intensity and area of the spot, and thereafter slowly declines. Turning off the spot abolishes the discharge.

If the small spot of light suddenly appears or disappears within the field of an ON-OFF cell, the discharge is short and occurs in both cases.

If the spot of light disappears from the field of an OFF cell, the discharge begins immediately, decreases slowly in frequency, and lasts a long time. It can be abolished promptly by turning the spot of light on again.

For all three sorts of field, sensitivity is greatest at the center of each field and least at the periphery.

Barlow (1953) extended Hartline's observations. He observed that the OFF cells have an adding receptive field, *i.e.*, the response occurs always to OFF at both center and periphery of that field, and that the effect of removing light from the periphery adds to the effect of a reduction of light at the center, with a weight decreasing with distance.

The ON-OFF cells, however, have differencing receptive fields. A discharge of several spikes to the appearance of light in the center is much diminished if a light is turned on in the extreme periphery. The same interaction occurs when these lights are removed. Thus, an ON-OFF cell seems to be measuring inequality of illumination within its receptive field. (Kuffler [1953] at the same time showed a similar mutual antagonism between center and periphery in each receptive field of ganglion cells in the eye of a cat, and later Barlow, Kuffler and Fitzhugh [1957] showed that the size of the cat's receptive fields varied with general illumination.) Barlow saw that ON-OFF cells were profoundly sensitive to movement within the receptive field. The ON cells have not been characterized by similar methods.

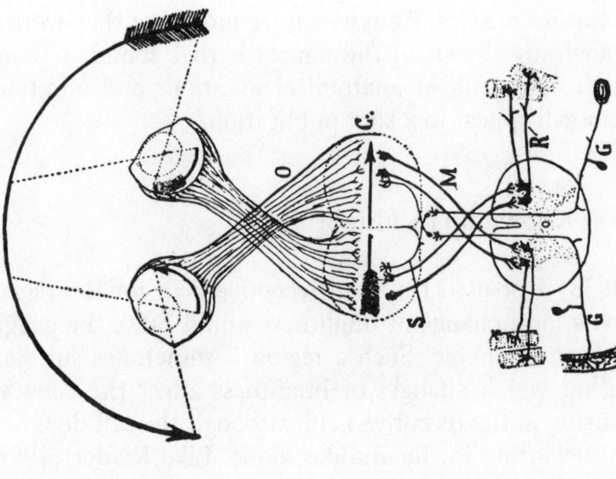

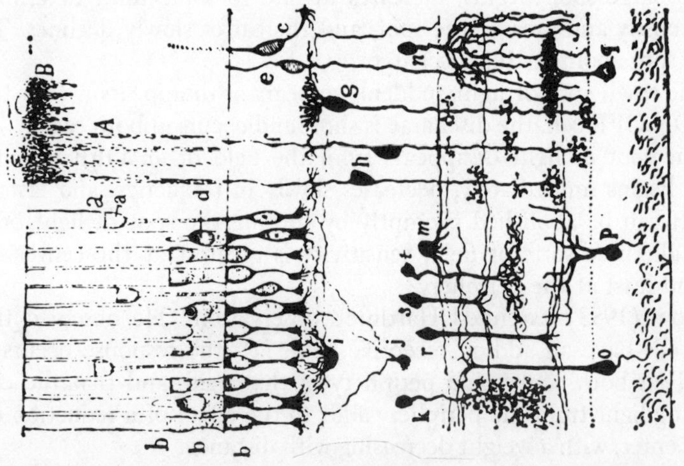

Fig. 1. (a) This is a diagram of the frog retina done by Ramon y Cajal over 50 years ago (1909-1911). The rods and cones are the group of elements in the upper left quarter of the picture. To their bushy bottom ends are connected the bipolar cells of the intermediate layer, for example, *f*, *g* and *h*. Lateral connecting neurons, called *horizontal* and *amacrine* cells, also occur in this layer, for example, *i*, *j* and *m*. The bipolars send their axons down to arborize in the inner plexiform layer, roughly the region bounded by cell *m* above and the bodies of the ganglion cells, *o*, *p* and *q*, below. In this sketch, Ramon has the axons of the bipolar cells emitting bushes at all levels in the plexiform layer; in fact, many of them branch at only one or two levels.

Compare the dendrites of the different ganglion cells. Not only do they spread out at different levels in the plexiform layer, but the patterns of branching are different. Other ganglion cells, not shown here, have multiple arbors spreading out like a plane tree at two or three levels. If the terminals of the bipolar cells are systematically arranged in depth, making a laminar operational map of the rods and cones in terms of very local contrast,

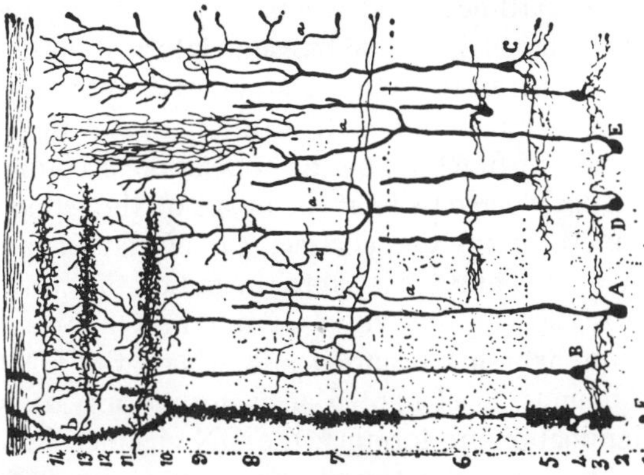

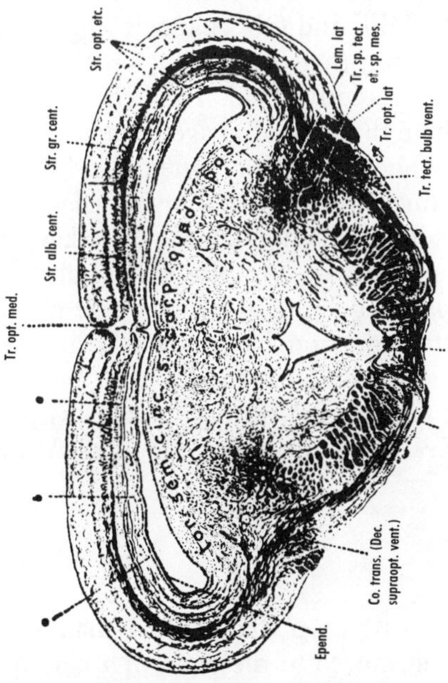


(c)

color, ON, OFF, etc., then the different shapes of the ganglion cells would correspond to different combinations of the local operations done by the bipolars. Thus would arise the more complex operations of the ganglion cells as described in the text. (b) This is Ramon y Cajal's diagram of the total decussation or crossing of the optic nerve fibers in the frog (1909-1911). He made this picture to explain the value of the crossing as preserving continuity in the map of the visual world. *O* is the optic nerve and *C* is the *superior colliculus* or *optic tectum* (the names are synonymous). (c) This is Ariens-Kapper's picture of the cross section of the brain of a frog through the colliculus, which is the upper or dorsal part above the enclosed space. (d) This is Pedro Ramon Cajal's diagram of the nervous organization of the tectum of a frog. The terminal bushes of the optic nerve fibers are labelled *a, b* and *c*. *A, B, C, D* and *E* are tectal cells receiving from the optic nerve fibers. Note that the axons of these cells come off the dendrites in stratum 7, which we call the *palisade* layer. The endings discussed in this paper lie between the surface and that stratum.

These findings of Hartline and Barlow establish that optic nerve fibers (the axons of the ganglion cells) do not transmit information only about light intensity at single points in the retina. Rather, each fiber measures a certain feature of the whole distribution of light in an area of the receptive field. There are three sorts of function, or areal operation, according to these authors, so that the optic nerve looks at the image on the retina through three distributed channels. In any one channel, the overlap of individual receptive fields is very great. Thus one is led to the notion that what comes to the brain of a frog is this: for any visual event, the OFF channel tells how much dimming of light has occurred and where; the ON-OFF channel tells where the boundaries of lighted areas are moving, or where local inequalities of illumination are forming; the ON channel shows (with a delay) where brightening has occurred. To an unchanging visual pattern, the nerve ought to become fairly silent after a while.

Consider the retinal image as it appears in each of the three distributed channels. For both the OFF and ON channels, we can treat the operation on the image by supposing that every point on the retina gives rise to a blur about the size of a receptive field. Then the OFF channel tells, with a long decay time, where the blurred image is darkened, and the ON channel tells with a delay and long decay where it is brightened. The third channel, ON-OFF, principally registers moving edges. Having the mental picture of an image as it appears through the three kinds of channel, we are still faced with the question of how the animal abstracts what is useful to him from his surroundings. At this point, a safe position would be that a fair amount of data reduction has in fact been accomplished by the retina and that the interpretation is the work of the brain, a yet-to-be unravelled mystery. Yet the nagging worries remain: why are there two complementary projections of equally poor resolution? Why is the mosaic of receptors so uselessly fine?

## Initial Argument

The assumption has always been that the eye mainly senses light, whose local distribution is transmitted to the brain in a kind of copy by a mosaic of impulses. Suppose we held otherwise, that the nervous apparatus in the eye is itself devoted to detecting certain patterns of light and their changes, corresponding to particular relations in the visible world. If this should be the case, the laws found by using small spots of light on the retina may be true and yet, in a sense, be misleading. Consider, for example, a bright spot appearing in a receptive field. Its actual and sensible properties include not only intensity, but the shape of its edge, its size, curvature, contrast, etc.

We decided then how we ought to work. First, we should find a way of recording from single myelinated and unmyelinated fibers in the intact optic nerve. Second, we should present the frog with as wide a range of visible stimuli as we could, not only spots of light but things he would be disposed to eat, other things from which he would flee, sundry geometrical figures, stationary and moving about, etc. From the variety of stimuli we should then try to discover what common features were abstracted by whatever groups of fibers we could find in the optic nerve. Third, we should seek the anatomical basis for the grouping.[1]

## *(ACTUAL) METHODS*

Using a variant of Dowben and Rose's platinum black-tipped electrode described in another paper of this issue, we then began a systematic study of fibers in the optic nerve. One of the authors (H. R. M.) had completed the electron microscopy of optic nerve in frogs (Maturana, 1958), and with his findings we were able to understand quickly why certain kinds of record occurred. He had found that the optic nerve of a frog contains about half a million fibers (ten times the earlier estimates by light microscopy). There are 30 times as many unmyelinated axons as myelinated, and both kinds are uniformly distributed throughout the nerve. The axons lie in small densely packed bundles of five to 100 fibers with about 100 A between axons, each bundle surrounded by one or more glial cells (Maturana, 1958). But along the nerve no bundle maintains its identity long, for the component fibers so braid between bundles that no two fibers stay adjacent. Thus the place a fiber crosses one section of the nerve bears little relation to its origin in the retina and little relation to where it crosses another section some distance away.

Fibers are so densely packed that one might suppose such braiding necessary to prevent serious interactions. On the other hand, the density makes the recording easier. A glial wall surrounds groups rather than single fibers, and penetration of the wall brings the tip among really bare axons each surrounded by neighbors whose effect is to increase the external impedance to its action currents, augmenting the external potential in proportion. Thus, while we prefer to use platinum black tips to improve the ratio of signal to noise, we recorded much the same population with ordinary sharp microelectrodes of bright Pt or Ag. The method records equally well from unmyelinated and myelinated fibers.

We used *Rana pipiens* in these experiments. We opened a small flap of bone either just behind the eye to expose the optic nerve, or over the brain to expose the superior colliculus. No further surgery was done except

[1] This program had started once before in our laboratory with A. Andrew (1955a, b) of Glasgow who unfortunately had to return to Scotland before the work got well under way. However, he had reported in 1957 that he found elements in the colliculus of the frog that were sensitive to movement of a spot of light (a dot on an oscilloscope screen) even when the intensity of the spot was so low that turning it on and off produced no response. In particular, the elements he observed showed firing upon movement away from the centers of the receptive fields, but not to centripetal movements. As will appear later, this sort of response is a natural property of OFF fibers.

to open the membranes of connective tissue overlying the nervous structure. The frog was held in extension to a cork platform and covered with moist cloth. An animal in such a position, having most of his body surface in physical contact with something, goes into a still reaction—*i.e.*, he will not even attempt to move save to pain, and except for the quick small incision of the skin at the start of the operation our procedure seems to be painless to him. With the animal mounted, we confront his eye with an aluminum hemisphere, 20 mils thick and 14 inches in diameter, silvered to a matte grey finish on the inner surface and held concentric to the eye. On the inner surface of this hemisphere, various objects attached to small magnets can be moved about by a large magnet moved by hand on the outer surface. On our hemisphere, 1° is slightly less than an eighth of an inch long. In the tests illustrated, we use as stimulating objects a dull black disk almost 1° in diameter and a rectangle 30° long and 12° wide. However, in the textual report, we use a variety of other objects. As an indicator for the stimulus, we first used a phototube looking at an image of the hemisphere taken through a camera lens and focussed on the plane of a diaphragm. (Later we used a photomultiplier, so connected as to give us a logarithmic response over about 4 decades.) Thus we could vary how much of the hemisphere was seen by the stimulus detector and match that area in position and size against the receptive field of the fiber we were studying. The output of this arrangement is the stimulus line in the figures.

## *FINDINGS*

There are four separate operations on the image in the frog's eye. Each has its result transmitted by a particular group of fibers, uniformly distributed across the retina, and they are all nearly independent of the general illumination. The operations are: (*1*) *sustained contrast detection*; (2) *net convexity detection*; (3) *moving edge detection; and* (4) *net dimming detection.* The first two are reported by unmyelinated fibers, the last two by myelinated fibers. Since we are now dealing with events rather than point excitations as stimuli, receptive fields can only be defined approximately, and one cannot necessarily distinguish concentric subdivisions. The fibers reporting the different operations differ systematically not only in fiber diameter (or conduction velocity) but also in rough size of receptive field, which ranges from about 2° diameter for the first operation, to about 15° for the last. The following description of these groups is definite.

### 1. Sustained Contrast Detectors

An unmyelinated axon of this group does not respond when the general illumination is turned on or off. If the sharp edge of an object either

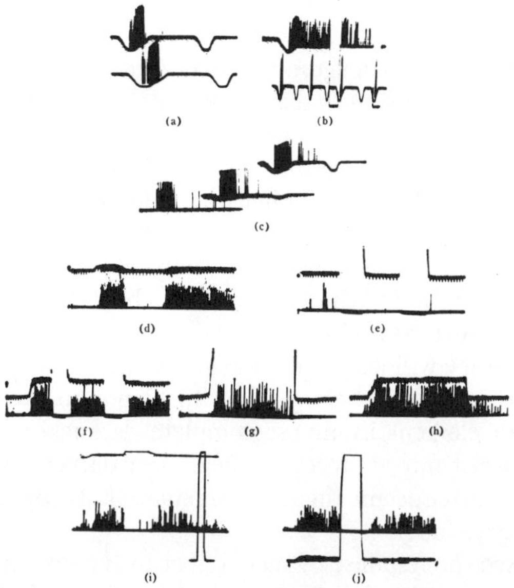

Fig. 2. (Operation 1)—contrast detectors. The records were all taken directly with a Polaroid camera. The spikes are clipped at the lower end just above the noise and brightened on the screen. Occasional spikes have been intensified by hand for purposes of reproduction. The resolution is not good but we think that the responses are not ambiguous. Our alternate recording method is by means of a device which displays the logarithm of pulse interval of signals through a pulse height pick-off. However, such records would take too much explanation and would not add much to the substance of the present paper. (a) This record is from a single fiber in the optic nerve. The base line is the output of a photocell watching a somewhat larger area than the receptive field of the fiber. Darkening is given by downward deflection. The response is seen with the noise clipped off. The fiber discharge to movement of the edge of a 3° black disk passed in one direction but not to the reverse movement. (Time marks, 20 per second.) (b) The same fiber shown here giving a continued response when the edge stops in the field. The response disappears if the illumination is turned off and reappears when it is turned on. Below is shown again the asymmetry of the response to a faster movement. (Time marks, 20 per second.) (c) The same fiber is stimulated here to show asymmetrical response to the 3° black object moved in one direction, then the reverse and the stimuli are repeated under a little less than a 3-decade change of illumination in two steps. The bottom record is in extremely dim light, the top in very bright light. (Time marks, 20 per second.) (d) In the bottom line, a group of endings from such fibers is shown recorded from the first layer in the tectum. A black disk 1° in diameter is moved first through the field and then into the field and stopped. In the top line, the receptive field is watched by a photomultiplier (see text) and darkening is given by upward deflection. (Time marks, 5 per second for all tectal records.) (e) OFF and ON of general illumination has no effect on these fibers. (f) A 3° black disk is moved into the field and stopped. The response continues until the lights are turned OFF but reappears when the lights are turned ON. These fibers are nonerasable. (g) A very large black square is moved into the field and stopped. The response to the edge continues so long as the edge is in the field. (h) The 3° disk is again moved into the field and stopped. When it leaves, there is a slight after-discharge. (i) A 1° object is moved into the field, stopped, the light is then turned off, then on, and the response comes back. The light is, however, a little less than 300× dimmer than in the next frame. Full ON and OFF are given in the rectangular calibration on the right. (j) The same procedure as in Fig. 2(i) is done under very bright light. The return of response after reintroducing the light seems more prolonged—but this is due only to the fact that, in Fig. 2(i), the edge was not stopped in optimal position.

lighter or darker than the background moves into its field and stops, it discharges promptly and continues discharging, no matter what the shape of the edge or whether the object is smaller or larger than the receptive field. The sustained discharge can be interrupted (or greatly reduced) in these axons by switching all light off. When the light is then restored, the sustained discharge begins again after a pause. Indeed the response to turning on a distribution of light furnished with sharp contrast within the field is exactly that reported by Hartline for his ON fibers. In some fibers of this group, a contrast previously within the field is "remembered" after the light is turned off, for they will keep up a low mutter of activity that is not present if no contrast was there before. That this is not an extraordinary sensitivity of such an element in almost complete darkness can be shown by importing a contrast into its receptive field after darkening in the absence of contrast. No mutter occurs then. This memory lasts for at least a minute of darkness in some units.

In Fig. 2 we see the response of such a fiber in the optic nerve. We compare these responses with full illumination (a 60-watt bulb and reflector mounted a foot away from the plane of the opening of the hemisphere) to those with less than 1/300 as much light (we put a variable resistance in series with the bulb so that the color changed also). We are struck by the smallness of the resulting change. In very dim light where we can barely see the stimulating object ourselves, we still get very much the same response.

## 2. Net Convexity Detectors

These fibers form the other subdivision of the unmyelinated population, and require a number of conditions to specify when they will respond. To our minds, this group contains the most remarkable elements in the optic nerve.

Such a fiber does not respond to change in general illumination. It does respond to a small object (3° or less) passed through the field; the response does not outlast the passage. It continues responding for a long time if the object is imported and left in the field, but the discharge is permanently turned off (erased) by a transient general darkness lasting 1/10 second or longer. We have not tried shorter obscurations.

The fiber will not respond to the straight edge of a dark object moving through its receptive field or brought there and stopped. If the field is about 7° in diameter, then, if we move a dark square 8° on the side through it with the edge in advance there is no response, but if the corner is in advance then there is a good one. Usually a fiber will respond indefinitely only to objects which have moved into the field and then lie wholly or almost wholly interior to the receptive field. The discharge is greater the greater the convexity, or positive curvature, of the boundary of the dark object until the object becomes as small as about ½ the width of the receptive field. At this point, we get the largest response on moving across that field, and a good, sustained response on entering it and stopping. As one uses smaller and smaller objects, the response to moving across the field begins to diminish at a size of about 1°, although the sustained response to coming in and stopping remains. In this way we find the smallest object to which these fibers respond is less than 3 minutes of arc. A smooth motion across the receptive field has less effect than a jerky one, if the jerks recur at intervals longer than ½ second. A displacement barely visible to the experimenter produces a marked increase in response which dies down slowly.

Any checked or dotted pattern (in the latter case, with dots no further apart than half the width of the receptive field) moved as a whole across the receptive field produces little if any response. However, if any dot within the receptive field moves differentially with respect to the back-

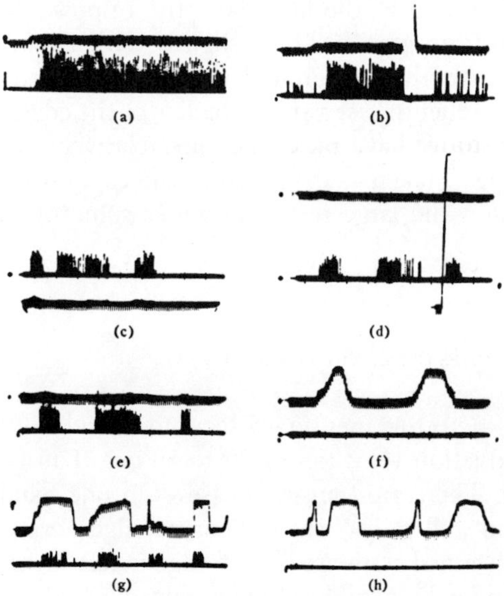

Fig. 3. (Operation 2)—convexity detectors. The photomultiplier is used, and darkening is an upward deflection. (a) These records are all from the second layer of endings in the tectum. In the first picture, a 1° black disk is imported into the receptive field and left there. (b) The same event occurs as in Fig. 3(a), but now the light is turned off then on again. The response is much diminished and in the longer record vanishes. These fibers are erasable. (c) The 1° disk, is passed through the field first somewhat rapidly, then slowly, then rapidly. The light is very bright. (d) The same procedure occurs as in Fig. 3(c), but now the light has been dimmed about 300×. The vertical line shows the range of the photomultiplier which has been adjusted for about 3½ decades of logarithmic response. (e) A 1° black disk is passed through the field at three speeds. (f) A 15° black strip is passed through at two speeds edge leading. (g) A 15° black strip is passed through in various ways with corner leading. (h) The same strip as in Fig. 3(g) is passed through, edge leading.

ground pattern, the response is to that dot as if it were moving alone. A group of two or three distinct spots enclosed within the receptive field and moved as a whole produce less direct response to movement and much less sustained response on stopping than if the spots are coalesced to a single larger spot.

A delightful exhibit uses a large color photograph of the natural habitat of a frog from a frog's eye view, flowers and grass. We can move this photograph through the receptive field of such a fiber, waving it around at a 7-inch distance: there is no response. If we perch with a magnet a fly-sized object 1° large on the part of the picture seen by the receptive field and move only the object we get an excellent response. If the object is fixed to the picture in about the same place and the whole moved about, then there is none.

Finally, the response does not depend on how much darker the object is than its background, so long as it is distinguishably so and has a clear-cut edge. If a disk has a very dark center and merges gradually into the grey of the background at the boundary, the response to it is very much less than to a uniform grey disk only slightly darker than the background. Objects lighter than the background produce almost no response unless they have enough relief to cast a slight shadow at the edge.

All the responses we have mentioned are relatively independent of illumination, and Fig. 3 taken as described in the caption shows the reactions to a 3° object and the large rectangle under some of the conditions described.

## General Comments on Groups 1 and 2

The two sorts of detectors mentioned seem to include all the unmyelinated fibers, with conduction velocities of 20 to 50 cm. The two groups are not entirely distinct. There are transition cases. On one hand, some convexity detectors respond well to very slightly curved edges, even so far as to show an occasional sustained response if that edge is left in the field. They may also not be completely erasable (though very markedly affected by an interruption of light) for small objects. On the other hand, others of the same group will be difficult to set into an indefinitely sustained response with any object, but only show a fairly long discharge, acting thereby more as detectors of edges although never reacting to straight edges. Nevertheless the distribution of the unmyelinated axons into two groups is very marked. Any fiber of either group may show a directional response—*i.e.*, there will be a direction of movement that may fail to excite the cell. For the contrast fibers, this will also appear as a nonexciting angle of the boundary with respect to the axis of the frog. Such null directions and angles cancel out in the aggregate.

## 3. Moving-Edge Detectors

These fibers are myelinated and conduct at a velocity in the neighborhood of 2 meters per second. They are the same as Hartline's and Barlow's ON-OFF units. The receptive field is about 12° wide. Such a fiber responds to any distinguishable edge moving through its receptive field, whether black

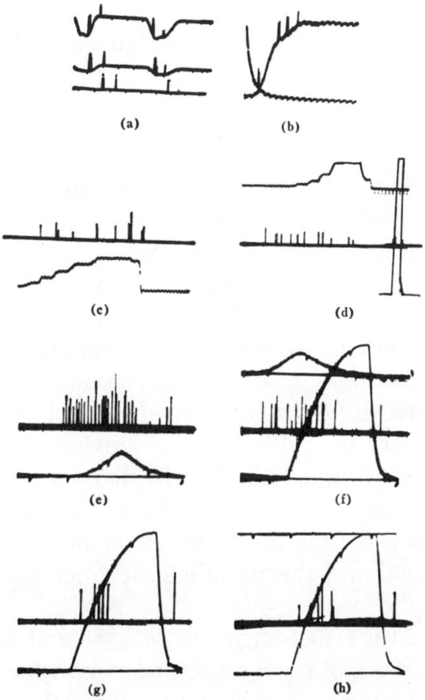


Fig. 4. (Operation 3)—moving-edge detectors. The first two pictures are taken from a single fiber in the optic nerve. (a) Shows a 7° black disk moving through the receptive field (the photocell was not in registration with the field). There is a response to the front and back of the disk independent of illumination. There is about a 300/1 shift of illumination between top and bottom of the record. Darkening is a downward deflection with the photocell record. (Time marks, 5 per second.) (b) OFF and ON of general lighting. (Time marks, 50 per second.) Note double responses and spacing. (c) This and succeeding records are in the third layer of endings in the tectum. Several endings are recorded but not resolved. Darkening is an upward deflection of the photomultiplier record. The response is shown to the edge of a 15° square moved into and out of the field by jerks in bright light. (d) The same procedure occurs as in Fig. 4(c), but in dim light. Calibration figure is at the right. (e) The response is shown to a 7° black disk passed through the receptive fields under bright light. The sweep is faster, but the time marks are the same. (f) The same procedure as for Fig. 4(e), but under dim light. The OFF and ON of the photomultiplier record was superimposed for calibration. (g) OFF and ON response with about half a second between ON and OFF. (h) Same as Fig. 4(g), but with 2 seconds between OFF and ON.

against white or the other way around. Changing the extent of the edge makes little difference over a wide range, changing its speed a great one. It responds to an edge only if that edge moves, not otherwise. If an object wider than about 5° moves smoothly across the field, there are separate responses to the leading and trailing edges, as would be expected from Barlow's formulation. These fibers generally show two or three regularly spaced spikes, always synchronous among different fibers to turning the light on or off or both. The response to moving objects is much greater than to changes in total illumination and varies only slightly with general illumination over a range of 1/300. The frequency of the discharge increases with the velocity of the object within certain limits (see Fig. 4).

## 4. Net Dimming Detectors

These are Hartline's and Barlow's OFF fibers. But they have some properties not observed before. They are myelinated and the fastest conducting afferents, clocked at 10 meters per second.[2] One such fiber responds to sudden reduction of illumination by a prolonged and regular discharge. Indeed, the rhythm is so much the same from fiber to fiber that in recording from several at once after sudden darkening, the impulses assemble in groups, which break up only after many seconds. Even then the activity from widely separated retinal areas seems to be related. We observe that the surface potential of the colliculus shows a violent and prolonged oscillation when the light is turned off. This oscillation, beginning at about 18 per second and breaking into 3 to 5 per second after several seconds, seems to arise from these fibers from the retina; the same record is seen when the optic nerve is severed and the recording electrode placed on the retinal stump. See Fig. 5.

The receptive field is rather large—about 15°—and works as Barlow describes. Darkening of a spot produces less response when it is in the periphery of the field than when it is at the center. The effect of a moving object is directly related to its size and relative darkness. The response is prolonged if a large dark object stops within the field. It is almost independent of illumination, actually increasing as the light gets dimmer. There is a kind of erasure that is complementary to that of group 2). If the general lighting is sharply dimmed, but not turned off entirely, the consequent prolonged response is diminished or abolished after a dark object passes through the receptive field. In this case, the reasons for erasure are apparent. Suppose one turns off the light and sets up a prolonged response. Then the amount of light which must be restored to interrupt the response gets less and less the longer one waits. That is, the sensitivity of the OFF discharge to the

[2] The even faster fibers, with velocities up to 20 meters per second, we presently believe to be the efferents to the retina, but although there is some evidence for this, we are not yet quite certain.

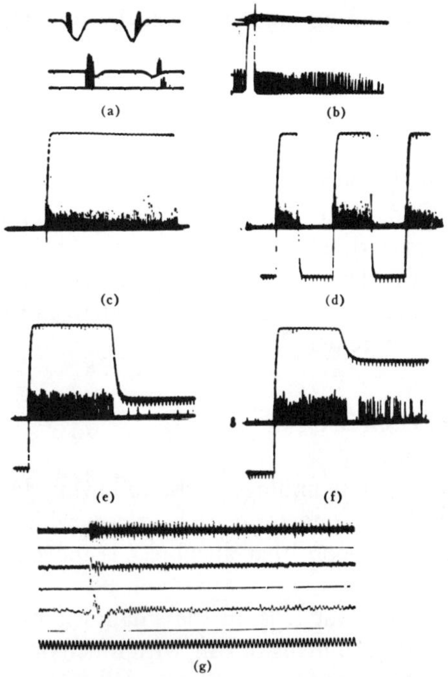

Fig. 5. (Operation 4)—dimming detectors. (a) This and the next frame are taken from a single fiber in the optic nerve. Here we see the response to a 7° black disk passing through the receptive field. The three records are taken at three illumination levels over a 300:1 range. In the phototube record, darkening is a downward deflection. (Time marks, 5 per second.) (b) OFF and ON of light. The OFF was done shortly after one sweep began, the ON occurred a little earlier on the next sweep. The fiber is silenced completely by the ON. (Time marks, 5 per second.) (c) In this and the next three frames, we are recording from the fourth layer of endings in the tectum. This frame shows the response to turning OFF the general illumination. (d) OFF and ON of light at regular intervals. (e) OFF then ON of the light to a lesser brightness. (f) OFF then ON of the light to a still lesser brightness. The level to which the ON must come to abolish activity decreases steadily with time. (g) The synchrony of the dimming detectors as described in the text. At the top are three or four fibers recorded together in the optic nerve when the light is suddenly turned off. The fibers come from diverse areas on the retina. In the second line are the oscillations recorded from the freshly cut retinal stump of the optic nerve when the light is suddenly turned off. In the third line are the oscillations recorded on the surface of the tectum, the visual brain, before the nerve was cut. Again the light is suddenly turned off. The last line is 20 cps. These records of synchrony were obviously not all made at the same time, so that comparing them in detail is not profitable.

ON of light increases with time. If we darken the general lighting only by a factor of 100, we also get a prolonged discharge. However, if we turn off the light completely a few seconds after the 100/1 dimming and then turn it back on to the same dim level, the discharge is increased by the second dimming and is completely or almost completely abolished by the relighting. The effect of moving a dark object through the field after dimming is to impose a second dimming pulse followed by brightening as the object passes.

### Others

Lastly, there is a small group of afferent fibers which does not seem to have distinct receptive fields. They each measure the absolute degree of darkness over a wide area with a long time constant. That is, the frequency of discharge is greater the darker it is. They have a complement in that some of the moving edge detectors have a resting discharge of very low frequency if the illumination is extremely bright.

## *DISCUSSION*

Let us compress all of these findings in the following description. Consider that we have four fibers, one from each group, which are concentric in their receptive fields. Suppose that an object is moved about in this concentric array:

(1) The contrast detector tells, in the smallest area of all, of the presence of a sharp boundary, moving or still, with much or little contrast.

(2) The convexity detector informs us in a somewhat larger area whether or not the object has a curved boundary, if it is darker than the background and moving on it; it remembers the object when it has stopped, providing the boundary lies totally within that area and is sharp; it shows most activity if the enclosed object moves intermittently with respect to a background. The memory of the object is abolished if a shadow obscures the object for a moment.

(3) The moving-edge detector tells whether or not there is a moving boundary in a yet larger area within the field.

(4) The dimming detector tells us how much dimming occurs in the largest area, weighted by distance from the center and by how fast it happens.

All of the operations are independent of general illumination. There are 30 times as many of the first two detectors as of the last two, and the sensitivity to sharpness of edge or increments of movement in the first two is also higher than in the last two.

## *RESULTS IN THE TECTUM*

As remarked earlier, the optic nerve fibers are all disordered in position through the nerve. That is, the probability that any two adjacent fibers look at the same region in the retina is very small. However, when the fibers terminate in the superior colliculus they do so in an orderly way such that the termini exhibit a continuous map of the retina. Each optic nerve crosses the base of the skull and enters the opposite tectus [Fig. 1(b)] via two bundles—one rostromedial, the other caudalateral. The fibers sweep out over the tectum in the superficial neuropil in what grossly appears to be a laminated way [Fig. 1(c)]. The detail of ending is not known, and there is some reason to think Pedro Ramon's drawing [9] is too diagrammatic [Fig. 1(d)], however well it fits with our data.

In any case, the outer husk of neuropil, roughly about half the thickness of the optic tectum, is formed of the endings of the optic fibers mixed with dendrites of the deeper lying cells, and in this felting lie few cell bodies.

We have found it singularly easy to record from these terminal bushes of the optic fibers. That is, if an electrode is introduced in the middle of one bush, the external potential produced by action currents in any branch increases in proportion to the number of branches near the electrode. Since the bushes are densely interdigitated everywhere, it is not difficult to record from terminal arbors anywhere unless one kills or blocks them locally, as is easily done by pressure, etc.

One may inquire how we can be sure of recording from terminal arbors, and not from cells and their dendrites. The argument is this. First, there are about four layers of cells in the depths of the tectum [Fig. 1(d)], and only their dendrites issue into the superficial neuropil wherein lie very few cells indeed. There are about 250,000 of these cells in all, compared to 500,000 optic fibers. In the outer thickness of the tectum, among the terminating fibers, almost every element we record performs one of the four operations characterizing the fibers in the nerve, and has a corresponding receptive field. Now as the electrode moves down from the surface in one track, we record 5 to 10 cells in the deepest half of the tectum. Not a single cell so recorded shows activity even remotely resembling what we find in the superficial neuropil. Among the cells, none show optic nerve operations, and the smallest receptive fields we find are over 30° in diameter. If the active elements in the upper layers are cells (one will see about 20 to 30 active elements in one electrode track before reaching the cell layer), which cells can they be? Or if they are dendrites, to what neurons do they belong? We regard these considerations as conclusive enough.

Figs. 2–5 show that the four operational groups of fibers terminate in four separate layers of terminals, each layer exhibiting a continuous map of the retina (we confirm Gaze's diagram of the projection [1958]) and all four maps are in registration. Most superficial lie the endings for the contrast detectors, the slowest fibers. Beneath them, but not so distinctly separate, are the convexity detectors. Deeper, and rather well separated, are the moving-edge detectors admixed with the rare and ill-defined axons that measure the actual level of darkness. Deepest (and occasionally contaminated with tectal cells or their axons) lie the dimming detectors. Thus the depth at which these fibers end is directly related to their speed of conduction.

Such an arrangement makes experiment easy, for all the fibers of one operation performed on the same field in the retina end in one place in the tectum and can be recorded as a group. It is very useful to see them this way, for then the individual variations among similar units cancel one another and only the common properties remain. We made the tectal records shown in the accompanying figures with a single electrode in two penetrations (to get decent separation of contrast and convexity detectors which lie just below the pia), to show how clear-cut the arrangement is.

## *CONFIRMATION OF SPERRY'S PROPOSAL*

The existence of a fourfold map of the retina in the tectal neuropil led us, naturally, to repeat Sperry's initial experiment on the regeneration of cut optic nerve (1951). Since the nerve is as scrambled as it can be originally, we saw no point in turning the eye around 180° but simply cut one nerve in a few frogs, separated the stumps to be sure of complete severance, and waited for about 3 months. At the end of this time, after it was clear that the cut nerves were functioning again, we compared the tectal maps of the cut and uncut nerves in some of them. We confirmed (as did Gaze [1959]) Sperry's proposal that the fibers grew back to the regions where they originally terminated in mapping the retina (Maturana et al., 1959). But we also found a restoration of the four layers with no error or mixing. In one frog, after 90 days, the fibers had grown back best at the entrance of the two brachia to the colliculus, and least at the center, yet there were no serious errors. The total area of retina communicating with one point of the collicular neuropil (*i.e*, the sum of the receptive fields of the fibers recorded from that point) had increased three or four times, from a diameter of about 15° to a diameter of about 30°. But there was no admixture of fibers with receptive fields in widely separated regions. In another frog, after 120 days, the area seen from one point was barely twice normal.

## *GENERAL DISCUSSION*

What are the consequences of this work? Fundamentally, it shows that the eye speaks to the brain in a language already highly organized and interpreted, instead of transmitting some more or less accurate copy of the distribution of light on the receptors. As a crude analogy, suppose that we have a man watching the clouds and reporting them to a weather station. If he is using a code, and one can see his portion of the sky too, then it is not difficult to find out what he is saying. It is certainly true that he is watching a distribution of light; nevertheless, local variations of light are not the terms in which he speaks nor the terms in which he is best understood. Indeed, if his vocabulary is restricted to types of things that he sees in the sky, trying to find his language by using flashes of light as stimuli will certainly fail. Now, since the purpose of a frog's vision is to get him food and allow him to evade predators no matter how bright or dim it is about him, it is not enough to know the reaction of his visual system to points of light. To get useful records from individual receptors (the rods and cones), assuming that they operate independently and under no reflex control, this stimulus may be adequate. But when one inspects responses that are a few nervous transformations removed from the receptors, as in the optic nerve, that same choice of stimulus is difficult to defend. It is equivalent to assuming that all of the interpretation is done further on in the nervous system. But, as we have seen, this is false.

One might attempt to measure numerically how the response of each kind of fiber varies with various properties of the successions of patterns of light which evoke them. But to characterize a succession of patterns in space requires knowledge of so many independent variables that this is hardly possible by experimental enumeration of cases. To examine the effect of curvature alone we should have to explore at least the response to all configurations of three spots moving in a large variety of ways. We would prefer to state the operations of ganglion cells as simply as possible in terms of whatever *quality* they seem to detect and, instead, examine the bipolar cells in the retina, expecting to find there a dissection of the operations into combinations of simpler ones performed at intermediate stages. For example, suppose that there are at least two sorts of rods and cones, one increasing its voltage with the log of light at one color, the other decreasing its voltage with the log of light at some other color. If bipolars connect to several contiguous rods or cones of opposing reactions and simply add voltages, some bipolars will register a large signal only if an appropriate contrast occurs. We have in fact found something of the sort occurring, for it seems that the inner plexiform layer of the retina is stratified to display several different local properties, one layer indicating local differences in intensity of light. Some of Svaetichin's (1958) data can be adduced here. The different dendritic distribution of the ganglion cells, as in Fig. 1(a), may signify that they extract differently weighted samples of simple local operations done by the bipolars, and it is on this that we are now working.

But there is another reason for a reluctance to make accurate measurements on the activity of ganglion cells in the intact animal. A significant efferent outflow goes to the retina from the brain. We now know to a certain extent how the cells in the tectum handle the four inputs to them which are described in this paper. There are at least two distinct classes of these cells, and at least one of them issues axons back into the optic nerve. We have recorded this activity there. Such axons enter the retina and we think some effects of their activity on the sensitivity of ganglion cells are noticeable.

The way that the retina projects to the tectum suggests a nineteenth century view of visual space. The image on the retina, taken at the grain of the rods and cones, is an array of regularly spaced points at each of which there is a certain amount of light of a certain composition. If we know the position of every point and the values of light at every point, we can physically reconstruct the image, and looking at it understand the picture. If, however, we are required to establish continuities within the picture only from the numerical data on position and light at independent points, it becomes a very difficult task. The retina projects onto the tectum in four parallel sheets of endings, each sheet mapping continuously the retina in terms of a particular areal operation, and all four maps are in registration. Consider the dendrite of a tectal cell extending up through the four sheets. It is looking at a point in the image on the retina, but that point is now seen in terms of the properties of its neighborhood as defined by the operations. Since the overlap of receptive fields within any operation is very great, it now seems reasonable to erect simple criteria for finding continuities. For example, if an area over which there is little change in the fourfold signature of a moving object is bounded by regions of different signature, it seems likely that that area describes the image of a single object.

By transforming the image from a space of simple discrete points to a congruent space where each equivalent point is described by the intersection of particular qualities in its neighborhood, we can then give the image in terms of distributions of combinations of those qualities. In short, every point is seen in definite contexts. The character of these contexts, genetically built in, is the physiological synthetic *a priori*. The operations found in the frog make unlikely later processes in his system of the sort described by two of us earlier (1947), for example, dilatations; but those were adduced for the sort of form recognition which the frog does not have. This work is an outgrowth of that earlier study which set the question.

## *CONCLUSION*

The output from the retina of the frog is a set of four distributed operations on the visual image. These operations are independent of the level of general illumination and express the image in terms of: (1) local sharp edges and contrast; (2) the curvature of edge of a dark object; (3) the movement of edges; and (4) the local dimmings produced by movement or rapid general darkening. Each group of fibers serving one operation maps the retina continuously in a single sheet of endings in the frog's brain. There are four such sheets in the brain, corresponding to the four operations, and their maps are in registration. When all axonal connections between eye and brain are broken and the fibers grow back, they reconstitute the original retinal maps and also arrange themselves in depth in the original order with no mistakes. If there is any randomness in the connections of this system it must be at a very fine level indeed. In this, we consider that Sperry (1951) is completely right.

We have described each of the operations on the retinal image in terms of what common factors in a large variety of stimuli cause response and what common factors have no effect. What, then, does a particular fiber in the optic nerve measure? We have considered it to be how much there is in a stimulus of that quality which excites the fiber maximally, naming that quality.

The operations thus have much more the flavor of perception than of sensation if that distinction has any meaning now. That is to say that the language in which they are best described is the language of complex abstractions from the visual image. We have been tempted, for example, to call the convexity detectors "bug perceivers." Such a fiber [operation 2] responds best when a dark object, smaller than a receptive field, enters that field, stops, and moves about intermittently thereafter. The response is not affected if the lighting changes or if the background (say a picture of grass and flowers) is moving, and is not there if only the background, moving or still, is in the field. Could one better describe a system for detecting an accessible bug?

## *REFERENCES*

Andrew, A. M. Report on frog colliculus. *Research Laboratory of Electronics, Massachusetts Institute of Technology*, Cambridge, Quarterly Progress Report, 1955, (a) 77-78.

Andrew, A. M. Action potentials from the frog colliculus. *Journal of Physiology*, 1955, *130:* (b)

Barlow, H. B. Summation and inhibition in the frog's retina. *Journal of Physiology*, 1953, *119*, 69-88.

Barlow, H. B., Fitzhugh, R., & Kuffler, S. W. Change of organization in the receptive fields of the cat's retina during dark adaptation. *Journal of Physiology*, 1957, *137*, 338-354.

Cajal, Pedro Ramón y. Histologie du Système Nerveux, Ramón y Cajal, Maloine, Paris, France, 1909-1911.

Gaze, R. M. The representation of the retina on the optic lobe of the frog. *Quarterly Journal of Physiology*, 1958, *43*, 209-214.

Gaze, R. M. Regeneration of the optic nerve in *Xenopus laevi*. *Journal of Physiology*, 1959, *146*, 40P.

Hartline, H. K. The response of single optic nerve fibres of the vertebrate eye to illumination of the retina. *American Journal of Physiology*, 1938, *121*, 400-415.

Hartline, H. K. The receptive field of the optic nerve fibres. *American Journal of Physiology*, 1940, *130*, 690-699.

Kuffler, S. W. Discharge patterns and functional organization of mammalian retina. *Journal of Neurophysiology*, 1953, *16*, 37-68.

Maturana, H. R. The fine structure of the optic nerve and tectum of anurans. An electron microscope study. Doctoral dissertation, Harvard University, Cambridge, Massachusetts, 1958.

Maturana, H. R. Number of fibers in the optic nerve and the number of ganglion cells in the retina of Anurans. *Nature*, 1959, *183*, 1406-1407.

Maturana, H. R., Lettvin, J. Y., McCulloch, W. S., & Pitts, W. H. Physiologigal evidence that cut optic nerve fibers in the frog regenerate to their proper places in the tectum. *Science*, 1959.

McCulloch, W. S., & Pitts, W. H. How we know universals. The perception of auditory and visual forms. *Bulletin of Mathematical Biophysics*, 1947, 9, 127-147.

Sperry, R. Mechanisms of neural maturation. In S. S. Stevens (Ed.), *Handbook of Experimental Psychology*, New York: Wiley, 1951.

Svaetichin, G., & MacNichol, E. F. Jr. Retinal mechanisms for chromatic and achromatic vision. *Annals of the New York Academy of Sciences*, 1958, *74*, 385-404.

*The reader will notice that McCulloch and Pitts, two of this paper's authors, specifically repudiate the sort of model for pattern processing they had proposed earlier (see in Part I, "How We Know Universals: The Perception of Auditory and Visual Forms"). Instead, this electrophysiological work argues strongly for a system of local property detectors, and the general view today is that pattern recognition, in vertebrates anyway, proceeds by such an initial step. It is not so easy, however, to see how such local properties, once detected, are "put together" into patterns, or Gestalten. On the whole that is a question that neurophysiologists have neglected, and probably one which their techniques of recording from single units are not well suited to solve. Thus, so far as stimulus equivalence is concerned, the results on the frog show how equivalence by coding can occur, and the argument for the biological utility of such coding is clearly presented, but we still are left with the larger question of pattern recognition as such.*

*The next paper proceeds another step up the evolutionary scale to a mammal, the cat, which has been widely used for experiments on visual*

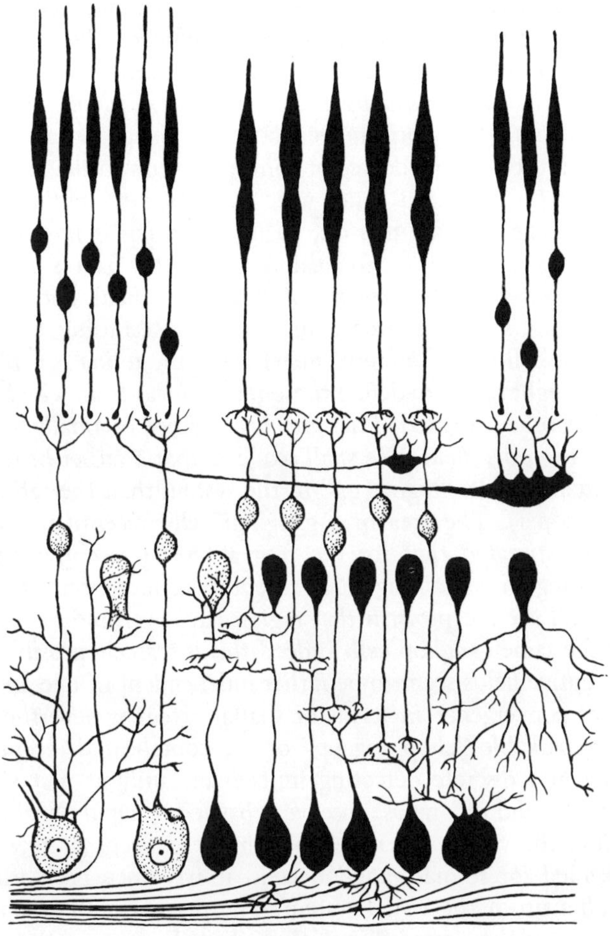

Fig. A

electrophysiology. The work reported is concerned entirely with the functional organization of the retina. Since it is important to know something of the retinal structure in mammals in order to get the main point of this paper, a diagram of the main anatomical features is given (Fig. A). Comparing this with the earlier diagram of the Frog's retina (p.308) we see that there is no very obvious difference in complexity, although such judgments must certainly be made with caution, at least on the basis of a couple of diagrams of this sort. At all events, this step within the vertebrate Order (from reptile to mammal) seems to involve little change in the peripheral organization. The major differences, as we shall later see, are in the more central neural structures and connections.

A glance at figure A indicates that one might expect to find a high degree of interaction between units in the retina, since connections exist which look as if they are there to expedite mutual influence. The ganglion cells look like the "collectors" of information from adjacent parts of the retina, and we know that in mammals there are always more photoreceptors (rods and/or cones) than optic nerve fibers (the axons of retinal ganglion cells) so there must be some degree of convergence on to the ganglion cells, unless some of the rods and cones were to serve no function—surely an unlikely hypothesis. What turns out to be surprising is not that there is some convergence, but that it is so great. Several of the papers in this section have already referred to the concept of a receptive field, and it would be as well to discuss it before proceeding further. Recording from a single retinal ganglion cell (or optic nerve fiber) while the retina is explored with a small spot of light serves to define those retinal areas from which the given ganglion cell can be activated. That area was defined originally as the given unit's retinal receptive field. We shall see later that a rather broader definition is required for cells "higher up" in the system than the retina (cf. also the previous paper). The area of a ganglion cell's receptive field is quite large; Barlow estimated that for the frog a typical receptive field might extend over a region containing 1,000 receptors or more, but of course it is unlikely that all the receptors in that region have even indirect connection to one and the same ganglion cell. Indeed this is scarcely possible since the different receptive fields seem to be rather independent of one another. But the degree of convergence in terms of spatial extent is nevertheless pretty large. The remarkable "chopping up" of the complicated receptor mosaic of the retina into discrete detecting units is certainly at first sight a surprising property, and one whose discovery has led to rapid developments in understanding the visual system. Although the concept of receptive field was first defined for retinal ganglion cells, it has since been extended to any cell higher up in the visual system. The properties of receptive fields will occupy us for the rest of this section; their discovery and extended investigation constitutes one of the most fruitful and exciting chapters in modern biological science.

Kuffler's paper, which follows immediately, is a milestone in the research on receptive field organization. He not only established the general outlines of the shape and extent of retinal receptive fields in the cat, but also defined and explored certain properties of mutual facilitation and antagonism between different areas within the same receptive field which have proved to be fundamental for further analysis and understanding of the system.

Certain parts of the paper are less relevant to our main purpose than others, and these as usual have been set in small type. There is also a certain amount of repetition from paper to paper mainly because the authors refer to the same classical source, or to each other, but this perhaps serves a useful pedagogical function and I have not attempted to reduce it by selective cutting from the originals.

# *Discharge Patterns and Functional Organization of Mammalian Retina*

S. W. KUFFLER

## *INTRODUCTION*

The discharges carried in the optic nerve fibers contain all the information which the central nervous system receives from the retina. A correct interpretation of discharge patterns therefore constitutes an important step in the analysis of visual events. Further, investigations of nervous activity arising in the eye reveal many aspects of the functional organization of the neural elements within the retina itself.

Following studies of discharges in the optic nerve of the eel's eye by Adrian and Matthews (1927, 1928), Hartline and his colleagues described the discharge pattern in the eye of the Limulus in a series of important and lucid papers (for a summary see Hartline, 1940). In the Limulus the relationship between the stimulus to the primary receptor cell and the nerve discharges proved relatively simple, apparently because the connection between sense cell and nerve fiber was a direct one. Thus, when stimulation is confined to one receptor the discharge in a single Limulus nerve fiber will provide a good indication of excitatory events which take place as a result of photochemical processes. Discharges last for the duration of illumination and their frequency is a measure of stimulus strength. Lately, however, it was shown by Hartline *et al.* (1952) that inhibitory interactions may be revealed when several receptors are excited. On the whole, the Limulus preparation shows many features which are similar to other simple sense organs, for instance, stretch receptors. In the latter, however, instead of photochemical events, stretch-deformation acts as the adequate stimulus on sensory terminals and is translated into a characteristic discharge pattern.

The discharge from the cold-blooded vertebrate retina (mainly frogs) proved much more complex. Hartline found three main types when recording from single optic nerve fibers: (i) "on" discharges, similar to those in

Reprinted from *Journal of Neurophysiology*, 1953.
This investigation was supported by a research grant from the National Institutes of Health, U. S. Public Health Service.

the Limulus, firing for the duration of the light stimulus, (ii) "off" discharges appearing when a light stimulus was withdrawn, and (iii) "on-off" discharges, a combination of the former two, with activity confined mainly to onset and cessation of illumination. The mammalian discharge patterns were studied in a number of species by Granit and his co-workers in the course of their extensive work on the physiology of the visual system (summaries in Granit 1947, 1948). On the whole, they did not observe any fundamental differences between frog and mammalian discharge types (see later).

The present studies were begun several years ago with the intention of examining the retinal organization and particularly processes of excitation and inhibition. As a first step, the discharge patterns were re-examined. It was assumed, in line with other workers, that the deviations in vertebrate eyes from the simple Limulus, or "on" discharge type, are due to the nervous structures and to their interconnections between the rod and cone layers on the one hand and ganglion cells on the other. Therefore, an extension of such studies should shed further light on the functional organization of the retina.

A preparation was used which approached fairly satisfactorily the "normal" state of the cat's eye. The discharge patterns reported by Hartline and those extensively studied by Granit were readily obtained. Single receptive fields—areas which must be illuminated to cause a ganglion cell to discharge—were explored with small spots of light and thereby some new aspects of retinal organization were detected. Specific receptive subdivisions, arranged in a characteristic fashion and connected to the common ganglion cells, seem to exist within each receptive field. This finding made it possible to study in detail some of the factors which normally contribute to the changing discharge pattern during vision. The present set-up also furnishes a relatively simple preparation in which the neural organization resembles the spinal cord and probably many higher centers of the nervous system. Many analogies have been found with discharge patterns in the spinal cord which are currently under study.

## *METHOD*

The experimental arrangement, particularly the details of the optical system, has been described in full in a preceding paper (Talbot & Kuffler, 1951). The main instrument, the "Multibeam Ophthalmoscope," consisted of a base which carried a holder in which the cat's head was rigidly fixed. Above the head, and also carried by the base, was the viewing-stimulating apparatus, which could be freely rotated and tilted. It contained three light sources with independent controls. This optical system was aligned with the cat's eye which thus was in the center of a spherical coordinate system and the eye's ordinary channels were used for illumination of the retina. One light provided adjustable background illumination and thereby determined the level of light adaptation. It was also used as a source for observation of the retinal structures. A maximal visual magnification of about 40 was obtained. The background illumination covered a circle of not less than 4 mm. (16° for the cat) in diameter, centered on the recording electrode. Two Sylvania glow-modulator tubes were used for stimulation of restricted areas of the retina. They illuminated patterns, mostly circles of varying diameter, which were imaged on the retina. The smallest light spots were 0.1 mm. in diameter on the retina. Thus, two images could be projected and their size and location varied independently on the retina. All three light sources used a common optical path, led into the eye through a pupil maximally dilated by Atropine or Neo-synepherine.

Complications from clouding of the cornea were prevented by the use of a glass contact lens, while the rest of the eye's optical system, lens and vitreous, remained intact. The circulation of the retina was under direct minute observation and whenever the general condition of the animal deteriorated this was readily noticed. The eye, as judged by its circulation and its discharge patterns, remained in good condition for the duration of the experiments which frequently lasted for 15-18 hours. Dial-urethane (Ciba) anesthesia (0.5 cc./kg.) or decerebration was used. The effect of anesthesia on the discharges is discussed later.

The eyeball was fixed by sutures to a ring which was part of the microelectrode manipulator. This fixation was generally satisfactory and breathing or minor body movement did not disturb the electrode position on ganglion cells. Sudden movements, however, such as coughing, jerking, etc., prevented continuous recording from single units. Occasionally a persistent slow nystagmus developed and, in order to abolish this movement, the tendons of extraocular muscles were severed at their insertions.

Microelectrodes were introduced into the eye protected by a short length of #19 hypodermic tubing which served to penetrate the scleral wall near the lambus. The unprotected electrode shaft, less than 1 mm. thick, then traversed the vitreous and made contact with the retinal surface and toward the tip it was drawn to a fine taper. The shadow of the electrode thus covered only a small portion of the receptive field. If hit by the narrow light beams the electrode shaft caused scattering. All these phenomena and the positions and imagery of the stimulating beams or patterns were directly observed during the experiments and thereby a subjective evaluation of illumination conditions could be formed.

Electrical contact with the retinal cells was made by 10-15 $\mu$ Platinum-Iridium wires which were pushed to the tip of the glass tubes. The metal was either flush with the surrounding glass jacket which was sealed around it, or it protruded several micra. The configuration of the electrode tip was purposely varied a good deal, especially when the ganglion discharge was to be blocked by pressure. The potentials varied in size, and the largest were around 0.6 mV. The position of the indifferent electrode could be anywhere on the cat's body. In technically satisfactory preparations no difficulty was encountered in finding ganglion cells in quick succession and individual units could be observed for many hours (see later).

The second beam of the oscilloscope was used as an indicator of the current flow through the Sylvania glow-modulator tubes. The current was proportional to the light output but the spectral distribution of the light varied with different current strength. Therefore, Wratten neutral filters were used when the white light of the stimulators had to be attenuated. For the purpose of the present experiments the wave length variation which occurred played no significant role in those cases where intensities were varied by current flow adjustment (see Figs. 7*III*, 8, 10). The accurate electronic control of the stimulating light sources made an adjustment of flash durations quick and convenient. The time base was also recorded on the second sweep by intensity modulation through a square-wave oscillator.

Illumination values are given in meter candles; the calibration was made for flux reaching the corneal surface above the pupil and calculated for the area which it covered on the retina. Losses within the eye's media are neglected. The maximal available background illumination was about 6000 meter candles at the retina and could be attenuated to any desired extent. Since 1 m.c. at the retina corresponds to 10 mL external brightness (see 31) the samples illustrated here were taken well within the photopic range. Discharge patterns were, however, also studied in the absence of background illumination. In most experiments the exploring spot's intensity was approximately 100 m.c.

## *RESULTS*

### 1. Some Characteristics of Single Unit Discharge

*Differentiation Between Ganglion and Axon Potentials.* As a recording electrode of 5–15 $\mu$ diameter at the tip made contact with the surface of the retina, a mass of potentials was usually recorded on illumination of the eye. Very light touch of the retinal surface rarely yielded differentiated single unit potentials. The latter could, however, be obtained with a slight further advance of the electrode, still without marked pressure against the tissue. Different degrees of "touch" and pressure were easily differentiated under close direct observation (see Method). The most common and most easily recorded potential seen in the retina was a polyphasic spike, starting with an initial positive deflection, similar to that shown in Figure 1*B*. Such potentials are generally set up by a small spot of light at some distance from the recording electrode. From this observation it follows that conduction to the recording lead has taken place and that the potential is derived from a nerve fiber. The polyphasic shape is typical of conducted potentials in a volume conductor. Similar potentials are familiar from recordings in other parts of the nervous system where microelectrodes are employed. The propagated potentials in nerve fibers could be used in the present studies, but they were small and could not be kept under the electrodes for prolonged periods. In contrast, potentials were recorded which always originated under the electrode tip (Fig. 1A). These were simpler and larger and usually started with a sharp negative inflection which was followed by a relatively smaller positivity. The potentials were generally about 0.3–0.4 msec. at the base, and their negative phase was of longer duration than in the potentials of Fig. 1*B*, where the whole triphasic complex is of a similar duration. The distortion of the real potential time course is due to the smallness of the effective interelectrode distance with the present electrodes. In a volume conductor the potentials which arise close to or under the electrodes start with a sharp negative inflection, as in Figure 1A. On such grounds this potential is likely to be a ganglion cell potential which lies in the vicinity of the electrode contact. Physiological tests furnish convincing evidence for such a conclusion. The area of the retina, which on illumination caused discharges in the "ganglion" cells, was found to be in the immediate neighborhood of the electrode tip; this also was the place where the lowest intensity light spot was effective in setting up discharges. As an exploring spot was moved further from the tip of the electrode, stronger stimuli were needed. The active unit lay in the approximate center of the "receptive field" (see later) and excitation apparently reached it

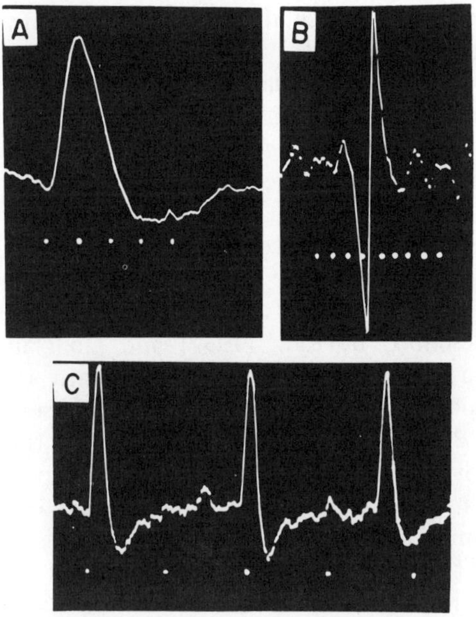


Fig. 1. Potentials from different retinal elements recorded with microelectrode. A: Ganglion cell discharge, caused by stimulation of retina in proximity of recording electrode. B: Nerve impulse in an axon, set up by retinal stimulation some distance from electrode. C: Three ganglion cell potentials from middle portion of a high-frequency discharge which is illustrated in Fig. 9c; potentials become progressively smaller at this rate. Negative deflexion of A and C 0.4 mV. and O.1 mV. in B. Time intervals in A and B 0.1 msec. and in C 1.0 msec. Note that ganglion potential can also start with small positive inflexion if recording electrode is somewhat shifted.

through converging pathways from its immediate neighborhood. Such an arrangement is typical of ganglion cells. Figure 1C illustrates three ganglion potentials which form part of the high-frequency discharge series of Figure 9*c*; the impulses follow at intervals of 2.0 and 1.7 msec. At these rates the potential heights decline.

It follows from the relationship between receptive area and recording electrode that one can distinguish between conducted potentials in axons and those arising from ganglion cells. The latter may, however, also show a more complex shape, presumably when the recording electrode is some distance away from the cell body. The present technique favors the selection of larger ganglion cells but the extent of this selection is not known (see Discussion). The findings agree with those of Rushton (1949), who by different methods showed the large single retinal discharges to arise from ganglion cells.

The potentials can also be easily distinguished by listening to their discharge in the loudspeaker. The ganglion potentials, which arise in the center of the receptive fields, have a lower pitch, apparently because of less high-frequency components than in the axon spike.

*Evidence for Single Cell Discharges.* The conventional criteria of single cell discharges are usually potentials of uniform size which arise at a sharp threshold and do not vary in a step-like fashion with fatigue or injury. Such criteria are generally sufficient to insure that potentials do not arise from several cells which fire in unison. In view of later findings, however, it is especially important to know that one really deals with single cell discharges.

The following procedures, which were incidental to many experiments, gave additional convincing evidence on this point.

(i) During *progressive pressure* which was obtained by advancing the recording electrode by means of a micrometer control, the ganglion cell discharge could frequently be blocked. Electrodes which had a relatively thick jacket flush with the platinum tip, were most convenient for such pressure blocks. By these procedures, potentials could be separated into two components. The first component was variable over a very wide range and its height depended on the amount of pressure, while the other varied much less. The small potential had the characteristics of a local potential which precedes propagated spikes as described by Katz (1937) and Hodgkin (1938). Accordingly, whenever such a "prepotential" was sufficiently reduced the spike disappeared abruptly. These events leading up to pressure block are illustrated in Figure 2. Pressure itself frequently stimulated the ganglion cells and the ensuing activity was usually photographed by exposing a fast recurring sweep until a required number of impulses was obtained. In Figure 2*a*, at the beginning of pressure, an inflexion marked by arrows is seen on the upper half of the rising phase. In *b* the two phases are more marked, the spike taking off from the beginning of the falling phase of the prepotential. In *c* a critical level is reached and at the first arrow a pure prepotential appears. The second arrow indicates two potentials which, by chance, were accurately superimposed; in one case the prepotential causes a spike, in the other it just fails to do so. In *d* the prepotential alone is seen. It should be noted that the time course of the potentials under pressure is slower than under normal (Fig. 1) conditions. This applies especially to the prepotential. While the microelectrodes give a distorted (shortened) time course of potentials, the difference between spike and prepotential seems significant. Decreasing the pressure restored the prepotential size and when it reached a critical height the spike suddenly reappeared; the process could then be repeated. With excessive pressure, however, the whole potential disappeared irreversibly. The constancy of the spike under such conditions of block, and recovery from block, confirm the assumption that it is derived from one ganglion cell only. It is unlikely that two cells should be so located in the vicinity of the electrode tip as to be affected in a quite similar and simultaneous manner. The origin of the variable prepotential was not studied in detail. It probably also originates in the ganglion cell, and such potentials may be set up there by the bipolars. It resembles some of the potentials obtained by Svaetichin (1951) in spinal ganglion cells. Similar potential sequences are also seen at neuromuscular junctions or ganglionic synapses with curare or fatigue blocks.

(ii) The *potential size* of impulses at high frequencies is further evidence that single cell discharges are recorded. In the eye discharge, frequencies of 200–700/sec. and more are quite common. During these high-frequency

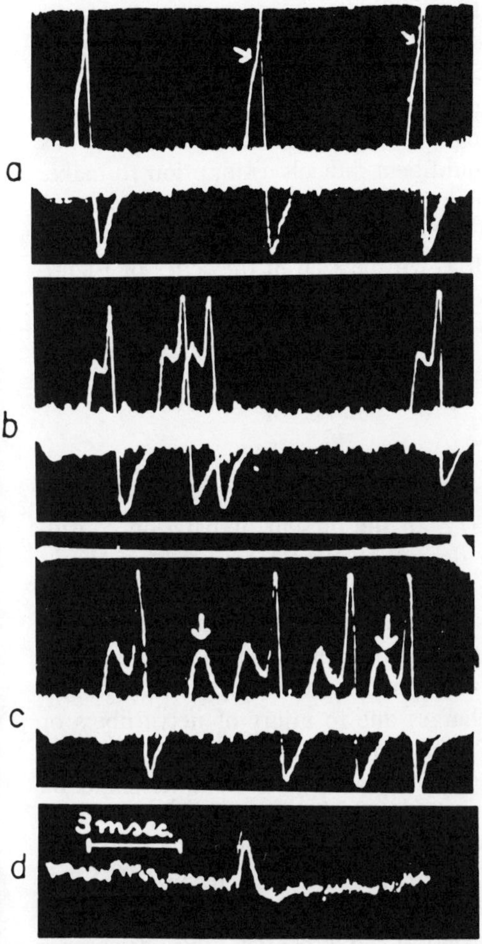


Fig. 2. Progressive pressure block of ganglion cell discharge. Exposures made with sweep recurring at high frequency. Four successive stages of pressure block. *a:* An initial inflexion (arrow) appears on upper portion of rising phase. *b:* A more discrete "prepotential" is seen. *c:* Prepotential is further reduced and occasionally (arrows) no spike appears. At second arrow a chance superposition of two apparently identical prepotentials occurred; one sets up spike, other fails to do so. *d:* spike is completely blocked, prepotential alone recorded on single sweep. Potential size in *a* is 0.3 mV.; note that also spike diminishes. Under progressive pressure potentials are of longer duration than normal (see Fig. 1).

bursts the potential size may decline, sometimes to about half of its original size. The decline is generally smooth in its progression and therefore cannot be due to one or two units dropping out during the discharge (Figs. 9, 10). If one cell ceased to fire the potential should abruptly decrease. Alternatively it could hardly be assumed that several units should be so closely coupled. Variability of potential size in single peripheral nerve fibers has been observed at frequencies around 500/sec. when recording stretch receptor discharges (Hunt and Kuffler, 1951). There seem to be some differences, however, in the potential height changes between axons and ganglion cells. The latter tend to show a fall in height at lower frequencies, a fact already studied by Renshaw in spinal motoneurons (1942). In the present instances (*e.g.*, Fig. 9) the ganglion cell probably fires near its physiological limit, each impulse following in the relative refractory period of the preceding one.

The most convincing test of single unit discharge, however, was a functional one revealed in the mapping of the receptive fields. As will be shown below, discharge patterns are distributed in a characteristic fashion within receptive fields (*e.g.*, Fig. 6). That more than one ganglion cell should happen to have identical receptive fields with such a great regularity as was found in the present experiments would be a difficult assumption to make. Moreover, one would have to postulate that the cells always gave coupled high-frequency discharges at near-limit rates without, even occasionally, separating. Further, interaction, such as will be seen in the series of Figure 8, where regular mutual suppression of discharges occurs, could hardly happen if one recorded simultaneously from two or more cells.

## 2. Spontaneous Retinal Activity

Spontaneous activity in the mammalian retina has been regularly observed by Granit in dark-adapted cats (1947). In the present preparation considerable background discharge was a dominant feature especially in dimly illuminated retinae (1–5 m.c. at the retina). In dark-adapted eyes it proved very difficult to investigate the detailed discharge patterns of single units, since they fired frequently at "resting" rates of about 20–30/sec. The "spontaneous" activity in the absence of illumination seems to be a normal feature for the following reasons: discharges due to injury of nerve fibers or ganglion cells under the recording lead, due to movement and pressure, could be excluded; spontaneous activity in many isolated units could be suppressed by illuminating the receptive fields some distance away from the recording lead (see also later); similarly, an electrode with a tip of 10–15 $\mu$, if gently placed near the middle of the optic disc, recorded massed spontaneous discharges which originated elsewhere, since illumination of the whole eye suppressed a great portion of the discharge; injury discharges along nerve fibers could not be expected to be modified by illumination in such a fashion.

Spontaneous activity was particularly pronounced in decerebrate animals, but was also regularly seen under Dial-urethane anesthesia. The latter seemed to reduce the activity. Similarly, intravenous Nembutal, in amounts such as 20 per cent of the anesthetic dose, had an immediate and prolonged effect in arresting or diminishing discharges from the retina. A similar effect with a slower onset was seen with intraperitoneal injections.

Since a great part of the present studies was done on cats under Dial-urethane the effect of the anesthetic will influence the findings to an unknown degree. All essential observations, however, were also repeated in decerebrate preparations.

As indicated above, spontaneous activity, when recorded from isolated dark-adapted units, was generally suppressed or decreased for varying periods after application of increased background illumination. In the course of light adaptation discharges usually returned gradually, or the slowed rates increased again. However, once a unit discharges in the light-adapted state, it is not possible to say how "spontaneous" the activity is.

Of particular interest are those discharges which were apparently not due to injury and were not appreciably modified by general illumination of the eye. No detailed study of their nature could be made since they were never recorded in complete isolation. It is possible that during a steady increased background illumination many units appear which have previously not discharged, while others drop out. Such switching of active units may make it impossible to decide whether certain units have been continuously active or not. This important aspect of retinal activity has yet to be explored. In many cats grouped discharges in numerous nerve fibers were seen. They could usually be suppressed by illumination of the eye, but again their origin was not studied.

While most features of "spontaneous" activity remain to be investigated, it is a noteworthy phenomenon, since it is upon such a high level of background activity that patterns of many visual events are superimposed. Rhythmic and "spontaneous" activity is common to the central nervous system in mammals and has also been observed in a variety of other visual systems (Adrian, 1937; Bernhard, 1940; Crescitelli & Jahn, 1939).

## 3. Extent of Receptive Fields of Cat's Retina

The receptive field of a single unit was defined by Hartline as the area of the retina which must receive illumination in order to cause a discharge in a particular ganglion cell or nerve fiber. Hartline (1938, 1940) was the first to study the physiological characteristics of receptive fields of single optic nerve fibers in frogs in a precise and thorough manner, by exploring the area with a small spot of light. Since the retina is composed of a group of overlapping receptive fields, the extent of these is of obvious interest. By charting the boundaries of an area over which a spot of light sets up impulses in a ganglion cell or in its nerve fiber, one will obtain the configuration of the receptive field. The field size depends on stimulus strength, the size of the exploring spot and the state of dark adaptation. The latter will largely determine the level of sensitivity of the area. For instance, if an exploring spot is made smaller, or if the level of background illumination is increased, the intensity of the spot has also to be increased in order to set up responses over as large an area as previously. The problems of determining receptive field sizes have been discussed in detail by Hartline (1940), and his results on frogs were found to apply equally to the mammalian retina.

The receptive field definition may be enlarged to include all areas in *functional* connection with a ganglion cell. In this respect only can the field size change. The anatomical configuration of a receptive field—all the receptors actually connected to a ganglion cell by some nervous pathways—is, of course, assumed to be fixed. As will be seen below, not only the areas from which responses can actually be set up by retinal illumination may be included in a definition of the receptive field but also all areas which show a functional connection, by an inhibitory or excitatory effect on a ganglion cell. This may well involve areas which are somewhat remote from a ganglion cell and by themselves do not set up discharges.

The optical conditions in the mammal present additional difficulties for mapping of receptive fields, as contrasted to those in the opened frog's eye. Because of the imperfections of the optical system, an appreciable amount of light scattering occurs and the images will be less sharply focussed. The most advantageous situation for the full exploration of the receptive fields, which approximates the anatomical receptive field boundaries, is complete dark adaptation. During this state, however, most units discharge spontaneously, making threshold determination or detection of changes in response patterns difficult. The mapping was mostly carried out in different states of light adaptation, and even under such conditions a "steady" state cannot be maintained. As implied in the term "adaptation," thresholds change, drifting towards a lower value, and discharge patterns may also vary correspondingly. Such changes seem to be part of normal events in the eye. In spite of these factors some relevant data of the size of receptive fields can be obtained.

Figure 3 illustrates a chart of a retinal region which contains receptors with connections which converge upon one ganglion cell and cause it to discharge. The exploring spot was 0.2 mm. in diameter and the background illumination approximately 10 m.c. The smallest inner area was obtained by an exploring spot, about five times threshold for a position near the electrode tip. If the spot was moved outside this area (5×), no discharges were set up. If the spot intensity was increased 10 times, by removing a Wratten neutral filter, and thus making it 50 times threshold, it caused discharges within the larger area (50×). Further increase in the stimulus strength to 500 times threshold expanded the receptive field on three sides (500×) while the demarcation line on the left remained practically unchanged. This may indicate that light scattering was not a very great factor in this particular mapping. Otherwise such a fixed portion of the boundary, in spite of an increase in stimulus intensity, could hardly be obtained. Frequently a receptive field as shown here was charted and then the exploring spot was further increased in strength. The field suddenly expanded several times and then generally no distinct boundary demarcation was obtained. It is thought that this was clearly due to scatter of light since a reduction of the stimulating spot size again resulted in a definite limit of the receptive field.

The present technique, using small exploring spots, is suited to detect

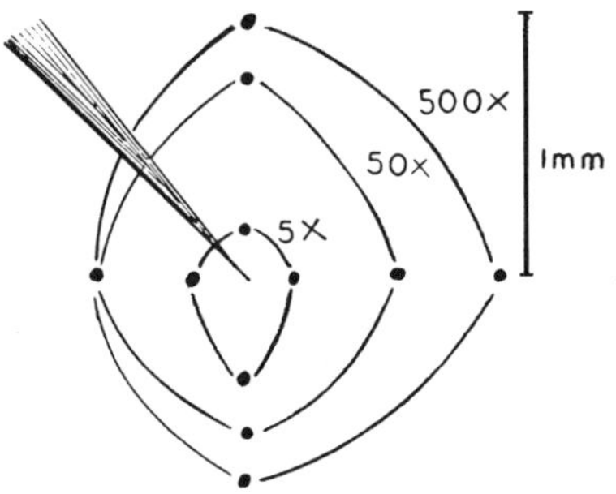


Fig. 3. Extent of receptive field obtained with exploring beam of 0.2 mm. in diameter at three different intensities. Electrode (shaded) on ganglion cell. Background illumination about 10 m.c. Inner line encloses retinal region within which light spot, about 5× threshold at electrode tip, sets up discharges. Other boundaries of field were mapped at intensity 50× and 500× threshold. Note that on left, receptive field does not expand appreciably as stimulating spot intensity is increased.

relatively dense concentrations of receptors which feed into a single ganglion cell, and therefore provides only an approximate estimate of the actual anatomical receptor distribution. Evidence suggests that the density of receptors beyond the receptive field limit (Fig. 3) may be insufficient to produce more than subthreshold effects on a ganglion cell (see Discussion). Stimulation with larger spots may overcome the difficulties and extend the receptive field into areas where the receptor concentration is low. By increasing the spot size, in fact, receptive fields apparently 3–4 mm. in diameter were found, but scatter of light makes those findings unreliable. The experiment should be done by the use of a great variety of illumination patterns near threshold intensities which would allow a more exclusive excitation of the "surround," while the central region is not illuminated. Most determinations in the present study were made in the region of the cat's tapetum, a highly reflecting region where the anatomical features of the retina can be observed with greater accuracy through the optical system. Further, the tip of the recording electrode can be seen, the stimulating spot can be followed, and in this way conditions can be checked by direct observation, provided the background illumination is sufficiently bright. The receptive field diameters varied between 0.8 and 2.0 mm. with the present method. Small ganglion cells may have fields of different extent. No determinations have been made in the periphery of the retina (see Discussion).

## 4. Stimulation of Subdivisions of Receptive Fields

*(a) Specific Areas within Receptive Fields.* In Hartline's (1938) experiments stimulation anywhere within a receptive field of the frog caused essentially the same discharge pattern in a given fiber; *i.e.*, either "on" "on-off" or pure "off" responses resulted. Accordingly the discharge type from the frog's receptive field seems relatively fixed (see, however, Discussion). This question was investigated in the present study.

It was found that the discharge patterns from ganglion cells whose re-

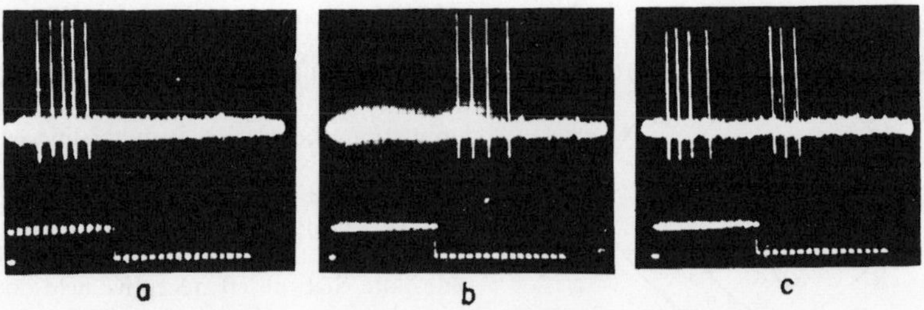


Fig. 4. Specific regions within receptive field. 0.2 mm. diameter light spot moved to three different positions within receptive field. Light flash to region near electrode tip in (a) causes only "on" discharges in ganglion cell, while same stimulus 0.5 mm. away is followed by "off" responses (b) and in an intermediate position an "on-off" discharge is set up (c). In this and subsequent records second beam signals intensity and duration of light flash; intensity modulation of 50/sec. gives time base. Impulses 0.5 mV.

ceptive fields were explored varied with the specific subdivisions which were illuminated. Figure 4 illustrates such findings. A light spot, 0.2 mm. in diameter, was moved to different positions, all within an area of 1 mm. in diameter. In Figure 4*a* a discharge appeared during illumination; this "on" response was of a transient nature and although stimulation was continued at the same intensity, the discharge ceased within less than one second (see Section 6). In Figure 4*b* when the light spot was moved 0.5 mm. from the first position no "on" discharge at all appeared and the response was of the pure "off" type, *i.e.*, discharges occurred after the cessation of illumination. At an intermediary position of the exploring spot, a combination of the first two responses resulted, and an "on-off" discharge is seen (*c*). All transitions in discharge patterns from those here shown were seen when the light spot of fixed intensity was moved to a number of positions within the receptive field, while the background illumination of the eye remained constant. Other illustrations of changes in discharge patterns with illumination of different areas within the receptive field are seen in Figures 7 and 8. Thus, the ratio and number of "on" or "off" discharges varied with the specific area which was illuminated. The changes in discharge type, caused by merely shifting an exploring spot, were not always striking in all units. To obtain the varied discharge patterns it was frequently necessary to change, in addition, the state of light adaptation, the stimulus intensity, or area of the stimulating light (see below).

It is concluded that within the receptive fields of single ganglion cells (or nerve fibers) there exist areas which can contribute differing discharge patterns. The discharge, as seen with stimulation of the whole receptive field, is the resultant of the contribution and interaction of all of these areas.

*(b) Distribution of Discharge Patterns in Receptive Fields.* All units had a central area of greatest sensitivity in which either the "on" or the "off" component predominated in the discharge pattern. Flashes of 0.5–1.0 sec.

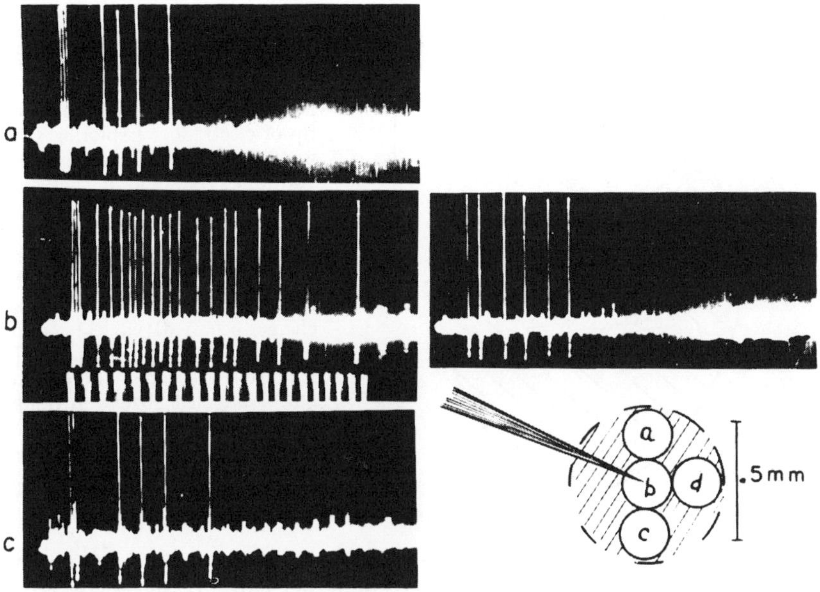


Fig. 5. Center portion of receptive field. Ganglion cell activity caused by circular light spot 0.2 mm. in diameter, 3-5 times threshold. Background illumination was about 30 m.c. Positions of light spot indicated in diagram. In *b* an "on" discharge persists for duration of flash. Intensity modulation at 20/sec. Movement of spot to positions *a, c,* and *d* causes lower frequency discharge which is not maintained for duration of light stimulus. Movement of spot beyond shaded area fails to set up impulses (see, however, extent of receptive field in similar unit with stronger stimuli in Fig. 6). Potential 0.5 mV.

duration, for instance, to subdivisions of an area of perhaps 0.5 mm. in diameter around the ganglion cell would give "on" responses only. Within this area the "on" frequency decreased as the spot was shifted away from the most sensitive region in the center. This is shown in Figure 5. A spot 0.1 mm. in radius was projected onto the retinal region around the tip of the recording electrode which was placed on a ganglion cell. In this and nearly all other experiments the region of electrode contact proved to be the most light-sensitive part of the receptive field. The area of lowest threshold and the geographical center of the receptive fields usually coincide. If the stimulating light spot was made 3–4 times threshold for the central location it evoked there a vigorous "on" response for the duration of illumination (Fig. 5*b*). A shift of the light spot, as illustrated in the scheme included in Figure 5, made it much less effective. The "on" discharges set up by the same stimulus became shorter and of lower frequency, and with further movement away from the center no discharges at all were set up. The boundaries of the receptive field with this relatively weak stimulus strength at a background of 30 m.c. are indicated by the broken circle.

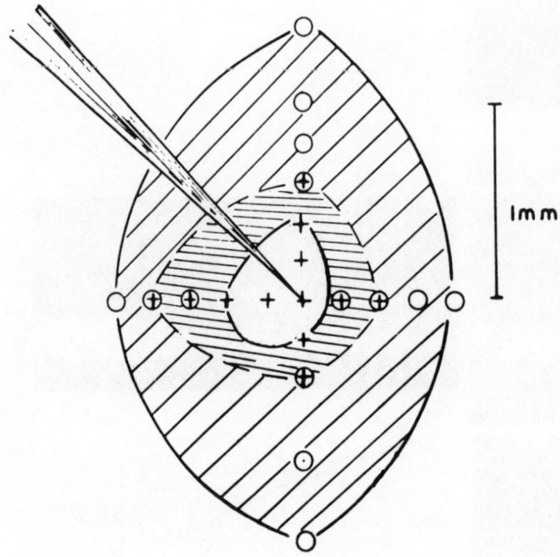


Fig. 6. Distribution of discharge patterns within receptive field of ganglion cell (located at tip of electrode). Exploring spot was 0.2 mm. in diameter, about 100 times threshold at center of field. Background illumination approximately 25 m.c. In central region (crosses) "on" discharges were found, while in diagonally hatched part only "off" discharges occurred (circles). In intermediary zone (horizontally hatched) discharges were "on-off." Note that change in conditions of illumination (background, etc.) also altered discharge pattern distribution (see text).

The records of Figure 5 show only a central area of a receptive field similar to the one which is within the inner circle of Figure 3. If the small exploring spot is made 100–1000 times threshold, a more complete picture of the discharge pattern distribution in receptive fields can be formed. The chart of Figure 6 was obtained from a unit under a background illumination of about 25 m.c. It is characteristic in a general way of the majority of units which have been studied. The crosses denote "on," the open circles "off" responses, and the "on-off" discharges are indicated by the cross-circle combinations. The different shaded areas give an approximate picture of the predominant areal organization within the receptive field, *i.e.*, of receptors and neural connections (see Discussion). The center-surround relationship may be the converse in other units, with the "off" responses predominating in the center; the area ratio between center and surround also fluctuates greatly. Further, the discharge pattern distribution shifts with changing conditions of illumination (see below).

Not in all units was the field laid out in a regular concentric manner as in Figure 6. The areas were frequently irregular. In some instances there appeared "gaps" between regions; *i.e.*, isolated spots in the periphery seemed to be functionally connected to a ganglion cell.

*(c) Factors Modifying Discharge Patterns and Size of Receptive Fields.* As indicated above, the discharge patterns arising in single receptive fields may vary, if conditions of illumination are altered. The four upper records of Figure 7 show "on" discharges produced by a 0.2 mm. diameter light spot. In the lower records is seen a corresponding series of "on-off" discharges which were obtained from the same unit by changing different parameters of illumination. In *I* the area of the stimulating spot was increased so as to include the whole receptive field and thereby the "on"

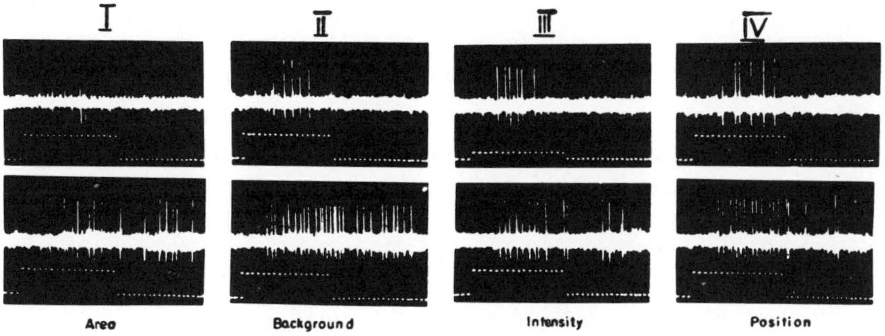


Fig. 7. Change in discharge pattern from "on" response (upper records) in single ganglion discharge into an "on-off" response (lower records). In I stimulating spot of 0.2 mm. diameter in central region of receptive field set up "on" discharge. Increasing spot diameter to 3 mm. set up more "on" impulses and brought in an "off" component. Same result was obtained in II by merely decreasing background illumination from 19 m.c. to 4 m.c. and in III by increasing stimulus spot intensity (intensity scale in III different). In IV exploring spot was shifted by about 0.4 mm. from central into more peripheral part of receptive field. Intensity modulation 50 p.s.

was converted into an "on-off" discharge. In *II* the same effect was obtained by decreasing the background illumination while leaving all other conditions unchanged. In *III* merely the intensity of the testing spot was increased, while in *IV* the spot was moved to another portion of the receptive field, without altering its intensity or area. It follows from these observations that a modification of any of these variables of light stimulation, alone or in combination, will in turn lead to modifications of the discharge pattern. In addition to the factors illustrated in Figure 7, the duration of stimulation also plays a role. The direction of the changes can usually be predicted. If, in a composite discharge pattern, one of the components—for instance, the "on" portion—predominates strongly, a reduction of stimulus strength will cause the relatively weak "off" fraction to disappear, while the "on" may be only little affected. The same result can generally be obtained by merely increasing the background illumination or reducing the area of the stimulating spot. Conversely, a combination of a weak "on" and a strong high-frequency "off" component can be changed into a pure "off" response by reducing the stimulus strength or increasing the background illumination intensity. Discharge patterns can frequently be altered by variation of background and stimulating light intensities even when the whole receptive field is illuminated. However, results are usually not as clear-cut as with fractional activation of the receptive field.

The *effect of background illumination* deserves more detailed analysis since it is one of the most potent factors in altering discharge conditions. As the background illumination is increased, the boundaries of the receptive fields "contract" and also the discharge pattern distributions change. The response type which is characteristic of the surround (diagonally hatched area of Fig. 6) tends to disappear and the pattern of the center (non-hatched region) will predominate. In fact, some units even with careful exploration, using small 0.1–0.2 mm. light spots under photopic conditions, gave only pure "on" or "off" responses within the limits of the receptive field which might be only 0.5 mm. in diameter. If the area of the stimulating spot was increased without changing its intensity—for instance, by illuminating a retinal patch 1 mm. in diameter—then the stimulus occasionally brought in an additional weak response which was characteristic of the "fringe" or surround. Thus, an "on" type of response would be converted into an "on-off" as the spot size was increased (see also Fig. 7*I*). The characteristic response of the surround could always be made evident by using a dim background, or after a short period (several minutes) of complete dark adaptation. Decreasing the background illumination first expanded the area from which center-type responses could be elicited, then brought in "on-off" responses around its boundary and eventually disclosed discharges which were characteristic of the surround. Whenever a careful search was made, both "on" and "off" components were seen in all receptive fields.

It should be noted that increased background illumination changed the receptive field in a similar manner in all units which were studied. The surround type of response, involving a presumably less dense contribution of receptors (see Discussion), was always suppressed first, independently of whether it consisted of a predominantly "on" or "off" response. This will have to be considered in discussions of the contribution of rods and cones to discharge patterns.

The great range of flexibility at the level of the single unit discharge is of particular interest, since all the factors which were found to affect the discharges play a role under normal conditions of vision.

## 5. Interaction of Different Areas Within Receptive Field

It may be presumed that one of the basic contributions of interneurons within the retina (cells between the photoreceptors and the ganglion cells which give rise to the optic nerve fibers) consists in modifying the pattern of discharges which are set up by excitation of rods and cones. The impulses emerging through the optic nerve show the result of a complex series of events which have taken place in the retina, such as spatial interaction and processes of facilitation and inhibition. These problems have already been considered by Adrian and Matthews in their classical investigations on the eel's eye (1927, 1928) and by Hartline in the early studies of the organization of the receptive field (1938, 1940a, 1940b). A wealth of data on the functional organization of the retina has also emerged from Granit's laboratory (1947, 1948, 1950).

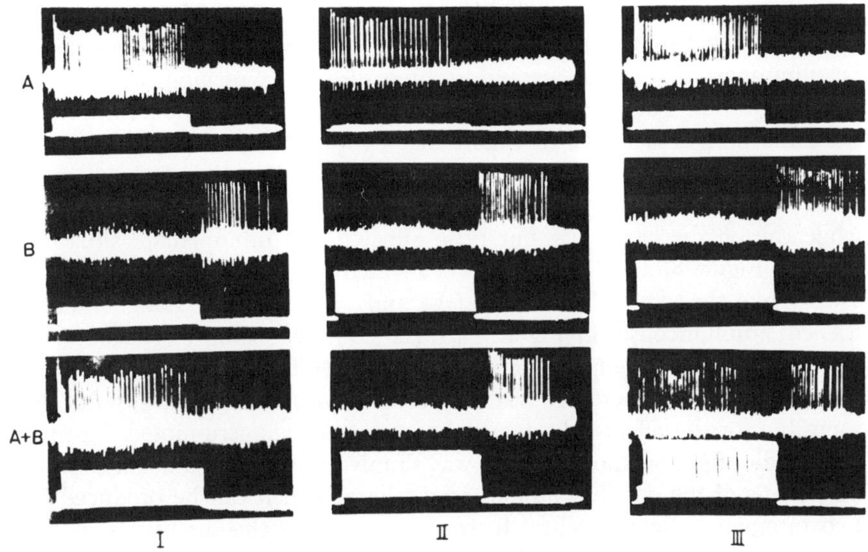


Fig. 8. Interaction of two separate light spots. Single ganglion cell discharge during background illumination of 20 m.c. Spot A, 0.1 mm. in radius, was placed in center of receptive field at tip of recording electrode. Spot B, 0.2 mm. in radius, was 0.6 mm. away in surround. Flashed separately they set up "on" (A) and "off" (B) responses. With a simultaneous flash, A+B in column I, "off" response was suppressed and at same time number of "on" discharges in A+B is slightly reduced as compared with A. In II, intensity of spot A was reduced, while spot B was increased (note flash strength indication on second beam). As a consequence B suppressed "on" discharge of A. In III, both spots were "strong." When flashed together (A+B) they reduced each other's discharges. Flash duration was 0.33 sec., potentials were 0.3 mV.

An additional approach is made possible by the present findings that certain areas within a single receptive field make a predominant "on" or "off" contribution to the discharge pattern. Two spots of light were projected onto the retina; each came from a separate light source, and the location, size, brightness and duration of illumination of both were controlled independently. The two light beams could be shifted on the retina in relation to each other and their temporal sequence was controlled electronically. There are numerous possible variants under which the experiments could be done. The first and simplest is illustrated in Figure 8. One of the exploring spots, (A), with a radius of 0.1 mm. was placed near the tip of the recording electrode in the center of the receptive field, and it caused a high-frequency "on" response during illumination. The other spot, (B), twice the diameter of the first, with its center 0.6 mm. from the ganglion cell and the recording electrode, was in the surround and set up a simple "off" discharge in this unit. When both spots were flashed on the retina simultaneously, the "off" response was suppressed (Fig. 8*I*, A+B). At the same time the number of "on" impulses was somewhat reduced as compared with the control response to stimulation of spot (A). Such situations could be produced regularly with two spatially separated light spots within a receptive field, *i.e.*, illumination of one area could suppress discharges arising from stimulation of another. The reverse situation from Figure 8*I* could be produced in the same unit as is shown in Figure 8*II*. Spot (A) was made less intense while (B) in the surround was made stronger. When these stimuli were given together (A+B), the "on" effect of (A) was completely suppressed, while the off discharge was but little affected. An intermediate situation between Figure 8*I* and *II* could also be created by altering the intensities so as to make the effects from spots (A) and (B) equally "strong." When flashed simultaneously in Figure 8*III* (A+B), they simply reduced each other's effect, setting up a relatively weak "on-off" response. In order to make certain that increased scatter of light with two spots was not responsible for the effects, the two light beams were superimposed. In such cases their effect on the discharge was simply additive. Figure 8 illustrates only a few of the possible variants in discharge which can be produced by two interacting light patches. Instead of changing the intensities of the stimulating spots, results similar to Figure 8 could also be obtained by merely varying the areas of spots (A) and (B) so as to produce the required amount of "on" or "off" discharge. Alternately, shifting the location of the light stimuli or altering the background illumination would balance the "on" and "off" relationship in any required direction.

In many experiments one light spot was fixed and the other was moved around it in the manner of a satellite. In this way a systematic study was made of the interacting regions within a receptive field. As might be expected from the above results, one could produce all combinations of response types and variants of the "on-off" ratio. Once the receptive field with its boundaries and discharge patterns within that area was plotted (see Fig. 6), the result of interaction of two spots could usually be predicted. It is worthy of note that in the present experiments not only the excitatory result of a light stimulus, such as an "on" discharge, could be inhibited, but also the "off" discharge—itself a consequence of inhibitory processes—could be suppressed. As a rule, then, when two light stimuli within the receptive field interact, *both* become modified, but if the effect of one is much "stronger" than the other, its discharge may not be appreciably affected.

Suppression of "off" responses could also be seen some time after stimulation of an "on" area. The time course of this inhibitory effect, presumably caused by persistent excitation after previous illumination, could be studied in the following manner. In units similar to that shown in Figure 8*I* the duration of the stimulus to the "on" area (A) could be progressively shortened while (B) was kept constant. It was found that beam (A) could suppress (B) for varying periods after (A) had been turned off. The time course of the inhibitory after-effect depended on the duration and intensity of (A). There was a transition from complete suppression of the "off" discharge to partial suppression and to a mere delay in the onset of the "off" discharge.

In these investigations it was surprising that frequently a ganglion cell, which gave an "off" effect, was largely unresponsive to stimulation of an "on" area during the period of the "off" discharge. Further, in the tests where the interaction of two "on" areas was studied, lack of addition of excitatory influences frequently developed. Since these observations on interaction phenomena have a bearing on functional organization of the retina a more thorough analysis will be presented in a separate publication.[1] Particularly the combination of spatial and temporal effects opens up some further approaches. These instances are mentioned here because they present a wider picture of factors which play a role in the production of discharge patterns. Further, they tend to explain some "anomalous" observations, such as lengthening of latent periods with stronger stimuli, or increased discharge frequencies with weaker ones (Figs. 11, 12).

## 6. Characteristics of "On" Discharge

(*a*) *Transient and Maintained "On" Response.* From analogies with the Limulus eye there may be reason to suspect that the maintained "on" response in mammals, which keeps discharging for long periods during illumination, is set up in receptors which have a fairly "direct" connection from photoreceptors to bipolars and to ganglion cells. On the other hand, the "on" which is part of the frequently occurring "on-off" type may be set up in units where the receptive field has different neuroanatomical connections.

In the preparations studied there were units which gave only the Limulus type of "on" response when the whole retina was stimulated under photopic or scotopic conditions. Under careful scrutiny, when restricted subdivisions of the receptive field were stimulated, with dim background illumination, it was always observed that these "on" units also received "off" contributions from the periphery (see Section 4). More frequent were those units which gave a transient "on" response lasting about 1–2 sec. with diffuse maintained retinal stimulation. These were generally followed by an "off" response, depending on the background illumination (see above). The most frequent units were those with "on-off" discharges, the "on" lasting 1 sec. or less. The following modifications of the transient "on" responses were of special interest because they revealed some further aspects of receptive field organization: (i) When the central portion of some receptive fields was illuminated by a spot of 0.1–0.2 mm. in diameter an "on" discharge resulted lasting for seconds, in several instances, even minutes. Either increasing

[1] These questions are discussed more fully in *Cold Spr. Harb. Symp. quant. Biol.*, 1952, *17*.

or decreasing the stimulus strength frequently shortened the duration of the "on" discharge. (ii) Moving the stimulating spot as little as 0.1–0.2 mm. from the center of the receptive field greatly shortened the discharge and at the same time the onset of the discharges could be delayed (Fig. 10b). Further, units were observed which gave a maintained "on" response at the center, "off" responses in the periphery and transient "on" responses coupled with "off" discharges in intermediate regions of the receptive field. This required the selection of an appropriate background illumination, stimulating intensity and size of the exploring spot. (iii) In some units a small central spot gave maintained "on" responses and, as the area of the illuminating patch was enlarged to include the surround, the discharge became of the transient type (see also 17). (iv) One isolated instance in which, however, the unit gave easily repeatable responses for several hours deserves mentioning. Under a background illumination of 10–20 m.c. the unit showed an "on" response which could not be maintained for longer than 1–2 sec. at any available intensity of the stimulating spot which was 0.2 mm. in diameter and directed onto the central region. When the background illumination was increased (60–100 m.c.) this discharge was converted into a maintained "on" type although the stimulus was of the same intensity as that which gave the shorter "on" response before. This situation was the reverse of the more common one since, by increasing the background illumination, a given stimulating intensity usually becomes less effective. One may surmise that in this unit the background illumination preferentially suppressed inhibitory influences from the "off" areas.

The above findings suggest the following interpretation: the maintained "on" discharge is converted into the transient type by activation of elements which converge onto the same ganglion cell from the periphery of the receptive field. Accordingly a unit which is so organized that it has a strong "on" center and a weak "off" surround will tend to give a well-maintained discharge even with illumination of the whole eye. The discharge will shorten in proportion to the peripheral "off" contribution. Such a view is also supported by the interaction experiments in which a simultaneous second spot in the surround weakens and shortens the discharge set up by the central one. The duration of the "on" discharge then will depend on how many "off" pathways to a ganglion cell are active in relation to the "on" fraction. It is realized that the inhibitory "off" action starts approximately simultaneously with the "on" action. Therefore, if both continued simultaneously at the same strength, one would expect merely a reduction of the "on" discharge frequency scale and not a shortening when a certain "off" component is added. Such a reduction of an "on" discharge is seen in Figure 8*III*. However, the "on" discharges which are generally observed start at a relatively high frequency which subsequently tends to decrease. With reduction of the stimulus strength producing such an "on" discharge, the initial high frequency will be reduced while the later discharge of lower frequency may drop out completely (see also Hartline, 1940a). Therefore a similar "weakening" of an "on" discharge by an inhibitory action may lead to a shortened "on" response. Further, the suppressing effect from "off" zones does not necessarily start with its full force, but may increase with prolonged stimulation as can frequently be seen in its action of stopping "off" discharges. The presence of inhibitory contributions in many pure "on" elements has already been shown by Donner and Willmer (1950).

(*b*) *Latent Period and Discharge Frequency of "On" Responses.* Generally one can cause increased excitation, as measured by frequency of response and shortened latent period, by (i) increased stimulus intensity, (ii) increase in stimulated area, (iii) decrease in background illumination (or increased dark adaptation), (iv) moving the stimulating spot toward the center of the receptive field.

A fairly typical effect of stimulus strength on the latent period and discharge frequency is seen in Figure 9. A spot 0.2 mm. in diameter was flashed at four different intensities onto the "on" center of a receptive field, increasing in steps of 10 from *a* to *d*, with the eye under a background illumination of about 2 m.c. This illustration is of particular interest because it shows how short the latent period can be and how high the discharge rate can become in the cat's retina even with moderate intensities of stimulation. In *a* the stimulus is near threshold and the latent period is 93 msec. In *b* the latency is 36 msec. and the average discharge rate for the first 8 impulses is about 180/sec. In *c* the discharge frequency is 300/sec. for the first 13 discharges and the latency is 22 msec. and in *d* a peak frequency of over 800/sec. is reached between the 4th and 10th impulse, the latency being 15 msec. This rate of discharge is much higher than is customarily obtained from nervous structures under physiological conditions. A pause as in *d* is common, both after "on" or "off" bursts. Increasing the area of stimulation within the center of the receptive field, starting with a relatively weak stimulus, also caused higher discharge frequency and latency shortening in this unit (see, however, below). The latent period of 15 msec. in Figure 9*d* is shorter than hitherto seen in mammals, presumably due to restriction of the stimulus to a predominantly "on" area (see below).

Figure 10 illustrates a unit which gave an "on" discharge lasting several seconds with illumination of the whole eye and a somewhat longer one with illumination confined to its "on" center. In *a* it showed a high-frequency initial burst of 575/sec. for the first 8 impulses with the potential size sharply declining (followed by a pause). The latent period of 15 msec. in *a* was lengthened and the discharge frequency and duration was reduced in the subsequent three records by the following: (i) in *b* the light spot of the same intensity as in *a* was moved from the center of the field by 0.1 to 0.2 mm.; (ii) in *c* with the light spot in the center again, the background illumination was increased; and (iii) in *d*, the stimulus in-

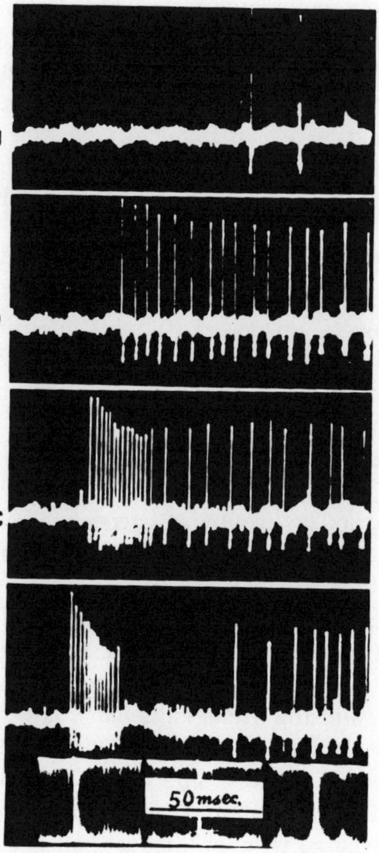


Fig. 9. Effect of stimulus strength on latent period and discharge frequency. 0.2 mm. diameter spot projected onto "on" center of a receptive field at illumination background of about 2 m.c. Between *a* and *d* stimulus was increased in steps of 10. Latent periods were 93, 36, 22 and 15 msec. Peak frequency in *d* was over 800/sec. Transient pause after a high-frequency burst occurred regularly, as did decline of potential size. Impulses 0.4 mV.

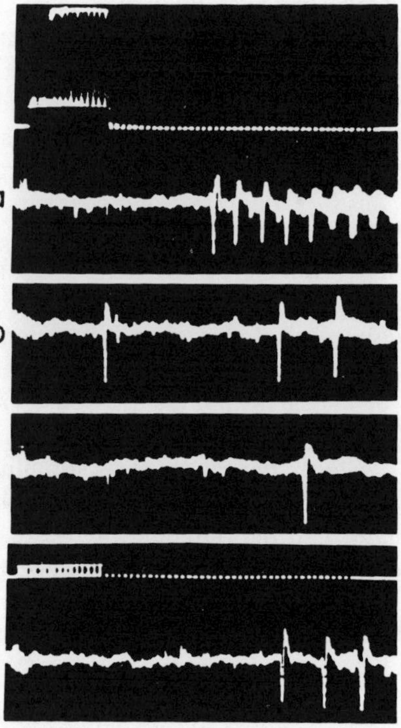


Fig. 10. Ganglion discharge with spot (0.2 mm. diam.) illumination. *a*: flash of 6.5 msec. in duration to center of receptive field set up response with initial frequency of 575/sec. and latent period of 15 msec. Prolonging illumination did not change latent period but caused an "on" response for 2–3 sec. *b*: same flash; image moved 0.1–0.2 mm. from central position. Latent period 21 msec., only two impulses set up. First impulse on sweep was "spontaneous" and not related to flash. *c*: same flash as *a*, but background illumination increased. Only one impulse set up. *d*: conditions as in *a*, but stimulus intensity decreased. Latent period 22 msec., discharge burst shorter. Effects seen in *b–d* were also obtained by shortening flash or reducing spot size. Intensity modulation 2000/sec.

tensity was reduced. Reducing the stimulating area or shortening the duration of the light flash (not illustrated) had a similar result as shown in *b–d*. The findings of Figures 9 and 10 are in general agreement with the early work of Adrian and Matthews (1927), Hartline (1938) and Granit (1947).

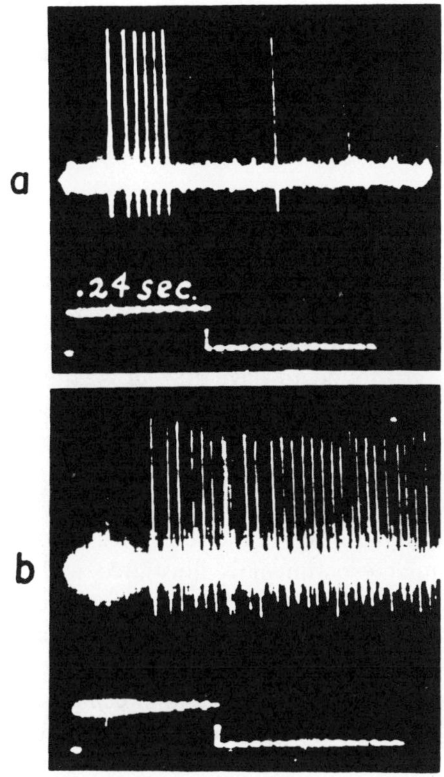


Fig. 11. "Anomalous" effect of change in stimulus area on latent period. *a*: ganglion discharge set up by 0.2 mm. diam. spot within central region of receptive field. *b*: spot size increased so as to include whole field. Note the greatly prolonged latent period of "on" component. Potentials 0.6 mV.

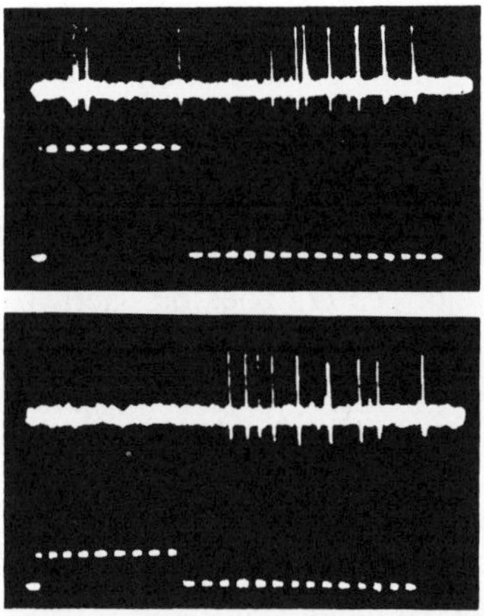

Fig. 12. "Anomalous" effect of change in stimulus intensity on discharge. Upper record: "on-off" ganglion discharge. Below: with stimulus intensity decrease "on" component drops out. Note, however, the shorter latent period and increased number of impulses in "off" discharge (see text). Frequency 50/sec.

Some notable exceptions to the general "rules" as discussed above were also observed—and, in fact, could frequently be produced by appropriately arranging the conditions of the experiment. Thus, in contrast to the usual results, the latent period of discharge was actually prolonged in the unit of Figure 11 when the area of stimulation on the retina was changed from a patch 0.2 mm. in diameter (a) to one of 3 mm. (b). Similarly, increasing the light intensity could have the same effect. One may assume that stimulation of the larger area brought in a strong "off" component from the surround, causing a delay in the "on" response. Such a situation could actually be produced frequently by stimulation of two separate small "off" and "on" areas. Another "exception" is seen in Figure 12 where an "on-off" response is converted into an "off" by reducing the stimulus strength. Surprisingly, however, the latent period of the "off" response is shorter and the number of impulses is greater with this weaker illumination (see also Donner & Willmer, 1950). Again, an explanation can be sought in the antagonism of "on" and "off" influences. The weaker stimulus, by failing to excite the "on" fraction, caused less inhibition of the "off" component. In all these "anomalous" instances it must be noted that a non-homogeneous population of receptors is activated and the discharge pattern depends on the proportion of "off"- and of "on"-oriented receptors which are excited.

## 7. "Off" Response

As appears from Section 4, no pure "off" units were found when the receptive fields were explored with small spots of light and suitable background illumination. Those units which gave an "off" response alone with illumination of the whole eye were always found to have an "off" center and "on" surround, while units giving "on-off" responses could have either type of center. The "off" activity of an area could be tested by the ability of a light stimulus to set up impulses when its intensity was reduced or the light turned off, or by the suppression of spontaneous activity.

The interaction between separate stimuli to "on" and "off" areas was shown in Figure 8; in Figure 13 a similar experiment is illustrated with both light stimuli to an "off" region. A Spot caused a strong "off" response by illumination of an area 0.2 mm. in diameter in the central portion of a receptive field, just about 0.1 mm. away from the area of lowest threshold at the electrode tip. The illumination was started before the sweep and only the cessation of the light signal appears on the record (marked by arrow). Grouped discharges similar to those in this figure were frequently seen and have been also noted by others during the "off" effect (Granit & Therman, 1935; Hartline, 1938). Spot B was the same distance from the electrode tip as A, but on the opposite side. This stimulus was shorter and by itself caused a briefer discharge (Fig. 13B). When B followed A, it suppressed the "off" discharge for the duration of its flash (Fig. 13A+B). When both stimuli were given to spot A in succession, the second ($A_2$) also suppressed the "off" impulses. $A_2$, being a shorter flash than the preceding A, set up a shorter "off" response than A alone. It is noteworthy, however, that the "off" discharges of A were not reinforced at the end of flash $A_2$. In this unit it seems that $A_2$ during its flash not only suppressed the impulses, but also the processes which "survived" after cessation of A. The inhibitory action of light on the "off" discharge by reillumination of the whole eye is well known from the work of Granit and Therman (1935) and Hartline (1938). Suppression of "off" discharges, set up in one region of the receptive field, by subsequent excitation of another "off" area is to be expected from the experiments on interaction (Section 5) and have also been seen by Hartline (1941).

The duration of the latent period of the "off" responses was studied, since it is a measure of the processes which have preceded the discharge. It is known that the latent period shortens and the discharge frequency in-

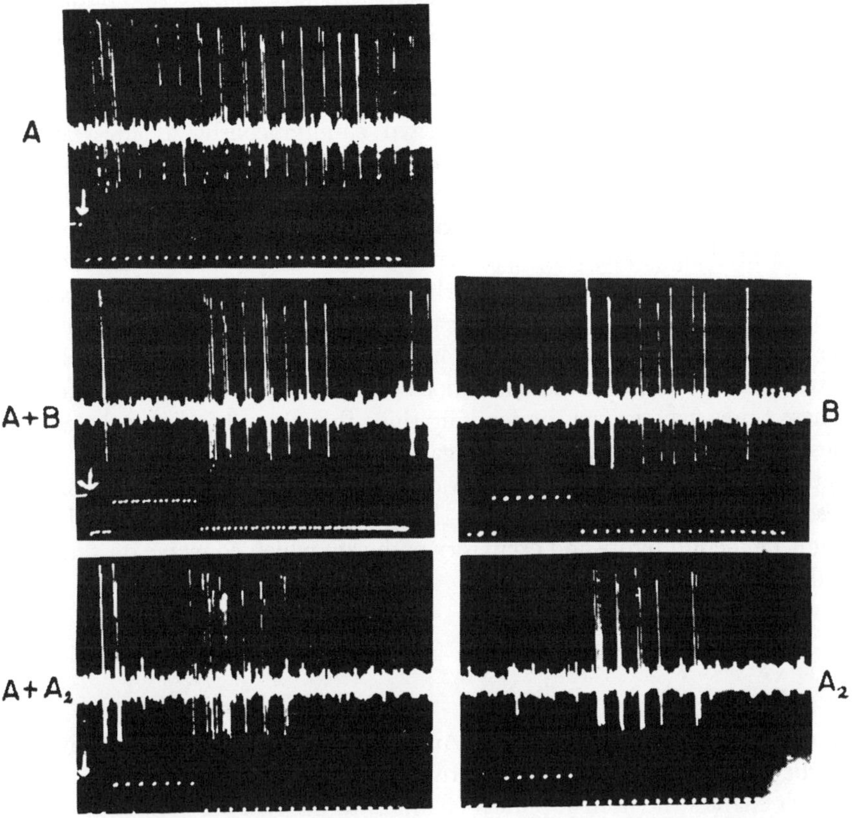


Fig. 13. Inhibitory action of light on "off" response. Light beams A and B projected onto separate areas, each 0.2 mm. in diameter, in central region of a receptive field near tip of recording electrode. Both regions give "off" responses only. Background 18 m.c. A: "Off" discharge produced following termination (arrow), at beginning of sweep, of stimulation by beam A. A+B: Beam B, applied during "off" discharge, suppresses impulses. B: spot B alone. A+A2: Stimulus to spot A ceases near beginning of sweep, as above, but same area is re-illuminated by second flash. Not only is there suppression of "off" discharges during flash of A2, but also subsequent "off" response duration is reduced as compared with A. A2: second flash of beam A alone. Note that "off" discharges set up in one region of receptive field can be suppressed by stimulation of another "off" region, or by restimulation of same area. The grouped discharges occurred in many units of this experiment. Time base 100/sec. in A+B, 50/sec. in all other records. Potentials 0.3 mV.

creases as a function of the intensity and duration of the preceding illumination (Granit, 1947; Hartline, 1940c). Again, however, exceptions to this rule occur. In some experiments latent periods as short as 10–15 msec., similar to the shortest periods for "on" discharges, could be seen. Another indication concerning the processes which are involved in inhibitory activity can be obtained from a determination of the time which is taken up between stimulation of the receptors and the first sign of suppression of activity at the ganglion cell level. Some conclusion may then be drawn regarding the mechanism of excitation spread within the retina. The speed and mode of this spread will be important in the competitive situation when both "on" and "off" areas are excited simultaneously, as must occur normally in the eye when stimulation is not confined to subdivisions of a receptive field. Such latent periods of inhibitory action are obtained by measuring the time it takes for a second flash (B or $A_2$ in Fig. 13) to suppress a discharge. The time between the onset of the "off" flash and the first suppressed impulse would clearly be the most accurate determination. This method will be most precise if the suppression is tested and measured on a well-maintained and regular high-frequency discharge. By such determinations the shortest latent periods of inhibition were around 10 msec. These times may, in fact, be too long since they do not indicate the actual onset of inhibitory action at the ganglion cell. The processes may start acting well before they become evident by their action of suppressing a discharge. Further information in this connection will be presented in a study of the inhibitory and excitatory pathways which converge on ganglion cells.

## *DISCUSSION*

*Sampling of units within retina.* An advantage of the present technique is the ease of recording retinal activity and the intactness of the eyeball which enables the normal optical channels to be used for illumination and observation. The method, however, will tend to select the potentials from the larger ganglion cells. On the other hand, since one generally can find suitable cells for recording within any small area of the retina, such as 1 square mm., it is quite likely that these cells can be smaller than the "giant" cells described by Rushton (1949). Further, nearly all the work was done on cells within a radius of about 5–8 mm. from the optic disc, particularly in the two quadrants above the disc within the highly reflecting region of the tapetum. No positive evidence has been found that within these areas there are specific subsections which give different discharge patterns. The cat has no fovea but there exists a region on the visual axis of the eye, called centralis (Chievitz, 1891), about 1–2 mm. temporal from the disc, which has an especially dense representation in the visual cortex (Talbot, personal communication). This region was included in the present studies and found to show no qualitative differences from other areas. No activity of bipolars has been recorded and therefore all the discharge patterns which are described, while derived from ganglion cells, represent also the discharges in the optic nerve fibers.

Since in each preparation the discharges from numerous units can be observed in quick succession, *e.g.*, 30–40 within an hour, it is possible to collect statistical data on discharge types. It was, however, found more informative to obtain detailed results from a relatively small number of units and frequently these were kept on the electrodes for 5–6 hours. Only those cases are presented which, at the present stage, seem more representative or important. The great majority of experiments were done well within photopic levels, with the background illumination between 1 and 50 m.c. All the essential features of discharge pattern behavior, however, were also present under scotopic conditions in the absence of background illumination. It should also be noted that in this study relatively short flashes were used and no "equilibrium" conditions were attained.

*Fluidity of Discharge Patterns.* The most outstanding feature in the present analysis is the flexibility and fluidity of the discharge patterns arising in each receptive field. Stability of discharge type can be obtained in the present preparations in units under certain conditions, especially with a relatively strong background illumination, when the surround is suppressed. A constant "on" or "off" response may then be seen even with spot illumination. Such stability, however, disappears when one or more of several parameters, such as the adaptation level, stimulus intensity, and area of illumination, are changed singly or in combination. In the absence of a fixed pattern from the whole receptive field, it does not appear accurate enough to speak of "on," "on-off" or "off" fibers in the cat's retina. The difference in retinal discharge pattern distribution between frog and cat is worthy of note, particularly since the analyses in frog were made by Hartline (1940a) with a well-controlled and accurate technique. Although he reported the discharge patterns in receptive fields fixed, he points out many exceptions and reports occasional units in which a change in discharge patterns did occur. He also presents data which may be interpreted to indicate the presence of inhibitory surrounds, such as a decline of discharge frequencies with strong stimuli or with large areas of excitation (Hartline, 1938, 1940b). The difference between cat and frog may turn out to be largely a quantitative one. A less flexible system of discharge in frogs may perhaps not be surprising. By using a different approach, such as pharmacological techniques (Granit, 1945) and passing current through the eye or varying the wave-length and intensity of the stimulating light, shifts in discharge patterns have already been observed by Granit and his colleagues. They also repeatedly pointed out the liability of certain portions of the discharges, particularly in connection with work concerning the on-off ratios (Donner & Granit, 1949; Granit, 1948, 1950). Donner and Willmer (1950), working with dark-adapted cats and stimulation of the whole retina, also observed a great range of variability in ganglion response patterns during stimulation at different intensities. They have shown that visual-purple-dependent receptors can give rise to both "on" and "off" discharge components.

*Functional Organization of Receptive Fields.* There seems to exist a very great variability between individual receptive fields and therefore a detailed classification cannot be made at present. Some features, however, of general organization were found common to all. In all fields there exists a central region giving a discharge pattern which is the opposite from that obtained in the periphery. The center may be either predominantly "off," the surround "on," or vice versa. A transitional zone is in between (see Fig. 6). The essential character of discharge within the centers cannot be changed by altering any of the parameters of illumination, *i.e.*, an "off" center cannot be converted into an "on" center. It must not be inferred, however, that the centers are quite uniform and receive no contribution which is characteristic of the surround. In view of the fixed nature of the center discharge, it may be convenient to classify receptive fields into "on" center and "off" center fields. In line with this the respective elements may be similarly designated as "on" center or "off" center units. No accurate record of distribution has been made in hundreds of units which were investigated. The "off" center units seemed to occur more frequently. Functionally the center and surround regions are opposed, the one tending to suppress the other. The ganglion cell is subjected to multiple influences from its receptive field and its discharge will express the balance between these opposing and interacting contributions. In view of the relative ease with which the peripheral receptive field contribution can be altered (see later), and thereby the balance within the unit changed, the discharge pattern fluidity is readily appreciated.

From a functional point of view, then, the important aspect of the present findings is not that one unit can give under special conditions either "on" or "off" responses but that there exists a mixture of contributing receptors, perhaps with their specific pathways (below). In proportion to their activation they can produce all shades of transitions from one response pattern to another. In any event, illumination of the whole receptive field will always produce a push-pull action as the opposing components are thrown into activity.

*Specific Neural Pathways.* The nervous organization of all the elements functionally connected to a ganglion cell constitutes an example of the complexity of the central nervous system, well known from the studies of Cajal (1933) and lately especially of Polyak (1941). It is natural that a specific organization should be suggested for excitatory and inhibitory pathways for which there is physiological evidence. Experiments seem to show (Fig. 6) that excitation of a certain number of receptors by restricted illumination causes one type of response only. Presumably a given pathway is utilized by a given group of receptors. The principal reason for a change in response type seems to be that either additional receptors have been brought in or receptors have been eliminated (see below). Suggestions as to the specific neural connections, based on present evidence, are clearly speculative and grossly simplified. One may think of a neural arrangement which parallels the roughly concentric functional pattern, with relatively uniform connection types between receptors in the center and the ganglion cell and a differing pathway set-up from the surround receptors to the ganglion cell. The in-between region may present the zone where the pathway types are more mixed than anywhere else. A correlation of greater significance between neural pathways and discharge patterns may perhaps be obtained from a study of animals with a fovea, *e.g.*, monkey, where the neuroanatomical connections are simpler and better known. It may be predicted, accordingly, that the foveal paths are associated with specific discharge behavior.

*Receptor Density in Receptive Fields.* Any given small area of the retina which has been studied presumably has a dense and fairly uniform receptor population (Polyak, 1941). Histological data also show that adjoining receptors, or even the same receptors, may have connections to different ganglion cells. Further, we know that the same receptor may connect to different ganglion cells in differing ways. This is the neuroanatomical basis for overlapping receptive fields. The present study gives some information about the density distribution of receptors which are *functionally* connected to one ganglion cell. The following type of experiment supports the assumption that the central portion of receptive fields hold a denser population of receptors per unit area than do the peripheral regions: units which have an "on" center and "off" surround, when tested with stimuli 100–1000 times threshold (Fig. 6), may be excited in their most sensitive central region by a 0.2 mm. diameter spot of near-threshold intensity. At this strength "on" discharges of quite short duration are evoked within a small central area (as Fig. 5). Such a small spot is well below threshold for the outlying portions of the receptive field. Placing a ground glass in front of the eye, thereby reducing, and in addition scattering, the light beam, will produce "on-off" or pure "off" responses. This suggests that receptors dispersed in peripheral regions have been reached and summation has occurred in their pathways leading to the ganglion cell. The experiment also shows that the receptors which contribute the "off" component do not have a lower threshold than those in the central "on" region. Threshold differences, however, within the receptor population are not contra-indicated by such results. Presumably because of the density of receptors, the center is found to be more sensitive when tested with small beams.

The scatter of receptors in the periphery makes obvious the difficulties of receptive field mapping with small light beams, since one has to assume that a sufficient number of receptors must be activated to evoke a ganglion cell discharge. Receptors, functionally connected but located in the periphery, will be missed and an error in underestimating the field size is likely to be made. When mapping is done in units with an "off" surround, while they show spontaneous activity, the field periphery can be delineated by the area over which a small spot will produce slowing or stoppage of firing. This method is more sensitive than the one described in Section 3 and receptive fields extending over 3–4 mm. (12–16° in cat), could occasionally be obtained. The effect of light scatter, however, could not be estimated closely enough to make these findings reliable.

The low density of receptors in the surround also makes readily understandable the observed shrinkage of receptive fields with augmented background illumination. If tested with a *small spot,* the dropping out of receptors by raised thresholds in the field surround will be of more consequence than in the dense central region, since the outer receptor family, being scattered, operates nearer to the margin for firing the ganglion cell. Even with illumination of the *whole field* the peripheral contribution, if it depends more on facilitation and summation, should be more affected if a portion of component pathways is put out of action. The background changes should affect an "on" or "off" surround equally, in line with present observations.

*Changes in Receptive Field Contribution to Ganglion Cells.* A special nervous organization of receptive fields alone could not account for all the observed discharge pattern changes under diverse conditions of illumination. There is a great body of evidence for a diversity of receptor properties in respect to thresholds, adaptation, wave-lengths, etc. For instance, in view of the changes in receptive field size at low or high levels of light adaptation, it is clear that under such changing conditions a largely differing set of receptors will be thrown into activity with a given stimulus. Hence, this alone will bring a different set of active connections with a ganglion cell into being. The differing connections, in turn, are likely to cause changes in discharge patterns. Since steady states cannot be attained, a shift in the active receptor population is likely to go on continuously even in the dark-adapted eye, as indicated by the background activity, unless the latter is entirely due to spontaneous rhythms in the neural elements.

*Psychophysical Aspects.* A transference of information about discharge patterns, as obtained here, to psychophysical data is obviously based on speculation. However, the data must be used with all their imperfections since they provide the components which form the basis of the message content reaching the higher centers. The most potent stimuli, those causing the greatest nervous activity, are relatively sudden changes. These may be either changes of the general illumination level or such changes as occur during movement of images (see also Hartline, 1948). In the latter case the antagonistic arrangement of central and peripheral areas within receptive fields seems important since the smallest shift can cause a great change in the discharge pattern. This should be advantageous in the perception of contrast and in acuity. In view of this the importance of small eye displacements, as would occur in any scanning movement, is clear. It should be noted that zonal gradients within fields, between center and surround, will change with different levels of adaptation as the receptive field shrinks or expands. It may also be tempting to consider in this connection well-known suppression phenomena like lateral inhibition which has been studied by many investigators. Particularly the interaction of two light patches with facilitation and inhibition as observed in humans over small distances on the retina may be considered in view of the extent of the cat's receptive field (Fry, 1934; Granit, 1930). It is clear, however, that even the smallest light beams used in the present experiments do excite a great number of ganglion cells through their overlapping receptive fields. It is not known how the latter are functionally related to each other. For instance, it would be of interest to know whether the same receptor can be connected to one ganglion cell through an excitatory and to another cell through an inhibitory pathway.

Regarding the information content carried by a single ganglion cell or its connected nerve fiber, the following two phenomena may be briefly considered: (i) If a ganglion cell can discharge at one time during illumination and then be converted into one which signals only when a light stimulus is withdrawn, one may assume that it does not carry merely the information which is suggested by a "simple" interpretation of the discharge pattern. The higher centers may receive identical impulse patterns in both cases. (ii) A unit giving "on-off" discharges in a given situation, according to a "simple" interpretation, sends information first about an increased and then about a decreased level of luminosity. The identical discharge pattern may, however, be evoked by turning a light on, and then instead of turning it off, one may further increase its intensity. Such fibers then merely signal change, but not necessarily the direction of change, such as brightness or darkness.

In view of the massive continued nervous activity in eyes "at rest" or during illumination it is difficult to think of information content in terms of single unit contributions. One may rather have to consider that groups of fibers modulate activity levels and patterns by superposition or substraction. The latter—for instance, transient cessation or diminution—is likely to be as meaningful as the opposite in terms of message content. Further, similar discharge patterns at different background illuminations may convey a different meaning, since they are superimposed on a different background activity. These examples merely illustrate some of the difficulties inherent in this type of analysis. They indicate that on the basis of the single unit discharge a 1:1 agreement between discharge patterns and information should not always be sought. At the same time it should be recalled that there is agreement between psychophysical measurements such as the visibility curves and the analogous curves, obtained in different mammals (Granit, 1947), or the Limulus (Hartline, 1940c), from nervous discharges.

In this study the influence of transient light changes on discharge patterns has been emphasized; in view of the importance of background activity the effect of steady levels of illumination on discharge behavior must be analyzed in great detail.

## *SUMMARY*

Discharge patterns from the unopened cat's eye have been studied by recording from single cells in the retina. Small electrodes, inserted behind the limbus, traversed the vitreous and made light contact with different regions of the retina. The normal optics of the eye were used for stimulation by two independently controlled light beams. Circular stimuli of various dimensions, duration and intensities were applied to different areas of the retina. A third light source provided the background illumination, determining the adaptation level, and also served for simultaneous direct observation of the fundus.

1. The discharges arising in nerve fibers and ganglion cells can be readily distinguished through differences in their time course and the location of their respective receptive fields. The present study was done on ganglion cell activity.

2. Ganglion cells can be blocked reversibly by pressure and the potentials can be split into "prepotentials" and "spikes."

3. Under dim background illumination and during dark adaptation the cat's retina is dominated by generalized spontaneous activity. The latter is reduced by illumination and anesthetics such as Dial or Nembutal. Certain discharges do not seem to be influenced appreciably by illumination. These observations are in general agreement with Granit's findings.

4. The configuration of receptive fields—those areas of the retina which must be illuminated to cause a discharge in a ganglion cell—were studied by exploration with small spots of light. The fields are usually concentric, covering an area of 1–2 mm., or possibly more, in diameter. The boundaries and extent of receptive fields cannot be delineated accurately. They shrink under high background illumination and expand during dark adaptation.

5. The discharge pattern from individual ganglion cells is not fixed. "On," "off" or "on-off" discharges can be obtained from one ganglion cell if specific zones within its receptive field are stimulated by small spots of light. The discharge pattern from a ganglion cell depends, amongst others, on the following factors: Background illumination and state of adaptation, intensity and duration of stimulation, extent and location of area which is stimulated within a receptive field. Each of these parameters can alter the discharge pattern by itself or in conjunction with the others.

6. The general functional organization of each receptive field is the following: There exists a central area of low threshold as tested by a small spot of light. The discharge pattern of the central region is the opposite of that

found in the periphery or surround. The center may give predominantly "off," the surround "on" discharges, or the reverse. An intermediary region gives "on-off" discharges. The units which carry discharges from "center on" or "center off" receptive fields may accordingly be classified as "on" center or "off" center units. A conversion of one type into another by changing conditions of illumination has not been possible.

Experiments indicate that receptors in the periphery of receptive fields are less dense per unit area than in the central regions.

7. Interaction of different regions within single receptive fields was studied by simultaneous excitation by two small beams of light. Depending on a number of factors, "off" areas may suppress the discharge from "on" regions, or vice versa. All degrees of mutual modification can be obtained. It is assumed that specific areas give rise to predominantly inhibitory or excitatory pathways to a given ganglion cell.

8. The discharge pattern of a ganglion cell, set up by illumination of an entire receptive field, depends on the summed effects of interacting pathways converging on the cell. The ratio of functionally opposing center and surround regions varies greatly in different receptive fields. Under diverse conditions of illumination the balance of active inhibitory and excitatory contributions changes within the same receptive field. This seems to be responsible for the varied discharge patterns.

9. The character of "on" components in discharge patterns was also studied. The maintained "on" response discharges for the duration of illumination while the transient "on" adapts quickly. Transitions between these two "on" types were found in the same receptive fields. It is suggested that the transient "on" discharges are the result of various amounts of addition by the "off" surround to the "on" center.

10. The latent periods of "on" or "off" responses were found to be shorter than hitherto observed, presumably because of more exclusive stimulation of their specific receptive areas. High discharge frequencies of 200–800/sec. were found to be within the normal range in the cat's eye.

11. Some "anomalous" observations, such as lengthened latent periods with increased stimulus intensities or higher frequency discharges with weaker stimuli, are interpreted in the light of receptive field organization.

## *REFERENCES*

Adrian, E. D. Synchronized reactions in the optic ganglion of Dysticus. *Journal of Physiology*, 1937, *91*, 66-89.

Adrian, E. D., & Matthews, R. The action of light on the eye. Part I. The discharge of impulses in the optic nerve and its relation to the electric changes in the retina. *Journal of Physiology*, 1927, *63*, 378-414.

Adrian, E. D., & Matthews, R. The action of light on the eye. Part III. The interaction of retinal neurones. *Journal of Physiology*, 1928, *65*, 273-298.

Bernhard, C. G. Contributions to the neurophysiology of the optic pathway. *Acta Physiologica Scandinavica*, 1940, *1*, Suppl. 1.

Cajal, S. Ramón y. La rétine des vertébrés. *Trab. Lab. Invest. biol. Madr.*, 1933, Suppl. 28.

Chievitz, J. H. Über das Vorkommen der Area centralis retinae in den vier höheren Wirbelthierklassen. *Anat. entw.-gesch. Monogr.*, 1891, 311-334.

Crescitelli, F., & Jahn, T. L. The effect of temperature on the electrical response of the grasshopper eye. *Journal of Cellular and Comparative Physiology*, 1939, *14*, 13-27.

Donner, K. O., & Granit, R. The effect of illumination upon the sensitivity of isolated retinal elements to polarization. *Acta Physiologica Scandinavica*, 1949, *18*, 113-120.

Donner, K. O., & Willmer, E. N. An analysis of the response from single visual-purple-dependent elements in the retina of the cat. *Journal of Physiology*, 1950, *111*, 160-173.

Fry, G. A. Depression of the activity aroused by a flash of light by applying a second flash immediately afterwards to adjacent areas of the retina. *American Journal of Physiology*, 1934, *108*, 701-707.

Granit, R. Comparative studies on the peripheral and central retina. I. On interaction between distant areas in the human eye. *American Journal of Physiology*, 1930, *94*, 41-50.

Granit, R. Some properties of post-excitatory inhibition studied in the optic nerve with micro-electrodes. *K. svenska VetenskAkad. Arkiv. Zool.*, 1945, *36*, 1-8.

Granit, R. *Sensory mechanisms of the retina*. London: Oxford University Press, 1947, 412.

Granit, R. Neural organization of the retinal elements, as revealed by polarization. *Journal of Neurophysiology*, 1948, *11*, 239-253.

Granit, R. The organization of the vertebrate retinal elements. *Ergebn. Physiol.*, 1950, *46*, 31-70.

Granit, R., & Therman, P. O. Excitation and inhibition in the retina and in the optic nerve. *Journal of Physiology*, 1935, *83*, 359-381.

Hartline, H. K. The response of single optic nerve fibers of the vertebrate eye to illumination of the retina. *American Journal of Physiology*, 1938, *121*, 400-415.

Hartline, H. K. The receptive field of the optic nerve fibers. *American Journal of Physiology*, 1940, *130*, 690-699. (a)

Hartline, H. K. The effects of spatial summation in the retina on the excitation of the fibers of the optic nerve. *American Journal of Physiology*, 1940, *130*, 700-711. (b)

Hartline, H. K. The nerve messages in the fibers of the visual pathway. *Journal of the Optical Society of America*, 1940, 30, 239-247. (c)

Hartline, H. K. The neural mechanisms of vision. *Harvey Lecture*, 1941, 37, 39-68.

Hartline, H. K., & Graham, C. H. Nerve impulses from single receptors in the eye. *Journal of Cellular and Comparative Physiology*, 1932, *1*, 277-295.

Hartline, H. K., Wagner, H. G., & MacNichol, E. F. Jr. The peripheral origin of nervous activity in the visual system. *Cold Spring Harbor Symposia on Quantitative Biology*, 1952, *17*, 125-141.

Hodgkin, L. A. The subthreshold potentials in a crustacean nerve fiber. *Proceedings of the Royal Society*, 1938, *B*, *162*, 67-121.

Hunt, C. C., & Kuffler, S. W. Stretch receptor discharges during muscle contraction. *Journal of Physiology*, 1951, *113*, 298-315.

Katz, B. Experimental evidence for a non-conducted response of nerve to subthreshold stimulation. *Proceedings of the Royal Society*, 1937, *B*, *124*, 244-276.

Polyak, S. L. *The retina*. Chicago: University of Chicago Press, 1941, 607.

Renshaw, B. Effects of presynaptic volleys on spread of impulses over the soma of the motoneuron. *Journal of Neurophysiology*, 1942, *5*, 235-243.

Rushton, W. A. H. The structure responsible for action potential spikes in the cat's retina. *Nature*, 1949, 164, 743-744.

Svaetichin, G. Analysis of action potentials from single spinal ganglion cells. *Acta Physiologica Scandinavica*, 1951, *24*, Suppl. 86.

Talbot, S. A. (personal communication).

Talbot, S. A., & Kuffler, S. W. A multibeam ophthalmoscope for the study of retinal physiology. *Journal of the Optical Society of America*, Dec. 1952 (in press).

*Kuffler's findings invite comparison with the papers of Ratliff and of Lettvin et al., on two major points. First of all, the matter of lateral inhibition: in Limulus the inhibitory interactions between ommatidia seem to be quite nonspecific in the sense that every ommatidium can influence (inhibit) every other one in its neighborhood, the degree of mutual influence depending only on their distance apart. The information about light intensity in one unit is available to influence the whole pattern of electrical responding in the optic nerve bundle. This is presumably an efficient arrangement, since there is just one optic nerve fiber to each ommatidium. In the mammalian eye, on the other hand, there are many more photoreceptor units than fibers (the ratio varies between species, but is generally between about 10:1 and 100:1) so the Limulus arrangement would not be possible. What is a general function over the whole eye in the simpler case now turns out to be a specialized function within each receptive field, but it is a function which still subserves the same computation, namely the detection of regions of sudden change in level of illumination at the retina. These "packets" of discrete information are preserved in the mammalian optic nerve, and relayed to higher centers—where we shall follow them shortly. Again, the system looks to be an efficient one for preserving essential features of the visual input. A new principle which appears with the receptive field organization is the mutual antagonism of "on" and "off" areas of receptive fields. The important role which this reciprocal inhibitory proc-*

ess plays in contour coding will become clear in the following two papers. The second comparison, with the findings of Lettvin et al., is also instructive. Kuffler's type of receptive field is far less specialized than those reported by Lettvin and his colleagues, although it should be said that Kuffler-type fields had earlier been reported by Hartline and Barlow for the frog. Kuffler's type of receptive field is probably not the only type that will eventually be identified for the cat retina, but at least nothing as specific as the frog's "bug detector" (net-convexity detector, or type 2) has been reported at the mammalian retinal level. What happens to the outputs of the cat's retinal ganglion cells? In the frog, it seems that four (or five) types of specific information are relayed to different layers of the tectum—that the information is preserved pretty much in the form of the "feature detection" language which is the retinal output. In the mammalian system, however, a much more complicated set of connections exists between retina and visual cortex, with extensive possibilities for interactions between the "packets" of information relayed from the retina. Our next paper, by Hubel and Wiesel, describes some of the stages of this process, and shows how the original information in the retinal output is transformed in various ways. As I have said earlier, this work is the single most important contribution to our understanding of the physiological basis for visual contour coding, and its impact on the field has been astounding.

In order to follow the paper more easily, a few introductory comments are in order. Figure B shows the general layout of a mammalian visual system in a very schematized way. It is the mammalian system in its most perfect form—that of man—but the general features are common to all mammals. The output from the retinas in the form of electrical pulses in individual optic nerve fibers, are relayed to certain midbrain structures known as the lateral geniculate bodies (l.g.b.s).[1] There they synapse with cells whose axons proceed to the primary visual, or striate, cortex in the occipital lobe. This cortical area has a layered structure, with many different types of neuron, and interconnecting fibers both within the area and to the neighboring so-called visual association areas. The structure is incredibly complex, so much so that one may be surprised that recording from single cells within it can be interpreted in any straightforward way, in terms of patterns of stimulation at the retina.

In man of the l.g.b.s. themselves have a sixfold layered structure, three layers receiving connections from the ipsilateral, three from the contralateral eye; the connectors are the axonial fibers of the retinal ganglion cells. Cells in the same positions in adjacent layers within the l.g.b. have inputs from closely corresponding areas of the two retinas, an arrangement which sug-

[1] Some of the fibers proceed directly to the *superior colliculus,* which is the structure corresponding to the optic tectum in the frog. We shall not follow them there, since relatively little is as yet known about their visual functions (cf., however, Schneider's paper in Part III).

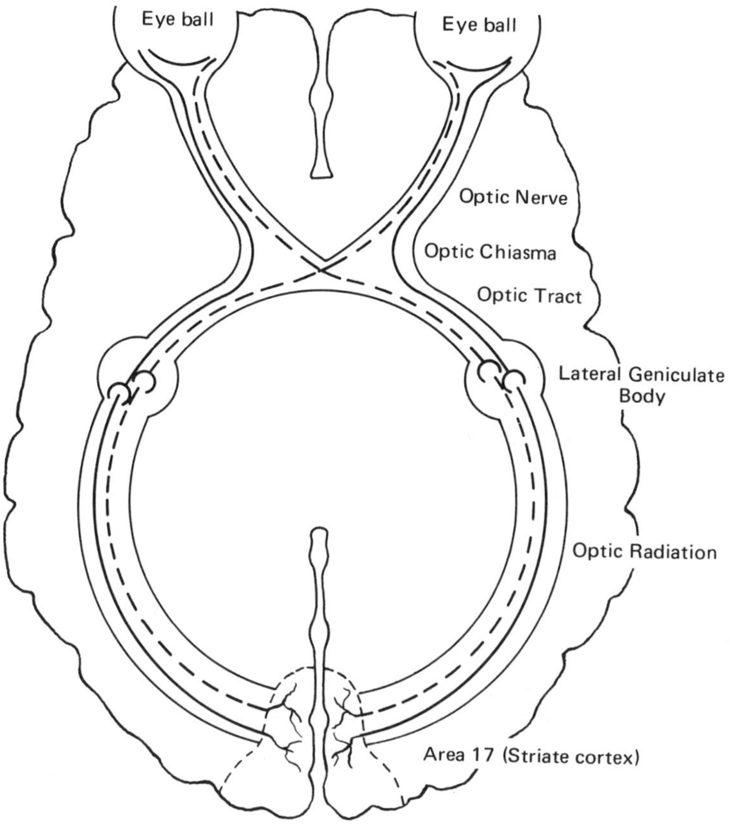


Fig. B

gests strongly that one of the l.g.b. functions is to "mix" inputs from the two eyes in a very specific way. The amount of crossing of fibers at the optic chiasma (Figure B) also varies greatly between species. At the lowest levels of vertebrate visual system there is complete decussation (crossing) of fibers (see Figure Ib, in the paper by Lettvin et al. in this section, p. 308), and at the mammalian level there is always some mixing, the very precise form in which two half-retinas are "represented" in each cerebral hemisphere, shown in figure B, being found only at the highest level. Similarly, within the mammalian group, there is much variation in the precision of the binocular mapping at the l.g.b.s., and also in the number of layers or laminations.

The major sites at which electrophysiological recordings are taken, retina, l.g.b. and cortex, are the places where one "level" of neurons synapses with a higher level. As a matter of fact, this rather precise division into "levels," at least until the cortex is reached, is itself quite remarkable. It is generally assumed that the places where major changes in the form of coded signals *occur are those where one level of neurons interconnect with another, and that the interplay of axonal orborizations and dendritic processes are the structural basis for such "computations". We have already seen several examples, particularly in the paper by Lettvin et al., of this sort of interpretation, and the evidence seems to bear it out very consistently.*

*Hubel and Wiesel's work is distinguished not only by the fact that they pioneered the investigation of sites "higher up" in the system than the retina, but also by the beautiful regularity—even simplicity—of the coding arrangements discovered.*

# Receptive Fields, Binocular Interaction and Functional Architecture in the Cat's Visual Cortex

D. H. HUBEL AND T. N. WIESEL

What chiefly distinguishes cerebral cortex from other parts of the central nervous system is the great diversity of its cell types and interconnexions. It would be astonishing if such a structure did not profoundly modify the response patterns of fibres coming into it. In the cat's visual cortex, the receptive field arrangements of single cells suggest that there is indeed a degree of complexity far exceeding anything yet seen at lower levels in the visual system.

In a previous paper we described receptive fields of single cortical cells, observing responses to spots of light shone on one or both retinas (Hubel & Wiesel, 1959). In the present work this method is used to examine receptive fields of a more complex type (Part I) and to make additional observations on binocular interaction (Part II).

This approach is necessary in order to understand the behaviour of individual cells, but it fails to deal with the problem of the relationship of one cell to its neighbours. In the past, the technique of recording evoked slow waves has been used with great success in studies of functional anatomy. It was employed by Talbot and Marshall (1941) and by Thompson, Woolsey and Talbot (1950) for mapping out the visual cortex in the rabbit, cat, and monkey. Daniel and Whitteridge (1959) have recently extended this work in the primate. Most of our present knowledge of retinotopic projections, binocular overlap, and the second visual area is based on these investigations. Yet the method of evoked potentials is valuable mainly for

Reprinted from *Journal of Physiology*, 1962.

detecting behaviour common to large populations of neighbouring cells; it cannot differentiate functionally between areas of cortex smaller than about 1 $mm^2$. To overcome this difficulty a method has in recent years been developed for studying cells separately or in small groups during long microelectrode penetrations through nervous tissue. Responses are correlated with cell location by reconstructing the electrode tracks from histological material. These techniques have been applied to the somatic sensory cortex of the cat and monkey in a remarkable series of studies by Mountcastle (1957) and Powell and Mountcastle (1959). Their results show that the approach is a powerful one, capable of revealing systems of organization not hinted at by the known morphology. In Part III of the present paper we use this method in studying the functional architecture of the visual cortex. It helped us attempt to explain on anatomical grounds how cortical receptive fields are built up.

## *METHODS*

Recordings were made from forty acutely prepared cats, anaesthetized with thiopental sodium, and maintained in light sleep with additional doses by observing the electrocorticogram. Animals were paralysed with succinylcholine to stabilize the eyes. Pupils were dilated with atropine. Details of stimulating and recording methods are given in previous papers (Hubel, 1959; Hubel & Wiesel, 1959, 1960). The animal faced a wide tangent screen at a distance of 1·5 m, and various patterns of white light were shone on the screen by a tungsten-filament projector. All recordings were made in the light-adapted state. Background illumination varied from $-1{\cdot}0$ to $+1{\cdot}0$ $\log_{10}$ cd/$m^2$. Stimuli were from 0·2 to 2·0 log. units brighter than the background. For each cell receptive fields were mapped out separately for the two eyes on sheets of paper, and these were kept as permanent records.

Points on the screen corresponding to the area centralis and the optic disk of the two eyes were determined by a projection method (Hubel & Wiesel, 1960). The position of each receptive field was measured with respect to these points. Because of the muscle relaxant the eyes usually diverged slightly, so that points corresponding to the two centres of gaze were not necessarily superimposed. In stimulating the two eyes simultaneously it was therefore often necessary to use two spots placed in corresponding parts of the two visual fields. Moreover, at times the two eyes were slightly rotated in an inward direction in the plane of their equators. This rotation was estimated by (1) photographing the cat before and during the experiment, and comparing the angles of inclination of the slit-shaped pupils, or (2) by noting the inclination to the horizontal of a line joining the area centralis with the optic disk, which in the normal position of the eye was estimated, by the first method, to average about 25°. The combined inward rotations of the two eyes seldom exceeded 10°. Since the receptive fields in this study were usually centrally rather than peripherally placed on the retina, the rotations did not lead to any appreciable linear displacement. Angular displacements of receptive fields occasionally required correction, as they led to an apparent difference in the orientation of the two receptive-field axes of a binoculary driven unit. The direction and magnitude of this difference were always consistent with the estimated inward rotation of the two eyes. Moreover, in a given experiment the difference was constant, even though the axis orientation varied from cell to cell.

The diagram of Text-fig. 1 shows the points of entry into the cortex of all 45 microelectrode penetrations. Most electrode tracks went no deeper than 3 or 4 mm, so that explorations were mainly limited to the apical segments of the lateral and post-lateral gyri (LG and PLG) and a few millimetres down along the adjoining medial and lateral folds. The extent of the territory covered is indicated roughly to Text-figs. 13-15. Although the lateral boundary of the striate cortex is not always sharply defined in Nissl-stained or myelin-stained material, most penetrations were well within the region generally accepted as 'striate' (O'Leary, 1941). Most penetrations were made from the cortical region receiving projections from in or near the area centralis; this cortical region is shown in Text-fig. 1 as the area between the interrupted lines.

Tungsten, micro-electrodes were advanced by a hydraulic micro-electrode positioner (Hubel, 1957, 1959). In searching for single cortical units the retina was continually stimulated with stationary and moving forms while the electrode was advanced. The unresolved background activity (see p. 129) served as a guide for determining the optimum stimulus. This procedure increased the number of cells observed in a penetration, since the sampling was not limited to spontaneously active units.

In each penetration electrolytic lesions were made at one or more points. When only one lesion was made, it was generally at the end of an electrode track. Brains were fixed in 10% formalin, embedded in celloidin, sectioned at 20 $\mu$, and stained with cresyl violet. Lesions were 50-100 $\mu$ in diameter, which was small enough to indicate the position of the electrode tip to the nearest cortical layer. The positions of other units encountered in a cortical penetration were determined by calculating the distance back from the lesion along the track, using depth readings corresponding to the unit and the lesion. A correction was made for brain shrinkage, which was estimated by comparing the distance between two lesions, measured under the microscope, with the distance calculated from depths at which the two lesions were made. From brain to brain this shrinkage was not constant, so that it was not possible to apply an average correction for shrinkage to all brains. For tracks marked by only one lesion it was assumed that the first unit activity was recorded at the boundary of the first and second layers; any error resulting from this was probably small, since in a number of penetrations a lesion was made at the point where the first units were encountered, and these were in the lower first or the upper second layers, or else at the very boundary. The absence of cell-body records

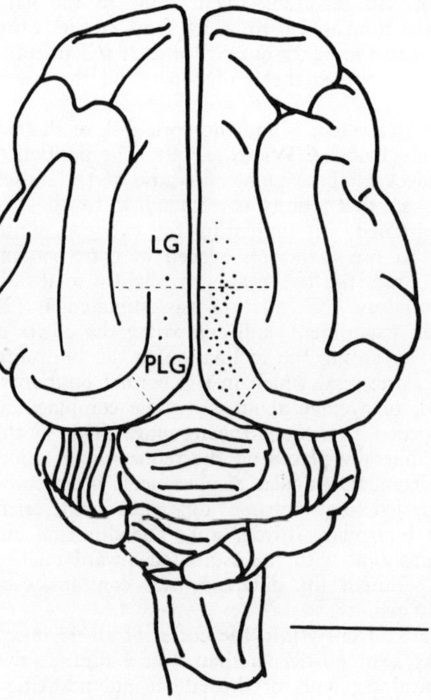


Text-fig. 1. Diagram of dorsal aspect of cat's brain, to show entry points of 45 micro-electrode penetrations. The penetrations between the interrupted lines are those in which cells had their receptive fields in or near area centralis. LG, lateral gyrus; PLG, post-lateral gyrus. Scale, 1 cm.

and unresolved background activity as the electrode passed through subcortical white matter (see Text-fig. 13 and Pl. 1) was also helpful in confirming the accuracy of the track reconstructions.

## Part I
## Organization of Receptive Fields in Cat's Visual Cortex: Properties of 'Simple' and 'Complex' Fields

The receptive field of a cell in the visual system may be defined as the region of retina (or visual field) over which one can influence the firing of that cell. In the cat's retina one can distinguish two types of ganglion cells, those with 'on'-centre receptive fields and those with 'off'-centre fields (Kuffler, 1953). The lateral geniculate body also has cells of these two types; so far no others have been found (Hubel & Wiesel, 1961). In contrast, the visual cortex contains a large number of functionally different cell types; yet with the exception of afferent fibres from the lateral geniculate body we have found no units with concentric 'on'-centre or 'off'-centre fields.

When stimulated with stationary or moving patterns of light, cells in the visual cortex gave responses that could be interpreted in terms of the arrangements of excitatory and inhibitory regions in their receptive fields (Hubel & Wiesel, 1959). Not all cells behaved so simply, however; some responded in a complex manner which bore little obvious relationship to the receptive fields mapped with small spots. It has become increasingly apparent to us that cortical cells differ in the complexity of their receptive fields. The great majority of fields seem to fall naturally into two groups, which we have termed 'simple' and 'complex'. Although the fields to be described represent the commonest subtypes of these groups, new varieties are continually appearing, and it is unlikely that the ones we have listed give anything like a complete picture of the striate cortex. We have therefore avoided a rigid system of classification, and have designated receptive fields by letters or numbers only for convenience in referring to the figures. We shall concentrate especially on features common to simple fields and on those common to complex fields, emphasizing differences between the two groups, and also between cortical fields and lateral geniculate fields.

### *RESULTS*

### Simple Receptive Fields

The receptive fields of 233 of the 303 cortical cells in the present series were classified as 'simple'. Like retinal ganglion and geniculate cells, cortical cells with simple fields possessed distinct excitatory and inhibitory subdivisions. Illumination of part or all of an excitatory region increased the maintained firing of the cell, whereas a light shone in the inhibitory region suppressed the firing and evoked a discharge at 'off'. A large spot confined to either area produced a greater change in rate of firing than a small spot, indicating summation within either region. On the other hand, the two types of region within a receptive field were mutually antagonistic. This was most forcefully shown by the absence or near absence of a response to simultaneous illumination of both regions, for example, with diffuse light. From the arrangement of excitatory and inhibitory regions it was usually possible to predict in a qualitative way the responses to any shape of stimulus, stationary or moving. Spots having the approximate shape of one or other region were the most effective stationary stimuli; smaller spots failed to take full advantage of summation within a region, while larger ones were likely to invade opposing regions, so reducing the response. To summarize: these fields were termed 'simple' because like retinal and geniculate fields (1) they were subdivided into distinct excitatory and inhibitory regions; (2) there was summation within the separate excitatory and inhibitory parts; (3) there was antagonism between excitatory and inhibitory regions; and (4) it was possible to predict responses to stationary or moving spots of various shapes from a map of the excitatory and inhibitory areas.

While simple cortical receptive fields were similar to those of retinal ganglion cells and geniculate cells in possessing excitatory and inhibitory subdivisions, they differed profoundly in the spatial arrangements of these regions. The receptive fields of all retinal ganglion and geniculate cells had one or other of the concentric forms shown in Text-fig. 2*A*, *B*. (Excitatory areas are indicated by crosses, inhibitory areas by triangles.) In contrast, simple cortical fields all had a side-to-side arrangement of excitatory and inhibitory areas with separation of the areas by parallel straight-line boundaries rather than circular ones. There were several varieties of fields, differing in the number of subdivisions and the relative area occupied by each subdivision. The commonest arrangements are illustrated in Text-fig. 2*C-G*: Table 1 gives the number of cells observed in each category. The departure of these fields from circular symmetry introduces a new variable, namely, the orientation of the boundaries separating the field subdivisions. This orientation is a characteristic of each cortical cell, and may be vertical, horizontal, or oblique. There was no indication that any one orientation was more common than the others. We shall use the term *receptive-field axis* to indicate a line through the centre of a field, parallel to the boundaries separating excitatory and inhibitory regions. The *axis orientation* will then refer to the orientation of these boundaries, either on the retina or in the visual field. Axes are shown in Text-fig. 2 by continuous lines.

Two common types of fields, shown in Text-fig. 2*C*, *D*, each consisted of a narrow elongated area, excitatory or inhibitory, flanked on either side by

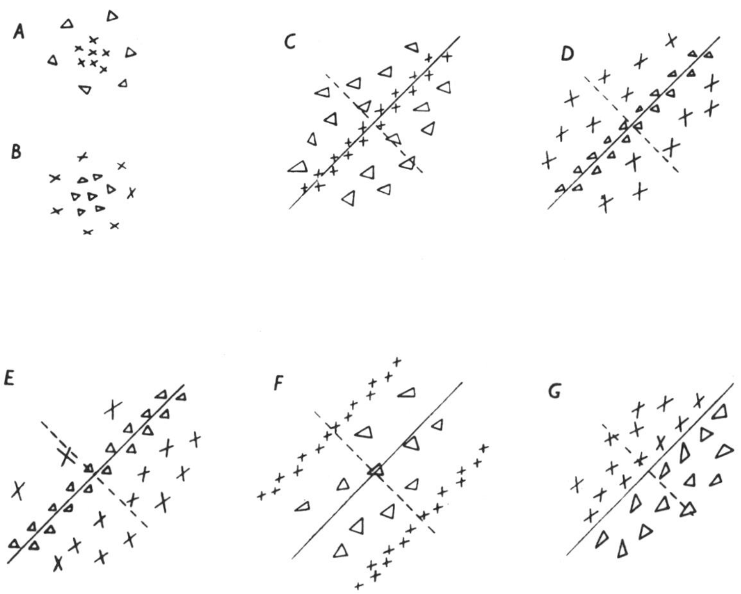


Text-fig. 2. Common arrangements of lateral geniculate and cortical receptive fields. A. 'On'-centre geniculate receptive field. *B.* 'Off'-centre geniculate receptive field. *C–G.* Various arrangements of simple cortical receptive fields. ×, areas giving excitatory responses ('on' responses); △, areas giving inhibitory responses ('off' desponses). Receptive-field axes are shown by continuous lines through field centres; in the figure these are all oblique, but each arrangement occurs in all orientations.

two regions of the opposite type. In these fields the two flanking regions were symmetrical, i.e. they were about equal in area and the responses obtained from them were of about the same magnitude. In addition there were fields with long narrow centres (excitatory or inhibitory) and asymmetrical flanks. An example of an asymmetrical field with an inhibitory centre is shown in Text-fig. 2E. The most effective stationary stimulus for all of these cells was a long narrow rectangle ('slit') of light just large enough to cover the central region without invading either flank. For maximum centre response the orientation of the slit was critical; changing the orientation by more than 5–10° was usually enough to reduce a response greatly or even abolish it. Illuminating both flanks usually evoked a strong response. If a slit having the same size as the receptive-field centre was shone in either flanking area it evoked only a weak response, since it covered only part of one flank. Diffuse light was ineffective, or at most evoked only a very weak response, indicating that the excitatory and inhibitory parts of the receptive field were very nearly balanced.

In these fields the equivalent but opposite-type regions occupied retinal areas that were far from equal; the centre portion was small and concentrated whereas the flanks were widely dispersed. A similar inequality was found in fields of type *F*, Text-fig. 2, but here the excitatory flanks were elongated and concentrated, while the centre was relatively large and diffuse. The optimum response was evoked by simultaneously illuminating the two flanks with two parallel slits (see Hubel & Wiesel, 1959, Fig. 9).

Some cells had fields in which only two regions were discernible, arranged side by side as in Text-fig. 2*G*. For these cells the most efficient stationary stimulus consisted of two areas of differing brightness placed so that the line separating them fell exactly over the boundary between the excitatory and inhibitory parts of the field. This type of stimulus was termed an 'edge'. An 'on' or an 'off' response was evoked depending on whether the bright part of the stimulus fell over the excitatory or the inhibitory region. A slight change in position or orientation of the line separating the light from the dark area was usually enough to reduce greatly the effectiveness of the stimulus.

Moving stimuli were very effective, probably because of the synergistic effects of leaving an inhibitory area and simultaneously entering an excitatory area (Hubel & Wiesel, 1959). The optimum stimulus could usually be predicted from the distribution of excitatory and inhibitory regions of the receptive field. With moving stimuli, just as with stationary, the orientation was critical. In contrast, a slit or edge moved across the circularly symmetric field of a geniculate cell gave (as one would expect) roughly the same response regardless of the stimulus orientation. The responses evoked when an optimally oriented slit crossed back and forth over a cortical receptive field were often roughly equal for the two directions of crossing. This was true of fields like those shown in Text-fig. 2*C*, *D* and *F*. For many cells, however, the responses to two diametrically opposite movements were different, and some only responded to one of the two movements. The inequalities could usually be accounted for by an asymmetry in flanking regions, of the type shown in Text-fig. 2*E* (see also Hubel & Wiesel, 1959, Fig. 7). In fields that had only two discernible regions arranged side by side (Text-fig. 2*G*), the difference in the responses to a moving slit or edge was especially pronounced.

Optimum rates of movement varied from one cell to another. On several occasions two cells were recorded together, one of which responded only to a slow-moving stimulus (1°/sec or lower) the other to a rapid one (10°/sec or more). For cells with fields of type *F*, Text-fig. 2, the time elapsing between the two discharges to a moving stimulus was a measure of the rate of movement (see Hubel & Wiesel, 1959, Fig. 5).

If responses to movement were predictable from arrangements of excitatory and inhibitory regions, the reverse was to some extent also true. The axis orientation of a field, for example, was given by the most effective orientation of a moving slit or edge. If an optimally oriented slit produced a brief discharge on crossing from one region to another, one could predict that the first region was inhibitory and the second excitatory. Brief re-

TABLE 1
SIMPLE CORTICAL FIELDS

| | *Text-fig.* | *No. of Cells* |
|---|---|---|
| (*a*) Narrow concentrated centres | | |
| (i) Symmetrical flanks | | |
| Excitatory centres | 2*C* | 23 |
| Inhibitory centres | 2*D* | 17 |
| (ii) Asymmetrical flanks | | |
| Excitatory centres | — | 28 |
| Inhibitory centres | 2*E* | 10 |
| (*b*) Large centres; concentrated flanks | 2*F* | 21 |
| (*c*) One excitatory region and one inhibitory | 2G | 17 |
| (*d*) Uncategorized | — | 117 |
| Total number of simple fields | | 233 |

sponses to crossing a very confined region were characteristic of cells with simple cortical fields, whereas the complex cells to be described below gave sustained responses to movement over much wider areas.

Movement was used extensively as a stimulus in experiments in which the main object was to determine axis orientation and ocular dominance for a large number of cells in a single penetration, and when it was not practical, because of time limitations, to map out every field completely. Because movement was generally a very powerful stimulus, it was also used in studying cells that gave little or no response to stationary patterns. In all, 117 of the 233 simple cells were studied mainly by moving stimuli. In Table 1 these have been kept separate from the other groups since the distribution of their excitatory and inhibitory regions is not known with the same degree of certainty. It is also possible that with further study, some of these fields would have revealed complex properties.

## Complex Receptive Fields

Intermixed with cells having simple fields, and present in most penetrations of the striate cortex, were cells with far more intricate and elaborate properties. The receptive fields of these cells were termed 'complex.' Unlike cells with simple fields, these responded to variously-shaped stationary or moving forms in a way that could not be predicted from maps made with small circular spots. Often such maps could not be made, since small round spots were either ineffective or evoked only mixed ('on-off') responses throughout the receptive field. When separate 'on' and 'off' regions could be discerned, the principles of summation and mutual antagonism, so helpful in interpreting simple fields, did not generally hold. Nevertheless, there were some

TABLE 2

COMPLEX CORTICAL RECEPTIVE FIELDS

| | *Text-fig.* | *No. of Cells* |
|---|---|---|
| (*a*) Activated by slit—non-uniform field | 3 | 11 |
| (*b*) Activated by slit—uniform field | 4 | 39 |
| (*c*) Activated by edge | 5-6 | 14 |
| (*d*) Activated by dark bar | 7-8 | 6 |
| Total number of complex fields | | 70 |

important features common to the two types of cells. In the following examples, four types of complex fields will be illustrated. The numbers observed of each type are given in Table 2.

The cell of Text-fig. 3 failed to respond to round spots of light, whether small or large. By trial and error with many shapes of stimulus it was discovered that the cell's firing could be influenced by a horizontally oriented slit ⅛° wide and 3° long. Provided the slit was horizontal its exact positioning within the 3°-diameter receptive field was not critical. When it was shone anywhere above the centre of the receptive field (the horizontal line of Text-fig. 3) an 'off' response was obtained; 'on' responses were evoked throughout the lower half. In an intermediate position (Text-fig. 3C) the cell responded at both 'on' and 'off'. From experience with simpler receptive fields one might have expected wider slits to give increasingly better responses owing to summation within the upper or lower part of the field, and that illumination of either half by itself might be the most effective stimulus of all. The result was just the opposite: responses fell off rapidly as the stimulus was widened beyond about ⅛°, and large rectangles covering the entire lower or upper halves of the receptive field were quite ineffective (Text-fig. 3*F*, G). On the other hand, summation could easily be demonstrated in a horizontal direction, since a slit ⅛° wide but extending only across part of the field was less effective than a longer one covering the entire width. One might also have expected the orientation of the slit to be unimportant as long as the stimulus was wholly confined to the region above the horizontal line or the region below. On the contrary, the orientation was critical, since a tilt of even a few degrees from the horizontal markedly reduced the response, even though the slit did not cross the boundary separating the upper and lower halves of the field.

In preferring a slit specific in width and orientation this cell resembled certain cells with simple fields. When stimulated in the upper part of its field it behaved in many respects like cells with 'off'-centre fields of type *D*, Text-fig. 2; in the lower part it responded like 'on'-centre fields of Text-fig. 2*C*. But for this cell the strict requirements for shape and orientation of the stimulus were in marked contrast to the relatively large leeway of the

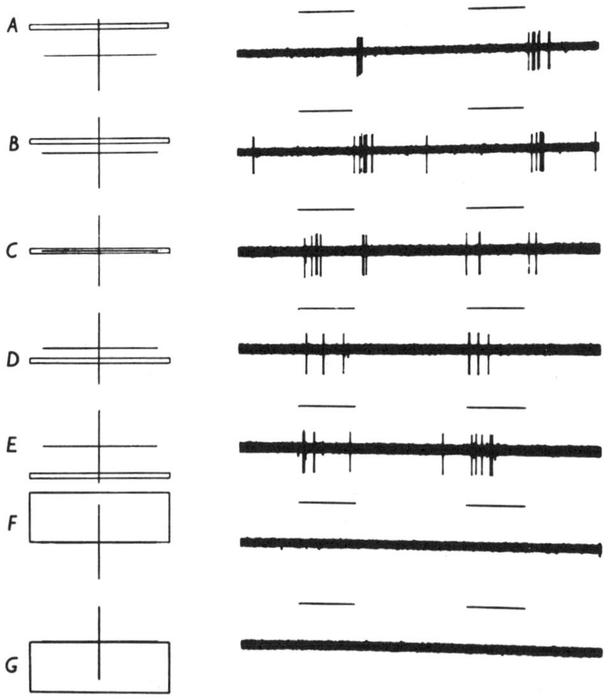


Text-fig. 3. Responses of a cell with a complex receptive field to stimulation of the left (contralateral) eye. Receptive field located in area centralis. The diagrams to the left of each record indicate the position of a horizontal rectangular light stimulus with respect to the receptive field, marked by a cross. In each record the upper line indicates when the stimulus is on. *A–E*, stimulus ⅛ × 3°, *F–G*, stimulus 1½ × 3° (4° is equivalent to 1 mm on the cat retina). For background illumination and stimulus intensity see Methods. Cell was activated in the same way from right eye, but less vigorously (ocular-dominance group 2, see Part II). An electrolytic lesion made while recording from this cell was found near the border of layers 5 and 6, in the apical segment of the post-lateral gyrus. Positive deflexions upward; duration of each stimulus 1 sec.

stimulus in its ordinate position on the retina. Cells with simple fields, on the other hand, showed very little latitude in the positioning of an optimally oriented stimulus.

The upper part of this receptive field may be considered inhibitory and the lower part excitatory, even though in either area summation only occurred in a horizontal direction. Such subdivisions were occasionally found in complex fields, but more often the fields were uniform in this respect. This was true for the other complex fields to be described in this section.

Responses of a second complex unit are shown in Text-fig. 4. In many ways the receptive field of this cell was similar to the one just described. A slit was the most potent stimulus, and the most effective width was again ⅛°. Once more the orientation was an important stimulus variable,

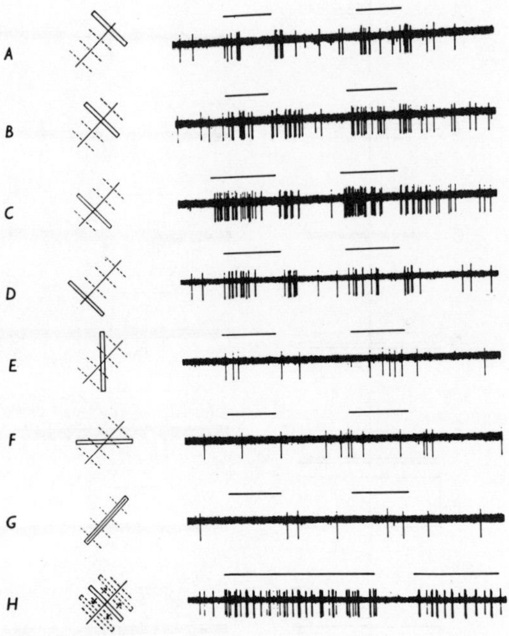


Text-fig. 4. Responses of a cell with a complex field to stimulation of the left (contralateral) eye with a slit ⅛ × 2½°. Receptive field was in the area centralis and was about 2 × 3° in size. *A–D*, ⅛° wide slit oriented parallel to receptive field axis. *E–G*, slit oriented at 45 and 90° to receptive-field axis. *H*, slit oriented as in *A–D*, is on throughout the record and is moved rapidly from side to side where indicated by upper beam. Responses from left eye slightly more marked than those from right (Group 3, see Part II). Time 1 sec.

since the slit was effective anywhere in the field as long as it was placed in a 10 o'clock–4 o'clock orientation (Text-fig. 4A–*D*). A change in orientation of more than 5–10° in either direction produced a marked reduction in the response (Text-fig. 4*E–G*). As usual, diffuse light had no influence on the firing. This cell responded especially well if the slit, oriented as in *A–D*, was moved steadily across the receptive field. Sustained discharges were evoked over the entire length of the field. The optimum rate of movement was about 1°/sec. If movement was interrupted the discharge stopped, and when it was resumed the firing recommenced. Continuous firing could be maintained indefinitely by small side-to-side movements of a stimulus within the receptive field (Text-fig. 4*H*). The pattern of firing was one characteristic of many complex cells, especially those responding well to moving stimuli. It consisted of a series of short high-frequency repetitive discharges each containing 5–10 spikes. The bursts occurred at irregular intervals, at frequencies up to about 20/sec. For this cell, movement of an optimally oriented slit was about equally effective in either of the two opposite directions. This was not true of all complex units, as will be seen in some of the examples given below.

Like the cell of Text-fig. 3 this cell may be thought of as having a counterpart in simple fields of the type shown in Text-fig. 2*C–E*. It shares with these simpler fields the attribute of responding well to properly oriented slit stimuli. Once more the distinction lies in the permissible variation in position of the optimally oriented stimulus. The variation is small (relative to the size of the receptive field) in the simple fields, large in the complex. Though resembling the cell of Text-fig. 3 in requiring a slit for a stimulus, this cell differed in that its responses to a properly oriented slit were mixed ('on-off') in type. This was not unusual for cells with complex fields. In contrast, cortical cells with simple fields, like retinal ganglion cells and lateral geniculate cells, responded to optimum restricted stimuli either with excitatory ('on') responses or inhibitory ('off') responses. When a

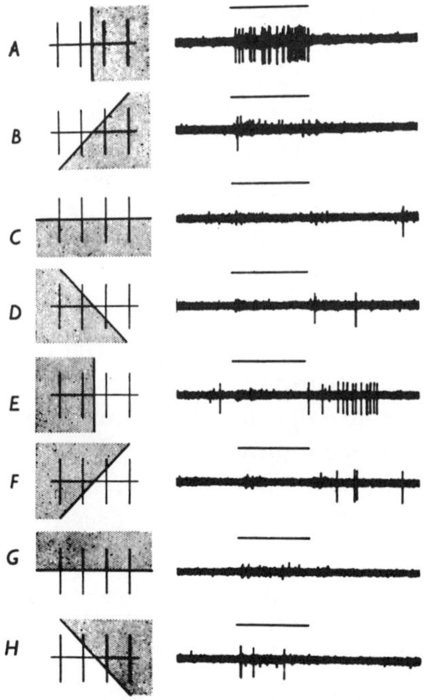


Text-fig. 5. Responses of a cell with a large (8 × 16°) complex receptive field to an edge projected on the ipsilateral retina so as to cross the receptive field in various directions. (The screen is illuminated by a diffuse background light, at 0·0 $\log_{10}$ cd/m$^2$. At the time of stimulus, shown by upper line of each record, half the screen, to one side of the variable boundary, is illuminated at 1·0 $\log_{10}$ cd/m$^2$, while the other half is kept constant.) *A*, vertical edge with light area to left, darker area to right. *B–H*, various other orientations of edge. Position of receptive field 20° below and to the left of the area centralis. Responses from ipsilateral eye stronger than those from contralateral eye (group 5, see Part II). Time 1 sec.

stimulus covered opposing regions, the effects normally tended to cancel, though sometimes mixed discharges were obtained, the 'on' and 'off' components both being weak. For these simpler fields 'on-off' responses were thus an indication that the stimulus was not optimum. Yet some cells with complex fields responded with mixed discharges even to the most effective stationary stimuli we could find. Among the stimuli tried were curved objects, dark stripes, and still more complicated patterns, as well as monochromatic spots and slits.

A third type of complex field is illustrated in Text-figs. 5 and 6. There were no responses to small circular spots or to slits, but an edge was very effective if oriented vertically. Excitatory or inhibitory responses were produced depending on whether the brighter area was to the left or the right (Text-fig. 5A, *E*). So far, these are just the responses one would expect from a cell with a vertically oriented simple field of the type shown in Text-fig. 2G. In such a field the stimulus placement for optimum response is generally very critical. On the contrary, the complex unit responded to vertical edges over an unusually large region about 16° in length (Text-fig. 6). 'On' responses were obtained with light to the left (*A–D*), and 'off' responses with light to the right (*E–H*), regardless of the position of the line separating light from darkness. When the entire receptive field was illuminated diffusely (*I*) no response was evoked. As with all complex fields, we are unable to account for these responses by any simple spatial arrangement of excitatory and inhibitory regions.

Like the complex units already described, this cell was apparently more concerned with the orientation of a stimulus than with its exact position in the receptive field. It differed in responding well to edges but poorly or not at all to slits, whether narrow or wide. It is interesting in this connexion that exchanging an edge for its mirror equivalent reversed the response, i.e. replaced an excitatory response by an inhibitory and vice versa. The ineffectiveness of a slit might therefore be explained by supposing that the opposite effects of its two edges tended to cancel each other.

As shown in Text-fig. 6, the responses of the cell to a given vertical edge were consistent in type, being either 'on' or 'off' for all positions of the edge within the receptive field. In being uniform in its response-type it resembled the cell of Text-fig. 4. A few other cells of the same general category showed a similar preference for edges, but lacked this uniformity. Their receptive fields resembled the field of Text-fig. 3, in that a given edge evoked responses of one type over half the field, and the opposite type over the other half. These fields were divided into two halves by a line parallel to the receptive-field axis: an edge oriented parallel to the axis gave 'on' responses throughout one of the halves and 'off' responses through the other. In either half, replacing the edge by its mirror image reversed the response-type. Even cells, which were uniform in their response-types,

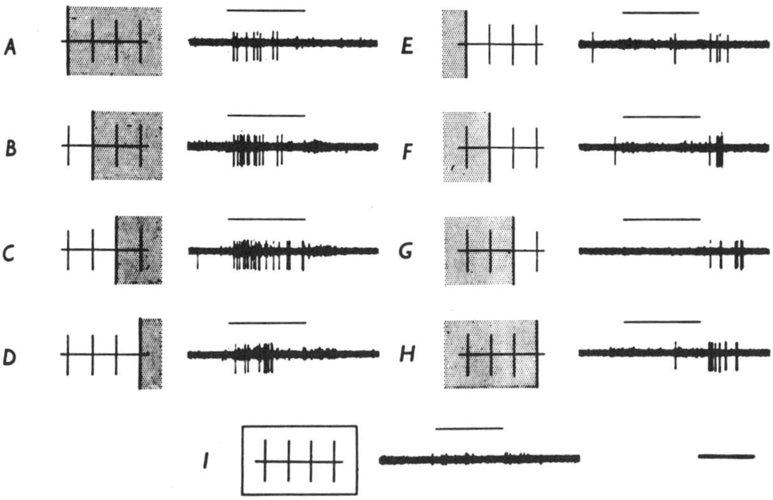


Text-fig. 6. Same cell as in Text-fig. 5. *A–H*, responses to a vertical edge in various parts of the receptive field: *A–D*, brighter light to the left; *E–H*, brighter light to the right; *I*, large rectangle, 10 × 20°, covering entire receptive field. Time, 1 sec.

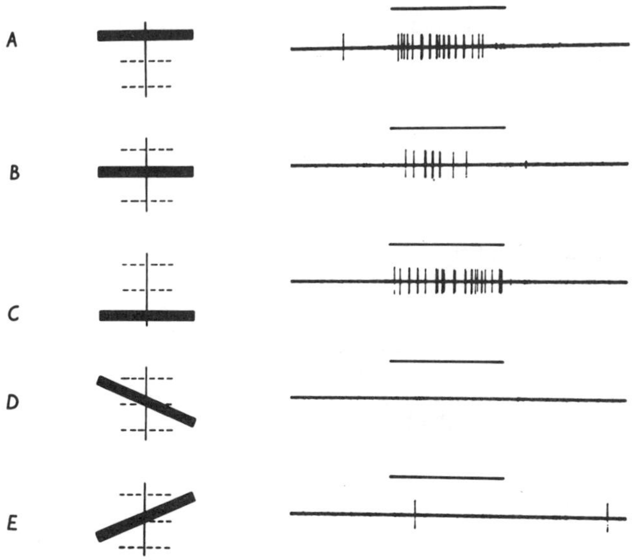


Text-fig. 7. Cell activated only by left (contralateral) eye over a field approximately 5 × 5°, situated 10° above and to the left of the area centralis. The cell responded best to a black horizontal rectangle ⅓ × 6°, placed anywhere in the receptive field (*A–C*). Tilting the stimulus rendered it ineffective (*D–E*). The black bar was introduced against a light background during periods of 1 sec, indicated by the upper line in each record. Luminance of white background, 1·0 $\log_{10}$ cd/m$^2$; luminance of black part, 0·0 $\log_{10}$ cd/m$^2$. A lesion, made while recording from the cell, was found in layer 2 of apical segment of post-lateral gyrus.

like those in Text-fig. 4–6, varied to some extent in the magnitude of their responses, depending on the position of the stimulus. Moreover, as with most cortical cells, there was some variation in responses to identical stimuli.

A final example is given to illustrate the wide range of variation in the organization of complex receptive fields. The cell of Text-figs. 7 and 8 was not strongly influenced by any form projected upon the screen; it gave only weak, unsustained 'on' responses to a dark horizontal rectangle against a light background, and to other forms it was unresponsive. A strong discharge was evoked, however, if a black rectangular object (for example, a piece of black tape) was placed against the brightly illuminated screen. The receptive field of the cell was about 5 × 5°, and the most effective stimulus width was about ⅓°. Vigorous firing was obtained regardless of the rectangle, as long as it was horizontal and within the receptive field. If it was tipped more than 10° in either direction no discharge was evoked (Text-fig. 7*D*, *E*). We have recorded several complex fields which resembled this one in that they responded best to black rectangles against a bright background. Presumably it is important to have good contrast between the narrow black rectangle and the background; this is technically difficult with a projector because of scattered light.

Slow downward movement of the dark rectangle evoked a strong discharge throughout the entire 5° of the receptive field (Text-fig. 8*A*). If the movement was halted the cell continued to fire, but less vigorously. Upward movement gave only weak, inconsistent responses, and left–right movement (Text-fig. 8*B*) gave no responses. Discharges of highest frequency were evoked by relatively slow rates of downward movement (about 5–10 sec to cross the entire field); rapid movement in either direction gave only very weak responses.

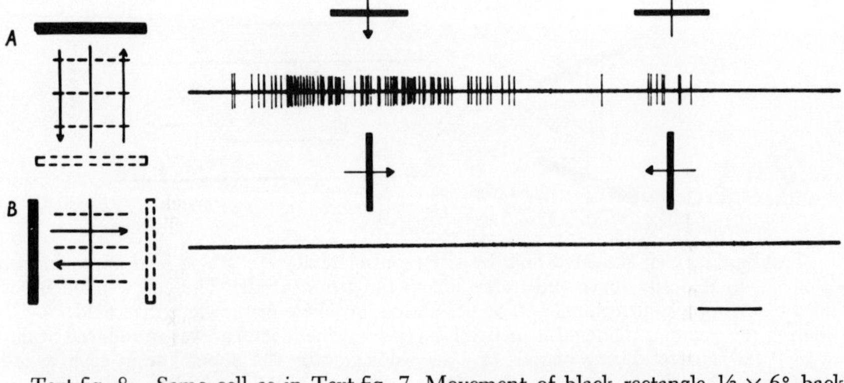


Text-fig. 8. Same cell as in Text-fig. 7. Movement of black rectangle ⅓ × 6° back and forth across the receptive field: *A*, horizontally oriented (parallel to receptive-field axis); *B*, vertically oriented. Time required to move across the field, 5 sec. Time, 1 sec.

Despite its unusual features this cell exhibited several properties typical of complex units, particularly the lack of summation (except in a horizontal sense), and the wide area over which the dark bar was effective. One may think of the field as having a counterpart in simple fields of type *D*, Text-fig. 2. In such fields a dark bar would evoke discharges, but only if it fell within the inhibitory region. Moreover, downward movement of the bar would also evoke brisker discharges than upward, provided the upper flanking region were stronger than the lower one.

In describing simple fields it has already been noted that moving stimuli were often more effective than stationary ones. This was also true of cells with complex fields. Depending on the cell, slits, edges, or dark bars were most effective. As with simple fields, orientation of a stimulus was always critical, responses varied with rate of movement, and directional asymmetries of the type seen in Text-fig. 8 were common. Only once have we seen activation of a cell for one direction of movement and suppression of maintained firing for the opposite direction. In their responses to movement, cells with complex fields differed from their simple counterparts chiefly in responding with sustained firing over substantial regions, usually the entire receptive field, instead of over a very narrow boundary separating excitatory and inhibitory regions.

## Receptive-Field Dimensions

Over-all field dimensions were measured for 119 cells. A cell was included only if its field was mapped completely, and if it was situated in the area of central vision (see p. 135). Fields varied greatly in size from one cell to the next, even for cells recorded in a single penetration (see Text-fig. 15). In Text-fig. 9 the distribution of cells according to field area is given separately for simple and complex fields. The histogram illustrates the variation in size, and shows that on the average complex fields were larger than simple ones.

Widths of the narrow subdivisions of simple fields (the centres of types *C*, *D* and *E* or the flanks of type *F*, Text-fig. 2) also varied greatly: the smallest were 10–15 minutes of arc, which is roughly the diameter of the smallest field centres we have found for geniculate cells. For some cells with complex fields the widths of the most effective slits or dark bars were also of this order, indicating that despite the greater overall field size these cells were able to convey detailed information. We wish to emphasize that in both geniculate and cortex the field dimensions tend to increase with distance from the area centralis, and that they differ even for a given location in the retina. It is consequently not possible to compare field sizes in the geniculate and cortex unless these variations are taken into account. This may explain the discrepancy between our results and the findings of

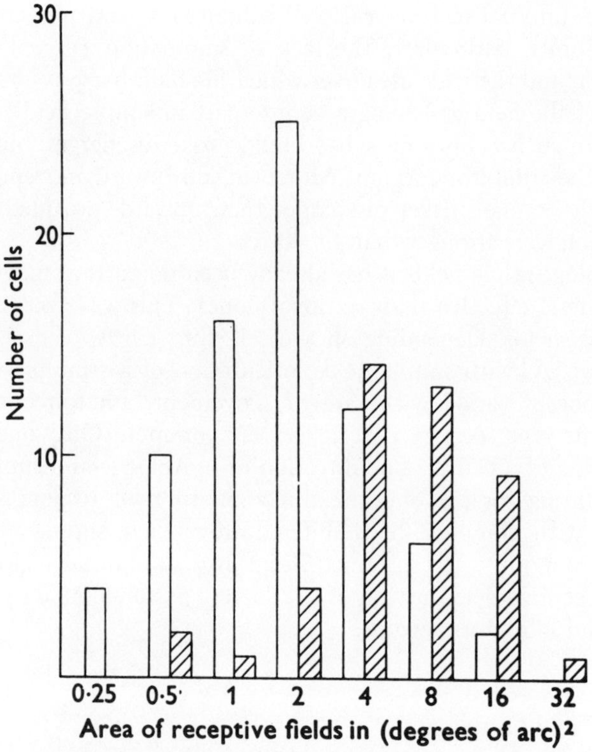


Text-fig. 9. Distribution of 119 cells in the visual cortex with respect to the approximate area of their receptive fields. White columns indicate cells with simple receptive fields; shaded columns, cells with complex fields. Abscissa: area of receptive fields. Ordinate: number of cells.

Baumgartner (see Jung, 1960), that 'field centres' in the cortex are one half the size of those in the lateral geniculate body.

## Responsiveness of Cortical Cells

Simple and complex fields together account for all of the cells we have recorded in the visual cortex. We have not observed cells with concentric fields. Except for clearly injured cells (showing extreme spike deformation or prolonged high-frequency bursts of impulses) all units have responded to visual stimulation, though it has occasionally taken several hours to find the retinal region containing the receptive field and to work out the optimum stimuli. Some cells responded only to stimuli which were optimum in their retinal position and in their form, orientation and rate of movement. A few even required stimulation of both eyes before a response could be elicited (see Part II). But there is no indication from our studies that the striate cortex contains nerve cells that are unresponsive to visual stimuli.

Most of the cells of this series were observed for 1 or 2 hr, and some were studied for up to 9 hr. Over these periods of time there were no qualitative changes in the characteristics of receptive fields: their complexity, arrangements of excitatory and inhibitory areas, axis orientation and position all remained the same, as did the ocular dominance. With deepening anaesthesia a cell became less responsive, so that stimuli that had formerly been weak tended to become even weaker or ineffective, while those that had evoked brisk responses now evoked only weak ones. The last thing to disappear with very deep anaesthesia was usually the response to a moving form. As long as any responses remained the cell retained the same specific requirements as to stimulus form, orientation and rate of movement, suggesting that however the drug exerted its effects, it did not to any important extent functionally disrupt the specific visual connexions. A comparison of visual responses in the anaesthetized animal with those in the unanaesthetized, unrestrained preparation (Hubel, 1959) shows that the main differences lie in the frequency and firing patterns of the maintained activity and in the vigour of responses, rather than in the basic receptive-field organization. It should be emphasized, however, that even in light anaesthesia or in the attentive state diffuse light remains relatively ineffective; thus the balance between excitatory and inhibitory influences is apparently maintained in the waking state.

## Part II
## Binocular Interaction and Ocular Dominance

Recording from single cells at various levels in the visual system offers a direct means of determining the site of convergence of impulses from the two eyes. In the lateral geniculate body, the first point at which convergence is at all likely, binocularly influenced cells have been observed, but it would seem that these constitute at most a small minority of the total population of geniculate cells (Erulkar & Fillenz, 1958, 1960; Bishop, Burke & Davis, 1959; Grüsser & Sauer, 1960; Hubel & Wiesel, 1961). Silver-degeneration studies show that in each layer of the geniculate the terminals of fibres from a single eye are grouped together, with only minor overlap in the interlaminar regions (Silva, 1956; Hayhow, 1958). The anatomical and physiological findings are thus in good agreement.

It has long been recognized that the greater part of the cat's primary visual cortex receives projections from the two eyes. The anatomical evidence rests largely on the observation that cells in all three lateral geniculate layers degenerate following a localized lesion in the striate area (Minkowski, 1913). Physiological confirmation was obtained by Talbot & Marshall (1941) who stimulated the visual fields of the separate eyes with small spots of light, and mapped the evoked cortical slow waves. Still unsettled, however, was the question of whether individual cortical cells receive projections from both eyes, or whether the cortex contains a mixture of cells, some activated by one eye, some by the other. We have recently shown that many cells in the visual cortex can be influenced by both eyes (Hubel & Wiesel, 1959). The present section contains further observations on binocular interaction. We have been particularly interested in learning whether the eyes work in synergy or in opposition, how the relative influence of the two eyes varies from cell to cell, and whether, on the average, one eyes exerts more influence than the other on the cells of a given hemisphere.

## *RESULTS*

In agreement with previous findings (Hubel & Wiesel, 1959) the receptive fields of all binocularly influenced cortical cells occupied corresponding positions on the two retinas, and were strikingly similar in their organization. For simple fields the spatial arrangements of excitatory and inhibitory regions were the same; for complex fields the stimuli that excited or inhibited the cell through one eye had similar effects through the other. Axis orientations of the two receptive fields were the same. Indeed, the only dif-

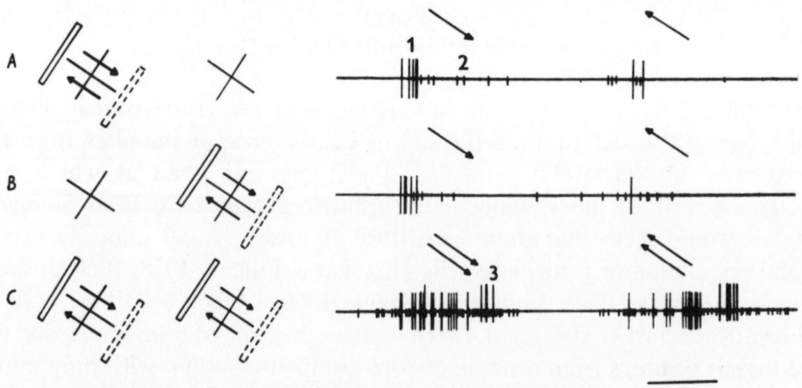


Text-fig. 10. Examples of binocular synergy in a simultaneous recording of three cells (spikes of the three cells are labelled 1–3). Each of the cells had receptive fields in the two eyes; in each eye the three fields overlapped and were situated 2° below and to the left of the area centralis. The crosses to the left of each record indicate the positions of the receptive fields in the two eyes. The stimulus was ⅛ × 2° slit oriented obliquely and moved slowly across the receptive fields as shown; *A*, in the left eye; *B*, in the right eye; *C*, in the two eyes simultaneously. Since the responses in the two eyes were about equally strong, these two cells were classed in ocular-dominance group 4 (see Text-fig. 12). Time, 1 sec.

ferences ever seen between the two fields were related to eye dominance: identical stimuli to the two eyes did not necessarily evoke equally strong responses from a given cell. For some cells the responses were equal or almost so; for others one eye tended to dominate. Whenever the two retinas were stimulated in identical fashion in corresponding regions, their effects summed, i.e. they worked in synergy. On the other hand, if antagonistic regions in the two eyes were stimulated so that one eye had an excitatory effect and the other an inhibitory one, then the responses tended to cancel (Hubel & Wiesel, 1959, Fig. 10A).

Some units did not respond to stimulation of either eye alone but could be activated only by simultaneous stimulation of the two eyes. Text-figure 10 shows an example of this, and also illustrates ordinary binocular synergy. Two simultaneously recorded cells both responded best to transverse movement of a rectangle oriented in a 1 o'clock–7 o'clock direction (Text-fig. 10A, B). For one of the cells movement down and to the right was more effective than movement up and to the left. Responses from the individual eyes were roughly equal. On simultaneous stimulation of the two eyes both units responded much more vigorously. Now a third cell was also activated. The threshold of this third unit was apparently so high that, at least under these experimental conditions, stimulation of either eye alone failed to evoke any response.

A second example of synergy is seen in Text-fig. 11. The most effective stimulus was a vertically oriented rectangle moved across the receptive

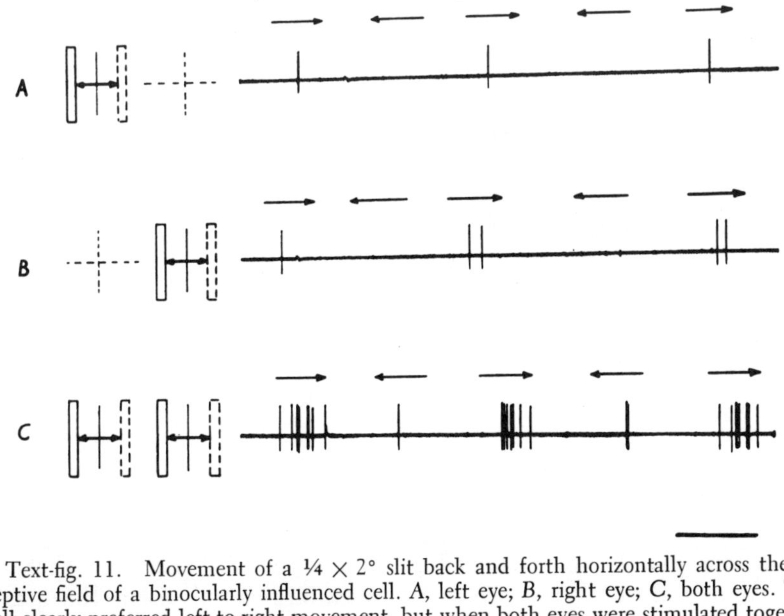


Text-fig. 11. Movement of a ¼ × 2° slit back and forth horizontally across the receptive field of a binocularly influenced cell. *A*, left eye; *B*, right eye; *C*, both eyes. The cell clearly preferred left-to-right movement, but when both eyes were stimulated together it responded also to the reverse direction. Field diameter, 2°, situated 5° from the area centralis. Time, 1 sec.

field from left to right. Here the use of both eyes not only enhanced the response already observed with a single eye, but brought into the open a tendency that was formerly unsuspected. Each eye mediated a weak response (Text-fig. 11*A*, *B*) which was greatly strengthened when both eyes were used in parallel (*C*). Now, in addition, the cell gave a weak response to leftward movement, indicating that this had an excitatory effect rather than an inhibitory one. Binocular synergy was often a useful means of bringing out additional information about a receptive field.

In our previous study of forty-five cortical cells (Hubel & Wiesel, 1959) there was clear evidence of convergence of influences from the two eyes in only one fifth of the cells. In the present series 84% of the cells fell into this category. The difference is undoubtedly related to the improved precision in technique of binocular stimulation. A field was first mapped in the dominant eye and the most effective type of stimulus determined. That stimulus was then applied in the corresponding region in the other eye. Finally, even if no response was obtained from the non-dominant eye, the two eyes were stimulated together in parallel to see if their effects were synergistic. With these methods, an influence was frequently observed from the non-dominant eye that might otherwise have been overlooked.

A comparison of the influence of the two eyes was made for 223 of the 303 cells in the present series. The remaining cells were either not sufficiently studied, or they belonged to the small group of cells which were only activated if both eyes were simultaneously stimulated. The fields of all cells were in or near the area centralis. The 223 cells were subdivided into seven groups, as follows:

| Group | Ocular dominance |
|---|---|
| 1 | Exclusively contralateral |
| 2* | Contralateral eye much more effective than ipsilateral eye |
| 3 | Contralateral eye slightly more effective than ipsilateral |
| 4 | No obvious difference in the effects exerted by the two eyes |
| 5 | Ipsilateral eye slightly more effective |
| 6* | Ipsilateral eye much more effective |
| 7 | Exclusively ipsilateral |

* These groups include cells in which the non-dominant eye, ineffective by itself, could influence the response to stimulation of the dominant eye.

A histogram showing the distribution of cells among these seven groups is given in Text-fig. 12. Assignment of a unit to a particular group was to some extent arbitrary, but it is unlikely that many cells were misplaced by more than one group. Perhaps the most interesting feature of the histogram is its lack of symmetry: many more cells were dominated by the contralateral than by the ipsilateral eye (106 vs. 62). We conclude that in the part of the cat's striate cortex representing central vision the great majority of cells are influenced by both eyes, and that despite wide variation in relative ocular dominance from one cell to the next, the contra-

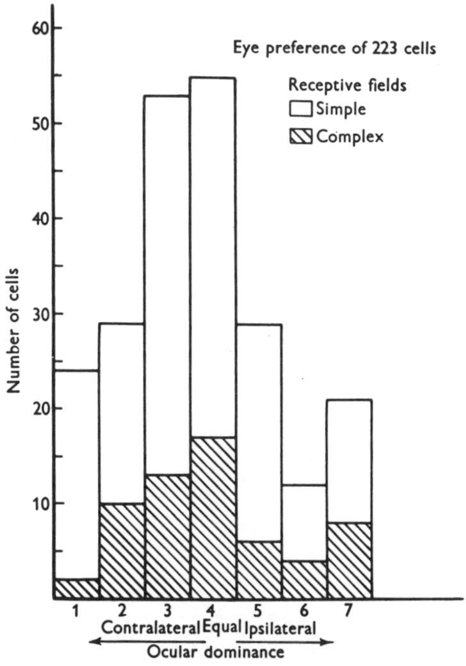


Text-fig. 12. Distribution of 223 cells recorded from the visual cortex, according to ocular dominance. Histogram includes cells with simple fields and cells with complex fields. The shaded region shows the distribution of cells with complex receptive fields. Cells of group 1 were driven only by the contralateral eye; for cells of group 2 there was marked dominance of the contralateral eye, for group 3, slight dominance. For cells in group 4 there was no obvious difference between the two eyes. In group 5 the ipsilateral eye dominated slightly, in group 6, markedly; and in group 7 the cells were driven only by the ipsilateral eye.

lateral eye is, on the average, more influential. As the shaded portion of Text-fig. 12 shows, there is no indication that the distribution among the various dominance groups of cells having complex receptive fields differs from the distribution of the population as a whole.

A cortical bias in favour of the contralateral eye may perhaps be related to the preponderance of crossed over uncrossed fibres in the cat's optic tract (Polyak, 1957, p. 788). The numerical inequality between crossed and uncrossed tract fibres is generally thought to be related to an inequality in size of the nasal and temporal half-fields, since both inequalities are most marked in lower mammals with laterally placed eyes, and become progressively less important in higher mammals, primates and man. Thompson *et al.* (1950) showed that in the rabbit, for example, there is a substantial cortical region receiving projections from that part of the peripheral contralateral visual field which is not represented in the ipsilateral retina (the 'Temporal Crescent'). Our results, concerned with more central portions of the visual fields, suggest that in the cat the difference in the number of crossed and uncrossed fibres in an optic tract is probably not accounted for entirely by fibres having their receptive fields in the temporal-field crescents.

## Part III
## Functional Cytoarchitecture of the Cat's Visual Cortex

In the first two parts of this paper cells were studied individually, no attention being paid to their grouping within the cortex. We have shown that the number of functional cell types is very large, since cells may differ in several independent physiological characteristics, for example, in the retinal position of their receptive fields, their receptive-field organization, their axis orientation, and their ocular-dominance group. In this section we shall try to determine whether cells are scattered at random through the cortex with regard to these characteristics, or whether there is any tendency for one or more of the characteristics to be shared by neighbouring cells. The functional architecture of the cortex not only seems interesting for its own sake, but also helps to account for the various complex response patterns described in Part I.

### *RESULTS*

Functional architecture of the cortex was studied by three methods. These had different merits and limitations, and were to some extent complementary.

(1) *Cells Recorded in Sequence.* The most useful and convenient procedure was to gather as much information as possible about each of a long succession of cells encountered in a micro-electrode penetration through the cortex, and to reconstruct the electrode track from serial histological sections. One could then determine how a physiological characteristic (such as receptive-field position, organization, axis orientation or ocular dominance) varied with cortical location. The success of this method in delineating regions of constant physiological characteristics depends on the possibility of examining a number of units as the electrode passes through each region. Regions may escape detection if they are so small that the electrode is able to resolve only one or two cells in each. The fewer the cells resolved, the larger the regions must be in order to be detected at all.

(2) *Unresolved Background Activity.* To some extent the spaces between

isolated units were bridged by studying unresolved background activity audible over the monitor as a crackling noise, and assumed to originate largely from action potentials of a number of cells. It was concluded that cells, rather than fibres, gave rise to this activity, since it ceased abruptly when the electrode left the grey matter and entered subcortical white matter. Furthermore, diffuse light evoked no change in activity, compared to the marked increase caused by an optimally oriented slit. This suggested that terminal arborizations of afferent fibres contributed little to the background, since most geniculate cells respond actively to diffuse light (Hubel, 1960). In most penetrations unresolved background activity was present continuously as the electrode passed through layers 2–6 of the cortical grey matter.

Background activity had many uses. It indicated when the cells within range of the electrode tip had a common receptive-field axis orientation. Similarly, one could use it to tell whether the cells in the neighbourhood were driven exclusively by one eye (group 1 or group 7). When the background activity was influenced by both eyes, one could not distinguish between a mixture of cells belonging to the two monocular groups (1 and 7) and a population in which each cell was driven from both eyes. But even here one could at least assess the relative influence of the two eyes upon the group of cells in the immediate neighbourhood of the electrode.

(3) *Multiple Recordings.* In the series of 303 cells, 78 were recorded in groups of two and 12 in groups of three. Records were not regarded as multiple unless the spikes of the different cells showed distinct differences in amplitude, and unless each unit fulfilled the criteria required of a single-unit record, namely that the amplitude and wave shape be relatively constant for a given electrode position.

In such multiple recordings one could be confident that the cells were close neighbours and that uniform stimulus conditions prevailed, since the cells could be stimulated and observed together. One thus avoided some of the difficulties in evaluating a succession of recordings made over a long period of time span, where absolute constancy of eye position, anaesthetic level, and preparation condition were sometimes hard to guarantee.

Regional variations of several physiological characteristics were examined by the three methods just outlined. Of particular interest for the present study were the receptive-field axis orientation, position of receptive fields on the retina, receptive-field organization, and relative ocular dominance. These will be described separately in the following paragraphs.

## Orientation of Receptive-Field Axis

The orientation of a receptive-field axis was determined in several ways. When the field was simple the borders between excitatory and inhibitory regions were sufficient to establish the axis directly. For both simple and complex fields the axis could always be determined from the orientation of the most effective stimulus. For most fields, when the slit or edge was placed at right angles to the optimum position there was no response. The receptive-field axis orientation was checked by varying the stimulus orientation from this null position in order to find the two orientations at which a response was only just elicited, and by bisecting the angle between them. By one or other of these procedures the receptive-field orientation could usually be determined to within 5 or 10°.

One of the first indications that the orientation of a receptive-field axis was an important variable came from multiple recordings. Invariably the axes of receptive fields mapped together had the same orientations. An example of a 3-unit recording has already been given in Text-fig. 10. Cells with common axis orientation were therefore not scattered at random through the cortex, but tended to be grouped together. The size and shape of the regions containing these cell groups were investigated by comparing the fields of cells mapped in sequence. It was at once apparent that successively recorded cells also tended to have identical axis orientations and that each penetration consisted of several sequences of cells, each sequence having a common axis orientation. Any undifferentiated units in the background responded best to the stimulus orientation that was most effective in activating the cell under study. After traversing a distance that varied greatly from one penetration to the next, the electrode would enter an area where there was no longer any single optimum orientation for driving background activity. A very slight advance of the electrode would bring it into a region where a new orientation was the most effective, and the succeeding cells would all have receptive fields with that orientation. The change in angle from one region to another was unpredictable; sometimes it was barely detectable, at other times large (45–90°).

Text-figure 13 shows a camera lucida tracing of a frontal section through the post-lateral gyrus. The electrode track entered normal to the surface, passed through the apical segment in a direction parallel to the fibre bundles, then through the white matter beneath, and finally obliquely through half the thickness of the mesial segment. A lesion was made at the termination of the penetration. A composite photomicrograph (Pl. 1) shows the lesion and the first part of the electrode track. The units recorded in the course of the penetration are indicated in Text-fig. 13 by the longer lines crossing the track; the unresolved background activity by the shorter lines. The orientations of the most effective stimuli are given by the directions of the lines, a line perpendicular to the track signifying a vertical orientation. For the first part of the penetration, through the apical segment, the field orientation was vertical for all cells as well as for the background activity. Fibres were recorded from the white matter and from the grey matter just beyond it. Three of these fibres were axons of cortical cells having fields

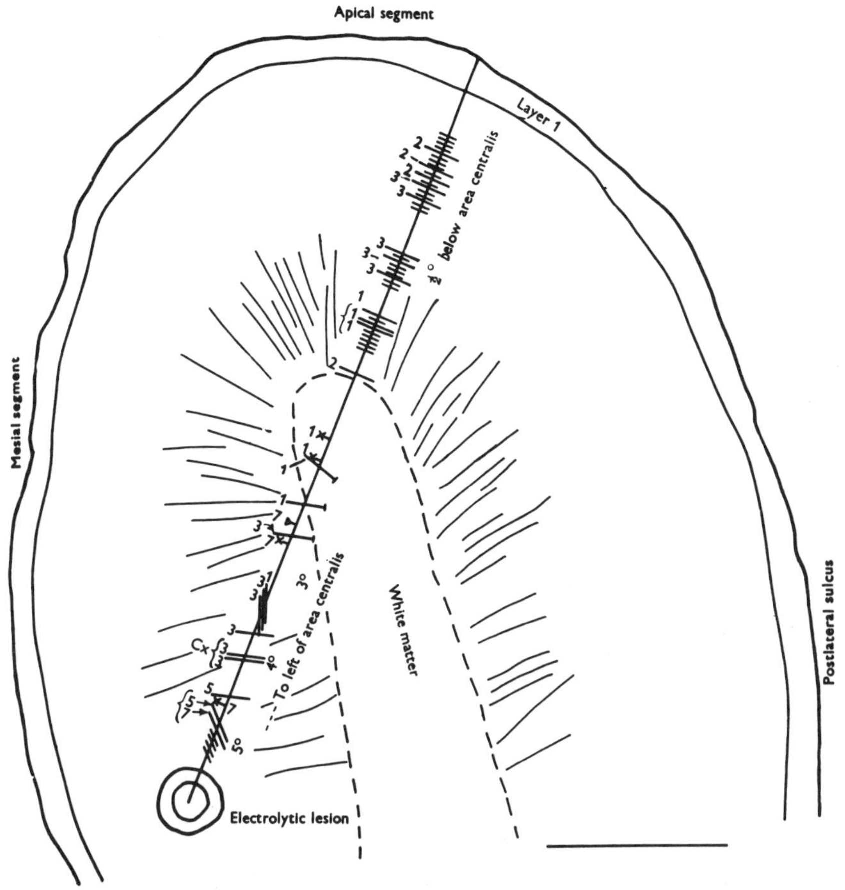


Text-fig. 13. Reconstruction of micro-electrode penetration through the lateral gyrus (see also Pl. 1). Electrode entered apical segment normal to the surface, and remained parallel to the deep fibre bundles (indicated by radial lines) until reaching white matter; in grey matter of mesial segment the electrode's course was oblique. Longer lines represent cortical cells. Axons of cortical cells are indicated by a cross-bar at right-hand end of line. Field-axis orientation is shown by the direction of each line; lines perpendicular to track represent vertical orientation. Brace-brackets show simultaneously recorded units. Complex receptive fields are indicated by 'Cx'. Afferent fibres from the lateral geniculate body indicated by x, for 'on' centre; Δ, for 'off' centre. Approximate positions of receptive fields on the retina are shown to the right of the penetration. Shorter lines show regions in which unresolved background activity was observed. Numbers to the left of the penetration refer to ocular-dominance group (see Part II). Scale 1 mm.

of various oblique orientations; four were afferent fibres from the lateral geniculate body. In the mesial segment three short sequences were encountered, each with a different common field orientation. These sequences together occupied a distance smaller than the full thickness of the apical segment.

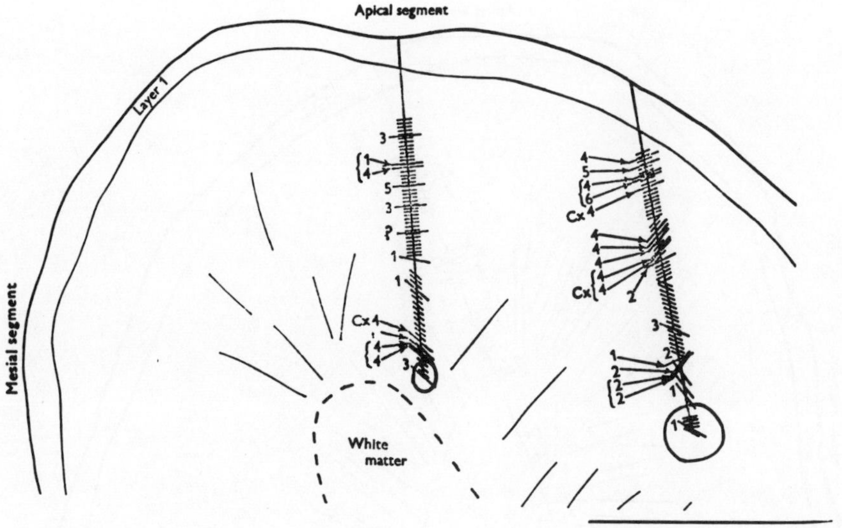


Text-fig. 14. Reconstructions of two penetrations in apical segment of post-lateral gyrus, near its anterior end (just behind anterior interrupted line in Text-fig. 1, see also Pl. 2). Medial penetration is slightly oblique, lateral one is markedly so. All receptive fields were located within 1° of area centralis. Conventions as in Text-fig. 13. Scale 1 mm.

In another experiment, illustrated in Text-fig. 14 and in Pl. 2, two penetrations were made, both in the apical segment of the post-lateral gyrus. The medial penetration (at left in the figure) was at the outset almost normal to the cortex, but deviated more and more from the direction of the deep fibre bundles. In this penetration there were three different axis orientations, of which the first and third persisted through long sequences. In the lateral track there were nine orientations. From the beginning this track was more oblique, and it became increasingly so as it progressed.

As illustrated by the examples of Text-figs. 13 and 14, there was a marked tendency for shifts in orientation to increase in frequency as the angle between electrode and direction of fibre bundles (or apical dentrites) became greater. The extreme curvature of the lateral and post-lateral gyri in their apical segments made normal penetrations very difficult to obtain; nevertheless, four penetrations were normal or almost so. In none of these were there any shifts of axis orientation. On the other hand there were several shifts of field orientation in all oblique penetrations. As illustrated by Text-fig. 14, most penetrations that began nearly normal to the surface became more and more oblique with increasing depth. Here the distance traversed by the electrode without shifts in receptive-field orientation tended to become less and less as the penetration advanced.

It can be concluded that the striate cortex is divided into discrete regions within which the cells have a common receptive-field axis orientation. Some of the regions extend from the surface of the cortex to the white matter; it is difficult to be certain whether they all do. Some idea of their shapes may be obtained by measuring distances between shifts in receptive-field orientation. From these measurements it seems likely that the general shape is columnar, distorted no doubt by any curvature of the gyrus, which would tend to make the end at the surface broader than that at the white matter; deep in a sulcus the effect would be the reverse. The cross-sectional size and shape of the columns at the surface can be estimated only roughly. Most of our information concerns their width in the coronal plane, since it is in this plane that oblique penetrations were made. At the surface this width is probably of the order of 0·5 mm. We have very little information about the cross-sectional dimension in a direction parallel to the long axis of the gyrus. Preliminary mapping of the cortical surface suggests that the cross-sectional shape of the columns may be very irregular.

## Position of Receptive Fields on the Retina

*Gross Topography*. That there is a systematic representation of the retina on the striate cortex of the cat was established anatomically by Minkowski (1913) and with physiological methods by Talbot and Marshall (1941). Although in the present study no attempt has been made to map topographically all parts of the striate cortex, the few penetrations made in cortical areas representing peripheral parts of the retina confirm these findings. Cells recorded in front of the anterior interrupted lines of Text-fig. 1 had receptive fields in the superior retinas; those in the one penetration behind the posterior line had fields that were well below the horizontal meridian of the retina. (No recordings were made from cortical regions receiving projections from the deeply pigmented non-tapetal part of the inferior retinas.) In several penetrations extending far down the mesial (interhemispheric) segment of the lateral gyrus, receptive fields moved further and further out into the ipsilateral half of each retina as the electrode advanced (Text-fig. 13). In these penetrations the movement of fields into the retinal periphery occurred more and more rapidly as the electrode advanced. In three penetrations extending far down the lateral segment of the post-lateral gyrus (medial bank of the post-lateral sulcus) there was likewise a clear progressive shift of receptive-field positions as the electrode advanced. Here also the movement was along the horizontal meridian, again into the *ipsilateral* halves of both retinas. This therefore confirms the findings of Talbot and Marshall (1941) and Talbot (1942), that in each hemisphere there is a second laterally placed representation of the contralateral half-field of vision. The subject of Visual Area II will not be dealt with further in this paper.

Cells within the large cortical region lying between the interrupted lines of Text-fig. 1, and extending over on to the mesial segment and into the lateral sulcus for a distance of 2–3 mm, had their receptive fields in the area of central vision. By this we mean the area centralis, which is about 5° in diameter, and a region surrounding it by about 2–3°. The receptive fields of the great majority of cells were confined to the ipsilateral halves of the two retinas. Often a receptive field covering several degrees on the retina stopped short in the area centralis right at the vertical meridian. Only rarely did a receptive field appear to spill over into the contralateral half-retina; when it did, it was only by 2–3°, a distance comparable to the possible error in determining the area centralis in some cats.

Because of the large cortical representation of the area centralis, one would expect only a very slow change in receptive-field position as the electrode advanced obliquely (Text-fig. 13). Indeed, in penetrations through the apex of the post-lateral gyrus and extending 1–2 mm down either bank there was usually no detectable progressive displacement of receptive fields. In penetrations made 1–3 mm apart, either along a parasagittal line or in the same coronal plane (Text-fig. 14) receptive fields again had almost identical retinal positions.

*Retinal Representation of Neighbouring Cells.* A question of some interest was to determine whether this detailed topographic representation of the retina held right down to the cellular level. From the results just described one might imagine that receptive fields of neighbouring cortical cells should have very nearly the same retinal position. In a sequence of cells recorded in a normal penetration through the cortex the receptive fields should be superimposed, and for oblique penetrations any detectable changes in field positions should be systematic. In the following paragraphs we shall consider the relative retinal positions of the receptive fields of neighbouring cells, especially cells within a column.

In all multiple recordings the receptive fields of cells observed simultaneously were situated in the same general region of the retina. As a rule the fields overlapped, but it was unusual for them to be precisely superimposed. For example, fields were often staggered along a line perpendicular to their axes. Similarly, the successive receptive fields observed during a long cortical penetration varied somewhat in position, often in an apparently random manner. Text-figure 15 illustrates a sequence of twelve cells recorded in the early part of a penetration through the cortex. One lesion was made while observing the first cell in the sequence and another at the end of the penetration; they are indicated in the drawing of cortex to the right of the figure. In the centre of the figure the position of each receptive field is shown relative to the area centralis (marked with a cross); each field was several degrees below and to the left of the area centralis. It will be seen that all fields in the sequence except the last had the same axis orientation; the first eleven cells therefore occupied the same column.

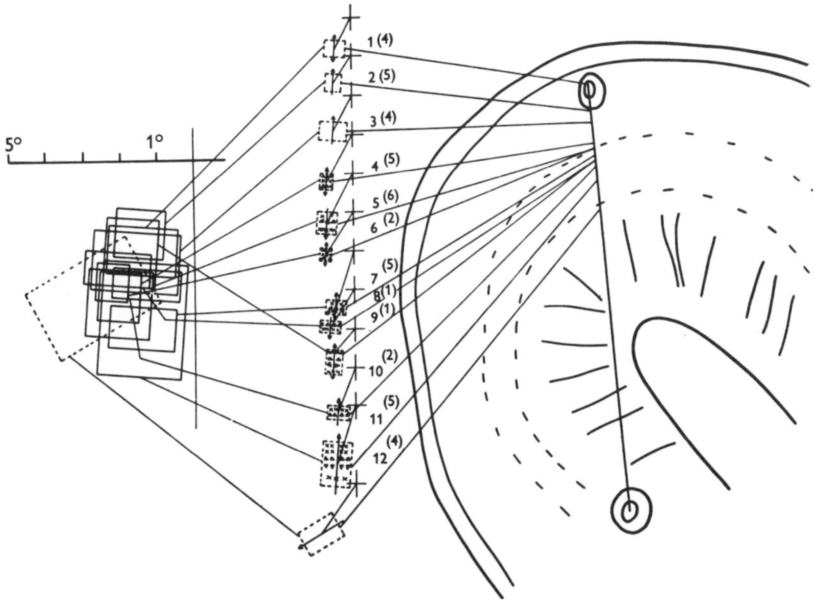


Text-fig. 15. Reconstruction of part of an electrode track through apical and mesial segments of post-lateral gyrus near its anterior end. Two lesions were made, the first after recording from the first unit, the second at the end of the penetration. Only the first twelve cells are represented. Interrupted lines show boundaries of layer 4.

In the centre part of the figure the position of each receptive field, outlined with interrupted lines, is given with respect to the area centralis, shown by a cross. Cells are numbered in sequence, 1–12. Numbers in parentheses refer to ocular-dominance group (see Part II). Units 5 and 6, 8 and 9 were observed simultaneously. The first three fields and the last were complex in organization; the remainder were simple. ×, areas giving excitation; △, areas giving inhibitory effects. Note that all receptive fields except the last have the same axis orientation (9.30–3.30 o'clock). The arrows show the preferred direction of movement of a slit oriented parallel to the receptive-field axis.

In the left part of the figure all of the receptive fields are superimposed, to indicate the overlap and variation in size. The vertical and horizontal lines represent meridia, crossing at the area centralis. Scale on horizontal meridian, 1° for each subdivision.

All but the first three and the last (cell 12) were simple in arrangement. Cells 5 and 6 were recorded together, as were 8 and 9.

In the left-hand part of the figure the approximate boundaries of all these receptive fields are shown superimposed, in order to indicate the degree of overlap. From cell to cell there is no obvious systematic change in receptive-field position. The variation in position is about equal to the area occupied by the largest fields of the sequence. This variation is undoubtedly real, and not an artifact produced by eye movements occurring between recordings of successive cells. The stability of the eyes was checked while studying each cell, and any tendency to eye movements would have easily been detected by an apparent movement of the receptive field under observation. Furthermore, the field positions of simultaneously recorded cells 5 and 6, and also of cells 8 and 9, are clearly different; here the question of eye movements is not pertinent.

Text-figure 15 illustrates a consistent and somewhat surprising finding, that within a column defined by common field-axis orientation there was no apparent progression in field positions along the retina as the electrode advanced. This was so even though the electrode often crossed through the column obliquely, entering one side and leaving the other. If there was any detailed topographical representation within columns it was obscured by the superimposed, apparently random staggering of field positions. We conclude that at this microscopic level the retinotopic representation no longer strictly holds.

## Receptive-Field Organization

*Multiple Recordings.* The receptive fields of cells observed together in multiple recordings were always of similar complexity, i.e. they were either all simple or all complex in their organization. In about one third of the multiple recordings the cells had the same detailed field organization; if simple, they had similar distributions of excitatory and inhibitory areas; if complex, they required identical stimuli for their activation. As a rule these fields did not have exactly the same retinal position, but were staggered as described above. In two thirds of the multiple recordings the cells differed to varying degrees in their receptive field arrangements. Two types of multiple recordings in which field arrangements differed seem interesting enough to merit a separate description.

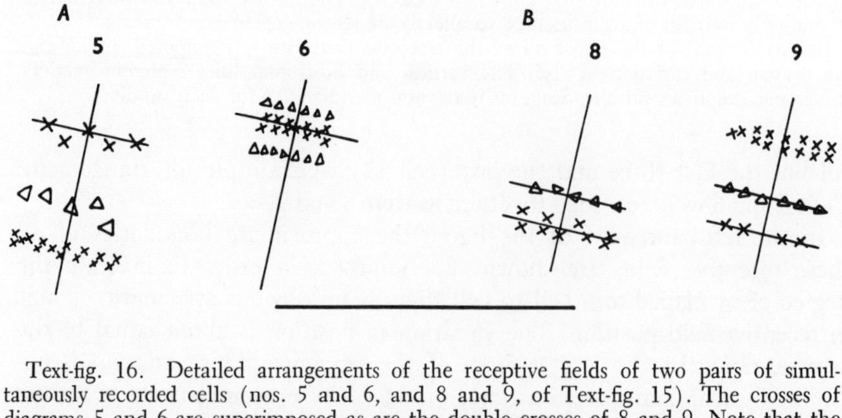


Text-fig. 16. Detailed arrangements of the receptive fields of two pairs of simultaneously recorded cells (nos. 5 and 6, and 8 and 9, of Text-fig. 15). The crosses of diagrams 5 and 6 are superimposed as are the double crosses of 8 and 9. Note that the upper excitatory region of 5 is superimposed upon the excitatory region of 6; and that both regions of 8 are superimposed on the inhibitory and lower excitatory regions of 9. Scale, 1°.

In several multiple recordings the receptive fields overlapped in such a way that one or more excitatory or inhibitory portions were superimposed. Two examples are supplied by cell-pairs 5 and 6, and 8 and 9 of Text-fig. 15. Their fields are redrawn in Text-fig. 16. The fields of cells 5 and 6 are drawn separately (Text-fig. 16*A*) but they actually overlapped so that the reference lines are to be imagined as superimposed. Thus the 'on' centre of cell 6 fell directly over the upper 'on' flank of 5 and the two cells tended to fire together to suitably placed stimuli. A similar situation existed for cells 8 and 9 (Text-fig. 16*B*). The field of 9 was placed so that its 'off' region and the lower, weaker 'on' region were superimposed on the two regions of 8. Again the two cells tended to fire together. Such examples suggest that neighbouring cells may have some of their inputs in common.

Cells responded reciprocally to a light stimulus in eight of the forty-three multiple recordings. An example of two cells responding reciprocally to stationary spots is shown in Text-fig. 17. In each eye the two receptive fields were also superimposed. The fields consisted of elongated obliquely oriented central regions, inhibitory for one cell, excitatory for the other, flanked on either side by regions of the opposite type. Instead of firing together in response to an optimally oriented stationary slit, like the cells in Text-fig. 16, these cells gave opposite-type responses, one inhibitory and the other excitatory. Some cell pairs responded reciprocally to to-and-fro movements of a slit or edge. Examples have been given elsewhere (Hubel, 1958, Fig. 9; 1959, Text-fig. 6). The fields of these cell pairs usually differed only in the balance of the asymmetrical flanking regions.

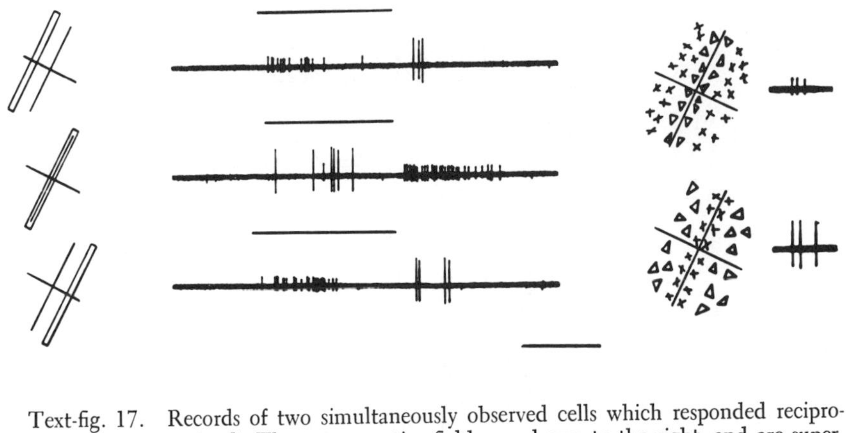

Text-fig. 17. Records of two simultaneously observed cells which responded reciprocally to stationary stimuli. The two receptive fields are shown to the right, and are superimposed, though they are drawn separately. The cell corresponding to each field is indicated by the spikes to the right of the diagram. To the left of each record is shown the position of a slit, ¼ × 2½°, with respect to these fields.

Both cells binocularly driven (dominance group 3); fields mapped in the left (contralateral) eye; position of fields 2° below and to the left of the area centralis. Time, 1 sec.

*Relationship Between Receptive-Field Organization and Cortical Layering.* In a typical penetration through the cortex many different field types were found, some simple and others complex. Even within a single column both simple and complex fields were seen. (In Text-fig. 13 and 14 complex fields are indicated by the symbol 'Cx'; in Text-fig. 15, fields 1–3 were complex and 4–11 simple, all within a single column.) An attempt was made to learn whether there was any relationship between the different field types and the layers of the cortex. This was difficult for several reasons. In Nissl-stained sections the boundaries between layers of the cat's striate cortex are not nearly as clear as they are in the primate brain; frequently even the fourth layer, so characteristic of the striate cortex, is poorly demarcated. Consequently, a layer could not always be identified with certainty even for a cell whose position was directly marked by a lesion. For most cells the positions were arrived at indirectly, from depth readings and lesions made elsewhere in the penetrations: these determinations were

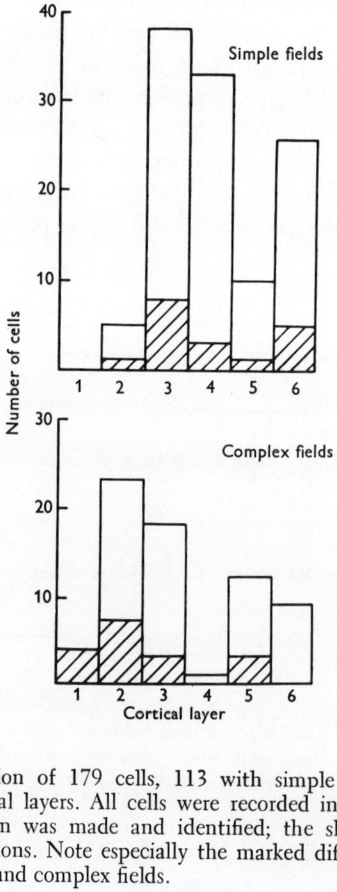


Text-fig. 18. Distribution of 179 cells, 113 with simple fields, 66 with complex, among the different cortical layers. All cells were recorded in penetrations in which at least one electrolytic lesion was made and identified; the shaded areas refer to cells marked individually by lesions. Note especially the marked difference in the occurrence, in layer 4, between simple and complex fields.

subject to more errors than the direct ones. Moreover, few of the penetrations were made in a direction parallel to the layering, so that the distance an electrode travelled in passing through a layer was short, and the error in electrode position correspondingly more important.

The distribution of 179 cells among the different layers is given in the histograms of Text-fig. 18. All cells were recorded in penetrations in which at least one lesion was made; the shaded portions refer to cells which were individually marked with lesions. As shown in the separate histograms, simple-field cells as well as those with complex fields were widely distributed throughout the cortex. Cells with simple fields were most numerous in layers 3, 4 and 6. Especially interesting is the apparent rarity of complex fields in layer 4, where simple fields were so abundant. This is also illustrated in Text-fig. 15, which shows a sequence of eight cells recorded from layer 4, all of which had simple fields. These findings suggest that cells may to some extent be segregated according to field complexity, and the rarity with which simple and complex fields were mapped together is consistent with this possibility.

## Ocular Dominance

In thirty-four multiple recordings the eye-dominance group (see Part II) was determined for both or all three cells. In eleven of these recordings there was a clear difference in ocular dominance between cells. Similarly, in a single penetration two cells recorded in sequence frequently differed in eye dominance. Cells from several different eye-dominance categories appeared not only in single penetrations, but also in sequences in which all cells had a common axis orientation. Thus within a single column defined by a common axis orientation there were cells of different eye dominance. A sequence of cells within one column is formed by cells 1–11 of Text-fig. 15. Here eye dominance ranged from wholly contralateral (group 1) to strongly ipsilateral (group 6). The two simultaneously recorded cells 5 and 6 were dominated by opposite eyes.

While these results suggested that cells of different ocular dominance were present within single columns, there were nevertheless indications of some grouping. First, in twenty-three of the thirty-four multiple recordings, simultaneously observed cells fell into the same ocular-dominance group. Secondly, in many penetrations short sequences of cells having the same relative eye dominance were probably more common than would be expected from a random scattering. Several short sequences are shown in Text-fig. 13 and 14. When such sequences consisted of cells with extreme unilateral dominance (dominance groups 1, 2, 6, and 7) the undifferentiated background activity was usually also driven predominantly by one eye, suggesting that other neighbouring units had similar eye preference. If cells of common eye dominance are in fact regionally grouped, the groups would seem to be relatively small. The cells could be arranged in nests, or conceivably in very narrow columns or thin layers.

In summary, cells within a column defined by a common field-axis orientation do not necessarily all have the same ocular dominance; yet neither do cells seem to be scattered at random through the cortex with respect to this characteristic.

## *DISCUSSION*

### A Scheme for the Elaboration of Simple and Complex Receptive Fields

Comparison of responses of cells in the lateral geniculate body with responses from striate cortex brings out profound differences in the receptive-field organization of cells in the two structures. For cortical cells, specifically oriented lines and borders tend to replace circular spots as the optimum stimuli, movement becomes an important parameter of stimulation, diffuse light becomes virtually ineffective, and with adequate stimuli most cells can be driven from the two eyes. Since lateral geniculate cells supply the main, and possibly the only, visual input to the striate cortex, these differences must be the result of integrative mechanisms within the striate cortex itself.

At present we have no direct evidence on how the cortex transforms the incoming visual information. Ideally, one should determine the properties of a cortical cell, and then examine one by one the receptive fields of all the afferents projecting upon that cell. In the lateral geniculate, where one can, in effect, record simultaneously from a cell and one of its afferents, a beginning has already been made in this direction (Hubel and Wiesel, 1961). In a structure as complex as the cortex the techniques available would seem hopelessly inadequate for such an approach. Here we must rely on less direct evidence to suggest possible mechanisms for explaining the transformations that we find.

The relative lack of complexity of simple cortical receptive fields suggests that these represent the first or at least a very early stage in the modification of geniculate signals. At any rate we have found no cells with receptive fields intermediate in type between geniculate and simple cortical fields. To account for the spatial arrangements of excitatory and inhibitory regions of simple cortical fields we may imagine that upon each simple-type cell there converge fibres of geniculate origin having 'on' or 'off' centres situated in the appropriate retinal regions. For example, a cortical cell with a receptive field of the type shown in Text-fig. 2C might receive projections

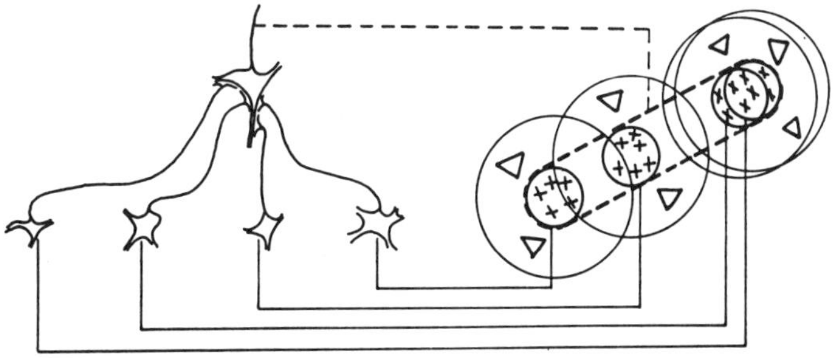

Text-fig. 19. Possible scheme for explaining the organization of simple receptive fields. A large number of lateral geniculate cells, of which four are illustrated in the upper right in the figure, have receptive fields with 'on' centres arranged along a straight line on the retina. All of these project upon a single cortical cell, and the synapses are supposed to be excitatory. The receptive fields of the cortical cell will then have an elongated 'on' centre indicated by the interrupted lines in the receptive-field diagram to the left of the figure.

from a group of lateral geniculate cells having 'on' field centres distributed throughout the long narrow central region designated in the figure by crosses. Such a projection system is shown in the diagram of Text-fig. 19. A slit of light falling on this elongated central region would activate all the geniculate cells, since for each cell the centre effect would strongly outweigh the inhibition from the segments of field periphery falling within the elongated region. This is the same as saying that a geniculate cell will respond to a slit with a width equal to the diameter of its field centre, a fact that we have repeatedly verified. The inhibitory flanks of the cortical field would be formed by the remaining outlying parts of the geniculate-field peripheries. These flanks might be reinforced and enlarged by appropriately placed 'off'-centre geniculate cells. Such an increase in the potency of the flanks would appear necessary to explain the relative indifference of cortical cells to diffuse light.

The arrangement suggested by Text-fig. 19 would be consistent with our impression that widths of cortical receptive-field centres (or flanks, in a field such as that of Text-fig. 2*F*) are of the same order of magnitude as the diameters of geniculate receptive-field centres, at least for fields in or near the area centralis. Hence the fineness of discrimination implied by the small size of geniculate receptive-field centres is not necessarily lost at the cortical level, despite the relatively large total size of many cortical fields; rather, it is incorporated into the detailed substructure of the cortical fields.

In a similar way, the simple fields of Text-fig. 2*D*–*G* may be constructed by supposing that the afferent 'on'- or 'off'-centre geniculate cells have their field centres appropriately placed. For example, field-type G could be formed by having geniculate afferents with 'off' centres situated in the region below and to the right of the boundary, and 'on' centres above and to the left. An asymmetry of flanking regions, as in field *E*, would be produced if the two flanks were unequally reinforced by 'on'-centre afferents.

The model of Text-fig. 19 is based on excitatory synapses. Here the suppression of firing on illuminating an inhibitory part of the receptive field is presumed to be the result of withdrawal of tonic excitation, i.e. the inhibition takes place at a lower level. That such mechanisms occur in the visual system is clear from studies of the lateral geniculate body, where an 'off'-centre cell is suppressed on illuminating its field centre because of suppression of firing in its main excitatory afferent (Hubel and Wiesel, 1961). In the proposed scheme one should, however, consider the possibility of direct inhibitory connexions. In Text-fig. 19 we may replace any of the excitatory endings by inhibitory ones, provided we replace the corresponding geniculate cells by ones of opposite type ('on'-centre instead of 'off'-centre, and conversely). Up to the present the two mechanisms have not been distinguished, but there is no reason to think that both do not occur.

The properties of complex fields are not easily accounted for by supposing that these cells receive afferents directly from the lateral geniculate body. Rather, the correspondence between simple and complex fields noted in Part I suggests that cells with complex fields are of higher order, having cells with simple fields as their afferents. These simple fields would all have identical axis orientation, but would differ from one another in their exact retinal positions. An example of such a scheme is given in Text-fig. 20. The hypothetical cell illustrated has a complex field like that of Text-figs. 5 and 6. One may imagine that it receives afferents from a set of simple cortical cells with fields of type G, Text-fig. 2, all with vertical axis orientation, and staggered along a horizontal line. An edge of light would activate one or more of these simple cells wherever it fell within the complex field, and this would tend to excite the higher-order cell.

Similar schemes may be proposed to explain the behaviour of other complex units. One need only use the corresponding simple fields as building blocks, staggering them over an appropriately wide region. A cell with the properties shown in Text-fig. 3 would require two types of horizontally oriented simple fields, having 'off' centres above the horizontal line, and 'on' centres below it. A slit of the same width as these centre regions would strongly activate only those cells whose long narrow centres it covered. It is true that at the same time a number of other cells would have small parts of their peripheral fields stimulated, but we may perhaps assume that these opposing effects would be relatively weak. For orientations other than horizontal a slit would have little or no effect on the simple cells, and would therefore not activate the complex one. Small spots should give only feeble 'on' responses regardless of where they were shone in the field. Enlarging the spots would not produce summation of the responses unless the enlargement were in a horizontal direction; anything else would result in invasion of opposing parts of the antecedent fields, and cancellation of the

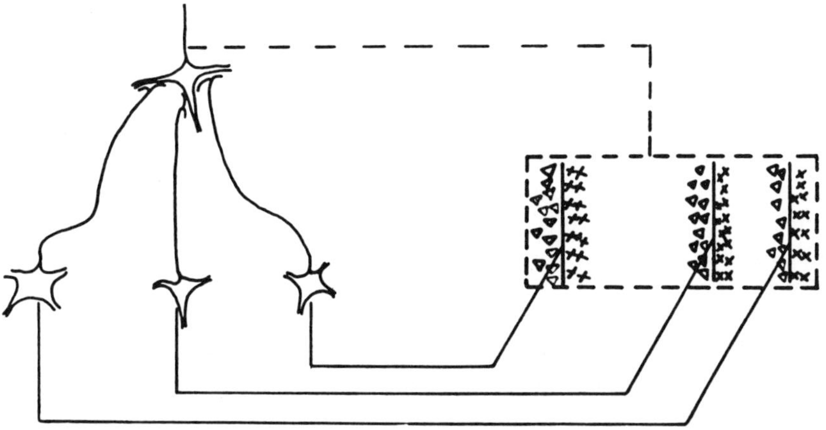

Text-fig. 20. Possible scheme for explaining the organization of complex receptive fields. A number of cells with simple fields, of which three are shown schematically, are imagined to project to a single cortical cell of higher order. Each projecting neurone has a receptive field arranged as shown to the left: an excitatory region to the left and an inhibitory region to the right of a vertical straight-line boundary. The boundaries of the fields are staggered within an area outlined by the interrupted lines. Any vertical-edge stimulus falling across this rectangle, regardless of its position, will excite some simple-field cells, leading to excitation of the higher-order cell.

responses from the corresponding cells. The model would therefore seem to account for many of the observed properties of complex fields.

Proposals such as those of Text-figs. 19 and 20 are obviously tentative and should not be interpreted literally. It does, at least, seem probable that simple receptive fields represent an early stage in cortical integration, and the complex ones a later stage. Regardless of the details of the process, it is also likely that a complex field is built up from simpler ones with common axis orientations.

At first sight it would seem necessary to imagine a highly intricate tangle of interconnexions in order to link cells with common axis orientations while keeping those with different orientations functionally separated. But if we turn to the results of Part III on functional cytoarchitecture we see at once that gathered together in discrete columns are the very cells we require to be interconnected in our scheme. The cells of each aggregate have common axis orientations and the staggering in the positions of the simple fields is roughly what is required to account for the size of most of the complex fields (cf. Text-fig. 9). That these cells are interconnected is moreover very likely on histological grounds: indeed, the particular richness of radial connexions in the cortex fits well with the columnar shape of the regions.

The otherwise puzzling aggregation of cells with common axis orientation now takes on new meaning. We may tentatively look upon each column as a functional unit of cortex, within which simple fields are elaborated and then in turn synthesized into complex fields. The large variety of simple and complex fields to be found in a single column (Text-fig. 15) suggests that the connexions between cells in a column are highly specific.

We may now begin to appreciate the significance of the great increase in the number of cells in the striate cortex, compared with the lateral geniculate body. In the cortex there is an enormous digestion of information, with each small region of visual field represented over and over again in column after column, first for one receptive-field orientation and then for another. Each column contains thousands of cells, some cells having simple fields and others complex. In the part of the cortex receiving projections from the area centralis the receptive fields are smaller, and presumably more columns are required for each unit area of retina; hence in central retina regions the cortical projection is disproportionately large.

## Complex Receptive Fields

The method of stimulating the retina with small circular spots of light and recording from single visual cells has been a useful one in studies of the cat's visual system. In the pathway from retina to cortex the excitatory and inhibitory areas mapped out by this means have been sufficient to account for responses to both stationary and moving patterns. Only when one reaches cortical cells with complex fields does the method fail, for these fields cannot generally be separated into excitatory and inhibitory regions. Instead of the direct small-spot method, one must resort to a trial-and-error system, and attempt to describe each cell in terms of the stimuli that most effectively influence firing. Here there is a risk of over- or underestimating the complexity of the most effective stimuli, with corresponding lack of precision in the functional description of the cell. For this reason it is encouraging to find that the properties of complex fields can be interpreted by the simple supposition that they receive projections from simple-field cells, a supposition made more likely by the anatomical findings of Part III.

Compared with cells in the retina or lateral geniculate body, cortical cells show a marked increase in the number of stimulus parameters that must be specified in order to influence their firing. This apparently reflects a continuing process which has its beginning in the retina. To obtain an optimum response from a retinal ganglion cell it is generally sufficient to specify the position, size and intensity of a circular spot. Enlarging the spot beyond the size of the field centre raises the threshold, but even when diffuse light is used it is possible to evoke a brisk response by using an intense enough stimulus. For geniculate cells the penalty for exceeding optimum spot size is more severe than in the retina, as has been shown by comparing responses of a geniculate cell and an afferent fibre to the same cell (Hubel and Wiesel, 1961). In the retina and lateral geniculate body there is no evidence that any shapes are more effective than circular ones, or that, with moving stimulus, one direction of movement is better than another.

In contrast, in the cortex effective driving of simple-field cells can only be obtained with restricted stimuli whose position, shape and orientation are specific for the cell. Some cells fire best to a moving stimulus, and in these the direction and even the rate of movement are often critical. Diffuse light is at best a poor stimulus, and for cells in the area of central representation it is usually ineffective at any intensity.

An interesting feature of cortical cells with complex fields may be seen in their departure from the process of progressively increasing specificity. At this stage, for the first time, what we suppose to be higher-order neurones are in a sense less selective in their responses than the cells which feed into them. Cells with simple fields tend to respond only when the stimulus is both oriented and positioned properly. In contrast, the neurones to which they supposedly project are concerned predominantly with stimulus orientation, and are far less critical in their requirements as regards stimulus placement. Their responsiveness to the abstraction which we call orientation is thus generalized over a considerable retinal area.

The significance of this step for perception can only be speculated upon, but it may be of some interest to examine several possibilities. First, neurophysiologists must ultimately try to explain how a form can be recognized regardless of its exact position in the visual field. As a step in form recognition the organism may devise a mechanism by which the inclinations of borders are more important than their exact visual-field location. It is clear that a given form in the visual field will, by virtue of its borders, excite a combination of cells with complex fields. If we displace the form it will activate many of the same cells, as long as the change in position is not enough to remove it completely from their receptive fields. Now we may imagine that these particular cells project to a single cell of still higher order: such a cell will then be very likely to respond to the form (provided the synapses are excitatory) and there will be considerable latitude in the position of the retinal image. Such a mechanism will also permit other transformations of the image, such as a change in size associated with displacement of the form toward or away from the eye. Assuming that there exist cells that are responsive to specific forms, it would clearly be economical to avoid having thousands for each form, one for every possible retinal position, and separate sets for each type of distortion of the image.

Next, the ability of some cells with complex fields to respond in a sustained manner to a stimulus as it moves over a wide expanse of retina suggests that these cells may play an important part in the perception of movement. They adapt rapidly to a stationary form, and continuous movement of the stimulus within the receptive field is the only way of obtaining a sustained discharge (Text-fig. 4*H*). Presumably the afferent simple-field cells also adapt rapidly to a stationary stimulus; because of their staggered fields the moving stimulus excites them in turn, and the higher-order cell is thus at all times bombarded. This seems an elegant means of overcoming a difficulty inherent in the problem of movement perception, that movement must excite receptors not continuously but in sequence.

Finally, the above remarks apply equally well to displacements of retinal images caused by small eye movements. The normal eye is not stationary, but is subject to several types of fine movements. There is psychophysical evidence that in man these may play an important part in vision, transforming a steady stimulus produced by a stationary object into an intermittent one, so overcoming adaptation in visual cells (Ditchburn and Ginsborg, 1952; Riggs, Ratliff, Cornsweet and Cornsweet 1953). At an early stage in the visual pathway the effect of such movements would be to excite many cells repeatedly and in turn, rather than just a few continuously. A given line or border would move back and forth over a small retinal region; in the cortex this would sequentially activate many cells with simple fields. Since large rotatory movements are not involved, these fields would have the same axis orientations but would differ only in their exact retinal positions. They would converge on higher-order cells with complex fields, and these would tend to be activated continuously rather than intermittently.

## Functional Cytoarchitecture

There is an interesting parallel between the functional subdivisions of the cortex described in the present paper, and those found in somatosensory cortex by Mountcastle (1957) in the cat, and by Powell and Mountcastle (1959) in the monkey. Here, as in the visual area, one can subdivide the cortex on the basis of responses to natural stimuli into regions which are roughly columnar in shape, and extend from surface to white matter. This is especially noteworthy since the visual and somatic areas are the only cortical regions so far studied at the single-cell level from the standpoint of functional architecture. In both areas the columnar organization is superimposed upon the well known systems of topographic representation—of the body surface in the one case, and the visual fields in the other. In the somatosensory cortex the columns are determined by the sensory submodality to which the cells of a column respond: in one type of column the cells are affected either by light touch or by bending of hairs, whereas in the other the cells respond to stimulation of deep fascia or manipulation of joints.

Several differences between the two systems will at once be apparent. In the visual cortex the columns are determined by the criterion of receptive-field axis orientation. Presumably there are as many types of column as there are recognizable differences in orientation. At present one can be sure that there are at least ten or twelve, but the number may be very large, since it is possible that no two columns represent precisely the same axis orientation. (A subdivision of cells or of columns into twelve groups according to angle of orientation shows that there is no clear prevalence of one group over any of the others.) In the somatosensory cortex, on the other hand, there are only two recognized types of column.

A second major difference between the two systems lies in the very nature of the criteria used for the subdivisions. The somatosensory cortex is divided by submodality, a characteristic depending on the incoming sensory fibres, and not on any transformations made by the cortex on the afferent impulses. Indeed we have as yet little information on what integrative processes do take place in the somatosensory cortex. In the visual cortex there is no modality difference between the input to one column and that to the next, but it is in the connexions between afferents and cortical cells, or in the interconnexions between cortical cells, that the differences must exist.

Ultimately, however, the two regions of the cortex may not prove so dissimilar. Further information on the functional role of the somatic cortex may conceivably bring to light a second system of columns, superimposed on the present one. Similarly, in the visual system future work may disclose other subdivisions cutting across those described in this paper, and based on other criteria. For the present it would seem unwise to look upon the columns in the visual cortex as entirely autonomous functional units. While the variation in field size from cell to cell within a column is generally of the sort suggested in Text-figs. 9 and 15, the presence of an occasional cell with a very large complex field (up to about 20°) makes one wonder whether columns with similar receptive-field orientations may not possess some interconnexions.

## Binocular Interaction

The presence in the striate cortex of cells influenced from both eyes has already been observed by several authors (Hubel and Wiesel, 1959; Cornehls and Grüsser, 1959; Burns, Heron and Grafstein, 1960), and is confirmed in Part II of this paper. Our results suggest that the convergence of influences from the two eyes is extensive, since binocular effects could be demonstrated in 84% of our cells, and since the two eyes were equally, or almost equally, effective in 70% (groups 3–5). This represents a much greater degree of interaction than was suggested by our original work, or by Grüsser and Grüsser-Cornehls (see Jung, 1960), who found that only 30% of their cells were binocularly influenced.

For each of our cells comparison of receptive fields mapped in the two eyes showed that, except for a difference in strength of responses related to eye dominance, the fields were in every way similar. They were similarly organized, had the same axis orientation, and occupied corresponding regions in the two retinas. The responses to stimuli applied to corresponding parts of the two receptive fields showed summation. This should be important in binocular vision, for it means that when the two images produced by an object fall on corresponding parts of the two retinas, their separate effects on a cortical cell should sum. Failure of the images to fall on corresponding regions, which might happen if an object were closer than the point of fixation or further away, would tend to reduce the summation; it could even lead to mutual antagonism if excitatory parts of one field were stimulated at the same time as inhibitory parts of the other. It should be emphasized that for all simple fields and for many complex ones the two eyes may work either synergistically or in opposition, depending on how the receptive fields are stimulated; when identical stimuli are shone on corresponding parts of the two retinas their effects should always sum.

Although in the cortex the proportion of binocularly influenced cells is high, the mixing of influences from the two eyes is far from complete. Not only are many single cells unequally influenced by the two eyes, but the relative eye dominance differs greatly from one cell to another. This could simply reflect an intermediate stage in the process of mixing of influences from the two eyes; in that case we might expect an increasing uniformity in the eye preference of higher-order cells. But cells with complex fields do not appear to differ, in their distribution among the different eye-dominance groups, from the general population of cortical cells (Text-fig. 12). At present we have no clear notion of the physiological significance of this incomplete mixing of influences from the two eyes. One possible hint lies in the fact that by binocular parallax alone (even with a stimulus too brief to allow changes in the convergence of the eyes) one can tell which of two objects is the closer (Dove, 1841; von Recklinghausen, 1861). This would clearly be impossible if the two retinas were connected to the brain in identical fashion, for then the eyes (or the two pictures of a stereo-pair) could be interchanged without substituting near points for far ones and vice versa.

## Comparison of Receptive Fields in the Frog and the Cat

Units in many respects similar to striate cortical cells with complex fields have recently been isolated from the intact optic nerve and the optic tectum of the frog (Lettvin, Maturana, McCulloch and Pitts, 1959; Maturana, Lettvin, McCulloch and Pitts, 1960). There is indirect evidence to suggest that the units are the non-myelinated axons or axon terminals of retinal ganglion cells, rather than tectal cells or efferent optic nerve fibres. In common with complex cortical cells, these units respond to objects and shadows in the visual field in ways that could not have been predicted from responses to small spots of light. They thus have 'complex' properties, in the sense that we have used this term. Yet in their detailed behaviour they differ greatly from any cells yet studied in the cat, at any level from retina to cortex. We have not, for example, seen 'erasable' responses or found 'convex edge detectors.' On the other hand, it seems that some cells in the frog have asymmetrical responses to movement and some have what we have termed a 'receptive-field axis.'

Assuming that the units described in the frog are fibres from retinal ganglion cells, one may ask whether similar fibres exist in the cat, but have been missed because of their small size. We lack exact information on the fibre spectrum of the cat's optic nerve; the composite action potential suggests that non-myelinated fibres are present, though in smaller numbers than in the frog (Bishop, 1933; Bishop and O'Leary, 1940). If their fields are different from the well known concentric type, they must have little part to play in the geniculo-cortical pathway, since geniculate cells all appear to have concentric-type fields (Hubel and Wiesel, 1961). The principal cells of the lateral geniculate body (those that send their axons to the striate cortex) are of fairly uniform size, and it seems unlikely that a large group would have gone undetected. The smallest fibres in the cat's optic nerve probably project to the tectum or the pretectal region; in view of the work in the frog, it will be interesting to examine their receptive fields.

At first glance it may seem astonishing that the complexity of third-order neurones in the frog's visual system should be equalled only by that of sixth-order neurones in the geniculo-cortical pathway of the cat. Yet this is less surprising if one notes the great anatomical differences in the two animals, especially the lack, in the frog, of any cortex or dorsal lateral geniculate body. There is undoubtedly a parallel difference in the use each animal makes of its visual system: the frog's visual apparatus is presumably specialized to recognize a limited number of stereotyped patterns or situations, compared with the high acuity and versatility found in the cat. Probably it is not so unreasonable to find that in the cat the specialization of cells for complex operations is postponed to a higher level, and that when it does occur, it is carried out by a vast number of cells, and in great detail. Perhaps even more surprising, in view of what seem to be profound physiological differences, is the superficial anatomical similarity of retinas in the cat and the frog. It is possible that with Golgi methods a comparison of the connexions between cells in the two animals may help us in understanding the physiology of both structures.

## Receptive Fields of Cells in the Primate Cortex

We have been anxious to learn whether receptive fields of cells in the monkey's visual cortex have properties similar to those we have described in the cat. A few preliminary experiments on the spider monkey have shown striking similarities. For example, both simple and complex fields have been observed in the striate area. Future work will very likely show differences, since the striate cortex of the monkey is in several ways different morphologically from that of the cat. But the similarities already seen suggest that the mechanisms we have described may be relevant to many mammals, and in particular to man.

## SUMMARY

1. The visual cortex was studied in anaesthetized cats by recording extracellularly from single cells. Light-adapted eyes were stimulated with spots of white light of various shapes, stationary or moving.

2. Receptive fields of cells in the visual cortex varied widely in their organization. They tended to fall into two categories, termed 'simple' and 'complex.'

3. There were several types of simple receptive fields, differing in the spatial distribution of excitatory and inhibitory ('on' and 'off') regions. Summation occurred within either type of region; when the two opposing regions were illuminated together their effects tended to cancel. There was generally little or no response to stimulation of the entire receptive field with diffuse light. The most effective stimulus configurations, dictated by the spatial arrangements of excitatory and inhibitory regions, were long narrow rectangles of light (slits), straight-line borders between areas of different brightness (edges), and dark rectangular bars against a light background. For maximum response the shape, position and orientation of these stimuli were critical. The orientation of the receptive-field axis (i.e. that of the optimum stimulus) varied from cell to cell; it could be vertical, horizontal or oblique. No particular orientation seemed to predominate.

4. Receptive fields were termed complex when the response to light could not be predicted from the arrangements of excitatory and inhibitory regions. Such regions could generally not be demonstrated; when they could the laws of summation and mutual antagonism did not apply. The stimuli that were most effective in activating cells with simple fields—slits, edges, and dark bars—were also the most effective for cells with complex fields. The orientation of a stimulus for optimum response was critical, just as with simple fields. Complex fields, however, differed from simple fields in that a stimulus was effective wherever it was placed in the field, provided that the orientation was appropriate.

5. Receptive fields in or near the area centralis varied in diameter from ½–1° up to about 5–6°. On the average, complex fields were larger than simple ones. In more peripheral parts of the retina the fields tended to be

larger. Widths of the long narrow excitatory or inhibitory portions of simple receptive fields were often roughly equal to the diameter of the smallest geniculate receptive-field centres in the area centralis. For cells with complex fields responding to slits or dark bars the optimum stimulus width was also usually of this order of magnitude.

6. Four fifths of all cells were influenced independently by the two eyes. In a binocularly influenced cell the two receptive fields had the same organization and axis orientation, and were situated in corresponding parts of the two retinas. Summation was seen when corresponding parts of the two retinas stimulated in identical fashion. The relative influence of the two eyes differed from cell to cell: for some cells the two eyes were about equal; in others one eye, the ipsilateral or contralateral, dominated.

7. Functional architecture was studied by (*a*) comparing the responses of cells recorded in sequence during micro-electrode penetrations through the cortex, (*b*) observing the unresolved background activity, and (*c*) comparing cells recorded simultaneously with a single electrode (multiple recordings). The retinas were found to project upon the cortex in an orderly fashion, as described by previous authors. Most recordings were made from the cortical region receiving projections from the area of central vision. The cortex was found to be divisible into discrete columns; within each column the cells all had the same receptive-field axis orientation. The columns appeared to extend from surface to white matter; cross-sectional diameters at the surface were of the order of 0·5 mm. Within a given column one found various types of simple and complex fields; these were situated in the same general retinal region, and usually overlapped, although they differed slightly in their exact retinal position. The relative influence of the two eyes was not necessarily the same for all cells in a column.

8. It is suggested that columns containing cells with common receptive-field axis orientations are functional units, in which cells with simple fields represent an early stage in organization, possibly receiving their afferents directly from lateral geniculate cells, and cells with complex fields are of higher order, receiving projections from a number of cells with simple fields within the same column. Some possible implications of these findings for form perception are discussed.

## *REFERENCES*

Bishop, G. H. Fiber groups in the optic nerve. *American Journal of Physiology,* 1933, *106,* 460-474.

Bishop, G. H., & O'Leary, J. S. Electrical activity of the lateral geniculate of cats following optic nerve stimuli. *Journal of Neurophysiology,* 1940, 3, 308-322.

Bishop, P. O., Burke, W., & Davis, R. Activation of single lateral geniculate cells by stimulation of either optic nerve. *Science,* 1959, *130,* 506-507.

Burns, B. D., Heron, W., & Grafstein, B. Response of cerebral cortex to diffuse monocular and binocular stimulation. *American Journal of Physiology,* 1960, *198,* 200-204.

Cornehls, U., & Grüsser, O.-J. Ein elektronisch gesteuertes Doppellichtreizgerät. *Pflügers Archiv für die gesamte Physiologie,* 1959, *270,* 78-79.

Daniel, P. M., & Whitteridge, D. The representation of the visual field on the calcarine cortex in baboons and monkeys. *Journal of Physiology,* 1959, *148,* 33.

Ditchburn, R. W., & Ginsborg, B. L. Vision with stabilized retinal image. *Nature,* 1952, *170,* 36-37.

Dove, H. W. Die Combination der Eindrücke beider Ohren und beider Augen zu einem Eindruck. *Mber. preuss. Akad., 1841,* 251-252.

Erulkar, S. D., & Fillenz, M. Patterns of discharge of single units of the lateral geniculate body of the cat in response to binocular stimulation. *Journal of Physiology,* 1958, *140,* 6-7.

Erulkar, S. D., & Fillenz, M. Single-unit activity in the lateral geniculate body of the cat. *Journal of Physiology,* 1960, *154,* 206-218.

Grüsser, O.-J., & Sauer, G. Monoculare und binoculare Lichtreizung einzelner Neurone im Geniculatum laterale der Katze. *Pflügers Archiv für die gesamte Physiologie,* 1960, *271,* 595-612.

Hayhow, W. R. The cytoarchitecture of the lateral geniculate body in the cat in relation to the distribution of crossed and uncrossed optic fibers. *Journal of Comparative Neurology,* 1958, *110,* 1-64.

Hubel, D. H. Tungsten microelectrode for recording from single units. *Science,* 1957, *125,* 549-550.

Hubel, D. H. Cortical unit responses to visual stimuli in nonanesthetized cats. *American Journal of Ophthalmology,* 1958, *46,* 110-121.

Hubel, D. H. Single unit activity in striate cortex of unrestrained cats. *Journal of Physiology,* 1959, *147,* 226-238.

Hubel, D. H. Single unit activity in lateral geniculate body and optic tract of unrestrained cats. *Journal of Physiology,* 1960, *150,* 91-104.

Hubel, D. H., & Wiesel, T. N. Receptive fields of single neurones in the cat's striate cortex. *Journal of Physiology,* 1959, *148,* 574-591.

Hubel, D. H., & Wiesel, T. N. Receptive fields of optic nerve fibres in the spider monkey. *Journal of Physiology,* 1960, *154,* 572-580.

Hubel, D. H., & Weisel, T. N. Integrative action in the cat's lateral geniculate body. *Journal of Physiology,* 1961, *155,* 385-398.

Jung, R. Microphysiologie corticaler Neurone: Ein Beitrag zur Koordination der Hirnrinde und des visuellen Systems. In D. B. Tower, and J. P. Schadé (Eds.), *Structure and function of the cerebral cortex.* Amsterdam: Elsevier Publishing Co., 1960.

Kuffler, S. W. Discharge patterns and functional organization of mammalian retina. *Journal of Neurophysiology,* 1953, *16,* 37-68.

Lettvin, J. Y., Maturana, H. R., McCulloch, W. S., & Pitts, W. H. What the frog's eye tells the frog's brain. *Proceedings of the Institute of Radio Engineers,* 1959, *47,* 1940-1951.

Maturana, H. R., Lettvin, J. Y., McCulloch, W. S., & Pitts, W. H. Anatomy and physiology of vision in the frog (*Rana pipiens*). *Journal of General Physiology*, 1960, *43* (Pt. 2), 129-176.

Minkowski, M. Experimentelle Untersuchungen über die Beziehungen der Grosshirnrinde und der Netzhaut zu den primären optischen Zentren, besonders zum Corpus geniculatum externum. *Arb. hirnanat. Inst.*, Zurich, 1913, 7, 259-362.

Mountcastle, V. B. Modality and topographic properties of single neurons of cat's somatic sensory cortex. *Journal of Neurophysiology*, 1957, 20, 408-434.

O'Leary, J. L. Structure of the area striata of the cat. *Journal of Comparative Neurology*, 1941, 75, 131-164.

Polyak, S. In H. Kluver (Ed.), *The vertebrate visual system*. Chicago: The University of Chicago Press, 1957.

Powell, T. P. S., & Mountcastle, V. B. Some aspects of the functional organization of the cortex of the postcentral gyrus of the monkey: a correlation of findings obtained in a single unit analysis with cytoarchitecture. *Johns Hopkins Hospital Bulletin*, 1959, *105*, 133-162.

Riggs, L. A., Ratliff, F., Cornsweet, J. C., & Cornsweet, T. N. The disappearance of steadily fixated visual test objects. *Journal of the Optical Society of America*, 1953, *43*, 495-501.

Silva, P. S. Some anatomical and physiological aspects of the lateral geniculate body. *Journal of Comparative Neurology*, 1956, *106*, 463-486.

Talbot, S. A. A lateral localization in the cat's visual cortex. *Federation Proceedings*, 1942, *1*, 84.

Talbot, S. A., & Marshall, W. H. Physiological studies on neural mechanisms of visual localization and discrimination. *American Journal of Ophthalmology*, 1941, *24*, 1255-1263.

Thompson, J. M., Woolsey, C. N., & Talbot, S. A. Visual areas I and II of cerebral cortex of rabbit. *Journal of Neurophysiology*, 1950, *13*, 277-288.

von Recklinghausen, F. Zum körperlichen Sehen. *Ann. Phys. Lpz.*, 1861, *114*, 170-173.

## *EXPLANATION OF PLATES*

### Plate 1

Coronal section through post-lateral gyrus. Composite photomicrograph of two of the sections used to reconstruct the micro-electrode track of Text-fig. 13. The first part of the electrode track may be seen in the upper right; the electrolytic lesion at the end of the track appears in the lower left. Scale 1 mm.

### Plate 2

A, coronal section through the anterior extremity of post-lateral gyrus. Composite photomicrograph made from four of the sections used to reconstruct the two electrode tracks shown in Text-fig. 14. The first part of the two electrode tracks may be seen crossing layer 1. The lesion at the end of the lateral track (to the right in the figure) is easily seen; that of the medial track is smaller, and is shown at higher power in *B*. Scales: A, 1 mm, *B*, 0·25 mm.

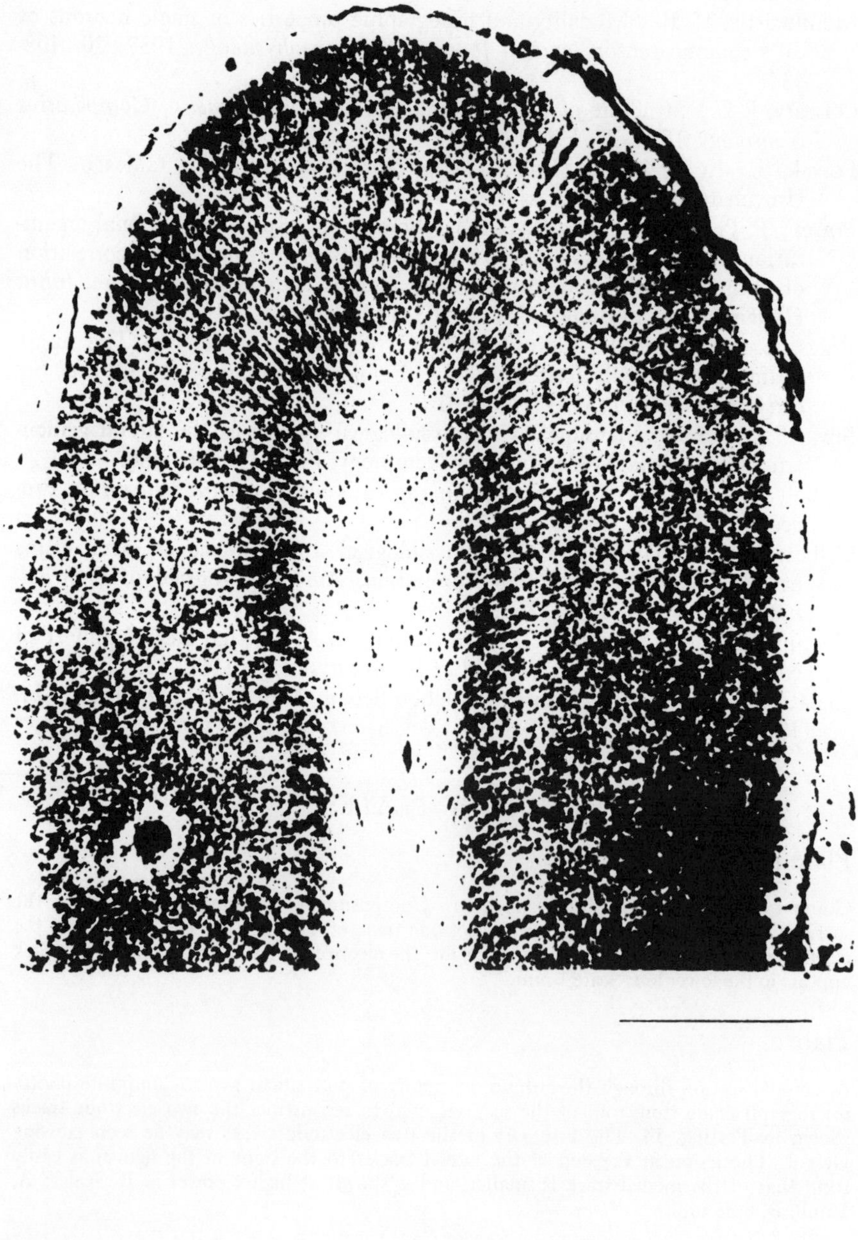

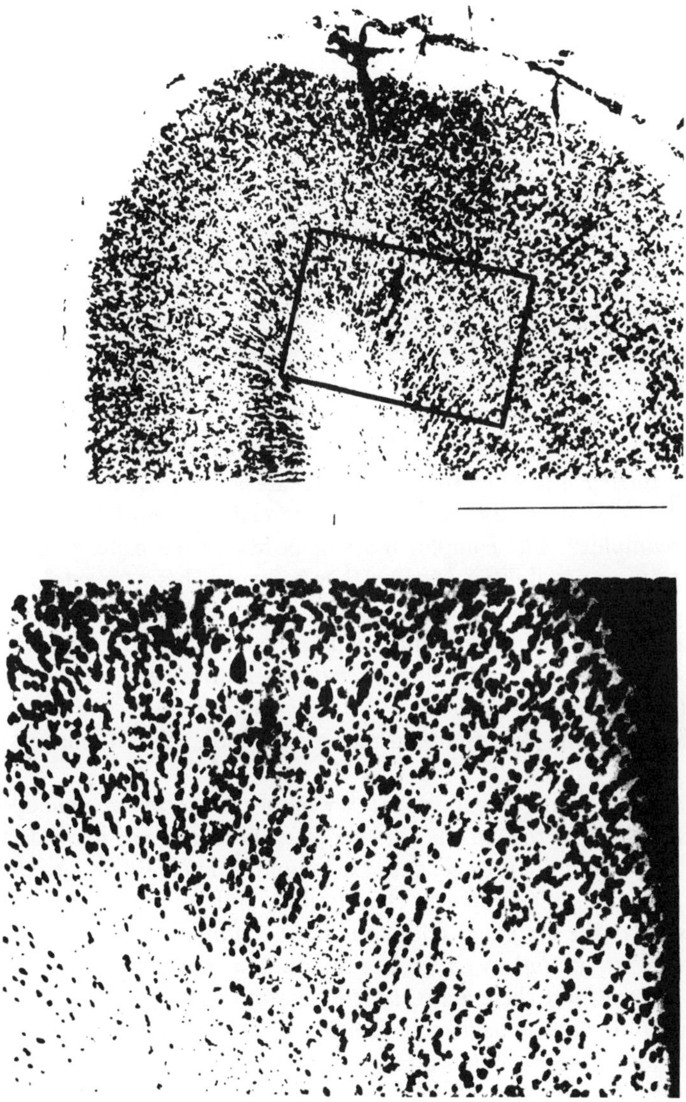

The justification for my earlier remarks about the importance of the discovery of interactions within receptive fields and the mutually antagonistic nature of "on" and "off" responses for further analysis of the coding system should by now be obvious. The only exception that has been discovered to the autonomy and independence of receptive field functions at a given level is the binocular mixing of "on" and "off" activity from corresponding fields in the two eyes. This fact leads directly to the final paper in this section which reports the successful search for units which encode binocular disparity, the cue to binocular depth detection (these terms are explained and discussed in the paper).

Before turning to that matter, there are some additional comments to make about Hubel and Wiesel's work. In the first place, they have shown that the system in all its essentials, as reported above, is present in very young kittens, as soon as their eyes open, so it must be a "built-in" innate property of the system (Hubel & Wiesel, 1963). Also, kittens deprived of pattern vision show more or less severe deficits in the coding system, depending on the time of deprivation and its duration: adult cats similarly deprived do not show the same deficits (Wiesel & Hubel, 1965), so that in its early history the system has to be used to maintain its efficiency. Exploring further into the visual association areas (areas 17 and 18) Hubel and Wiesel (1965) have discovered still more elaborate units which they call "hypercomplex." The complex units described in the paper presented here offer exciting possibilities because they suggest a basis for contour equivalence under changes of position (see also "A Coupled System for Coding and Learning in Shape Discrimination" in Part II), but the "hypercomplex" units are not so easy to interrupt in terms of stimulus equivalences, since they code for very specific features. A full discussion of this point would take us too far afield, but the interested reader will find such a discussion in Dodwell (1970b, Ch. III).

A very important question to ask is whether the receptive field coding system is specific to the cat, or whether it is more general; if the latter, it is important to inquire how general. Hubel and Wiesel (1968) have discovered essentially the same system in the monkey, and various pieces of evidence suggest that the system is common to all mammals, at least in all its essentials. Part of that evidence is the common basic form of mammalian visual systems, but there are scattered electrophysiological findings on other species, and some behavioral evidence (see Part III) which supports the notion. Since the form and arrangement of coding seems to depend essentially on a specific type of retinal organizations as well as on the presence of the higher structures—l.g.b.s. and visual cortex—it does not seem particularly plausible to suppose that just this sort of processing system exists in lower animal types. At least there is as yet no evidence for it.

One final point: since publication of Hubel and Wiesel's 1962 article a number of investigators have looked for other special property detectors in the mammalian retina and elsewhere and with some success. For instance, Barlow, Hill and Levick (1964) showed that there are ganglion cells in the rabbit retina which are differentially sensitive to movement in particular directions, and our next paper gives another example. Also there have been some reports that the receptive fields are less tidily organized than was originally reported. For instance, Spinelli (1966) reports finding cortical units with a variety of less regular features (when plotted with a moving light spot) than those demonstrated by Hubel and Wiesel. These findings raise the question of whether the Hubel–Wiesel system is unique, and whether it could form the basis for a reliable contour coding process. My answer—and it will not be agreed to by some—is that a considerable majority of the cortical units discovered have the sorts of property described by Hubel and Wiesel, so that even if other "feature detectors" are discovered (who knows, perhaps even detectors as specific as some of those reported by Lettvin et al.) the major properties of the overall system are probably correctly described by them. If some of the units have less regular receptive fields than Hubel and Wiesel originally claimed, or as we can say, are more "noisy" or unreliable as detectors, this should not matter since there are large numbers of such units which, operating simultaneously, can guarantee reliable performance. Again, a more thorough discussion of these points can be found in Dodwell (1970b). I believe that the major problems which Hubel and Wiesel's findings raise for the psychology of stimulus equivalence and pattern recognition are of a different kind, and I will touch on these at the end of the section.

Our last paper in the section is a prime example of scientific detective work. The authors argue that a particular type of feature detector should be there within the contour coding system, and set about demonstrating its presence in a workmanlike manner.

# *The Neural Mechanism of Binocular Depth Discrimination*

H. B. BARLOW, C. BLAKEMORE,
AND J. D. PETTIGREW

*1. Binocularly driven units were investigated in the cat's primary visual cortex.*

*2. It was found that a stimulus located correctly in the visual fields of both eyes was more effective in driving the units than a monocular stimulus, and much more effective than a binocular stimulus which was correctly positioned in only one eye: the response to the correctly located image in one eye is vetoed if the image is incorrectly located in the other eye.*

*3. The vertical and horizontal disparities of the paired retinal images that yielded the maximum response were measured in 87 units from seven cats: the range of horizontal disparities was 6•6°, of vertical disparities 2•2°.*

*4. With fixed convergence, different units will be optimally excited by objects lying at different distances. This may be the basic mechanism underlying depth discrimination in the cat.*

## *INTRODUCTION*

The image formed by a single eye is a two-dimensional projection of the three-dimensional world which entirely lacks representation of those distances in the three-dimensional world that are possibly of greatest survival value to an animal, namely the distances of the external objects from the eye. It is true that the third dimension of apparent depth can be added to the visual image of a single eye by using a number of indirect cues, such as the angular subtense of an object of known size, motion parallax, accommodative effort, and the obscuration of distant objects by nearer ones. However, these cues can only be utilized in special circumstances, and most of them require rather complex image-processing. In animals where the

Reprinted from *Journal of Physiology*, 1967.

visual fields of the two eyes overlap the situation becomes much more favourable, for between them the different projections on the two retinae now contain much more direct cues to the distances of the features of the image. Wheatstone (1838) demonstrated that these cues from binocular parallax could be used and this ability has been the subject of the extensive psychophysical investigations described by Ogle (in Davson, 1962).

One can distinguish two important steps that must be taken in order to employ these cues. The first is the selection of those parts of the two images that belong to each other in the sense that they are images of the same feature in three-dimensional space. The second is the assessment of the small displacements in the relative positions of these paired parts that result from binocular parallax and provide the cue to depth. This communication describes the possible neural mechanism whereby these two operations are performed in the cat's brain. A suggestion made by Pettigrew (1965) is supported, and further evidence will be found in other papers (Nikara, Bishop and Pettigrew, 1967, and Pettigrew, Nikara and Bishop, 1967a, b).

*Vertical and Horizontal Disparities.* In order to facilitate discussion of the displacements caused by parallax it is customary to take one retinal locus as a reference point, and for this the centre of each fovea in man, or area centralis in the cat, is naturally chosen. The position of a small part of the image in the right eye is defined by the angles from this reference point, $H_R^\circ$ measured horizontally, and $V_L^\circ$, measured vertically, preferably using the co-ordinate system proposed by Bishop, Kozak and Vakkur (1962). Now the position, $H_L^\circ$, $V_L^\circ$, of the paired counterpart in the left eye is found, and the *horizontal disparity* is defined as the difference between $H_R^\circ$ and $H_L^\circ$, the *vertical disparity* as the difference between $V_R^\circ$ and $V_L^\circ$. If one imagines a cat with the area centralis of each eye trained exactly on some point in space, then the images from all features lying on the circle through this point and the two anterior nodal points of the eyes will, by definition, have zero horizontal disparity. In studies on human binocular vision this is called the Vieth–Müller Circle. Points on the images from a feature lying inside this circle will have what is termed *convergent or crossed disparity*: points further away will have *divergent or uncrossed disparity*. Vertical disparities will occur because of slight differences in elevation of the eyes, and also because the linear magnification for the two eyes can be significantly different for objects lying at a distance which is only a few multiples of the interocular separation. However, the range of vertical disparities for features lying at reasonable viewing distances is much less than the range of horizontal disparities.

*Anatomy and Physiology.* Isaac Newton was the first to propose partial decussation of the optic nerve fibres in binocular mammals (Polyak, 1957, reviews the early investigations). The optic tract of one side receives information from the contralateral visual hemi-fields of both eyes. Although neurones from the two retinae lie near each other at the relay in the lateral geniculate nucleus, there is apparently little interaction in the primary visual pathway until the cortex is reached, for single neurones with a binocular input are rarely found at the geniculate (Bishop, Burke, Davis and Hayhow, 1958), whereas the majority of cells in the striate cortex can be binocularly driven. Hubel and Wiesel (1962) have described how cortical neurones respond only to the appropriate specific stimulus or trigger feature. Diffuse light or darkness will be ineffective, whereas a moving dark bar, bright slit, or edge, if correctly orientated, will cause a neurone to respond vigorously. Any stimulus will only cause a response in the small fraction of neurones that are appropriately 'tuned,' i.e. those which respond to the right trigger feature, at the right orientation and position.

Now one can see that this might provide the basis for performing the first of the two operations postulated above, namely the identification of the parts of the two images corresponding to a single feature in object space. Clearly the number of identical trigger features in a small part of the monocular image is likely to be low: hence similar features, lying in the same approximate region of the image in each eye, can safely be assumed to belong to the same object. For example, a black line of a particular orientation in one image should be associated with the black line of the same orientation at the most nearly corresponding position in the other image because both are likely to be images of the same object.

Hubel and Wiesel (1962) said that the receptive field and appropriate stimulus for a cortical neurone was the same for each eye, and that the inputs from the two eyes summated when the two stimuli were correctly located. They thought that the receptive fields always lay in corresponding regions in the two retinae—presumably at zero disparity—but variations in disparity might have been obscured by residual eye movements in their preparation. We therefore thought it possible that different cortical neurones might require different horizontal disparities for optimal response: the trigger feature might have to lie at a specific distance from the cat and this distance might be different in different neurones, even with an unvarying convergence position of the eyes. If that were so, then these cortical neurones would be performing both of the operations required for binocular stereopsis. A particular neurone would respond optimally to only one of a variety of features (dark bar, light slit or edge) over only a fraction of the whole range of possible orientations, and over only a fraction of the possible range of distances. It would certainly require a very large number of neurones to cover the full range of possible stimulus features not only in variety and orientation, but also in position and depth. However, since there is in fact an enormous number of neurones in the primary visual cortex compared with the number of incoming fibres, the idea cannot be rejected on this score.

To test this conjecture we need to find out first if the stimulus must have a specific disparity to excite a particular neurone, and if excitation with

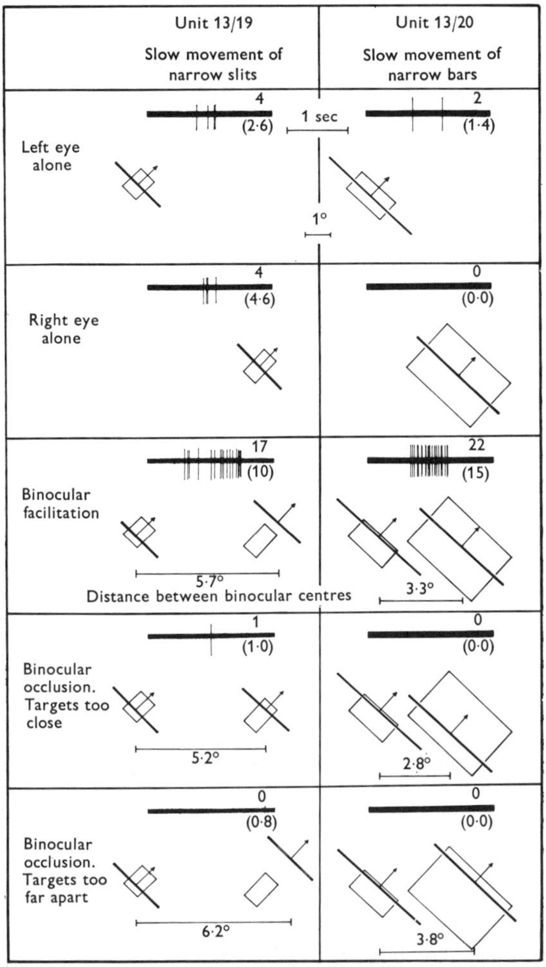


Fig. 1. Binocular interactions showing that facilitatory responses occur at different disparities in two cortical neurones from the same cat. The units were studied consecutively, their receptive fields lay close together in the visual field, and their axis orientations were the same. For each unit five stimulus conditions are illustrated—monocular stimulation for each eye alone, and three examples of binocular stimulation. Each box contains a sample record (retouched for reproduction, positive deflection downward) with the number of spikes in that sample and the average number for five repetitions in parentheses. The positions of the stimuli and the minimum response fields on the tangent screen are illustrated diagrammatically. Eye torsion and elevation have been corrected, but no correction has been made for the divergence of the visual axes or the separation of the two eyes. The projections of the areae centrales would be separated by about 6·4° in this diagram. Minimum response fields were plotted with a bright slit for both units, but binocular facilitation showed up better with a dark bar for unit 13/20, and these responses were chosen for this illustration. Slits and bars were 3 min of arc wide and several degrees long. Optimum facilitation occurs at 5·7° separation of targets for unit 13/19, 3·3° separation for unit 13/20. These were estimated to be equivalent to 0·7° and 3·1° of convergent disparity.

different disparities results in a substantially lower response. Qualitative evidence for this is provided in Fig. 1, and quantitative evidence is given in another paper (Pettigrew *et al.*, 1967b). Secondly, we must find out if there exists, from neurone to neurone, a variation in the horizontal disparity required for optimal stimulation. Without such variation it might be held that binocular facilitation, such as is shown in Fig. 1, serves simply to improve the signal/noise ratio. But, if there exists variation of optimum horizontal disparity, then it follows that objects at different distances will optimally excite different neurones; consequently the neurones that respond can give cues to the depths of the features activating them. The aim of this investigation was to determine whether the binocular receptive fields of single cortical neurones all have the same disparity, or whether there is variation from neurone to neurone.

## *METHODS*

We recorded the action potentials of single neurones in the primary visual cortex of adult cats, using methods that are already well established. The animal's head was firmly held in a stereotaxic frame with the horizontal Horsley–Clark plane tilted so that the visual axes were approximately horizontal. The animal was anaesthetized with 80% nitrous oxide and 20% oxygen, paralysed by continuous infusion of a relaxant mixture described below, artificially respired, and maintained thermostatically at 36° C. The characterization of each neural unit took 1–6 hr, and it was desirable to study as many as possible in each preparation. Long survival was therefore important for the success of this experiment, and with the methods employed good units could be obtained over a period as long as 6 days.

It is clear that eye movements would hopelessly mar the results and special precautions were taken to prevent them. First, a mixture of gallamine triethiodide (Flaxedil) at 5 mg/kg.hr with d-tubocurarine at 0•5 mg/kg.hr was infused continuously; higher dosages of curare often reduce arterial blood pressure by more than 20 mm Hg, and the life expectancy is drastically reduced. Eye-movements were found to be about 6 min of arc/hour (Rodieck, Pettigrew, Bishop & Nikara, 1967), but since this was still enough to be troublesome, the eyes were held mechanically by stretching and drying the conjunctivae on metal rings attached to flexible arms (Fleximount tool holders) which could be locked in any position. In addition an open pneumothorax was made and cervical sympathectomy performed. Slipping of the contact lenses or correcting lenses can cause apparent image movements, and this was carefully prevented.

In order to test the adequacy of these precautions the optic disks were viewed ophthalmoscopically through transparent extensions of the tangent screen (see below), and their projections were carefully plotted several times during each experiment. In early experiments movements were observed, but when the above precautions were taken these projections did not change position perceptibly. Also, no change in the position of the borders of the tiniest receptive fields could be detected during the 1–6 hr of study.

When the eyes are fixed to rings one can no longer directly use the method developed in Sydney, based on the results of Bishop *et al.* (1962), to infer the approximate positions of the visual axes from the separation of the blind spot projections in the relaxed cat. Therefore the optic disks were always plotted, in the manner described above, before the eyes were manipulated, and the approximate horizontal distances from the blind spots to the visual axes were calculated, so that this information could be used to estimate the projections of the areae centrales after the eye positions had been changed.

It was also necessary to measure the torsion of the eyes caused by the relaxant and by fixing to the rings. This was estimated in two ways: (1) photographs of the slit-like entrance pupils were made in the unrestrained cat and after attachment of the eyes to rings. (2) In the majority of centrally located units the receptive field axis orientation could be accurately determined for each eye; the mean difference between them was attributed to torsion. These two estimates agreed well with each other in each cat. Similarly an approximate estimate of the difference in elevation of the two eyes could be made from the heights of the blind spot projections.

Special care was taken to preserve good optics: the corneae were covered with contact lenses, the pupils were dilated with phenylephrine (Neosynephrine) and atropine, 3 mm artificial pupils were used, and we applied the appropriate spherical refractive correction, establishing this by retinoscopy and direct ophthalmoscopy.

To provide the visual stimuli an overhead projector cast an image from behind on to a translucent tangent screen placed 114 cm from the eyes. A 45° Perspex (lucite) reflector produced an identical image on a horizontal board. Receptive fields were plotted on paper sheets positioned accurately on this board. A wide variety of visual stimuli could be produced by cutting or punching card masks and moving them by hand over the stage of the projector. As seen by the cat the luminance of the bright parts of these stimuli was about 500 cd/m$^2$, the dim background about 50 cd/m$^2$.

Because of the interocular separation and divergence of the visual axes the receptive fields were always well separated on the tangent screen, and it was easy to explore each separately: to exclude one eye completely an occluder was placed in front of it.

The current experiments did not extend beyond 15° eccentricity, and the majority of receptive fields were between 5° and 10°. This had the advantage of simplifying the calculations by making it permissible to assess disparities solely in terms of linear separations on the tangent screen. The errors caused by this simplification were calculated for the unit with the greatest eccentricity, and were found to be negligible.

## *RESULTS*

Preliminary experiments taught us whereabouts in the cortex to place the electrode in order to record from neurones in the part of area 17 receiving its input from the central region of the visual field. The evidence that we were not recording in area 18, which lies next to 17, is as follows: (*a*) we inserted the electrode in area 17 according to the maps of Otsuka and Hassler (1962) and Hubel and Wiesel (1965): (*b*) we recorded a majority of units which, in most respects, fit Hubel and Wiesel's description of 'simple' cells: (*c*) if we moved laterally we obtained units which had much more complex properties: (*d*) if we moved medially we obtained units whose receptive fields lay more peripherally in the contralateral field of vision. There can therefore be little doubt that we were recording in the primary visual cortex.

We searched for the receptive fields by moving thin black bars, thin white slits, or black-white edges, of various orientations through the visual field. We found only minor divergences from Hubel and Wiesel's description (1962) of the units found in area 17. Out of 137 units 112 could be binocularly driven, although only 87 of these were plotted reliably enough to analyse the disparities. When a unit was found each eye was first studied independently. The axis orientation was established and two lines were marked parallel to this axis, marking the beginning and end of the response to a moving slit, bar, or edge, whichever was the most effective. These two lines form the primary borders of the plot. Lateral borders were determined by shifting laterally the continuously oscillating stimulus, maintaining the axis of orientation, until the end of the target had moved out of the field and no constant response could be elicited. This procedure was performed on both sides, and the resultant rectangular area we have called the *minimum response field*: regions outside this area affect the neurone but the influences are either subthreshold, or inhibitory and hence difficult to detect against a slow maintained discharge. Minimum response fields plotted in this way varied greatly in size, the smallest being about 3 min $\times$ 5 min, the largest about 6·5° $\times$ 6·5°. The fields for the two eyes were not necessarily the same size, the dominant eye tending to have the larger field. For reasons given below we think these minimum response fields give an approximate guide to the centres of the retinal areas which connect to a cortical neurone, but they do not by any means indicate the full extent of these areas. However, the plots were quite reproducible; repeat determinations indicated that the primary borders could be placed with an accuracy of 5–15 min, the lateral borders about 10–20 min. Reproducibility varied greatly from unit to unit.

For testing the hypothesis we need to know the positions of the stimulus for each eye where maximal binocular facilitation of the response is obtained. The centres of the minimum response fields provide a useful guide to these positions, but maximal facilitation was often obtained when the stimuli were not exactly centred on the minimum response fields, and, in a few of the smaller fields, the optimal position actually lay outside the monocular plot (for an example see Fig. 1 below). For this reason, when a minimum response field had been plotted for each eye, binocular interaction was examined by simultaneously stimulating the eyes with a pair of slits, bars, or edges, of the appropriate orientation, moved in synchrony. This is illustrated in Fig. 1. Owing to the divergence of the visual axes in our preparation the two minimum response fields lay several inches apart on the tangent screen, and the synchronously moving targets initially were separated by about the same amount. Variation of this separation varies the horizontal disparity of the binocular excitation; this corresponds to a change in depth of a single target when the visual axes are directed towards some fixed point, as they would be in an unanesthetized cat with normal muscular tonus. At some critical separation of the stimuli a maximum facilitation of the response was noted (see Fig. 1), and the positions of these optimally separated targets were marked with a line on their respective monocular response fields at the peak of the binocular response, judged by ear. The point on this line where the normal would pass through the centre of the monocular minimum response field was called the *binocular centre*, and our analysis has been performed on these positions. The average distance

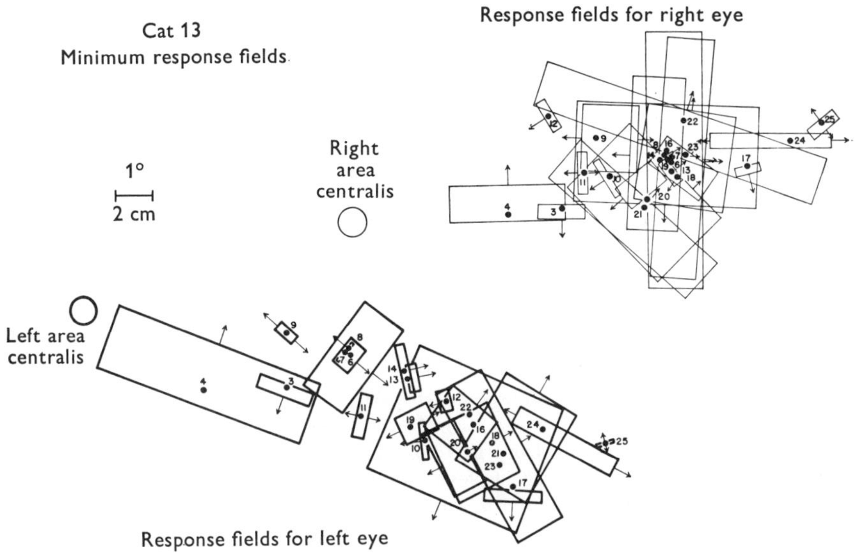


Fig. 2. A reconstruction of the minimum response fields for all the binocularly driven units studied in cat 13 as they appeared on the screen. For each unit there are two rectangular plots, not necessarily of the same size, with arrows to indicate the preferred directions of movement. Directionally-selective units have one arrow, bi-directional units two. The estimated projections of the areae centrales are shown and it is apparent that the visual axes are divergent. All the units in this cat were recorded from the left hemisphere and hence the minimum response fields occupy the contralateral visual hemi-field. The intorsion of the eyes, much more in the left than in the right, is reflected in the tilting of the two arrays of fields with respect to each other. In or near each minimum response field is the number of the unit and a dot representing the position of the binocular centre for that eye.

of the binocular centre from the centre of the minimum response field was 12 min in the 87 units (174 fields), and in fourteen of the smaller minimum response fields it actually lay just outside the monocular plot.

Figure 2 shows the minimum response fields of all the binocularly driven units studied in one cat. The fields are each numbered, and appear as rectangles of varying size and orientation in two groups, one for the right eye and one for the left. In, or near, each rectangle is a black dot, representing the binocular centre. These are reproduced as they appeared on the tangent screen facing the cat; the next problem is how to calculate the disparities.

*Data Reduction.* Ideally one would like to mark the exact position of the area centralis of each eye on Fig. 2, together with the true verticals and horizontals for the eyes in their normal positions, with no torsion. It would then be a simple matter to measure the position of each field in each eye in terms of azimuth and elevation, and obtain horizontal and vertical disparities by taking the differences. Unfortunately it is extremely difficult to determine the position of the area centralis in the cat: it cannot be ac-

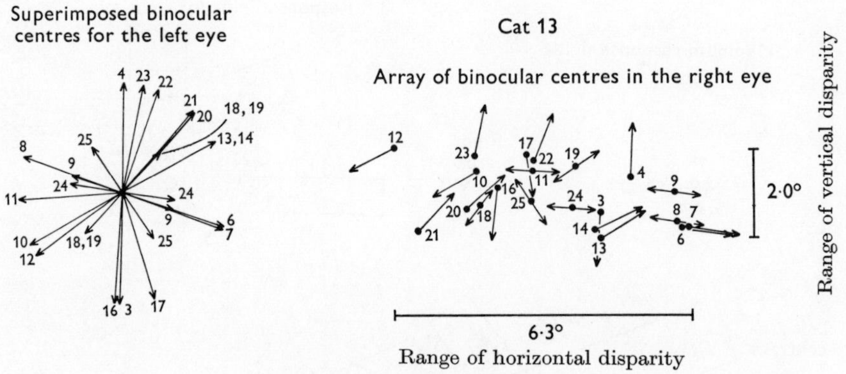


Fig. 3. Range of horizontal and vertical disparities of twenty-one cortical neurones in one cat. The positions of the receptive field centres for maximum binocular facilitation were determined on the tangent screen, and then shifted to correct for torsion and the difference in elevation of the two eyes. The directions and amounts of movement required to superimpose all the binocular centres of the receptive fields in the left eye were measured, and each right eye field was then shifted in a parallel direction by the same amount as its left eye counterpart. Arrows show the directional selectivity of the units, half length arrows indicating bi-directional responses. In this figure the dots at the tails of the arrows show the shifted positions of the binocular centres: they are superimposed in the left eye, and the scatter of the right eye dots shows the distribution of disparities.

TABLE 1. Spread of vertical and horizontal disparities in seven individual cats and results pooled by two alternative methods

| | Horizontal disparity | | Vertical disparity | | |
|---|---|---|---|---|---|
| Cat no. | Total range in degrees | Standard deviation in degrees | Total range in degrees | Standard deviation in degrees | No. of units studied |
| 6 | 2·4 | 1·2 | 0·4 | 0·21 | 3 |
| 7 | 2·9 | 0·85 | 1·6 | 0·45 | 9 |
| 8 | 4·2 | 0·94 | 1·5 | 0·38 | 19 |
| 9 | 4·7 | 1·5 | 2·2 | 0·75 | 12 |
| 10 | 3·9 | 1·4 | 0·9 | 0·36 | 6 |
| 11 | 5·7 | 1·6 | 1·1 | 0·34 | 17 |
| 13 | 6·3 | 1·9 | 2·0 | 0·62 | 21 |
| Pooled: areae centrales superimposed | 7·9 | 1·8 | 2·8 | 0·55 | 87 |
| Pooled: individual means superimposed | 6·6 | 1·5 | 2·2 | 0·51 | 87 |

curately located ophthalmoscopically, and we have made estimates based on the separation of the optic disks in the relaxed cat, using methods developed in P. O. Bishop's laboratory. However, the primary question we are trying to answer is not the absolute disparity of a single neurone, but whether the disparities are all the same. This question can be answered if many neurones are investigated in a single preparation, where the projections of the area centralis of each eye, wherever they may be, are always in the same place. For this reason we are not too upset by large errors in determining the position of the area centralis.

Figure 3 shows the result of adjusting the positions of the response fields in Fig. 2 by three operations. First, the response fields were swung around the area centralis to correct for the estimated torsion of each eye; the figure shows that the left eye had more torsion (see Methods). Next, the right fields were lowered to correct for the greater elevation of the right area centralis compared with the left. Finally, the linear displacements required to superimpose all the binocular centres of the left eye were measured, and these same displacements were applied to each of the corresponding right eye centres. The result is of course to make all the left eye centres coincide, and if the disparities were always equal the right eye centres would also coincide. It is abundantly clear that they do not, for these centres lie in an oval with 6·3° horizontal spread and 2° vertical spread. The 3 to 1 difference is worth emphasizing, for if the spread of disparities arose as a result of accumulated errors of our original estimates and the various corrections, there is no reason why the horizontal errors should so greatly exceed the vertical.

In Fig. 3 the direction of motion giving the greatest response is also indicated by an arrow; half length arrows signify bi-directional units. It might be thought that the disparities would be associated with their directional specificity, either because of errors associated with time lags, or possibly for some functional reason, but there is no evidence for this.

In six other cats sufficient neurones were isolated to estimate the horizontal and vertical spread of disparities. The total range and the unbiased estimate of standard deviation are used as measures of this spread in Table 1 which shows the results for all seven cats. There is no doubt that the spread of horizontal disparities greatly exceeds the spread of vertical disparities.

Figures 4 and 5 show the information from seven preparations combined in two different ways. In the histograms of Fig. 4 we have measured all disparities using the estimated positions of the two areae centrales as the reference points of zero disparity. Note the asymmetry of the distribution of horizontal disparity, with more convergent than divergent disparity. Note also that the ranges (2·8° vertical disparity and 7·9° horizontal disparity) exceed those of individual cats, probably because the error in locating the areae centrales is extending them. In Fig. 5 the results from separate preparations have been combined by superimposing the means of the individual histograms on the assumption that the mean vertical disparity is zero, and the mean horizontal disparity is the same in all preparations; for this figure it was assumed to be zero. As would be expected the spread is reduced, and becomes comparable with that of individual cats. In this figure we have also indicated the disparities of the estimated positions of the areae centrales of each cat, having defined the mean separation of binocular centres as zero disparity. The scatter of apparent disparities of the areae centrales

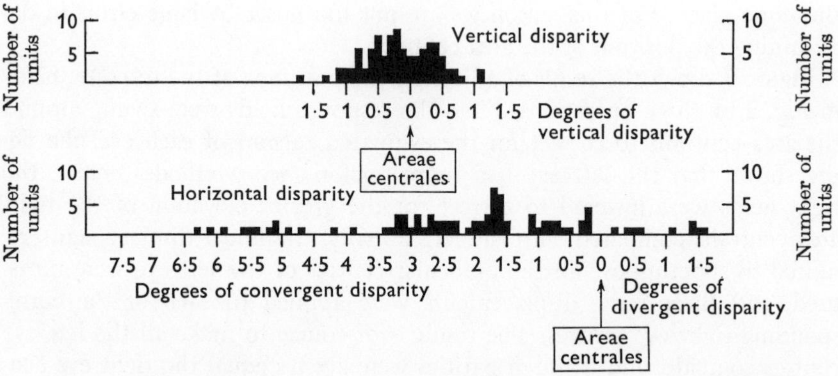


Fig. 4. Histograms of horizontal and vertical disparities of the binocular centres for 87 units in seven cats. The positions of the two areae centrales were estimated in each cat, and their vertical and horizontal separations were assigned zero disparity in that cat. If the horizontal angular separation of the binocular centres was less than the areae centrales, the unit had convergent disparity; if greater, the unit had divergent disparity. These units would be optimally stimulated by objects lying closer than, or beyond, the fixation point in the normal cat.

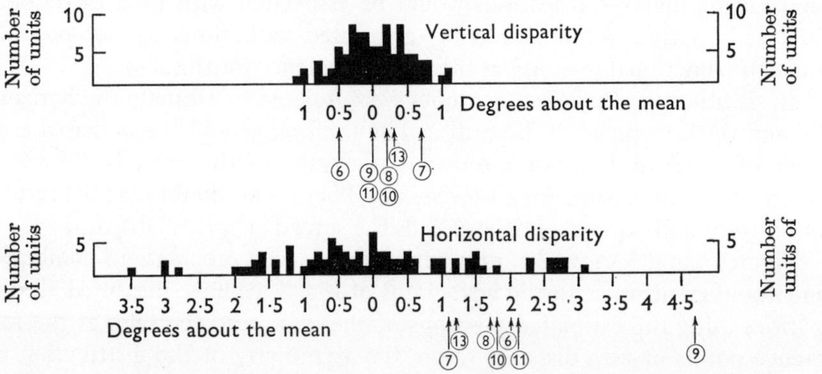


Fig. 5. Histograms of horizontal and vertical disparities with means superimposed. In Fig. 4 the results from different cats were combined by measuring disparities relative to the areae centrales, but since the estimate of area centralis position is subject to considerable error, Fig. 4 may indicate too wide a spread of disparities. In this figure the mean vertical and horizontal angular separations of the binocular centres for each cat have been assigned zero disparity and these reference points have been superimposed. This gives a more conservative estimate of the range of disparities than Fig. 4. Below the scale of each histogram are seven circles containing the identifying numbers of the cats. Arrows from these circles indicate the horizontal and vertical separations of the estimated areae centrales with respect to the mean disparities of the binocular centres. Much of the dispersion of these estimates is likely to be caused by errors in estimating the position of the area centralis.

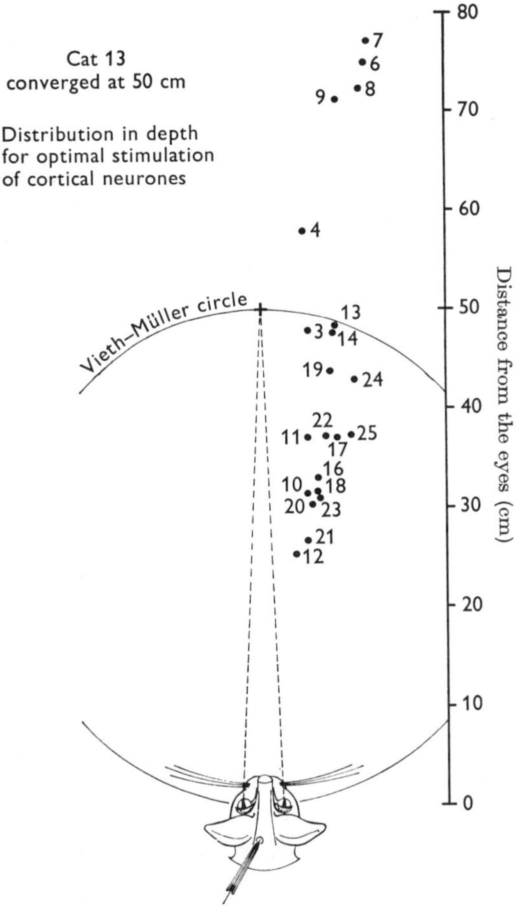


Fig. 6. Distribution in depth of positions for optimal stimulation of the units studied in cat 13. After the corrections for torsion and elevation had been made the array of binocular centres in both eyes was moved until the estimated visual axes were converged on a point 50 cm from the eyes. Each numbered dot shows the horizontal position and depth in space an object would have to occupy in order for its retinal images to fall on the binocular centres in the two eyes for that unit. These points are, then, the optimal positions in space, projected on to the horizontal plane, for the trigger features of the cortical cells.

is probably caused by errors of the procedure for estimating their positions, and we therefore believe that the histograms in Fig. 5 give a better representation of the actual disparities of cortical neurones than Fig. 4.

One must bear in mind the possibility that the mean disparity of cortical neurones varies with the eccentricity of their receptive fields in the visual field. Our data are not adequate to decide if there is a constant association between mean disparity and eccentricity, but there is certainly a big spread of disparities at all eccentricities. In Fig. 6 the data from cat 13 are displayed to show at what distance and horizontal position in space a stimulus should be applied to excite optimally each neurone, if the areae centrales are converged on a point 50 cm from the eyes.

## *DISCUSSION*

Figure 1 shows that the retinal images of a trigger feature must be correctly placed in both eyes to evoke the most vigorous response, and that incorrect positioning, equivalent to a disparity in the retinal images inappropriate for that particular neurone, results in a much smaller response. Furthermore, the results shown in Figs. 3–6 prove that different neurones require different disparities. It follows that, with fixed convergence, objects at different distances will excite different neurones. This provides a plausible basis for binocular depth discrimination and stereopsis, but of course there remains a lot to discover about how this depth information, segregated in different primary cortical cells, is subsequently sorted out by higher order visual neurones.

The 7° spread of horizontal disparities is very large compared with the disparity threshold required for stereopsis—only about 10 sec in man. Few estimates have been made of the upper limit for obtaining stereopsis, but Rashbass and Westheimer (1961) obtained definite convergent or divergent human eye movements for up to 5° of convergent or divergent disparity. Obviously, such movements require, at some stage, the detection of depth. In view of this finding the range does not appear unreasonable, nor does the greater spread towards convergent disparities indicated in Fig. 4, because of the geometric situation: if the eyes of cat 13 were converging on a point at 147 cm, the divergent spread would go to infinity, the convergent to 39 cm.

This discovery of surprising specificity of response at an early level in the visual system fits in with the trend of recent discoveries on the visual systems of vertebrates and invertebrates, where the trigger features are often amazingly specific, even at precortical levels (Barlow, 1953; Lettvin, Maturana, McCulloch & Pitts, 1959; Maturana & Frenk, 1963; Waterman & Wiersma, 1963; Barlow, Hill & Levick, 1964; Waterman, Wiersma & Bush, 1964). Furthermore, there is an indication that the mechanism of achieving this specificity may be similar, for it will be seen in Fig. 1, and even better in the work with post-stimulus time histograms (Pettigrew *et al.*, 1967b) that one eye 'vetos' the response of the other eye when the disparity is incorrect. Thus it may be another example of the kind of mechanism proposed by Barlow and Levick (1965) to account for directional selectivity in ganglion cells of the rabbit retina: here it was thought that selectivity was achieved by horizontal cells vetoing the response of bipolar cells.

Can the range of vertical disparities shown in Figs. 3 and 4 be explained by errors in our measurements and corrections? We think it is too big for this: perhaps variable vertical disparity is required to compensate and correct for vertical errors in the cat's eye movement control system, and for the vertical image disparities that inevitably arise at short viewing distances in the peripheral retina.

It is interesting to compare the action of the primary visual neurones in the cat's cortex with the mechanism for stereopsis proposed by Julesz (1961, 1965). In his experiments with random dot stereograms he found no evidence for monocular pattern recognition, on either a macroscopic or microscopic scale, preceding the binocular analysis that yields the impression of depth. He postulates a point by point comparison for varying disparities, or degrees of lateral shift of one of the fields, and he thinks a depth impression results when a zone of similarity between the two fields is revealed by a particular lateral shift. On his scheme the recognition that two regions belong to each other, and can yield a depth cue by their disparity, depends solely upon detecting point by point similarity. On the other hand our results suggest that the cat's cortex uses a less general, more specific, method; it appears to use primitive feature filtering to recognize similarity and thus decide upon the appropriate pairing up of the parts of the two eye fields.

One should be wary of assuming that these results on the cat apply *in toto* to man. It was suggested above that two operations were required for stereopsis: recognition of some feature in each image, and assessment of the disparities of these features caused by binocular parallax. It would not be at all surprising if man, with well developed colour vision, uses different features from the cat. And in other respects there may also be important differences, for Rashbass and Westheimer (1961) have shown that convergence movements in man are exquisitely controlled. Possibly the cat, a hunting animal, surveys a wide range of depth at low accuracy, whereas man, a sophisticated toolmaker, surveys a narrow band at high accuracy, varying the position of the band with his convergence movements.

## *REFERENCES*

Barlow, H. B. Summation and inhibition in the frog's retina. *Journal of Physiology*, 1953, *119*, 69-88.

Barlow, H. B., Hill, R. M., & Levick, W. R. Retinal ganglion cells responding selectively to direction and speed of image motion in the rabbit. *Journal of Physiology*, 1964, *173*, 377-407.

Barlow, H. B., & Levick, W. R. The mechanism of directionally selective units in rabbit's retina. *Journal of Physiology*, 1965, *178*, 477-504.

Bishop, P. O., Burke, W., Davis, R., & Hayhow, W. R. Binocular interaction in the lateral geniculate nucleus—a general review. *Transactions of the Ophthalmological Society of Aust.*, 1958, *18*, 15-35.

Bishop, P. O., Kozak, W., & Vakkur, G. J. Some quantitative aspects of the cat's eye: axis and plane of reference, visual field co-ordinates and optics. *Journal of Physiology*, 1962, *163*, 466-502.

Davson, H. *The eye.* Vol. 4. New York and London: Academic Press, 1962, 209-417.

Hubel, D. H., & Wiesel, T. N. Receptive fields, binocular interaction and functional architecture in the cat's visual cortex. *Journal of Physiology*, 1962, *160*, 106-154.

Hubel, D. H., & Wiesel, T. N. Receptive fields and functional architecture in two non-striate visual areas (18 and 19) of the cat. *Journal of Neurophysiology*, 1965, *28*, 229-289.

Julesz, B. Binocular depth perception and pattern recognition. In C. Cherry (Ed.), *Information theory. 4th London Symposium.* London: Butterworth, 1961, 212-224.

Julesz, B. Some neurophysiological problems of stereopsis. In P. W. Nye (Ed.), *Proceedings of the Symposium on Information Processing in Sight Sensory Systems.* Pasadena: California Institute of Technology, 1965.

Lettvin, J. Y., Maturana, H. R., McCulloch, W. S., & Pitts, W. H. What the frog's eye tells the frog's brain. *Proceedings of the Institute of Radio Engineers*, 1959, *47*, 1940-1951.

Maturana, H. R., & Frenk, S. Directional movement and horizontal edge detectors in the pigeon retina. *Science, N.Y.*, 1963, *142*, 977-979.

Nikara, T., Bishop, P. O., & Pettigrew, J. D. Analysis of retinal correspondence by studying receptive fields of binocular single units in cat striate cortex. *Experimental Brain Research*, 1968, *6*, 353-372.

Otsuka, R., & Hassler, R. Über Aufbau und Gliederung der corticalen Sehsphäre bei der Katze. *Arch. Psychiat. NervKrankh.*, 1962, *203*, 212-234.

Pettigrew, J. D. Binocular interaction on single units of the striate cortex of the cat. Thesis submitted for the degree of B.Sc. (Med.) in the Department of Physiology, University of Sydney.

Pettigrew, J. D., Nikara, T., & Bishop, P. O. Responses to moving slits by single units in cat striate cortex. *Experimental Brain Research*, 1968, *6*, 373-390.

Pettigrew, J. D., Nikara, T., & Bishop, P. O. Binocular interaction on single units in cat striate cortex: simultaneous stimulation by single moving slit with receptive fields in correspondence. *Experimental Brain Research*, 1968, *6*, 391-410.

Polyak, S. *The vertebrate visual system.* Chicago: University of Chicago Press, 1957, 109-110.

Rashbass, C., & Westheimer, G. Disjunctive eye movements. *Journal of Physiology*, 1961, *159*, 339-360.

Rodieck, R. W., Pettigrew, J. D., Bishop, P. O., & Nikara, T. Residual eye movements in receptive-field studies of paralyzed cats. *Vision Research*, 1967, *7*, 107-110.

Waterman, T. H., & Wiersma, C. A. G. Electrical responses in decapod crus-

tacean visual systems. *Journal of Cellular and Comparative Physiology,* 1963, *61,* 1-16.
Waterman, T. H., Wiersma, C. A. G., & Bush, B. M. H. Afferent visual responses in the optic nerve of the crab, Podophthalmus. *Journal of cellular and comparative Physiology,* 1964, *63,* 135-155.
Wheatstone, C. Contributions to the physiology of vision. Part the first: On some remarkable and hitherto unobserved phenomena of binocular vision. *Philosophical Transactions of the Royal Society,* II, 1838, 371-394.

*The main point of this section has been to demonstrate, by means of some of the major papers, how detailed investigation of the structure and function of the visual system has been made possible in recent years, mainly by improvements in the technology of electrode implantation and recording. It was also intended to give at least some feeling for the comparative anatomy of visual systems, and for the different types of neurophysiological coding which occur, culminating in the hierarchical receptive field organization found in mammalian visual systems.*

*We have seen the outlines of the major features of a contour coding system at the neurophysiological level, the demonstration that at least some additional special property detectors are to be found, and the promise that in all probability others will turn up in due course. The positive contributions of this neurophysiological work to our questions about pattern recognition are obvious enough. What of its limitations, if any?*

*The main limitation to my mind—and perhaps really the only one—is that the single unit recording technique seems to be restricted to the discovery of specific feature detectors, and this is only a step, as I have said before, in the process of pattern detection, stimulus classification and recognition. It is not necessarily true that single unit recording be limited in this way, yet it seems in fact to be true. For example, at some time the recognition of the equivalence of two patterns (say, of two triangles) must involve the integration of information about two or more contours in different orientations; yet there is extremely little evidence, if any, in the single unit work to indicate that this is a function of the receptive field coding system, even at the hypercomplex level. I have argued elsewhere (Dodwell, 1970b) that integration of different sorts of information from the receptive field system is quite probably achieved only through perceptual learning (cf. also my paper in Part II). This is speculative, but consistent I believe with the presently available evidence. The important general topic of perceptual learning, and how it is related to questions about stimulus equivalence, has been dealt with extensively in another book of readings (Dodwell, 1970a).*

*Perhaps it will seem, after reading this part, that the neurophysiologists have rather captured the field, and there is little enough left for the psychologist to do in it. But the arguments of the previous paragraph are arguments against that position. The sorts of questions about perception which the psychologist is equipped to answer certainly includes a range of items which is wider than that tackled by neurophysiologists. Perhaps we should look forward to the day when the typical experimental situation in either field will involve contributions from experts in both disciplines.*

# V

# MACHINES, MODELS, AND COMPUTER SIMULATION

*This final part of the book is devoted to a topic which has recently gained considerable importance in the psychology of perception and one whose contributions are likely to increase in the future. The title for the part suggests two closely related topics, but in fact there are really three. First, someone may have ideas about pattern recognition which suggest a mechanical, electrical, or similar analogue, that is a machine (in a general sense of machine) which embodies the principles on which pattern recognition is supposed to operate. Building such machines can be instructive both in clarifying and making more rigorous our thinking about the system it is designed to model, and perhaps also in suggesting new properties of the system which are worth investigating. The first paper, by Uttley, is of this sort. Second, it is possible to model a system by computer simulation (usually on a general-purpose digital computer with some special input device), which means devising a program to carry out the operations which are thought to be carried out in the real system. In principle these two ways of doing things are really equivalent, since what can be embodied in a special-purpose machine can be represented in a computer program, and vice versa. Historically, the building of machines preceded the devising of programs, and to a large extent the latter has now supplanted the former. The second paper, by Grimsdale et al., is an outstanding example of computerized methods of pattern recognition. It was not designed, however, to model specifically any particular biological system or process, but rather to solve a general problem about how patterns might be recognized. Third, ideas may flow, as it were, in the opposite direction. That is to say, general concepts from systems engineering, control theory, and the like may be applied to psychological problems, with a view to suggesting novel ways of solving them. The third paper, by MacKay, is largely of this sort.*

*The first two papers in this part were originally published before the neurophysiological work on contour coding had been reported. If the search for understanding of pattern recognition is to be and remain a truly co-operative venture among different disciplines, as it should be, we would certainly expect the neurophysiological findings to influence the makers of machine analogies and computer simulations, as well as psychologists. This* has happened to some extent, an early example being the application of local property detectors of the Hubel and Wiesel type to perceptron models for pattern recognition (Rosenblatt, 1962). It is true to say, however, that the neurophysiological findings can be applied only at a rather peripheral level in the input to such a system; they imply a degree of structure and pattern preprocessing already anticipated in the Grimsdale et al. paper, but have relatively little to suggest about the important question of how detected features are "assembled" into patterns (see Dodwell, 1970b, for further discussion of this point).

The early workers in the field of computer modeling nearly all assumed, as did many physiologists and psychologists, that the "wiring up" of the organism's central nervous system, and particularly within the brain, must be initially fairly random. The idea was that a high degree of specificity, initial structure, and organization in such a complicated organ as the brain, with its billions of potential connections (in man) must be inherently improbable, and biologically and psychologically unsound too, since the fact that organisms display perceptual learning in their early lives indicates that the system is plastic rather than "pre-wired" and fixed. An initially rather random arrangement which was organized through "experience" seemed to fit the bill. Yet the "random" machines were not very successful as pattern recognizors. The neurophysiological demonstration of a built-in detector (or pattern processing) system shows that the assumption of initial randomness was wrong, and using the principle of built-in detectors, it turns out in fact, can lead to better pattern recognition results with machines. Rather than quote papers to illustrate this point, we shall turn our attention in the final selection to the very difficult and important question of pattern "assembly," that is to say, to the problem of how the detected features are integrated into pattern categories. Again Grimsdale et al. were considerably ahead of the field in their treatment of this topic, some important later proposals being essentially extensions of their ideas (e.g., Clowes, 1967; Sutherland, 1968; Sutherland's paper is the most extensive and detailed attempt so far made to reconcile psychological findings with a computer model of this sort). The final selection is a paper by Stevens and Halle on speech perception. This may seem to be a very radical departure from the general plan of the book, but the paper is included for two reasons: (1) it indicates a different approach to the question of pattern assembly, and (2) it illustrates very clearly how close the problems of pattern recognition in speech are to the problems of visual recognition. It seems very probable that the communality of problems will lead increasingly to attempts to subsume both forms of behavior within a common conceptual framework. Neisser's Cognitive Psychology is an important contribution to such a development (see also Minsky, 1969).

The first selection, by Uttley, gives his basic ideas on hierarchical classification systems, and on how such a signal classifier might be embedded in *the nervous system. Subsequently these ideas were extended to incorporate a form of memory, in the so-called conditional probability computer (Uttley, 1958, 1959). Although space limitations preclude the possibility of quoting from those later papers, the central themes have been incorporated in a model already described in "A Coupled System for Coding and Learning in Shape Discrimination" in Part II.*

# *The Classification of Signals in the Nervous System*

A. M. UTTLEY

## *INTRODUCTION*

For a long time the behaviour and construction of machines have been compared with those of nervous systems; but the principles of known machines seem insufficient and methods of describing the activity of complicated parts of a nervous system are inadequate because of a lack of suitable analogies. In consequence, and also because the search may well be for many new principles, it is often difficult to discover what forms of behaviour are determined by what parts of a nervous system.

One approach has been to construct machines whose behaviour resembles that of animals in some respects. Specialised digital computers have been designed to solve logical problems (McCallum & Smith, 1951); universal digital computers have been programmed to solve such problems (Uttley, 1951), in particular to play chess (Shannon, 1950). Such machines have been programmed to learn (Oettinger, 1952). It is unlikely that structural resemblances could be seen between nervous systems and such machines, simply because they are universal; their structure permits all possible behavioural phenomena and so can contain no clue to the structure of a special machine. But the nervous system is a mechanism with special properties which are associated with a particular structure.

A number of principles have been suggested to explain the behaviour of animals. Wiener (1949) has emphasised the principle of feedback; but this, in itself, cannot contribute to plasticity; the relation between the input and the output of a servo-mechanism is invariant. The afferent feedback from

Reprinted from *EEG and Clinical Neurophysiology* (Appendix omitted), 1954.

sense organs can give rise to plasticity only if a learning principle is invoked.

Learning in an animal is seen in its simplest form in the conditioned reflex; such behaviour has been imitated in a number of machines (Ashby, 1953; Grey Walter, 1953). Grey Walter (1951) has enumerated a number of their essential requirements, and Mackay (1950) has pointed out that an essential operation is the computation of transition probabilities.

Yet another principle is that of "trial-and-error", seen in the random panic movements of animals in unfamiliar situations, e.g., cats in cages with latched doors; an accidental success in opening a door to obtain food tends to be repeated by virtue of a learning principle. The trial-and-error principle has been introduced into special machines (Ashby, 1948); also it has been programmed into universal computers.

When the designer of automatic machines considers the problem of animal behaviour, he finds himself in a peculiar and unfamiliar dilemma. In his normal work he never starts to design a machine without first knowing what mathematical equations are to be solved by the machine, what functions are to be computed, or what operations are to be performed. For example, memory, for him, is the storage of numbers; he cannot begin to design a "remembering" machine without first asking the question: "What numbers shall I store?"; and to this there is no very clear answer from biology. To postulate that synapses have the nature of variable resistances or switches and to consider the consequences is to enter the field of computer design, but by a method of thought that is the reverse of that of a machine designer, who always starts with a specification and deduces the necessary structure. The method of this paper is to concentrate attention on a small facet of animal behaviour, to suggest an explanatory hypothesis, and to deduce from it the principles of design of a mechanism capable of such behaviour. It must be for the biologist to consider whether the structure of the machine resembles that of any part of a nervous system. The element of behaviour chosen for consideration is that part of the stimulus-response activity which is generally known as pattern recognition.

The attitude of the physiologist to this problem may be illustrated by one or two quotations from Dr. E. D. Adrian's Anniversary Address to the Royal Society (1952). Referring to the olfactory organ he says: "It is still too early to give a definite decision, but it looks very much as though discrimination depends in the main on difference in the general distribution of excitation over the whole organ; in the spatial and temporal pattern set up by the arrival of different kinds of molecule . . . You will see that studies of the olfactory organ place the emphasis more on the whole pattern of discharge from it than on the reactions of the individual receptor, though these certainly determine the pattern. . . . And when we consider the flavours of food, the nerves of taste and all the sensory endings in the mouth will be involved as well to give the composite pattern which we recognise as that to be expected from, for instance, an anchovy or a banana." From this point of view pattern recognition depends on the analysis of signals in sensory fibres.

The question to be considered will be put in the following particular form. What kind of mechanism could distinguish the pattern of nervous activity set up by a banana from that set up by an anchovy? Consider another question of similar form. What kind of mechanism could distinguish a soldier who was married and had three children, from one who was unmarried and a bricklayer? To this second question there is an immediate answer. If the soldier is *represented* by holes in a punched card, then a sorting machine can distinguish two such cards, or rather it can distinguish the patterns of electrical activity set up by the holes in two such cards. An examination will therefore be made of the fundamental principles of a card sorting machine, of its essential structure and the actions of which it is capable.

## *CLASSIFICATION MECHANISMS*

A card sorter operates on the principle of classification, which is defined in the following way: "A set (or class or aggregate) of objects is to be thought of not as a heap of things specified by enumerating its members one after another, but as something determined by a property, which can be used to test the claim of any object to be a member of the set." (Newman, 1951). It is important to note that there can be only one of two possible results of the above test; a property is either possessed or not possessed.

A class of objects can contain a sub class which is determined by a set of properties; *a set of properties will be called a pattern.* Although the words "class" and "set" have the same meaning, the former word will be used in this paper when referring to objects, and the latter when referring to properties.

In the machine the object to be classified is a card, and its elementary

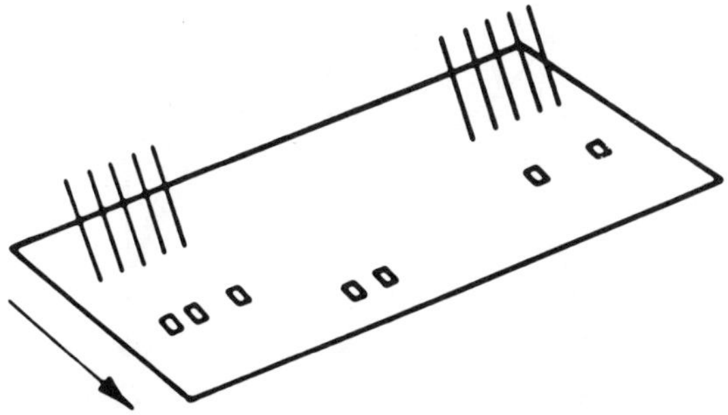

Fig. 1. A punched card and a row of brushes which can test a row of positions simultaneously.

property is that of possessing a hole in a particular position. The card travels under a row of wire brushes, any one of which is electrified if a hole passes it; such a card and hole-testing mechanism is shown in figure 1. Each brush will be said to provide an *input* to the classification mechanism. To distinguish a particular set of holes in a single row, the corresponding inputs can be arranged to control an *indicating unit* which will operate only if all the inputs are in the active state *simultaneously*. A point to be considered later arises from the fact that delay mechanisms are required if the pattern of holes to be analysed is contained in more than one row, that is, a temporal pattern. For analysis in respect of all possible classes in a machine, it would be necessary for the inputs to be combined in all possible ways, each combination operating an indicating unit of common design; the connections for a 3 input machine are shown in figure 2. If there were $n$ inputs there would have to be $2^n$ indicating units; in practical machines $n$ may be as large as 1000, but the need for very large numbers of units does not arise because the connections between inputs and units are changed to suit the problem in hand. The extent to which classification can be complete in a mechanism with *fixed connections* depends on the number of units that it is feasible to construct; nervous tissue would appear to be far less limited in this way than man-made mechanisms.

In comparing a classification machine with a nervous system, attention must be drawn not to the punched cards but to the electrical pulses they produce; essentially it is these which are the *properties* upon which classification is based. The soldier is transformed into a card and the card into

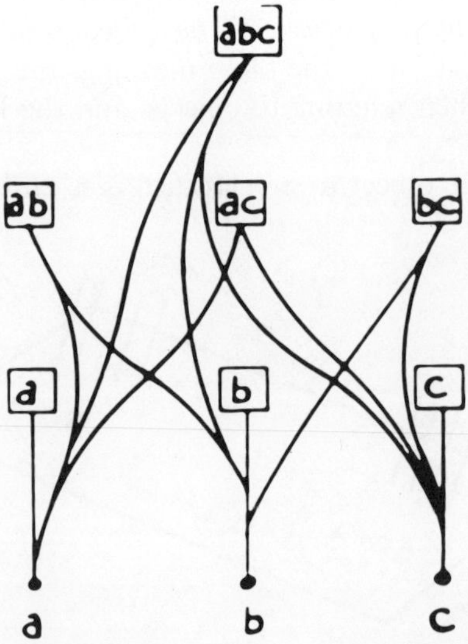


Fig. 2. A three input classification mechanism capable of distinguishing all possible classes simultaneously. Dots represent inputs, squares indicating units.

sets of pulses; but the card is only a convenient intermediate storage system for input data. It is not suggested that there is any corresponding storage of signals from receptors in a nervous system. *If a nervous system contains a classification mechanism then the elementary property of the external world upon which that classification is based is that of producing a state of activity in one of the fibres which is an input to the mechanism.*

Considering the behaviour of a classification machine, perhaps the most important feature is the ability to produce the same reaction or response to all objects of a certain class; this can occur only if the objects possess common properties and activate common inputs. Disjunct patterns could never give rise to the same response.

There are two further important features of the behaviour of classification machines; firstly, recognition is instantaneous and without error; secondly, there is no variation in behaviour, no learning or forgetting as a result of past experience; one reason for this is that there is no storage of the effects of past acts of classification.

The recognition by a bird of an egg regardless of its exact markings can be explained on the basis of classification; but this principle cannot explain a common reaction to stimuli from different sensory modes, or even from the same light stimulus falling on different areas of a retina. This extended form of recognition is the subject of a further paper (Uttley, 1954a).

## *CLASSIFICATION IN A NERVOUS SYSTEM*

In some areas of a nervous system connections appear to follow a discernible plan; a motor nerve may control a group of muscles; there may be a closed loop in the neural elements of a reflex system; there may be projection from a receptor area to a higher level. But in other areas no such plan can be found; in many neural bodies each efferent fibre appears to be influenced by many afferent fibres, and each afferent fibre appears to influence many efferent fibres; the situation exists in extreme form in cerebral cortex.

*The hypothesis will here be made that in such areas fibre growth is largely random.* Consider, for example, the structure of the primary visual area of the cat. The optic radiation contains specific afferent fibres which enter the visual area and arborise at about the fourth layer. Here they are in the presence of a dense population of neurons each with a dendritic system whose fibre density falls off exponentially with distance (Sholl, 1953); the axonal system of each specific afferent therefore comes close to the dendrites of various cortical neurons. *Assuming that connections are formed as a result of this chance proximity*, it can be shown that a classification system will arise to some extent; the treatment is static, there is no discussion of ontogenetic or other variation in the distribution of connections.

If a fibre *a* enters a neural body of the above structure, then about it there will be a cluster of neurons with only one connection to it; there will be a similar cluster for a second fibre *b*. Some neurons will be members of both clusters; these might be labelled (*ab*) neurons, the remaining neurons of the two clusters being labelled (*a*) and (*b*) neurons respectively. If all these neurons are to perform the function of indicating units in a classification mechanism, then

(i) An (*a*) neuron must fire if there is an impulse in the *a* axon to which it has one connection; similarly for (*b*).

(ii) An (*ab*) neuron must fire if impulses arrive at it simultaneously from *a* and *b* axons, but not if an impulse arrives from only one.

These conditions would not appear to be in accord with physiological facts. Consider therefore the hypothesis that a neuron fires if the post-synaptic potential rises to some multiple (say 10) of that produced by a single pre-synaptic impulse (Eccles, 1953).

The single afferent fibre *a* will have different numbers of connections to different neurons in its neighbourhood; the average number depends on the density of arborisation of the fibres and this will be discussed below. Neurons with less than ten connections will be inoperative and will not be discussed. Consider for the moment only those neurons with ten connections to the fibre *a*; all will function correctly as (*a*) indicating units. In a similar way there will be (*b*) indicating units. If the *a* and *b* axonal systems overlap there will be neurons with the following 9 arrangements of connection to *a* 1 2 3 4 5 6 7 8 9
to *b* 9 8 7 6 5 4 3 2 1 ; all will function correctly as (*ab*) indicating units since they will fire only if there are impulses in the *a* and *b* fibres simultaneously. The same argument can be applied for any number of afferent fibres up to 10 but, still considering only those neurons with 10 connections, classification will be impossible for sets of more than 10 fibres (patterns of more than 10 properties). The classification discussed here will be called *direct classification* because it is effected by neurons which are directly connected to the input fibres.

A second effect arises because the above neurons themselves possess axonal systems. Consider one neuron correctly labelled an (*a*) unit because it possesses ten connections to the *a* axon; then about it there will be a cluster of other neurons whose dendrites possess 10 connections to its axonal system; these too will function correctly as (*a*) units; they will be said to possess *indirect connections of the first order* to axon *a*, because they are connected to it via one intermediate neuron.

Consider now 2 neurons A and *B* with direct connections to afferent fibres as in table 1. Neuron A will indicate for the set (abcdefg) since it fires if all these inputs are active but not if some are inactive; similarly neuron *B* is an (fghijk) unit. The connections are shown in figure 3A. It will be possible for a neuron *a* to possess say six connections to A and four to *B*; this neuron

TABLE 1

| *Afferent Fibre* | *Neuron A* | *Neuron B* |
|---|---|---|
| a | 2 | |
| b | 2 | |
| c | 2 | |
| d | 1 | |
| e | 1 | |
| f | 1 | 2 |
| g | 1 | 2 |
| h | | 2 |
| i | | 2 |
| j | | 1 |
| k | | 1 |

will therefore be an (abcdefghijk) unit. In a similar way any of the original sets of up to 10 inputs can be combined in any number up to 10; in consequence there will arise a process of *classification of sets of sets.* The whole process can be repeated indefinitely, for higher orders of indirect connections; it will be called *indirect classification.*

This argument would be of little value if it could not be put upon a quantitative basis. The average number of connections between the mat of axonal fibres and the dendrites of a neuron may not be 10; even if it is, what will be the effect of neurons with greater numbers of connections?

Even though it is not known how many synapses there are between any axonal system and a neighbouring dendritic system, it is possible to calculate the number of times that these systems approach to within a given distance $s$ of each other (Uttley, 1954b). The necessary elementary geometry and statistics could be used equally well to calculate the number of times that a set of telephone wires touched the twigs in passing through an apple orchard. The assumption is therefore made that *if an axon and a dendrite grow to within a critical distance s (centre to centre) then a growth process is initiated whereby a synapse is formed.*

In what follows the term *fibre density* is defined as the length of fibre per unit volume. If all fibres were parallel this quantity would also be the number of fibres per unit cross sectional area; in this case the reciprocal of the square root of the density would be the mean separation of fibres. These notions are illustrated in figure 3B.

Sholl (*loc. cit.*) has shown that, except for apical dendrites, $D$ the dendritic density of a neuron in the striate area of the cat obeys the law

$$D = a \exp(-r/r_o)$$

$$\text{For stellate cells} \quad a = \exp(-5.89)$$

$$r_o = 31.2\mu$$

(The quantity $r_o$ used here is equal to the quantity $1/k$ of Sholl).

If the mean density of an axonal mat is $\overline{A}$, then it can be shown (Uttley,

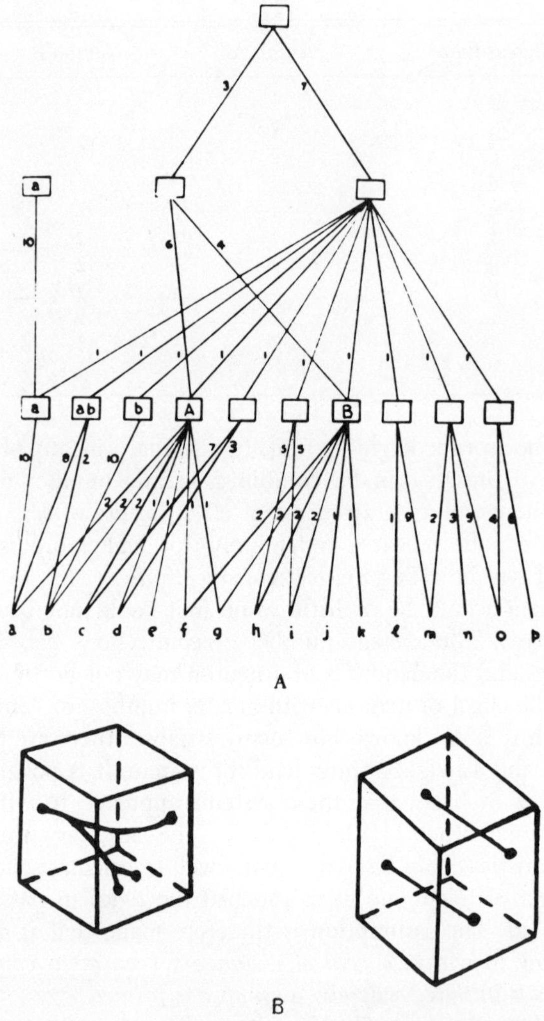


Fig. 3. A. Classification in sets of sets, no set containing more than ten elements. The number of connections to any unit is shown. B. The notion of fibre density.

*loc. cit.*) that N the average number of synapses formed with a neuron of the above form is given by the relation

$$N = 32ar^3{}_o s\overline{A}$$

For the above values of $a$ and $r_o$, $N$ will be ten if s $\overline{A} = 0.0037\ \mu^{-1}$. For example if s $= 2\ \mu$, then the mean separation of axonal fibres must be $23.2\mu$. Under these conditions it can be shown that about one in 8 neurons will possess 10 connections to the axonal system; they will be said to possess a *relative density* P(1) whose value is ⅛.

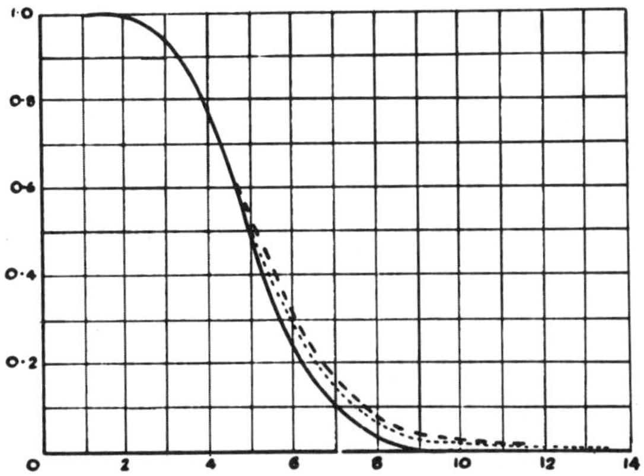


Fig. 4. The relative density of neurons which classify a set of r inputs. Ord. relative density. Abs. number of inputs. The full line includes all neurons with ten connections to an axonal mat. The dotted line includes those neurons with more than ten connections and which classify unambiguously. The broken line also includes those neurons which classify ambiguously. It is suggested that this function is related to the probability of a subject distinguishing a pattern of *r* objects.

The curve of figure 4 must therefore be modified in two ways. Because of the additional neurons which classify correctly, the curve will approach zero asymptotically instead of when $r = 11$. This is shown qualitatively by the dotted line in figure 4. If the relative density of the ambiguous neurons is included, the curve is raised still further; this is shown qualitatively by the broken line of figure 4.

## Indirect Classification

Now consider neurons which are embedded in the axonal fibres of the directly connected neurons. The argument of the previous section can be applied; there may be a region of the axonal mat which consists entirely of axonal fibres from 2 directly connected neurons *A* and *B*. The density of neurons with 10 connections to this material, and with at least one connection to A and one to *B* will be $\frac{P(2)}{P(1)}$; as before; in general, the function $\frac{P(r)}{P(1)}$ of figure 4 will describe the relative density of indicators of a set of *r sets of inputs.*

The argument can be extended for indirect connections of any order; it suggests a reason why, in psychological experiments to distinguish sets of objects, the results obtained are independent of the nature of the objects, for example whether they be dots, letters or words.

Hunter and Sigler (1940) have determined the total light energy E that there must be in a visual presentation of dots for correct discrimination of the pattern on 50 per cent of occasions. One can test the hypotheses that discrimination depends on an adequate number of indicator neurons firing, and that this number is proportional to $E$ and to $\frac{P(r)}{P(1)}$, the relative density of the neurons which act as indicators of the pattern. The product $\frac{E.P(r)}{P(1)}$ is given in table III on an arbitrary scale for different values of $r$; it does appear to be reasonably constant.

## Direct Classification

Now suppose that a large number of afferent fibres enter the population of neurons to form an axonal mat whose mean density $\overline{A}$ is such as to make the average number of connections to an embedded neuron equal to 10. In one region of the mat all the axons may arise from a single afferent fibre $a$, and here the relative density of $(a)$ indicators will be $P(1)$.

In another region of the mat the constituent axons may arise from two fibres $a$ and $b$. Any neuron which possesses 10 connections to the 2 fibres with at least one to each will act as an indicator of the set of inputs $(ab)$; it can be shown the density of such neurons will be a maximum if the 2 fibre systems have equal densities $A/2$; consider this situation.

The number of ways in which the 10 connections can be made to the $a$ or $b$ systems is $2^{10}$, and all will have equal probabilities; 2 of these ways will be of 10 connections to $a$ and 10 to $b$; the remaining ways will give rise to $(ab)$ indicators. Consequently if $P\ (2)$ is the relative density of these indicators

$$\frac{P(2)}{P(1)} = \frac{2^{10} - 2}{2^{10}}$$

By an extension of the argument it can be shown that if a region of the mat consists of $r$ afferent fibre systems, each of density $A/r$, then $P(r)/P(1)$ equals

$$\frac{r^{10} - {}_rC_1\,(r-1)^{10} + {}_rC_2\,(r-2)^{10} \ldots + (-1)^{r-1}{}_rC_{r-1}}{r^{10}}$$

This function is the relative density of neurons which can act as indicators of sets of $r$ inputs. If the system being considered does exist in nervous tissue, then the function describes the relative probability that an animal can distinguish a set or pattern of $r$ items. Values of this function are given in table 2, and graphically as the continuous line in Figure 4; they do appear to accord with known psychological facts.

Now consider neurons with more than 10 connections; the relative density of neurons with q connections is the Poisson function $\frac{e^{-N}N^{q}}{q\,!}$ which decreases as q increases above N.

N has been taken to be 10.

TABLE 2

| $r$ | $(P(r)/P(1)$ |
|---|---|
| 1 | 1 |
| 2 | 0.998 |
| 3 | 0.950 |
| 4 | 0.781 |
| 5 | 0.522 |
| 6 | 0.272 |
| 7 | 0.106 |
| 8 | 0.030 |
| 9 | 0.0047 |
| 10 | 0.0003 |
| 11 | 0 |

Consider first the neurons with 11 connections; their relative density will be 0.114. The majority of their connective arrangements will give rise to correct classification; but about 1 in $2^{11}$ of them can possess one connection to each of 11 fibres. Such neurons will fire if any 10 of these fibres are active simultaneously; in consequence they will act as *ambiguous indicating units.* There will be a similar effect for neurons with greater numbers of connections but because of the Poisson law their numbers will decrease rapidly as the number of connections increases. It would be possible to avoid the second of the above hypotheses if in the psychological experiment the energy were kept constant; the probability of a correct discrimination could then be compared directly with $P(r)/P(l)$.

In order to determine to what absolute extent indirect classification can occur consider only the $(a)$ units. For every neuron with 10 direct connections to the $a$ axon let there be an average number of $m$ neurons with 10 first order indirect connections to the $a$ axon as in figure 3A. Then because of a non linear effect, each of the latter neurons will activate more than $m$ neurons with second order indirect connections. Nevertheless, if the process continues indefinitely, the total number of $(a)$ indicators will remain finite if $m$ has less than a critical value. The value of $m$ depends on:

TABLE 3

| $r$ | $E.P(r)/P(1)$ |
|---|---|
| 2 | 4.4 |
| 3 | 5.6 |
| 4 | 5.0 |
| 5 | 4.4 |
| 6 | 2.5 |
| 7 | 6.6 |

(i) The parameters of the dendritic system of the neuron which have been determined by Sholl (*loc. cit.*).
(ii) Similar parameters of the axonal system of the neuron.
(iii) The critical distance to within which an axon and a dendrite must approach in order to form a synapse.
(iv) The mean volume density of the neurons; this has been determined (Sholl, *loc. cit.*; Mitra, 1953).

It is possible to calculate the value of $m$ for simple forms of axonal system (Uttley, *loc. cit.*).

If $m$ is small the whole effect will be negligible, but as m approaches the critical value it will be greatly magnified; if this value is exceeded and physically it is quite possible, then all neurons will be ($a$) units, all will be ($b$) units, so all will be ($ab$) units, and so on. In other words everything will fire everything. A structure of quite different properties emerges; if there is an impulse in a single afferent fibre, a wave of activity will pass through the whole structure, its velocity depending on synaptic and transmission time delays (Beurle, 1954). Because there is a refractory period after each neuron has fired, there is the possibility of a maintained oscillation in such a structure (Uttley, 1954c). But the property of classification will have been lost.

## Economy of Indicators

If there are $n$ inputs to a classification mechanism there are $2^n$ different sets of these inputs. For complete classification there should be an indicator for each set; for example, if there were a million specific afferent fibres in a cortex, the number of indicators should be $2^{1000000}$, which is about $10^{333,000}$. But if classification is limited to that of sets of sets, with a practical limit of 8 elements for a set, then the required number of indicators is enormously reduced, as the following approximate argument shows. A million inputs form 125,000 sets of eight; for complete classification of each of these sets $2^8$ indicators will be required; the total number required for this direct classification will be 32,000,000. Next the 125,000 sets of inputs can form 15625 sets of sets; they will require ⅛ (32,000,000) indicators for complete first order indirect classification. If the process is continued indefinitely the total number of indicators will be 32,000,000 $(1 + \frac{1}{8} + \frac{1}{64} \ldots)$ which is about 37,000,000.

In general, if there are $n$ inputs and sets are limited to contain $q$ elements, the number of required indicators is about $\frac{n.2q}{q^{-1}}$; so the number of required indicators is proportional to the number of inputs.

Applying this formula for the above example one finds that had the number of elements in a set been limited not to 8 but to 16, then the required number of indicators would have risen to 4360,000,000.

## *THE FORM OF INPUT SIGNALS TO A CLASSIFICATION MACHINE*

An input signal to a classification machine conveys the information that a property either is or is not possessed, so only two states of the signal are distinguished; these states could be "signal present" and "signal absent." It would appear that if a signal were present its form could vary in a number of ways, though no effect need be produced in the machine by this variation. But for a mechanism based on the hypothesis that a neuron fires if the p.s.p. exceeds some multiple of a quantum p.s.p. a principle of summation is introduced, so all signals must be constant in form.

### Constancy of Form

This requirement is met if the signal consists of a single pulse such as is produced, for example, by an on-off cell in a retina (Barlow, 1953) it is also met if the signal consists of a volley of pulses whose number is reasonably constant. But it is not met if the signal consists of a pulse train of varying frequency; this form exists widely in nervous systems, pulse frequency providing a variable analogue measure of the intensity of a stimulus.

The problem of controlling a machine suited to binary inputs by means of signals which vary continuously is often met in engineering; it is solved by interposing an *analogue-digital converter* in which a single analogue input controls a number of binary outputs. .To take a simple example, it might be arranged that the $r^{th}$ binary output of a converter was active if the input variable $x$ met the condition $x \geqslant r - l$. Such a converter would be acceptable in a calculating machine since the measure of the input signal would not be lost; but it might be too good for a nervous system which is notoriously bad at measuring the intensity of stimuli. Coding in a nervous system is considered further in the next section.

### Simultaneity and Temporal Pattern

The voltage waveforms on the brushes of a card sorter take the form of figure 5a; they are constant not only in amplitude but duration. They are also simultaneous, like chords on a piano, and classification occurs, i.e., indicating units operate, during each chord. If only the condition of constant

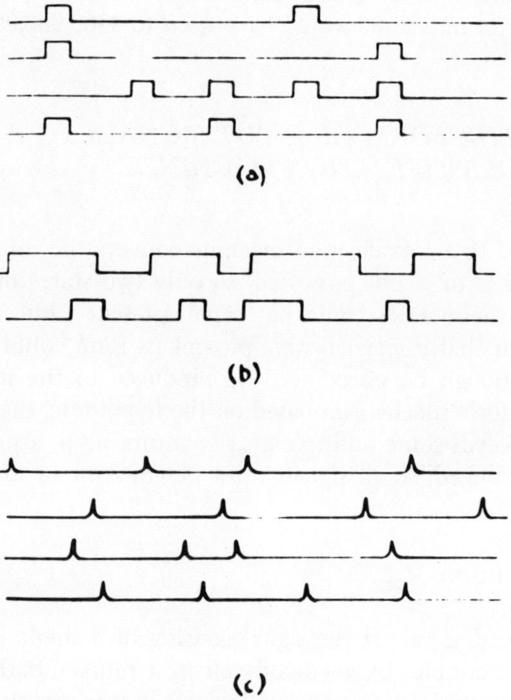


Fig. 5. Input signals to a classification mechanism.
(a) Waveforms from a punched card; signals constant in amplitude and duration.
(b) Waveforms constant in amplitude only. Upper signal from an *a* input; lower signal from a *b* input.
(c) Waveforms after differentiation and separation into *on* and *off* signals; reading downwards they are A *on*, A *off*, B *on* and B *off*.

amplitude were met, signals would take the form of figure 5b. The classification machine could still operate satisfactorily with such inputs, but its indicators would refer only to pattern of the form *a and b* occurring simultaneously; there would be no indicator to distinguish such a pattern from, say, *a occurred before b*. Additional indicators are required in a machine if temporal patterns are to be distinguished.

If the *a* and *b* waveforms of figure 5b are examined it can be seen that the idea of *a before b* is not a clear one. What distinguish the different (*ab*) patterns are the temporal relations between the instants when signals go "on" and "off". It is therefore necessary that these binary waveforms be *differentiated;* and if "a on" is to be distinguished from "a off", each of these occurrences must provide its own input to a classification mechanism.

If then, inputs are to be variable in form (e.g., amplitude or pulse frequency) and in duration, and if temporal patterns are to be distinguished, there must be *coding mechanisms* interposed between the inputs and the

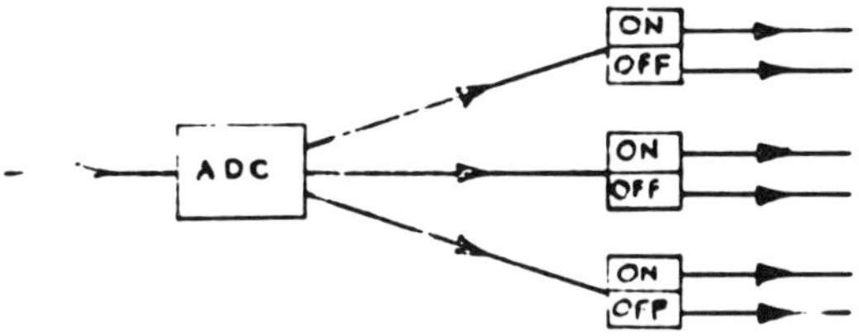


Fig. 6. Transformation of a variable signal into signals which can form inputs to a classification mechanism. After the analogue-digital converter ADC signals have the form of figure 5b; after the *on* and *off* mechanisms they have the form of figure 5c.

classification mechanism as in figure 6. First there must be analogue-digital converters; then there must be "on" and "off" mechanisms; and these coding mechanisms could not be interposed in the reverse order. The waveforms of figure 5b will now have been transformed into those of figure 5c. A third and final transformation is required to ensure that such signals arrive at indicators simultaneously.

It is necessary to consider only two such signals, say "a on" and "b off"; for convenience they will be referred to as the *j* and *k* inputs. Suppose first that the mechanism is to distinguish only three different temporal patterns,

(j before k) written as (j′k),
(j and k simultaneously) written as (jk)
(j after k) written as (jk′);

then there must be a separate indicator for each pattern. There must be a delay in the connection from the *j* input to the (*j′k*) indicator and from the *k* input to the (*jk′*) indicator; the arrangement for the three indicators is shown in figure 7A. Suppose that the delay is of duration $\delta$, that the signal is a pulse of duration $\tau$ and that the *k* pulse starts at a time *t* after the start of the *j* pulse, (t algebraic). Then the (*j′k*) unit will operate if

$$\delta + \tau > t > \delta - \tau,$$

the (*jk*) will operate if

$$\tau > t > -\tau,$$

the (*jk′*) unit will operate if

$$-\delta + \tau > t > -\delta - \tau;$$

these time relations are shown in figure 7B. If *t* exceeds $\delta + \tau$ in absolute value, pattern relations cannot arise. If some indicator is to operate for all lower values of t then $\delta$ must not exceed $2\tau$.

The signals *j*, *j delayed*, *k* and *k delayed* may be regarded as separate inputs which can be combined in all possible ways in a classification mecha-

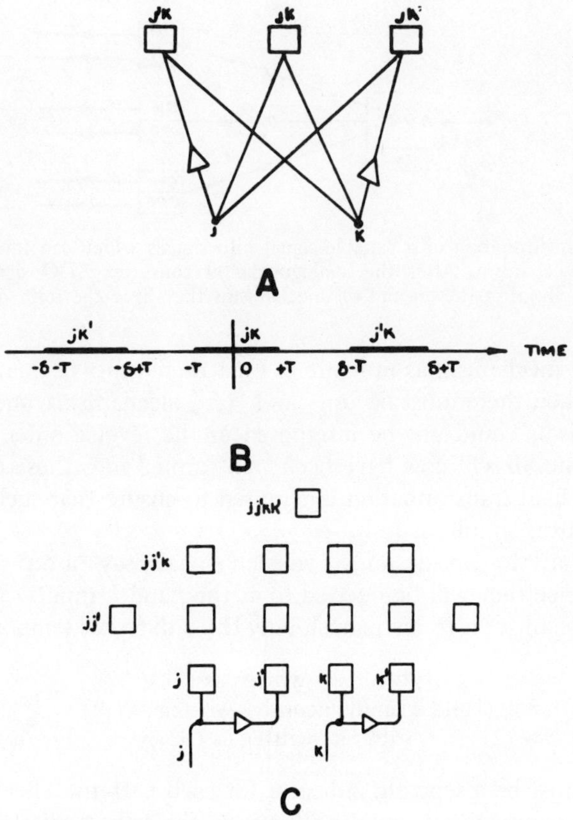


Fig. 7. A. An extended form of classification mechanism with three indicators to distinguish the temporal patterns *j before k, j and k simultaneous,* and *j after k.* Triangles represent delays.
B. Time relations between signals for the operation of the three indicators. The delay is of duration $\delta$; the signal is a pulse of duration $\tau$; the $j$ signal starts at a time $t$ before the $k$ signal.
C. A mechanism to distinguish the patterns of figure 8.

nism. This system takes the form of figure 7C. The 15 indicators distinguish the following patterns:

(j), (j′), (k), ((k′);
(jj′), (kk′), (jk), (j′k), (j′k′), (k′);
(j′kk′), (jkk′), (jj′k′), (jj′k);
(jj′kk′).

Of these patterns ($j'$), ($k'$) and ($j'k'$) are repeats of ($j$), ($k$) and ($jk$); so the delay mechanism invoked for the recognition of temporal pattern, also has the nature of a short term storage system. Omitting the repeated patterns, the others are represented by means of musical notation in figure 8; the introduction of the delay mechanism has made it possible for the classification machine to distinguish all these patterns.

Fig. 8. Temporal patterns which can be distinguished if the mechanism of figure 7A is extended to contain indicators for all possible combinations of the signals *j*, *j delayed*, *k* and *k delayed*.

A mechanism to demonstrate these facts can be simply constructed with 12 relays (it is briefly described in the Appendix to original paper: Ed.)

So far only the temporal relations *before*, *simultaneous* and *after* have been considered; these can be analysed in greater detail by means of an extended mechanism. For example, if there is a multiple delay for each input as in figure 9, a *variable* time delay can be analysed in respect of a finite number of classes.

If a temporal pattern of pulses occurs at the input to a multiple delay, it is coded into a spatial pattern which travels down the delay line; at a particular set of points in the line the whole pattern becomes available *simultaneously* for analysis by a classification mechanism; an example is given in figure 9. The delay line also stores the pattern during the time that it exists in the line.

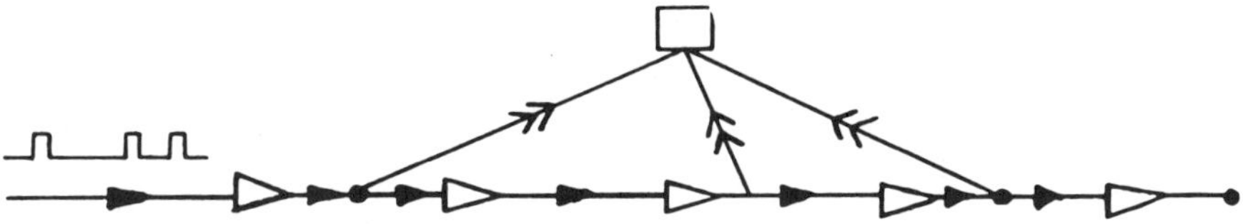

Fig. 9. A multiple delay line for distinguishing degrees of temporal separation between two input signals, and for distinguishing different temporal patterns in a single input signal; a temporal pattern is transformed into a moving spatial one. Double arrows indicate simultaneous signals to indicator.

Such a mechanism has the nature of the analogue-digital converter already suggested for the classification of variable intensities. But again there is the danger that such a mechanism can be too good to explain the psychological facts; in the multiple delay unit there is little loss of information of the quantitative measure of time intervals. Nevertheless some system with multiple outputs involving time delays would seem essential.

## *CODING IN A NERVOUS SYSTEM*

It has been shown that there are three stages in the transformation of a variable signal into one suitable for a classification machine; firstly there must be analogue-digital conversion, then there must be differentiation, and lastly there must be multiple delays. Could such transformations be occurring in nervous systems? The engineer would prefer them to be carried out in three separate units, but this would not be absolutely necessary. In a nervous system, there might be a progressive change in signal form through a larger number of bodies, but it should still be possible to observe the three principles at work though they might occur in overlapping phases. In this connection one may note the general arrangement in afferent pathways of first, second and third order neurons.

To detect such transformations it is necessary to examine the form of signals in fibres. If there is analogue-digital conversion there should be a tendency for the form of signals to change from one of variable pulse frequency to one in which there is either no activity or a constant state of activity. Such a change does appear to occur to a considerable extent in the cochlear nucleus of the cat. Galambos and Davis (1943) found that an increase in intensity of a stimulus (a pure tone) from 10 db above threshold to 20 db above threshold increased the discharge rate in an afferent fibre to the nucleus almost threefold; but Hilali and Whitfield (1953) found that a similar increase in intensity only increased the discharge rate in an efferent fibre by between 20 and 100 per cent; the two relations are shown in figure 10. Similarly, for variation in the frequency of the stimulus, there is a tendency for the discharge rate to vary less in efferent fibres than in afferent fibres of the nucleus (Whitefield, 1953). The two relations are shown in figure 11.

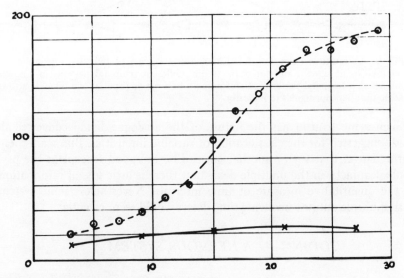

Fig. 10. The tendency towards analogue-binary conversion in the cochlear nucleus in respect of intensity of sine wave stimulus.

Ordinate. Fibre pulse rate. Abscissa. Intensity of stimulus.

Broken line characteristic of afferent fibre (Galambos & Davis, 1943).

Full line characteristic of efferent fibre (Hilali & Whitfield, 1953).

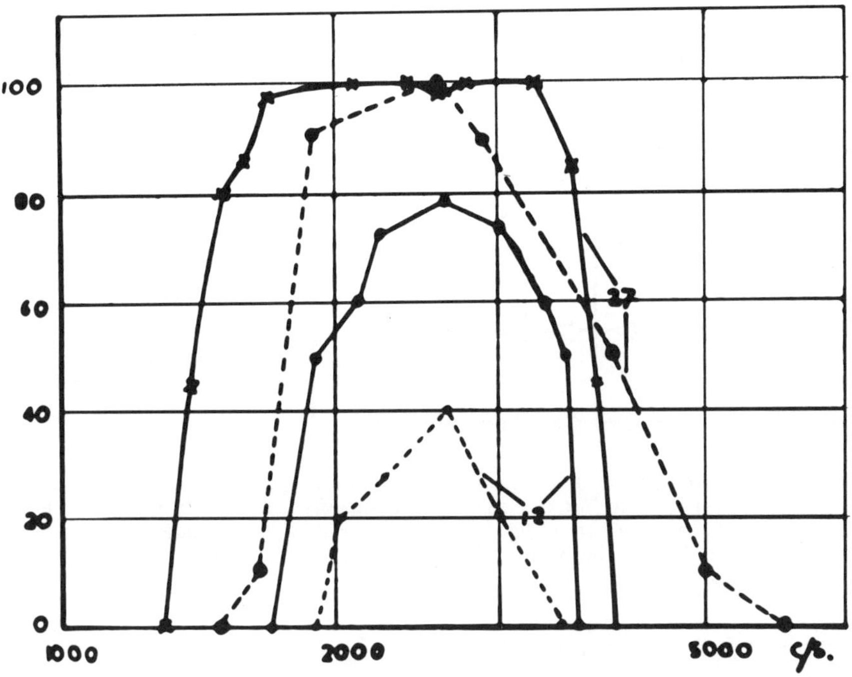


Fig. 11. The tendency towards analogue-binary conversion in the cochlear nucleus in respect of frequency of sine wave stimulus. Ord. Fibre pulse rate as % of max. Abs. Frequency of stimulus. Broken line characteristic of afferent fibre. Full line characteristic of efferent fiber. (Whitfield, 1953.)

The requirement of differentiation is partly met by the phenomenon of adaptation, a ubiquitous property of living tissue. An increased discharge at the onset of a stimulus can be seen in the records of Galambos and Davis for afferent fibres to the cochlear nucleus, and in those of Hilali and Whitfield for efferent fibres. But there should also be fibres in which there are increased discharges when stimuli cease, if such occurrences are to form elements of temporal patterns.

The requirement of a multiple delay is met by a long chain of neurons but not by a short ring alone; in the latter there will be ambiguity of time measurement because there will be no means of distinguishing the number of times that a wave of activity has gone round. Figure 3A shows the way connections will form in a population of neurons; at the left hand side of the diagram it can be seen that a chain of ($a$) neurons is produced. It is possible, therefore, that such a system can meet the two requirements of classification and delay.

In a multiple delay a single input pulse produces activity for a finite time, and such a phenomenon has been observed by de Lisle Burns (1951) in experiments on blocks of isolated cortex; the activity lasts for several seconds.

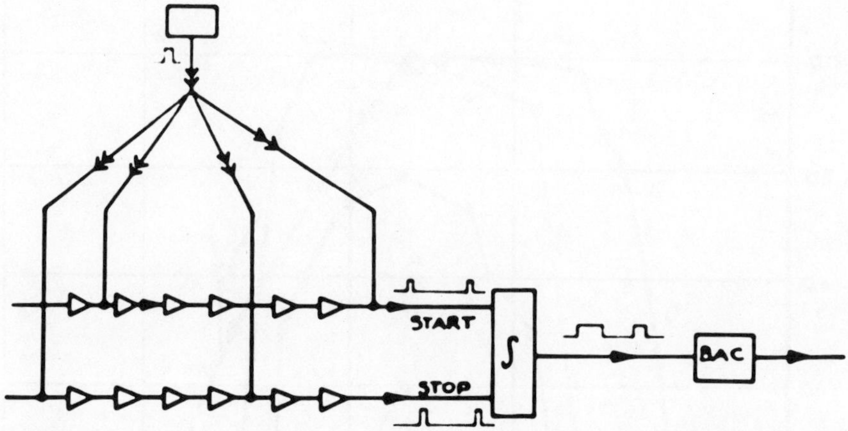


Fig. 12. The necessary transformations of a single output pulse from a classification mechanism if it is to give rise to a signal whose intensity varies with time. After the delay line signals have the form of figure 5c; after the *start stop* mechanisms they have the form of figure 5b; after the Binary Analogue Converter, BAC, the signal can be of variable intensity.

Psychological experiments by Blakely (1953) on the human discrimination of time intervals between clicks show that the departure from Weber's law begins to occur for intervals of the order of 3 sec.

## Coding From a Classification Mechanism

It is no part of this paper to discuss the synthesis of efferent patterns, but it may be pointed out that the ouput from a classification mechanism is the binary signal from an indicating unit. If such outputs are to determine patterns of signals to motor units, and if the signals are to be pulse trains of variable frequency, then the coding mechanisms may be the converse of those discussed for afferent signals; they are shown in figure 12. First there must be a multiple delay line with a parallel input from the classification mechanism and a serial output of short pulses. Next there must be a principle of *integration;* instead of the *on-off* mechanism there must be a *start-stop* mechanism. The need for this has been pointed out by Craik (1945). Finally there must be *binary-analogue conversion.*

## *SUMMARY*

A machine for sorting punched cards operates on the principle of classification; the objects (cards) possess properties (holes) and any set of such properties, called a pattern, determines a class of card. In the machine, cards are distinguished by the temporal and spatial patterns of electrical activity set up in a row of brushes which detect the holes as the cards move by. Consider only one row of holes, so that temporal patterns do not arise; a spatial pattern of signals is distinguished if the corresponding brushes are connected to an indicator which can operate only if all these brushes are electrified. To distinguish all possible spatial patterns simultaneously indicators would have to be connected to inputs in all possible ways. This system of connections arises naturally if inputs and indicators are connected at random. To distinguish temporal patterns additional delay mechanisms must be included.

If a nervous system contains a classification mechanism then the elementary property of the external world upon which that classification is based is that of producing a state of activity in one of the fibres which is an input to the mechanism.

The inputs and indicators of the machine are compared to the afferent fibres and neurons of cerebral cortex; it is suggested that synapses between them are formed if, by chance, axons and dendrites approach to within some critical distance; if this is so a classification mechanism can arise to a considerable extent. If it is assumed that a neuron fires only if some critical number q of pre-synaptic impulses occur simultaneously, it can be shown that the cortical neurons which are directly connected to specific afferent fibres can act as indicators for sets of input signals not exceeding $q$ in number. Neurons which are connected to the above neurons can classify in respect of sets of signals, but no set can exceed $q$ in number; the process can continue indefinitely.

The relative density of the neurons which can act as indicators of a set of r elements can be calculated; it accords quite well with the results of psychological experiments.

The input signals to a classification mechanism are of standard intensity and duration; if the machine is to be controlled by signals which are pulse trains of variable frequency, their necessary transformation can be deduced; there is evidence that such transformations do occur, for example, in the cochlear nucleus.

## *REFERENCES*


Adrian, E. D. Address of the President. *Proceedings of the Royal Society, Series B.*, 1952, *139*, 289-299.

Ashby, W. R. Design for a brain. *Electrical Engineering*, 1948, *20*, 379-383.

Barlow, H. B. Action potentials from the frog's retina. *Journal of Physiology*, 1953, *119*, 58-68.

Beurle, R. I. Activity in a block of cells capable of regenerating pulses. *Radar Research Establishment Memorandum,* 1954, No. 1042.

Blakely, W. The discrimination of short empty temporal intervals. Ph.D. Thesis, University of Illinois Library, 1933.

Burns, B. D. Some properties of isolated cerebral cortex. *Journal of Physiology,* 1951, *112,* 156.

Craik, K. J. W. Theory of the human operator in control systems. *British Journal of Psychology,* 1947, 38, 56-61.

Eccles, J. C. *The neurological basis of mind.* Oxford: Oxford University Press, 1953, 132.

Galambos, R., & Davis, H. The response of single auditory nerve fibres to acoustic stimulation. *Journal of Neurophysiology,* 1943, 6, 39-57.

Garrett, H. E., & Schneck, M. R. *Psychological tests.* New York: Harper, 1933.

Hilali, S., & Whitfield, I. C. Responses of the trapezoid body to acoustic stimulation with pure tones. *Journal of Physiology,* 1953, *122,* 158-171.

Hunter, W. S., & Sigler, M. The span of visual discrimination as a function of time and intensity of stimulation. *Journal of Experimental Psychology,* 1940, 26, 160-179.

MacKay, D. M. *Symposium on information theory.* London, 1950, 194-195.

McCallum, D. M., & Smith, J. B. Mechanical reasoning. Logical computers and their design. *Electrical Engineering,* 1951, 23, 126-133.

Mitra, N. L. A comparative study of neuron types in the mammalian neocortex. Ph.D. Thesis. University of London Library, 1953.

Newman, M. H. A. *Elements of the topology of plane sets of points.* Oxford: Oxford University Press, 1951.

Oettinger, A. G. Programming a digital computer to learn. *Philosophical Magazine,* 1952, 43, 1243-1263.

Shannon, C. E. Programming a computer to play chess. *Philosophical Magazine,* 1950, *41,* 256-275.

Sholl, D. A. Dendritic organisation in the neurons of the visual and motor cortices of the cat. *Journal of Anatomy,* 1953, 87, 387-406.

Uttley, A. M. Les machines à calculer et la pensée humaine. *Colloque Internationale C.R.N.S., Paris,* 1951, 465-473.

Uttley, A. M. Conditional probability machines and Conditioned Reflexes. *Radar Research Establishment Memorandum,* 1954, No. 1045. (a)

Uttley, A. M. The probability of neural connections. *Radar Research Establishment Memorandum,* 1954, No. 1048. (b)

Uttley, A. M. The stability of a uniform population of neurons. *Radar Research Establishment Memorandum,* 1954, No. 1049. (c)

Walter, W. Grey. Les machines à calculer et la pensée humaine. *Colloque Internationale C.R.N.S., Paris,* 1951, 407-421.

Walter, W. Grey. *The living brain.* London: Duckworth, 1953, 4212.

Whitfield, I. C. Auditory nerve patterns and their relation to the cortical response. *Proceedings of the XIX. International Physiological Congress, Montreal,* 1953, 885.

Wiener, N. *Cybernetics.* New York: Wiley, 1948.

A criticism which has been leveled more than once at Uttley's type of system is that it is potentially too complete: if a nervous system were to compute or classify all the different possible combinations of input patterns, given the number of photoreceptors on a retina, the required system would be astronomically large. However, it is now clear what the correct answer to that objection is, if the system is held to model vertebrate vision: there is a good deal of predigestion or preprocessing of patterns of spatial information before input to the central nervous classificatory system. This gives a very drastic reduction in the number of classifying units. A suggestion of how this reduction could be achieved was given in the model described in my paper in Part II, and we now have forceful evidence, in the form of neurophysiological specification of contour coding, that such preprocessing really does occur in higher visual forms at least.

The next paper is the sole representative of a computer pattern recognition system, but an important one. Ironically enough, Grimsdale and his colleagues were not interested in attempting to model any biological pattern recognizer, and yet their ideas turned out to be a good deal closer to a successful model of the mammalian pattern recognition system than the ideas of others, who started out with the objective of designing such a model explicitly in mind. This of course does not mean that the paper presents a completely sucessful model; nevertheless it is striking that "feature detection" was arrived at as a rational solution for problems of pattern recognition and equivalence independently of the discovery of "feature detection" as a property of visual systems. As was indicated earlier, Grimsdale et al. were also among the first to tackle the problem of pattern recognition as a process of "Gestalt formation", that is, as a question of how the individual elements or features are assembled, or integrated into a single pattern.

# A System for the Automatic Recognition of Patterns

R. L. GRIMSDALE, F. H. SUMNER,
C. J. TUNIS, AND T. KILBURN

*The paper describes a new method for the automatic recognition of patterns. The method may be applied to any form of spatial pattern, but in the present instance, patterns consisting of line figures are considered. The pattern is presented to a flying-spot scanner connected to a digital computer. The shape of the pattern is analysed and a statement is prepared describing the basic features of the pattern. The pattern is then recognized by comparing this statement with a number of others already stored in the computer which relate to named patterns. Patterns are recognized independently of the angle at which they are presented to the scanner, and may be of any size provided that limits imposed by the resolution of the scanner are not exceeded. The average time to recognize a character is 60 seconds with the system programmed on a medium-speed computer. Special-purpose equipment built to perform certain of the stages of the process, together with the use of higher-speed computers now envisaged, will reduce this time by at least a thousandfold.*

*If a new pattern is presented to the machine, it will indicate its inability to recognize the pattern, but by giving the machine the name of the pattern, it may become one of the standard patterns which it can subsequently recognize. All the patterns recognized by the machine are hand-drawn and consist of such symbols as the capital letters of the alphabet and numerals, although the system is in no way limited to any special set of characters. Using exactly the same method but with an increase in the degree of complexity, it will be possible for machines to read handwriting.*

*Special allowances are made for imperfections in the patterns, including breaks and general ill-definition. Where there is some confusion and an unknown pattern resembles two or more of the standard patterns, the relative degrees of similarity of the unknown to each of these standard patterns is printed out by the machine.*

Reprinted from *Proceedings of the Institute of Electrical Engineers,* 1959.

## *INTRODUCTION*

Automatic recognition of characters—printed or handwritten—is becoming increasingly important. The paper describes a system for automatic pattern recognition. The distinction between a "character" and a "pattern" is important because both a Gothic and an Arabic A may be considered to be the same character but are entirely different patterns. A less extreme example of this is the symbols **4** and ***4***.

The system at present is restricted to line figures, although it could be adapted to solid ones. The pattern is fed into the computer using a flying-spot scanner and is represented within the machine as a two-dimensional array of points in the store (Fig. 1). The pattern is examined by a programmed scan which starts as a television-type scan until part of the pattern is found. The scan then changes to follow the particular part of the figure, the scan progressing essentially in a vertical direction. This mechanism produces a description of the part of the figure, giving details of the length, slope and curvature. This part is then removed and descriptions are obtained of the remaining parts. A further process assembles the parts of the figure as scanned into more basic sections which are to form the "statement." The statement is then compared with the statements of the patterns "known" to the machine. A considerable degree of flexibility is included in

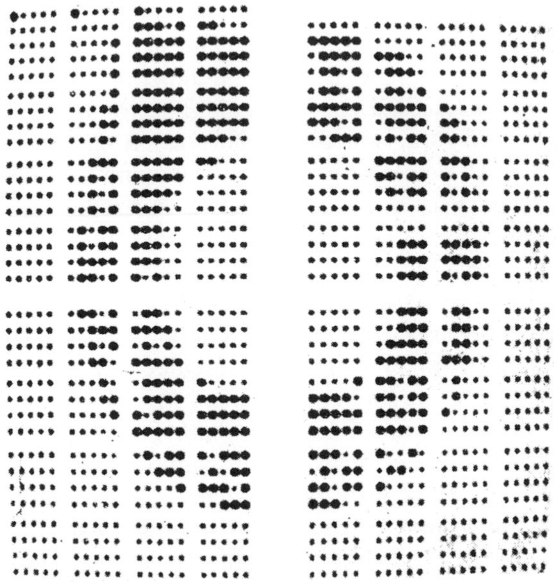

Fig. 1. Computer console display of stored pattern.

this recognition section, and the statement referring to the unknown pattern need not be identical with a particular statement of a known pattern, but need only be nearly identical.

The system can thus produce a statement for an unknown pattern which subsequently becomes one of the known statements. In this way the machine can "learn" new patterns.

The present system differs from the majority of methods (Bailey & Norris, 1957; Chow, 1957; Dineen, 1955; Greanias et al., 1956; Kirsch et al., 1957; Loeb, 1953, p. 317, p. 322; Magnetic ink, 1965; Shepard, Bargh, & Heasly, 1957) which have been devised or produced for character recognition, because it obtains a description of the shape of the figure. The majority of the other methods involve a geometrical comparison of the unknown figure with a set of standard figures. The simplest one (Shepard, Bargh, & Heasly, 1957) uses a rotating disc and an optical system with a photocell to measure the amount of agreement. It is not always realized that with such systems the amount of disagreement between the unknown and the standard figures is just as important as the amount of agreement. This is particularly evident in the comparison between the symbols **C** and **O**.

Other methods, (Bailey & Norris, 1957; Dineen, 1955; Greanias et al., 1956; Kirsch et al., 1957) including the present one, involve some sort of scanning, either by a vertical bank of photocells moving horizontally, or by a flying-spot scanner and a single photocell. Such scanning systems are employed for economic reasons, although a two-dimensional array of photosensors, as in the human eye, would give higher speeds.

The use of figures printed with magnetic ink (Magnetic ink, 1965) is being extensively developed in America. The figures are magnetized and passed under a single magnetic head. The number of symbols which can be distinguished by this method is severely limited, to about 12. The figures must be of a special form and differ somewhat from normal typescripts, particularly if a small degree of rotation of the figure is to be allowed.

One system (Greanias, et al., 1956) uses a flying-spot scanner with vertical scanning lines. As the scanning point passes over the figure, the position, number and length of the intersections of the figure by the scan are recorded. The figure is recognized by details of these intersections.

Another system involves the use of a flying-spot scanner to divide the pattern area into a matrix of 10 by 10 points (Bailey & Norrie, 1957). The information (black or white points) contained in this matrix is used to activate a set of logical circuits. These test both for the concurrence of observed black areas with those of a standard symbol, and for the concurrence of white areas. Displacement of the character is allowed for by the use of a "pre-scan," which positions the scan relative to the character. The number of symbols handled is limited, and rotation of the characters is not tolerated, but the method is very fast.

One of the difficulties inherent in the process of scanning symbols

Fig. 2. Enlarged typewritten character.

printed on paper is the poor quality encountered in practice. Fig. 2 shows an enlarged symbol printed by a normal typewriter. When the blurring and mutilation which the symbol may suffer in its subsequent history are superimposed, it becomes apparent that any processing of the scanner output must take account of these imperfections. This problem is considered in the paper; it has also been considered in a different way at M.I.T. (Selfridge, 1955) Another approach to the problem of pattern recognition is one in which a conditional probability machine is used (Uttley, 1956, p. 277).

## *GENERAL DESCRIPTION OF THE SYSTEM*

The operation is performed in a number of stages, each of which will be considered in detail. The pattern is first transferred from paper to the store of the computer. The pattern is then examined by a programmed scan. The result of the scan is to produce descriptions of segments of the figure, i.e., divisions which are conveniently produced by the scanning process, and are not necessarily true divisions. The vertical and horizontal lines comprising a letter **L** might be regarded as true divisions. The scanning process also includes measures to allow for figure imperfections, dirt on the paper, and other forms of "noise."

In the "assembly" part of the programme which follows, the segments of the figure obtained in the scan are analysed and connected, wherever appropriate, into true figure parts; a description is given of the length and slope of straight-line parts and the length and curvature of curved portions. The scan and assembly sections of the programme together produce the "statement," which gives a complete description of the figure. This description is independent of the orientation and size of the figure, the lengths of the various parts being given relative to one another. It is, in effect, a coded representation of the pattern. It may be regarded as a one-dimensional pattern which consists of symbols chosen from a restricted range. For example, there is one symbol to represent a straight-line portion and another to represent a curved portion. In the "recognition" section which follows, a comparison is made between the one-dimensional pattern or statement describing the unknown pattern and the statements already stored within the computer, together with the names of the patterns they describe. A considerable time would be wasted if every stored statement had to be examined; to prevent this, an automatic classification system is provided; this examines the stored statements and arranges them into classes according to common features. As an example, all statements describing figures with, say, four ends would be grouped together; then, at an early stage in the recognition process, a statement referring to an unknown pattern which had four ends would be compared with the statements which are members of the "four ends" class.

The criterion for a successful comparison is that there must be a certain measure of agreement between the "unknown" statement and the statement referring to the pattern with which it is to be identified. This must be substantially greater than the agreement between the unknown statement and any of the other stored statements. The relative importance of the features embodied in the statements, used in assessing the measure of the agreement, may be stated by the programme designer or may be acquired by the system as the result of "experience." In this case it will be necessary to measure the time to search for the required stored statement, using various classification systems, and to give a high score to those which yield a minimum. On subsequent searches, classification systems with a high score will be used first.

## The Scan

The object of this part of the scheme is to produce a form of geometrical description of the figure; such a description will not be ideal, but will provide sufficient and convenient information for the assembly programme to process into the statement. One of the difficulties with the scanning of an actual pattern is that the quality is often very poor and may undergo further deterioration in the transfer to the computer using the flying-spot scanner. The other difficulty is that, to achieve greatest speed, it is best to programme the computer to perform what is basically a horizontal scan. Vertical or nearly vertical lines may then be readily examined, but horizontal lines present more difficulty. It would be desirable to provide special facilities in the computer or in some special-purpose equipment for easier vertical scanning. The whole of the pattern is examined, although this amounts to examining the edges after testing that the particular horizontal portion of the pattern has an adequate amount of "black" or figure points between the edges.

The Manchester Mark I Computer has been used for this work and so it has been convenient to choose a raster size of $40 \times 64$. The picture area is then represented in the machine by 64 forty-digit lines. Points on the pattern appear as points on these lines; this is illustrated in Fig. 1. Scanning is conveniently done from right to left along the horizontal lines of this stored pattern area, and from bottom to top. The scanning programme operates by analysing the pattern into "groups." Broadly, a group is defined as a two dimensional collection of pattern points, the horizontal extent of which displays no sudden changes on successive lines. Examples of groups are shown in Fig. 3. In *a*, group 1 consists of the lower vertical portion. Group

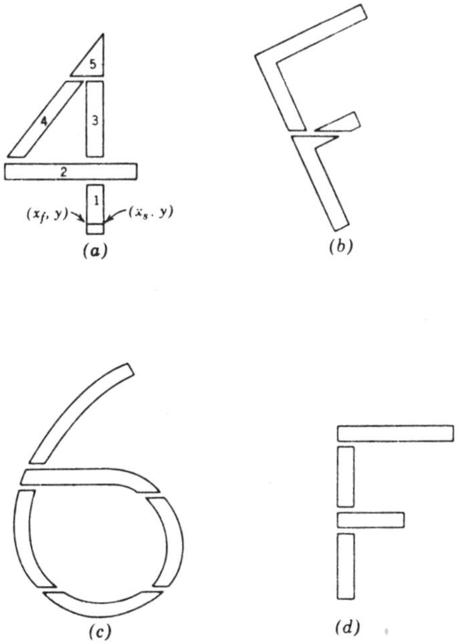


Fig. 3. Examples of groups.

2 is taken as a new group because the horizontal length of its sets of points is much greater than the corresponding length for group 1. Similarly, groups 3 and 4 are separately identified. The junction of these two forms a new and distinct group, No. 5. Further examples of group formations are shown in *b* and *c*. It is clear that the groups into which a pattern is analysed by the scan will depend on the orientation of the pattern with respect to the scanning lines. Fig. 3*d* shows the group formation of the pattern at *b* for a different orientation. However, the assembly programme which follows will yield identical statements for *b* and *d*.

For purposes of description it is convenient to refer to a particular portion of a pattern on one scanning line as a "section." In Fig. 3*a*, the section is completely described by the co-ordinates of its extremities, $(x_s, y)$, $(x_f, y)$.[1] There may, of course, be more than one section per scanning line, but each will belong to a different group.

The scanning programme has a number of significant features:

(*a*) NOISE FIGURE. This allows for the absence of points from any particular section, due to irregularities or imperfections of the pattern. It also prevents the inclusion into a group of spurious points due to dust or dirt on the pattern or to flying-spot scanner noise.

(*b*) INTERNAL AND GAP COUNTS. When a particular section has been found, it is tentatively assumed that there will be similar sections on lines above. However, owing to imperfections there may be a complete, or almost complete, absence of points on one or more of the lines; such gaps must be tolerable, and for this reason the gap count is provided. The interval count is similar to the gap count in that it allows for the presence of an excessive number of points on one or more of the lines. The interval and gap counts are related to the noise figure, and this is set automatically by the programme to one of three values according to whether the pattern is considered to be small, medium or large. As a future development, the noise figure will be adjusted automatically if the imperfections of the figure result in its being divided into too many groups.

(*c*) QUICK LOOK. This is a section of the scanning programme which simulates a form of curve following. By the use of existing machine logical functions, it enables a simple group to be quickly followed; it is based on the assumption that the position of a section on the next line to be considered will be predictable from information of an existing group. When complications appear, such as the intersection of two groups, this section of the programme will be abandoned for a more elaborate examination in the section of the programme known as "detailed scan."

(*d*) DETAILED SCAN. The features of this part of the programme are illustrated below.

[1] It is implied that the space between $x_s$, and $x_f$ is filled with pattern points. However, in view of the provision of the noise figure (q.v.), it is not essential that every digit position between $x_s$, and $x$ should contain a point.

*A Sample Scan.* The action of the scanning programme and the formation of groups is illustrated here with reference to Fig. 4. The noise figure, the allowable gap count and the allowable interval count are all assumed to have the value 2. Scanning begins on the bottom line ($y = 0$) under the control of the "master" section of the scanning programme and proceeds from right to left.

Lines on which the number of points is less than the noise figure are ignored, and when the first line to be considered is found, lines below this one will not be referred to again. The first line to be examined here is $y = 11$, and it is examined point by point for pattern points. This results in a description of the section as $x_s = 24$, $x_f = 20$ and $y = 11$, and these values are recorded.

The section is presumed to be a member of a possible group, and if further sections of this group are to be found, they will lie on the line above in roughly the same range. Accordingly, the points $x_s + 5$, $x_s + 6$ and $x_f - 5$, $x_f - 6$ on the next line are first examined. If there are no pattern points at these positions, the quick-look section of the programme is entered; otherwise the slower detailed-scan section is used.

The quick-look routine examines only the points between $x_s + 5$ and $x_f - 5$ on the line above, and the beginning and end of the section on line 12 are rapidly found.

A section is defined as a collection of pattern points on a line which is continuous, i.e., which has no gap greater than the noise figure; thus the section on line 12 is defined by $x_s = 24$ and $x_f = 20$. This new section is now compared with the previous section of line 11, to establish whether both are members of the same group. The tests used are given below.

(*a*) OVERLAP TEST. Two sections on consecutive lines are members of the same group only if the range ($x_s$ to $x_f$) of one includes the range of the other.

```
  xxxxxxxx              xxxxxx                   xxxxx
   xxxxxx             xxxxxx               xxxxx
    (i)                 (ii)                     (iii)
```

Thus the sections at (i) and (ii) are accepted as members of the same group while those at (iii) are not.

(*b*) LENGTH TEST. The length ($x_s - x_f$) of a proposed section is compared with that of the last member section of the group, and the section is accepted if its length is within a given range of the member section.

(*c*) EDGE CONTINUITY TEST. If two sections are to be members of the same group, at least one of the edges must be continuous.

```
  xxxxxxxxxxx        xxxxxxxxxxx
      xxx              xxxxx
     (iv)               (v)
```

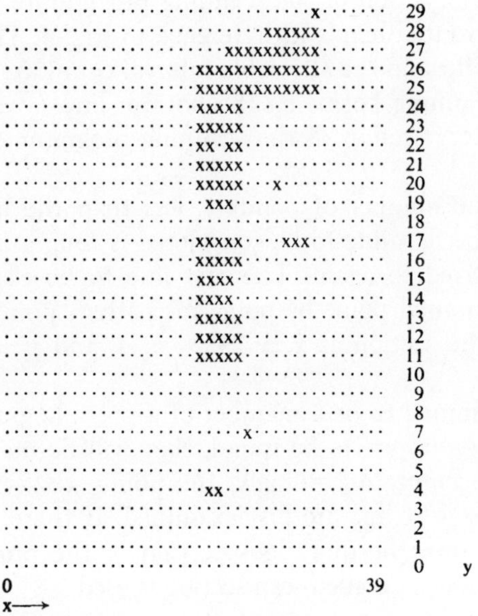


Fig. 4.

Thus sections at (iv) are not accepted as members while those at (v) are. The situation at (v) arises for straight lines making a small angle with the direction of the scanning lines.

The noise figure in use is taken into account in all the tests, and all tests must be successful for a new section to be accepted as a member of the current group.

The sections on lines 11 and 12 (Fig. 4) are clearly members of the same group, as are the sections on lines 13, 14, 15 and 16, and this is established by the quick-look routine. However, the presence of the points $x = 29$—$31$ on line 17 is noted when the points $x_s + 5$, $x_s + 6$ are examined as a preliminary to the quick-look routine; as a result, the detailed-scan routine is entered instead of the quick-look routine.

Detailed scan considers the points at $x = 29$, 30, and 31 as a complete section since the nearest neighbour on the line ($x = 24$) is more than two points (= noise figure) distant. This section fails to qualify as a member of the current group, being rejected by the overlap test. The remainder of the line is then examined for further sections. That between $x = 20$ and $x = 24$ is found and accepted as a group member.

As each member section is accepted, its co-ordinates ($x_s$, $x_f$) are entered in a list. In addition, the difference between these co-ordinates and those of the previous section are calculated and retained until a new section is found. Thus the ($x_s$, $x_f$) for the last two sections are always available.

No points are found on line 18 and a gap count of 1 is noted. The values of $x_s$, $x_f$ and the co-ordinates for line 18 are interpolated, using the current $x_s$, $x_f$ values and the co-ordinates of the last section member of the group. Thus, the gap is temporarily filled in, and the quick-look routine can examine the correct range on line 19 for further sections. That on line 19 is accepted and the gap count is reset to zero. If, however, no sections belonging to the group are found on lines 19 and 20, the gap count will be increased to 3, and since this is larger than the allowable value, the group is deemed to be terminated.

The presence of the point at $x = 28$ on line 20, being more than 2 points (= noise figure) from its nearest neighbour, results in the quick look being abandoned, and a detailed scan is performed on that line. The point ($x = 28$) is rejected as a possible group member, and the remaining points are examined and accepted as a section belonging to the current group, as are the sections on lines 21–24.

The section on line 25 is rejected by the length test as a member of the current group. An interval count of 1 is recorded. The interval count operates in a similar manner to the gap count and is successively increased to 2 and 3 on lines 26 and 27. The value of 3 exceeds the allowable interval count, and the group is terminated. The master section of the scanning programme is then reentered.

At this time the group is described by a list of $x_s$, $x_f$ values preserved in the high-speed store of the computer, and by the lines on which it begins and ends. A test for triviality is first applied, to determine whether the group is worth "remembering" as a component of the pattern. The criterion for rejection is the size of the group, and the test is included to eliminate stray groups not belonging to the pattern, such as ink spots which are too large to be ignored by the application of the noise figure. The current group is accepted, and its points are removed from the pattern to prevent reconsideration.

The group data must now be averaged to remove small irregularities in the edges of the group. The smoothing thus produced is necessary for a later stage in the information analysis, when the values of $x_s$, $x_f$ are effectively differentiated to find the slopes and curvatures of the group edges. The averaging process consists in replacing the individual values of $x_s$ by average values of $x_s$ taken four at a time. This is, of course, also done for the $x_f$ values. The averaged and unaveraged edges of a group are shown in Fig. 5. Groups with less than four lines cannot be treated in this way and are labelled to receive special attention; groups with less than six lines are also labelled because they too require special treatment in later stages.

The group considered in this sample scan is, however, averaged since it is 14 lines high. The total data pertaining to it are now stored away and the co-ordinates of its beginning and end sections $(x_s, x_f, y_b)$, $(x_s, x_f, y_e)$, together with the position in which it is stored, are noted in a group directory.

```
xxxxxx         xxxxxxx
xxxxxx         xxxxxxx
xxxxxx         xxxxxxx
xxxxxxxxx      xxxxxxx
xxxxxx         xxxxxxx
xxxxxx         xxxxxx
xxxxxx         xxxxxx
xxxxxx         xxxxxx
xxxxxx         xxxxxx
xxxxx          xxxxxx
xxxxxx         xxxxxx
xxxxxx         xxxxxx
xxxxxx         xxxxx
xxxxxx         xxxxx
xxxx           xxxxx
xxxxxx         xxxxx
xxxxxx         xxxxx
xxxxx          xxxxxx
xxxxxx         xxxxx
               xxxxx
xxxxx          xxxxx
xxxxxx         xxxxx
xxxxxx         xxxxx

 Unaveraged     Averaged
   Edges          Edges
```

Fig. 5.

The scanning process recommences on line 11 and the section $x_5 = 29$, $x_S = 31$ is found on line 17. This is tentatively assumed to be a new group. Failure to find further section members on lines 18–20 results in this group being deemed trivial.

Scanning begins again on line 17 and the section on line 25 is found and assumed to be the beginning of another group. The process is continued until all sections have been removed from the pattern area.

## Assembly

It is the purpose of the assembly programme to process the information concerning the individual groups obtained from the scan programme and to produce a simple coded representation—the statement—describing the pattern. This is done in two parts; in the analysis section a description is obtained of the lengths, slopes and curvatures of the various groups comprising the pattern; the synthesis section, which follows, determines the relationship between the individual groups and prepares a table of joins.

*Analysis.* The particular nature of the scan programme produces two types of groups which it is convenient to identify separately. These are horizontal and non-horizontal groups. A horizontal group is one which has its length directed along the scanning lines. The sections at the ends of these groups (i.e., at the top and the bottom of the groups) may be rejected as members of the group, by virtue of the length test; a special examination is therefore performed, and those adjacent horizontal groups which overlap sufficiently are combined and redescribed as a single horizontal group.

The remainder of the description of the analysis programme applies essentially to non-horizontal groups, but, of course, where appropriate, a similar treatment is given to horizontal groups.

The scan programme prepares a table of values of $x_s$ and $x_f$, the starting and finishing abscissae for each section of the groups. The $x_s$ and $x_f$ values are treated separately at first, and since the processes are identical, only the treatment for $x_s$ values is given. The column of values in the $x_S$ column is differenced to obtain the $\Delta x_s$ values and these are subsequently differenced to obtain $\Delta\Delta x_s$. The values of $\Delta\Delta x_s$ are now smoothed; this proves necessary because, for patterns with irregular edges, the action of effectively differentiating twice accentuates these irregularities, and the general tendencies become masked.

A further column is produced giving values of the cumulative second differences, $\Sigma\Delta\Delta x_s$. This new column, at any line, represents the total change of slope of the group edge from the first line of the group to the present line. For a straight-edged group, the entries in this column will, ideally, all be zero; for a curve, the successive entries will display either a gradual increase or decrease.

When the nature of the trend of the cumulative-sum column changes, there will have been a change in the nature of the group edge, say from curve to straight line. In order to detect these changes, two further columns are formed. These are headed Last Increase and Last Decrease and represent respectively the number of lines since the last increase in the cumulative-sum column and the number since the last decrease. When the nature of the group edge changes, a zero entry will be made in one of these columns, in which the entries have previously been increasing steadily. The change is considered significant if the value preceding the zero is greater than a value $b$, where $b$ is some fraction of the total length of the group. Such changes serve to divide the group edge into "edge-sub-elements," which are separate straight-line or curved portions of the edge.

The next stage is one of correlating the edge-sub-elements obtained for the two edges of a group, to form its "elements." This is done in the following manner.

Using this end co-ordinates, the length and overall slope of each sub-element may be calculated. The lengths of the first left-hand edge and right-hand edge sub-elements are compared and their difference in length ($\Delta L$) is noted. If the right-hand edge-sub-element is longer, its length is compared with the combined lengths of the first two left-hand edge-sub-elements. If the difference in length is now larger than $\Delta L$, the first edge-sub-element on the right is compared in other respects (slope and curvature) with the first edge-sub-element on the left. If the difference in length is smaller than $\Delta L$, however, a tentative combination of the first three left-hand edge-sub-elements is made, and the process of length comparison is repeated. Thus the edge-sub-elements of either edge are matched with respect to length before a more detailed comparison is made. Further, the matching is such as to attempt to combine the sub-elements of one edge, if the other edge has a simple description.

The slope and curvature of the matched sub-elements of the two edges are now compared. If these are in general agreement, an element of the group is formed. The average length, slope and curvature of the two edge descriptions, as given by the sub-elements, is recorded, together with the end co-ordinates $(x_s, x_f, y_b)$, $(x_s, x_f, y_e)$ of the element.

If the slopes of the matched sub-elements do not agree, any combined sub-element is broken down into its components and these are individually tested for agreement with the slope and curvature of the sub-element of the opposite edge. If agreement is obtained, group elements are formed; if not, "abnormal elements" are produced. Examples of abnormal elements are shown in Fig. 6; these are elements (*a*) 2, (*b*) 2 and (*c*) 1. Fig. 6*b* illustrates a case where the two sub-elements of the right-hand edge are tentatively combined in order to match the length of the single sub-element of the left-hand side. But the overall slopes disagree and the right-hand side is broken down into its components, sub-elements 1 and 2.

If the matching sub-elements agree with respect to overall slope, but not with respect to curvature, no attempt is made to break down the combined sub-elements (if indeed, there are any) and an abnormal element is formed. Fig. 7 illustrates a group with edges of differing curvature. This case will be detected by the slopes comparison and thus described as two elements, one of which, 2, is abnormal.

Abnormal elements due to different edge slopes are described by the average length of the two edges and by both edge slopes. These are used at a later stage in joining groups to one another, when slopes must be

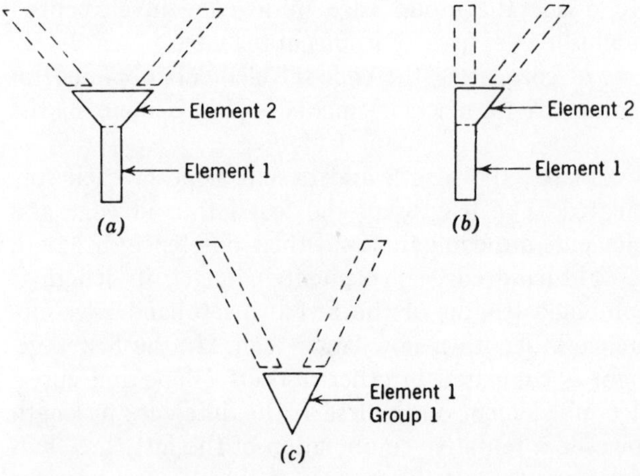


Fig. 6. Abnormal elements.

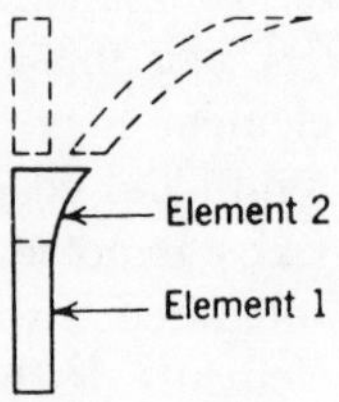


Fig. 7.

TABLE 1. Table of joins

| | BT | | | TB | | | TT | | | BB | | |
|---|---|---|---|---|---|---|---|---|---|---|---|---|
| | R | L | C | R | L | C | R | L | C | R | L | C |
| Group 0 | – | – | – | 2 | – | – | – | – | – | – | – | – |
| Group 1 | – | – | – | – | 2 | – | – | – | – | – | – | – |
| Group 2 * | 0 | 1 | – | 4 | 6 | – | – | – | – | – | – | – |
| Group 3 * | – | – | – | – | – | – | – | – | – | – | – | – |
| Group 4 | 2 | – | – | 7 | – | – | – | – | – | – | – | – |
| Group 5 * | – | – | – | – | – | – | – | – | – | – | – | – |
| Group 6 | – | 2 | – | – | 7 | – | – | – | – | – | – | – |
| Group 7 | 4 | 6 | – | – | – | – | – | – | – | – | – | – |

* Groups 2, 3, 5 are combined and designated "Group 2."

BT bottom-top join.
TB top-bottom join.
TT top-top join.
BB bottom-bottom join.
R right join.
L left join.
C centre join.

The numbers in the columns refer to the adjoining groups.

matched. Abnormal elements due to different curvatures are described by the average length, slope and curvature of the two edges involved. All abnormal elements are specially labelled for future identification.

*Synthesis.* The groups of the pattern are now described in terms of their elements. The present section determines the relationship between individual groups, and a table of their joins to one another is prepared. Some of the various joins that can occur are shown in Fig. 8 and a sample table of joins for the *R* pattern of Fig. 9 is given in Table 1. The four columns of the table of joins correspond to:

Joins from the bottom of the current group to the top of another (BT joins).

Joins from the top of the current group to the bottom of another (TB joins).

Joins from top to top (TT joins).

Joins from bottom to bottom (BB joins).

There is a row for each group and the numbers of the groups to which it joins are in appropriate columns. These signify whether the join concerned is to the right, left or centre, as illustrated in Fig. 8.

It may be seen that provision is made to record only a limited number of joins. This restricts the current application to relatively simple patterns, but it is not a fundamental limitation of the method used.

When there is no adjoining group at one end of a given group, this group is said to have a "figure end." The nature of these ends is determined, and

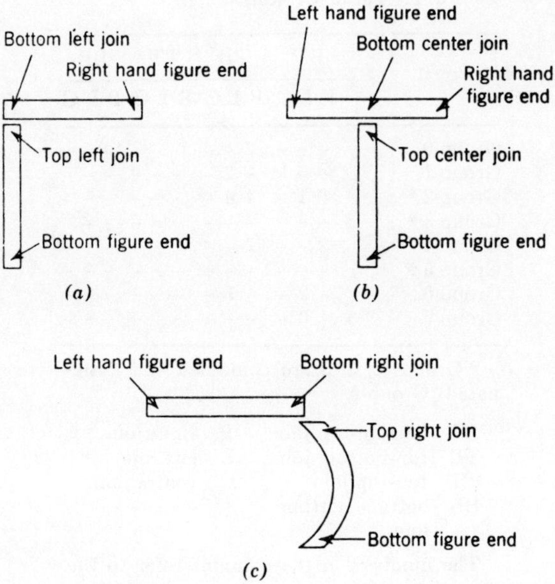


Fig. 8. Types of joins and ends.

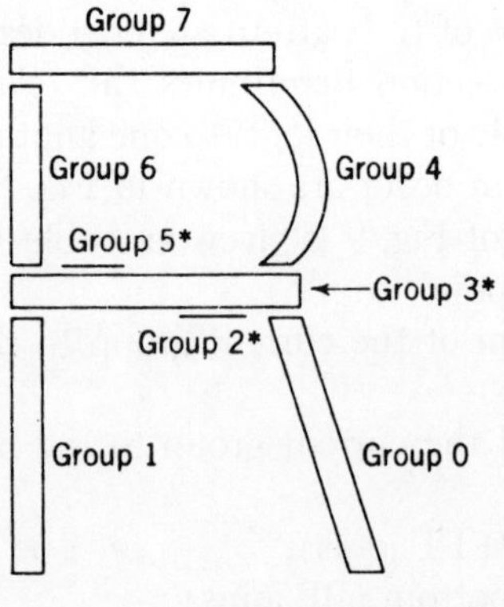


Fig. 9. Groups of an R pattern. *Groups 2, 3, and 5 combined and designated as "Group 2."

the types of ends possessed by a group are denoted by a label in the group directory. Types of ends are shown in Fig. 8.

With the group connections established, the group elements may be examined in detail to eliminate those which have been introduced by the interaction of two groups or the presence of figure ends. Types of these

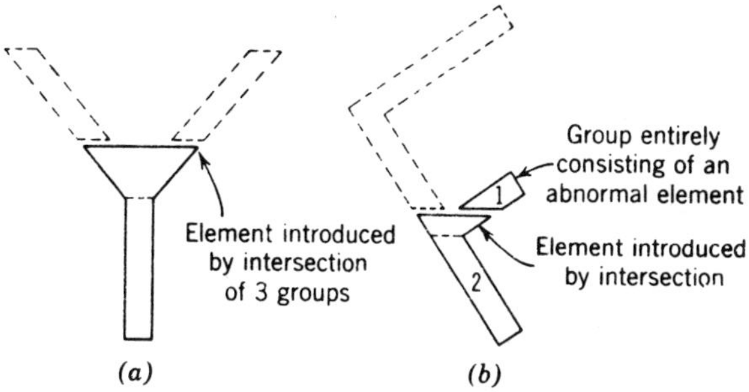


Fig. 10.

elements are illustrated in Fig. 10. Groups which consist entirely of abnormal elements, such as that shown in Fig. 11, are also examined further. These will carry labels signifying bottom or top intersections as a result of the previous classifying process. If these groups do, in fact, join to two other groups (appropriately), they themselves are effectively removed from the directory, and the two adjacent groups are denoted as joining each other in the table. Group 1 in Fig. 10*b* will also consist entirely of an abnormal element. It is not a true intersection, however, since it joins only one other group of the pattern. The final element of group 2 is an abnormal one and thus both its edge slopes are preserved. This applies equally to group 1. With the information concerning the nature of the join of group 1 to group 2, appropriate slopes may be compared to verify a proper match. If this is

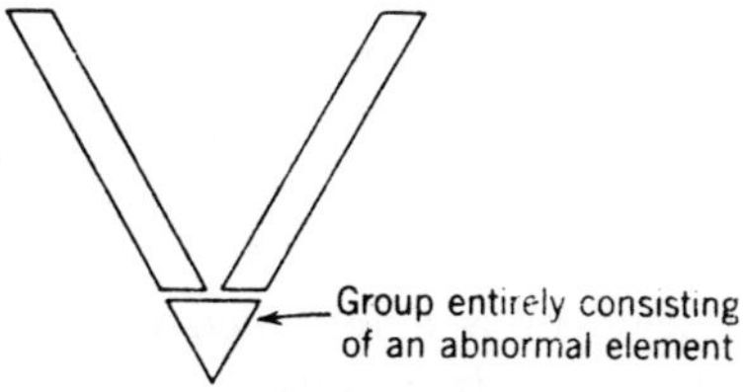


Fig. 11.

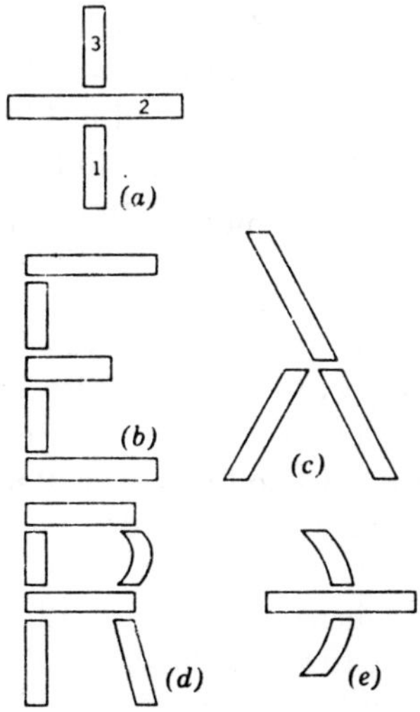


Fig. 12. Examples of division into groups.

successful, group 2 is redescribed as a straight-line group having a figure end and a slope equal to the average matched slopes.

The information concerning abnormal elements is not required after the group connections have been made and groups obscured by figure ends have been reconstructed. Accordingly, abnormal elements are removed from the group descriptions, their lengths being added to those of adjacent elements, as part of a general condensation process which is performed on the group descriptions. Elements with similar slopes and curvatures are combined and any remaining trivial elements are removed.

The various groups comprising the pattern have been analysed and described and their interrelations noted. However, these groups are a consequence of the internal scanning process of the machine and do not necessarily represent the simplest description of the pattern. For example, the pattern of Fig. 12*a* is broken up into three groups with group 1 having a top centre join to group 2 and group 3 having a bottom centre join to group 2. A simpler description of this pattern is obtained if groups 1 and 3 are combined to form a new group which crosses group 2.

The object of the main part of the synthesis section of the programme is to form the "segments" of the pattern, segments being defined as the components of the simplest description of the pattern. Since groups are not always identical with pattern segments, some combinations of the groups may be required. Further examples where this is necessary are given in Figs. 12*b–e*.

Broadly speaking, the synthesis takes place in two phases. The first is synthesizing groups which have been separated owing to intervening or adjoining groups. The second is synthesizing groups which are members of curved segments and which have been separated owing to the nature of the scanning process. Examples of the first type are shown in Figs. 12*a, b, c* and *e*, and of the second in Fig. 12*d*.

The next process to be carried out is the compression and coding of the information concerning the segments of the pattern and their interrelationship, to form the statement.

The slopes ascribed to curved segments are determined in a convenient manner; these remain unaltered, as the direction they define is unique with respect to the remainder of the pattern. This is not the case for "horizontal" groups, as is shown in Figs. 13*a* and *b*. The line at *a* will have a slope of 170°, while that at *b* will have a slope of 10°, yet they may be the same line rotated through 20°. The result will be that, if the segment is part of a larger pattern (Figs. 13*c* and *d*), its relative slope with respect to other segments will be radically changed by rotating the pattern slightly. This is not the case, however, if the slope of the segment is determined by the direction of travel from its end—if it possesses one. It is thus convenient at this stage to redefine the slopes with respect to the end wherever possible; this serves an additional purpose, as will be seen from consideration of

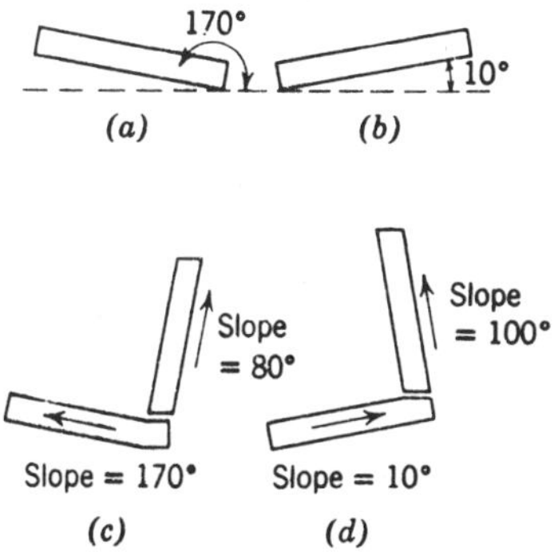


Fig. 13. Definition of slope.

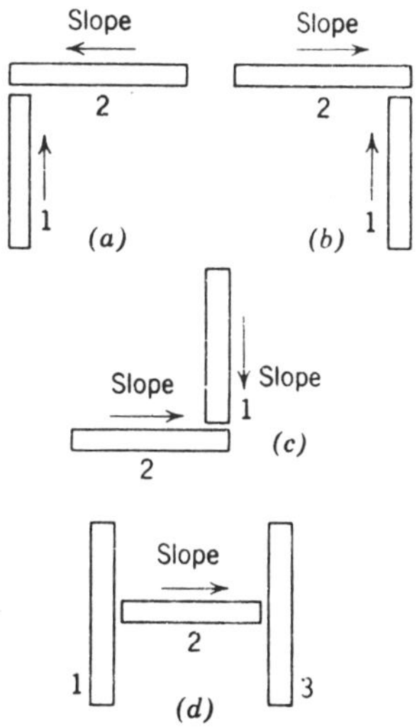


Fig. 14. Definition of slope using figure ends.

Figs. 14*a*, *b* and *c*. For if each of the lines of the patterns shown has a slope as determined from their ends, the type of joins they possess, i.e. whether left or right, top or bottom, need not be specified.

This cannot, of course, apply to straight-line segments having no figure ends or two figure ends. With the latter, allowance is made in the recognition process to tolerate 180° differences in the slopes of these particular segments.

The slopes of all segments, which have hitherto been in degrees to permit detailed comparisons, are adjusted to have one out of 32 possible values. The total length of the pattern is calculated, and the length of each segment is normalized again to have one of 32 values. The entire data concerning the pattern segments are now coded into 40 binary digits. This is the representation used at present, and it will suffice only for relatively simple patterns such as the English alphabet capitals and numerals. A small increase in the coded data will allow the unique description of more complex patterns. The 40-digit coded representation gives the length, slope and curvature of the segment, together with details of the ends and joins to other segments.

The set of 40-digit representations forms the statement for the pattern.

## *RECOGNITION*

The main object of the present work is the recognition of patterns, but it is anticipated that the method will be applied to character identification; the distinction between pattern recognition and character identification has already been mentioned in the Introduction—it is that several patterns may be used to represent the same character. The present section is primarily concerned with pattern recognition.

The machine has available a list of standard pattern statements which is extended as the machine learns new patterns. The problem involved in pattern recognition consists essentially of selecting one of the standard pattern statements which agrees sufficiently well with the statement relating to the unknown pattern. Two systems have been devised for performing this operation, the second being an improved and more versatile method; both have been used and they are now described, with some suggestions for further systems.

## Recognition—System 1

The first stage is to determine the number of segments in the unknown pattern statement. A reference segment is now chosen out of those forming the unknown pattern statement. This segment should preferably be one which does not involve any ambiguity in the slope. Thus it should be a straight-line segment which has one end as a figure end; failing this, a curved segment is chosen; if neither of these is available, a straight-line segment with two or no figure ends is selected. In this latter case a label is attached to the reference segment to indicate the possibility of a 180° ambiguity in slope. The reference segment is the one to which the slopes of all the other segments of the unknown pattern are referred so that the pattern may be described independently of its particular orientation.

A corresponding segment must now be found in the standard pattern statement selected from the stored list. To do this a number of tests are applied; these tests, which are applied to the reference segment and each of the standard pattern segments, allow

(*a*) No difference in the number of figure ends or joins.

(*b*) A difference of up to one quadrant in the specification of a curved segment.[2]

(*c*) No difference in the number of elements.

After these tests have been satisfied, a further test is applied which allows a difference in length between the two segments proportional to the length of one of the segments involved. If no suitable segment is found in the standard pattern, another standard is chosen. When the segment corresponding to the reference segment is found, the difference in slope $\Delta S_p$ between the two segments is determined. An attempt is then made to match each segment in the unknown pattern with each segment of the standard pattern. To do this, the above tests are applied, together with a

[2] Curved segments are specified in terms of the number of quadrants they occupy.

test to compare the slopes of the corresponding segments in which due allowance is taken of the $\Delta S_p$ value. If these conditions are fulfilled, segments in the standard pattern statement are rearranged and renumbered to match the unknown pattern statement. When this is done, the joins of the segments are compared and these must agree. That is, if group 2 of the unknown has a side join to group 1, the same must apply to groups 2 and 1 of the standard pattern. If the joins agree, the unknown pattern has been identified and the "name" of the successful standard pattern is printed out. If the joins do not agree, a new standard pattern is considered, and if the pattern cannot be identified with any of the standard patterns, the machine will indicate failure and await further instructions. If required, the unknown pattern may become a new standard pattern.

## Recognition—System 2

Recognition system 1 is limited in scope and requires complete agreement at certain stages. System 2 has a greater degree of flexibility and uses an improved directory system to give rapid selection of the standard pattern statements.

After the statement for the unknown pattern has been found, as at the end of the Section entitled "Synthesis," a 40 digit "key word" for the pattern is formed. The key word is made up of 8 blocks of 5 digits giving in turn the numbers of segments, straight-line segments, one-segment curves, two-segment curves, 3 or more segment curves, ends, side joins and crosses.

In the first stage of the recognition process of system 2, the key word for the unknown pattern is formed and compared with all the key words for the standard patterns, and the degree of agreement with each is noted.

The statement whose key word gave the maximum score is now compared in detail with the statement for the unknown pattern. The unknown pattern statement is first modified, if necessary, so that it has the same number of segments as the standard pattern. All such modifications are noted, as they affect the final score. If these modifications are so severe that an excessive adverse score is incurred, the particular standard pattern is rejected and another chosen.

All standard patterns which have obtained more than a certain score are now compared, one by one, in greater detail with the unknown pattern. One segment of the unknown pattern is chosen; this should be preferably the longest straight-line segment having one figure end, or, failing this, the longest curved line. This segment is compared with the first segment of the standard pattern. A score is obtained which is based on the agreement of number of ends, side joins, crosses and length. If the score is sufficiently high, the difference in slope is determined and recorded. The remaining segments of the unknown and standard patterns are compared in all possible combinations using the difference in slope already found. A total score of agreement is accumulated. This is now repeated taking the same original segment of the unknown pattern with the second of the standard pattern. Again the difference in slope is calculated, and the total scores for all the other segments taken with each other in the various possible combinations are determined.

The whole procedure is repeated with all the patterns whose key words showed reasonably high agreement with the unknown pattern key word.

If one of the standard patterns shows a sufficiently large amount of agreement with the unknown, and this agreement is much greater than the agreement of the unknown with any other standard pattern, the name of the best standard pattern is printed out; otherwise the machine indicates that there is some confusion between two or more patterns. As with system 1, there is the facility that if the pattern is not recognized it can be made into a new standard pattern.

## Future Developments

It is possible to envisage a number of interesting systems which could be included in future recognition schemes. One of these may be used in the recognition process when applied to character identification. When a large number of standard pattern descriptions are stored within the machine, time may be wasted in choosing suitable standard patterns to be compared with the unknown. Accordingly a classification system more detailed than that described for Recognition System 2 would be desirable.

It is intended that such a classification system will develop after a large number of standard patterns have been recorded in the store. The significant features are then determined. These are the features which are special to some but not all patterns; for example, classes might be formed of patterns with 4 ends or patterns with 3-segment curves. The unknown patterns are examined to find which significant features they possess; the appropriate class is then selected, and a more detailed examination is performed to differentiate between the members of the group.

A further development to facilitate both the classification process and to improve the speed of the system is to employ some special-purpose equipment to perform the scanning of the pattern on the paper. The scanner should be capable of performing certain special operations like curve-following under direct control of the computer. One of the parts of the programme which occupies a large amount of time is the scanning procedure which determines the slope and curvature of the parts of the figure. The computer at present examines the pattern in rather too great detail, and it would be preferable if the scanner could indicate if there were more than a certain number of picture points in a certain region. In this way the scanner could indicate general trends.

## *CONCLUSIONS*

The system described has been tested and has operated successfully on a large range of patterns. The computer is first supplied with a library of standard patterns consisting of all the capital letters of the alphabet and the numerals. These standard patterns are drawn in white on a black background, a typical example being shown in Fig. 15. Each standard pattern is presented to the scanner in the vertical position, and the computer obtains a statement which describes the essential features of the pattern. The computer is given the name of each standard pattern as it is presented, and it stores the statement for each pattern together with its associated name in its library. Owing to the limited resolution of the flying-spot scanner, the patterns which the internal scanning system of the machine operates with are not so well defined as in Fig. 15*a* but appear as in Fig. 15*b*. It is patterns of this form which the machine has to process in the recognition system.[3]

Having been given a library of standard patterns, the machine is capable of recognizing all of them when subsequently presented, independently of the orientation. Shifts in the vertical or horizontal directions, provided the pattern remains in the field of the scanner, also present no difficulty. The computer prints the name of the pattern, the difference between the angle at which this pattern is presented and the angle at which the standard pattern was presented. When the presented pattern resembles two or more

(*a*) (*b*)

Fig. 15. Pattern reproduction: *a*, original character as presented to the scanner; *b*, digital representation of character.

[3] These figures have been prepared by the computer using a teleprinter; they are copies of the two-dimensional array which appears in the store at the beginning of the process.

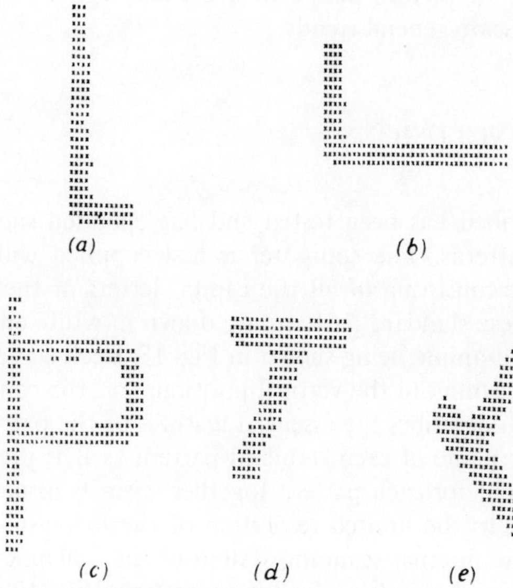


Fig. 16. Deformed characters which can be recognized.

standard patterns, the names of these are printed and with each there is a number to indicate the degree of agreement or certainty.

Using the same library of standard patterns, the machine is capable of recognizing a range of other patterns. A group of these is shown in Fig. 16. They have the same general form as the standard patterns, but not their precise shape. Fig. 10*e* illustrates a case where the machine indicates uncertainty. The pattern could either be the letter **T**, with the join not central, or a poorly drawn letter **L**. When this pattern is presented, the machine prints the following:

| | | |
|---|---|---|
| **L** | 320 | 30 |
| **T** | 140 | 45 |

The figures following the letters give, in the first column, the angle of the pattern from the vertical measured in degrees in the anti-clockwise direction, and in the second column, the measure of certainty of the particular answer. If great significance is placed on ends in the scoring system used by the recognition part of the system, as occurred in the present case, the **T** is the more probable pattern. If, however, greater importance had been attached to the angles of rotation of the patterns, the **L** answer would have been the more probable.

The system can also deal with patterns of various thickness (Fig. 17). The thin-line patterns are simple to analyse and recognize, but thick-line patterns present difficulties to recognition machines in general. The present

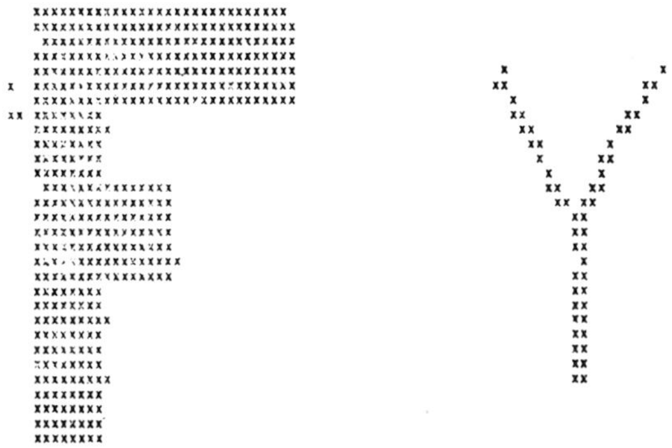

Fig. 17. Examples of thick and thin characters.

system successfully recognizes thick figures, provided they can be adequately resolved by the scanner. It is a feature of the internal scanning mechanism that the whole of the figure is examined. Whereas information is only recorded about the edges of the figure, all the space between the edges is scanned, and it is implicit in the information given about the edges of the figure that the figure is solid. Thus when the **F** pattern shown in Fig. 18 is scanned, it is broken into segments in the same way as for a thin-line figure. The system as at present arranged fails to obtain correct statements for a few curved figures at certain angles, because there are insufficient scanning lines to determine the curvature, as illustrated in Fig. 18. Nevertheless, when an incorrect description has been obtained, the recognition programme still succeeds in giving a name to the pattern in certain cases. This difficulty can be overcome either by increasing the resolution of the scanner or by a process of first reducing the thick figure to a thin one. The effect of such a reduction is shown in Fig. 19.

The patterns need not be perfectly regular, and various imperfections

Fig. 18.

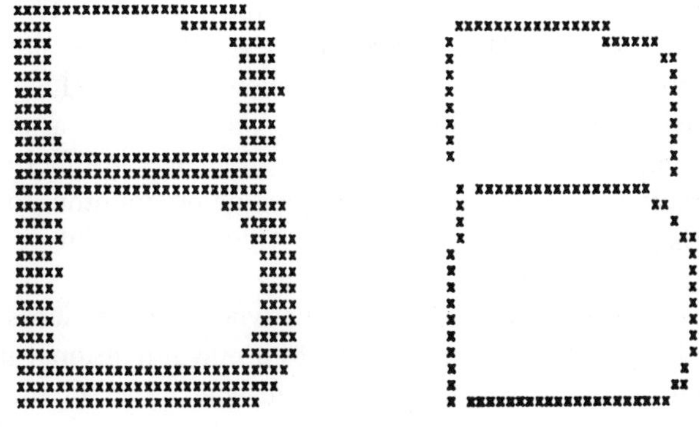

Fig. 19. Reduction of a thick to a thin character.

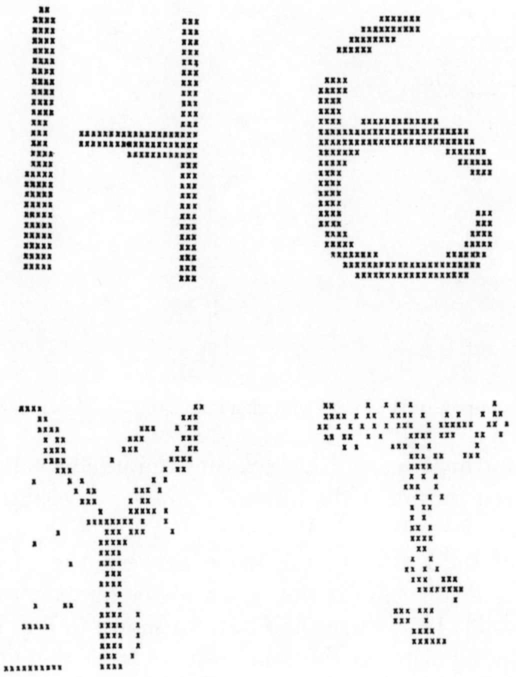

Fig. 20. Broken or noisy characters.

such as breaks, ragged edges and dirt on the paper are tolerated. The bad patterns in Fig. 20 are all recognized, again using the library of standard patterns for comparison. There are two reasons for this recognition: first, there is an averaging process and mechanism for ignoring breaks in the pattern, controlled by the noise figure (see above: "The Scan"); secondly, the information is reduced to statements describing lines and curves. There is thus a preliminary recognition procedure in the scanning process, in that straight and curved lines are recognized from ill-defined patterns.

Whilst the method may be applied to the recognition of any pattern, there are certain restrictions in the present system. It can deal with the small letters of the English alphabet, the Greek alphabet and other similar sets of symbols, such as those shown in Fig. 21, but it fails with symbols having a large amount of detail. The system as arranged breaks down with complex patterns because the scanner has insufficient resolving power and there is not provision, in the present programme, for enough groups. Both these restrictions can be easily removed in future systems based on the same principles.

An important concept in the whole recognition system is the reduction of a two-dimensional pattern to a one-dimensional pattern. This reduction occurs in the scanning process in which the statements are prepared. The statements take the form of one-dimensional patterns, and it is these

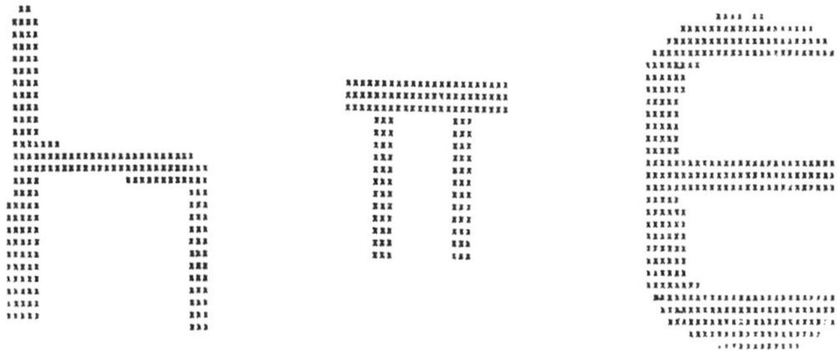

Fig. 21.

statements which are compared with those referring to the standard library patterns in the recognition section of the system. This is of twofold importance: first, the production of the statement is a process which is unaffected by the rotation of the pattern, or by variations in its size or precise form; secondly, the recognition problem is reduced to one of comparing one-dimensional patterns. This reduction makes the comparison possible in a reasonable time, which is particularly important when the library of standard patterns becomes large.

The whole operation is performed by a programme on a medium-speed digital computer. The programme has approximately 4000 instructions, and the time to recognize a pattern is of the order of 60 seconds, depending on the complexity of the pattern and the size of the library.

This time may be reduced by performing certain sections of the programme with special equipment. For example, the scanning of the pattern is a slow process on a digital computer and could be considerably speeded up. The time taken could be further reduced by performing the programme on higher-speed computers now being built. The reduction in time on such a machine would be by a factor of a thousandfold at least.

The present system can, in principle, be used for the recognition of handwriting. It would be necessary to extend the programme so that a greater number of groups could be handled, and provision would have to be made for dealing with complete words. With bad handwriting, interpretation is only possible, even for human readers, by using the context.

## *REFERENCES*

Bailey, C. E., & Norrie, G. O. Automatic reading of typed or printed characters. British Institution of Radio Engineers Convention on Electronics in Automation, June 1967.

Chow, C. K. Optimum character recognition system using decision functions. *Wescon Convention Record,* Pt. 4, 121.

Dineen, G. P. Programming pattern recognition. *Proceedings of the Western Joint Computer Conference*, Los Angeles, March 1955.

Greanias, E. C., Hoppel, C. J., Kloomok, M., & Osborne, J. S. The design of the logic for the recognition of printed characters by simulation. *Proceedings I.E.E.*, November 1956, *103B* (3, Paper No. 2149M), 456.

Kirsch, R. A., Cahn, L., Ray, C., & Urban, G. H. Experiments in processing pictorial information with a digital computer. *Proceedings of the Eastern Joint Computer Conference*, 1957, 221.

Loeb, J. Communication theory of transmission of simple drawings. In *Communication theory*. London: Butterworths Scientific Publications, 1953.

Magnetic ink character recognition. The technical Sub-Committee on Mechanization of Check Handling of the American Bankers Association. *Computers and Automation*, 1956, 5, 10.

Selfridge, O. G. Pattern recognition and modern computers. *Proceedings of the Western Joint Computer Conference*, Los Angeles, March 1955.

Shepard, D. H., Bargh, D. F., & Heasly, C. C. A reliable character sensing system for documents prepared on conventional business devices. *Wescon Convention Record*, 1957, Pt. 4, 111.

Uttley, A. M. Temporal and spatial patterns in a conditional probability machine. In *Automata studies*. Princeton, N.J.: Princeton University Press, 1956.

*Although the two papers quoted are quite old, they embody many (if not most) of the themes which run through the literature on computer simulation of pattern recognition. Inevitably there are some serious omissions, for instance Selfridge's "Pandemonium" which is now something of a classic in the field (Selfridge, 1959). This paper is reprinted in Uhr (1966) and Dodwell (1970a), in the former case along with a number of other important papers on computer simulations. "Pandemonium" is in fact an early example of a generalized model for pattern recognition, which consists of a system of feature detectors arranged hierarchically within a computation and decision network. Because it is so generally described, it can be thought of more as a proposal for the sort of arrangement that it would be sensible to consider, rather than as a specific model for any one form of pattern recognition. Indeed, Selfridge makes somewhat the same point himself. In this sense "Pandemonium" assumes the fact of stimulus equivalence in pattern processing, and does not contribute specific solutions to the problem.*

*The next selection, by MacKay, is a fine example of the ways in which concepts developed in physics, engineering, and control theory can be applied fruitfully to questions about perception. Most of the arguments are on a fairly general level, but are still rather specific in the messages they convey, not the least important of which is that there are potential dangers inherent in the uncritical application of mechanical analogies of human behavior.*

# *Ways of Looking at Perception*

D. M. MAC KAY

I take my brief to be to "stir the pot," so to speak, in the hope that its various ingredients may be better brought into contact with one another in our minds. At the outset I should like to make a remark which I hope will not be thought to be provocative, but which may serve to keep us on our toes. The kinship of interest between designers of automata and theorists of perception has, I think we would all agree, led to a remarkably fruitful series of interactions; but there are subtle differences of emphasis between the two sides which have also, I think, tended toward a confounding of a distinction that is useful in thinking of the application of the study of perception to the problems of automation. I mean the distinction between perception as experience, as becoming aware of features of the world, and perception as observable behavior, as the manifestation of input-output coordination. Perception becomes a subject of scientific observation as a result of rather a long chain of reasoning which we tend to forget. A percept can be thought of as a current constraint on the organization of action by the perceiver. What I perceive becomes a datum for my calculation of any action or reaction to which its presence is relevant. The observable evidence of my having perceived it is usually, therefore, the correlation observed in my behavior between input and output, provided that I am suitably motivated to display this. (Anyone who experiments on perception knows that the real problem is to make sure that the subject is, in fact, motivated to display the coordination in which we are interested.)

Typical perceptual tasks are those of discrimination, classification, matching; and in each case the study is conducted by trying to ensure that the subject is motivated to perform an action whose form will reflect the form of the feature which we want him to perceive. Because such input-output correlations are often required for practical purposes, there is then a temptation to take any device which shows the appropriate correlation between input and output as *ipso facto* a possible explanatory model of perceptual processes in a living organism, so reducing the problem of perception to a problem of discriminative, classificatory public behavior, leaving out the

Reprinted from *Models for the Perception of Speech and Visual Form*, 1967.

awkward questions of motivation to action and the experience of the perceiving agent. I want to suggest that as the study of perception advances we will need to sharpen this distinction between perception and mere input-output coordination, because it will become more and more questionable which features of perception, particularly in the human case, are relevant and necessary in an automaton to do the kinds of jobs we might describe as "input-output coordination."

To see that this distinction is one of fact and not merely of linguistic convention, it is only necessary to remind ourselves of all the bodily processes which come into the category of input-output coordination (the matching of the diameter of the pupil to the intensity of light, for example) yet are unaccompanied by conscious perception. Similarly, there are many processes of an artificial kind which are discriminatory, classificatory, and so on, where it would seem to be a little perverse to speak of perception. A sieve, for example, will receive an input and will nicely classify it into categories according to size, but few of us would regard it as *perceiving* what it handles. Throughout the world there are in fact any number of more complex natural processes which can be regarded as classificatory, but which it would be very odd indeed to call perceptual. For example, wherever water dribbles from the end of a rain pipe or the edge of a rock and the wind is blowing, the heavier drops are deflected a short distance, and the smaller drops a greater distance. So here is "classification" going on—but who would be so animistic as to call it an instance of perception?

What I am suggesting, then, is that in our models the mere appearance of internal configurations which match or correspond 1 for 1 to features of the environment, though it may be a necessary feature of any model of perception, does not *ipso facto* guarantee that perceiving is going on in these models, nor that what is going on is in any sense an adequate model of what goes on in peoples' nervous systems when they perceive. In other words, we must take into account not only the physical correlate of *classification*, but also the correlate of *action* and the planning of action, and the part played by the percept in the planning of action. All of these would have to make their appearance in our model before we could even begin to advance it as a candidate for the explanation of perception.

## *THE ORGANIZATION OF ACTION*

Action may be defined as activity in view of ends. The familiar skeleton map of Figure 1 summarizes the essential features. An effector system E has a repertoire of activities within the field F. Information as to the current state of F is supplied via a receptor system R. The problem of the organization of action is to secure a running selection from the repertoire

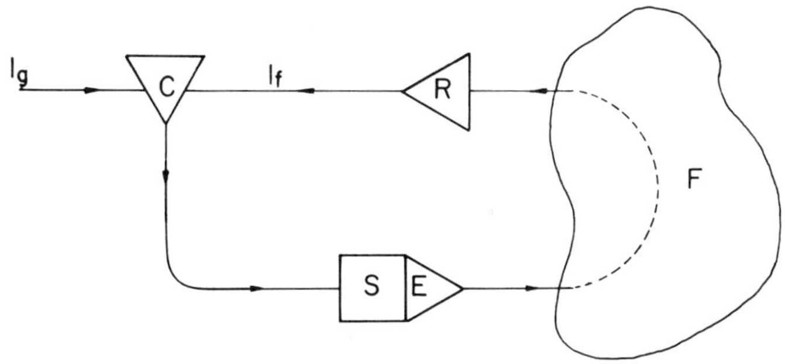


Fig. 1. Basic flow map for goal-directed activity.

of E which is best calculated to achieve current ends (goal-pursuit, norm-holding, threat-avoidance) on the basis of current and past information. It is a dual problem, then, that confronts us. We have, on the one hand, to secure within this system an internal representation of the external world, the data on which action is to be based. Secondly, and perhaps less often noticed, there has to be some system concerned with the ordering of goal priorities in situations of conflict between incompatible goals. In other words, the organization of action has two aspects, the indicative and the normative; the representation of what is the case, and the representation of what shall be pursued and in what order of priority.

## *ORGANIZATION TO PROFIT FROM REDUNDANCY*

In this context, then, we can think of *perception* as the organism's *adaptive response to redundancy* in the pattern of demands and constraint imposed upon it by the field in which it is active. The field is not purely random, but structured. The structure is responsible for redundancy in the pattern of demand (actual or conditional) flowing in upon the organism via its receptive system R.

The general outline of the scheme of Figure 1 is very familiar, but it may serve to focus our ideas, and we may as well stick to the conventional example of the thermostat, because I do not think it leaves out anything that matters for our purpose. Here E is a heater, R a thermometer, sending an indication ($I_f$) of the temperature of the field to an evaluator C, which compares it with an "indication of goal" ($I_g$). In the simplest situation there is a continual selective operation by the evaluator C upon the repertoire of E, calculated to minimize the disparity between $I_f$ and $I_g$. Suppose now that the pattern of demand for selective action shows some regularity, due for example to the alternation of day and night. Then, of

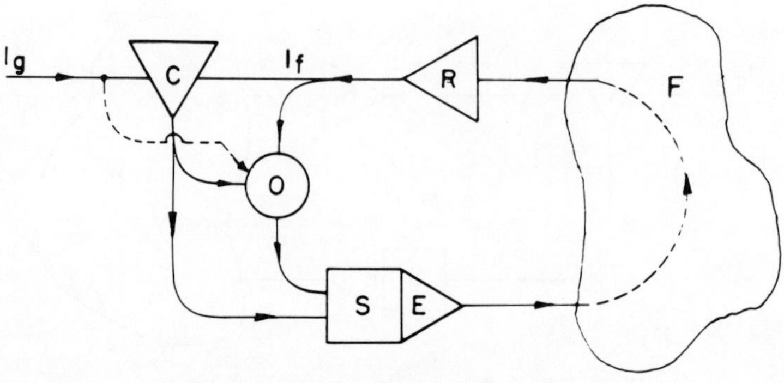


Fig. 2. Flow map with "feedforward".

course, the selective operation upon E could in principle be partly prefabricated; and we could imagine incorporating an organizer (O) in the system (see Figure 2), which replicates those components of the selective operation that are predictable on the basis of this regularity (MacKay, 1951, 1956a, 1956b). This organizer may in part act upon feedforward from the receptive system (for example, a second thermometer outside the building, registering ambient temperature); or it may simply abstract from the output of the evaluator the regular features that become predictable; but in either case this organizer, which prefabricates as much of the selective operation as matches the regularity of the demand, in a sense *represents* internally the regular feature in the outside world to which it is adaptive.

Indication of goal ($I_g$) is here supplied by an open terminal, so to speak, and is normally set by the housewife. Now if the housewife wants the system to respond as quickly as possible, she would not necessarily do best by merely moving the indicator of $I_g$ to the new setting. She could usually do better by also precomputing the extent to which the heater ought to be turned up or down, and setting it roughly to match her demand, leaving the evaluator to make the fine adjustments. So we require for the purpose a feedforward from $I_g$ into the organizing system in addition to the feedback which comes by way of the field and $I_g$, and any feedforward supplied by the thermometer sampling the temperature of the outside environment. What I want to point out is the importance of the proper balance of feedforward and feedback in this continual process of adaptation to the redundant features of the pattern of demand.

## *META-ORGANIZATION*

So far our system has been a slave. It depends on an outside source for its goal-specification. Before we can begin to approximate to an autonomous

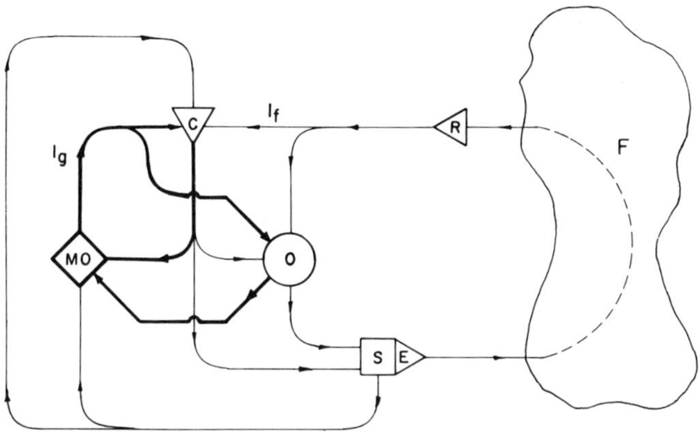


Fig. 3. Addition of "meta-organizing" system (heavy lines) to evaluate and modify organizing activity.

cognitive agency, we must introduce a second system, MO, whose function is to determine and order the priorities of the goals to be pursued (Figure 3). We may term this the *meta-organizing* system (MacKay, 1966). In the case of our thermostat (Figure 1) the meta-organizing function would normally be exercised by the housewife, who might for example adjust the goal-temperature according to her current activity, or her household's state of health, or the size of the fuel bill, and so forth; but it is not difficult to envisage a mechanical system taking her place. Here, of course, the goal-adjustment required is simple and one-dimensional, but the principle can be extended to a goal-hierarchy of any complexity. In each case there has to be a flow of information from the meta-organizer (MO) into the evaluator, setting the criteria of evaluation. Again, for this to function with greatest efficiency, we will want feedforward from the meta-organizing system into the organizer. We also will require feedback from the internal field of activity of the meta-organizing system, analogous to the feedback from the external field of activity to the organizing system. So we end up with a hierarchic organization, in which the job of goal pursuit is organized by a system which treats the internal organizing network as its field of action, receiving feedback from it and supplying feedforward as well as acting directly on its goal-settings. Finally, of course, the meta-organizing system must receive from the evaluator an indication of the effectiveness of its current programming, i.e., the data which are relevant to a change of goal priority. To take a simple example, an organism may be pursuing some simple goal, say intake of food, when it receives some indication of a threat. As a result the goal of eating is set aside in favor of flight, the threat-avoidance program. This kind of goal-switching process, and the computations behind it, count as meta-organizing activity.

One further point. As a result of the evaluator's stirring up the organizing system, the organizing system will set in motion events in the field of activity which will be reflected in the input to the evaluator. One way of evaluating the success of the program is then for the evaluator to compare key features of what is coming in with what was programmed to be produced by the effector system. For this we require an input to the evaluator from the output and/or the input to the appropriate effectors. This is analogous to what von Holst (1950) called the "efference copy": the copy of what is meant to be produced in the sensory input as a result of effector action. We shall have more to say of this later.

## *DEVELOPMENT OF THE ORGANIZING SYSTEM*

We have now sketched a network in which we can say that *action* occurs, *calculated in view of a representation of the external world* and of a hierarchic *goal structure* which the system itself generates and adapts in its meta-organizing system.

In concrete terms of what goes on in the nervous system, this raises many questions. First of all there is the question of the way the organizing system itself gets organized. Clearly it would be possible to prefabricate it; but to prefabricate the organizing system (the system which in effect, we remember, represents the regular features of the external world) would of course be to run into the danger of irremediable *category blindness*. Only predetermined categories could be taken into account by the system. If a new category became relevant which the designer had not thought of, the system would never grasp it, so to speak. So, although some prefabrication will obviously be useful in an organism living in our world, which has indeed many universal regularities, we would expect also to find some use for a more flexible approach. In addition to having some prefabricated general principles of organization, the organizing system should also be *adaptive*, able for example to assemble trial organizers, and later if necessary dismantle or set them aside according to the outcome of their use. This amounts to suggesting that within the organizing system there must be a region that we could call a "workshop" (MacKay, 1959b); a region in which trial subroutines can be constructed and run, perhaps run ahead of time, and their outcomes then evaluated by the meta-organizing system, for potential usefulness in securing particular ends.

Secondly, there is the problem of keeping the whole system up-to-date; and here, at last, is where we make contact again with our topic of perception. What I am suggesting is that in the context of this skeleton model, we can define the correlate of perception as the activity of *keeping up-to-date* the organizing system that implicitly represents the external world, by an internal matching response to the current impact of the world upon the receptive system. Once again, perception as an updating activity may be carried on either (a) through the action of prefabricated filters which extract from the input the necessary clues to select the appropriate state of the internal organizing system, and/or (b) through a process of self-guided modification of the internal state of the organizing system to match the incoming data: e.g., by "backing off" the incoming data in such a way that an isomorphism is developed between the principles of generation of the internal back-off signal and the structure of the external percepta to which the internal state is a match (MacKay, 1951, 1956b).

I do not want now to go into detail. The purpose of this introduction has been to sketch the context in which the relative merits of (a) "filtering" and (b) "matching" (or as some Americans call it, "analysis by synthesis") can be rationally discussed—not, I would emphasize, as rivals, but as complementary principles to be adopted in different proportions. A bank of filters covering all possible features would of course offer the speediest way of keeping a system up-to-date; but to be comprehensive it must be extremely large and hence inefficiently employed. A self-matching mechanism, on the other hand, can be extremely compact, but it may be slow, and it is limited (by the number of its degrees of freedom) as to the number of features it can "track" at a time. (This, by the way, is also a notorious characteristic of human perception.)

Consider for example a system required to respond differentially to different frequencies of input. On the filter principle a bank of n filters will be needed, with a response time only of the order of $1/\Delta f$ ($\Delta f =$ bandwidth). On the "matching" principle we need only a single servo-operated sine wave generator plus comparator, the system hunting until it matches the incoming frequency. The economy of the second is obvious, but also its slowness and its limitation to one signal at a time. Our choice between the two would clearly depend on the size of n, and on the value we place on the different costs of equipment and time. The first could be important, in spite of the bulkiness or the multiplicity of the elements required, where relatively little prior information was available as to the nature and number of the features to be matched simultaneously; whereas conversely, where it is known that only one or two degrees of freedom will be needed, the second, self-matching process is likely to be more efficient. In the perception of speech, for example, where the ensemble of commands for generating speech is relatively limited, and the elements form a sequence ordered by few parameters, there may be more to be said for a self-molding adaptive, matching-response model than, for example, in the perception of shape. In most cases, however, (speech included) we might expect maximum efficiency to be derived from a combination of the two principles, using a number of self-matching generators guided by rough clues from filters.

## *PHYSIOLOGICAL EVIDENCE*

Most people will be familiar with the physiological evidence which has begun to temper speculation in this field, so on this I will be brief. It is now over five years since the physiologists Hubel and Wiesel (1963), Barlow and Hill (1963), and Lettvin and others (1959) began to discover in the visual system networks of cells which were selectively responsive to such features as the direction of a contour, motion of a contour, rate of change of brightness, curvature of contour, and things of that kind. More recently Evans and Whitfield (1964) and others have found somewhat analogous gradient detectors in the auditory system. So it is now pretty generally agreed that any perceptual model of the visual or auditory system had better assume the existence of banks of filters in the input to the organizing system, permitting a preliminary extraction of cues to which the internal organizing process has to match itself.

## *PSYCHOLOGICAL EVIDENCE*

Let me now refer to some striking psychological indications that seem to point in the same direction. The first concerns the adaptive response of the visual system to fields of near parallel lines. Figure 4, for ex-

Fig. 4. "Ray" pattern which evokes complementary images.

ample, has a high degree of contour-directional redundancy. After looking at it for a while and looking away, one sees a curious pattern of wavy *circles*. With Figure 5 on the other hand, one sees wavy *radial* streamers as an afterimage. A general description, then, would be that exposure to near-parallel lines in one direction, the visual system seems to be hypersensitized to a direction roughly *orthogonal* to the direction of the stimulus. This led (for once, in advance of the physiological evidence) to the suggestion (MacKay, 1957) that in the visual system there might be networks specifically sensitive to direction, and capable of adapting to direction in the kind of way that our color-sensitive mechanisms tend to adapt to color, so that complementary *directions* tend to be seen after exposure to a given direction just as complementary colors tend to be seen after exposure to a given color.

It turns out to be possible to reveal and study tendencies of this sort continuously by using as a "neutral" test stimulus a random succession of randomly patterned figures which we call "visual noise". This can be generated electronically on a television tube (MacKay, 1957) or photographically with a cine film of random fields such as photographs of sandpaper or distributions of confetti (Wilson, 1960). When superimposed on Figures 4 and 5, the randomness largely disappears, the "noise" being seen as organized into a totally different pattern, in the one case a kind of rotating rosette, and in the other a set of radial streamers (MacKay, 1957, 1961). So here we have what looks like good evidence that the visual system is in-

Fig. 5. "Target" pattern.

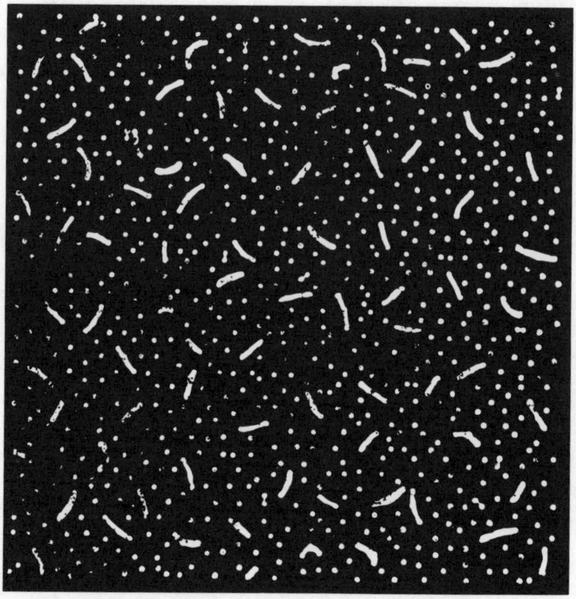

Fig. 6. An impression of the "maggot" effect.

deed hypersensitive to directions contrasting as strongly as possible with the directions of contour that are present in excessively large numbers.

Another related phenomenon recently discovered with the same tool we call, for want of a better term, the "maggot" effect (Fiorentini & MacKay, 1965). When each frame of a random noise sequence is followed by a blank flash at a certain interval of the order of 25 msec, then even without any superimposed line pattern, the "noise" takes on a linear structure, as if the screen were filled with short maggotlike objects (Figure 6). Tentatively our interpretation is that by this particular rhythm, namely a flash following each frame with a delay of the order of 25 msec, we must be "presensitizing" certain elements in the visual perceptual mechanism which are sensitive to contour, so that subjective contours are spuriously generated when none are objectively present in the stimulus. We are still working on this one and finding interesting correlates in the evoked potentials (MacKay & Fiorentini, 1966).

One other illustration will show the sort of data that are accumulating on this general topic of the visual pattern-filter mechanisms. Figure 7 shows a "noise" pattern which is reasonably random. After a few seconds' fixation of a particular point, subjects report spontaneously that the appearance of randomness diminishes, and may even be replaced by a periodic structure. Displacing the fixation point by a few degrees at once reveals the magnitude of the change that has taken place (MacKay, 1964). Once again we are only beginning to investigate this, but it looks like evidence

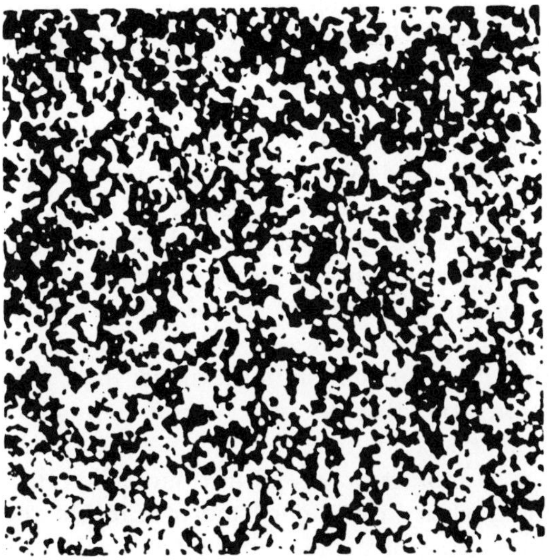

Fig. 7. A sample of "visual-noise."

of adaptation in yet another filter mechanism, whose function is to signal or abstract *inhomogeneities* in distribution. We cannot blame this on ordinary adaptation to brightness, because the phenomenon is visible with all-or-none patterns, in which brightness adaptation presumably leaves the geometrical distribution unchanged in form. It may be significant that patterns like newsprint, which has, of course, a high degree of redundancy already, show this effect much less strongly.

To summarize thus far, what I am suggesting is that we should think of the modeling of perception, not in terms of an exclusive choice between filtering and internal adaptive matching by the internal replication of the input, but in terms of the interaction of both. The foregoing demonstrations would seem to indicate that perception is indeed a *synthetic* activity, but one guided by *cues* extracted by the filter mechanisms; what we see has many elements which come from the structure within rather than from the stimulus without.

## *THE PROBLEM OF PERCEPTUAL STABILITY*

If our image of the perceived world is implicitly embodied in our state of organization to cope with it, it may be expected to be naturally *stable*. The perception of change will be an updating response triggered only by a *significant degree of mismatch* between the incoming indications and the internal criteria of evaluation adopted in the light of the action currently programmed. As a concrete illustration of the implications of this way of looking at perception, I should like to turn to the problem of the stability of the perceived world in the face of transformations of the input caused by voluntary actions.

Take first the tactile case. Suppose it is dark and we are exploring a surface with the palm of our hand. We use our arm muscles to move our palm around the tactile world, thus giving rise to all manner of rubbing sensations—sensations of relative motion between the surface and the palm. But we do not in consequence perceive the object under our palm as in motion. On the contrary, if the object under our palm were, let us say, a trolley mounted on a rail so that as we moved our palm the trolley followed, it would be the *absence* of motion signals under those circumstances that would supply information that the trolley was in motion. The motion signals generated by tactile exploration, then, do not have to be *canceled* or suppressed in any way in order to prevent us from feeling that a stationary object is in motion, when we run our hand over it. On the contrary, they are *evaluated* as evidence of stability, in the light of criteria appropriate to the fact that we have organized an exploratory movement.

In terms of Figure 3, we may say that the meta-organizing system has set up as a goal the exploration of the object by palm movement. Some kind of information flow from the effector to the evaluator is of course necessary in any model if the evaluator is to interpret the incoming signals properly; but the point I want to make is that this information need not have either the complexity or the accuracy that would be required in order to *cancel* the incoming motion signals. All it has to do is to attach the appropriate *significance* to them as evidence for a static, stable representation of this object. We may assume that some internal representation of my tactile world fills out in detail as I explore: but unless I make contact with an actually moving surface the motion signals generated by my exploration are only confirmatory of the validity of my stationary world-model, and not destructive of it.

Very briefly, I should like to suggest that the same logic seems to apply to the much-discussed problem of the stability of the visual world: that using my eye muscles to throw my retina around the visual scene can be regarded as analogous to using my arm muscles to throw my palm around the tactile world. It is true that there are many differences, in proprioceptive inputs and so forth, between the two cases; but there would seem to be no more reason to expect that the visual motion signals generated by voluntary eye movement should be canceled or suppressed, than the friction signals from the palm. What is necessary, once again, is rather that the flow of information from the eye-movement system should modify the criteria of *evaluation* of these signals, so that they become indications of the stability of the visual world rather than the contrary (MacKay, 1959a, 1962).

A number of simple demonstrations help, I think, to support this view of the matter. If we close one eye and press very lightly on the open eyelid at the corner, the visual world of course appears to move. The impression of motion is irresistible. If we look closely, however, we find that the region around the fixation point appears to move *more* than the peripheral region; and in fact with very small movements we may not feel that the periphery is moving at all, but only the region around the fixation point. If we now do the same while viewing Figure 4, an interesting feature emerges. In addition to the displacement of the center, we see a sort of "rubber-sheet" distension and contraction of the field, perpendicular to the direction of motion (MacKay, 1960). For example, if the image is displaced from left to right, the regions at "3 o'clock" and "9 o'clock" seem to perform a fan-wise expansion or contraction. Suppose now that a vertical marker of some sort is introduced halfway along, say, the "3 o'clock" ray. At once the rubbery expansion in its vicinity ceases, although in the symmetrical region at 9 o'clock (without a marker) it is still present.

In each case what we see, I suggest, can be interpreted as the result of a mismatch of the evaluatory criteria: but these anomalies illustrate the thesis that our internal representation of the world is affected only in proportion as there is *information* to justify a change. On this principle, it is not surprising that when the visual image is displaced, we normally see the central region, which stimulates an area rich in detectors, as "moving" more than the periphery. Again, in the absence of significant mismatch of a particular feature of the visual representation, no change in that feature is perceived. We do not see a displacement of Figure 4 as a whole, because the translation of a contour along itself gives no information; but we do perceive expansion corresponding to any change in separation of the contours. On the other hand, given a marker in the orthogonal direction, we see displacement but no expansion.

Let me mention one further striking illustration. If a small steadily glowing lamp is viewed against a background lit stroboscopically at about five flashes per second, and the same eye-pressing experiment is repeated, a dramatic dissociation takes place (MacKay, 1958). With sufficiently gentle displacements, the lamp is seen to move, although the background remains stationary; yet the lamp is not seen to move *relative* to the background! Once again, the change perceived is the minimum justified by the optical evidence, however *intellectually* impropable or absurd that change may be.

A particular moral of these demonstrations for our present purpose is that whatever the principle on which our visual world is kept stable, it cannot be a matter of some global transformation of the incoming optical pattern of the sort familiar, for example, in a shipborne radar system. On board ship, to preserve a "true north" map on the radar screen, the incoming radar picture is subjected to a rotation which exactly cancels any rotation produced when the ship's head turns. There is a sensory gyro that signals the amount of ship-rotation to a "compensator," which "subtracts out" this rotation and so ensures the stability of the display. What I am suggesting is that we cannot plausibly use that kind of model for at least the more complicated effects of exploratory changes in the direction of our eyes, or indeed, of any of our sensory surfaces. Many experimental results under various pathological conditions and abnormal conditions, as with anaesthetized eye-muscles or stabilized retinal images, may indeed be *qualitatively* the same on either a "cancellation" or an "evaluation" model; but the quantitative accuracy required in the information channels is quite different (MacKay, 1959a, 1962). In our model (Figure 3), the information supplied from the effector system (whether derived from its input or output) need have an accuracy comparable only with the accuracy of the criterion of evaluation, which can be no greater than the accuracy of the *effector* system. In the radar case, on the other hand, the cancellation must be carried out with accuracy comparable with the resolving power of the *receptive* system if no instability is to be detected. In the case of the visual and tactile senses, such accuracies in the "efference copy" would seem to be physiologically improbable, if not unattainable; and in any case, on the view I have advanced, they are unnecessary.

## *THE DISTINCTION BETWEEN PERCEPTION AND SENSORIMOTOR COORDINATION*

May I now return to the point made at the outset, that the discovery of a satisfactory model of coordination between sensory input and motor output may not necessarily settle the question of *perception* which is associated with it. Perception, in the sense of the subjective experience of the perceiver, is something that we have seen may even embody mutually incompatible components. In addition to the demonstrations I have mentioned, let me remind you of the familiar "waterfall illusion" for example. After watching a moving surface and looking away, one sees a stationary surface as *both* moving *and* yet not changing its position. Such mutually incompatible components in perception could not result in any coherent motor coordination. Hence the importance, as I see it, of keeping sharp and clear the distinction between modeling mechanisms of sensorimotor coordination, and finding models to explain perception as conscious experience. Many perplexing problems of the perceptual theorist may be bypassed if all we want to do is to design an automaton to make adequate use of sensory input.

Does this distinction help at all to clarify or give a sharper meaning to the old question of the neural *location* of perceptual activity as such? We are all inclined, I think rightly, to be wary of such questions, feeling that they may be as silly as to ask for the "location of triangularity" among the dots of a triangle. I want to suggest, however, that in the light of our operational model such an answer would be a little too short. In principle it is operationally meaningful to imagine ourselves gaining access to the flow-system of Figure 3, and blocking or clamping various channels so as to isolate particular sub-systems. It would then be possible to stimulate on each side of the isolating barrier, and discover which activity had a perceptual correlate according to the testimony of the subject. There is thus an operational meaning in asking where the neural activity takes place which is correlated with perception, as distinct from sensorimotor coordination. The suggestion that emerges from our model when one looks into it (MacKay 1956a, 1966), is that whereas much sensorimotor coordination is likely to be cortically mediated, the basic correlate of perception as such, of *consciousness* of the external world, would be activity evoked in the meta-organizing system by sensory stimulation: activity molded and elaborated by the activity of the (presumably cortical) organizing system that matches the sensory input "on behalf of" the meta-organizer. If then we venture to ask where in the nervous system are the minimum necessary elements for conscious awareness, it may well be that we will have to look not in the great massive market place of the cerebral cortex, where demands are met by subroutines matched to them, but rather in a much smaller normative meta-organizing system, perhaps (who knows?) in the limbic system, where the priorities and policies of the whole traffic are determined and kept up-to-date (MacKay, 1956a, 1966).

## *CONCLUSION*

In relation to the main purpose of this conference, the point I would stress in summary is that in most of our artifacts the work of conscious, normative meta-organization is intended to be performed by somebody else. Normally we design our automata to subserve ultimate goals which are not autonomously determined: they are set by ourselves. Most of our automata need not, and normally should not, have any autonomous meta-organizing system; so they lack an essential feature of conscious agency. Hence the suggestion that not all features of models of human perception which try to do justice to the *experienced* aspects of it are necessarily relevant to the design of artifacts required to develop mere sensorimotor coordination. Conversely, there is no guarantee that the most effective solution of this design problem need have any claim on the attention of psychologists. In other words, oddly enough, automaton designers with an interest in the perception of speech and visual form might do well to ignore, in the first instance, those aspects of the psychological theory of perception that are primarily concerned with perceiving; for perceiving is something that their automata may not be required to do.

## *REFERENCES*


Barlow, H. B., & Hill, R. M. Evidence for a physiological explanation of the waterfall phenomenon and figural after-effects. *Nature*, 1963, *200*, 1345-1347.

Evans, E. F., & Whitfield, I. C. Classification of unit responses in the auditory cortex of the unanaesthetized and unrestrained cat. *Journal of Physiology*, 1964, *171*, 476-493.

Fiorentini, A., & MacKay, D. M. Temporal factors in pattern vision. *Quarterly Journal of Experimental Psychology*, 1965, *17*, 282-291.

Hubel, D. H., & Wiesel, T. N. Shape and arrangement of columns in cat's striate cortex. *Journal of Physiology*, 1963, *165*, 559-567.

Lettvin, J. Y., Maturana, H. R., McCulloch, W. S., & Pitts, W. H. What the frog's eye tells the frog's brain. *Proceedings of the Institute of Radio Engineers*, 1959, *47*, 1940-1951.

MacKay, D. M. In search of basic symbols. In von Foerster (Ed.), *Transactions 8th conference on cybernetics 1951*. New York: Joseph Macy, Jr., Foundation, 1951.

MacKay, D. M. The epistemological problem for automata. In C. E. Shannon, & J. McCarthy (Ed.), *Automata studies*. Princeton: Princeton Univer. Press, 1956, pp. 235-251.(a)

MacKay, D. M. Towards an information-flow model of human behavior. *British Journal of Psychology*, 1956, *47*, 30-43.(b)

MacKay, D. M. Moving visual images produced by regular stationary patterns. *Nature*, 1957, *180*, 849-850.

MacKay, D. M. Perceptual stability of a stroboscopically lit visual field containing self-luminous objects. *Nature*, 1958, *181*, 507-508.

MacKay, D. M. The stabilization of perception during voluntary activity. In *Proceedings of the fifteenth international congress of psychology, 1957*. Amsterdam: North-Holland, 1959, pp. 284-285.(a)

MacKay, D. M. Operational aspects of intellect. In Nat. Phys. Lab. Sympos. No. 10, 1958, *Mechanization of thought processes*. London: HMSO., 1959, pp. 37-52.(b)

MacKay, D. M. Modelling of large-scale nervous activity. In J. W. L. Beament (Ed.), Soc. exp. Biol. Sympos. No. 14, *Models and analogues in biology*. London: Cambridge Univer. Press, 1960. Pp. 192-198. (Amer. ed., New York: Academic Press, 1960.)

MacKay, D. M. Interactive processes in visual perception. In W. A. Rosenblith (Ed.), *Sensory communication*. New York: M.I.T. Press and Wiley, 1961, pp. 339-355.

MacKay, D. M. Theoretical models of space perception. In C. A. Muses (Ed.), *Aspects of the theory of artificial intelligence*. New York: Plenum, 1962, pp. 83-104.

MacKay, D. M. Dynamic distortions of perceived form. *Nature,* 1964, *203,* 1097.

MacKay, D. M. Cerebral organization and the conscious control of action. In J. C. Eccles (Ed.), *Brain and conscious experience.* New York: Springer-Verlag, 1966, pp. 422-445.

MacKay, D. M., & Fiorentini, A. Evoked potentials correlated with a visual anomaly. *Nature,* 1966, *209,* 787-789.

von Holst, E., & Mittelstaedt, H. Das Reafferenzprinzip. *Naturwissenschaften,* 1950, *37,* 464.

Wilson, J. P. The response of the visual system to spatially repetitive stimuli. Unpublished doctoral thesis, University of London, 1960.

*The final selection for this collection considers problems of stunning complexity, compared to the level of analysis and explanation of phenomena considered in earlier sections. It gives a taste of the sorts of problem that will have to be tackled if visual processing is to be understood in any complete way, but makes relatively little contribution to the specific "low level" problem of stimulus equivalence which has mainly been discussed here, since such equivalences are assumed a priori for the Stevens-Halle type of model. As I said earlier, the paper is included to give some sense of perspective on our major topic, and to show that the problems of pattern recognition extend well beyond the conventional boundaries of visual perception.*

# *Remarks on Analysis by Synthesis and Distinctive Features*

K. N. STEVENS AND M. HALLE

Lastly, I am to take notice, that there is so great a Communication and correspondency between the Nerves of the Ear, and those of the Larynx, that whensoever any sound agitates the Brain, there flow immediately spirits towards the Muscles of the Larynx, which duely dispose them to form a sound altogether like that, which was just now striking the Brain. And although I well conceive, that there needs some *time* to facilitate those motions of the Muscles of the Throat, so that the Sounds, which excite the Brain the first time, cannot be easily expressed by the Throat, yet notwithstanding I doe as well conceive, that by virtue of repeating them it will

Reprinted from *Models for the Perception of Speech and Visual Form,* 1967.

come to pass, that the Brain, which thereby is often shaken in the same places, sends such a plenty of spirits through the nerves, that are inserted in the Muscles of the Throat, that at length they easily move all the cartilages, which serve for that action, as 'tis requisite they should be moved to form Sounds like those, that have shaken the Brain.

(de Cordemoy, G. A *philosophical discourse concerning speech*. London: J. Martin, 1668.)

Some years ago we proposed a model of speech perception that we called "analysis by synthesis" (Halle & Stevens, 1959; Halle & Stevens, 1962; Stevens, 1960). This model postulated that the perception of speech involves the internal synthesis of patterns according to certain rules and a matching of these internally generated patterns against the pattern under analysis. We suggested, moreover, that the generative rules utilized in the perception of speech were in large measure identical with those utilized in speech production, and that fundamental to both processes was an abstract representation of the speech events.[1] The aim of the present paper is to explore certain aspects of our model in greater detail than in earlier papers with the hope that we might initiate discussion that might lead toward a deeper understanding of the perception of speech.

## *THE ROLE OF SEGMENTS AND FEATURES IN SPEECH PRODUCTION*

We begin by reviewing some of the evidence in favor of the view that an abstract representation of the speech event and a set of appropriate generative rules are involved in the process of speech production. Let us consider first the purely physiological aspect of speech production and examine from this point of view the English utterances *spy*, *sty*, and *sky*. It is immediately obvious that these three utterances resemble one another in certain striking respects; in fact, the sequences of gestures that are required to produce these words are all but identical. First a narrow constriction is created by the tongue immediately behind the teeth, through which air is blown from the lungs without exciting the vocal cords. This is followed by complete blocking of the vocal tract, causing an interruption of the air flow and a simultaneous buildup of pressure behind the point of closure, the vocal cords remaining inactive all this time. Next, the blockage is released suddenly, and more or less simultaneously with the release the vocal cords remaining inactive all this time. Next, the blockage is released

[1] It should be evident that our model is similar to that discussed sometime ago by Professor D. M. MacKay (1951) which he has subsequently refined in later papers, including the presentation at this symposium. The ideas underlying analysis by synthesis have a much longer history, however, going back to rationalist theories of perception.

suddenly, and more or less simultaneously with the release the vocal cords begin to vibrate; the vocal tract, which previously had been blocked, is then made to assume a relatively unconstricted open shape. At the beginning of this opening phase the tongue is far back in the mouth, narrowing the top part of the pharynx; then the tongue is moved forward and upward towards the roof of the mouth where it remains to the end of the gesture. The difference between the three utterances are due solely to the differences in the placement of the blockage: in *spy* the blockage is at the lips, in *sty* it is just behind the teeth, and in *sky* it is back in the mouth in the rear of the soft palate.

The preceeding, seemingly quite naturalistic description of the vocal-tract behavior, however, suggests a quantization of the gestures which is not always directly observable. In our description we have talked about features of the vocal-tract gesture such as the degree of narrowing, location of the narrowing, and vibration of the vocal cords as if these were entirely independent of one another. We have also imposed a temporal segmentation on the gesture by describing it in terms of features that are ordered with respect to each other in a sequence. In sum, our description has proceeded as if the events we described consisted of temporally delimited segments which are complexes of features.

The foregoing is, of course, the traditional manner of describing speech, and originally it was believed to be an accurate statement of what could be observed directly. Since the first X-ray motion pictures of speech were produced some 30 years ago, however, serious questions have been raised with regard to the correctness of this belief. It has become quite obvious by now that in the actual speech events the discreteness of the segments and of the features is blurred or totally obliterated, so that it is frequently impossible to isolate the segments and features in the actual event. We are thus faced with the difficulty that, though on the one hand speech can be described in very satisfactory fashion in terms of segments and features, the latter do not seem to be directly present in the observable speech event.

We believe that there is a fairly straightforward resolution of this difficulty; namely, to recognize explicitly that characterizations of speech in terms of segments and features are not more or less naturalistic records of particular physical events but are rather abstract representations of classes of events. The features and segments which appear in the abstract representation are related in an explicit manner to different overt attributes of the speech event; this relationship need not, however, be one-to-one nor need it necessarily preserve the discreteness of the features and the segments. We may regard the segments and features of the abstract representation as instructions for particular types of behavior of the speech-generating mechanism. When these instructions are executed, the interaction between different physiological structures, each possessing its own sluggish response characteristics, will naturally produce a quasi-continuous gesture in which the discrete instructions initiating the gesture are no longer always discernible as distinct components.

The actual practice of phoneticians conforms quite precisely to the view just proposed that the phonetic transcription is an abstract representation of instructions to the vocal tract. It is explicit already in A. M. Bell's *Visible Speech* (1867), and accounts for the constant recurrence in phonetic studies of remarks such as the following taken from P. Ladefoged's recent study of West African languages (1964) [our italics—KS/MH]: "But although instrumental techniques were used extensively in the course of this study, I would like to stress that *an equally important part of the work consisted of simply* observing and *imitating informants.* As a result of an experimental approach, I was often able to select the most appropriate out of a number of conflicting hypotheses about the way in which a particular sound was made; and occasionally instrumental data revealed a new articulatory possibility which I had not thought of before. Nevertheless, I am still sure that 'instrumental phonetics is, strictly speaking, not phonetics at all. It is only a help . . . The final arbiter in all phonetic questions is the trained ear of the practical phonetician.' (Sweet, 1911.) For those of us who are not as skilled as Sweet, instrumental phonetics may be a very powerful aid and of great use in providing objective records on the basis of which we may verify or amend our subjective impressions. *But even the most extensive array of instruments can never be a substitute for the linguist's accurate observation and imitation of an informant.*"

Evidence concerning the nature of the abstract framework of segments and features that underlies the generation of speech is based not only on observations of the behavior of the vocal mechanism and on auditory impressions of speech sounds but also on observations of the way the segments and features play a role in other aspects of language (Halle, 1964; Jakobson, Fant, & Halle, 1952). It is a well-known fact that every language possesses specific constraints on the sequence of segments that can constitute a well-formed utterance. The most natural framework for characterizing these constraints is provided by the same set of features as those characterizing the motor behavior. Thus, for instance, there is in English a restriction on the appearance of nasals before stops: we get /m/ before /p/ or /b/; /n/ before /t/ or /d/; and /n/ before .k. or /g/. For example, *trump, rombic, hint, hinder, think, finger* are English words, but sequences such as *thimk, trunp,* or *tringt* are simply not English. It is all but self-evident that the nasal must be identical with the following stop consonant in the features of diffuseness and gravity (traditionally referred to as the point of articulation); but this characterization involves in an essential way features that are correlated with specific articulatory properties of speech.

Another area where features play an obvious role is in the determining of the phonetic shape of grammatical elements (morphemes) in different contexts. Thus, for instance, the past tense suffix of English regular verbs is (a) /id/ if the verb ends in /t/ or /d/; (b) /t/ if the verb ends in any voiceless segment except /t/; and (c) /d/ if the verb ends in any voiced segment except /d/. We note that in (b) and (c) the choice between the voiced /d/ or the voiceless /t/ as the past tense signal depends on the presence of the same feature in the last segment of the verb stem. This again is an instance where a higher level regularity can be accounted for in a natural fashion in terms of the feature framework utilized for characterizing the vocal-tract behavior.

Examples of the preceding type are so numerous and widespread that there can be little doubt that features and segments are the (abstract) entities that underlie the entire phonology of every language, and not only its lowest stage, the vocal-tract gestures. The discovery of important regularities on the more abstract levels of the phonology of a language will, therefore, be taken as prima-facie evidence of the existence of a given feature. In fact, it is reasonable to suggest that a feature that plays a role in the phonology of a language must also have plausible articulatory and acoustic correlates, although our lack of knowledge of the physiological processes of speech may prevent such correlates from being immediately evident to us. Indeed, examination of the phonology may well provide indirect evidence that can lead to a better understanding of the organization and control of speech gestures.

As a case in point, we may cite the feature *diffuse* in vowels, which in the framework that we have adopted replaces in part the traditional phonetic feature of tongue height. As will be recalled, the traditional phonetic frameworks distinguish at least three degrees of tongue height: high, middle, and low. Instead, in the feature system that we have adopted here, we distinguish diffuse (high) vowels such as /i/ and /u/, from the rest which are nondiffuse. The latter are sub-categorized into compact such as /a/ or /ɔ/ and noncompact such as /o/ or /e/.

A particularly good example of the utilization of the feature diffuse-nondiffuse is provided by modern standard Russian where, in unstressed position, nondiffuse vowels coalesce into /a/ after "hard" (nonpalatalized) consonants, and into /i/ after "soft" (palatalized or palatal) consonants. The diffuse vowels /i/ and /u/ on the other hand, remain distinct in unstressed as well as in stressed position. Since stress in Russian may fall on different vowels of a word in different grammatical forms, the variations in position of stress are paralleled also by variations in vowel quality, as indicated in the following examples:

*after "hard" consonants*

| | | |
|---|---|---|
| /v'al/ (nom.sg) | /val'i/ (nom.pl.) | "wave" |
| /v'ɔl/ (nom.sg.) | /val'i/ (nom.pl.) | "ox" |

/e/ appears only after "soft" consonants

*after "soft" consonants*

| | | |
|---|---|---|
| /vz,'al/ (masc.sg.) | /vz,il'a/ (fem.sg) | "took" |
| /v,'ol/ (masc.sg.) | /v,il'a/ (fem.sg.) | "led" |
| /st,'en/ (gen.pl.) | /st,in'a/ (nom.sg.) | "wall" |

But no change in vowel quality is observed in

| | | |
|---|---|---|
| /bl,'ul/ (masc.sg.) | /bl,ul'a/ (fem.sg.) | "observed" |
| /p,'il/ (masc.sg.) | /p,il'a/ (fem.sg.) | "drank" |

From the point of view of articulation, this feature is correlated with a maximally narrow (for vowels) constriction being placed in the front part of the buccal cavity. (It is this placement which ensures the production of a maximally low first formant—the well-known acoustical correlate of this feature.) At first sight such an articulatory correlate lacks the immediate appeal and plausibility of such other universally recognized features as nasality, voicing, or labialization. There seems to be no single anatomical structure which can be said to be in control of the execution of this feature. In producing diffuse vowels we can make a constriction either with the lips or with the forward part of the tongue, and it is by no means obvious why these two different organs should form a single functional unit. Cineradiographic data show, however, that a constriction of this type must be accompanied by a raised mandible. It is entirely possible, then, that such a gesture provides a single articulatory correlate of the feature diffuse. An alternative argument might be that the lips and forward part of the tongue are involved in one of the basic types of instinctive behavior in all mammals —sucking. We find it, therefore, not hard to believe that the formation of a constriction in the forward portion of the buccal cavity should constitute a single functional control unit in the process of speech production.

Our view of the speech-production process, therefore, may be summarized as follows. The speaker of a language has stored in his memory an abstract representation of lexical items of the language. These representations consist of segments which themselves are complexes of features. The representations can, therefore, be pictured as abstract two-dimensional matrices in which the columns represent the strings of segments and the rows different features. The syntactic component of the language establishes the order in which different lexical items appear in the sentence as well as the relationship between the items in the string. The string of matrices is then operated on by a set of rules which transform the matrices into sets of instructions for vocal-tract behavior. Ultimately the execution of these instructions produces the acoustical signal. While these instructions bear a close relationship to the articulatory behavior they elicit and to the acoustical properties of the utterances produced by it, there is no implication that the acoustic output must be necessarily decomposible into sequences of discrete segments or that instructions or features are directly recoverable from the signal. We *are* asserting that the acoustical output is a joint function of the abstract representation, the rules of the language and the dynamics of the vocal tract, but we do not mean to imply that this is a linear function of the segments in the abstract representation; nor is there any reason to suppose that it must be so. As a result it cannot be recoverable from the signal by simple techniques of signal analysis.

## *THE ROLE OF SEGMENTS AND FEATURES IN SPEECH PERCEPTION*

We should like to suggest that in speech perception the acoustic signal is decoded into an abstract representation identical to that already described, i.e., a representation in terms of segments and features. Furthermore, we would like to argue that in decoding an input signal into such a representation, the listener brings to bear the same phonological rules as those in generating the signal from the abstract representation.

That such a representation plays a role in speech perception is strongly suggested by the fact that normal speakers of a language understand without apparent difficulty utterances in a fairly wide range of dialects. This obvious fact would be quite inexplicable if we assumed that utterances are identified solely by means of direct classification of successive segments of the acoustical signal or by comparison of the input signal against an inventory of stored patterns, for the dialectal differences that do not inhibit comprehension are precisely differences in the inventory of the sounds. If, on the other hand, we assume that dialectal differences in the sounds are due to the fact that a given abstract representation of a speech event is actualized in accordance with *different* phonological rules, then the performance of the normal speakers becomes at once understandable. Having listened to a relatively small sample of utterances in a dialect different from his own, the speaker of a language is evidently able to determine the modifications of a few phonological rules of the dialect as compared with those in his own dialect. He is then able to utilize these rules to identify correctly combinations of elements or words he has never heard before in that dialect.

Consider, for example, the case of one of our children who says /sing/ instead of /sin/. Such an error is not uncommon among 4 to 6-year-olds; it is also quite interesting from a theoretical point of view. Observe first that the child could not possibly be mimicking anyone in its environments since no one in its surroundings speaks English with this sort of an accent (which is characteristic, however, of certain partially foreign milieus of our bigger cities). Since imitation has to be excluded for lack of a model, we must look for another explanation. We should like to propose that the child does not primarily mimic its parents but rather tries to establish the rules that govern the speech of its parents and utilizes these rules to construct utterances of its own. Since the child is new at it, he will occasionally fail to establish a rule correctly or he may overlook a rule altogether. He will then produce utterances that are at variance with those of his parents.

Viewed in this light the pronunciation of /sing/ for /sin/ is no longer an inexplicable curiosity. As observed above, the nasal /n/ has a peculiar distribution in English. It occurs on the one hand, before /g/ or /k/ (e.g., *finger, Lincoln*), where it is the only admissible nasal consonant; and, on the other hand, it is found in word final position but never at the beginning of the word. The facts just listed can most economically be described by saying that mature speakers of English obey the following two rules, which incidentally have to be applied in the order indicated:

1. A nasal consonant assimilates the place of articulation of the following stop consonant.
2. Final /g/ is deleted in word final position following a nasal consonant.

The child who utters /sing/ is evidently using the first of these rules but does not invoke the final rule. Likewise, when he listens to and identifies the word he must again be invoking these rules and be decoding the sound into the abstract representation /s + ɪ + nasal + g/ for in English every word final velar nasal must derive from a sequence of /nasal + g/.

An example that is, perhaps, more striking is the case, described by J. Applegate (1961), of the "secret language" spontaneously created by some children in Cambridge, Massachusetts. The difference between the grammar of this "language" and standard English consisted of two ordered rules: (a) in a word containing several identical stop consonants, all but the first of these is replaced by a glottal stop; and (b) all continuants are replaced by the cognate stops. As a result of these two rules, we find in the language of the children the following deviations from standard English:

| | | | |
|---|---|---|---|
| /ba?iy/ | Bobby | /ded/ | does |
| /di?/ | did | /takt/ | talks |
| /day?/ | died | /teykt/ | takes |
| /pey?r/ | paper | /dayd/ | dies |
| /key?/ | cake | /payp/ | fife |

It is evident that these children are using the same abstract representation for these words as their peers, since they understand both standard English and their secret language. In generating and in perceiving utterances in the secret language, they simply impose a slight modification on the rules of standard English.

## *MODELS OF SPEECH PRODUCTION AND PERCEPTION*

In order to render our remarks more concrete, we have attempted to schematize the processes involved in speech production and perception in terms of block diagrams. A representation of the speech production system is shown in Figure 1. The abstract representation of an utterance in matrix

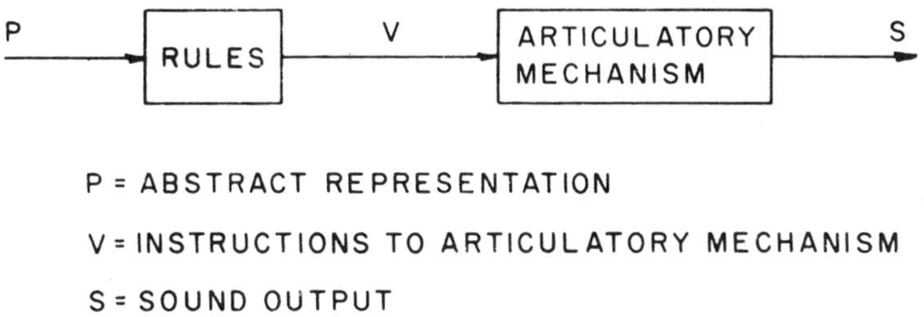


Fig. 1. Model of the speech-generating process, showing the transformations from the abstract discrete representation P to the articulatory instructions V to the sound S.

form is denoted by the symbol P at the left. As we have observed, a set of rules operates on this representation to yield instructions to the vocal mechanism, which are designated by V. These instructions cause appropriate activity in the articulatory mechanism, which generates the output sound S. We assume that included in the vocal system are the various auditory, tactile, and other feedback paths; the operation of the vocal mechanism may, of course, be very much dependent upon these feedback paths.

It is important to emphasize that in the model of Figure 1 we do not equate the instructions V with movements of the articulatory structures. Rather, we regard the patterns V to be actualized in the form of appropriate sequences of motor commands only after certain motor skills have been acquired. Thus, for example, a given set of instructions V that occur in an utterance of a certain language may require that the talker actualize a series of gestures with the tongue and lips, but he may not in fact be able to realize the proper sequence of movements, and consequently may speak the language with an accent. One can make an analogy with a person who observes a tennis game and then tries to play with no further practice. Obviously when he attempts to transform his observations into motor commands he cannot perform as well as a skilled player, even though he is generally aware of what is involved.

We now add to the model the capability of perceiving speech as well as generating it, as shown in Figure 2. Thus an input sound S' is processed by

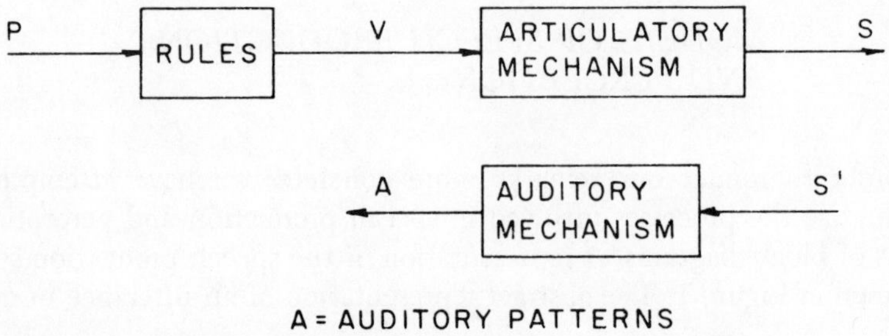


Fig. 2. Model of the articulatory mechanism and of the speech-generating process.

the auditory mechanism to yield auditory patterns, which we designate by A. The transformation that the auditory mechanism applies to S' is not understood in detail. At one time it was thought that the auditory system had the properties of a bank of filters, and that the auditory patterns A were much like the patterns produced by a sound spectrograph. However, recent neurophysiological studies on sensory systems of lower animals—studies like those of Lettvin, Maturana, McCulloch, and Pitts (1959) on the visual system of the frog, and of Frishkopf and Goldstein (1963) on the frog's auditory system—suggest that fairly complex processing takes place fairly near the periphery. We would expect, therefore, that the auditory patterns A constitute a much more radical transformation of the input than a simple frequency analysis of the type performed by a sound spectrograph.

It is evident, furthermore, that these auditory patterns have close ties with articulatory activity, since we can produce an articulatory movement with instructions V and observe the consequences at the level of A.[2] A listener can also observe the utterances of others who are using the same phonological rules. Knowing the P → V transformations that the talker is using, he can make some estimate of the V → A transformation between the instructions V of the talker and his own auditory patterns A. The attraction of the suggestion that there is a close correspondence between A– and V– patterns resides in the fact that the abstract features of P would then be related in a direct way not only to the articulatory instructions V but also to the auditory patterns A. In this view, therefore, speech would be anchored equally in the motor and in the auditory system of man.

Consideration of the general model up to this point indicates that we all

[2] F. A. Hayek (1963) has discussed in more general terms instances in which "correspondence (is) established between movement patterns which are perceived through different sense modalities." [p. 326]. He postulates that "the recognition of a correspondence between patterns made up of different sensory elements presupposes a mechanism of sensory pattern transfer, that is, a mechanism for the transfer of the capacity to discern an abstract order or arrangement from one field to another." [p. 327]

carry around with us (a) the abstract representation of the entities of our language; (b) the rules that operate on features or groups of features in this abstract representation to yield instructions to the articulatory mechanism; and (c) a description in some form of the transformation between articulatory instructions and auditory patterns. This latter transformation is presumably independent of language and depends only on the physiological and anatomical characteristics of the auditory and articulatory mechanisms.

We have already argued that speech perception involves decoding of the signal into an abstract representation P that is identical with that used by the talker. The question that remains therefore, is: What is the process whereby the auditory patterns A corresponding to an utterance are converted into the abstract representation P? We have given examples to suggest that a direct segmentation and classification of segments at the level of A cannot yield the representation P, and that somehow the phonological rules that are used in speech production must be employed by the listener in the decoding operation. We propose the analysis-by-synthesis model as a possible description of this decoding from A to P.

The principle features of this model are shown in Figure 3. We observe outside the large dashed box the components and levels we have already discussed: the abstract representation P, the phonological rules, the patterns V that give rise to motor commands, and the auditory patterns A. We have included also a short-time memory in which these auditory patterns can be stored. We postulate first that the auditory patterns that result

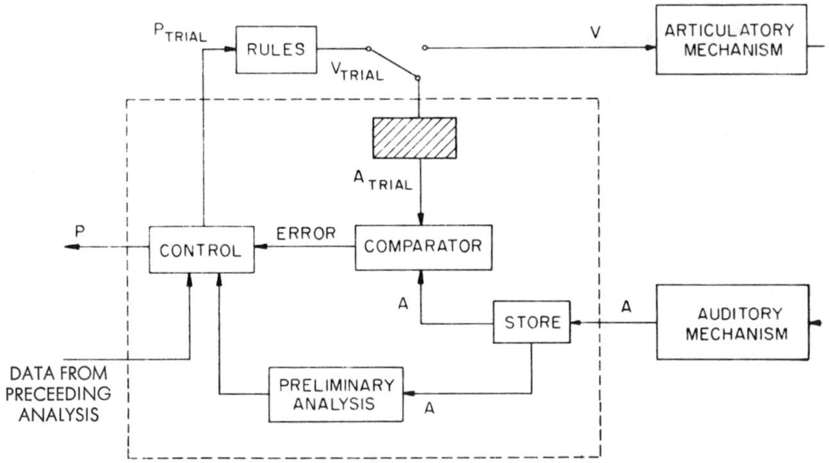


Fig. 3. Model for the speech-generating and speech-perception process. (The dashed line encloses components of a hypothetical analysis-by-synthesis scheme for speech perception. The shaded component indicates the capability of the model for effecting transformations between articulatory instructions and auditory patterns.)

from an acoustic speech signal at the ears undergo some *preliminary analysis,* and as a consequence of this preliminary analysis, together with contextual information derived from analysis of adjacent portions of the signal, an hypothesis is made in a control component concerning the abstract representation of the utterance. This hypothesized sequence of units, which we have labeled $P_{trial}$, is then operated on by the phonological rules (the same ones that are used in the generation of speech) to yield a pattern $V_{trial}$. During speech production, this pattern would normally give rise to motor commands that would lead to articulatory activity and sound generation. During speech perception, however, this path is inhibited, and instead an equivalent auditory pattern $A_{trial}$ is derived from $V_{trial}$, as indicated by the shaded box in the figure. This computed pattern is compared with the pattern under analysis. If there is agreement between the two patterns, then the trial sequence of elements was correct and this sequence is read out for processing at higher levels. If there is a difference between the patterns, the control component takes note of this error and assembles a new trial sequence of units. This process continues until the trial abstract representation gives a match at the comparator, in which case the correct output sequence is established as P.

Since we have recognized that the output of the auditory mechanism may already be in a form that is closely related to the features of the abstract representation, it may frequently, or indeed usually, happen that the initial trial for P is the correct result. When contextual information supplements that provided by the direct analysis, then the probability of obtaining a correct guess on the first trial is further enhanced. In spite of the fact that a correct output sequence may frequently be obtainable even before a matching is attempted, we would suggest that the matching process is always employed as a check. That is, we suggest that normal speech perception can proceed only through active participation of the listener—he makes hypotheses on the basis of direct analysis and contextual information and he then verifies these hypotheses through an internal replication and matching procedure, though we expect that the criteria employed in the matching operation may not always be very stringent.

We should emphasize that Figure 3 represents a model of the perception of speech and is not, of course, a model of auditory perception in general.[3] It is a particular mode of perception that is, so to speak, "switched in" whenever a listener attempts to understand a speech signal that reaches his ears. Since the output P of the speech perception model is in terms of segments and features it is categorial; indeed, when a listener is operating in the speech perception mode we suggest that he is always performing a categorization of the input. This tendency of a listener to categorize lin-

[3] Although, as D. M. MacKay suggests in his paper at this symposium, it may well be that all types of perception involve an internal replication and matching process of the type discussed here.

guistic stimuli has been demonstrated in a number of studies (see Liberman, Cooper, Harris & MacNeilage, 1962, and references cited therein). For example, Liberman, Harris, Hoffman, & Griffith (1957) showed that a series of consonant-vowel syllables in which the starting frequencies of the second formant for the initial stop consonant are arranged along a continuum are perceived not as a continuously changing sequence of sounds but rather as a series of syllables whose initial consonants change in a stepwise fashion from /b/ to /d/ to /g/. (However, in a similar series of experiments with isolated vowel stimuli characterized by formant frequencies spaced along a continuum, perception tended to be continuous rather than categorial [Stevens, Öhman, Studdert-Kennedy, and Liberman, 1964].) It would appear that in an experimental situation in which these isolated vowels are the stimuli, the listener utilizes a nonspeech mode of perception in which categorial responses are not required.)

Fundamental to the proposed model of speech perception is the requirement that in order to understand the speech of a talker a listener must know the phonological rules that the talker is using to transform the abstract representation in articulatory instructions. It must be emphasized that knowing these rules is not equivalent to being able to generate speech in the language or dialect used by the talker. One does *not* need to possess in detail the motor skills that are required to transform V-patterns into sound in order to understand the utterances of the talker. In the model of Figure 3 these motor skills are considered to be part of the articulatory mechanism, and thus are not directly involved in speech perception. Thus the learning of a new language is in large measure acquisition of the phonological rules (and, of course, the lexicon, and syntactic, and semantic rules) and *not* asquisition of certain motor skills. Such skills are required only if one wishes to speak the language with perfect native accent. Effective command of a language often falls far short of this aim.

## *REFERENCES*

Applegate, J. Phonological rules of a subdialect of English. *Word*, 1961, *17*, 186-193.

Bell, A. M. *Visible speech: The science of universal alphabetics*. London: Simpkin, Marshall, 1867.

Frishkopf, L. S., & Goldstein, M. H., Jr. Responses to acoustic stimuli from single units in the eighth nerve of the bullfrog. *Journal of the Acoustical Society of America*, 1963, 35, 1219-1228.

Halle, M. On the bases of phonology. In J. A. Fodor and J. J. Katz (Eds.), *The structure of language: Readings in the philosophy of language*. Englewood Cliffs, N.J.: Prentice-Hall, 1964, 324-333.

Halle, M., & Stevens, K. N. Analysis by synthesis. In W. Wathen-Dunn and

L. E. Woods (Eds.), *Proceedings of the seminar on speech compression and processing*. Vol. 2. AFCRC-TR-59-198, USAF Camb. Res. Ctr., 1959, Paper D7.

Halle, M., & Stevens, K. N. Speech recognition: A model and a program for research. *IRE Transactions PGIT*, 1962, *IT-8*, 155-159.

Hayek, F. A. Rules, perception, and intelligibility. *Proceedings of the British Academy*, 1963, *47*, 321-344.

Jakobson, R., Fant, C. G. M., & Halle, M. Preliminaries to speech analysis. *M.I.T. Acoustical Laboratory Technical Report*, 1952, No. 13. Cambridge: M.I.T. Press, 1965.

Ladefoged, P. *A phonetic study of West African languages*. Cambridge: Cambridge University Press, 1964, xviii.

Lettvin, J. Y., Maturana, H. R., McCulloch, W. S., & Pitts, W. H. What the frog's eye tells the frog's brain. *Proceedings of the Institute of Radio Engineers*, 1959, *47*, 1940-1959.

Liberman, A. M., Cooper, F. S., Harris, K. S., & MacNeilage, P. F. A motor theory of speech perception. *Proceedings of the speech communication seminar*. Vol. 2. Stockholm: Royal Institute of Technology, 1962.

Liberman, A. M., Harris, K. S., Hoffman, H. S., & Griffith, B. C. The discrimination of speech sounds within and across phoneme boundaries. *Journal of Experimental Psychology*, 1957, *54*, 358-368.

MacKay, D. M. Mindlike behaviour in artifacts. *British Journal for the Philosophy of Science*, 1951, *2*, 105-121.

Stevens, K. N. Toward a model for speech recognition. *Journal of the Acoustical Society of America*, 1960, *32*, 47-55.

Stevens, K. N., Öhman, S. E. G., Studdert-Kennedy, M., & Liberman, A. M. Crosslinguistic study of vowel discrimination. *Journal of the Acoustical Society of America*, 1964. *36*, 1989. (Abstract)

Sweet, H. Phonetics. In *Encyclopedia Britannica*. Vol. 21. (11th ed.) Cambridge: Cambridge University Press, 1911.

*To return to terra firma after such a heady flight, I shall reiterate the fact that the two specific contributions to the questions of stimulus equivalence and classification in this section, the papers by Uttley and by Grimsdale et al., are both fairly old. The reader may be surprised that they should be chosen to represent a "young" field where active developments can be expected, particularly in view of the rapid advances in computer technology of recent years. There have, of course, been very many proposals for pattern recognition by machine, specifically by computer; an expert a short time ago guessed at perhaps as many as 2,000. Yet not a great deal in the way of genuinely new ideas has turned up recently. I am certainly not claiming that all this work is without value, rather that most of the important and interesting basic ideas were contained in comparatively early papers—and the experts in the field seem to feel that this is so too. An important exception to this rather sweeping generalization is to be found in some of the models* reported in Minsky (1969) which make use of the new heuristic programming devices.

The power and versatility of recent computer methods cannot be denied, but it is well worth enquiring to what extent they have been used successfully to model biological pattern recognition systems. My own belief, argued in some detail elsewhere (Dodwell, 1970b), is that really fruitful new results in this area will now only come about by much closer cooperation between scientists in the different fields. The general problem of pattern recognition by machine is no longer of burning interest, just as Lashley's problem of stimulus equivalence no longer holds the center of attention. The reason is the same in both cases. The problem has been solved. What is required, if machine analogy and computer simulation are to contribute to the understanding of visual pattern recognition, is a much more deliberate attempt to model specific types of visual system (or subsystem) with certain well-defined properties, and to do this in ways which make sense to the physiologist and psychologist as well as to the computer scientist. There have been as yet almost no developments of this sort.

Compared with the situation two decades ago, say, there is undoubtedly more interchange now among different disciplines, yet the very close communality of interest amongst scientists of different sorts who work on pattern recognition argues for even stronger cooperation.

## CONCLUSION

To conclude this book of readings, an attempt to summarize the main lines of investigation, to give some idea of the shape of the field in capsule form, seems appropriate. In doing this my own judgments about what the important points are will be involved, but this is inevitable; as I argued earlier, an attempt to outline a clear position should have the advantage of giving the reader something to attack—or defend—and this is better than feeling lost in a maze of uninterpretable and confusing facts. At least I hope I have helped to avoid that danger.

First, I have tried to demonstrate the multidisciplinary nature of research on pattern recognition, even if the disciplines still work to a large extent within their own separate compartments. Thus we have seen that physiologists, biologists, biophysicists, computer scientists, and psychologists have all made important contributions to the field, and this list is not exhaustive. The sorts of problems dealt with in these different disciplines overlap to a large extent, and we have seen evidence in several cases of convergence on a common type of solution, which is an encouraging sign.

Second, the major concepts and findings seem to me to be as follows:

1. There is ample evidence for specific visual stimulus coding operations

in all levels of animal life with recognizably differentiated eyes and nervous systems that have been studied. The evidence shows that the forms of coding vary, perhaps quite widely, between very different types of visual system, but this is scarcely surprising. The degree of anatomical and physiological complexity also varies greatly, both at the primary receptive (retinal) level and even more in the central structures and connections.

2. There are two sorts of change of organization which are correlated with progress up the phylogenetic scale towards higher forms. The first of these is the increase in hierarchical structure, accompanied by the receptive field type of organization, found in vertebrate systems: here the relationship between structure and function is clear, the multilevel processing arrangements only occurring in mammalian visual systems so far as we know. Although the point is not conclusively established, it also seems very possible that at the higher level the coding system is less specialized, and therefore more flexible, than at the lower (consider the differences between receptive field types in frog and cat, as the primary example). The second sort of change, in going from the lower to higher animal types, is the increasingly important part that perceptual learning and development come to play, a point made very forcefully by Hebb some years ago. The point has not been well documented in this book, but it is one which is pretty firmly established. In my opinion perceptual learning requires that we postulate further steps in the hierarchical arrangements for coding, steps which at present are not open to investigation by direct physiological methods.

3. Behavioral experiments, with human subjects and with animals, yield results which are consistent with what is known of neurophysiological coding systems, at least at the level of simple pattern, or pattern-element, recognition. Whether more complicated pattern recognition behavior (which we have touched on but briefly) is similarly consistent or not it is difficult to say. But at the higher levels, particularly in humans, perceptual learning and other factors like attention and interest play such an important role that it might be impossible to give a definite answer to that question.

4. The coding (pattern processing) and hierarchical classificatory schemes are used in some, but not all, machine pattern-recognition systems, and in some but not all psychological models. This is a point where the convergence of ideas from different disciplines is perhaps more clearly illustrated than elsewhere, since some of the ideas were proposed as rational means for solving the general problems of stimulus equivalence and pattern recognition even before the neurophysiological results were known.

Obviously, in this summary I have emphasized the neurophysiological discoveries, which I think are of very great importance for the field. However, a reminder of some of the cautionary remarks made earlier is in order. The findings offer us some insight into the coding system at its lowest level, and they refer primarily to the vertebrate, and particularly the mammalian system so far as receptive field organization and hierarchical structure are concerned. While the correlations between structure and function look promising, we should be particularly aware, in formulating psychological models of pattern recognition, that a model now needs to be tailored to a particular type of system, and over-generalized models are perhaps rather unrealistic. Continuity may be sought in some principle of operation of a coding system, such as the principle of lateral interaction and inhibition, but not in the detailed structure and operation of models.

I believe that the most fruitful line of inquiry and development in this field, for psychologists, is to continue to look for pattern-recognition behavior which supports the receptive-field principle, and also to find ways of investigating—and modeling—the integration of such coding with more general aspects of pattern recognition. As I have said several times now, the coding operations can be but the first step in the development of true pattern recognition.

This brings us back to the question with which we originally started: How do organisms categorize events in their environment? We have seen that so far only limited answers to that question have been obtained. While we now have rather good concepts for dealing with problems of stimulus equivalence, at least at a low level of categorization, we are still not far along the way towards being able to specify pattern dimensions, towards what Attneave (1954) called a "psychophysics of form." And such specifications are surely needed in order to be able to model pattern recognition processes adequately. Even then, we should only have dealt with some part of the larger issues raised by Klüver in our first paper. Stated in modern guise, we can say that we have started to unravel the mysteries of the input side of an elaborate cognitive system, but there are many questions about categorization, choice, concept identification and so on which must naturally follow, but which we have only briefly touched on here. We can argue, however, that without a good understanding of the initial input categorization, of "simple" pattern recognition, those other questions cannot be definitely answered.

# Bibliography


Adrian, E. D., & Matthews, R. The action of light on the eye. I. Impulses in optic nerve. *Journal of Physiology*, 1927, *63*, 378-414.

Andrews, D. P. Perception of contour orientation in the central fovea. Part I: short lines. *Vision Research*, 1967, *7*, 975-997. (a)

Attneave, F. Some informational aspects of visual perception. *Psychological Review*, 1954, *61*, 183-193.

Attneave, F., & Arnoult, M. D. The quantitative study of shape and pattern perception. *Psychological Bulletin*, 1956, *53*, 452-471.

Barlow, H. B., Hill, R. M., & Levick, W. R. Retinal ganglion cells responding selectively to direction and speed of image motions in the rabbit. *Journal of Physiology*, 1964, *173*, 377-407.

Clowes, M. B. An hierarchical model of form perception. In W. Wathen-Dunn (Ed.), *Models for the perception of speech and visual form*. Cambridge, Mass.: M.I.T. Press, 1967.

Deutsch, J. A. A system for shape recognition. *Psychological Review*, 1962, *69*, 492-500.

Dodwell, P. C. Shape recognition in rats. *British Journal of Psychology*, 1957, *48*, 221-229.

Dodwell, P. C. Coding and learning in shape discrimination. *Psychological Review*, 1961, *68*, 373-382.

Dodwell, P. C. Anomalous transfer effects after shape discrimination training in the rat. *Psychonomic Science*, 1965, *3*, 97-98.

Dodwell, P. C. *Perceptual learning and adaptation*. London: Penguin Books, 1970. (a)

Dodwell, P. C. *Visual pattern recognition*. New York: Holt, Rinehart & Winston, 1970. (b)

Dodwell, P. C. Anomalous transfer effects after pattern discrimination training in rats and squirrels. *Journal of Comparative and Physiological Psychology*, 1970, *71*, 42-51. (c)

Hartline, H. K., & Graham, C. H. Nerve impulses from single receptors in the eye. *Journal of Cellular & Comparative Physiology*, 1932, *1*, 277-295.

Hebb, D. O. *The organization of behavior*. New York: Wiley, 1949.

Held, R. A neural model for labile sensori-motor coordinations. *Biological Prototypes and Synthetic Systems*, 1962, *1*, 71-74.

Held, R. Dissociation of visual functions by deprivation and rearrangement. *Psychologische Forschung*, 1967, *31*, 338-348.

Held, R. Two modes of processing spatially distributed visual stimulation. In P. O. Schmitt (Ed.), *The neurosciences: second study program*. New York: The Rockefeller University Press, 1971.

Hinde, R. A. *Animal Behavior: a synthesis of ethology and comparative psychology*. New York: McGraw-Hill, 1966.

Honig, W. K. (Ed.) *Operant behavior: areas of research and application*. New York: Appleton-Century-Crofts, 1966.

Hubel, D. H., & Wiesel, T. N. Receptive fields of cells in striate cortex of very young visually inexperienced kittens. *Journal of Neurophysiology*, 1963, *26*, 994-1002.

Hubel, D. H., & Wiesel, T. N. Receptive fields and functional architecture in two non-striate visual areas (18 and 19) of the Cat. *Journal of Neurophysiology*, 1965, *28*, 229-280.

Hubel, D. H., & Wiesel, T. N. Receptive Fields and Functional Architecture of Monkey Striate Cortex. *Journal of Physiology*, 1968, *195*, 215-243.

Hull, C. L. *A behavior system*. New Haven: Yale University Press, 1952.

Lashley, K. S. Functional interpretation of anatomic patterns. In *Patterns of organization in the central nervous system*. Baltimore: Williams & Wilkins, 1952.

Lashley, K. S., Chow, K. L., & Semmes, J. An examination of the electrical field theory of cerebral integration. *Psychological Review*, 1951, *58*, 123-136.

Minsky, M. *Semantic information processing*. Cambridge, Mass.: M.I.T. Press, 1969.

Mittelstaedt, H. Control systems of orientation in insects. *Annual Review of Entomology*, 1962, *7*, 177-198.

Neisser, U. *Cognitive psychology*. New York: Appleton-Century-Crofts, 1967.

Rosenblatt, F. A comparison of several Perception models. In M. C. Yovits, G. T. Jacobi, & G. D. Goldstein (Eds.), *Self-organizing systems 1962*. Washington, D.C.: Spartan Books, 1962.

Selfridge, O. G. Pandemonium: a paradign for learning. In *Mechanization of thought processes*. London: H.M.S.O., 1959.

Spence, K. W. The nature of discrimination learning in animals. *Psychological Review*, 1936, *43*, 427-449.

Sperry, R. W., Miner, N., & Myers, R. E. Visual pattern perception following subpial slicing and tantalum wire implantations in the visual cortex. *Journal of Comparative and Physiological Psychology*, 1955, *48*, 50-58.

Spinelli, D. N. Visual receptive fields in the cat's retina: complications. *Science*, 1966, *152*, 1768-1769.

Sutherland, N. S. Shape discrimination and receptive fields. *Nature*, London, 1963, *197*, 118-122.

Sutherland, N. S. Outlines of a theory of visual pattern recognition in animals and man. *Proceedings of the Royal Society*, B, 1968, *171*, 297-317.

Uhr, L. (Ed.) *Pattern recognition*. New York: Wiley, 1966.

Uttley, A. M. A theory of the mechanism of learning based on the computation of conditional probabilities. *Proceedings of the First International Congress on Cybernetics*. Paris: Gauthier-Villars, 1958.

Uttley, A. M. The design of conditional probability computers. *Information and Control*, 1958, *2*, 1-24.

Wiesel, T. N., & Hubel, D. H. Extent of recovery from the effects of visual deprivation in kittens. *Journal of Neurophysiology*, 1965, *28*, 1060-1072.

Young, J. Z. A *Model of the brain*. Oxford: Clarendon Press, 1964.

# Subject Index

# Author Index